ACTIONS OF ALCOHOL

VOLUME II

ACTIONS OF ALCOHOL

VOLUME I

BIOCHEMICAL, PHYSIOLOGICAL AND
PSYCHOLOGICAL ASPECTS

VOLUME II

CHRONIC AND CLINICAL ASPECTS

ACTIONS OF ALCOHOL

VOLUME II

CHRONIC AND CLINICAL ASPECTS

by

HENRIK WALLGREN

*Research Laboratories of the Finnish State Alcohol Monopoly (Alko),
and the Department of Physiological Zoology, University of Helsinki,
Helsinki (Finland)*

and

HERBERT BARRY, III

*Department of Pharmacology, School of Pharmacy, University of Pittsburgh,
Pittsburgh, Pennsylvania (U.S.A.)*

ELSEVIER PUBLISHING COMPANY

AMSTERDAM – LONDON – NEW YORK

1970

ELSEVIER PUBLISHING COMPANY
335 JAN VAN GALENSTRAAT
P.O. BOX 211, AMSTERDAM, THE NETHERLANDS

ELSEVIER PUBLISHING CO. LTD.
BARKING, ESSEX, ENGLAND

AMERICAN ELSEVIER PUBLISHING COMPANY, INC.
52 VANDERBILT AVENUE
NEW YORK, NEW YORK 10017

LIBRARY OF CONGRESS CARD NUMBER: 70–135479
STANDARD BOOK NUMBER: 0-444-40902-5
WITH 9 ILLUSTRATIONS AND 8 TABLES.

PRINTED IN THE NETHERLANDS

Contents

VOLUME II
CHRONIC AND CLINICAL ASPECTS

Volume II, Part C
Voluntary Consumption and Chronic Effects

Chapter 8. Voluntary Selection of Alcohol, p. 403

Chapter 9. Prolonged Exposure to Alcohol, p. 479

Volume II, Part D
Applications to Clinical and Other Topics

Chapter 10. Drug Actions in Relation to Alcohol Effects, p. 621

Chapter 11. Understanding and Treatment of Alcoholics, p. 715

Chapter 12. Conclusions, p. 797

VOLUME I

BIOCHEMICAL, PHYSIOLOGICAL AND PSYCHOLOGICAL ASPECTS

Part A. General Introduction

Part B. Acute Effects of Alcohol

Abbreviations

ADH	alcohol dehydrogenase
AGN	alcohol gaze nystagmus
ALA	8-aminolaevulinate
CCC	citrated calcium carbimide
CFF	critical fusion frequency
DAF	delayed auditory feedback
DRL	differential reinforcement for low rate
ECG	electrocardiogram
ER	endoplasmic reticulum
FFA	free fatty acids
GABA	γ-aminobutyric acid
GOT	glutamic oxaloacetic transaminase
GPT	glutamic pyruvic transaminase
GSR	galvanic skin response
5-HIAA	5-hydroxyindoleacetic acid
5-HT	5-hydroxytryptamine
LADH	liver alcohol dehydrogenase
LD	lactic dehydrogenase
LSD	lysergic acid diethylamide
MMPI	Minnesota Multiphasic Personality Inventory
NCPCA	National Center for the Prevention and Control of Alcoholism
OCT	ornithine–carbamyl transferase
PAD	pralidoxime, pyridine-2-aldoximedodecyl iodide
PAN	positional alcohol nystagmus
REM	rapid eye movement
ROM	roving ocular movements
SGOT	serum glutamic oxaloacetic transaminase
SGPT	serum glutamic pyruvic transaminase
SOCT	serum ornithine–carbamyl transferase
TAT	thematic apperception test
WHO	World Health Organization

Volume II, Part C

Voluntary Consumption and Chronic Effects

Chapter 8

Voluntary Selection of Alcohol

This chapter begins the volume on chronic and clinical aspects of the actions of ethyl alcohol. The experiments reviewed in the present chapter provide suitable introductory material for the topics of the subsequent chapters. Voluntary choice between alcohol and a nonalcoholic beverage is usually tested throughout a span of several days, weeks, or months. This procedure involves chronic intake of alcohol and chronic effects, which are reviewed in Chapter 9. Experiments on voluntary consumption are necessary for comprehensive study of the clinical problems associated with alcohol. These include physical pathology caused by chronic alcohol intake (Chapter 9), relationships of alcohol to other drugs and effects of congeners in alcoholic beverages (Chapter 10), and the alcoholic's chronic craving for liquor (Chapter 11). However, there are severe limitations in the applicability of this chapter to the chronic and clinical aspects reviewed in the subsequent chapters. Nearly all the experiments on voluntary selection of alcohol have been conducted on laboratory animals, in order to obtain prolonged control and measurement of the subject's choice of beverage. These experiments have failed to provide the desired model for studying the development and manifestations of alcoholism, because voluntary intoxication and pathological craving for liquor have not been dependably induced in laboratory animals. However, the animal experiments aid in the analysis of the problem by permitting identification of several factors which affect drinking.

Three principal types of action of alcohol may be distinguished: its pharmacological effects, its nutritional effects, and its odor and taste. The present chapter, more than any of the others, includes each of these actions and thus is related to the topics reviewed in all of the other chapters. In

Volume I, alcohol has been described principally as a pharmacological agent, and the present chapter reviews evidence that the drug effect constitutes an important incentive for voluntary consumption of alcohol and also sets a stringent limit on the quantity consumed. Since an amount of alcohol sufficient to produce pharmacological effects also includes a substantial number of calories, alcohol is a food as well as a drug. The nutritional aspect of alcohol is an important determinant of voluntary consumption, reviewed in the present chapter; the physiological effects of prolonged intake, discussed in Chapter 9, are largely due to nutritional actions. Voluntary consumption is also influenced by the odor and taste of alcohol and of the other fluid or fluids in which it is diluted.

Experiments on voluntary selection of alcohol constitute the most recent of the major areas of research reviewed in these two volumes. For several decades after the original report (Richter, 1926), this research technique was very seldom used. A thorough review of the topic by Mardones (1960) contained a total of 54 bibliographical references; a subsequent, general review of alcohol effects (Mardones, 1963) included some further references on "appetancy for ethanol." Since 1961, publications on this topic have accelerated, as noted in a review by Lester (1966). Some of the topics have been included in a review by Schuster and Thompson (1969). Good information on various aspects of alcohol selection is also available in reviews by Rodgers and McClearn (1962a) and Rodgers (1967), in a series of articles in an issue of *Psychosomatic Medicine* devoted to the topic of alcoholism (Forsander, 1966; Mello and Mendelson, 1966; Myers, 1966; Rodgers, 1966; Schlesinger *et al.*, 1966), and in a monograph by Eriksson (1969a).

Most of the experiments reviewed in this chapter were well designed and conducted on an adequate number of subjects, perhaps due to their prevalent recency. However, in most cases the value of the information is impaired by ambiguity and incompleteness of the information on alcohol intake. The beverage is usually described in terms of the percentage alcohol concentration, but many experimenters fail to specify whether the alcohol percentage was in terms of volume (v/v) or weight (w/v). Barry and Wallgren (1968) pointed out that the same percentage solution contains 25% more alcohol calculated on a w/v than on a v/v basis. A more frequent ambiguity, which fortunately has a smaller potential for error, is whether the percentage is in terms of 95% alcohol or 100% (absolute) alcohol. Mardones (1960) stated that the reported percentage alcohol usually refers to v/v in relation to the 95% concentration which is generally the undiluted fluid. However, not all experimenters adhere to these meanings, and it is unfortunate that they do not all give the information needed for accurate specification of the amount of alcohol in the fluid. A more prevalent and serious omission is the information on the amount of alcohol consumed. In tests of a choice between alcohol and water, some experimenters report the consumption of alcohol as a percentage of total fluid, without providing information on the quantity of alcohol intake. Most experimenters fail to report the average body weight of the animals, which is needed for calculating the daily intake in g/kg and relating this figure to acute alcohol effects and metabolic capacity. It is also desirable to report intake of solid food in order to compare this measure with the caloric intake in the form of alcohol, but most experimenters do not use the nonspillable containers necessary for recording food consumption. In the present chapter, alcohol consumption is described when possible in terms of g alcohol/kg body weight/day in order to enhance comparability with the measure of alcohol dose used in the other chapters. Unfortunately, most of the published data limit the description to g alcohol/day.

A. Characteristics of the beverages

The most frequently used choice procedure is to provide a continuous supply of solid food and two bottles of fluid, one containing alcohol and the other without alcohol. Experiments on the effects of different concentrations of alcohol solution provide the basic data on alcohol intake as a function of the quantity of fluid the animal must consume to obtain a particular dose of alcohol. Another type of variation in the test situation is to provide a multiple choice among several alcohol concentrations or to provide a third fluid in addition to water and an alcohol solution. The choice between an alcoholic and nonalcoholic beverage may also be affected by additional substances included in one or both fluids.

(1) Concentration of alcohol

In a choice between alcohol and water, most experimenters have characterized the animal's behavior as preference or aversion for alcohol, depending on whether consumption of the alcohol solution was more or less than half the total intake from both bottles. However, reports of the fluid intake from both the alcohol and water bottle have usually enabled calculation of the amount of alcohol intake in grams per day. A number of experimental

References p. 468

findings give evidence that the amount of alcohol voluntarily consumed by the animal remains highly stable with different concentrations of alcohol and under other conditions which alter the amount of fluid intake.

Fig. 8–1 summarizes findings of three different reports, in normal rats under normal choice conditions, on percentage of fluid consumption from the alcohol rather than water bottle (*top graph*) and alcohol intake in g/ day (*bottom graph*). In each study the animals were tested with progressively increasing concentrations. Kahn and Stellar (1960) reported on a group of 12 rats, Goodrick (1967) on a total of 80 rats divided among 6 ages (1–24 months), and Myers and Holman (1967) on a group of seven rats. In each of these studies, alcohol was preferred at low concentrations, but the high concentrations caused an apparent aversion for alcohol. The amount of alcohol intake per day progressively increased as the concentrations rose

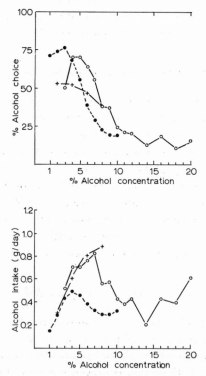

Fig. 8–1. Choice between water and progressively increasing alcohol concentrations in three experiments on rats. ●– –●, Kahn and Stellar (1960); +––+, Goodrick (1967); ○——○, Myers and Holman (1967).

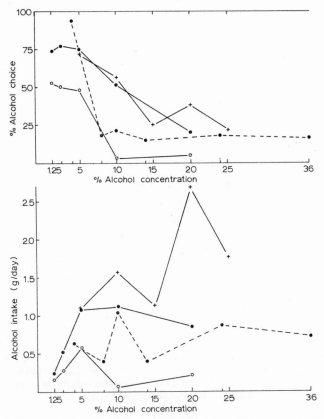

Fig. 8–2. Choice between water and several alcohol concentrations tested in different groups of rats in three experiments. ● – – – ●, Hausmann (1932); + —— +, Mendelson and Mello (1964); ●——●, Myers (1962) G-4 strain; ○——○, Myers (1962) Wistar strain.

above the initial, lowest levels, but contrary to the data on percentage alcohol choice there was no consistent decrease in the amount of consumption at the highest alcohol concentrations. Fig. 8–2 summarizes in the same manner findings of three studies in which different groups of rats were used for tests of the choice between water and different alcohol concentrations. The data reported by Hausmann (1932) are for the initial 10-day choice test with one rat at each concentration. Myers (1962) gave a single 22-hour test in a novel environment, comparing a Wistar albino strain with a G–4 nonalbino strain of rats; the data shown are for 8 animals of each strain tested at each alcohol concentration, averaging results with two environ-

References p. 468

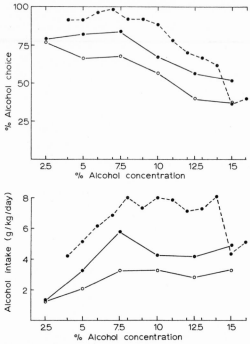

Fig. 8–3. Choice between water and several alcohol concentrations tested in different groups of rats in two experiments which included data on alcohol intake in g/kg/day. ● – – ●, Dicker (1958); ●——●, Eriksson (1969) heavy-drinking strain; ○——○, Eriksson (1969) light-drinking strain.

mental temperatures (18° and 27 °C). Mendelson and Mello (1964) tested groups of four albino rats, each with a choice between a single concentration of alcohol and water for 99 consecutive days. In common with the results shown in Figure 1, high concentrations caused apparent avoidance of alcohol, measured by percentage of alcohol choice, but no consistent change in amount of alcohol intake.

Although the groups of animals shown in Figs. 8–1 and 8–2 differed widely in amount of alcohol consumption, each group stabilized at a fairly consistent average quantity when the alcohol concentration was sufficiently high to permit this consumption with a normal amount of total fluid intake. It would be interesting to compare their daily amount of voluntary alcohol consumption with the daily metabolic capability in the rat, which averages approximately 7.2 g/kg/day (Chapter 2, Table 7). Unfortunately, these experimenters did not provide the information on body weight of the animals.

Assuming that the average body weight was approximately 300 grams, the asymptotic daily intake of about 2 g/day in one of the studies (Mendelson and Mello, 1964) signified more than 6 g/kg/day, a level which is close to the average maximal capacity to metabolize the drug. Fig. 8–3 shows both the percentage alcohol choice and the alcohol consumption in g/kg/day in two studies which included the information needed for these calculations. Dicker (1958) gave 8 rats an ascending series of alcohol concentrations, with one to four days at each concentration. Their maximal alcohol consumption was close to the metabolic capability in rats. Eriksson (1969a) tested six concentrations in a random sequence, each for four days, in 24 rats divided into two strains selected and bred for several generations for high and low consumption. Data reported on male and female rats of each strain are averaged together. Alcohol consumption was somewhat below the metabolic capacity, even in the drinker strain, especially as the metabolic capacity of these rats was found to be at the unusually high level of approximately 9.6 g/kg/day (Eriksson and Malmström, 1967).

Other findings also give evidence that the amount of alcohol consumption remains fairly constant when the alcohol concentration is high enough so that the animal can obtain its preferred daily quantity of alcohol with a normal amount of total fluid intake. Assuming a constant amount of total fluid intake, data reported by Cicero and Myers (1969) on average alcohol choice as percentage of total fluid intake by six rats, with alcohol concentrations from 2 to 30%, indicate a fairly constant amount of alcohol intake, with a tendency for an increase rather than decrease as concentration increased from 12% to 30%. Marfaing-Jallat (1964), in a comparison of 15 drinker with 15 nondrinker rats each given four-day tests of choice between water and an ascending series of alcohol concentrations, reported that for both groups of rats the alcohol choice in relation to total fluid intake was approximately one-third as high for the 15.8% concentration as for the 5% concentration. Thomas (1969), in an experiment on two strains of mice, likewise showed a decrease in percentage alcohol choice to about one-third the former level when the alcohol concentration was increased from 10% to 30%. A drastic decrease in alcohol choice resulting from a small increase in concentration may be characteristic of some individuals, or groups of animals under some conditions, but this behavior pattern in a "typical" rat shown by Richter (1941) and in one of three rats reported by Cicero and Myers (1968) might be attributable to the tendency for experimenters to select such clear-cut responses as typical instances.

References p. 468

It is evident that the measure of amount of alcohol intake is more stable at different concentrations than the measure of alcohol choice as a percentage of total fluid intake. Amount of intake in g/day or preferably g/kg/day has the further advantage of closer correspondence to other measures of alcohol dose. Variations in this quantitative measure are likely to conform satisfactorily to the normal distribution of scores, whereas percentage alcohol choice is limited to the range of scores between 0 and 100%. Brewster (1968, 1969) reported on the use of an arc–sine transformation of scores for percentage alcohol choice so that the values close to 0 and 100% would have variances similar to the values close to 50%. The general problem of alcohol consumption as a function of concentration has been discussed by Myers and Eriksson (1968). In several studies the amount of alcohol intake has been shown to be fairly constant with a wide range of concentrations at about 7.5% and above, so that a single alcohol concentration may suffice for comparing different strains or other experimentally varied conditions. Most of the studies reviewed later in this chapter provided a choice between water and a single alcohol concentration, usually 10%. Comparison of several different concentrations multiplies the number of animals which must be tested or the amount of time required for the tests. However, the demonstrations of a constant amount of alcohol intake, regardless of the concentration, have mostly been limited to one species (the rat) and to a certain set of test conditions, in a choice between water and an alcohol solution.

(2) Multiple and alternative choices

In several studies the animals were given a choice among several concentrations of alcohol instead of only one. Eriksson (1969a) used this multiple-choice procedure in the same heavy-drinking and light-drinking rats whose choice between water and a single alcohol concentration is shown in Fig. 8–3. The results of the multiple-choice procedure, tested subsequently, are shown in Fig. 8–4. In both strains the total consumption from all the alcohol bottles greatly exceeded the consumption from the water bottle. The drinker strain showed greater preference for the higher alcohol concentrations measured by percentage choice. However, the measure of alcohol intake shows a rather stable amount at alcohol concentrations between 7.5 and 12.5%. The total amount of intake from the five bottles of alcohol solutions averaged 4.9 g/kg/day for the drinker strain and 2.9

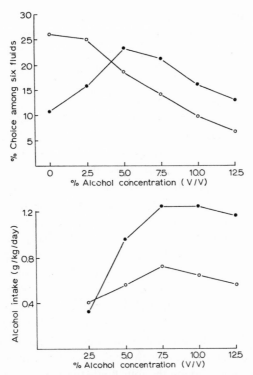

Fig. 8–4. Concurrent choice between water and several alcohol concentrations in a heavy-drinking and light-drinking strain of rats. ●——●, heavy-drinking strain; ○——○, light-drinking strain. (Eriksson, 1969a)

g/kg/day for the nondrinker strain. These amounts agree very closely with the intake of 4.9 g/kg/day by the drinker strain and 3.3 g/kg/day by the nondrinker strain shown in Fig. 8–3 for the choice between water and a 7.5% alcohol solution (the midpoint of the five choices between 2.5 and 12.5%).

Uniformity of alcohol intake with different concentrations has not been found in tests of multiple choice with other species. A few studies with mice have also been conducted with several different concentrations of alcohol presented simultaneously. Rodgers and McClearn (1962b) offered mice, housed in groups, a choice among seven fluids: water and alcohol concentrations ranging from 2.5 to 15%. Two strains of mice drank similar proportions of liquid from all of the bottles, which means an increasing amount consumed with increased concentrations. The other two strains consumed very little from any of the alcohol bottles. Fuller (1964), in a study of four strains of mice and six hybrid combinations, housed in groups, offered a choice among six alcohol concentrations, ranging from 0.5 to 16%. Strains with low alcohol preference appeared to drink approximately a constant amount in g/day from each bottle, whereas strains with high alcohol preference consumed progressively more in g/day as the concentration increased. Arvola and Forsander (1963) conducted both two-choice and multiple-choice tests on male and female hamsters. Fig. 8–5 shows the comparison between the two types of test, with the two sexes averaged together. With increasing concentrations, alcohol intake in g/day progressively increased in the two-choice tests but decreased in the multiple-choice test. The average intake of 1.3 g/day in the multiple-choice test was substantially higher than in any of the two-choice tests. The animals were housed in groups in the multiple-choice tests and individually in the two-choice tests, but this difference would be expected to have the opposite effects on alcohol consumption according to data reviewed later in this chapter (pp. 418–419). Data reported by Anderson and Smith (1963), on choice by monkeys among water and three alcohol concentrations (5, 10, 20%), indicated that the decreasing percentage choice of higher concentrations resulted in a closely similar amount of alcohol consumption from the three alcohol cups in a series of tests with small amounts of fluid offered, but in continuous free choice among the four fluids the monkeys drank very little of the 20% solution.

A technique for determining the amount of alcohol consumed in preference to other attractive alternatives is to provide a third fluid, containing sucrose or some other substance, in addition to water and an alcohol solution. Lester and Greenberg (1952) reported that a sucrose solution of 11.5% w/v as the third choice greatly reduced consumption of a 10% alcohol solution by rats. A third choice of a non-nutritive, sweet-tasting substance (saccharin) or a liquid fat solution decreased alcohol intake by about 50%, which was a smaller effect. However, some other experimenters have found smaller effects of a third solution consisting of a sugar solution. Mardones *et al.* (1955) found that alcohol consumption by rats was decreased approximately 50% by a third choice of 10–70% sucrose or 10 or 30% glucose. When a solution of B vitamins was offered as a third choice, a large quantity was consumed but there was no significant effect on alcohol intake. Parisella and Pritham (1964) found that rats consumed a large quantity of 8% alcohol, in spite of a third choice of 10% sucrose. The alcohol intake by one of

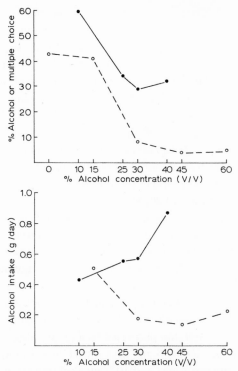

Fig. 8–5. Choice between water and a single alcohol concentration compared with choice between water and several alcohol concentrations in hamsters. ●——●, two choice; ○ – – – ○, multiple choice. (Arvola and Forsander, 1963)

their groups (3–4 months old) averaged 8.2 g/kg/day, and more than 50% of the total fluid consumption was from the alcohol bottle. In mice, Iida (1960) found that consumption of a 15% alcohol solution was decreased by a third choice of glucose, fructose, and sucrose but not other sugars. However, interpretation of the results is complicated by the fact that elevated alcohol consumption was induced by pretreatment with carbon tetrachloride. Rodgers and McClearn (1964) reported that a strain of mice (C57BL) showed a marked preference for a 15% sucrose solution over water and a 10% alcohol solution, but their daily alcohol intake under this condition (1.2 ml of the 10% solution) was at the fairly high level of 3.2 g/kg, assuming an average body weight of 30 g. In general, most of these studies show that animals continue to consume substantial quantities of alcohol even when an attractive third choice is available.

References p. 468

(3) Additional components of the fluids

In a choice between water and an alcohol solution, the two fluids differ from each other with respect to taste, pharmacological effects, and caloric value. The effects of these characteristics on the choice of alcohol have been tested and to some degree specified by experiments in which other substances were added to one or both fluids.

Eriksson (1969a) tested for 40 days the choice between a 10% alcohol solution and water in 72 rats, equally divided between heavy-drinking and light-drinking strains. He showed that alcohol consumption was increased by experimental variations in the taste of the alternative fluids, either adding a non-nutritive sweet substance (0.0034% saccharin) to the alcohol or adding a bitter substance (0.002% quinine sulfate) to the water. Both treatments combined had a greater effect on alcohol choice than either one alone. These effects were similar in both strains, and the heavy-drinking strain reached a peak choice of 93–95% of their fluid from the alcohol bottle. Their daily alcohol intake of 12–14 g/kg appeared to exceed the average metabolic capacity for this strain (Eriksson and Malmström, 1967). The total amount of fluid consumption remained rather stable, but it was increased by the addition of saccharin to the alcohol and decreased to a greater degree by the addition of quinine to the water. Rodgers and McClearn (1964) reported that in mice, tested for choice between water and 10% alcohol, increasing concentrations of sucrose added to the alcohol (2–16%) progressively increased the amount of alcohol consumed. A similar effect was found in nine strains, differing in baseline alcohol choice. Assuming a body weight of 30 g, the nine mouse strains averaged together consumed 11.2 g/kg/day in a 16% sucrose solution, which is close to the metabolic capacity in the mouse of 13.2 g/kg/day (Chapter 2, Table 7). One of the strains (C57BL) consumed 18.7 g/kg/day, although studies reviewed later in the present chapter (p. 435) indicate little difference among strains in rate of alcohol metabolism. In a subsequent experiment, Rodgers et al. (1967) reported that after 50 weeks of choice between water and the combination of 10% alcohol with 16% sucrose, consumption of sweetened alcohol reached even higher levels. The C57BL/10J strain consumed 24.5 g/kg/day, assuming 30 g body weight. In both experiments, a limiting effect of metabolic capability for alcohol is suggested by the finding that in a choice between water and 16% sucrose, the animals drank much larger quantities of the sucrose solution when alcohol was not included in it.

The joint effects of alcohol and another substance on choice can be studied more precisely when the alternative fluid contains the other substance without alcohol. Dethier (1961) found that in a choice between a solution of 0.4% sucrose and both the sucrose and ethanol, blowflies drank more of the solution containing alcohol in concentration of 0.004% to 4%. Anosmic blowflies did not show this preference for the ethanol solution, and at higher alcohol concentrations all the insects preferred the sucrose solution without ethanol. Several experimenters have tested choice between an alcohol solution and water with 1% salt added to both fluids (Iida, 1957; Zarrow et al., 1960; Aschkenasy-Lelu, 1965). Forsander et al. (1958), in a test of effects of Nadisan, added the same amount of this drug to both the alcohol solution and water. Mirone (1959) tested effects of various spices added to the drinking fluid of male and female mice given water or a 10% alcohol solution as the only fluid. The data indicated that the addition of cloves (0.005%), anise oil (0.001%) and nutmeg (0.001%) decreased consumption of water but increased consumption of alcohol.

Mendelson and Mello (1964), in an experiment on long-term choice between water and several alcohol concentrations, included in Fig. 8–2, tested the reasonable hypothesis that alcohol might be more delectable to rats if presented in the form of beverages customarily drunk by humans instead of in a water solution. Groups of animals given a choice between water and bourbon whisky, diluted to the concentrations of 5–25%, did not differ consistently in consumption from the groups which chose between water and the same alcohol concentrations in water. In tests of a choice between ethanol in water and diluted bourbon whisky, the same animals generally preferred the ethanol in water. Aschkenasy-Lelu (1958) found that a group of 12 rats given a choice between 5% alcohol in the form of red wine and water drank less alcohol than a group of 12 rats given a choice between 5% ethanol and water. Similarly, Aschkenasy-Lelu (1960b) showed that rats preferred a 10% ethanol solution to the same alcohol concentration in the form of wine. Richter (1953) showed comparisons between female rats which received 8%, 10%, or 24% alcohol in water as their sole fluid and male rats which received wine (12.5% alcohol) or beer (4.4% alcohol) as their sole fluid. A much larger amount of fluid was consumed in the form of beer than wine, but the two groups were closely similar in weight gain and in caloric intake, both from dry food and from their alcoholic fluid. The 8% and 10% alcohol solutions appeared to have effects closely similar to those of the wine, but in addition to the sex differences the animals differed in age and in duration of the experimental procedure.

References. p. 468

B. Other determinants of alcohol consumption

Alcohol concentration and the components of the fluids are only some of the most obvious determinants of alcohol consumption in choice tests. The present section reviews several determinants of alcohol consumption not included in the other sections of this chapter. This portion of the review begins with a discussion of methodological variables which should be controlled in all experiments on voluntary alcohol consumption. A review of attempts to induce voluntary intoxication presents information on a topic of special importance because of its clinical application to the development of addictive drinking in human alcoholics. A summary of effects of prior exposure to alcohol likewise may provide evidence concerning the development of tolerance and dependence on alcohol. The final topic of this section, detectability of alcohol solutions, provides information on the influence of the taste and odor of alcohol on voluntary consumption in a choice situation.

(1) Techniques and variables in choice tests

The positions of the alcohol and water bottles may influence the consumption of the fluids. Gillespie and Lucas (1958) reported that for 80% of the rats tested, the choice between water and a 15% alcohol solution was influenced by the positions of the two liquids. The few animals which did not show a position preference were for the most part the ones which drank the smallest quantities of alcohol. The liquids tended to be preferred when partially separated from the food bin by a partition, rather than adjacent to the food. Kahn (1969) has reported that in mice, given a choice between water and a 3% alcohol solution, alcohol consumption was generally affected by position preference. It is desirable to place the liquids symmetrically, not only with respect to the food but also with respect to other distinctive features of the environment, including illumination and exposure to the room. Albino rats prefer the fluid in the darker location and at the back of the cage. A less commonly recognized form of preference is between different drinking tubes, presumably due to differences in width of aperture, reported by Korn (1960). Systematic alternation of tubes, independently of positions of the two liquids, was reported by Korn (1960) and by Kahn and Stellar (1960).

Many experimenters interchange the positions of the water and alcohol solutions every day. This procedure eliminates error due to position preference but has the disadvantage that the animal must relearn the positions of the fluids every day. Korn (1960) reported higher alcohol consumption by rats whose alcohol solutions were always presented in the same location and drinking tube than by rats given both the alcohol solution and water in the two locations and drinking tubes according to a daily randomized sequence. Since fluid intake is generally recorded once a day, it is necessary to keep the fluids in the same positions for two days in order to obtain data on the effect of the change in position on the animal's choice. Some experimenters change the positions of the fluids only once every several days (McClearn and Rodgers, 1959, 1961) or once a week (Eriksson, 1969a).

An important procedural control, when two or more animals are tested, is for the equivalent cage position to be the location of alcohol for half the animals and of water for the others. Richter (1941) established an equal choice between two water bottles, followed by tests in which one of the bottles, always in the same position, was changed to an alcohol solution. This may lead to ambiguous findings, because the animal might respond to the change in the contents of a bottle in a particular position, perhaps selecting it because of curiosity or else avoiding it because of fear of the novel substance. Myers and Holman (1966) attempted to minimize position preference by including a third, empty bottle, so that the water and alcohol bottles could be shifted among three positions. However, any decrease in position preference attained by this procedure would probably be due to confusing the animal rather than improving validity of the choice. A more effective use of three bottles to test stability of choice would be to present water in two bottles with alcohol in the third bottle for half the animals and alcohol in two bottles with water in the third bottle for the other animals.

Most experimenters ignore the potential error due to loss of fluid by spillage, evaporation, and change in air pressure. In an experiment reported by Fuller (1964), the tubes were kept as full of fluid as possible in order to minimize the amount pumped out by changes in atmospheric pressure. Measurements of fluid in water bottles attached to empty cages revealed an average loss of 0.1 ml per tube per day, and the reported data were corrected by this constant value. However, this procedure does not detect spilling of fluid due to jiggling of the tube by the animal. In a study of choice by hamsters between water and a single alcohol solution, Arvola and Forsander (1963) reported rather large amounts of fluid loss. A much higher percentage of 25–40% alcohol was spilled than of 10% alcohol or water.

Average spillage ranged from 22% to 52% with these higher alcohol concentrations. In a multiple-choice experiment, Rodgers and McClearn (1962b) reported that loss by leakage and evaporation varied between 0 and 1 ml per cylinder per day. In two strains of mice the recorded consumption of the various alcohol concentrations, varying between 0.3 and 1.0 ml per day, could have been due entirely to these factors. It is obviously important to fasten the bottles securely in order to minimize fluid loss due to jiggling. Evaporation can be minimized by the use of a narrow opening at the end of the tube, and leakage can be minimized by placing the opening at the top of the receptacle, in the form of a cup rather than a spout. A tube with these characteristics has been described by Eriksson (1969a).

Since environmental temperature has definite effects on food and water consumption, it would be reasonable to expect effects on alcohol intake. Eriksson (1969a) tested effects of three environmental temperatures (5, 22, 32 °C), each for a two-week period, on choice by rats among water, 5% alcohol and 10% alcohol. Warmer temperatures increased fluid and decreased food intake. The highest temperature caused less increase in alcohol than water intake, and increasing temperature also enhanced preference for 5% in comparison with 10% alcohol. These findings suggest a greater relative preference for alcohol in a cold environment. Further evidence for this effect is a brief report by Emerson et al. (1952) that hamsters consumed more alcohol in extreme cold and less in extreme heat. Also, Zarrow et al. (1960) found that cold temperature of 2–5 °C increased choice of 10% alcohol, although even under this condition a fluid choice of glucose was preferred to alcohol. Contrary to these findings, Myers (1962), in an experiment included in Fig. 8–2, reported less alcohol consumption by rats tested in a cold environment (18 °C) than in a hot environment (27 °C). However, these temperatures were only slightly outside the range of comfort and the test was a single, 22-h session in a novel situation. It seems likely that the effects of temperature on alcohol intake are mediated by the dietary and metabolic reactions to the temperature.

An important aspect of the animal's environment is its housing condition, whether isolated or aggregated, spacious or crowded. There have been very few experimental tests of effects of these conditions on alcohol consumption. Rats have usually been housed individually whereas mice have usually been housed in groups during choice tests. Rodgers and Thiessen (1964), in a comparison between aggregated and isolated mice, found that aggregation decreased water consumption and thus increased alcohol preference measured by percentage of total fluid consumption, but the amount of alcohol intake remained constant. This gives further evidence for the conclusion, stated earlier in this chapter, that the measure of amount of alcohol intake, independent of the amount of fluid consumption, has the advantage of greater stability. Wilson (1969) reported more consumption of a 5.5% alcohol solution by rats housed alone rather than in groups, but the difference was rather small. Brown (1968) found more consumption of a 5% alcohol solution by mice housed individually rather than in groups of four.

The method and conditions of presentation of alcohol solutions, and the measurements and expressions of amounts consumed, should be considered carefully in relation to the aims of the study, whether metabolic, pharmacological, or behavioral. For instance, genetic study requires a reproducible measure of the phenotype whereas psychological or physiological analysis may be furthered by identification of environmental conditions or physiological changes which alter drinking.

(2) Attempts to induce voluntary intoxication

Comprehensive study of the addictive behavior of chronic, excessive alcohol consumption would be facilitated if a behavioral pattern resembling that of human alcoholics could be elicited in laboratory animals. In spite of widespread recognition of this research need, and many attempts to accomplish it, little evidence has been reported on the development of addictive voluntary alcohol consumption in laboratory animals. Failure to induce addictive drinking has been emphasized in reviews by Mardones (1960, 1963), Lester (1966) and Barry (1968). Animals generally avoid the repeated intoxications over a prolonged time period which appear necessary for development of dependence on alcohol. Chapter 9 of the present volume (p. 508) mentions the difficulty of inducing the withdrawal state in animals and refers to reports on self-administration of drugs by infusion. Deneau et al. (1969) have recently reported that monkeys chronically self-infused alcohol in daily amounts up to 8.6 g/kg. Periods of abstinence for several days were characteristic in spite of severe withdrawal symptoms, in contrast to steady, addictive self-infusion of morphine and pentobarbital.

A variety of ingenious procedures have been used to induce animals to consume large quantities of alcohol, and they may be important in showing conditions under which alcohol consumption is increased, even if only on a short-term basis, as well as providing useful information for future attempts to induce addictive drinking. Large daily quantities of alcohol are consumed by animals whose sole source of fluid is an alcohol solution. Chapter 9 (p. 482 and Table 9–1) reviews a number of studies in which this procedure was used. Although animals are willing to consume alcohol up to the limit of their metabolic capacity before curtailing their fluid intake, they apparently avoid intoxication. The normal mode of drinking water is to take small sips at frequent intervals, and this behavior pattern is accentuated when the drinking fluid is an alcohol solution. Sohler *et al.* (1969) observed this effect in rats given a 40% alcohol solution as their sole fluid. Another adaptive response of these animals was to lick the fluid at a considerable distance from the tip of the tube, allowing considerable evaporation of alcohol when the drop of fluid remained there for several minutes.

A source of error in reports on alcohol consumption is indicated in a comment by Sohler *et al.* (1969) that if the fluid consumed by the rats had contained 40% ethanol, the alcohol intake would have been at the impossibly high level of 24 g/kg/day, whereas blood alcohol levels were only about 0.02%. Lester and Greenberg (1952) reported that under choice conditions which resulted in consumption of large amounts of alcohol, the blood levels in their rats averaged only 0.0065%, with a range from zero to 0.031%. In unpublished observations by one of the present authors (H.W.), the maximum blood alcohol levels in a choice situation reached the much higher level of 0.12%. Unfortunately, blood alcohol levels have seldom been measured in experiments on voluntary alcohol consumption.

The quantity of alcohol consumption can be enhanced when sucrose is added to the alcohol solution, as in some experiments reviewed earlier in the present chapter. Various types of physiological pathology, resembling symptoms of human alcoholics, have been found in mice or rats after prolonged consumption of a sweetened alcohol solution as their sole fluid (Rodgers *et al.*, 1967; Porta *et al.*, 1969) or in a choice between the sweetened alcohol solution and water (Rodgers *et al.*, 1967). However, even in these cases acute intoxication has not been reported.

A more effective technique for inducing intoxication is to deprive the animal of fluid except for a limited period, such as one hour per day, during which the alcohol solution is available. Newman and Lehman (1938) demonstrated development of tolerance in dogs forced to drink intoxicating quantities of alcohol by this technique (Chapter 9, p. 499). However, thirsty rats tend to reduce their fluid intake rather than accept intoxicating quantities of alcohol (J. H. Mendelson, *personal communication*). In an unpublished experiment by one of the present authors (H.W.), chicks which ordinarily drink water by filling their crop were given an alcohol solution. They rapidly learned to avoid this habitual behavior and instead drank small quantities of the fluid after their initial experience of filling their crop with an intoxicating dose. Terroine and Rochette (1946) reported that after deprivation of all nourishment for two days, rats given a choice between water and a 10% alcohol solution consumed large amounts of alcohol but showed no evidence of inebriation. Enhanced consumption of an alcohol solution was induced in rats by deprivation of liquid or food or both, in a number of experiments reviewed later in the present chapter (pp. 448–450). However, intoxicating effects have seldom been observed in these situations.

One of the most promising techniques for inducing voluntary alcohol intoxication is to use an experimental schedule in which hungry animals, which are rewarded for lever pressing by the occasional delivery of a dry food pellet, will drink large quantities of fluid if it is available. Lester (1961), by making a 5.6% w/v alcohol solution the only fluid available in this situation, induced nine rats to consume sufficient alcohol to become definitely intoxicated, with blood alcohol levels reaching 0.2%. Freed (1968) reported that five rats drank sufficient quantities of a 5.6% w/v alcohol solution during a one-hour session with this procedure to give rise to blood alcohol levels ranging from 0.10 to 0.25%. Holman and Myers (1968) reported that six rats consumed approximately 1 g/kg in a 3.5-h test session, which should be sufficient for intoxicating effects. In accordance with data reviewed earlier in the present chapter, the amount of alcohol intake remained approximately the same in a series of daily tests with progressively increasing alcohol concentrations from 3% to 20%. The high alcohol consumption was apparently due largely to the food intake and the availability of an alcohol solution as the sole fluid rather than the schedule of food presentation, because in a subsequent test of the same rats, given the entire food ration at the beginning of the 3.5-h session, alcohol intake was about half the former quantity in tests with low concentrations and equal to the former quantity in tests with high concentrations. The animals apparently learned to avoid extreme intoxication, according to a further finding in a subgroup of 3 rats, given the same alcohol concentration in their home cage as in the test situation. As the alcohol concentration increased on successive days, these animals drank progressively more during the 20.5 h in the home cage, in relation to their consumption during the 3.5-h test session.

Several experimenters have trained rats to drink ethanol as a means of obtaining food reward or relief from punishment. Mello and Mendelson (1964, 1965) induced rats to consume substantial quantities of an alcohol solution when the reward of milk was earned by licking the tube of the alcohol bottle many times at a fast rate. Keehn (1969) trained four hungry rats to drink a 10% (w/v) alcohol solution in order to obtain food. Alcohol consumption was high under this condition and also in subsequent sessions in which food was delivered at regular intervals. In one instance, an alcohol consumption of 4.6 g/kg during a 30-minute session was shown to give rise to a blood alcohol concentration of 0.21% at 15 min after the session. However, the consumption was due to a desire for fluid rather than for the alcohol, because in tests with a saccharin solution also available, this was preferred almost to the exclusion of the alcohol solution. Senter and Persensky (1968) trained 14 rats, while deprived of food and liquid, to drink a 7% alcohol solution in response to a warning signal in order to avoid painful shock and obtain a food pellet. In 14 subsequent days of choice between water and 7% alcohol solution, without food deprivation, choice of alcohol as percentage of total fluid intake was higher in a group of seven rats which remained in the test apparatus, with continuing presentation of the warning signal but shocks omitted, than in a group of seven rats returned to their home cages. Unfortunately, the authors did not report the amount of alcohol consumed either in the training or test stage. Ramsay and Van Dis (1967) trained three rats to escape and avoid painful shock by drinking a 10% alcohol solution in milk. The amount of alcohol consumption during 30–45 min test sessions varied from 0.8 to 2.5 g/kg. This experimental report differed from most of the others not only by providing information on alcohol intake in g/kg but also by including the observation that the animals showed signs of drunkenness.

In general, large amounts of voluntary alcohol consumption can be induced by a variety of methods. Animals appear to avoid intoxication, so that the voluntary, repeated drunkenness found in many humans is difficult to reproduce in laboratory animals. However, intoxication would be expected from the large amounts of alcohol consumption reported in some of the experiments. Some of the techniques for measuring intoxication, reviewed in Chapter 7, could profitably be used in these experiments. A commendable instance of this was the use of the tilted plane test by Sohler *et al.* (1969).

(3) Prior exposure to alcohol

Since animals are wary of drinking novel, strong-tasting fluids, prior exposure to alcohol may be expected to increase the amount consumed in choice tests. Therefore, experimenters should provide a habituation period or else continue the choice test long enough to allow the consumption to stabilize. Studies of the effects of prior exposure to alcohol may identify this effect and provide useful information to experimenters about the duration and type of habituation required. A further aspect of such studies, with important clinical implications, is the possibility that prolonged exposure to alcohol may give rise to tolerance and habituation, indicated by an increase in voluntary consumption of the alcohol solution.

Richter (1957b) stated that rats which had previously avoided a 10% alcohol solution would nearly always drink moderate amounts in choice between alcohol and water, after a few days in which alcohol was the only fluid available. A systematic test of this effect was reported by Eriksson (1969a). A group of 10 rats given a 5% alcohol solution as the only fluid for 10 days drank more alcohol in subsequent choice tests between the 5% alcohol solution and water than two groups of 10 rats which had been given the choice during the prior 10 days also. The difference between these groups remained stable throughout 20 days. An initial period of an alcohol solution as the only fluid was routinely used by Eriksson (1969a) as a means of obtaining a stable and high level of alcohol consumption. Longer durations of exposure to alcohol as the sole fluid also increase alcohol consumption in subsequent choice tests. Parisella and Pritham (1964) found that rats given an alcohol solution rather than water for four weeks drank more alcohol in subsequent testing of choice among 8% alcohol, 15% sucrose, and water. The difference was more consistent at the end than at the beginning of four weeks of choice tests. Further evidence for this effect is found in rats (Myers and Holman, 1967) and in chimpanzees (Fitz-Gerald et al., 1968).

The effect appears to be enhanced when the prior exposure is at an early age or for a prolonged duration. Clay (1964) found a higher percentage of alcohol choice in rats which received an alcohol solution as their sole fluid from weaning (at 19 days of age) until the choice tests began at 60 days of age. Rodgers and McClearn (1962a) showed a similar effect in mice, although the increase in alcohol consumption above that of control animals developed only in some individuals. In two separate experiments on mice,

References p. 468

Mirone (1952, 1958) found the same effect of post-weaning exposure to alcohol and also gave evidence for the same effect of pre-weaning exposure to alcohol by the further finding of higher alcohol consumption in choice tests by progeny of alcohol-fed than of water-fed parents. Aschkenasy-Lelu (1960b) reported more consumption of a 10% alcohol solution in choice tests of rats which had received the same alcohol solution rather than water as their sole drinking fluid for the preceding five months. Wallgren and Forsander (1963) found much more consumption of a 10% alcohol solution in choice tests of rats at two and a half years of age after one year of receiving the same alcohol solution rather than water as their sole fluid.

Prior exposure to alcohol also increases alcohol consumption when the animals have been deprived of food and fluid at the time of the choice test. Myers (1961a) trained rats to press three levers for food, water, and an alcohol solution. Animals given a 5% alcohol solution rather than water for 10, 30, or 90 previous days pressed the lever for a 5% alcohol solution more often in the 1-h choice tests. Myers and Carey (1961), in a similar test with an increased or decreased alcohol concentration each day, found greater preference for the alcohol lever in rats whose fluid had been restricted to a 5% or 20% alcohol solution for 120 rather than 30 previous days. With the use of a novel technique for pretreating the animals with alcohol, Myers (1963) found that 10 days of infusion of minute quantities of ethanol ($1-3\mu l$ of a 5% or 10% solution) into the cerebral ventricles, once every 15 min, increased the rat's choice of the lever which delivered an alcohol solution. This effect increased progressively with higher quantities infused and persisted for at least several days after the ethanol infusion was discontinued. The maximum quantity of alcohol administered (less than 0.1 g/kg in a rat weighing 300 g) was negligible metabolically and systemically, but the concentration at the site of infusion would probably have reached temporarily a level as high as 0.3%. Myers (1966) showed the amount of alcohol consumed in grams during the choice tests. Assuming a body weight of 300 grams, average alcohol intake reached an intoxicating level of over 2 g/kg from a 20–30% solution after infusion of 3 μl of a 10% solution every 15 min. However, Koz and Mendelson (1967) found no effect of intraventricular ethanol infusion on alcohol consumption by two monkeys, given free access to the 10% alcohol solution, water, and food throughout.

Senter et al. (1968) found little change in percentage choice of a 6% alcohol solution by 20 rats during 26 weeks beginning at three and a half months of age, but a progressive increase in alcohol consumption, during

repeated or continued choice tests, has been reported by several experimenters in rats (Moore *et al.*, 1952a; Powell *et al.*, 1966; Eriksson and Malmström, 1967; Veale and Myers, 1969) and in mice (Rodgers and McClearn,
1962a). In the absence of an appropriate control group, this change could
be attributed to the effects of advancing age, increased duration of exposure
to alcohol, or general habituation to the test situation. Experiments on
effects of age, reviewed later in this chapter (p. 444), generally show
decreased alcohol consumption by older animals. It is plausible although
not proven that the increase in alcohol consumption during choice tests
represents a further effect of exposure to ethanol.

Although an increase in voluntary alcohol consumption due to prior
exposure to this drug has been demonstrated convincingly under a variety
of conditions, there is little evidence for development of addictive dependence
on alcohol in laboratory animals. A striking increase in alcohol consumption
by dogs, after prolonged administration of large alcohol doses, was reported
by Baïsset and Montastruc (1962). A 20% alcohol solution and water were
available throughout the experiment. During six months, while three animals
were given a daily alcohol dose of 3.2 g/kg, divided into four administrations per day, alcohol consumption decreased slightly whereas water intake
greatly increased, due to the diuretic action of alcohol. When alcohol
administrations were discontinued, alcohol consumption greatly increased.
This enhanced alcohol consumption was related to the diuretic action,
because subsequent administration of an antidiuretic hormone (posthypophyseal extract, 10 units per day) decreased alcohol consumption, and in
another group of three dogs, given the antidiuretic hormone during administration of alcohol, there was a much smaller increase in water consumption during the six-month treatment and no increase in alcohol consumption
afterward. Richter (1953, 1957b) found no evidence for craving for alcohol
in rats after a number of weeks during which their drinking fluid was
restricted to an alcohol solution. However, he reported evidence for pathological addiction in three wild rats limited to 10% alcohol according to one
account (1953, 1957b) or in two wild rats limited to 20% alcohol according
to another account (1957a). When water was again made available after 40
days, they progressively drank more alcohol and less water and food until they died approximately 30 days later. In an attempt to repeat this experiment, Eimer and Senter (1968) found that during restriction to a 20%
alcohol solution, domestic hooded rats drank more than wild pack rats
although the difference was small in terms of body weight (approximately

References p. 468

11.6 g/kg for the domestic rats and 7.6 g/kg for the wild rats). When the choice tests were commenced the consumption of the domestic rats decreased greatly whereas the consumption of wild rats decreased only slightly. This reversal gives some evidence that the more emotional wild rats were more susceptible to an enhanced voluntary consumption of alcohol as a result of prior forced consumption. A brief mention was made by Eggleton (1941) of a colleague's technique for addicting cats and dogs to alcohol by restricting their fluid intake to a solution of milk with gradually increasing concentrations of alcohol.

There is evidence that after exposure to alcohol, an interval without alcohol may result in an increased choice of alcohol when this fluid is reintroduced. Sinclair and Senter (1967) found that after four weeks of choice by rats between water and a 7% alcohol solution, alcohol consumption was enhanced when one-week choice periods alternated with one-week "alcohol deprivation" periods in which water was the only fluid available. The increase in alcohol consumption was greatest on the first day of choice after the one-week periods of water. In a subsequent experiment, Sinclair and Senter (1968) found that six days of "alcohol deprivation" increased alcohol consumption in choice tests in groups of rats previously exposed to the choice between water and 7% alcohol for 7 to 21 days but not in those exposed for only one day. A similar effect was previously reported in rats by Le Magnen (1960), Le Magnen and Marfaing-Jallat (1962) and Nichols and Hsiao (1967). This effect suggests a tendency for rats to regulate their alcohol intake over an extended period, with a compensatory increase following enforced cessation. The absence of any addictive craving in this situation is indicated by a finding (Le Magnen, 1960) that the increase in alcohol consumption is abolished or reversed if the animals are subjected to food deprivation during the preceding interval when alcohol is absent.

Contrary to the usual effects of prior exposure to alcohol, consumption of alcohol as the sole fluid in a concentration of 10% (Williams et al., 1949) or 12% (Veale and Myers, 1969) decreased alcohol choice in a subsequent choice test. These findings might indicate avoidance caused by forced consumption of aversively high concentrations of ethanol. Myers (1961a) reported that alcohol choice was increased after a 10–90 day period of a 5% but not 20% alcohol solution as the sole fluid. Myers and Carey (1961) reported greater alcohol choice at intermediate concentrations in a group of rats given a choice between water and a progressively higher concentration on successive days than in a group given a choice between water and a progressively decreasing alcohol concentration. Thomas (1969) likewise found that mice consumed more alcohol in choice tests with an ascending rather than descending series of concentrations. Korn (1960) similarly reported higher consumption by rats given a slowly increasing sequence of concentrations, from 0.01 to 15% in 50 days, rather than in a random sequence, but the difference might be attributable to the uniform location of the alcohol solution and tube for the former group, as discussed earlier in the present chapter (p. 417). Thiessen and Rodgers (1965) found that five days of intraperitoneal injection of 1 ml of a 10% alcohol solution in mice (more than 2 g/kg, assuming 30 g body weight) decreased alcohol consumption in a subsequent choice test.

(4) Detectability of alcohol

Some experiments on choice of water and an alcohol solution have included concentrations which were so low that a consistent preference or aversion of the alcohol bottle might provide useful evidence for ability to detect very weak solutions. Richter (1941) showed in a "typical" rat no consistent preference for the water or alcohol solution at concentrations of 0.01% to 1.60%. Thomas (1969) found no preference for water or alcohol by three strains of mice in choice tests with alcohol concentrations of 0.01% or below; one of the strains (DBA/2) preferred water to alcohol concentrations of 0.1% and above. However, detection of very low alcohol concentrations has been demonstrated by other experimenters. Kahn and Stellar (1960) reported that rats reliably preferred the alcohol solution with concentrations as low as 0.04%. Their careful controls included alternating not only the positions of the bottles but also the tubes on the bottles. Marfaing-Jallat (1964) reported that nondrinker rats showed aversion for alcohol at concentrations of 0.005% to 0.158%. Dethier (1961) found in blowflies a strong preference for an alcohol solution at concentrations of 0.006% to 6% v/v (0.001 M to 1 M). The preference for very weak alcohol solutions apparently depends on the odor, because no difference in consumption between water and low alcohol concentrations was found in anosmic rats (Richter, 1957b; Kahn and Stellar, 1960) and anosmic blowflies (Dethier, 1961). The odor of alcohol also provides a mechanism for aversion of higher concentrations according to reports that the peak alcohol preference is at a higher concentration in anosmic than normal rats (Richter, 1957b; Kahn and Stellar, 1960) and that removal of the olfactory bulbs increased consumption of a 10% alcohol solution by a strain of mice (BALB/c) which normally chose very little alcohol at this concentration (Rodgers and McClearn, 1962a). Dicker (1958) reported that methylpentynol carbamate, a drug which dulls the taste, temporarily increased consumption of a 20% alcohol solution by six rats which had previously refused it, while abolishing consumption of the 20% alcohol by two other rats. Terroine and Rochette (1946), in a series of studies on a small number of rats, found that a weaker alcohol solution was preferred over a stronger one, even in a choice between 1% and 2% concentration and even when both solutions were in bouillon soup rather than water. Additions of substances to mask the odor of alcohol (scatol or essence of orange) generally diminished but failed to abolish the preference for the weaker alcohol solution, but this series of experiments was inconclusive because the same substance was not added to both fluids. Fitz-Gerald et al. (1968), in an experiment on monkeys, reported evidence that a 10% alcohol solution was more effectively disguised in grape juice than in orange or grapefruit juice. Tests with an ethanol and vodka solution showed no evidence for a detectable difference.

Considerably higher thresholds for detecting odor or taste of alcohol have been reported with other techniques of measurement. In studies of olfactory acuity, measured in rats trained to avoid the alcohol solution by electric shock punishment, the threshold for detection was 3.6% v/v (Eayrs and Moulton, 1960) or approximately 1.5–2% v/v (Moulton and Eayrs, 1960). The concentration of alcohol vapor in the air, also reported in these studies, was much lower. Hellekant (1965a) reported that an alcohol solution of 9.2% v/v (1.6 M) placed on the tongue of rats was the minimal concentration sufficient to depress efferent neural activity, whereas in a choice between water and alcohol the first sign of rejecting alcohol was observed at a concentration of 8.6% v/v (1.5 M). The same concentrations increased neural activity of dogs and especially of cats (Hellekant, 1965b), whereas in the rat the increase in neural activity required a much higher concentration and was much weaker. Diamant et al. (1963) studied the neural response to alcohol applied to the tongue of a human and a dog. In humans, alcohol concentrations exceeding 6% v/v (1 M) were necessary to elicit a strong neural response to the taste stimuli (Diamant et al., 1965). In a test of taste discrimination in 13 humans between water and alcohol (Diamant et al., 1963), the median threshold detectability was at a concentration of 2.9% v/v (0.5 M). Wilson (1969) reported that the mean threshold for detecting the difference between alcohol and water, based on 167 observations in humans, was at a concentration of 2.4%. This was generally described as a sweet taste in both studies, although a bitter taste was sometimes reported, especially at higher concentrations. According to Wilson (1969), a concentration of 13.6% was the average threshold for a burning taste. In an earlier experiment, Richter (1941) studied taste threshold in 240 humans, including 72 children 4–10 years of age. The laboratory alcohol was redistilled over citric acid to eliminate its bitter taste. Most of the subjects were able to distinguish it from water at 2% and were able to recognize the taste of alcohol at 3%. The majority of the subjects disliked the taste in concentrations above 10–15%, but a substantial proportion of them preferred it to water even in concentrations as high as 50%. The results were apparently closely similar for adults and children. In another study on humans (Dolcetta and Stella, 1956), the majority of a group of newborn premature babies violently refused to swallow four drops of cognac. An equivalent group of babies generally accepted, but with disgust, four drops of cognac diluted in white wine. Both of these alcohol concentrations were undoubtedly above the level at which rats have generally been found to drink more from the alcohol than from the water bottle.

Detection of the taste, odor, or effects of alcohol has also been demonstrated by training animals to avoid the fluid which has unpleasant effects. In a choice between water and an alcohol solution, rats learned to decrease their consumption of the fluid which had been associated with punishment by electric shocks (Korman and Stephens, 1960) and loud noise (Korman et al., 1962), and mice likewise learned to avoid the fluid which had been associated with irradiation (Peacock and Watson, 1964). These procedures are similar to aversion training of human alcoholics (Chapter 10, p. 675). Treatment with disulfiram (Antabuse), which in humans causes a toxic reaction to alcohol (Chapter 11, p. 762), decreased alcohol choice by mice (Schlesinger et al., 1966). Mice given a choice among water, ethyl alcohol, and methyl alcohol drank large amounts of ethyl alcohol but early learned to avoid methyl alcohol, although the two alcohols are closely similar in taste (Loiseleur and Petit, 1947). Chapter 9 (p. 483) reports evidence that when experimentally produced diabetes insipidus in rats provides an incentive to avoid the diuretic action of alcohol, fluid intake is decreased by the addition to the drinking fluid of an alcohol concentration as low as 0.3% v/v. Learning to detect the pharmacological effect of alcohol, without the experience of its taste or odor, has been demonstrated by training rats to perform differential responses on the basis of whether they have been injected intraperitoneally with alcohol or saline (Chapter 7, p. 382). In animals trained to differentiate between saline and an alcohol dose of 1.2 g/kg, the ED_{50} dose was 0.50 g/kg (Kubena and Barry, 1969).

C. Genetic, sex, and individual differences

Large individual differences in amount of alcohol consumption are found in almost any sample of human drinkers. Experiments on laboratory animals provide a valuable opportunity for specifying genetic or other constitutional determinants of variations in voluntary consumption. Comparisons between different inbred strains of rats and mice may indicate effects of stable, long-established, genetic differences in animals of the same species which are similar in most respects. The ability of strains to interbreed permits experiments on hybrids, specifying much more precisely the genetic basis for differences in alcohol consumption. Rodgers (1967) and Rodgers and McClearn (1962a) have summarized some of the experiments by them and their colleagues on inbred strains of mice. Even more precise specification of genetic determinants, differentiating animals of the same inbred strain, is possible by comparisons between offspring of rats and mice which differ in alcohol consumption. Mardones (1960) and Eriksson (1969a) have reported on development of strains of rats which differ in this characteristic. Their designations "nondrinker" and "drinker" rats are misleading, in view of evidence reviewed earlier in this chapter that the daily amount of voluntary alcohol intake is largely independent of concentration. The terms "drinker" and "nondrinker" are based on the distinction between alcohol preference and alcohol avoidance in choice tests with a particular concentration. These differentiated strains are more accurately described by the designations, used in this chapter, of "light-drinking" and "heavy-drinking." Whatever terminology is used, some specific determinants of alcohol consumption may be indicated by studies of other behavioral and physiological characteristics of these strains or of other strains which also differ in alcohol consumption. Comparisons between males and females, and among different species, provide information on other genetically determined differences which may be related to differences in alcohol consumption. This section concludes with a review of studies in which individual differences in alcohol consumption are related to various potential determinants, including metabolism of ethanol, behavioral and emotional characteristics, and physiological condition. Some of these potential determinants, such as age, comprise a complex group of characteristics, no one of which can be identified as the cause of difference in alcohol consumption. However, the information about a wide variety of constitutional attributes related to alcohol consumption may be expected to lead to some important and valid conclusions about determinants of voluntary alcohol consumption.

(1) Strains of rats and mice

The existence of genetic determinants of alcohol consumption has been demonstrated in two ways: by comparisons between inbred strains of the same species found to differ in alcohol consumption, and by selective breeding of animals for differences in drinking habits. Myers (1962) reported higher alcohol consumption by G-4 than by Wistar albino rats. Van Steenkiste (1964) reported higher alcohol consumption by Wistar than by London Black rats. Reed (1951) studied six rat strains, most of them of Wistar origin, in various stages of inbreeding ranging from the 16th generation to more than a hundred generations of inbreeding. The smallest variation in alcohol preference was found in the strain inbred for 16 generations. This has been regarded as evidence that genetic factors contribute very weakly to the regulation of drinking. However, even morphologic characteristics may show a large degree of variation in highly inbred animal strains. Since Reed's (1951) study gives incomplete details of the experimental procedures and does not contain appropriate statistical analyses of the data, the observation remains rather inconclusive.

The existence of many well-established strains of mice has provided greater opportunity for genetic studies in that species. Rodgers (1967) has rank-ordered 15 mouse strains or sublines in percentage choice of an alcohol solution in relation to total fluid consumption. Other comparisons of mouse strains in choice tests have been reported by McClearn and Rodgers (1959), Rodgers and McClearn (1962a, b; 1964), and Thomas (1969). Remarkably similar strain differences have been found by this group of investigators and also by independent experimenters (Fuller, 1964; Eriksson and Pikkarainen, 1968). The same strain differences have generally been found in tests of simultaneous choice among several alcohol concentrations (Rodgers and McClearn, 1962b; Fuller, 1964), with sweetened alcohol solutions (Rodgers and McClearn, 1964), after stressful procedures (Thiessen and Rodgers, 1965) and in tests after deprivation of food (Rodgers et al., 1963) and fluid (Thiessen and McClearn, 1965; Fuller, 1967). Alcohol consumption is by far the highest in the C57 mouse and in closely related strains, such as C58; C3H and R111 are intermediate; A and BALB are low; DBA is lowest.

Studies of hybrids between different strains have yielded important information about the genetic basis for strain differences in alcohol consumption. McClearn and Rodgers (1961) reported intermediate alcohol preference by offspring of C57BL and low-preference strains (C3H/2, A/2, BALB/c, DBA/2N, with a tendency to be more similar to the low-preference parent. A finding of intermediate scores in two generations of hybrids between C57BL and A, without the extreme low or high alcohol preferences of the source strains, gave evidence for a polygenic determinant of alcohol consumption. However, their statistical analyses were incomplete, representing conclusions based only on average consumption in the various generations. Brewster (1968), by a statistical reanalysis of the data, concluded that 82% of the variation in ethanol preference was due to genetic factors, which were transmitted polygenically. McClearn and Rodgers (1961) concluded absence of "maternal effects" from a finding that mice with a C57BL mother and C3H/2 father did not differ reliably in alcohol preference from mice with a C3H/2 mother and C57BL father, but there were only six animals in each group and the offspring of C57BL mothers showed slightly higher average preference, as would be expected from a maternal effect. Eriksson (1968) reported an apparent but not statistically significant maternal effect in mice. Rodgers and McClearn (1962a) presented further data on hybrids between different strains. Cross-fostering studies showed that the strain differences in alcohol preference were not due to strain differences in maternal behavior or in nutrition between birth and weaning. Thomas (1969) found that the alcohol preference of hybrids between C57BL and DBA/2 mice was intermediate but slightly lower than the midparent. Backcrosses indicated that any dominance of one strain was weak. Fuller (1964), in tests of hybrids among four mouse strains, found intermediate alcohol consumption, with evidence for stronger effects of the parent strain with more extreme high or low alcohol score. In four out of six hybrid strains the offspring resembled the parent with lower alcohol preference. Brewster (1968), by a statistical reanalysis of the data, concluded that some parental strains were dominant over the others and calculated an 86% influence of genetic factors. In a later study by Fuller (1967), hybrid offspring of C57BL/6 and DBA/2 mice were intermediate between their parents in alcohol consumption during fluid deprivation. As in the earlier study (Fuller, 1964), the hybrids were more similar to the alcohol-preferring C57BL/6 parent. Eriksson (1970), in a preliminary report of extensive cross-breeding studies in C57 and CBA mice, estimated that the heritability of alcohol consumption was 74% in females and 92% in males.

Brewster (1968) reported on a cross-breeding experiment on the 29th generation of two strains of Wistar, albino rats (Maudsley Nonreactive and Reactive). The Nonreactive parental strain consumed more alcohol in choice tests; the hybrid offspring were similar in alcohol intake to the Nonreactive, alcohol-preferring parent. The dominance of the alcohol-preferring parent was statistically reliable for the measure of amount of alcohol intake but not for the measure of preference for the 5% alcohol solution in relation to total fluid intake. Heritability was polygenic and accounted for 71% of the variance in alcohol intake and 72% of the variance in alcohol preference; these values for rats are high but lower than for mouse strains. In accordance with Eriksson's (1968) findings in mice, alcohol intake and preference of the offspring were slightly more closely related to that of the mother than father, but this maternal effect was not statistically significant.

Long-established, inbred strains which differ in alcohol consumption are likely to differ also in a wide variety of other characteristics. A more precise specification of the genetic basis for differences in alcohol consumption has been sought by breeding animals of the same inbred strain for differences in alcohol consumption, thus developing new strains which are selected on this basis. Mardones (1960) showed sample pedigrees for 15 generations of rats bred for low and high consumption of a 10% alcohol solution in tests of free choice between this fluid and water. A reliable differentiation between the strains occurred within the first few generations.

A sample pedigree showed that according to the criteria of less than 1.5 g/kg/day for the light-drinking strain and 4.6 g/kg/day or more for the heavy-drinking strain, greater homogeneity was attained in the light-drinking strain. Eriksson (1968; 1969a) has reported on the development of differentiated light-drinking and heavy-drinking strains of rats from a Wistar, albino stock. In the eighth generation, average alcohol consumption in tests of choice between a 10% solution and water averaged 5.8 g/kg/day for the heavy-drinking and 1.9 g/kg/day for the light-drinking strain (Eriksson, 1968). Similar results, found in tests with several alcohol concentrations (Eriksson, 1969a), are summarized earlier in the present chapter (Figures 3 and 4). The differences between the two strains accounted for 66% of the variance in alcohol consumption. Dominance of the light-drinking characteristic is indicated by greater homogeneity of alcohol consumption by the light-drinking strain (Eriksson, 1969a), in agreement with the report by Mardones (1960). Heritability, calculated from hybrids between the strains, was higher for females (0.37) than for males (0.26), suggesting sex-linked inheritance (Eriksson, 1968). A similar coefficient of heredity (0.41) was reported by Mardones *et al.* (1953) for the fifth generation of their light-drinking and heavy-drinking strains of rats. Subsequently, Eriksson (1969b) reported on 177 offspring of 19 pairs of parents, selected from the tenth generation of his light-drinking and heavy-drinking strains. The correlations of drinking scores between offspring and parents were only moderately high and were higher for percentage choice of alcohol in relation to total fluid intake than for amount of alcohol consumption. The highest correlations were between mother and female offspring, giving further evidence for sex-linked inheritance.

The important question of why the newly developed rat strains differ in alcohol consumption might be answered by identifying other characteristics which differentiate these strains. Thus far only a few such characteristics have been discovered, and they do not provide plausible explanations for the differences in alcohol consumption. In a comparison of the rat strains developed by Mardones (1960), Segovia-Riquelme *et al.* (1956, 1962) found no significant difference in oxidation of ethanol and ethanol metabolites. Subsequently, Segovia-Riquelme *et al.* (1964) reported more rapid metabolism of radioactively tagged glucose and gluconate to carbon dioxide in the heavy-drinker than light-drinker strain, but this has no obvious implication for ethanol metabolism and as pointed out by Lester (1966) the authors did not control for differences in voluntary alcohol intake prior to the test of metabolism. The data reported by Mardones (1960) showed lower body weights in the heavy-drinking strain, but the difference was not reliable. However, Eriksson (1969a) also found lower body weights in his heavy-drinking strain, and this difference was statistically reliable. This difference, in conjunction with the larger intake of solid food by the heavy-drinking strain, suggests a higher level of general metabolism, while higher total fluid consumption by the heavy-drinking strain is probably attributable to the diuretic action of their higher alcohol intake (Eriksson, 1968). Another observation was greater sucess in breeding the heavy-drinking than light-drinking strain (Eriksson, *personal communication*). The differences between these strains in alcohol consumption appear to be remarkably consistent under various test conditions, including choice among multiple alcohol concentrations and addition of saccharin to the alcohol solution and quinine to the water (Eriksson, 1969a).

Some suggestive correlates with alcohol consumption have been reported in rats selectively bred for other characteristics. Nichols and Hsiao (1967) bred rats for difference in consumption of an 0.5% w/v morphine solution, in a choice test two weeks after prolonged forced intake of addicting amounts. When animals of the third generation were subjected to similar procedures, with a 10% alcohol solution instead of morphine, the strain bred for "addiction liability" to morphine consumed more alcohol in a choice test after two weeks of no alcohol. Whether or not the authors' interpretation of "addiction liability" is accepted, their finding indicates a common genetic basis for willingness to consume relatively large amounts of either morphine or alcohol. Higher alcohol consumption by the Maudsley Nonreactive than Reactive strain of rats (Brewster, 1968) suggests a positive relationship of alcohol choice with the lower fearfulness, greater activity and superior learning ability characteristic of the Nonreactive strain. Subsequently, Brewster (1969) reported partially contrary results for the Maudsley strain but also found higher alcohol consumption by a Roman strain characterized by superior performance of a shock-avoidance response. Similarly, Clay (1964) found higher alcohol choice by rats whose parents had responded more flexibly and successfully to a difficult and stressful discrimination problem.

In mice, the extensively studied strain differences in alcohol consumption have been related to strain differences in other characteristics. Schlesinger (1966) has summarized findings of a number of studies. McClearn (1963) reported in five strains an inverse relation between their alcohol preference and duration of sleeping time after intraperitoneal injection of 3.4 g alcohol/kg. Kakihana et al. (1966) also found this difference in a comparison between C57BL and BALB/c mice. These findings are not attributable to a generalized difference in sensitivity to ethanol. The strains did not differ in the interval from injection to losing their righting reflex, nor in brain alcohol levels at 100 and 140 min after injection. Reports by Rodgers (1966), Schlesinger (1966), and Wilson (1967) also indicate no large or consistent strain differences in rate of ethanol disappearance. Whitney and Whitney (1968) found that an intraperitoneally injected dose of alcohol caused a higher percentage of deaths in C57BL/1 mice than in four strains characterized by low alcohol preference. Hybrids were intermediate in mortality. The reported dose was impossibly high (160 g/kg), but the reasonable quantity of 16 g/kg is obtained from the assumption that the mice were given 0.4 ml. of 50% v/v ethanol per 10 g instead of per g. In other experiments, the alcohol-preferring strain has shown superior metabolic adjustment to moderate doses of ethanol. Kakihana et al. (1968b) reported that 0.8 g/kg caused a smaller and less prolonged increase in plasma corticosterone levels of C57BL/10J than of DBA/2J mice. Schlesinger et al. (1966) found that injection of alcohol gave rise to lower blood acetaldehyde levels in C57BL than in DBA/2 mice. Pretreatment with disulfiram (Antabuse) increased blood acetaldehyde and retarded ethanol metabolism to a greater degree in the C57BL than DBA/2 strain. Rodgers et al. (1963), by measuring weight loss under a diet of insufficient solid food, found that drinking fluid of 10% alcohol rather than water had a greater beneficial effect on C57BL mice than on any of the other five strains tested. The strain with the next highest alcohol preference (R111) was the only other one which showed a reliable beneficial effect of alcohol as the drinking fluid.

Evidence has been reported for higher levels of liver ADH activity in strains with greater alcohol preference. Rodgers et al. (1963) found a perfect rank order correlation in six strains of mice between alcohol preference during restricted intake of solid food and LADH activity. Schlesinger (1966) reported further evidence for a positive relationship between alcohol preference and LADH. In different experiments, LADH activity was higher in C57BL mice than in C3H (Wilson et al., 1961), in DBA/2 (McClearn et al., 1964) and in CBA (Eriksson and Pikkarainen, 1968). These strain differences suggest general metabolic differences but they are not attributable to a specific difference in alcohol metabolism, because LADH activity is generally not the rate-limiting step in alcohol metabolism (Chapter 3, p. 96), as is further indicated by the lack of consistent strain differences in rate of alcohol disappearance. Sheppard et al. (1968) reported that in comparison with the low-preference DBA strain, C57BL mice showed 30% more alcohol dehydrogenase activity but 300% more aldehyde dehydrogenase activity. In a test for a different type of metabolic difference, Rodgers and Lewis (1963) found that glucose was present and glucurone absent in the livers of each of three mouse strains which differed in alcohol preference.

Strain differences in diverse other attributes may provide suggestive evidence about characteristics related to differences in alcohol preference. In accordance with similar findings in rats, reviewed earlier, C57BL mice had lower body weights than the low-preference strain, in a comparison with R111 mice (Thiessen and McClearn, 1965) and in a comparison with

CBA mice (Eriksson and Pikkarainen, 1968). Thomas (1969) commented that DBA/2 mice, which are lowest in alcohol preference, are difficult to breed and rear to maturity. However, Fuller (1967) stated that females of the DBA/2J and of the highest-preference strain (C57BL/6J) are superior in fertility to C3HeB/FeJ and A/J females. Thiessen *et al.* (1967) reported that the high average daily consumption of 16–23 g alcohol/kg body weight by C57BL mice had no adverse effect on their fertility or on the survival of their pups. Other studies indicate superior vigor or boldness of C57 mice. Thiessen and Rodgers (1965) reported much more fighting by C57BL than by R111 mice when they were put into groups prior to any alcohol consumption. More active and bolder exploratory behavior was found in C57 mice than in low-preference strains (Thompson, 1953; Fredericson, 1953; McClearn, 1959, 1960). Green and Meier (1965), in a review of a number of strain differences, reported that C57 mice showed longer survival times after radiation and were insensitive to the depressant effect of chlorprom-azine. However, in other studies of strain differences in exploratory behavior (Bruell, 1964) and in learning and performance (Bovet *et al.*, 1968, 1969), sublines of the C57 strain differed among themselves and were not consistently different from the other strains tested. Data presented by Thiessen and Nealey (1962) on five mouse strains and by Thiessen (1964) on six mouse strains indicated that most of the physiological and behavioral measures showed little correlation with voluntary alcohol consumption.

Techniques in behavioral genetics are now sufficiently advanced to permit systematic study of heritable factors in drinking. Such studies should include reliable determination of the phenotype, appropriate biometric methods, and suitable mating procedures. The methods required are discussed for instance in Bruell's (1964) paper and in a book edited by Hirsch (1967). Other differences between strains may be entirely unrelated to the drinking, especially when the genetic selection originally was made for other traits than alcohol consumption. By crosses between strains, inheritance of alcohol consumption can be compared with inheritance of other characteristics enabling detection of features genetically linked with the regulation of drinking. With respect to the genetic mechanisms involved in the control of drinking, there is already evidence for differences among strains of mice (McClearn and Rodgers, 1961; Fuller, 1964; Eriksson, 1970) and rats (Mardones *et al.*, 1953; Brewster, 1968, 1969; Eriksson, 1968).

References p. 468

(2) Species and sex differences

In contrast to the substantial number of studies comparing alcohol preference in different strains of rats and mice, there has been little research on other genetic determinants of alcohol consumption. Genetically determined differences are found among different species, and within the same species and strain between males and females. Comparisons between species and sexes involve a wide variety of different characteristics, no one of which can be identified with certainty as the determinant of differences in alcohol consumption. Nevertheless, useful information may be obtained by comparing alcohol consumption in different species and in the two sexes.

The preceding review of strain differences in rats and mice emphasizes differences in alcohol consumption within each species rather than differences between these species. Mardones (1960), in a review of studies on mice and rats, showed that mice generally consumed more alcohol in relation to body weight. This difference may be attributed to the higher rate of ethanol metabolism in the mouse (Chapter 2, Table 7). However, greater variability has been seen among strains of mice than rats. Figs. 1–3 of the present chapter indicate that alcohol concentrations of 5% or even higher are not avoided by rats, and many of the animals drink more alcohol than water at these concentrations. However, one strain of mouse (DBA/2) avoids alcohol at a concentration as low as 0.05% (Thomas, 1969).

Several experimenters have reported high alcohol preference in hamsters. Emerson *et al.* (1952) found very high voluntary consumption of 10% alcohol by hamsters and deer mice, whereas little alcohol was consumed by cotton mice and usually by albino rats of Sprague–Dawley strain. Aschkenasy-Lelu (1960b), with a choice between water and a 5% alcohol solution, found the highest daily alcohol consumption by hamsters (5.2 g/kg); the consumption was much lower in mice (2.4 g/kg) and still lower in rats (1.4 g/kg). Arvola and Forsander (1961), with a choice between a 10% alcohol solution and water in six species, found that the golden hamster was the only one which drank larger amounts of the alcohol solution than water. The other species, in descending order of alcohol preference, were the rabbit, hedgehog, albino rat, albino mouse, and guinea pig. Consumption of several alcohol concentrations by the hamster, studied by Arvola and Forsander (1963), was summarized in Fig. 8–5. Estimating the average body weight at 100 grams, the alcohol intake by hamsters, with a choice between a 40% solution and water, averaged more than 8 g/kg/day. The high consumption of alcohol by this species might be due to the fact that hamsters are desert animals, accustomed to bitter tasting substances, so that their aversion of the strong taste of alcohol might be minimal.

There may be particular value in the study of alcohol consumption by species which more closely resemble humans in size and in cortical development. Nevertheless, very few experimenters have tested alcohol consumption in such species. Baïsset and Montastruc (1962) reported that dogs consumed only about 0.4 g/kg/day in a choice between a 20% alcohol solution and water. After 6 months of administration of 6.4 g/kg/day, their voluntary intake increased to about 4 g/kg/day. Large amounts of daily alcohol consumption by primates have been reported in the few studies on these animals most closely related to humans. During prolonged choice between a 15% alcohol solution and water, Mello and Mendelson (1966) found wide variation in alcohol consumption by four rhesus macaque monkeys, up to a maximum of 6.1 g/kg/day. Koz and Mendelson (1967) found that during prolonged periods of free choice between a 10% alcohol solution and water, average daily alcohol consumption by two rhesus speciosa monkeys ranged from 4 to 8 g. The authors did not report the body weights of the animals. Clark and Polish (1960) reported that during choice between a 20% alcohol solution and water, average alcohol intake by two rhesus monkeys ranged from approximately 0.7 to 2.3 g/kg/day. Anderson and Smith (1963) reported on choice tests in Macaca nemestrina (Pigtail) monkeys. The data indicated substantial amounts of alcohol consumption although some of the tests were preceded by fluid deprivation, which would be expected to enhance preference for water over alcohol. Consumption of intoxicating amounts of alcohol was reported by Fitz-Gerald *et al.* (1968), who offered to chimpanzees and orangutans a fruit juice (grape, orange, or grapefruit), with or without the addition of a 10% concentration of ethanol or vodka. The alcohol greatly decreased the amount of juice consumed, but in the brief drinking period, averaging 10 min, alcohol consumption often exceeded 1 g/kg. Intoxication was observed in several of the chimpanzees.

A consistent finding, in all species of vertebrates tested in the laboratory, is the avoidance of intoxicating doses of alcohol. However, an attractive concentration of alcohol induces drinking to intoxication in flies, according to data on blowflies reported by Dethier (1961) and on other species of flies cited in that article. This one study on blowflies, also cited earlier in the present chapter (p. 427), is an example of the wide variety of available species, most of which have never been tested for alcohol consumption.

References p. 468

Reports on sex differences in alcohol preference have been rather conflicting. The valid comparison is for alcohol intake in relation to body weight, so that the experimenter should report both the amount of alcohol consumption and the average weights of the animals. Since males are usually heavier, and also may consume less fluid due to their lower surface/volume ratio, equal alcohol intake in g/kg/day may require a much higher percentage choice of alcohol by males in relation to total fluid intake. These factors may partly account for the higher percentage alcohol choice in male rats reported by Clay (1964) and the larger amount of alcohol consumption in male hamsters reported by Arvola and Forsander (1963). Fitz-Gerald *et al.* (1968), in presentations of a single beverage containing 10% alcohol, found that male chimpanzees drank almost twice as much alcohol as females whereas male and female orangutans drank the same amount, in comparisons between males and females with approximately equalized body weights. In choice tests with rats, Schadewald *et al.* (1953) found that males consumed more alcohol in g/kg/day but Aschkenasy-Lelu (1960c), Eriksson and Malmström (1967), Brewster (1969), and Eriksson (1969a) found that females consumed more alcohol in g/kg/day. Eriksson and Malmström (1967) also found faster alcohol elimination in female rats, and Eriksson (1969a) reported that the sex difference in alcohol consumption was greater in the heavy-drinking than in the light-drinking strain of rats, in accordance with the expectation that the faster metabolism in females would be a more influential determinant when alcohol intake was at a high level. In mice, Mirone (1952) reported higher alcohol consumption by males but Eriksson and Pikkarainen (1968) found higher alcohol consumption by females in g/kg/day, and this sex difference was greater in the alcohol-preferring strain (C57BL) than in the CBA strain, again giving evidence that the faster metabolism in females is more influential when alcohol intake is at a high level. A tendency for higher alcohol preference in females than males of the C57BL strain, but not of low-preference strains, was found under limited food rations (Rodgers *et al.*, 1963) but not in other choice tests (McClearn and Rodgers, 1961). This finding has been confirmed by Eriksson (1970).

Most experimenters on rats and mice have found little sex difference in alcohol consumption (*e.g.* Mardones, 1960; Rodgers and McClearn, 1962a). Differences between males and females may be influenced by a variety of conditions which generally have not been tested systematically in both sexes. The alcohol intake of females is affected by the stage of the reproductive cycle. Studies of this variable are reviewed in the present chapter (p. 445).

(3) Other individual differences

The final portion of the present section, on constitutional determinants, reviews studies of individual differences in alcohol consumption without a known genetic basis for the differences and without differential treatment of the animals. Eriksson (1969a, b) has emphasized the large amount of variability in the voluntary alcohol consumption of rats, unexplained by genetic differences. Senter *et al.* (1968) demonstrated stable individual differences in alcohol choice by rats throughout 26 weeks of testing with a 5% solution and water. In the following review, the characteristics of the animals related to alcohol consumption include various types of influence, including metabolic, dietary, emotional, and physiological conditions. Since these characteristics were not directly manipulated by the experimenter, direct cause-and-effect relationships cannot be proven. Even in the case of variables which produce obvious differences in the animals, such as stages of the reproductive cycle and advancing age, the natural occurrence of these variations involves a wide variety of characteristics which might be the determinants of alcohol consumption. In spite of the limitation on conclusiveness, however, these studies may provide useful evidence about variables related to voluntary alcohol consumption.

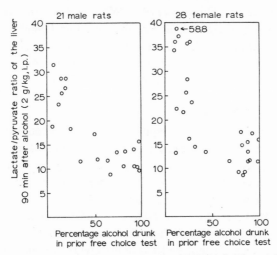

Fig. 8–6. Lactate/pyruvate ratio of liver 90 min after alcohol injection related to preceding choice in tests with water and a 10% concentration of alcohol, in 21 male and 28 female rats. The data for males are from Forsander (1966).

Evidence for less metabolic disturbance caused by a high fat load was found in a report by Forsander and Salaspuro (1962) that rats with high rather than low prior choice of alcohol excreted smaller amounts of ketone bodies after oral administration of fat. Subsequently, Forsander (1966) found that another group of rats with high rather than low prior alcohol choice responded to an intraperitoneal dose of ethanol (2 g/kg) with less elevation of the lactate/pyruvate ratio in the liver. This indication of less metabolic disturbance in heavy drinkers is portrayed in Fig. 8–6 for 21 male and 28 female rats. These data suggest that a high degree of susceptibility to metabolic disturbance prevents heavy drinking in some individuals. An interesting feature of both the ketone excretion and the lactate/pyruvate ratios is that all the heavy drinkers showed evidence for slight metabolic disturbance whereas the light drinkers included a wide range of variation in metabolic disturbance. In these metabolic characteristics the light drinkers were more heterogeneous, and the animals with apparent metabolic capability for heavy drinking included a wide range of variation in alcohol choice. Presumably some other factor, such as a preference or aversion for nutritional or pharmacological actions of alcohol, accounted for the fact that heavy alcohol consumption was found in some of these metabolically capable animals.

Some other relationships with voluntary alcohol consumption may indicate metabolic factors. Thiessen et al. (1967) reported a positive correlation between alcohol intake and liver size in mice. Iida (1960) found elevated glucurone level in mice with high "craving" for alcohol. Clay (1964) found that rats with a high percentage choice of alcohol drank more fluid, perhaps due to a diuretic effect, and female heavy drinkers were lower in body weight, in agreement with differences among strains of mice and rats, reviewed earlier (pp. 434–436).

The nutritional rather than metabolic aspect of alcohol appears to be influential in some studies of individual differences in alcohol consumption. In two experiments on a total of 48 rats, those which voluntarily consumed more alcohol in choice tests showed a higher average aversion threshold to quinine in the water (Le Magnen and Marfaing-Jallat, 1961; Marfaing-Jallat, 1964). However, Eriksson (1969a) found little differential effect of quinine in heavy-drinking and light-drinking strains of rats. An inverse relationship between alcohol and sugar preference was indicated by a rat which consumed the least sucrose in a choice between 10% sucrose and water but consumed a large amount of alcohol in a choice between 10%

alcohol and water (Williams *et al.*, 1955). Le Magnen and Marfaing-Jallat (1962) found that rats with higher alcohol preference, in a choice between a 6% w/v solution and water, consumed more alcohol and less food when the solid food was limited to a carbohydrate diet. However, the rats with different alcohol preferences showed little difference in choice among a carbohydrate, protein, and fat diet, both with and without availability of the alcohol solution. Under most of the test conditions the former differences in alcohol choice almost disappeared. According to several studies of humans, reviewed in Chapter 11 (p. 737), heavy drinkers consume low quantities of sweets.

Some individual differences in emotional reactivity may be related to the amount of incentive for obtaining the sedative effects of alcohol. Lagerspetz (1964) found that in choice tests more aggressive mice drank larger amounts of both 10% alcohol and water. Dember and Kristofferson (1955) found that rats with high alcohol consumption tended to show a short latency of onset of audiogenic seizure in response to a high-pitched sound. Duveau *et al.* (1966) likewise found higher alcohol consumption in mice which were more susceptible to audiogenic seizure, but this difference was short of statistical significance, and a reliably larger amount of water was consumed by the susceptible than refractory animals. Clay (1964) found no correlation between alcohol choice and susceptibility to audiogenic seizure in rats. Korn (1960) reported that a different test of emotionality, the number of trials required before the animal ceased urinating or defecating in a novel, brightly illuminated arena, was positively correlated with alcohol choice in rats. Adamson and Black (1959) reported that the most efficient shock-avoidance performance was achieved by rats which were intermediate in alcohol choice, presumably because they were intermediate in degree of tension. However, in a similar, unpublished experiment by Wallgren and Savolainen, with 34 rats, no systematic relationship was found between alcohol choice and shock-avoidance performance.

In several experiments, high preference for alcohol was related to greater vigor or superior performance, but as in tests of emotionality reviewed above, the evidence is not very consistent. Tobach (1957) found that in rats alcohol consumption was positively correlated with amount of locomotor exploratory activity in a novel, brightly illuminated arena but not correlated with a number of other behavioral tests. However, Clay (1964) found no correlation between alcohol choice and learning of a difficult discrimination and a complex maze. In an experiment on 28 mentally defective human children, Zucchi and Santangelo (1956) reported that when wine was made available at meals, the more vivacious children drank more, whereas the apathetic ones drank less, and there was no relationship between consumption and degree of mental deficiency.

Advancing age involves changes in metabolic, nutritional, emotional, and general physiological condition. Measurement of alcohol choice as a percentage of total fluid intake may show a misleading increase in older animals because of their higher body weight and lower fluid consumption. Wallgren and Forsander (1963) found higher percentage alcohol choice by rats at 29 than at 7 months of age, but because of lower fluid consumption and heavier body weight the older animals consumed less alcohol in g/kg/day. Eriksson (1969a) likewise found in rats higher percentage alcohol choice but lower consumption in g/kg/day at six than at two months of age. Parisella and Pritham (1964) tested four age groups of rats (1–2, 3–4, 10–15, 20–24 months) in a choice among 8% alcohol, 5% w/v sucrose and water. They reported that the percentage choice of alcohol was highest at 3–4 months and lowest at 1–2 months, but in terms of body weight alcohol consumption was highest in the youngest animals (10.4 g/kg/day) and was progressively lower in each older age group. Alcohol consumption in terms of body weight at 3–4 months was only slightly lower than at 1–2 months and much higher than at the older ages, whereas both sucrose and water consumption were much lower at the three oldest ages than at 1–2 months. Goodrick (1967) tested choice between an alcohol solution (2, 4, 6, or 8%) and water by groups of rats at six ages (1, 3, 5, 10, 15, 24 months). Both percentage choice and amount of consumption of alcohol were highest at 5 months and lowest at 15 months. Body weights were not reported, but if they were similar to those reported by Parisella and Pritham (1964), alcohol intake in g/kg/day decreased progressively with older age from 1 to 15 months. Evidence for a similar inverse relationship between age and alcohol consumption in BALB/c mice is a report by Kakihana and McClearn (1963) that the percentage choice of alcohol, in a test between a 10% solution and water, was higher at 1–2 than at 3–5 months of age. However, neither fluid intake nor body weight was reported. Fitz-Gerald *et al.* (1968), who allowed chimpanzees one hour to drink from a single bottle containing a 10% alcohol solution, found much less consumption by two old animals (40–49 years) than by animals 10–39 years old, while juveniles (4–9 years) were intermediate. Their body weights were not reported, but it seems likely that the youngest animals consumed the most alcohol in g/kg.

Alcohol consumption, in common with many other behavioral and physiological responses, varies greatly at different stages of the female reproductive cycle. Female rats consume less alcohol during the estrous than diestrous phase of their cycle (Aschkenasy-Lelu, 1960a,c). Thiessen *et al.* (1966) reported that the normally high alcohol consumption by C57 mice increases during pregnancy, but apparently less than body weight, whereas during lactation alcohol consumption gradually increases to double the normal amount, followed by an abrupt return to normal after weaning. Thiessen *et al.* (1967) showed that on the tenth day after birth, average alcohol intake of the lactating mother was 23 g/kg/day compared with 16 g/kg/day for control mice. A species difference may be indicated by reports (Emerson *et al.*, 1952; Carver *et al.*, 1953) that alcohol consumption by female hamsters decreases near the end of gestation and during lactation.

D. Physiological and emotional factors

This section reviews experiments on various nutritional, metabolic, hormonal, and emotional determinants of voluntary alcohol consumption. These diverse factors were all studied by comparing alcohol consumption in groups of animals or under conditions which were equated in all respects except for one or more experimentally manipulated treatments. The complex interrelationships among variables may obscure the specific determinant of alcohol consumption, because an experimentally induced change in nutrition, hormonal secretions, or emotional condition causes changes in all of the other variables. Nevertheless, the experimental manipulations and control conditions, in the experiments reviewed in the present section, help to identify and specify determinants of alcohol consumption. The variables discussed in the present section include many which were tested in studies reviewed in the preceding section, and some of those observations and measurements of constitutional differences are more conclusively verified by the controlled experiments reviewed in the present section.

The effects of nutritional condition and other physiological variations on alcohol consumption have been reviewed thoroughly by Mardones (1960) and by Aschkenasy-Lelu (1960b). Experiments on drinking for sedative effects have been discussed under the heading "stress and anxiety" by Lester (1966). This last topic has been characterized by a meager amount of good research prior to Lester's review, and several good experiments have been published subsequently.

(1) Nutritional condition

The effects of nutritional condition on alcohol intake are partly attributable to the fact that alcohol, as a source of calories, affects the animal's
nutritional condition. Forsander (1966) has suggested that the animal's real
choice is between the two calorie sources (solid food and alcohol) rather
than between alcohol and water. As a source of energy which is rapidly
metabolized and not stored, ethanol resembles the carbohydrates more than
proteins and fat. On the other hand, ethanol and fat share certain metabolic
characteristics, notably low requirement of thiamine (vitamin B_1), whereas
this vitamin is important for oxidation of carbohydrates (Wertz *et al.*, 1951;
Forsander, 1966). In rats, daily ethanol consumption of 4 g/kg, which is
typical for the studies summarized in Fig. 3, provides 28 kcal/kg. This
comprises about one third of the daily basal metabolism (Chapter 2, Table
11). The dietary importance of this alcohol intake is enhanced by its special
metabolic characteristics, in particular because alcohol may consume nearly
all of the catabolic activity of the liver (Chapter 3, p. 108). Since alcohol
consumption is determined partly by the amount of solid food intake and
by the components of the diet, these items of information should be recorded
and reported. Unfortunately, they are usually described adequately only
when these dietary features are experimentally manipulated.

An inverse relationship between alcohol and carbohydrate consumption
was suggested by a report that a diet with higher carbohydrate content
resulted in less alcohol choice by rats (Lester and Greenberg, 1952). However, subsequent experiments have indicated that other dietary components
have more important effects on alcohol consumption. An experiment by
Mardones *et al.* (1955), summarized by Mardones (1960), showed a tendency
for more alcohol intake by rats on a low carbohydrate diet than on the
basic or high carbohydrate diet. Mirone (1957), in an extensive test with
various diets in a total of 384 mice, of the alcohol-preferring C57 strain,
found no consistent effect of a high-carbohydrate diet. A comparison
between two low-carbohydrate diets showed that alcohol consumption was
increased by the one high in protein and decreased by the one high in fat.
Alcohol consumption was also higher with her "Basal Diet L" than with
Purina chow which was lower in fat, higher in carbohydrate and in general
less nutritious. Eriksson (1969a), in a comparison among several diets, found
the lowest alcohol consumption by rats with the one high in fat. Both the
high-carbohydrate and the optimum diet resulted in higher alcohol intake

than the standard diet, which was higher in protein content than any of the others. Further evidence that alcohol consumption is inversely related to fat or protein rather than carbohydrate intake was obtained by LeMagnen and Marfaing-Jallat (1962) with the interesting technique of permitting rats a free, continuous choice among these dietary components. The availability of a 6% alcohol solution in addition to water increased carbohydrate intake and decreased consumption of fat and protein. When the animals were divided into subgroups, each limited to one of the three dietary components, alcohol consumption was substantially increased only by the fat and protein diets, and with them only in animals whose alcohol consumption was initially low. With a single dietary component and a 20% alcohol solution as the sole drinking fluid, carbohydrate consumption was decreased the least and protein consumption was decreased the most, whereas matching the amount of food intake with a balanced diet showed that consumption of the 20% alcohol solution as the sole fluid was decreased least by the protein diet. Similarly, Regnault and Aschkenasy-Lelu (1963) found that in rats given a choice between an alcohol solution and water, alcohol consumption was slightly increased by a diet without proteins but was decreased in a group of animals limited to the same quantity of a balanced diet.

Much more research effort has been devoted to the relationship of alcohol consumption to specific nutritional deficiencies, especially thiamine and other B vitamins. Attempts to explain alcoholism in humans in terms of such deficiencies are discussed in Chapter 11 (p. 728). Mardones (1960) reviewed a number of experiments showing that a variety of nutritional deficiencies increased voluntary alcohol consumption by laboratory animals. He suggested the existence of an unidentified factor "N", present in yeast, liver, and meat, as the principal nutrient which reduced appetite for alcohol. Thiamine deficiency might be expected to increase alcohol consumption because carbohydrate utilization becomes difficult in thiamine deficiency whereas alcohol metabolism is not affected. Intake of alcohol actually helps to conserve thiamine (Wertz et al., 1951). A suggestive observation (Wertz et al., 1951) was that thiamine-deficient rats would voluntarily drink enough of a 25% alcohol solution, offered as the only fluid, to cause unconsciousness of several hours' duration. However, the aggregate results of several experiments do not indicate a consistent or specific effect of thiamine deficiency on alcohol consumption in tests of choice between an alcohol solution and water. Westerfeld and Lawrow (1953) found that the increase in alcohol consumption by rats on a thiamine-deficient diet was less than by a matched control group restricted to the same amount of food intake without a thiamine deficiency. This gave evidence that the increase in alcohol consumption was not caused directly by the thiamine deficiency but instead was due to the reduced food intake by animals on a thiamine-deficient diet. Purdy and Lee (1962), with a similar paired-feeding technique and the unusually high alcohol concentration of 15% w/v (19% v/v), found a tendency for alcohol intake to be higher in thiamine-deficient than control rats whereas alcohol intake tended to be lower in riboflavin-deficient than control rats. The restriction in food intake, due to vitamin deficiency on the paired-feeding, caused an increase in alcohol consumption which was larger than the differences between the paired animals. In a strain of mice, obtained from crosses of four strains with low alcohol preference, Brown (1969) found an increase in alcohol consumption on diets deficient in niacin, thiamine, or pyridoxine but no effect of deficiency in pantothenic acid. This effect was greater in females than males, perhaps due to greater capability of females to drink large amounts of alcohol when they have the incentive to do so, discussed earlier in the present chapter (p. 440). However, Rodgers (1967) reported no reliable effect of thiamine deprivation on alcohol choice by a strain of mice, and the animals on the deficient diet tended to consume less instead of more alcohol than the controls. Senter and Sinclair (1968) reported a rapid and large increase in alcohol consumption by a group of rats on a thiamine-deficient diet when this vitamin was included in the 7% alcohol solution. No effect of adding thiamine to the alcohol solution was found in a group whose diet included sufficient amounts of this vitamin.

When other substances are added to either the alcohol solution or the food, it is necessary to consider the possibility that the alcohol choice is due to a change in the relative palatability of the choices. Rogers *et al.* (1955) reported that the addition of 100 mg glutamine to the diet of rats decreased their choice of a 10% alcohol solution whereas intraperitoneal injection of 50 mg had no effect. In a subsequent experiment (Rogers *et al.*, 1956), alcohol consumption was decreased by addition to the food of glutamine whereas several other amino acids (glutamic acid, monosodium glutamate, asparagine, glycine) had no effect. This gives evidence that glutamine has a unique effect, but it could be due either to a dietary action or to a gustatory characteristic, enhancing palatability of the food.

Since vitamin deficiency generally causes reduced food intake, pair-fed controls are required to determine which factor causes the effect on alcohol intake. Such controls are lacking in a study by Williams *et al.* (1955), showing higher consumption of 10% alcohol by rats on a vitamin-poor diet than by a group on a vitamin-rich diet. An effect of the lowered food intake is suggested by the finding that in a prior choice test between a 10% w/v sucrose solution and water, the animals on the vitamin-poor diet consumed a larger amount of sucrose. Restriction of food intake would be expected to increase alcohol intake, not only as a source of calories but also because a diet which is limited in quantity, without specific deficiencies, shifts metabolism toward utilization of fats rather than carbohydrates. A rather severe limitation of diet appears necessary to cause substantial changes in alcohol consumption. Westerfeld and Lawrow (1953) found that with a choice between 10% alcohol and water, rats greatly increased their alcohol consumption when their solid food was restricted to 50% of the former quantity. A group of rats restricted to 75% of their former food consumption gained weight and did not increase their consumption of the 10% alcohol solution. Marfaing-Jallat (1963) and Royer and Lamarche (1965) reported increases in choice of an alcohol solution by rats when the food rations were limited to 50% of the previous consumption. Aschkenasy-Lelu (1960b) reported that choice of an alcohol solution increased during three days of food deprivation. This effect was larger in male than female rats and occurred in male but not female mice. Rodgers and McClearn (1962a) reported that food deprivation increased alcohol choice by a strain of mice with high alcohol preference (C57BL) whereas there was less effect on the alcohol choice of four strains which even when satiated show lower alcohol preference.

Evidence has been reported that alcohol choice decreases below the normal level during a period of increased food consumption following dietary restriction. Aschkenasy-Lelu (1960b) showed this effect in rats during five days following three days of food deprivation. Brady and Westerfeld (1947) reported that when vitamin supplements were added to a deficient diet, alcohol consumption decreased abruptly, followed by a rise. Senter and Sinclair (1968) showed lower alcohol choice in two groups of rats after a change from a thiamine–deficient to a nutritious diet than in two groups given the nutritious diet continuously. Wilson et al. (1969) found that when a choice between an alcohol solution and water was given, less alcohol was consumed by rats which had been subjected to one of four restricted feeding schedules for more than two months previously than by rats which had never been deprived of food. LeMagnen (1960) reported that instead of the usual increase in alcohol consumption by rats, after the 6% alcohol solution had been removed for 20 days, alcohol consumption was below normal if the removal of the alcohol solution coincided with restriction of food to 50% of the normal amount. This effect depended on rather severe food restriction, because it was not found with 75% of the normal rations, but it did not depend on abnormally high food consumption after the deprivation period because the alcohol consumption was likewise below normal when the food was limited to 100% of the normal amount.

Since deprivation of either food or water diminishes the voluntary intake of the other substance, water deprivation has many physiological effects in common with food deprivation. However, in a choice between an alcohol solution and water, thirsty animals would be expected to prefer the pure water to the liquid with food properties. Rick and Wilson (1966) found that in choice tests for 24 h between an alcohol solution and water, larger amounts of both fluids were drunk following 24 h of fluid deprivation than when the alcohol solution had been the sole fluid. A comparison of groups given different alcohol concentrations (2, 4, 8, 16%) showed that the fluid deprivation increased the percentage choice of the three lowest solutions and decreased the percentage choice of the highest one. Thiessen and McClearn (1965) obtained evidence for an adverse effect of thirst on alcohol choice in mice by limiting the test to one hour after 23 hours fluid deprivation. The lower percentage choice of the 10% alcohol solution under this condition, combined with the lower daily fluid consumption, resulted in much lower alcohol intake in g/kg/day than with continuous free choice. However, the decrease can be explained by the fact that after 23 hours fluid deprivation the average amount of alcohol consumed in one hour, approximately 2 g/kg, was a heavily intoxicating dose. Fuller (1967), with even more stringent limitation on availability of fluids, found that mice consumed more alcohol in a choice between an 8% concentration and water if the fluids were presented for five 1-min intervals, spaced one hour apart, than if they were presented for a single five-minute period. This difference, which developed only in the last three of the five test days, might be due to lower thirst levels in the later 1-min drinks. Data reported by Anderson and Smith (1963) showed less alcohol preference when monkeys had been deprived of fluid for 24 or 48 h. Comparisons between two strains of mice, by Thiessen and McClearn (1965) and by Fuller (1967), showed that the usual difference in alcohol preference was reduced in choice tests following fluid deprivation. This was probably due to consumption of a highly intoxicating dose under this condition, even by the strain with normally low alcohol preference.

(2) Other physiological variations

The effects of dietary conditions on alcohol consumption must be mediated by metabolic, hormonal, or other physiological functions which interact with each other and with the behavior of alcohol consumption in regulating the internal environment of the intact organism. Experimental manipulation of particular physiological functions may provide much information on the mechanisms by which alcohol consumption is regulated. However, because of the complex interactions among the regulators we should expect instances of ambiguous and contradictory results from experiments which seemingly alter the same function. This expectation has been amply fulfilled in the experiments reviewed below.

A disturbance of ethanol metabolism is indicated by the highly toxic effect of even small amounts of alcohol on humans who have been pretreated with disulfiram (Antabuse). The use of this drug as a deterrent to drinking in alcoholics is discussed in Chapter 11 (p. 762), and the physiological mechanisms for the toxic interaction of disulfiram with ethanol are discussed in Chapter 10 (pp. 675–677). Pretreatment with disulfiram decreases voluntary alcohol consumption by rats (Harkness et al., 1953). A daily disulfiram dose of 15 mg/kg administered orally caused a drastic decrease in alcohol consumption which had been elevated by restricting the food intake of the rats (Royer et al., 1962). Two hypoglycemic sulfonamides (chlorpropamide and phenbutamide) had similar but weaker effects. In three strains of mice, Schlesinger et al. (1966) found only a moderate decrease in alcohol consumption with a daily disulfiram dose (100 mg/kg, injected intraperitoneally) which was sufficient to cause marked inhibition of ethanol metabolism and a large increase in acetaldehyde levels. Hillbom (1967) reported that voluntary alcohol consumption by rats on a low protein, high fat diet was greatly decreased by deficiency of choline chloride and was increased by adding large amounts of this substance to the food. Although this effect could be due to an aversive gustatory characteristic of choline chloride, making the alcohol solution relatively more attractive, a more plausible explanation is based on the author's finding that the choline-deficient rats developed fatty livers, which may give rise to toxic levels of acetaldehyde if alcohol is ingested in metabolically significant amounts. However, this assumed rise in acetaldehyde has not yet been proven (cf. Chapter 9, p. 528).

Several drugs, used primarily for their antibiotic activity, have effects on alcohol consumption which have been attributed to changes in alcohol metabolism. Metronidazole (Flagyl), used as a trichomonacide, has a weak but apparently definite action of reducing craving for liquor in human alcoholics (Chapter 11, pp. 763–764) and decreasing voluntary alcohol consumption by rats (Campbell *et al.*, 1967). Chapter 10 (pp. 678–679) reviews evidence that metronidazole inhibits alcohol metabolism. Mendelson *et al.* (1965) reported that puromycin, an antibiotic which interferes with protein synthesis, decreased consumption by rats of a 10% alcohol solution, when it was the only fluid and also in a choice between the alcohol solution and water. Assays of LADH activity indicated that puromycin prevented the adaptive increase found in the control animals after several weeks of a 10% alcohol solution as the only fluid. Mardones (1960) suggested that a gradual decrease in alcohol consumption by rats treated with thioctic acid is due to the need for this substance by certain intestinal microorganisms which aid in the metabolism of acetaldehyde. Evidence in support of this theory was a finding that succinylsulfathiazole, an antibacterial agent, prevented this effect of thioctic acid on alcohol consumption. Other agents with important actions on bacteria have effects on alcohol consumption which are not readily explained but are suggestive. Rogers *et al.* (1955, 1956) reported a decrease in alcohol consumption by rats when their food included large amounts of glutamine, which is a necessary substance in the nutrition of *Streptococcus haemolyticus*. Nash *et al.* (1952) reported a marked increase in alcohol consumption by rats when infection was treated by sulfonamides.

Rodgers (1967) has suggested that the amount of voluntary alcohol consumption is primarily determined by variations in alcohol metabolism, but the complex physiological changes associated with alcohol metabolism may cause increased alcohol consumption under conditions which impair alcohol metabolism. One such condition is liver cirrhosis (Chapter 9, p. 524); production of this disease in rats by injections of carbon tetrachloride caused a large increase in voluntary alcohol consumption to a level of 6.6 g/kg/day (Sirnes, 1953). The author suggested that the alcohol may function to conserve thiamine, which is poorly utilized in chronic liver injury. This finding thus may indicate the motivation for the alcoholic's continued excessive drinking after he has already suffered liver damage. Iida (1958, 1960) likewise found that daily administration of carbon tetrachloride to mice caused a large increase in voluntary alcohol consumption. However, further experiments on mice (Iida, 1958) showed that alcohol consumption was increased by some hepatotoxic agents (chloroform, methyl alcohol, phosphorus) but not by others (allyl formate, DL-ethione), and there was no correlation between the increase in alcohol consumption and the amount of liver damage. The elevated alcohol consumption during administration of carbon tetrachloride was reduced by injections of ascorbic acid. Iida (1958, 1960) suggested that alcohol may alleviate a disturbance in glucose metabolism of a damaged liver. Rodgers (1967) stated that surgical removal of portions of the liver and periodic fuming with carbon tetrachloride did not markedly increase alcohol consumption by the strains of mice tested.

Fluid intake is affected by dietary, hormonal, and other physiological conditions. A diuretic effect of ethanol is well established (Chapter 4, p. 165). Baïsset and Montastruc (1962) reported a decrease in voluntary alcohol consumption by dogs when they were treated with an antidiuretic hormone. This suggests an aversive effect of the diuretic action of alcohol when fluid excretion is inhibited by an antidiuretic. Eriksson (1967) has reported that in rats the amount of alcohol consumption was not affected by the increased fluid intake caused by addition to the food of a diuretic drug (Dichlotride or Hygroton). Since the choice of alcohol as percentage of fluid intake decreased under this condition, the measure of alcohol consumption in g/kg/ day was thereby shown to be more stable than percentage preference. In spite of the tendency for a constant amount of alcohol consumption, also shown in Figs. 1–3 of the present chapter, the regulation of fluid intake apparently supersedes the appetite for alcohol. In Figs. 1–3, rats consumed less alcohol in g/kg/day at very low concentrations instead of increasing their fluid intake to maintain a constant level of alcohol consumption.

Rather inconsistent effects on alcohol consumption have been reported with experimental manipulations of hormonal secretions which regulate the general metabolic level. The contradictory findings may be due to the fact that general increase in metabolism tends to enhance rate of alcohol metabolism but also may enhance disturbances caused by the metabolism of this drug. For example, the hypoglycemic effect of alcohol can be more severe when the animal's glycogen reserves are consumed at a higher rate (as in hyperthyroidism), or if gluconeogenesis is inactive because of a high dietary intake of preformed glucose (Chapter 3, p. 112). This may be the basis for observations by Richter (1957b) of an inverse relationship between alcohol and sugar intake. Forsander et al. (1958) found that in rats alcohol consumption was increased by insulin or Nadisan, which induce hypoglycemia, and was drastically decreased by alloxan, which produces diabetes. Mardones and Segovia (cited acc. to Mardones, 1960) reported that partial pancreatectomy decreased alcohol consumption, and insulin increased alcohol consumption by these rats but not by normal animals. A decrease in alcohol consumption by rats daily administered two hypoglycemic sulfamides (Royer *et al.*, 1962) is attributable to specific metabolic interactions of these drugs with alcohol. The effect of these two compounds was rather small and gradual, and no effect was found with glybuthiazol or with a sufficient dose of insulin to cause convulsions in some of the rats. Zarrow *et al.* (1960) reported that alloxan diabetes increased alcohol consumption, but the amount of alcohol intake remained small and a large increase in water consumption resulted in a decrease in choice of alcohol as a percentage of fluid intake.

The thyroid gland is one of the most important regulators of the general metabolic level. Richter (1956) reported that addition of thyroid powder to the food reduced alcohol consumption, whereas rats which were made hypothyroid by removal of the thyroid gland increased their consumption of alcohol. He gave evidence that hyperthyroid rats are unable to metabolize alcohol adequately, thus explaining the avoidance of alcohol when thyroid powder was added to the diet. The more severe hypoglycemic response to ethanol in hyperthyroidism (Chapter 3, p. 112) provides a further mechanism for an aversive effect of ethanol. LeMagnen (1960) suggested that a decrease in voluntary alcohol consumption by rats after an interval of restricted food rations and no alcohol solution, reviewed earlier in the present chapter (p. 449), was due to a hyperthyroid response to the increase in food rations. In support of this hypothesis, the author reported that the alcohol consumption in this situation tended to increase in thyroidectomized rats. However, most other experimenters have reported conflicting effects. Zarrow and Rosenberg (1953) reported that alcohol consumption of rats was increased by adding to their food a daily dose of propyl thiouracil, which decreases thyroid functioning, but thyroidectomy did not increase alcohol consumption, and the high alcohol intake during thiouracil treatment was not reduced by administration of thyroxine. Mardones (1960) pointed out that the bitter taste of the thiouracil might have made the food less palatable, thus inducing the animals to obtain more of their calories from the alcohol. Aversive taste might also have accounted for the finding by Prieto *et al.* (cited acc. to Mardones, 1960) that the addition of thyroid powder to the diet increased alcohol consumption. Mardones and Segovia (cited acc. to Mardones, 1960) reported that administration of thyroxine increased alcohol consumption. Zarrow *et al.* (1960) found no effect of intraperitoneally injected thiouracil on alcohol consumption by rats when nearly all of their fluid intake was from a 10% glucose solution. Mirone (1957) found that an iodine deficient diet decreased alcohol consumption by mice. Mäenpää and Forsander (1966) likewise reported that alcohol consumption was decreased by an iodine-deficient diet in rats, but the effect was small and limited to the first few days after the dietary change. Another group showed a similar decrease in alcohol consumption after enrichment of the diet with iodine, giving evidence that the change in diet had a temporary inhibitory effect on alcohol consumption. In general, there is more consistent evidence for a decrease in alcohol consumption due to thyroid excess than for either an increase or decrease in alcohol consumption due to thyroid deficiency. Failures to find decreased alcohol consumption during hyperthyroidism might be caused by the nutritional deficiencies often associated with this condition.

Several experiments agree well in giving evidence for a positive relationship of alcohol consumption to adrenocortical activation. Zarrow et al. (1960) reported that alcohol consumption was increased by the stressors of cortisone or formaldehyde injection and prolonged exposure to a very cold environment. Under these conditions a third liquid choice of a glucose solution was consistently preferred to the 10% alcohol solution. Alcohol consumption was not decreased after adrenalectomy, but the 1% salt solution added to both the alcohol and water bottles may have counteracted the effect of adrenalectomy. Aschkenasy-Lelu (1965) found that in normal rats, adding a 1% salt concentration to both the water and the 10% alcohol solutions more than doubled consumption from both bottles without altering the percentage of total fluid selected from the alcohol bottle. In spite of this effect of 1% salt added to the fluids, Aschkenasy-Lelu (1965) and Mardones and Segovia (cited acc. to Mardones, 1960) found a decrease in alcohol consumption after adrenalectomy. Aschkenasy-Lelu (1965) also found that injections of corticosterone and desoxycorticosterone increased the alcohol consumption of adrenalectomized rats to normal levels. Adverse effects of intense adrenocortical activation on alcohol consumption may be indicated by the further findings that in intact rats corticosterone injections had little effect and injections of epinephrine slightly decreased alcohol consumption. Consistent with these findings is an experiment on mice (Iida, 1957), showing that the consumption of alcohol was increased by daily injections of 1% saline (10 ml/kg), corticosterone, and desoxycorticosterone but was decreased by a higher dose of desoxycorticosterone. Myers and Veale (1968) reported that alcohol choice in rats was reduced by administration of α-methyl-ptyrosine, which depletes brain catecholamines, and p-chlorophenylalanine, which selectively depletes levels of serotonin, a closely related amine.

Mardones (1960) reviewed several prior experiments showing slight and inconsistent effects of gonadectomy or injection of male sex hormones on alcohol consumption but a tendency for alcohol consumption to be decreased by injection of some female hormones (diethylstilbestrol and estradiol but not progesterone). Subsequent experiments have confirmed these conclusions. Zarrow et al. (1960) and Aschkenasy-Lelu (1960c) found little effect of gonadectomy on alcohol consumption in both sexes. Eriksson (1969c) found slightly but reliably lower alcohol consumption by ovariectomized than control rats. Aschkenasy-Lelu found little effect of testosterone injections (1960c) but a decrease in alcohol consumption after injections of diethylstilbestrol in intact (1958, 1960a) and gonadectomized (1960c) female rats and in intact male rats (1960a). Since this estrogenic hormone is normally elevated during the estrous stage of the female cycle, this effect is consistent with the decreased alcohol consumption in female rats during estrous, cited earlier in the present chapter (p. 445). Eriksson (1969c) found that a contraceptive hormone combination greatly decreased alcohol consumption both in ovariectomized and control female rats.

In spite of the importance of the central, sedative action of alcohol as an incentive for drinking in humans, there has been rather little research on the effects of other drugs with primarily central actions on alcohol consumption by laboratory animals. Rogers and Pelton (1958) tested effects of seven clinically used drugs, added to the food, on alcohol consumption in rats. An increase in alcohol consumption by the animals given promazine was attributable to aversion to the taste of this drug in the food. None of the other drugs had a reliable effect, although one (meprobamate) was also observed to have an aversive taste. A report that the addition of coffee to a poor quality diet increased alcohol consumption in rats (Register et al., 1967) might also be due to aversive taste of the coffee. Myers and Cicero (1968) found that a tranquilizing drug (tybamate, 20 mg/kg injected intraperitoneally) increased alcohol consumption in 4-h choice tests but a higher dose of tybamate (40 mg/kg) had no consistent effect. In an earlier experiment (Myers, 1963), two tranquilizers (meprobamate and hydroxyphenamate, both injected intraperitoneally in a dose of 80 mg/kg) increased choice of the alcohol solution. Moore et al. (1952b) found that daily injection of amphetamine (4 mg/kg) decreased alcohol consumption by most of their rats, but increased it in the case of the two animals with the highest pre-treatment alcohol consumption. LeMagnen (1958) reported increased consumption of a 6% alcohol solution by rats after 24 days of amphetamine administration. However, the increase could be accounted for by a caloric deficiency, because the food ration was reduced by 15% during the methamphetamine administration; a control group, given the same reduction in their food ration without the drug, showed almost as large an increase in alcohol consumption. Kakihana et al. (1968a) reported that administration of goldthioglucose, a drug which causes hyperphagia, decreased alcohol consumption by C57BL mice, which normally show a high preference for alcohol. The authors attributed this effect to hypothalamic damage but noted that liver changes and gastric distress might also have been involved. Myers and Veale (1969) found that alcohol consumption in rats was increased by intraventricular infusion of small amounts of acetaldehyde, paraldehyde, or methanol. This indicates lack of specificity of an earlier finding (Myers, 1963) that alcohol consumption was increased by intraventricular infusions of ethanol. Cicero and Myers (1969) reported that intraventricular injection of carbachol, which increases consumption of water, decreased consumption of an alcohol solution (4–12%) which was the only fluid available. Therefore, under these conditions alcohol was chosen as a food or a drug rather than as a substitute for water.

(3) Drinking for sedative effects

Chapter 7 has reviewed extensive evidence in experimental animals that alcohol relieves fear and in particular reduces the avoidance component of an approach-avoidance conflict. Therefore, it seems reasonable to expect that animals might learn to increase their alcohol consumption in order to obtain these effects. However, the doses which effectively alleviate fear are generally at an intoxicating level, above the amount that animals are willing to consume voluntarily under normal conditions. Further difficulties in learning to drink for sedative effects include the delayed pharmacological action, the unpleasant effects of excessive quantities, the necessity to consume large volumes of fluid in order to obtain the alcohol in a palatable dilution, and the tendency for stressful situations to inhibit consummatory behavior. In spite of these obstacles, experiments on several species of laboratory animals have given good evidence that stressful situations elicit an increase in alcohol consumption (Barry and Buckley, 1966).

Masserman and Yum (1946) reported an increase in alcohol choice by cats which had been made "neurotic" by receiving air blasts or shock whenever they approached a box containing food. Most of the animals in this conflict situation chose the plain milk more often than the milk containing alcohol, but normal cats almost always avoided the alcohol solution and in the test situation the alcohol choice gradually diminished within a few weeks as "normal" behavior became reestablished. A probable aid in training the cats to drink alcohol was that they had previously experienced relief from the neurotic symptoms under the influence of an alcohol dose administered orally or intraperitoneally. Chapter 7 (p. 359) reviews that phase of the experiment. In a subsequent article, Masserman (1957) further described the training procedures which successfully induced voluntary alcohol consumption in about half of 18 neurotic cats. The experimental procedures were rather complex and variable, and the article by Masserman and Yum (1946) omitted some important items of information, notably the amount of alcohol solution or milk consumed in the choice test. However, this initial experiment yielded generally convincing evidence that laboratory animals may drink to obtain the sedative effects of alcohol. Other experimenters have provided further evidence that conflict situations may increase alcohol consumption. Ahlfors (1969) found increasing choice of a 15% alcohol solution instead of water by hungry rats during 4-h sessions in which they received painful electric shock whenever they approached the food cup. This experiment, which was reviewed in detail by Barry (1969), lacked a control for the possibility that the rats learned to obtain calories from the alcohol solution instead of the food. Nevertheless, the apparent consumption of an intoxicating dose, in this situation, is an interesting finding. Von Wright et al. (1970) subjected hungry rats to similar conflict tests for 24-h periods with continuous availability of water, a 10% alcohol solution, and also a liquid food solution with sufficient quinine added to reduce the consumption to an amount equal to the alcohol solution. In addition to this control for consumption of alcohol as a non-punished source of calories, the experiment included control animals which obtained the solid food without punishment. The experimental animals, punished by shock for obtaining the solid food, were divided into a strong-shock and weak-shock group. Alcohol consumption during the test session increased in the high-shock animals but not in the weak-shock or control animals.

In these conflict tests, the increased alcohol consumption occurred in the stressful situation, presumably with the incentive for alleviating the fear and avoidance of the shock. If the animal is subjected to inescapable shocks, the stressful situation tends to decrease all consummatory behavior, including alcohol intake. However, there is evidence that alcohol consumption may be elevated after the stressful experience. Von Wright *et al.* (1970) found that in contrast to the effect of conflict, which increased alcohol consumption only in the test situation, rats subjected to severe, inescapable shocks in a similar situation generally showed little change in alcohol consumption during the 24-h test, but many of them drank a larger amount of alcohol in the home cage throughout a number of days afterward. Mild, inescapable shocks had little effect on alcohol consumption. Casey (1960) reported that in rats, tested for choice between a 16% alcohol solution and water, alcohol consumption increased during 16 days of inescapable shocks but increased further to a peak at about two weeks after termination of the shocks. Brown (1968) reported that in mice housed individually, alcohol consumption was elevated during two weeks when they were subjected to rapid spinning for 5 or 20 min per day. The alcohol consumption undoubtedly did not occur while the animals were spun and therefore is a further example of a post-stress effect. However, alcohol consumption decreased to normal during two weeks after cessation of spinning, and the effect of the spinning was not found in animals housed in groups of four, presumably due to greater resistance to the stress effect. Williams (1959) reported briefly a finding that alcohol choice by rats increased during the stressor of flashing lights and jangling cowbells day and night near their cages.

When animals are trained to perform a shock-avoidance response, most of their food and liquid consumption generally occurs during rest periods rather than during the avoidance schedule. Therefore, increases in alcohol intake are attributable to changes in consummatory behavior after, rather than during the test session. Clark and Polish (1960) subjected two rhesus monkeys to 56 days of 1-h shock-avoidance sessions alternating with 1-h rest periods. Consumption of a 20% alcohol solution was increased, both when it was the only fluid available and in a choice with water. Alcohol consumption decreased gradually during 56 days after termination of the shocks. Mello and Mendelson (1966) subjected two rhesus monkeys to 6-h sessions of shock avoidance, or receiving the shocks which the other monkey failed to avoid, alternating with 6-h rest periods. The results were inconclusive but showed a tendency for higher alcohol consumption on days when the animal performed the avoidance response than on days when it received inescapable shocks or the warning signals without shocks. Cicero *et al.* (1968) tested daily consumption of an alcohol solution and water by rats subjected

References p. 468

to 2-h sessions of shock avoidance alternating with 6-hour rest periods. Alcohol consumption was not affected by this schedule but increased in 4 rats which were given unavoidable shocks, each preceded by a warning signal, during the shock-avoidance sessions. Myers and Cicero (1968) replicated this effect of unavoidable shocks but also found an increase in alcohol consumption caused by the preceding shock-avoidance schedule, in a group of 12 rats. Myers and Cicero (1969) found that the unavoidable shocks, during a shock-avoidance schedule, increased alcohol consumption during 4 h of choice test, including an hour before and an hour after the daily 2-h test session. The hypothesis that alcohol consumption increases after but not during the stress sessions is compatible with an earlier finding by Myers and Holman (1967) that alcohol consumption by rats was not affected by inescapable shocks delivered without rest periods throughout the 14 days of tests for choice between the alcohol solution and water.

In some other experiments, increases in alcohol consumption are attributable to stress but complex or unusual procedures allow other interpretations. Clay (1964) found higher percentage choice of alcohol by rats which performed a series of stressful tasks, but the concurrent food deprivation of these animals might have accounted for their difference from the controls in alcohol choice. Myers (1961a), in a lever-pressing choice among food, water, and a 20% alcohol solution, found that selection by rats of the alcohol response was enhanced when no food or liquid was delivered. This was attributed to the stressful frustration of nonreward, and in a further study (Myers, 1961b), elimination of this alcohol preference by meprobamate was attributed to the tranquilizing action of that drug. Senter and Persensky (1968) reported that after rats had been trained to drink a 7% alcohol solution in order to avoid painful shocks, a group which remained in the test apparatus with the warning signals presented but no shocks showed a higher percentage choice of the alcohol solution throughout 2 weeks than a group returned to their home cages.

A few experimenters have reported that stressful procedures failed to increase alcohol consumption. Masserman (1959) stated that monkeys refused to drink an alcohol solution in the same type of conflict situation which elicited alcohol consumption by cats. Miller (1956) reported failure to induce cats to drink an alcohol solution in a situation similar to that of Masserman but involving fear without conflict. Powell et al. (1966) reported that 2-min sessions of inescapable shock five times per day tended to increase alcohol consumption in female rats but had the opposite effect on males.

There are very few experimental reports of a decrease in alcohol consumption as a result of stressful procedures. Rodgers and Thiessen (1964) reported that the presumed stressful effects of aggregation decreased percentage choice of alcohol in mice, but isolation may be a more severe stressor, as suggested in the experiment by Brown (1968) reviewed on p. 459. Thiessen and Rodgers (1965) found that several stressful procedures decreased subsequent alcohol choice by mice, but the stressors were of rather brief duration and in a different situation from the choice test.

Alcohol consumption seems to be increased only after a prolonged and severe stressor, but such powerful stimulation tends to inhibit all consummatory behavior. This may account for some of the inconsistent findings and the tendency for alcohol consumption to increase only after the stress session. Nevertheless, several experiments have given strong evidence that certain stress situations result in elevated alcohol consumption. It is plausible to attribute this effect to the desire for obtaining the sedative action of this drug, but other explanations are possible. For example, Williams (1959) suggested that stress leads to increased alcohol consumption by aggravating the dietary deficiency which, according to his theory, is the cause of excessive drinking. The hormonal and other physiological responses to stressors may affect not only the pharmacological or nutritional effects of alcohol but also the metabolic reactions and the animal's sensitivity to its taste.

E. Summary

In a number of different experiments under various conditions, with continuous choice between an alcohol solution and water, the percentage alcohol choice in relation to total fluid consumption generally decreased progressively with increasing concentrations above 7.5% v/v. The amount of alcohol consumption by rats in g/day was rather constant at the same alcohol concentrations, indicating stable regulation of the amount of intake rather than aversion for high concentrations. When the alcohol solution is sufficiently dilute, the animal usually consumes most of its fluid from the alcohol bottle but does not increase its fluid intake sufficiently to maintain its preferred level of alcohol consumption. Different experiments show great variations in the average amount of alcohol consumption, and in some groups of rats the alcohol intake in g/kg/day seems to be close to the rat's metabolic capability. Calculation of the intake is made difficult by the fact that some experimenters report only the percentage alcohol choice without reporting the amount of fluid consumption from the alcohol and water bottles, and many of the experimenters who do report amount of alcohol consumption fail to report the body weights of the animals. Ambiguities in many reports are whether the percentage alcohol concentration is calculated as v/v or w/v and whether the percentage is of a 100% or 95% concentration.

The procedure of offering a simultaneous choice among three or more fluids has generally shown little effect on the regulation of daily alcohol intake. In comparison with a two-choice test, the total amount of alcohol consumption in a choice among several concentrations was the same in rats but somewhat higher in hamsters. The availability of a sweet-tasting liquid decreases alcohol consumption but in most experiments this effect is only moderate. Alcohol consumption can be substantially increased by adding sucrose to the alcohol or by adding quinine to the water. There is little evidence for preference of beer, wine or diluted whisky over the same concentration of ethyl alcohol in water.

Choice between the alcohol and water bottle may be affected by position preferences, especially if the bottles differ in proximity to the food bin or other environmental features. In order to control and detect position preferences, the locations of the alcohol and water bottles should be interchanged occasionally, but frequent changes may impair the stability of the choice response and decrease the amount of alcohol consumed. Tests of other environmental variations have given evidence for higher alcohol consumption in very cold temperatures and by animals housed alone rather than in groups.

Under most experimental conditions, animals voluntarily consume only small or moderate quantities of alcohol, maintaining the blood alcohol concentration at a very low level. Unlike humans, laboratory animals seem to be highly resistant to voluntary intoxication and to the development of addictive dependence on alcohol. Consumption of intoxicating quantities has generally been induced only when alcohol is the sole fluid presented and the animals are thirsty or subjected to special conditions. Methods for inducing heavy alcohol consumption include a food reinforcement schedule which elicits high fluid consumption and a requirement to drink the alcohol solution in order to obtain food or to escape from painful shocks. There is little evidence that intoxication can be induced for prolonged periods or repeatedly by these or any other procedures.

Previous exposure to alcohol generally results in a marked and prolonged increase in alcohol consumption. Experimenters should provide a period of exposure, for example by giving an alcohol solution as the only fluid, in order to obtain a high and stable level of alcohol consumption in choice tests. The effect on alcohol consumption seems to be greater if the exposure begins at an early age or is continued for several months. In a few cases such procedures seem to have resulted in damaging excess of alcohol consumption instead of the prevalent pattern of well regulated intake, but pathological responses of this type have been difficult to induce in laboratory animals. Infusion of small amounts of ethanol into the ventricles of the brain has been reported to increase alcohol intake. After a period of exposure to alcohol, an interval during which it is absent generally seems to enhance subsequent alcohol consumption, but this "alcohol deprivation" effect is not attributable to the development of addictive craving. Although prior exposure to alcohol generally increases subsequent consumption, forced exposure to aversively high concentrations may have the opposite effect. The amount of alcohol consumption is greater if the alcohol concentration on successive days is progressively increased instead of decreased.

Some experiments on choice between an alcohol solution and water have given evidence for detectability of the alcohol solution at concentrations below 0.1 %. Experiments with anosmic rats and blowflies have shown that the odor of alcohol is an important determinant of preference at low concentrations and aversion at higher concentrations. Various techniques for measuring the detectability threshold, applied to animals and humans, have generally indicated that the weakest alcohol concentrations which can be reliably detected are approximately 2–3 %.

A number of experiments have demonstrated stable differences in alcohol consumption of several inbred strains of mice. In particular, C57BL black mice consistently show the highest choice of alcohol whereas DBA mice almost completely avoid alcohol solutions. When strains which differ in alcohol preference are crossbred, the offspring are generally intermediate in this respect. Alcohol preference seems to be a polygenic characteristic with a high degree of heritability in mice. Development of heavy-drinking and light-drinking strains of rats from the same inbred stock has indicated that in this species the heritability of alcohol preference is lower and appears to be sex-linked. The heavy-drinking strain is more heterogeneous in alcohol choice and gives evidence for a higher level of general metabolism, although no difference in rate of alcohol metabolism has been found. In comparisons among long-established, inbred strains of rats and mice, those with higher

References p. 468

alcohol preference generally seem to show greater vigor and boldness. There is evidence for superior metabolic and behavioral adjustment to the effects of alcohol by the high-preference C57 mouse strain, although rate of ethanol metabolism is no higher than in mouse strains with low alcohol preference. The C57 strain has a high rate of liver alcohol dehydrogenase activity, but this probably indicates superiority in general metabolism rather than in specific ability to metabolize ethanol. In addition to the information already obtained, much more can be learned about determinants of alcohol consumption as a result of identification of strain differences, establishment of new light-drinking and heavy-drinking strains, cross-breeding experiments, and statistical analysis of genetic characteristics.

The few comparisons made among species indicate the highest alcohol preference in hamsters, which may be attributed to tolerance for strong-tasting substances in this desert species. Alcohol consumption in g/kg is generally higher in mice than rats, but one mouse strain avoids alcohol at all detectable concentrations whereas rats generally show preference or at least no aversion for alcohol at concentrations up to about 5%. The few studies on primates indicate a rather high level of voluntary alcohol consumption, in tests of continuous choice, and chimpanzees have been observed to drink an intoxicating amount of an alcoholic beverage presented for a brief time.

Consumption by males and females should be compared in terms of g/kg; reports of percentage choice of the alcohol solution or intake in ml/day tend to overestimate consumption by males, which are heavier and drink less fluid in relation to their body weight. Reports on sex difference in alcohol consumption are conflicting. Some experimenters have found higher alcohol consumption by female rats and mice, especially in heavy-drinking strains, attributable to a higher rate of ethanol metabolism in females. Other experimenters have found lower alcohol consumption by female rats and mice, attributable to a sharply decreased amount of alcohol intake during the estrous stage of their reproductive cycle. Alcohol consumption rises above the normal level during lactation.

Experiments on rats, mice, and chimpanzees have shown that alcohol consumption in g/kg/day is inversely related to age. Comparisons among strains, and studies of individual differences among rats or mice of the same strain, sex, and age, have generally agreed in showing that higher alcohol consumption is characteristic of animals which are lighter, superior in performance, and more emotionally reactive, with a higher activity level both metabolically and behaviorally.

Greater metabolic tolerance for alcohol in rats with higher alcohol preference is indicated by findings of less excretion of ketone bodies after oral administration of fat and less elevation of the lactate/pyruvate ratio in the liver after injection of ethanol. In this respect the animals with low alcohol preference are more heterogeneous, including some with and some without the apparent metabolic capability for heavy alcohol consumption. The degree of metabolic disturbance rather than rate of ethanol elimination appears to be the limiting factor. These data suggest that a low degree of metabolic tolerance prevents heavy drinking in some individuals. Other physiological or emotional variations may account for the fact that some but not all the animals with the metabolic capability choose to drink heavily. There is evidence in both humans and laboratory animals that individuals with a high preference for alcohol show a low preference for sugar and sweetened foods.

Contrary to expectations based on the inverse relationship between alcohol and sugar preference, variations in the carbohydrate content of the diet appear to have no consistent effect on alcohol consumption. However, several experiments on rats and mice indicate an inverse relationship between the fat or protein content of the diet and alcohol consumption. High fat intake may be expected to impair metabolic tolerance to alcohol whereas high protein intake may supply nutritional substances, in particular thiamine (vitamin B_1), which are necessary for metabolism of carbohydrates and thus permit the animal to consume more calories from that source. Claims that alcohol consumption is specifically increased by thiamine deficiency are only partially supported by experiments with paired-fed controls, which show that the increase in alcohol consumption is primarily due to the general nutritional deficiency or the reduced food intake in thiamine-deficient animals. Restriction of food intake without specific dietary deficiencies increases alcohol intake, but a rather severe decrease in solid food is necessary to cause this effect. The increase in alcohol consumption is attributable not only to the incentive for obtaining the calories available in the alcohol solution but also to a shift in metabolism toward utilization of fats rather than carbohydrates. A further example of a nutritional determinant is that alcohol consumption decreases below the normal level during a period of increased food intake, due to preceding food deprivation or removal of a nutritional deficiency.

In tests of choice between an alcohol solution and water after fluid deprivation, alcohol preference is decreased as would be expected, but the effect is rather small, perhaps because a water-deprived animal eats very little food and thus becomes hungry also. Thirsty mice have been reported to drink heavily intoxicating amounts of alcohol in a brief choice test.

Alcohol consumption is affected by various metabolic conditions. Disulfiram (Antabuse), which causes an aversive reaction to alcohol in humans, has been shown to decrease voluntary alcohol consumption in rats and mice. Metronidazole (Flagyl), which gives evidence for weakly aversive interaction with alcohol in humans, also decreases alcohol consumption by rats. Effects of some other antibiotics on alcohol consumption have been attributed to their actions on intestinal flora which participate in alcohol metabolism. Responses to disturbance in liver function are indicated by a decrease in alcohol consumption when fatty livers are induced by choline chloride and increase in alcohol consumption when liver cirrhosis, induced by carbon tetrachloride, impairs utilization of thiamine.

Hormonal secretions which regulate general metabolic level tend to have opposite effects on alcohol consumption, because increases in metabolism tend to enhance rate of alcohol metabolism but also may enhance disturbances caused by the metabolism of this drug. Alcohol consumption is increased by insulin, producing hypoglycemia, and decreased by the hyperglycemic, diabetic effect of alloxan. Experimental manipulations of thyroid function have generally shown that hyperthyroidism decreases alcohol consumption, but thyroid deficiency seems to have inconsistent effects. Alcohol consumption generally is increased by adrenocortical activation, induced by cortical hormone administration, by various physiological stressors, or by addition of salt to the diet. Conversely, alcohol consumption is decreased by adrenalectomy and by administration of drugs which deplete brain catecholamines and 5-hydroxytryptamine.

Alcohol consumption is decreased by administration of estrogen, in agreement with the decrease in alcohol consumption found during the estrous stage of the female reproductive cycle. Drugs with primarily central actions have not shown consistent effects on alcohol consumption. In some studies, addition of the drug to the food or to the drinking fluids raises the possibility that the effect on alcohol consumption could be due to a change in the palatability of the food or fluids. Findings of changes in alcohol consumption due to drugs infused into the ventricles of the brain could be due to local, toxic effects rather than the systemic, pharmacological actions.

Several experiments have given evidence for increase in alcohol consumption in several species of animals subjected to conflict or other stressful experiences. Alcohol consumption is increased during conflict between approach and avoidance of food, whereas alcohol consumption generally increases only in the rest period after exposure to an inescapable stress situation. The few experiments on monkeys suggest a large increase in alcohol consumption by these animals in response to stressful experiences. Reports of difficulties in reproducing the increase in alcohol consumption may be due to the fact that the stressors tend to decrease all consummatory behavior. The experiments in general give evidence that alcohol consumption may be increased by a desire to obtain its sedative effects, in a stressful situation. However, other interpretations are possible on the basis of the metabolic or nutritional rather than pharmacological actions of alcohol.

REFERENCES

ADAMSON, R. AND BLACK, R. (1959). Volitional drinking and avoidance learning in the white rat. *J. Comp. Physiol. Psychol. 52*, 734–736.

AHLFORS, U. G. (1969). Alcohol and conflict; A qualitative and quantitative study on the relationship between alcohol consumption and an experimentally induced conflict situation in albino rats. *Alcohol Research in the Northern Countries* Vol. 16, Helsinki. 77 pp.

ANDERSON, W. D. AND SMITH, O. A., JR. (1963). Taste and volume preferences for alcohol in *Macaca nemestrina*. *J. Comp. Physiol. Psychol. 56*, 144–149.

ARVOLA, A. AND FORSANDER, O. (1961). Comparison between water and alcohol consumption in six animal species in free-choice experiments. *Nature 191*, 819–820.

ARVOLA, A. AND FORSANDER, O. A. (1963). Hamsters in experiments of free choice between alcohol and water. *Quart. J. Studies Alc. 24*, 591–597.

ASCHKENASY-LELU, P. (1958). Action d'un oestrogène sur la consommation spontanée d'une boisson alcoolisée chez le rat. *Compt. Rend. Acad. Sci. 247*, 1044–1047.

ASCHKENASY-LELU, P. (1960a). Action inhibitrice d'une hormone oestrogène sur la consommation spontanée d'alcool par le rat. *Rev. Franc. Etud. Clin. 5*, 132–138.

ASCHKENASY-LELU, P. (1960b). L'alcoolisation chronique expérimentale. Influence exercée par divers facteurs physiologiques sur la consommation spontanée d'alcool chez les animaux de laboratoire. *Ann. Nutrition et Aliment. 14*, 101–133.

ASCHKENASY-LELU, P. (1960c). Relation entre l'effet inhibiteur des oestrogènes sur la consommation d'alcool du rat et leur action génitale. *Arch. Sci. Physiol. 14*, 165–174.

ASCHKENASY-LELU, P. (1965). Surrénales et consommation préférentielle d'alcool chez le rat. *Arch. Sci. Physiol. 19*, 231–245.

BAÏSSET, A. AND MONTASTRUC, P. (1962). Effet de l'hormone antidiurétique sur le besoin d'alcool créé par l'habitude. *Compt. Rend. Soc. Biol. 156*, 945–948.

BARRY, H., III (1968). Sociocultural aspects of alcohol addiction. In: A. WIKLER, Ed., *The Addictive States. Res. Publ. Assoc. Nerv. Ment. Dis. 46*, 455–471.

BARRY, H., III (1969). Review of Ahlfors, U. G. (1969). *Quart. J. Studies Alc. 30*, 1081–1083.

BARRY, H., III AND BUCKLEY, J. P. (1966). Drug effects on animal performance and the stress syndrome. *J. Pharm. Sci. 55*, 1159–1183.

BARRY, H., III AND WALLGREN, H. (1968). A further note on preparing alcohol solutions. *Quart. J. Studies Alc. 29*, 176–178.

BOVET, D., BOVET-NITTI, F. AND OLIVERIO, A. (1968). Memory and consolidation mechanisms in avoidance learning of inbred mice. *Brain Res. 10*, 168–182.

BOVET, D., BOVET-NITTI, F. AND OLIVERIO, A. (1969). Genetic aspects of learning and memory in mice. *Science 163*, 139–149.

BRADY, R. A. AND WESTERFELD, W. W. (1947). The effect of B-complex vitamins on the voluntary consumption of alcohol by rats. *Quart. J. Studies Alc. 7*, 499–505.

BREWSTER, D. J. (1968). Genetic analysis of ethanol preference in rats selected for emotional reactivity. *J. Heredity 59*, 283–286.

BREWSTER, D. J. (1969). Ethanol preference in strains of rats selectively bred for behavioral characteristics. *J. Genet. Psychol. 115*, 217–227.

BROWN, R. V. (1968). Effects of stress on voluntary alcohol consumption in mice. *Quart. J. Studies Alc. 29*, 49–53.

BROWN, R. V. (1969). Vitamin deficiency and voluntary alcohol consumption in mice. *Quart. J. Studies Alc. 30*, 592–597.

BRUELL, J. H. (1964). Inheritance of behavioral and physiological characters of mice and the problem of heterosis. *Am. Zoologist 4*, 125–138.

CAMPBELL, B., TAYLOR, J. A. T. AND HASLETT, W. L. (1967). Anti-alcohol properties of metronidazole in rats. *Proc. Soc. Exptl. Biol. Med. 124*, 191–195.

CARVER, J. W., NASH, J. B., EMERSON, G. A. AND MOORE, W. T. (1953). Effects of pregnancy and lactation on voluntary alcohol intake of hamsters. *Federation Proc. 12*, 309. (Abstract.)

CASEY, A. (1960). The effect of stress on the consumption of alcohol and reserpine. *Quart. J. Studies Alc. 21*, 208–216.

CICERO, T. J. AND MYERS, R. D. (1968). Selection of a single ethanol test solution in free-choice studies with animals. *Quart. J. Studies Alc. 29*, 446–448.

CICERO, T. J. AND MYERS, R. D. (1969). Preference-aversion functions for alcohol after cholinergic stimulation of the brain and fluid deprivation. *Physiol. Behav. 4*, 559–562.

CICERO, T. J., MYERS, R. D. AND BLACK, W. C. (1968). Increase in volitional ethanol consumption following interference with a learned avoidance response. *Physiol. Behav. 3*, 657–660.

CLARK, R. AND POLISH, E. (1960). Avoidance conditioning and alcohol consumption in rhesus monkeys. *Science 132*, 223–224.

CLAY, M. L. (1964). Conditions affecting voluntary alcohol consumption in rats. *Quart. J. Studies Alc. 25*, 36–55.

DEMBER, W. N. AND KRISTOFFERSON, A. B. (1955). The relation between free-choice alcohol consumption and susceptibility to audiogenic seizures. *Quart. J. Studies Alc. 16*, 86–95.

DENEAU, G., YANAGITA, T. AND SEEVERS, M. H. (1969). Self-administration of psychoactive substances by the monkey. A measure of psychological dependence. *Psychopharmacologia 16*, 30–48.

DETHIER, V. G. (1961). The role of olfaction in alcohol ingestion by the blowfly. *J. Insect Physiol. 6*, 222–230.

DIAMANT, H., FUNAKOSHI, M., STRÖM, L. AND ZOTTERMAN, Y. (1963). Electrophysiological studies on human taste nerves. In: *Olfaction and taste*, Y. ZOTTERMAN, Ed., Pergamon Press, Oxford. Pp. 193–203.

DIAMANT, H., OAKLEY, B., STRÖM, L., WELLS, C. AND ZOTTERMAN, Y. (1965). A comparison of neural and psychophysical responses to taste stimuli in man. *Acta Physiol. Scand. 64*, 67–74.

DICKER, S. E. (1958). The effects of methylpentynol on ethanol drinking and on water metabolism in rats. *J. Physiol. (London) 144*, 138–147.

DOLCETTA, B. AND STELLA, L. (1956). Accettazione e rifiuto delle bevande alcooliche nei prematuri. (Acceptance and refusal of alcoholic beverages by premature babies.) *Atti XI Congr. Psicol. Ital.* 329–330. (Abstr. *Quart. J. Studies Alc.* 1958, *19*, 678.)

DUVEAU, A., DAHAN, G. AND COSNIER, J. (1966). Consommations d'eau et d'alcool de souris sensibles ou réfractaires à la crise audiogène. *Compt. Rend. Soc. Biol. 160*, 791–794.

EAYRS, J. T. AND MOULTON, D. G. (1960). Studies in olfactory acuity. I. Measurement of olfactory thresholds in the rat. *Quart. J. Exptl. Psychol. 12*, 90–98.

EGGLETON, M. G. (1941). The effect of alcohol on the central nervous system. *Brit. J. Psychol. 32*, 52–61.

EIMER, E. O. AND SENTER, R. J. (1968). Alcohol consumption in domestic and wild rats. *Psychonomic Sci. 10*, 319–320.

EMERSON, G. A., BROWN, R. G., NASH, J. B. AND MOORE, W. T. (1952). Species variation in preference for alcohol and in effects of diet or drugs on this preference. *J. Pharmacol. Exptl. Therap. 106*, 384. (Abstract.)

ERIKSSON, K. (1967). Effect of two diuretic drugs on liquid consumption and free choice of alcohol in albino rats. *Nature 213*, 316–317.

ERIKSSON, K. (1968). Genetic selection for voluntary alcohol consumption in the albino rat. *Science 159*, 739–741.

ERIKSSON, K. (1969a). Factors affecting voluntary alcohol consumption in the albino rat. *Ann. Zool. Fennici 6*, 227–265.

ERIKSSON, K. (1969b). The estimation of heritability for the self-selection of alcohol in the albino rat. *Ann. Med. Exptl. Fenniae 47*, 172–174.

ERIKSSON, K. (1969c). Effects of ovarectomy and contraceptive hormones on voluntary alcohol consumption in the albino rat. *Japan. J. Studies Alc. 4*, 1–5.

ERIKSSON, K. (1970). Genetical analysis of the voluntary alcohol consumption in mice under quinine–saccharine motivation. *J. Clin. Lab. Invest.* Suppl., in press.

ERIKSSON, K. AND MALMSTRÖM, K. K. (1967). Sex differences in consumption and elimination of alcohol in albino rats. *Ann. Med. Exptl. Fenniae 45*, 389–392.

ERIKSSON, K. AND PIKKARAINEN, P. H. (1968). Differences between the sexes in voluntary alcohol consumption and liver ADH-activity in inbred strains of mice. *Metabolism 17*, 1037–1042.

FITZ-GERALD, F. L., BARFIELD, M. A. AND WARRINGTON, R. J. (1968). Voluntary alcohol consumption in chimpanzees and orangutans. *Quart. J. Studies Alc. 29*, 330–336.

FORSANDER, O. A. (1966). Metabolism of rats as related to voluntary alcohol consumption. *Psychosom. Med. 28*, 521–528.

FORSANDER, O. AND SALASPURO, M. (1962). Voluntary ethanol consumption as related to ketone bodies metabolism in rats. *Life Sciences 9*, 467–470.

FORSANDER, O., KOHONEN, J. AND SUOMALAINEN, H. (1958). Physiological alcohol consumption. *Quart. J. Studies Alc. 19*, 379–387.

FREDERICSON, E. (1953). The wall-seeking tendency in three inbred mouse strains (*Mus musculus*). *J. Genet. Psychol. 82*, 143–146.

FREED, E. X. (1968). Effect of self-intoxication upon approach-avoidance conflict in the rat. *Quart. J. Studies Alc. 29*, 323–329.

FULLER, J. L. (1964). Measurement of alcohol preference in genetic experiments. *J. Comp. Physiol. Psychol. 57*, 85–88.

FULLER, J. L. (1967). Effect of drinking schedule upon alcohol preference in mice. *Quart. J. Studies Alc. 28*, 22–26.

GILLESPIE, R. J. G. AND LUCAS, C. C. (1958). An unexpected factor affecting the alcohol intake of rats. *Canad. J. Biochem. Physiol. 36*, 37–44.

GOODRICK, C. L. (1967). Alcohol preference of the male Sprague-Dawley albino rat as a function of age. *J. Gerontol. 22*, 369–371.

GREEN, E. L. AND MEIER, H. (1965). Use of laboratory animals for the analysis of genetic influences upon drug toxicity. *Ann. N. Y. Acad. Sci. 123*, 295–304.

HARKNESS, W. D., JOHNSTON, C. D. AND WOODARD, G. (1953). Methods to evaluate in rats the antipathy to alcohol produced by Antabuse and related compounds. *Federation Proc. 12*, 328–329.

HAUSMANN, M. F. (1932). The behavior of albino rats in choosing food and stimulants. *J. Comp. Psychol. 13*, 279–309.

HELLEKANT, G. (1965a). Electrophysiological investigation of the gustatory effect of ethyl alcohol. I: The summated response of the chorda tympani in the cat, dog and rat. *Acta Physiol. Scand. 64*, 392–397.

HELLEKANT, G. (1965b). Electrophysiological investigation of the gustatory effect of ethyl alcohol. II: A single fibre analysis in the cat. *Acta. Physiol. Scand. 64*, 398–406.

HILLBOM, M. (1967). The effect of choline chloride on the voluntary alcohol consumption of the albino rat. *Japan. J. Studies Alc. 2*, 111–114.

HIRSCH, J., Ed. (1967). *Behavior-genetic analysis.* McGraw-Hill, New York. 522 pp.

HOLMAN, R. B. AND MYERS, R. D. (1968). Ethanol consumption under conditions of psychogenic polydipsia. *Physiol. Behav. 3*, 369–371.

IIDA, S. (1957). Experimental studies on the craving for alcohol: I. Alcoholic drive in mice following administration of saline. *Japan. J. Pharmacol. 6*, 87–93.

IIDA, S. (1958). Experimental studies on the craving for alcohol. II. Alcoholic drive in mice following administration of hepatotoxic agents. *Japan. J. Pharmacol. 8*, 70–74.

IIDA, S. (1960). Experimental studies on the craving for alcohol. III. The relationship between alcoholic craving and carbohydrate metabolism. *Japan. J. Pharmacol. 10*, 15–20.

KAHN, A. J. (1969). Site selection and the response to ethanol in C3H mice; Passive acceptance versus active attraction. *Quart. J. Studies Alc. 30*, 609–617.

KAHN, M. AND STELLAR, E. (1960). Alcohol preference in normal and anosmic rats. *J. Comp. Physiol. Psychol. 53*, 571–575.

KAKIHANA, R. AND MCCLEARN, G. E. (1963). Development of alcohol preference in BALB/c mice. *Nature 119*, 511–512.

KAKIHANA, R., BROWN, D. R., MCCLEARN, G. E. AND TABERSHAW, I. R. (1966). Brain sensitivity to alcohol in inbred mouse strains. *Science 154*, 1574–1575.

KAKIHANA, R., BUTTE, J. C. AND NOBLE, E. P. (1968a). Effects of goldthioglucose on alcohol consumption in C57BL mice. *Life Sciences 7*, 825–832.

KAKIHANA, R., NOBLE, E. P. AND BUTTE, J. C. (1968b). Corticosterone response to ethanol in inbred strains of mice. *Nature 218*, 360–361.

KEEHN, J. D. (1969). "Voluntary" consumption of alcohol by rats. *Quart. J. Studies Alc. 30*, 320–329.

KORMAN, M. AND STEPHENS, H. D. (1960). Effects of training on the alcohol consummatory response in rats. *Psychol. Rep. 6*, 327–331.

KORMAN, M., KNOPF, I. J. AND LEON, R. L. (1962). Alcohol as a discriminative stimulus: A preliminary report. *Texas Repts. Biol. and Med. 20*, 61–63.

KORN, S. J. (1960). The relationship between individual differences in the responsivity of rats to stress and intake of alcohol. *Quart. J. Studies Alc. 21*, 605–617.

KOZ, G. AND MENDELSON, J. H. (1967). Effects of intraventricular ethanol infusion on free choice alcohol consumption by monkeys. In: *Biochemical factors in alcoholism*, R. P. MAICKEL, Ed., Pergamon Press, Oxford. Pp. 17–24.

KUBENA, R. K. AND BARRY, H., III (1969). Generalization by rats of alcohol and atropine stimulus characteristics to other drugs. *Psychopharmacologia 15*, 196–206.

LAGERSPETZ, K. (1964). Studies on the aggressive behavior of mice. *Ann. Acad. Sci. Fennicae* Series B, *131*, 1–131.

LE MAGNEN, J. (1958). Apparition de l'alcoolisme chez le rat blanc à la cessation d'un traitement prolongé par la D'amphétamine. *J. Physiol. (Paris) 50*, 371–374.

LE MAGNEN, J. (1960). Étude de quelques facteurs associés à des modifications de la consommation spontanée d'alcool éthylique par le rat. *J. Physiol. (Paris) 52*, 873–884.

LE MAGNEN, J. AND MARFAING-JALLAT, P. (1961). Le rôle des afférences buccales dans le déterminisme des consommations spontanées d'alcool chez le rat. *J. Physiol. (Paris) 53*, 407–408.

LE MAGNEN, J. AND MARFAING-JALLAT, P. (1962). L'interaction entre les consommations spontanées d'alcool éthylique et de divers régimes alimentaires chez le rat blanc. *Arch. Sci. Physiol. 16*, 179–192.

LESTER, D. (1961). Self-maintenance of intoxication in the rat. *Quart. J. Studies Alc. 22*, 223–231.

LESTER, D. (1966). Self-selection of alcohol by animals, human variation, and the etiology of alcoholism; A critical review. *Quart. J. Studies Alc. 27*, 395–438.

LESTER, D. AND GREENBERG, L. A. (1952). Nutrition and the etiology of alcoholism; The effect of sucrose, saccharin and fat on the self-selection of ethyl alcohol by rats. *Quart. J. Studies Alc. 13*, 553–560.

LOISELEUR, J. AND PETIT, M. (1947). L'éthylisme expérimental de la souris. *Compt. Rend. Soc. Biol. 141*, 568–569.

MÄENPÄÄ, P. H. AND FORSANDER, O. A. (1966). Influence of iodine deficiency on free choice between alcohol and water in rats. *Quart. J. Studies Alc. 27*, 596–603.

MARDONES, J. (1960). Experimentally induced changes in the free selection of ethanol. *Int. J. Neurobiol. 2*, 41–76.

MARDONES, J. (1963). The alcohols. In: *Physiological Pharmacology*, W. S. ROOT AND F. G. HOFMANN, Eds. Academic Press, New York; Vol. 1, pp. 99–183.

MARDONES, J., SEGOVIA, N. AND HEDERRA, A. (1953). Heredity of experimental alcohol preference in rats. II. Coefficient of hereaity. *Quart. J. Studies Alc. 14*, 1–2.

MARDONES, J. SEGOVIA-RIQUELME, N., HEDERRA, A. AND ALCAÍNO, F. (1955). Effect of some self-selection conditions on the voluntary alcohol intake of rats. *Quart. J. Studies Alc. 16*, 425–437.

MARFAING-JALLAT, P. (1963). Différences interdividuelles de la consommation spontanée d'éthanol par le rat blanc dans diverses situations expérimentales. *J. Physiol. (Paris) 55*, 296–297.

MARFAING,-JALLAT, P. (1964). Nouvelles données sur le rôle des afférences buccales dans le déterminisme des consommations spontanées d'alcool chez le rat. *Compt. Rend. Soc. Biol. 158*, 2049–2053.

MASSERMAN, J. H. (1957). Stress situations in animals and the nature of conflict. In: *Neuropharmacology, Transactions of the Third Conference*, H. A. ABRAMSON, Ed., Josiah Macy, Jr. Foundation, New York. Pp. 147–167.

MASSERMAN, J. H. (1959). Behavioral pharmacology in animals. In: *Neuro-psychopharmacology*, P. B. BRADLEY, P. DENIKER AND C. RADOUCO-THOMAS, Eds., Elsevier, Amsterdam; Vol. 1, pp. 97–107.

MASSERMAN, J. H. AND YUM, K. S. (1946). An analysis of the influence of alcohol on experimental neuroses in cats. *Psychosom. Med. 8*, 36–52.

McCLEARN, G. E. (1959). The genetics of mouse behavior in novel situations. *J. Comp. Physiol. Psychol. 52*, 62–67.

McCLEARN, G. E. (1960). Strain differences in activity of mice: Influence of illumination. *J. Comp. Physiol. Psychol. 53*, 142–143.

McCLEARN, G. E. (1963). Genetic differences in the effect of alcohol upon behaviour of mice. In: *Alcohol and Road Traffic*, J. D. J. HAVARD, Ed., British Med. Assoc., London. Pp. 153–155.

McCLEARN, G. E. AND RODGERS, D. A. (1959). Differences in alcohol preference among inbred strains of mice. *Quart. J. Studies Alc. 20*, 691–695.

McCLEARN, G. E. AND RODGERS, D. A. (1961). Genetic factors in alcohol preference of laboratory mice. *J. Comp. Physiol. Psychol. 54*, 116–119.

McCLEARN, G. E., BENNETT, E. L., HEBERT, M., KAKIHANA, R. AND SCHLESINGER, K. (1964). Alcohol dehydrogenase activity and previous ethanol consumption in mice. *Nature 203*, 793–794.

MELLO, N. K. AND MENDELSON, J. H. (1964). Operant performance by rats for alcohol reinforcement; A comparison of alcohol-preferring and nonpreferring animals. *Quart. J. Studies Alc. 25*, 226–234.

MELLO, N. K. AND MENDELSON, J. H. (1965). Operant drinking of alcohol on a rate-contingent ratio schedule of reinforcement. *J. Psychiat. Res. 3*, 145–152.

MELLO, N. K. AND MENDELSON, J. H. (1966). Factors affecting alcohol consumption in primates. *Psychosom. Med. 28*, 529–550.

MENDELSON, J. H. AND MELLO, N. K. (1964). Ethanol and whisky drinking patterns in rats under free-choice and forced-choice conditions. *Quart. J. Studies Alc. 25*, 1–25.

MENDELSON, J. H., MELLO, N. K., CORBETT, C. AND BALLARD, R. (1965). Puromycin inhibition of ethanol ingestion and liver alcohol dehydrogenase activity in the rat. *J. Psychiat. Res. 3*, 133–143.

MILLER, N. E. (1956). Effects of drugs on motivation: The value of using a variety of measures. *N.Y. Acad. Sci. 65*, 318–333.

MIRONE, L. (1952). The effect of ethyl alcohol on growth, fecundity and voluntary consumption of alcohol by mice. *Quart. J. Studies Alc. 13*, 365–369.

MIRONE, L. (1957). Dietary deficiency in mice in relation to voluntary alcohol consumption. *Quart. J. Studies Alc. 18*, 552–560.

MIRONE, L. (1958). The effect of ethyl alcohol on growth and voluntary consumption of alcohol by successive generations of mice. *Quart. J. Studies Alc. 19*, 388–393.

MIRONE, L. (1959). Water and alcohol consumption by mice. *Quart. J. Studies Alc. 20*, 24–27.

MOORE, W. T., MOORE, B. M., NASH, J. B. AND EMERSON, G. A. (1952a). Effects of maze running and sonic stimulation on voluntary alcohol intake of albino rats. *Tex. Rep. Biol. Med. 10*, 59–65.

MOORE, W. T., MOORE, B. M., NASH, J. B. AND EMERSON, G. A. (1952b). Effect of amphetamine sulfate on voluntary choice of alcohol in albino rats. *Tex. Repts. Biol. and Med. 10*, 406–413.

MOULTON, D. G. AND EAYRS, J. T. (1960). Studies in olfactory acuity: II. Relative detectability of *n*-aliphatic alcohols by the rat. *Quart. J. Exptl. Psychol. 12*, 99–109.

MYERS, A. K. (1962). Alcohol choice in Wistar and G-4 rats as a function of environmental temperature and alcohol concentration. *J. Comp. Physiol. Psychol. 55*, 606–609.

MYERS, R. D. (1961a). Changes in learning, extinction, and fluid preferences as a function of chronic alcohol consumption in rats. *J. Comp. Physiol. Psychol. 54*, 510–516.

MYERS, R. D. (1961b). Effects of meprobamate on alcohol preference and on the stress of response extinction in rats. *Psychol. Reports 8*, 385–392.

MYERS, R. D. (1963). Alcohol consumption in rats: Effects of intracranial injections of ethanol. *Science 142*, 240–241.

MYERS, R. D. (1966). Voluntary alcohol consumption in animals: Peripheral and intracerebral factors. *Psychosom. Med. 28*, 484–497.

MYERS, R. D. AND CAREY, R. (1961). Preference factors in experimental alcoholism. *Science 134*, 469–470.

MYERS, R. D. AND CICERO, T. J. (1968). Effects of tybamate on ethanol intake in rats during psychological stress in an avoidance task. *Arch. Intern. Pharmacodyn. 175*, 440–446.

MYERS, R. D. AND CICERO, T. J. (1969). Effects of serotonin depletion on the volitional alcohol intake of rats during a condition of psychological stress. *Psychopharmacologia 15*, 373–381.

MYERS, R. D. AND ERIKSSON, K. (1968). Ethyl alcohol consumption: Valid measurement in albino rats. *Science 161*, 76–77.

MYERS, R. D. AND HOLMAN, R. B. (1966). A procedure for eliminating position habit in preference-aversion tests for ethanol and other fluids. *Psychonomic Sci. 6*, 235–236.

MYERS, R. D. AND HOLMAN, R. B. (1967). Failure of stress of electric shock to increase ethanol intake in rats. *Quart. J. Studies Alc. 28*, 132–137.

MYERS, R. D. AND VEALE, W. L. (1968). Alcohol preference in the rat: Reduction following depletion of brain serotonin. *Science 160*, 1469–1471.

MYERS, R. D. AND VEALE, W. L. (1969). Alterations in volitional alcohol intake produced in rats by chronic intraventricular infusions of acetaldehyde, paraldehyde or methanol. *Arch. Intern. Pharmacodyn. 180*, 100–113.

NASH, J. B., MOORE, W. T. AND EMERSON, G. A. (1952). Effects of sulfonamides on voluntary choice of 10% v/v alcohol by albino rats. *J. Pharmacol. Exptl. Therap. 106*, 408. (Abstract)

NEWMAN, H. W. AND LEHMAN, A. J. (1938). Nature of acquired tolerance to alcohol. *J. Pharmacol. Exptl. Therap. 62*, 301–306.

NICHOLS, J. R. AND HSIAO, S. (1967). Addiction liability of albino rats: Breeding for quantitative differences in morphine drinking. *Science 157*, 561–563.

PARISELLA, R. M. AND PRITHAM, G. H. (1964). Effect of age on alcohol preference by rats. *Quart. J. Studies Alc. 25*, 248–258.

PEACOCK, L. J. AND WATSON, J. A. (1964). Radiation-induced aversion to alcohol. *Science 143*, 1462–1463.

PORTA, E. A., KOCH, O. R. AND HARTROFT, W. S. (1969). A new experimental approach in the study of chronic alcoholism. IV. Reproduction of alcoholic cirrhosis in rats and the role of lipotropes *versus* vitamins. *Lab. Invest. 20*, 562–572.

POWELL, B. J., KAMANO, D. K. AND MARTIN, L. K. (1966). Multiple factors affecting volitional consumption of alcohol in the Abrams Wistar rat. *Quart. J. Studies Alc. 27*, 7–15.

PURDY, M. B. AND LEE, J. G. (1962). The effect of restricted food intake, thiamin deficiency and riboflavin deficiency on the voluntary consumption of ethanol by the albino rat. *Quart. J. Studies Alc. 23*, 549–556.

RAMSAY, R. W. AND DIS, H. VAN (1967). The role of punishment in the aetiology and continuance of alcohol drinking in rats. *Behav. Res. Therap. 5*, 229–235.

REED, J. G. (1951). A study of the alcoholic consumption and amino acid excretion patterns of rats of different inbred strains. *Texas Univ. Publ. 5109*, 144–149.

REGISTER, U. D., MARSH, S. R., THURSTON, C. E., HORNING, M. C. AND HARDINGE, M. G. (1967). Effect of diet on consumption of alcohol in rats. *Federation Proc. 26*, 693. (Abstract.)

REGNAULT, M. AND ASCHKENASY-LELU, P. (1963). Effets de la privation de protéines alimentaires sur la consommation préférentielle d'alcool chez le rat. *J. Physiol. (Paris) 55*, 324.

RICHTER, C. P. (1926). A study of the effect of moderate doses of alcohol on the growth and behavior of the rat. *J. Exptl. Zool. 44*, 397–418.

RICHTER, C. P. (1941). Alcohol as food. *Quart. J. Studies Alc. 1*, 650–662.

RICHTER, C. P. (1953). Alcohol, beer and wine as foods. *Quart. J. Studies Alc. 14*, 525–539.

RICHTER, C. P. (1956). Loss of appetite for alcohol and alcoholic beverages produced in rats by treatment with thyroid preparations. *Endocrinology 59*, 472–478.

RICHTER, C. P. (1957a). Decreased appetite for alcohol and alcoholic beverages produced in rats by thyroid treatment. In: *Hormones, Brain Function, and Behavior*, H. HOAGLAND. Ed., Academic Press, New York. Pp. 217–220.

RICHTER, C. P. (1957b). Production and control of alcoholic cravings in rats. In: *Neuropharmacology; Transactions of the Third Conference*, ABRAMSON, H. A., Ed., Josiah Macy, Jr., Foundation, New York. Pp. 39–146.

RICK, J. T. AND WILSON, C. W. M. (1966). Alcohol preference in the rat; Its relationship to total fluid consumption. *Quart. J. Studies Alc. 27*, 447–458.

RODGERS, D. A. (1966). Factors underlying differences in alcohol preference among inbred strains of mice. *Psychosom. Med. 28*, 498–513.

RODGERS, D. A. (1967). Alcohol preference in mice. In: *Comparative Psychopathology*, J. ZUBIN AND H. HUNT, Eds., Grune and Stratton, New York. Pp. 184–201.

RODGERS, D. A. AND LEWIS, U. J. (1963). Relationship of liver content of glucose and glucurone to ethanol preference of inbred mice. *Japan. J. Pharmacol. 13*, 125–126.

RODGERS, D. A. AND McCLEARN, G. E. (1962a). Alcohol preference of mice. In: *Roots of behavior*, E. L. BLISS, Ed., Harper, New York. Pp. 68–95.

RODGERS, D. A. AND McCLEARN, G. E. (1962b). Mouse strain differences in preference for various concentrations of alcohol. *Quart. J. Studies Alc. 23*, 26–33.

RODGERS, D. A. AND McCLEARN, G. E. (1964). Sucrose versus ethanol appetite in inbred strains of mice. *Quart. J. Studies Alc. 25*, 26–35.

RODGERS, D. A. AND THIESSEN, D. D. (1964). Effects of population density on adrenal size, behavioral arousal, and alcohol preference of inbred mice. *Quart. J. Studies Alc. 25*, 240–247.

RODGERS, D. A., McCLEARN, G. E., BENNETT, E. L. AND HEBERT, M. (1963). Alcohol preference as a function of its caloric utility in mice. *J. Comp. Physiol. Psychol. 56*, 666–672.

RODGERS, D. A., WARD, P. A., THIESSEN, D. D. AND WHITWORTH, N. S. (1967). Pathological effects of prolonged voluntary consumption of alcohol by mice. *Quart. J. Studies Alc. 28*, 618–630.

ROGERS, L. L. AND PELTON, R. B. (1958). Effect of behavior-altering drugs on alcohol consumption by rats. *Tex. Repts. Biol. and Med. 16*, 133–136.

ROGERS, L. L., PELTON, R. B. AND WILLIAMS, R. J. (1955). Voluntary alcohol consumption by rats following administration of glutamine. *J. Biol. Chem. 214*, 503–506.

ROGERS, L. L., PELTON, R. B. AND WILLIAMS, R. J. (1956). Amino acid supplementation and voluntary alcohol consumption by rats. *J. Biol. Chem. 220*, 321–323.

ROYER, R. AND LAMARCHE, M. (1965). Une méthode expérimentale d'étude de l'activité antialcool type Antabuse. *Arch. Intern. Pharmacodyn. 156*, 306–318.

ROYER, R., DEBRY, G. AND LAMARCHE, M. (1962). Recherches expérimentales sur les réactions vasomotrices à l'alcool après administrations de quelques sulfamides hypoglycémiants. *Thérapie 17*, 989–997.

SCHADEWALD, M., EMERSON, G. A., MOORE, W. T. AND MOORE, B. M. (1953). Voluntary preference for alcohol of white rats after gonadectomy. *Federation Proc. 12*, 364–365. (Abstract.)

SCHLESINGER, K. (1966). Genetic and biochemical correlates of alcohol preference in mice. *Am. J. Psychiat. 122*, 767–773.

SCHLESINGER, K., KAKIHANA, R. AND BENNETT, E. L. (1966). Effects of tetraethylthiuramdisulfide (Antabuse) on the metabolism and consumption of ethanol in mice. *Psychosom. Med. 28*, 514–520.

SCHUSTER, C. R. AND THOMPSON, T. (1969). Self administration of and behavioral dependence on drugs. *Ann. Rev. Pharmacol. 9*, 483–502.

SEGOVIA-RIQUELME, N., VITALE, J. J., HEGSTED, D. M. AND MARDONES, J. (1956). Alcohol metabolism in "drinking" and "non-drinking" rats. *J. Biol. Chem. 223*, 399–403.

SEGOVIA-RIQUELME, N., CAMPOS, I., SOLODKOWSKA, W., GONZÁLES, G., ALVARADO, R. AND MARDONES, J. (1962). Metabolism of labeled ethanol, acetate, pyruvate, and butyrate in "drinker" and "nondrinker" rats. *J. Biol. Chem. 237*, 2038–2040.

SEGOVIA-RIQUELME, N., CAMPOS, I., SOLODKOWSKA, W., FIGUEROLA-CAMPS, I. AND MARDONES, J. (1964). Glucose and gluconate metabolism in "drinker" and "nondrinker" rats. *Med. Exp. 11*, 185–190.

SENTER, R. J. AND PERSENSKY, J. J. (1968). Effects of environment on ethanol consumption in rats after conditioning. *Quart. J. Studies Alc. 29*, 856–862.

SENTER, R. J. AND SINCLAIR, J. D. (1968). Thiamin-induced alcohol consumption in rats. *Quart. J. Studies Alc. 29*, 337–341.

SENTER, R. J., EIMER, E. O. AND RICHMAN, C. L. (1968). Intersubject and intrasubject variability in the consumption of alcohol. *Psychonomic Sci. 10*, 165–166.

SHEPPARD, J. R., ALBERSHEIM, P. AND McCLEARN, G. E. (1968). Enzyme activities and ethanol preference in mice. *Biochem. Genet. 2*, 205–212.

SINCLAIR, J. D. AND SENTER, R. J. (1967). Increased preference for ethanol in rats following alcohol deprivation. *Psychonomic Sci. 8*, 11–12.

SINCLAIR, J. D. AND SENTER, R. J. (1968). Development of an alcohol-deprivation effect in rats. *Quart. J. Studies Alc. 29*, 863–867.

SIRNES, T. B. (1953). Voluntary consumption of alcohol in rats with cirrhosis of the liver; A preliminary report. *Quart. J. Studies Alc. 14*, 3–18.

SOHLER, A., BURGIO, P. AND PELLERIN, P. (1969). Changes in drinking behavior in rats in response to large doses of alcohol. *Quart. J. Studies Alc. 30*, 161–164.

STEENKISTE, J. VAN (1964). Contribution à l'étude des différences d'appétence alcoolique de deux races de rats de laboratoire. *J. Physiologie (Paris) 56*, 457–458.

TERROINE, T. AND ROCHETTE, J. (1946). Instinct, expérience ou hasard dans le libre choix de rats, entre une ration normale et une ration alcoolisée. *Arch. Intern. Pharmacodyn. 72*, 191–205.

THIESSEN, D. D. (1964). Population density, mouse genotype, and endocrine function in behavior. *J. Comp. Physiol. Psychol. 57*, 412–416.

THIESSEN, D. D. AND MCCLEARN, G. E. (1965). Thirst and alcohol preference of inbred strains of mice. *J. Comp. Physiol. Psychol. 59*, 436–438.

THIESSEN, D. D. AND NEALEY, V. G. (1962). Adrenocortical activity, stress response and behavioral reactivity of five inbred mouse strains. *Endocrinology 71*, 267–270.

THIESSEN, D. D. AND RODGERS, D. A. (1965). Alcohol injection, grouping, and voluntary alcohol consumption of inbred strains of mice. *Quart. J. Studies Alc. 26*, 378–383.

THIESSEN, D. D., WHITWORTH, N. S. AND RODGERS, D. A. (1966). Reproductive variables and alcohol consumption of the C57BL/Crgl female mouse. *Quart. J. Studies Alc. 27*, 591–595.

THIESSEN, D. D., WHITWORTH, N. AND RODGERS, D. A. (1967). Reproductive functions and metabolic capacity as determinants of alcohol preference in C57BL female mice. *J. Comp. Physiol. Psychol. 63*, 151–154.

THOMAS, K. (1969). Selection and avoidance of alcohol solutions by two strains of inbred mice and derived generations. *Quart. J. Studies Alc. 30*, 849–861.

THOMPSON, W. R. (1953). The inheritance of behaviour: behavioural differences in fifteen mouse strains. *Canad. J. Psychol. 7*, 145–155.

TOBACH, E. (1957). Individual differences in behavior and alcohol consumption in the rat. *Quart. J. Studies Alc. 18*, 19–29.

VEALE, W. L. AND MYERS, R. D. (1969). Increased alcohol preference in rats following repeated exposures to alcohol. *Psychopharmacologia 15*, 361–372.

WALLGREN, H. AND FORSANDER, O. (1963). Effect of adaptation to alcohol and of age on voluntary consumption of alcohol by rats. *Brit. J. Nutr. 17*, 453–457.

WERTZ, A. W., HORN, P. S. VAN AND LLOYD, L. E. (1951). The effect of the ingestion of alcohol on the storage and excretion of thiamine. *J. Nutrition 43*, 181–191.

WESTERFELD, W. W. AND LAWROW, J. (1953). The effect of caloric restriction and thiamin deficiency on the voluntary consumption of alcohol by rats. *Quart. J. Studies Alc. 14*, 378–384.

WHITNEY, G. D. AND WHITNEY, Y. (1968). Ethanol toxicity in the mouse and its relationship to ethanol selection. *Quart. J. Studies Alc. 29*, 44–48.

WILLIAMS, R. J. (1959). *Alcoholism: The Nutritional Approach.* Univ. of Texas Press, Austin. x + 118 pp.

WILLIAMS, R. J., BERRY, L. J. AND BEERSTECHER, E., JR. (1949). Biochemical individuality. III. Genetotrophic factors in the etiology of alcoholism. *Arch. Biochem. 23*, 275–290.

WILLIAMS, R. J., PELTON, R. B. AND ROGERS, L. L. (1955). Dietary deficiencies in animals in relation to voluntary alcohol and sugar consumption. *Quart. J. Studies Alc. 16*, 234–244.

WILSON, A. S., BERNSTEIN, L. AND TURRELL, E. S. (1969). Alcohol selection in rats with different early feeding experiences. *Quart. J. Studies Alc. 30*, 566–570.

WILSON, C. W. M. (1969). An analysis of the mechanisms involved in the taste for drink. In: *Scientific basis of drug dependence*, H. STEINBERG, Ed., J. and A. Churchill, London. Pp. 221–242.

WILSON, E. C. (1967). Ethanol metabolism in mice with different levels of hepatic alcohol dehydrogenase. In: *Biochemical factors in alcoholism*, R. P. MAICKEL, Ed., Pergamon Press, New York. Pp. 115–124.

WILSON, E. C., RESPESS, J. C., HOLLIFIELD, C. AND PARSON, W. (1961). Studies of alcohol metabolism in mice which preferentially consume ethanol. *Gastroenterology 40*, 807–808. (Abstract.)

WRIGHT, J. M. VON, PEKANMÄKI, L. AND MALIN, S. (1970). Effects of conflict and stress on the intake of alcohol in rats. *Quart. J. Studies Alc.*, in press.

ZARROW, M. X. AND ROSENBERG, B. (1953). Alcoholic drive in rats treated with propyl thiouracil. *Amer. J. Physiol. 172*, 141–146.

ZARROW, M. X., ADUSS, H. AND DENISON, M. E. (1960). Failure of the endocrine system to influence alcohol choice in rats. *Quart. J. Studies Alc. 21*, 400–413.

ZUCCHI, M. AND SANTANGELO, F. (1956). Accettazione e rifiuto delle bevande alcooliche in un gruppo di bambini con deficienza mentale di vario grado. (Acceptance and refusal of alcoholic beverages in a group of children with mental deficiencies of various degrees.) *Arch. Psicol. Neurol. Psichiat. 17*, 1009–1021. (Abstr. *Quart. J. Studies Alc.* 1958, *19*, 342.)

Chapter 9

Prolonged Exposure to Alcohol

Repeated doses of a drug may have effects which differ greatly from the acute effects of a single dose. The development of dependence on alcohol and the onset of medical complications, after repeated or prolonged intoxication, are major criteria for alcoholism, and therefore of special importance. Most of the experimental work on effects of prolonged alcohol consumption relates implicitly or explicitly to some aspect of alcoholism. The present chapter is primarily concerned with the contribution of controlled experiments to the description and understanding of the effects of prolonged exposure to alcohol. These studies form a part of the background necessary for evaluation of the causes and treatments of alcoholism. Portions of the vast clinical and pathological literature on alcoholics provide supplementary information and enable us to point out areas in which the conclusions from experimental findings agree or disagree with clinical observations of alcoholics.

Each of the sections of this chapter contains much material which pertains to the effects of excessive drinking and the symptoms of alcoholism. The first section, on nutritional aspects, reviews the consequences of the fact that alcohol is the only commonly used drug which is a substantial source of calories. These nutritional aspects are involved in the development of organ pathologies associated with alcoholism, which are discussed in subsequent sections of the chapter. The second section reviews pharmacological aspects of the effects of prolonged alcohol consumption on the central nervous system. The topics covered are tolerance and the withdrawal syndrome. The third section discusses possible metabolic factors in tolerance and dependence. The next two sections deal with the development of organic pathological alterations. Most of the material concerns the liver, where nearly all alcohol is metabolized and where cirrhosis is an important consequence of excessive alcohol consumption. Diseases of the central nervous system and of various other organs and tissues are reviewed in the final section prior to the summary.

A. Nutritional aspects

Alcohol doses sufficient for pharmacological effects also comprise a substantial amount of calories. Chapter 3 reviews the mechanisms for metabolism and utilization of this energy source. Some theories of the etiology of alcoholism, reviewed in Chapter 11, are based on this nutritional property of alcohol. Contrary to such theories, the present authors believe that the pharmacological effects of alcohol account for the attraction of alcoholic beverages, both for normal drinkers and for alcoholics. We think it illogical to view alcoholism as a phenomenon conceptually apart from drug dependence in general. Consequently, we are skeptical about theories that emphasize the singular properties of alcohol as a nutrient, instead of placing the problem of alcoholism into the general context of drug abuse.

The antecedents of alcoholism are extremely difficult to identify, whereas consequences of alcohol use are more readily accessible to experimental study. It is evident that nutritional deficiencies arising from prolonged, excessive alcohol consumption are important factors in the development of organ pathologies. The nutritional aspects of prolonged alcohol use are the first ones discussed in this chapter, not to emphasize them in relation to other aspects but because of the non-specific, pervasive effects of nutritional deficiencies. Therefore, repetition is avoided by dealing with this topic prior to the discussion of the different categories of organ systems in the subsequent sections of this chapter.

Nutritional aspects of alcoholism have been reviewed by several contributors to a symposium of the British Nutrition Society (*Proc. Nutr. Soc. 14*, 93–129, 1955). Olson (1964) has written a valuable review on nutrition and alcoholism which includes discussion of metabolic aspects and of the mechanisms by which dietary deficiencies may contribute to organic lesions in alcoholics. A recent review of the metabolism and utilization of alcohol is by Trémolières *et al.* (1967).

(1) Alcohol as a source of calories

Bjerre (1899), Atwater and Benedict (*e.g.*, 1902, and Carpenter, 1915; cited acc. to Houssay, 1955) demonstrated that total energy expenditure in human subjects remained unchanged if ethanol was included in their diet, and that utilization of other sources of energy decreased in proportion to the energy derived from ethanol. Later, Carpenter and Lee (1937) showed that ethanol decreased the utilization of carbohydrates and lipids with little influence on protein metabolism. Similar findings were reported by Richter (1953). The early calorimetric work has been reviewed by Carpenter and Lee (1937) and Mitchell and Curzon (1940). In spite of the conclusive evidence that energy derived from ethanol substitutes fully for energy from other substrates, the public has repeatedly been told that energy from ethanol is totally lost as heat. One reason for this erroneous belief has been the fact that the rate of alcohol metabolism is not augmented by exposure to cold or by muscular work. The explanation for this is that the metabolic rate of the principal site of alcohol oxidation, the liver, is not affected by acute cold exposure or by muscular exercise (*cf.* Chapter 3). The continuing discussion and some recent conflicting reports prompted Barnes *et al.* (1965) and Pawan (1968) to re-investigate the topic in human subjects, and previous results were confirmed.

The partial oxidation of ethanol to acetate in the liver results in release of one third of the chemical energy from ethanol available to the body and covers at least 75 % of the energy need of the liver (Leloir and Muñoz, 1938; Lundquist *et al.*, 1962; Forsander, 1963; Tygstrup *et al.*, 1965). The acetate derived from ethanol with the remaining two thirds of the available energy is mainly oxidized in tissues other than the liver and naturally contributes to their energy balance. The mean elimination rate is 0.1 g ethanol/kg body weight per h (2.4 g ethanol/kg body weight per day). With release of 7 kcal from each g of ethanol, a person weighing 70 kg would derive about 1100 kcal from ethanol within 24 h. Since the human basal energy requirement is about 1650 kcal per day for a body weight of 70 kg, about two thirds of this amount may be supplied by ethanol if it is continuously present and metabolized. Close to half of the requirement in sedentary work (about 2500 kcal during 24 h) can thus be supplied by ethanol. As discussed by Forsander (1963) and Hartroft (1967), these are important facts in any consideration of the effects of ethanol on the human organism. Unfortunately, the share of ethanol combustion in the energy balance of the body has been grossly underrated in some authoritative treatises on alcoholism (Kennedy and Fish, 1959).

Table 2–11, in Chapter 2, includes a compilation of data on the percentage share of ethanol in the metabolism of humans and various common laboratory animals. During oxidation of ethanol the major contribution of this substrate to the total metabolism of the body, in all of the species listed, obviously must have consequences for the metabolism in general. Since ethanol is simply and elegantly metabolized without digestion, it has been advantageously used in parenteral nutrition (Wilkinson, 1955; Thorén, 1963, 1964). However, the metabolic limitations and also the pharmacological properties of intoxicating doses preclude administration of the entire caloric requirement in the form of ethanol.

(2) Effects on growth and reproduction

The combined calorigenic and pharmacological properties of ethanol are clearly seen in its effects on the growth of the developing organism. Experiments on effects of prolonged alcohol administration on this simple and basic measure of biological action are summarized in Table 9–1. This coverage is generally limited to investigations with a sufficiently large number of animals to yield statistically valid results. As might be expected, there is most information on the laboratory rat.

Adult rats on a normal laboratory diet drink approximately 8–10 ml of water per 100 g of body weight per day. Consumption of such a volume of 10% v/v alcohol as the sole drinking fluid brings the amount of alcohol per day, 6–8 g/kg body weight, close to the animals' capacity of elimination and supplies about 35% of the calories. As the data in Table 9–1 indicate, no harmful effects have been found with a nutritious diet. The same conclusion is obtained from some less rigorous but longer-lasting experiments than those presented in the table, in which the calorie consumption of experimental animals has been recorded (Richter, 1926, 1941, 1953; Mirone, 1965b) or restricted (e.g., Zarrow et al., 1962). In recent work with liquid diets to rats as the only source of both nutrients and fluid, 36% of the calories given as alcohol did not retard growth and even permitted cure of liver pathology induced by deficient diets (Takada et al., 1967).

When the only source of fluid contains alcohol substantially in excess of 10% v/v, the necessity for remaining within the capacity for alcohol metabolism curtails the fluid intake. The resultant dehydration appears to be the main cause of growth retardation (Morgan *et al.*, 1957). Dehydration is also the most likely explanation of the hematuria, the damage to the epithelial cells of the renal proximal tubuli, and the enlarged kidneys observed by Orten *et al.* (1967) in rats receiving 20 or 40% alcohol as their sole source of fluid. In diabetes insipidus induced experimentally in rats, addition of alcohol to the drinking fluid even in low concentration (0.3% v/v) diminishes the fluid intake (Lambert *et al.*, 1965).

When intoxicating doses of alcohol are administered repeatedly to young rats, their growth is retarded by amounts which are well tolerated when consumed voluntarily in the drinking fluid (Mallov, 1955; Kokata and Furutoku, 1956; Figueroa and Klotz, 1962a). This differential effect was recently demonstrated in an experiment by Wallgren *et al.* (1967) in which alcohol and other calorie intake were kept equal by means of a pair-feeding technique. Intoxicating doses of alcohol evidently interfere with utilization of calories for growth. Gastric disturbance, alterations in endocrine and autonomic regulatory functions, or changes at the level of metabolic regulation are some possible mechanisms for this effect.

Effects of chronic alcohol administration on measures of general biological function, other than growth, have received rather sporadic and unsystematic attention. Numerous studies of the effects on reproductive performance were performed in the first three decades of this century. Transmission of any adverse effects of alcohol to the offspring could not be demonstrated (see *e.g.* Hanson *et al.*, 1928). According to Mirone (1952), 5% ethanol as sole source of fluid decreases fecundity in male mice but does not affect females. This experimental finding agrees with studies on sexual functions reviewed in Chapter 4 (p. 180), and with observations of sexual activity of alcoholic patients. Aschkenasy-Lelu (1958) reports that in rats prolonged consumption of 10% v/v alcohol does not prevent reproduction but increases the mortality of the puppies. Pilström and Kiessling (1967) found no disturbances of reproduction in rats given 15% alcohol as their sole fluid. There was no postnatal growth and a high incidence of mortality in the pups when the mothers continued to drink alcohol, whereas pups which were suckled by control females grew normally. Alcohol evidently blocked secretion of oxytocin from the posterior lobe of the hypophysis (Chapter 4, p. 182), thereby preventing milk ejection and causing the pups to starve (Pilström and Kiessling, 1967). In mice, voluntary ingestion even of large quantities of alcohol does not prevent females from rearing young successfully (Thiessen *et al.*, 1966). Blignaut (1965) gave mice of nine consecutive generations

TABLE 9–1

EFFECTS OF PROLONGED ALCOHOL INTAKE ON GROWTH

Species	Age (weight)	Dosage of alcohol	Way of administration	Food regimen	Duration of expt.	Final weight or weight change	Comment	Authors
Rat	5 weeks	5% v/v	Sole fluid	Ad lib., protein 21.8 or 15.3%	29 days	Alcohol groups faster weight gain, difference greater with more dietary protein	—	Pelaez et al. (1949)
Rat	Juvenile	5 or 10%	Sole fluid	Normal 12 g/day	129–157 days	Controls 261 g 5% 331 g 10% 364 g	—	Zarrow et al. (1962)
Rat	Young	10%	Sole fluid	Normal ad lib.	163 days	Control rats gained 34% of initial weight, alcohol rats 44%	—	Newman and Lehman (1938)
Rat	540 days	10% v/v	Sole fluid	Normal ad lib.	350 days	Weights unchanged	—	Wallgren and Forsander (1963)
Rat	150–160 g	10% v/v	Sole fluid	Normal ad lib.	150 days	Alc. + 69 g Control + 80 g ($P < 0.01$)	Food and fluid cons. smaller in alcohol group. Weight gain/100 g food 14.2 g in controls, 18.2 g in alcohol group	Aebi and von Wartburg (1960)
Rat	Adult	10%	Sole fluid	Normal ad lib.	185 days	Weights not affected	Food intake diminished	von Wartburg and Röthlisberger (1961)
Rat	Young	10%	Sole fluid	Normal ad lib.	7 months	2–6 months, no effects; 7 months, alcohol group less wt. gain	—	Aschkenasy-Lelu (1957)
Rat	30 days	10%	Sole fluid	Normal ad lib.	7 months	Growth retardation	—	Aschkenasy-Lelu and Guérin (1960)
Rat	30 days	10%	Sole fluid	Normal ad lib.	2 months	No sign. effect	—	Aschkenasy-Lelu and Guérin (1960)

Animal	Age	Concentration	Administration	Diet	Duration	Effect	Remarks	Reference
Rat	30 days	10%	Sole fluid	Normal ad lib.	6 months	No sign. effect	—	Aschkenasy-Lelu and Guérin (1960)
Rat	Young males (200–250 g)	10% v/v	Sole fluid	Normal ad lib.	13 weeks	Some growth retardation	Growth in proportion to caloric intake unaffected	Chauhan and Doniach (1968)
Rat	45–55 g	12%	Sole fluid	Normal ad lib.	24 weeks	About 10% lower final weight in alcohol than in water group	During first 6 weeks, alc. group grew more slowly, but utilized calories for growth slightly better than controls	Newell et al. (1964)
Rat	Weanling	15% v/v	Sole fluid	Purina chow partial pair-feeding	Up to 27 weeks	Slightly slower growth than in controls, similar to isocalorically fed animals receiving glucose instead of alcohol	—	Scheig et al. (1966)
Rat	30 days	8% v/v, 10% v/v, 16% v/v	Sole fluid	Normal ad lib., measured	270 days	All groups total caloric intake and growth similar	—	Richter (1926)
Rat	Adult	8% v/v, 10% v/v, 16% v/v, 24% v/v	Sole fluid	Normal ad lib.	30 days	24% group, initial decrease, then normal again	—	Richter (1941)
Rat	Adult	8% v/v, 10% v/v, 16% v/v, 24% v/v	Sole fluid	Normal ad lib.	265 days	Weights well maintained in all groups	Out of 8 animals in groups, 4 died in the one on 24% alcohol, none in the others	Richter (1953)
Rat	Young males 100 g	5, 10, 20%	Sole fluid	Normal ad lib.	10–11 months	Growth retarded with all concentrations	—	Meek et al. (1967)

TABLE 9–1 (continued)

Species	Age (weight)	Dosage of alcohol	Way of administration	Food regimen	Duration of expt.	Final weight or weight change	Comment	Authors
Rat	80–100 g	Controls 10% 3 weeks 15% 2 weeks 20% 1 week	Sole fluid	Normal ad lib.	6 weeks	During 10%, no difference, with 15 and 20%, growth retardation	Dehydration apparently cause of growth retardation. No lasting effect since period of rapid growth followed imm. after alcohol	Lee et al. (1964)
Rat	100–120 g	20%	Sole fluid	Normal ad lib.	40 weeks	No significant difference	Food intake 20% reduced, growth comparable to controls	Dajani et al. (1963)
Rat	75–175 g	36% of calories as alc.	Liquid diet as only source of food and water	Isocaloric	24 days	Daily weight gain 2.28 g on sucrose, 1.79 g on alc.	Increased water requirement after alc. not taken into account	Lieber et al. (1965)
Rat	80 males 200–250 g	10% v/v to 40 rats	Sole drinking fluid. Additionally 2, 2.5, 3, 3.5, 4 g per os daily in weekly increments, for last 7 weeks 4.5 g/kg	Lab. chow ad lib.	12 weeks	Final weight similar in alcohol and control group	12 animals of alcohol group died, survivors appeared healthy	Hawkins et al. (1966)
Rat	Young	5–6 g/kg/day	Stomach tube twice daily	Liquid diet with 22% alcohol calories	30 days	Retardation of growth	—	Mallov (1955)
Rat	Young females	2.4 g/kg	I.p. 3 times a week	Normal ad lib.	16 weeks	Growth ceased	Diarrhea	Figueroa and Klotz (1962a)
Rat	About 140 g	5–6 g/kg/ two days	Water control, dilute alcohol or same quantity as 25% alc by	High fat-low protein isocaloric for pair-fed groups	6 months	No difference betw. controls and group on dilute alcohol, group intoxicated	—	Wallgren et al. (1967)

Animal	Age	Dose	Route	Diet	Duration	Effect	Notes	Reference
					every other day	grew significantly less		
Rat	20 days	Daily anesthesia	Inhalation	Normal ad lib.	100 days	Growth retardation	—	Hanson et al. (1928)
Rat	28 days	Daily anesthesia	Inhalation	Normal ad lib.	100 days	Growth retardation	—	MacDowell (1922)
Mouse	Young	5%	Sole fluid	Normal ad lib.	12–15 months	No clear effect on growth	—	Mirone (1952)
Mouse	Growing	10%	Stomach tube daily	Normal ad lib.	(?)	Doses larger than 0.2 ml for first 5 g and 0.1 ml for every additional 5 g of body weight retarded growth	—	Kokata and Furutoku (1956)
Mouse	Young	10.5% as wine	Sole fluid	Normal ad lib.	6 months	First 4 months, better growth alc. group, after 4 months growth retardation	—	Sautet et al. (1960)
Mouse	Weanling	15%	Sole fluid	Purina chow ad lib.	Up to 12 months	No effect on growth rate or final weight	—	Mirone (1965a, b)
Hamster	Young	20%	Sole fluid	Normal ad lib.	(?)	Growth retarded	Food and fluid intake diminished, apparently state of water deprivation induced	Morgan et al. (1957)
Chicken	7 weeks	7%	Sole fluid	Normal or low protein, high or normal cholesterol	18 weeks	In no condition was growth affected	—	Nikkilä and Ollila (1959)
Chicken	Newly hatched	Control, light alc., heavy alc.	By tube into esophagus	Normal ad lib.	16 weeks	Males Females 954 891 1023 940 879 832	—	Elhardt (1930)

20% alcohol solution as sole drinking fluid at age 8 to 16 weeks, with appropriate water controls. Fertility was not affected, but alcohol caused increased mortality, particularly in the sixth generation. General activity and nervous functioning were disturbed particularly in the males. In the tenth generation, when no alcohol was given, the disturbances persisted in offspring of the mice given alcohol.

The use of cell and tissue cultures is a potentially powerful technique which has seldom been used for study of chronic alcohol effects. Both nutritional and pharmacological effects of alcohol are involved in the growth and survival of cell and tissue cultures, or of intact organisms. Speidel (1937) observed microscopically effects of alcohol on the nerves in the tail of tadpoles. With less than 0.5% alcohol, the tadpoles lived "indefinitely" without sign of injury. More concentrated solutions appeared especially to affect the myelin sheaths. Growth at the ending of regenerating nerve fibers was also inhibited. McLaughlin et al. (1964) have reported effects of alcohol on embryonic development in chicks, but without any indication of the concentrations reached and the duration of the action. Parker et al. (1950) measured the effect of alcohol on survival time of chick embryo mesenchymal cells. No toxicity appeared at concentrations below 2% and 0.1–0.5% even prolonged survival. Growth, estimated on basis of multiplication and outgrowth of fibroblasts, was stimulated by concentrations between 0.25 and 0.5%, was similar to that of the controls at 1%, and was progressively inhibited with higher concentrations until 5% completely suppressed cell migration. These cell types thus were stimulated at concentrations that would strongly interfere with functioning of the central nervous system. Trowell (1965) has found that ethanol in 1% concentration is not toxic to lymphocytes in lymph node cultures, and cites work by Schrek (1947) according to which a concentration of 9.2% ethanol is not toxic to lymphocytes.

Pace and Frost (1948) found that growth and oxygen consumption of the large amoeba *Pelomyxa* were curvilinearly related to alcohol concentration, growth being maximally stimulated at 5 mM (0.023%) and respiration at 10 mM (0.046%). Conjugation of a *Paramecium* ciliate had a maximum 6 times above the control rate at 0.046% concentration. The greater sensitivity of these protozoans as compared with the avian embryonal cells may partly be related to their mode of movement. The functioning of cilia, however, is not necessarily sensitive to ethanol. Rang (1960) found that about 0.8 M (3.7% w/v) ethanol was required for 50% inhibition of motility in a *Paramecium*. The movements of the cilia of the ependymal cells lining the central canal and ventricles of the mammalian central nervous system are not affected by ethanol at 1.7 M (7.8% w/v) concentration (Hild, 1957, cited by Murray, 1965). In a paper which gives a review of prior work on the ciliotoxic effects of ethanol, Dalhamn *et al.* (1967) report that in rabbit trachea maintained *in vitro*, ciliary movement ceases at a concentration of about 4% of ethanol in the tissue. Buetow and Padilla (1963) found that ethanol was superior to acetate as a source of carbon for two acetate flagellates, *Astasia longa* and *Euglena gracilis*. Population density increased when the concentration of ethanol was raised up to 0.2 M (0.92% w/v). In a recent report, Levedahl and Wilson (1965) compared growth rate of a flagellate on succinate, acetate, or alcohol at low levels as the carbon source, the initial concentration ranging from 1 to 5 mM. Ethanol was the most effective of these nutrients for production of cell mass. Why alcohol in low concentrations often tends to stimulate growth is not known.

(3) Ethanol in the caloric budget of alcoholics

Normally, the metabolic and caloric impact of ethanol is restricted to passing episodes without any major significance. Prolonged use can change the picture radically. The share of ethanol in the calorie balance of alcoholics was measured by Mendelson and La Dou (1964) in a controlled situation for a period of 24 days. During days 5–18 of the experiment, 2100 kcal a day were obtained from alcohol and 1800 kcal from food. During the last 6 days, the proportions were about 2800 kcal from alcohol and 1100 from food, a strikingly high rate of alcohol consumption.

Jellinek (1955) has contributed an interesting analysis of official statistics, showing that a small segment of the population performs most of the drinking. In the U.S.A. in 1950, alcoholics constituted 8.8% of the men but drank 46.7% of the alcohol. The mean daily intake by alcoholics slightly exceeded the average capacity of humans to metabolize alcohol. Therefore, substantial numbers of the alcoholics greatly exceed that average quantity not only occasionally, but continuously for long periods of time. The same conclusion is obtained from Fegiz' data, cited by Jellinek (1955), which show that the consumption of wine by some Italian men exceeds 3 liters a day, *i.e.*, more than 2400 kcal, and from a theoretical distribution of consumption rates worked out for the population of France by Ledermann (1952), and for that of Canada by De Lint (1968).

References p. 583

The average rate of ethanol clearance estimated from the rate of fall of blood alcohol (Widmark's β-value) is 0.015% per h, corresponding to an elimination of about 160 g alcohol per day on the basis of 70 kg body weight. However, the values in some cases are substantially higher, owing to individual differences. By direct determinations on 4 subjects, Newman *et al.* (1952) found elimination rates of approximately 215–310 g/24 h. De Lint and Schmidt (1965) obtained a closely similar estimate of 300 g alcohol per day for maximal individual consumption, with data on individual purchases of cheap wine in an urban community. Forsander (1963) quotes figures in Jolliffe *et al.* (1936) according to which severe alcoholics consumed 450 g alcohol daily for extended periods. According to Goldberg (1963b), Fennelly *et al.* (1964) and Brigden and Robinson (1964), heavy drinkers and alcoholics have maintained intakes equivalent to 400 g of absolute alcohol daily for periods of several months. Dietetic investigations in France indicate that there are alcoholics who continuously satisfy more than half of their calorie need through alcohol, consuming quantities of wine equivalent to 400–450 g of absolute alcohol a day (Delore *et al.*, 1959). Self-reported values by 120 French alcoholics ranged from approximately 165 to close to 800 g per day (Sadoun *et al.*, 1965). In a population of alcoholics studied by Neville *et al.* (1968), more than half of the subjects reported consumption above 160 g alcohol per day, and maximal values were about 500 g. Mechanisms which might raise the capacity of alcoholics to metabolize ethanol are discussed below (pp. 519–522).

When an average capacity to metabolize alcohol is put into continuous use, the alcohol satisfies approximately half of the calorie requirement in moderate activity. Higher rates of alcohol oxidation, such as those cited above, increase its metabolic role. The consequent restriction of food consumption automatically creates risks of malnutrition. The extent of the risk is increased in most alcoholics by poor quality of the food consumed and by generally low standards of living. Gross deficiency may occur more commonly among wine drinkers with heavy daily alcohol consumption than among alcoholics whose excessive drinking is in the form of occasional benders. The very poor physical condition of some wine drinkers is illustrated by the data on protein loss in Table 9–2. Even when overt deficiencies are not seen, there is no doubt that a condition of suboptimal nutrition is the rule among alcoholic patients. Their diet is always poorly balanced because as shown in Table 9–3, alcoholic beverages do not furnish significant amounts of any protective nutrient, with the exception that some types of

TABLE 9–2

CONSUMPTION OF CALORIES (EXCLUSIVE OF ALCOHOL) AND NITROGEN DURING 6
MONTHS OF UNCOMPLICATED UNDERNUTRITION AND DURING UNDERNUTRITION
COMBINED WITH ALCOHOLISM

(Acc. to Le Breton and Trémolières, 1955)

	Undernutrition	Undernutrition + alcoholism
kcal/day	1500–1700	1550–1700
Nitrogen (g/day)	8	8
Reduction of "active" body mass	20–25%	20–45%
	Rehabilitation period of 8 weeks	
kcal/day	3000–4000	3000–4000
Nitrogen (g/day)	18–21	18–30
Nitrogen retention (g/day)	3–6	3–15

TABLE 9–3

NUTRITIONAL VALUE OF SOME ALCOHOLIC BEVERAGES

(Data from Leake and Silverman, 1966)

	kcal/l	Protein (g/l)	Thiamine (mg/l)	Ribo-flavin (mg/l)	Pyridoxine (mg/l)	Niacin (mg/l)
Beer, lager	446	0.63–6.2	0.02–0.06	0.3–1.2	0.4–0.9	5–20
Red wine	795	—	—	—	—	—
White wine, dry	754	—	0–0.24	0.06–0.22	0.22–0.82	—
White wine, sweet	914	—	—	—	—	—
Sherry	1300	—	0.05	0.11	0.19	0.88
Port wine	1613	—	0.13	0.24	0.64	2.0
Vermouth	1500	—	—	—	—	—
Vodka	2200–2500	—	—	—	—	—
Whisky	2600	—	—	—	—	—
Cognac	2400	—	—	—	—	—
Daily requirement	—	—	(1 mg)	(1.5 mg)	(1–2 mg)	(10 mg)

beer may satisfy the daily requirement of niacin (Gebauer, 1959). Beers may
also provide magnesium and some wines iron. Consumption of any alcoholic
beverage thus shifts the balance between caloric intake and protective
nutrients in an unfavorable direction. However, when drinking is intermittent, periods of poor nutrition during drinking are to some extent
compensated by more adequate nutrition during sobriety (Olson, 1964;
Neville *et al.*, 1968). The next section of this chapter discusses the further
question of whether alcohol interferes more directly with the body's utilization of protective nutrients than merely by substition for other food-stuffs.

References p. 583

(4) Vitamin balance

The high incidence of vitamin deficiencies among alcoholics has been abundantly documented in clinical literature, reviewed by Jolliffe (1942), Sinclair (1955) and Olson (1964). Various signs of vitamin deficiency in alcoholics are discussed by Leevy and Baker (1968). Vitamin supplementation is commonly but rather randomly applied in the treatment of alcoholics. A basis for more rational methods in this sector of therapy could be obtained through studies of the character of the deficiencies and the mechanisms by which they arise. Insufficient intake is an indirect factor, shown above to be important. Olson (1964) has pointed out that the alcoholic should be more likely to develop signs of deprivation of water-soluble vitamins because fat-soluble vitamins are better stored. Possible mechanisms for the deficiency would be a direct action of alcohol on intestinal resorption, on tissue binding and storage, on metabolism, or on excretory loss of the vitamins. Studies of vitamin-B utilization have shown no consistent impairment due to alcohol intake. Alcohol delayed the onset of thiamine deficiency in rats (Lowry *et al.*, 1942b) and pigeons (Westerfeld and Doisy, 1945). French (1966a) found indications of a reduced requirement of thiamine and an increased requirement of pyridoxine in prolonged experiments with rats. A later study (French and Castagna, 1967) led to the conclusion that the worsening effect of ethanol on pyridoxine deficiency probably is due to some indirect effect rather than enhanced requirement for the vitamin. However, effects of ethanol on thiamine metabolism have also been reported. In prolonged experiments with rats receiving ethanol solution as sole fluid, Kiessling and Tilander (1961) found that the thiamine content of the cytoplasmic fraction of liver tissue had decreased significantly after seven months, and Konttinen *et al.* (1967b) found that thiamine was significantly lowered in the blood of rats after a year. According to Kiessling and Tilander (1961), supernatant of liver tissue from rats that had consumed 15% alcohol for 10–12 months dephosphorylated thiamine at a higher rate than supernatant from control animals. This observation is compatible with increased losses.

Observations of alcoholics have shown no consistent evidence for a direct effect of alcohol on thiamine utilization. Sinclair (1955) stated that alcohol causes a marked depression of thiamine phosphorylation in the liver, and speculates on the mechanism of this purported inhibition. However, the claim is based on two reports (Sinclair, 1939; Goodhart and Sinclair, 1939) which only show decreased concentration of thiamine and depressed cocarboxylase activity in the blood of alcoholics suffering from polyneuritis. These findings give no evidence that alcohol directly depresses thiamine phosphorylation. Levels of various B-complex vitamins have been found to be lowered in the serum (Ungley, 1938; Sinclair, 1939; Bang, 1945; Leevy et al., 1965) and urine (Jokivartio and Okko, 1947; Pluvinage and Lelus, 1962) of alcoholics. According to Leevy and Baker (1963) and Leevy et al. (1965), however, serum and liver tissue levels are lowered only in cases of manifest tissue damage. This is probably a consequence of poor nutrition rather than a direct effect of the alcohol. Delaney et al. (1966) found no correlation between plasma thiamine, plasma and erythrocyte magnesium, and plasma lactate in alcoholics. Rutter (1966) has reported a deficiency in alcoholics of capacity to convert nicotinic acid to nicotinamide. This may be a sequel of pyridoxine deficiency and consequent disturbance of trans-aminations.

Studies of less prolonged administration of alcohol likewise show no consistent impairment of vitamin B utilization. Leevy and Baker (1963) reported that in rats acute ethanol intoxication caused a decrease only in cerebral folic acid, whereas in the liver, folic acid increased and pantothenic acid decreased slightly but statistically significantly. Otherwise, vitamin levels were unchanged. In rats, a transient increase in excretion of thiamine has been seen on change to a regimen with 10% v/v alcohol as sole fluid, and a likewise transient retention on return to water a few days later (Suoma-lainen, 1963; Oura et al., 1963; Konttinen et al., 1967a). A loss induced by ethanol was suggested. Butler and Sarett (1948) observed excretion of thiamine after alcohol in humans and gave the alternative explanation of decreased requirement as thiamine is needed in the metabolism of carbo-hydrate but not in that of alcohol. The same result can be found with changes from a carbohydrate to a fat regimen and vice versa (Holt and Snyderman, 1955). However, these short-term experiments involving only excretion studies are inconclusive. The same applies to absorption studies, actually based on excretion in urine and stools of labeled thiamine administered orally, which suggests deficient absorption in alcoholics (Thomson et al., 1968, cited acc. to Leevy and Baker, 1968; Tomasulo et al., 1968). Only complete balance and turnover studies can give a reliable picture of the actual changes. The tentative conclusion that alcohol does not increase requirements for thiamine, and may indeed have a sparing effect, is supported by the observation that in alcoholic subjects, alcohol consumption did not increase the need for thiamine over a certain basic requirement (Neville et *al.*, 1968). Leevy and Baker's (1968) suggestion that alcohol might increase the need for thiamine seems to be based on an erroneous interpretation of a metabolic scheme.

Macrocytic anemia, often encountered in association with liver cirrhosis in alcoholics, is a condition reproduced also in rats (Dube and Kumar, 1962; Wallgren *et al.*, 1967). Herbert *et al.* (1963) demonstrated that this condition correlated with folic acid deficiency but were unable to conclude from their data whether this was due to deficient diet or to alcohol directly interfering with folic acid metabolism or absorption. Sullivan and Herbert (1964) found that alcohol prevented folic acid from stimulating the formation of red blood cells. They concluded that alcohol inhibited the metabolism of folic acid. Bertino *et al.* (1965) have shown that alcohol in a concentration of 1.9% v/v significantly inhibits the action of folic acid in causing transfer of one-carbon units to nucleic acids in rat bone marrow and liver. Tetrahydrofolate formase was the only enzyme likely to be involved that was found to be inhibited by a corresponding concentration of ethanol. Halsted *et al.* (1967) found that in alcoholic subjects acute ingestion of alcohol had no effect whereas consumption of alcohol over a time period corresponding to a drinking debauch inhibited the absorption of folic acid. Alcohol therefore gives evidence for causing insufficient dietary intake, decreased absorption, and interference with metabolism of folic acid. Clinical studies by Klipstein and Lindenbaum (1965) indicate that alcohol may increase the requirement for folic acid owing to hyperactivity of the bone marrow as a consequence of gastrointestinal bleeding, hypersplenism or hemolysis. However, Ralli *et al.* (1959) found no evidence that alcohol (15% in the drinking fluid) increased the requirement of rats for folic acid, measured by growth, nitrogen balance, liver nitrogen, and liver fat under vitamin B_{12}-deficiency.

There are only a few studies on effects of alcohol on utilization of other vitamins. Decreased urinary excretion of vitamin C, suggestive of incipient deficiency, has been reported in male alcoholic patients (Lester *et al.*, 1960). However, Forbes and Duncan (1953) found that alcohol given in intoxicating doses three times a week did not accelerate development of scurvy in guinea pigs receiving a scorbutigenic diet. Clausen *et al.* (1940) found that in the dog, administration of ethanol was followed by a rise in the concentration of circulating vitamin A. Lee and Lucia (1965) have studied the mechanism by which ethanol causes mobilization of vitamin A. The results of Clausen *et al.* were confirmed with both adrenalectomized and pancreatectomized dogs. In perfusion experiments with rat livers, release of vitamin A was increased by addition of 0.05 % ethanol to the perfusion medium. In accordance with this direct effect of alcohol on the liver, promoting release of vitamin A, Zahorska *et al.* (1955) have reported decreased storage of vitamin A in livers of rats receiving 20 % ethanol as sole drinking fluid. According to Bakumenko (1957), the metabolism of vitamin K and the prothrombin synthesis of the liver are impaired in chronic alcoholism.

These experimental and clinical studies lead to the tentative conclusion that alcohol has no major direct effects on vitamin metabolism. A nonspecific deficiency in nutrition is thus the dominant factor in malnutrition of alcoholics. Consequently, multiple deficiencies should usually occur and the symptoms should resemble those in other conditions associated with chronic malnutrition.

B. Effects on the central nervous system

The acute effects of alcohol have been reviewed in earlier chapters. Chronic effects on the central nervous system involve the important problems of tolerance and the withdrawal syndrome which are closely connected with the development of alcoholism. These aspects are reviewed in the present section whereas pathology of the nervous system is discussed in connection with the review of tissue pathology at the end of this chapter. Three main categories of study are included in this review: animal experiments on changes in the nervous system as a consequence of prolonged alcohol administration; true experiments on human subjects who are usually patients under treatment for alcohol or drug dependence; and controlled, clinical studies on patients. A point of terminology, in discussions of the condition of alcoholism, is that we have avoided as far as possible use of the words "addiction" and "addict". We have followed the recommendation of WHO (Eddy *et al.*, 1965) to speak of *dependence*, considering the alcohol-type of dependence to be a special instance of drug dependence. A thought-provoking discussion on methodological and conceptual problems involved in the study of drug dependence has been edited by Kalant and Hawkins (1969).

(1) Tolerance

Development of tolerance to the effects of various foreign agents is a general biological phenomenon of obvious adaptive significance. One aspect of differences in tolerance is seen in variation among individuals in the

References p. 583

functional impairment caused by a particular concentration of ethanol in the blood, discussed in Chapter 7 (p. 353). An important and often difficult task is to distinguish between psychological compensatory mechanisms and true "tissue tolerance". The former implies learning to function more efficiently during the influence of alcohol, the latter a change in the nervous system leading to improvement of physiological functioning in the presence of a given concentration of alcohol. In the present section, evidence concerning development of true tolerance to alcohol is reviewed.

Evidence for development of tolerance during a single episode of intoxication has been reviewed briefly by Wieser (1965). On the topic of tolerance developed after prolonged administration of ethanol, Newman (1941) has contributed an important review. Recent brief reviews are due to Fraser (1957), Seevers and Deneau (1963), and Wieser (1965).

Development of tolerance during a single episode of intoxication is indicated by greater impairment at a given blood alcohol level in the ascending than in the descending phase of the curve. This has been demonstrated in controlled studies of various psychomotor and psychological tests performed on human subjects (Mellanby, 1919; Eggleton, 1941; Goldberg, 1943; Alha, 1951; Bschor, 1951, 1952). In all of these investigations, maximal blood alcohol levels were low or moderate, in the range 0.1–0.2%. According to Alha et al. (1957), differences were found when the blood alcohol levels were below 0.15%, whereas they disappeared at higher blood alcohol levels.

There is evidence that the results may be partly explained by an "overshoot" of the concentration of alcohol in the brain during the absorption phase, so that the concentration found in the blood is less than the amount concurrently affecting the brain. Eggleton (1941) noted that the difference was more marked when the blood alcohol rose rapidly than slowly, and Alha (1951) and Bschor (1951, 1952) found that maximal impairment preceded the peak blood alcohol level. However, these factors do not seem sufficient to account for the entire decrease in effect of alcohol during the descending phase of the curve. Further evidence for tolerance was reported by Mirsky et al. (1941) with rabbits and human subjects administered alcohol in quantities giving rise to symptoms of inebriation. When the blood alcohol level was then maintained, the symptoms again disappeared within 4–10 h at blood alcohol levels higher than those at which they first appeared. Rosenbaum (1942) demonstrated similar phenomena in humans. Maynert and Klingman (1960) found in experiments with dogs that the blood alcohol level at which signs of intoxication disappeared, during the declining portion of the curve, was highest after the largest (2.5 g/kg) of four different doses administered in random order.

Electroencephalographic recordings give further evidence for development of true tissue tolerance. Mirsky *et al.* (1941) found that alcohol-induced EEG-depression in rabbits again disappeared although the blood alcohol levels were maintained or even raised. Gorzym *et al.* (1957) also reported return of the EEG of rabbits to normal while the blood alcohol was still high. Studies on humans have given less convincing evidence. Caspers and Abele (1956) reported equivalent effects on the human EEG at 0.03–0.04% higher blood alcohol levels in the descending than in the ascending phase of the blood alcohol curve, but Holmberg and Mårtens (1955) found the largest effect when the blood alcohol was falling. According to von Hedenström and Schmidt (1951), the correlation between blood alcohol and EEG alterations was much closer during rising than during falling blood alcohol, suggesting great individual variability in tolerance. It should also be noted that whereas motor functions tend to show evidence for tolerance, sensory deficits may be equal or even larger in the phase of descending than ascending blood alcohol curve (Goldberg, 1943, 1963a; Rauschke, 1954; Holmberg and Mårtens, 1955).

The development of tolerance in humans, after prolonged exposure to alcohol, has generally been tested by comparing acute alcohol effects on people with different drinking habits. One of the first and most important studies is by Goldberg (1943) who also reviewed earlier investigations. His subjects, classified as abstainers, moderate drinkers and heavy drinkers, gave clear evidence for difference between the groups in tests for sensory, motor and psychological function (Table 9–4). Holmberg and Mårtens (1955) found that alcohol caused slightly more disturbance of EEG and ECG, and more pronounced ataxia in hospital attendants than in alcoholic patients. Mizoi *et al.* (1963) found an electromyographic response to disappear at blood alcohol levels of 0.012–0.082% in 12 "virtual non-drinkers", 0.072–0.120% in 11 "moderate drinkers" and 0.131–0.139% in 3 "heavy drinkers".

These studies on subjects with different experience of drinking give strong evidence for tolerance but the objection can always be raised that they may represent samples of the population with a difference existing prior to drinking. Therefore, essential corroborative evidence is provided by studies showing the development of tolerance.

In one such study, by Adams and Hubach (1960), normal subjects drank alcohol daily for 20 days. The changes in EEG initially caused by ethanol,

TABLE 9–4

MEAN BLOOD ALCOHOL VALUES (% w/v) AT DISAPPEARANCE OF THE EFFECT OF
ALCOHOL ON VARIOUS TYPES OF PERFORMANCE IN SUBJECTS WITH DIFFERENT
EXPERIENCE OF ALCOHOL

(From Goldberg, 1943)

Test	Abstainers (n = 10)	Moderate drinkers (n = 17)	Heavy drinkers (n = 10)
Flicker test	0.039	0.064	0.091
Corneal test	0.026	0.040	0.088
Standing steadiness (ordinary Romberg)	0.052	0.069	0.120
Standing steadiness (modified Romberg)	0.044	0.059	0.110
Finger–finger test	0.037	0.065	0.097
Subtraction test	0.057	0.097	0.100
Bourdon test (letters correctly marked)	0.060	0.071	0.071
Bourdon test (number of letters read)	0.057	0.071	0.089
Average blood alcohol	0.047	0.067	0.096

particularly in the alpha activity, gradually disappeared. The use of normal human subjects is often precluded by ethical, social and other considerations; therefore, most other studies on the development of tolerance in humans have been with alcoholic or drug-dependent patients. Isbell et al. (1955) and Wikler et al. (1956) found that although blood alcohol levels of former narcotic addicts remained high or became further elevated during alcohol intake for a number of days, disturbance of the EEG tended to decrease in degree or remain stationary, as did also the degree of overt inebriation. The fact that the effect was quantitatively rather weak may have been due to tolerance developed prior to the experiment. Similarly, Mendelson and La Dou (1964) and Talland et al. (1964a) found a decrease in the disturbance caused by sustained elevated blood alcohol. Motor skills and attention actually improved with blood alcohol levels up to well above 0.1%, and return to the basal level occurred at blood alcohol levels as high as 0.2% for some functions. These findings give convincing evidence for increased tolerance, but the patients' previous history of drug dependence or heavy drinking precludes conclusions as to whether similar sustained drinking would lead to a similar degree of tolerance in normal subjects.

Data on the development of tolerance in subjects whose entire alcohol intake has been controlled are obtainable only in animal experiments. Development of tolerance has usually been measured by behavioral tests. Since the same individuals must be tested repeatedly it is imperative to use tests not influenced by the repetition, or to control for practice effects. The experimental and control groups should be equalized not only in exposure to the tests but also in the alcohol or nondrug condition associated with each exposure. This point is illustrated by an experiment reported by Chen (1968). Alcohol injections were given to rats before or after test sessions, for three sessions, followed by a fourth in which all animals were injected before the session. Tolerance to the general depressant action of alcohol was evident in all the rats. Skilled performance, on the contrary, was much less affected in the animals accustomed to perform under the influence of alcohol.

Tolerance to alcohol was convincingly demonstrated by Lévy (1935a, b, c) in rats, given progressively increasing doses of alcohol over periods of 47 to 152 days. The dose required for liminal anesthesia increased by about 25% and the minimal fatal dose increased by about 10%. Newman and Card (1937) and Newman and Lehman (1938) found that dogs forced to ingest intoxicating quantities of alcohol twice daily for periods of more than 3 months were clearly less affected than the controls.

Ahlquist and Dille (1940) administered daily doses of 1.5 g alcohol/kg i.p. to rabbits and found increased tolerance within 15 to 25 days as evidenced by a shortened period of loss of the righting reflexes. Troshina (1957) has reported that in the test of time for hanging on a rod, rats showed tolerance after only 4 days of administration of approximately 3.5 g/kg by stomach tube. Hogans et al. (1961) found that in rhesus monkeys, the periods required for development of behavioral tolerance ranged from 4 to 11 days in different individuals. Hatfield (1966) used the righting reflex to determine tolerance in rats, given daily i.p. injections of 2.5 g alcohol/kg. Tolerance was found after the tenth treatment in females and after the fifteenth treatment in males.

In contrast to the gradual development of tolerance to most drugs is the claim that tolerance is demonstrable in mice on the second administration of alcohol (Vollmer, 1932). Eickholt et al. (1967) report that the principal increase in tolerance of rats occurs from the first to the second administration of alcohol. The explanation for this finding may be an early phase of unspecific resistance to the alcohol effect, due to the stress of handling and intoxication. Likewise, in experiments that involved administration three times per week to previously untreated rats, it was found that tolerance appeared to be raised after one and two weeks also in water controls (Scheinin, personal communication). After three weeks (10 doses of alcohol), the alcohol-treated animals became clearly less affected by a given dose of alcohol than the controls, thereby indicating the development of genuine alcohol tolerance. It is interesting to note that Kalant and Grose (1967) have reported that slices of cerebral tissue, in which normally release of acetylcholine during incubation is inhibited by alcohol in the medium, become resistant to this effect if taken from tolerant animals. When 5 g alcohol per kg was given daily to rats, this resistance appeared after two weeks' treatment although behavioral tolerance was evident after one week. The emergence of resistance to the inhibition of acetylcholine-release may be a reflection of true tolerance.

In rats, tolerance has been found to develop in similar fashion in the cold (0–5 °C) as at room temperature (Leung et al., 1966). In a test for motor coordination, the cold-adapted animals were affected more by alcohol than the animals kept at room temperature.

The degree of tolerance to alcohol is less than that developed for morphine and barbiturates. On the other hand, in contrast to morphine the tolerance to alcohol develops even without sustained presence of the drug. This indicates a residual "carry-over" effect of alcohol persisting for some time after the drug has been completely eliminated. In rats tested by means of the tilted plane test (Wallgren and Lindbohm, 1961) or a conditioned avoidance response (Wallgren and Savolainen, 1962) tolerance developed when alcohol in a dose of 5 or 3 g/kg p.o. was given every other day for a total of ten doses. In these experiments, it was not established how soon tolerance might have been induced, but Scheinin's previously cited results show that development of tolerance with three doses per week requires approximately ten doses, or three weeks. It is not clear whether tolerance develops more rapidly when alcohol is administered daily.

It is to be expected that blood and brain alcohol must be raised above some minimal level for tolerance to develop. In rats, voluntarily regulated intake of 10 % v/v alcohol given as single source of fluid has not been found to shorten alcohol-induced sleeping time after 163 days on the regimen (Newman and Lehman, 1938). In male rats similarly maintained for 350 days, Wallgren and Forsander (1963) did not find increased tolerance as measured by the tilting plane test. In the study of Wallgren et al. (1967), a quantity of alcohol which produced tolerance when administered in an intoxicating dose every other day had no effect when given diluted in the drinking fluid. In mice, on the contrary, tolerance has been reported after only 19 days with 9.5 % alcohol as sole fluid (Hiestand et al., 1952), measured by toxicity of 1 ml of 48 % alcohol injected i.p. However, the highly irritating concentration of alcohol used in their toxicity test introduces severe local tissue damage (Barry and Wallgren, 1968), so that the differential mortality of the experimental and control groups might have been due to differential responses to this local damage instead of signifying differential tolerance in the central nervous system.

Evidence for development of tolerance is also conflicting in studies with administration of small amounts of alcohol rather than voluntary intake. Malméjac and Plane (1956) studied the effect of alcohol given in small doses on a conditioned salivary response in dogs. Initially, there was a hyperactivity at 0.03–0.04% concentration of alcohol in the blood, but after daily administration for 1–2 weeks, tolerance developed since the response disappeared. A study by Moskowitz and Wapner (1964), which includes the criticism that Troshina (1957) failed to control for practice effects, does not show tolerance in the test for hanging time on a rod after 0.84 g alcohol/kg was administered by stomach tube 3 times a week for $4\frac{1}{2}$ months. Moskowitz and Wapner (1964) also used an escape–avoidance test for measuring tolerance and found after 30 weeks that control animals under 0.96 g of alcohol/kg showed a clear increase in avoidance latency over the first 3 of 20 successive trials, but for the remaining 17 trials performed at the same level as the experimental animals. Since the dose was so low, it is possible that the initial effect on avoidance latency was overcome by an arousal effect in the control animals. Arousal is known to counteract effects of small and medium doses of alcohol (Chapter 7, p. 367). With a similarly small dose of alcohol (1 g/kg 6 times a week i.p.), Kinard and Hay (1960) showed a definite tolerance in rats after 9 weeks by measuring performance in the rotarod test.

The results cited are not sufficient to establish clearly for dogs, rats, or mice which is the minimal dosage regimen inducing tolerance. For other species, no data are available. A relationship between the size of the doses administered and the resulting degree of tolerance might be expected, and has indeed been demonstrated. Allan and Swinyard (1949) have shown that up to a certain dosage, increase in the amount of alcohol administered in each dose will augment the degree of tolerance. Maynert and Klingman (1960) obtained similar results in their studies on tolerance following administration of single doses. Repeated administration seems to induce the most marked tolerance to dosage of intermediate size. The only published evidence for an increase in lethal dosage known to us are the studies by Lévy (1935a, b, c) and by Hiestand *et al.* (1952), cited above.

References p. 583

Once tolerance has been induced, the duration of further maintenance of the condition apparently has little effect on the extent of tolerance. Thus, Wallgren *et al.* (1967) found the same degree of tolerance in rats at months 3 and 6 of a prolonged experiment. However, regression analysis of Scheinin's results also suggested that maximal tolerance was not reached within 7 weeks. As yet, no study has established definitely the time required to build up maximal tolerance, nor its extent. There is only fragmentary information on the duration of acquired tolerance. Newman and Card (1937) found that in habituated dogs alcohol tolerance had returned to the initial level after 7 months of abstinence. Ahlquist and Dille (1940) found tolerance to persist for 4 but not 6 days in rabbits when daily administration of alcohol for 15–25 days was discontinued. According to Hasebe (1961), tolerance in rabbits induced by daily administration for 16 weeks persisted for 16 further weeks, but the validity of the claim is not well substantiated in the report. In the experiments with dogs, cited above, Malméjac and Plane (1956) found that 2 weeks' abstinence caused return of the initially hyperactive salivary response at low blood alcohol levels. According to Hatfield (1966), tolerance persisted for more than 9 days in female and more than 11 days in male rats. According to LeBlanc *et al.* (1969), "maximal" tolerance to alcohol developed in rats after 3 weeks' daily administration of ethanol, was reduced within one week of withdrawal, then appeared to be subnormal for a short time, and returned to the normal level within 3 to 4 weeks after the last alcohol dose had been given.

With respect to the mechanisms involved, early investigations demonstrated conclusively that the tolerance was not due to decreased tissue levels of alcohol caused by decreased absorption, altered distribution, or increased rate of elimination (Lévy, 1935a, b, c; Newman and Lehman, 1938; reviews by Newman, 1941; Goldberg, 1943; Elbel and Schleyer, 1956). In fact, some investigators have reported a tendency for higher levels of alcohol in the blood and brain of tolerant animals (Lévy, 1935b; Newman and Lehman, 1938; Troshina, 1957). There is no doubt that an altered resistance of the central nervous system is involved. Evidence which eliminates the possibility of learning factors or psychological compensation is embodied in many studies (Lévy, 1935b; Ahlqvist and Dille, 1940; Allan and Swinyard, 1949; Hiestand *et al.*, 1952; Hasebe, 1961; Wallgren and Lindbohm, 1961; Wallgren and Savolainen, 1962; Hatfield, 1966). The nature of the change, however, is not known. Central nervous system activity may be measured directly by EEG recording. In the experiments on humans mentioned above

(Adams and Hubach, 1960; Isbell *et al.*, 1955; Wikler *et al.*, 1956), diminution of the effects of alcohol on EEG recordings from the scalp paralleled the development of behavioral tolerance. Contrary to this is the finding (Hogans *et al.*, 1961) that when behavioral tolerance was evident in monkeys, the effect of alcohol on EEG recorded from electrodes implanted in the cerebral cortex was as marked as on the first alcohol day. Part of the reason for this discrepancy may be that Hogans *et al.* (1961) worked in the initial period of unspecific tolerance. Also, there is the possibility that development of tolerance is tied to changes in deeper structures rather than in the cortex.

Takemori (1961) has shown much less effect of morphine on respiration *in vitro* of potassium-stimulated cerebral tissue from rats which have become tolerant to morphine than from control animals. Wallgren and Lindbohm (1961) could not detect any difference between control and behaviorally tolerant rats, in measurements of the effect of ethanol (0.5% v/v) on the respiration of electrically stimulated cerebral cortex tissue. In view of this finding, it is not surprising that Mendelson and Mello (1964) found no significant differences in the effects of 750 mM (4.40% v/v) ethanol on the potassium-stimulated respiration of cerebral cortex of rats with high or low preference for alcohol in a free selection situation. We may expect these relatively crude measures to show tolerance to morphine but not to ethanol, because of the great quantitative difference in the extent of tolerance to these two drugs.

(2) Physical dependence

Acquired increase in tolerance and physical dependence are the two most clearly recognized biological entities involved in development of "addiction" to drugs acting on the central nervous system. Seevers and Deneau (1963) stress that tolerance is a less specific and more prevalent form of biological adjustment to a drug. Seevers and Deneau (1963) suggest the following definition of physical dependence: "the state of latent hyperexcitability which develops in the cells of the central nervous system of higher mammals following frequent and prolonged administration of the morphine-like analgesics, alcohol, barbiturates, and other depressants is termed *physical dependence* and becomes manifest subjectively and objectively as specific symptoms and signs, the *abstinence syndrome* or the *withdrawal illness*, upon abrupt termination of drug administration".

Seevers and Deneau (1963) state that "the most prevalent form of physical

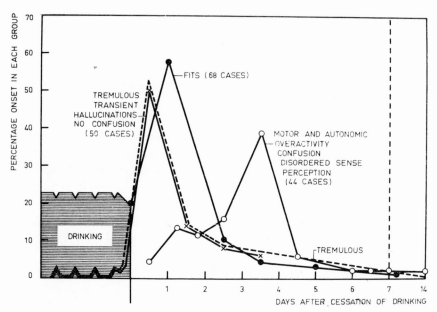

Fig. 9–1. Relation of onset of acute neurologic disturbances to cessation of drinking.
(Acc. to Victor and Adams, 1953.)

dependence is that which occurs to ethyl alcohol". The occurrence of a
withdrawal illness in alcoholism was recognized by Magnus Huss in 1849.
According to Hubach (1963) and Wieser (1965), it was generally known
among physicians in the last century. After the year 1900, the concept
gradually fell into oblivion. Reports by Piker (1937), Figurelli (1958) and
Lundquist (1959) typify the opinions of many psychiatrists who view
delirium tremens and rum fits as consequences of direct toxicity of alcohol.
Nielsen (1965) emphasizes that alcohol is not a completely effective antidote.
He also thinks that cessation of drinking is a sign of the incipient illness
and not its cause. Only gradually has it become re-established that abstinence,
or at least a sharp reduction in drinking, is necessary to precipitate the
condition. Clinical reports, including those by Kalinowsky (1942), Lehman
(1955), Allgén *et al.* (1957), Daniels and Ohler (1959), Victor and Hope
(1958), Johnson (1961) and Bührer (1964) have established that the typical
abstinence symptoms develop after withdrawal of alcohol, either during the
decrease of blood alcohol or even after total elimination of the alcohol from
the body. The symptoms in mild cases include tremor, excessive perspiration,
nervousness, weakness and gastric distress, anorexia, hyperreflexia and

insomnia, a condition commonly called "the shakes"; with increasing severity the blood pressure, heart rate and body temperature are elevated with visual or auditory hallucinations, disorientation, and in some cases convulsions (Victor and Adams, 1953; Isbell *et al.*, 1955; Johnson, 1961; Cutshall, 1965). The most severe symptoms form the syndrome of delirium tremens, with or without convulsions (rum fits). Hubach (1963) describes a triad of symptoms in the full-blown withdrawal syndrome: delirium, clouding of consciousness, and cerebral convulsive activity. An acute alcohol withdrawal illness has been reported for newborn human infants delivered by mothers with delirium tremens (*e.g.*, Nichols, 1967).

An extremely important clinical study is that by Victor and Adams (1953) who carefully evaluated the relation between termination of drinking and the appearance of various symptoms in a large number of patients. A diagrammatic representation of their results (Fig. 9–1) very convincingly demonstrates that the syndrome results form the withdrawal of alcohol.

Clinical observations do not clearly establish the role of alcohol withdrawal in precipitating the abstinence syndrome because the effects are partly obscured by complicating factors such as nutritional deficiencies, electrolyte disturbance, liver disease, exhaustion of the pituitary-adrenal system, and brain pathology. It is obviously important in clinical practice to identify and treat any physical complication in alcoholic patients. However, it is absolutely necessary for an understanding of the pharmacological properties and potential of alcohol to establish clearly whether or not a withdrawal syndrome occurs and is due to specific reversible changes in the nervous system. Controlled studies on physically fit subjects maintained on adequate nutrition are important for a conclusive answer to this question.

Isbell *et al.* (1955) have reported the first well-conducted experiment on prolonged drinking and sudden withdrawal. The subjects were ten healthy men, all former morphine addicts, who were maintained in the maximum state of intoxication compatible with ambulatory management for 6–13 weeks, followed by abrupt termination of the alcohol. The average daily intake varied from 199 to 365 g alcohol (approximately 3–5 g/kg). Convulsions and delirium did not occur while high blood alcohol was maintained. Mild symptoms were briefly seen in three of the four subjects who withdrew early from the experiment. The remaining six subjects, who drank for 48–87 days, all developed tremors, marked weakness, nausea, vomiting, diarrhea, hyperreflexia, fever, and hypertension at withdrawal. Two had seizures, three had frank delirium, two more had transient hallucinations, and only one escaped both delirium and hallucinations. All this became evident in spite of an adequate diet and multiple vitamin supplements. The symptoms began to appear before blood alcohol was zero. Three months after the termination of drinking, no evidence of residual impairment was seen in physical, psychiatric, psychological, laboratory, and electroencephalographic examinations.

The study has been criticized on the ground that the subjects were former morphine addicts. However, this cannot obscure the fact that severe symptoms became manifest on *withdrawal of alcohol*. Jellinek (1959, 1960) has rightly put great emphasis on these results. Mendelson *et al.* (1964) have contributed another highly important study. Ten male alcoholics selected from a correctional institution received alcohol for 24 days, beginning with increasing dosage for 5 days, then 300 g alcohol daily for 14 days, and finally 400 g daily for 5 days. Only during the last 5 days was intoxication gross and blood alcohol high. This period was followed by abrupt withdrawal. Probably because of the short duration of the drinking, withdrawal was followed by relatively mild symptoms such as tremor, deficits in orientation and memory, and hallucinosis. Only two subjects lacked signs of the withdrawal syndrome. This study convincingly demonstrated that the frequency of symptoms rises abruptly on withdrawal.

These controlled studies on human subjects show very clearly hyperactivity in the central nervous and autonomic nervous systems following alcohol withdrawal. They demonstrate unequivocally the development of physical dependence on alcohol. In contrast with the morphine abstinence syndrome, a severe alcohol abstinence syndrome develops only after a very heavy and prolonged intake of the drug (Seevers and Deneau, 1963). Also, morphine-type drugs prevent development of similar symptoms as long as a moderate level is maintained in the organism, whereas mild symptoms such as tremor, dizziness, perspiration, and even occasional hallucinations and seizures may appear during drinking of alcohol (Johnson, 1961; Mendelson and La Dou, 1964), although apparently only during a fall in blood alcohol.

Tremor is a variable phenomenon, partly under direct control from higher centers and thus subject to the influence of mood and conscious efforts. However, Carrie (1965) has clearly demonstrated a larger amplitude of finger tremor in alcoholic patients than in normal controls. None of his patients showed neurological abnormalities or alcoholic psychosis. In most instances, they had abstained from alcoholic beverages for seven days prior to testing. Analyses of individual differences indicated that among alcoholics, as well as among nonalcoholic subjects, emotional disorder was associated with an increase in tremor amplitude.

In contrast to the often violent physical signs of withdrawal, EEG-changes are rather mild. Few observations have been reported, partly because of the difficulties in eliminating artifacts, including effects of tremor. Isbell *et al.* (1955) and Wikler *et al.* (1956) found that between the 16th and the 33rd hour of abstinence, the percentage of alpha activity decreased and bursts of slow waves were observed. Withdrawal of alcohol differs in this as in many other ways from withdrawal of morphine-type drugs. Withdrawal of barbiturates causes a condition largely resembling the alcohol abstinence syndrome (Seevers and Deneau, 1963), but the EEG-changes are much more marked (Wikler *et al.*, 1956). Recording from subcortical structures might reveal a different picture. A recent attempt toward fundamental neurophysiological investigation of the withdrawal phenomenon has been performed by Gross *et al.* (1964). Of 4 patients with delirium, two with auditory hallucinations had a slower evoked response to auditory stimulation than the two others. Evidence was found that sensory disturbances may contribute to the emergence of hallucinations (Gross *et al.*, 1963; Saravay and Pardes, 1967; Sabot *et al.*, 1968). Gross and associates (*e.g.* Gross *et al.*, 1966; references in Gross, 1967) have also provided interesting data on sleep disturbances and EEG in the withdrawal state and particularly report deficiency in the delta sleep. The observations on effects of ethanol on activated sleep in normal subjects cited in Chapter 6 (p. 282) were somewhat ambiguous. The large amounts of alcohol generally consumed by alcoholics may cause more consistent disturbances which in turn may contribute to the agitation of the withdrawal state and the physiological need for compensatory reactions. Carlsson and Häggendal (1967) found that in the withdrawal phase, the plasma level of noradrenaline increased, indicating sympathetic activation.

Alcohol may precipitate latent epileptic conditions, and "alcoholic epilepsy" is the subject of a fairly extensive literature (*e.g.*, Marinacci, 1956; Jellinek, 1960). Interpretation is often difficult because of incomplete information concerning the patients. Convulsive activity during alcohol withdrawal may develop in patients who have not previously shown evidence of seizure patterns in their EEG's (Isbell *et al.*, 1955; Marinacci, 1956; Weiss *et al.*, 1964b).

A barrier to progress in investigation of the neuropharmacological basis of the withdrawal syndrome has been the difficulty to induce the state in laboratory animals. One of the problems has been to ensure maintenance of severe intoxication without using methods of administration which by themselves is poorly tolerated. Neither gastric intubation nor intraperitoneal injection is suitable for this purpose, and these techniques also make it very laborious to maintain high alcohol concentrations in small laboratory animals because of their rapid rates of ethanol elimination. Several studies (Richter, 1926; Zarrow et al., 1962; Denenberg et al., 1961; Newell et al., 1964; Wallgren et al., 1967) gave no evidence of abstinence symptoms in the animals, possibly because the conditions of administration were not sufficiently severe. Borlone et al. (1966) studied effects of alcohol administered on a continuous basis to cats on the electric activity of the cerebral cortex and thalamic nuclei. During administration of alcohol (0.4 to 2.4 g/kg every 8 h during 14 days), amplitude and frequency of the thalamic rhythm increased. After withdrawal of alcohol, no changes were seen except that in one cat, the thalamic rhythm was augmented. McQuarrie and Fingl (1958), however, demonstrated hyperexcitability in mice, evidenced by decreased electroshock convulsive threshold, after a 14-day period during which alcohol had been administered every 8 h in a dose of 1.8 g/kg.

Some recent developments seem very promising. Techniques for self-administration through implanted cannulae by lever-pressing have yielded very interesting information on development of pharmacological dependence in animals (Weeks, 1964). The self-administration techniques have been successfully used with rhesus monkeys in tests for administration of several drugs, including ethanol (Deneau et al., 1969). Four of five monkeys initiated administration of ethanol, but one discontinued after a month. The others maintained intoxication for months, with alcohol intake reaching a maximal level of 8.6 g/kg/day over a period of a week. Abrupt discontinuation of the alcohol gave rise to a full blown withdrawal illness including convulsions. Goldenberg and Korolenko (1963) have reported signs of an alcohol withdrawal syndrome in dogs. Likewise, Essig and Lam (1968) have reported convulsions and symptoms suggesting hallucinations in dogs on withdrawal of alcohol which was administered through cannulae implanted in the stomach. This technique seems promising and has been used for experiments on therapy (Chapter 11, p. 746), but it has the drawback of causing gastric ulcerations. A very interesting technique has been described by Freund (1969). He deprived mice of food so that severe weight reduction occurred. The animals were then given a liquid diet containing 35% of the calories as ethanol as sole source of food and fluid. On this regimen, many animals maintained intoxication for 4 days and developed withdrawal symptoms, even terminating in fatal convulsions, on abrupt withdrawal of ethanol from the diet. Maintenance of high concentrations of ethanol in the tissues was facilitated by slow rates of ethanol elimination, known to occur in fasted animals (Chapter 3, p. 99). The short duration of the period for induction of withdrawal symptoms seems surprising but may be related to the high rate of physiological processes in mice. Chronic administration of alcohol in intoxicating quantities to animals is the subject of a more general discussion in Chapter 8 (pp. 419–422).

Essig and Lam (1968) as well as Freund (1969) stress the importance of a suitable animal model for development of effective therapy. Even more important is the possibility opened up for experimental study of the neural mechanisms involved in the manifestation of withdrawal symptoms. The complex clinical picture presented by chronic alcoholics has led to many theories of an indirect and multifactorial origin of the abstinence syndrome. Wieser (1965) reviews a number of these theories which include suggestions that malnutrition and disturbance of cerebral circulation (Yamashita, 1962) or respiratory infections, circulatory disturbances, and liver complications (Coda, 1961) are important factors in the pathogenesis of delirium tremens. There has also been a search for correlations between liver damage and delirium tremens (Allgén et al., 1958; Allgén, 1966), but no consistent association has been found (Pergola and Cachin, 1957; Lundquist et al., 1959). According to Kennedy and Fish (1959), Marzi has also contributed evidence that delirium tremens is not related to liver disease. The investigations of Isbell et al. (1955) and of Mendelson and associates (Mendelson, 1964), cited above (pp. 505–506), showed withdrawal symptoms in healthy subjects without evidence of liver disease. Also no consistent correlation has been found between altered electrolyte or water balance and the symptoms of dependence.

These observations illustrate the recurrent problem of how to distinguish phenomena related specifically to physical dependence from more general disturbances. It seems well established (Seevers and Deneau, 1963) that physical dependence on depressant drugs in general involves all the major structures of the central nervous system. The multifarious symptoms of alcohol withdrawal give the same impression. The symptomatology very impressively shows a disequilibrium of the central regulation of autonomic functions. There is, however, no single instance in which the exact mechanism of physical dependence on a drug is known. In the case of alcohol, the brain structures involved have not been identified and analyzed, nor has the mechanism been elucidated on the cellular or subcellular level. The concept of drug-receptor interaction has stimulated pharmacological research in many ways (Schueler, 1960; Ariëns, 1964) and plays an important role in hypotheses concerning dependence on morphine-type drugs (Seevers and Deneau, 1963; Collier, 1968). But in the case of the small, structurally simple ethanol molecule which apparently is neither bound nor metabolized to any significant extent in the brain, such phenomena do not seem to be involved.

Some hypotheses purporting to explain neural dependence on alcohol are conjectures based on single aspects of alcohol effects which have not been integrated into the general body of knowledge of the effects of alcohol. Thus Leevy and Baker (1963) have suggested that delirium tremens might be due to cellular dependence on the effects of increased NADH which is markedly raised during ethanol intoxication only in the liver and not in the brain. The hypothesis also fails to account for the similarities between alcohol and barbiturate withdrawal. Armstrong and Gould (1955) suggested that vitamin deficiencies would cause ethanol in place of carbohydrate to be forced on the central nervous system as an alternative source of nutrition. However, alcohol cannot be considered a source of nutrition for brain tissue (Chapter 5, p. 227). Also, Isbell et al. (1955) and Mendelson and La Dou (1964) have clearly shown that withdrawal symptoms may occur even when generous vitamin supplies are given. Following an old suggestion that delirium is caused by cerebral edema and by accumulation of a hypothetical toxin, Adriani and Morton (1968) studied cerebrospinal fluid pressure and composition in patients with alcoholic withdrawal disease. Neither increased pressure of the cerebrospinal fluid nor abnormalities in its composition could be detected.

Unfortunately, our limited knowledge of how alcohol acts on the nervous system prevents formulation of very specific testable proposals. However, certain concepts appear to explain important features of the known phenomena. Hubach (1963) described the abstinence syndrome as an overshoot occurring when normal excitability is restored in a central nervous system which has been under prolonged influence of an agent that suppresses the excitability. Whereas the formulation describes the situation well in a general way, it does not include any specification of the actual mechanism except that it involves the central nervous system. Weiss et al. (1964a), on the basis of observations of retinal functions during prolonged alcohol intoxication, suggested that alcohol affects differently the threshold of inhibitory and excitatory components in the retina. They extended this hypothesis from the retina to the entire central nervous system. Referring to the work of McQuarrie and Fingl (1958), they stated that "it may thus be assumed that excitatory components recover more rapidly than inhibitory components on withdrawal after chronic administration, and thus may account for the tremulousness, hallucinoses, convulsions, hyperreflexia, tachycardia, insomnia, and delirium". This is an attractive hypothesis which also serves to stress the importance of exploring the possible differential sensitivity to alcohol of excitatory and inhibitory pathways in the central nervous system.

The observations cited in the preceding paragraph raise the question of whether the development of physical dependence affects synaptic functioning and might be reflected in changes in the metabolism and function of transmitter or moderator substances within the central nervous system. There is little evidence for a specific sensitivity of the synaptic region to the effects of alcohol (Chapter 5). Effects of alcohol on synaptic function in the central nervous system have not been studied adequately. Although a change affecting the neurons more generally seems to be indicated, the possibility of alterations in transmitter levels, function, or metabolism should be systematically explored, with particular attention given to regional changes within the central nervous system.

The structures involved in the excitation cycle of the neuronal membrane, which appear to be primary targets for the depressant action of ethanol, are also likely to be involved in the development of physical dependence. Continuous exposure to ethanol may induce compensatory reactions to the depressing action on those structures, perhaps even involving alterations of their molecular arrangement or changes in the balance of the enzymic reactions which maintain normal reaction patterns. In any case, hyperactivity would be expected to follow disappearance of alcohol if a compensation for the depressant action of alcohol has occurred within the excitable structures. This hyperactivity would gradually diminish during readjustment to the alcohol-free condition. A suggestion that ethanol might induce formation of hallucinogenic alkaloids in the brain (Collins and Cohen, 1968) seems unnecessarily conjectural and also disregards the real information which after all is available concerning the way ethanol acts.

An important remaining question is whether development of tolerance bears any direct relationship to physical dependence. At least a superficial difference is that tolerance becomes evident with rather widely spaced doses whereas withdrawal symptoms have been seen only after prolonged, heavy consumption with continuous presence of alcohol.

(3) Hangover and its relation to physical dependence

It is remarkable that hangover has been so widely neglected as a subject of serious study. Some brief reviews (Lolli, 1946; Himwich, 1956; an anonymous editorial in J.A.M.A., 1961) describe the general symptoms and relate them to the known effects of acute alcohol intoxication. A book of impressive size by Karpman (1957) deals only with psychiatric aspects. The symptoms of hangover include a number of rather general disturbances such as ion and water shift, hypoglycemia, gastritis, and thirst. Elevated blood lactate and acetaldehyde have been suggested as causes (Himwich, 1956), but during hangover acetaldehyde and lactate are not elevated whereas pyruvate is (Ogata et al., 1966). The hypoglycemia is a rather impressive metabolic finding, which has been studied in persons apprehended for intoxication (Vartia et al., 1960) and experimentally in normal human subjects (Ogata et al., 1966). The larger the dose of alcohol the more marked is hypoglycemia, which also seems to correlate with other symptoms of hangover. Subjective feelings of fatigue are typical. Direct involvement of the central and autonomic nervous systems is indicated by additional symptoms, including headache, vertigo, positional nystagmus, pallor, sweating, nausea, tremor, elevated heart rate, and hyperexcitability. Courville (1955) suggests cerebral edema as a possible cause of the hangover symptoms. This hypothesis is contradicted by Adriani and Morton's (1968) report that in patients with acute alcohol withdrawal illness, the cerebrospinal fluid pressure was not increased.

All the symptoms of hangover combine with hyperexcitability to define a state which resembles a mild abstinence syndrome. The similarity even extends to the fact, known since antiquity, that alcohol seems to be the most effective remedy for hangover. Rauschke (1954) tested whether sleep or exercise would assist in restoring normal sensory reaction time in the post-drinking phase and found neither one effective, whereas renewed administration of alcohol shortened the reaction time to optic and acoustic stimuli.

A striking neural change associated with the hangover state is the reversal of the positional nystagmus caused by alcohol intoxication (Chapter 6,

p. 306; Goldberg, 1963a; Aschan *et al.*, 1964). This phenomenon has been seen only in humans. Goldberg (1963a) found that subjective feelings of drowsiness and fatigue were at a maximum when blood alcohol had decreased to very low values and even to zero, and that these feelings as well as the more specific hangover symptoms of dizziness, vertigo, nausea and vomiting coincided with the maximal intensity of the second phase of the positional alcohol nystagmus. Rauschke (1954) and Holmberg and Mårtens (1955) also have observed that sensory deficit and drowsiness are great in relation to motor disturbance during the late phases of intoxication. These differential effects persist even after complete elimination of alcohol. Fatigue, which often results from lack of sleep associated with many normal drinking situations, cannot explain these experimental findings. The symptoms of the hangover state appear to counteract the increased tolerance which is seen in the decrease in motor disturbance while the blood alcohol level is falling.

We may tentatively conclude that the hangover state contains an element of the withdrawal syndrome and thus provides information about physical dependence on alcohol. None of the systematic experiments indicates how the peak of the hangover symptoms is related to the elimination of alcohol. Complete disappearance does not seem to be a required condition. The symptoms apparently tend to become manifest during the descent of blood alcohol, perhaps at higher concentrations after the peak has been higher, although this has not been definitely established. The second phase of positional alcohol nystagmus may begin during presence of some alcohol in the organism, but always continues for several hours after disappearance of the alcohol (Goldberg, 1963a; Aschan *et al.*, 1964).

Other studies indicate a high degree of resistance to detrimental effects of hangover. Flynn (1958) (Chapter 4, p. 168) studied electrolyte and water balance in human subjects administered 2.5 ml of whisky/kg (approximately 1/g alcohol/kg) in repeated tests on alternating days. The most striking finding was dehydration which reached its maximum after disappearance of the headache and other symptoms. Water consumption increased by 50–90% on alcohol days. Flynn concluded that his physiological measures could not explain the phenomenon of hangover, and he suggested that the symptoms may be caused by toxic effects of alcohol on the central nervous system. The few studies of psychomotor performance during hangover indicate that any impairments are small compared with the preceding stage of acute intoxication. Lundgren (1947) tested lumbermen working after consumption of 250 ml of spirits (about 1 g alcohol/kg) in the preceding evening. Pulse rate was 13% higher, blood pressure 3% higher, and work output less efficient. Takala *et al.* (1958) in an experiment on healthy male students, administered 1.4 g alcohol/kg as beer or brandy. The peak blood alcohol had an average value of 0.152% after brandy, 0.124% after beer. There was no change in perceptual speed or dexterity, tested after overnight rest. The only decrement was in some intellectual functions, after beer. Karvinen *et al.* (1962) gave 30 humans an average dose of 1.67 g alcohol/kg in the evening and measured their physical performance the next morning. Performance on a bicycle ergotometer was impaired and heart rate was increased both during rest and during work. Other tests (hand grip, back lifting, jumping) were not significantly affected. Psycho-motor performance was measured in humans while they were subjected to hypoxia, 10 hours after consumption of beverage equivalent to 105 ml absolute alcohol in the evening (Carroll *et al.*, 1964). Subjective symptoms of hangover included headache, increased task fixation, unsteadiness, fatigue and dehydration with thirst, but performance in the task was not significantly affected. The short duration of the observations (only 15 min) may in part explain the lack of an effect.

Our knowledge of hangover, as of alcohol dependence, is severely limited by inability thus far to demonstrate and test the condition in laboratory animals. A prolonged physiological change in mice after intoxication has been reported by Ammon *et al.* (1965). Coenzyme A in the brain required 20 hours after injection of 4.1 g ethanol/kg to return to normal, and cerebral lactate was depressed even after 40 hours. McQuarrie and Fingl (1958) demonstrated decreased electroshock seizure threshold in mice after disappearance from the body of a single alcohol dose of 4 g/kg, administered orally.

(4) Acute intoxication of alcoholics

During the successive stages of alcoholism, intoxication becomes an increasingly urgent desire and usually an increasingly prevalent condition. Observations of characteristics of alcoholics have been tested in experiments on acute effects of alcohol. Evidence for the distinction between inability to abstain and inability to stop drinking was reported by Marconi *et al.* (1967). Hospitalized alcoholics were permitted to drink any amount of alcohol they desired in a test after four or more days of abstinence. In accordance with their clinical classifications, seven intermittent alcoholics all drank a larger quantity of alcohol in this situation than did six inveterate alcoholics. In a well-controlled experiment, Merry (1966) obtained self-ratings of craving for alcohol from 9 loss-of-control patients in a series of tests after alcohol or placebo beverages. The patients, who were led to believe the drinks were nonalcoholic, did not report any increase in craving after drinking a small quantity of alcohol (approximately 0.15 g/kg). However, an alcohol dose of approximately 0.3 g/kg in the same situation did elicit reports of craving. Experimental observations of amnesia in alcoholics have been reported by Diethelm and Barr (1962a, b). More than twenty hospitalized patients were administered approximately 1.0 g/kg intravenously, giving rise to blood alcohol levels above 0.15%. Several of the patients had no memory for certain of their statements, actions and especially emotions evoked during intoxication. The authors claimed that each instance of amnesia was related to a conflicted and highly emotional topic, generally representing a release of repressed memories or actions under the influence of alcohol. Some of the patients were not amnesic; these generally had a vague, inexact recollection of events associated with the drunken episode, rather than complete obliteration of certain specific memories.

Acquisition of tolerance to high doses of alcohol, and of dependence in heavy drinkers and alcoholics, has been discussed in prior sections of this chapter. After physical dependence on alcohol has been established, the craving for alcohol may be due partly to a desire for relief of the withdrawal symptoms. However, several experiments have given evidence that alcohol may improve the performance of alcoholics, after sufficiently lengthy abstinence for recovery from any withdrawal symptoms. Tripp et al. (1959), with measures of motor control over handwriting, found that the performance of alcoholics was improved by an alcohol dose (1.0 g/kg) which had a detrimental effect on nonalcoholic subjects. One of their measures of improvement was decreased pressure, and similarly Kissin et al. (1959) found that 0.8 g/kg alcohol decreased the writing pressure exerted by alcoholics. In a study of alcoholics during sustained, heavy intoxication for a number of days, performance in tests of motor skills (Talland et al., 1964a) and of attention (Talland et al., 1964b) remained unimpaired at blood alcohol levels below 0.15% or 0.2%. These studies, and measurements of critical flicker fusion (Weiss et al., 1964), gave evidence for improved performance under the influence of alcohol, but there was no control for improvement due to practice during the progressively increasing alcohol consumption. However, a comparison of alcohol with control sessions by Docter et al. (1966) provided a convincing demonstration that a low dose of alcohol (0.4 g/kg) improved performance of alcoholics in a task which required sustained attention for 50 minutes. Cutter (1969) asked subjects to estimate their probability of future success in a game. After a low dose of alcohol (0.2 g/kg), the influence of a specified qualification ("very lucky" or "very unlucky") was increased in the alcoholic but decreased in the nonalcoholic subjects. This seems to indicate that alcohol improved the appropriate response by alcoholics to the experimenter's instructions, although the author of the article interpreted the results as expressing conflicting attitudes toward drinking in alcoholics.

Rather variable findings have been reported in experimental studies of acute intoxication on the moods and emotions of alcoholics. Mello (1968) has reviewed a number of such studies. Drinking produces a more normal or elevated emotional state in alcoholics according to several experimental studies. Fleetwood (1955) combined assessment of the emotional state of psychiatric patients with biological assay of hormones in the blood. Substances resembling acetylcholine were found to be associated with anxiety, whereas substances resembling epinephrine were associated with feelings of resentment. In the blood of alcoholics, high levels of the resentment factor were found, and these were lowered after ingestion of alcohol. This suggestion of a special type of emotional state of alcoholics is interesting but has not been confirmed in later, independent studies. Kissin *et al.* (1959) reported that alcohol (0.8 g/kg) alleviated tension in alcoholics, measured by various physiological tests and handwriting pressure. Docter and Bernal (1964), in an experiment on two alcoholics, given 1.5 g alcohol/kg daily for 14 days, found an increase in pulse rate and stimulant effects on EEG and rapid eye movements. Docter *et al.* (1966) likewise found stimulant effects of alcohol on heart rate, EEG and rapid eye movement of alcoholics given a total of 1.2 g/kg alcohol in five portions at 1–15 minute intervals, but some of these changes were maximal even after the first portion. Contrary to these positive effects, Mendelson *et al.* (1964) reported that prolonged consumption by alcoholics of a regulated, large dose of alcohol gave rise to anxiety, depression, and psychopathic tendencies. In a comparison of alcoholics with nonalcoholics during a similar period of prolonged, regulated consumption, McGuire *et al.* (1966) found that the alcoholics expressed expectations of pleasure, excitement and relief beforehand. During the drinking they believed that their mood and social relationships became better and more pleasing, whereas observations often suggested the opposite. Mendelson and Stein (1966) suggested that the raised serum cortisol levels observed in alcoholics during drinking may indicate increased anxiety. Anxiety of alcoholics also increased under a schedule which permitted them to earn alcohol at a self-determined rate (McNamee *et al.*, 1968; Tamerin and Mendelson, 1969).

The increased anxiety seen in alcoholics during the later stages of prolonged drinking might be due to their increasing physical dependence and anticipation of the forthcoming withdrawal symptoms. Requests for larger amounts or more frequent drinks (Mendelson *et al.*, 1964) or increases in consumption on a self-selection schedule (McNamee *et al.*, 1968) have been noted at the later stages. However, the emotionally disinhibitory effects of the chronic intoxication, leading to expression of unpleasant feelings and variability of emotion, are emphasized by Tamerin and Mendelson (1969). In contrast to these aversive reactions at the later stage, Tamerin and Mendelson (1969) reported an initial pleasurable reaction to alcohol in all of their subjects. Other experimental studies of moods of alcoholics show similarly conflicting effects. Vanderpool (1969) reported that alcoholics expressed more adverse evaluation of themselves in responses to questionnaire items while intoxicated. With the use of a technique for intravenous infusion of alcohol, Mayfield and Allen (1967) and Mayfield (1968a) found that alcohol improved the mood of alcoholics, though less than that of depressed patients, but Mayfield (1968b) found adverse effects on mood, especially with the higher of two alcohol doses. Pollack (1966) reported that alcoholics when under the influence of alcohol gave less expressive responses in a sentence completion test. An anxiety-alleviating effect of alcohol might be inferred from a report (Menaker, 1967) that anxiety of alcoholics, tested by self-descriptions of mood, was higher if they were anticipating a drink than if they had drunk a small dose of alcohol.

It seems likely that the emotional responses of alcoholics to intoxication are greatly influenced by the situation. Most of the studies indicate beneficial effects shortly after drinking, especially if the quantity is small or moderate, whereas adverse effects on mood occur after prolonged consumption of large amounts. Conclusiveness of the findings is limited by the small number of subjects used in most of the experiments, because there is great variability among alcoholics in their accounts of how they experience the effects of alcohol. More comparisons are needed between gamma and delta alcoholics, or other categories of alcoholics.

References p. 583

C. Metabolic and physiological changes after prolonged
intake of alcohol

It has been established that behavioral tolerance to alcohol is due to increased tolerance of the nervous system rather than a more rapid rate of elimination. However, the evidence for very high rates of alcohol metabolism in some alcoholics has sustained interest in the question of whether metabolic adaptation may become manifest as an increased capacity to metabolize alcohol. Two other questions arise from the special characteristics of alcohol metabolism. The first is whether the organism, and particularly the liver, somehow compensates for and minimizes the metabolic changes during oxidation of ethanol. The second is whether the diminished utilization of nutrients other than alcohol may result in maladaptive changes, thereby impairing the capacity to handle normal food.

Physiologically, the marked and sometimes violent vegetative disturbance of alcohol withdrawal raises the question of the nature of the disturbance of homeostatic mechanisms. Improved understanding should aid us to find means of restoring the equilibrium. We may also ask whether prolonged use of alcohol leads to a changed reaction to the drug which may give it a new significance. Notwithstanding the importance of getting reliable answers to such questions, the work in the area has been rather unsystematic and often based on conjectures lacking a solid foundation in knowledge about the effects of alcohol. The difficulties are undoubtedly great. In work on humans rigorous control is impossible and the possible approaches are restricted whereas the complex features of human alcoholism have not been reproduced in animals.

(1) Induced changes in rate of alcohol metabolism

There are three principal sources of information on effects of chronic administration on alcohol metabolism: observations on humans, animal studies, and elimination of alcohol in relation to liver disease.

(a) Observations on humans

In most of the studies cited by Elbel and Schleyer (1956), elimination rates determined by blood alcohol curves were compared in groups classified according to their reported alcohol habits. In a few instances, experimental induction of changes was attempted by repeated daily administration of alcohol. The final conclusion was that the studies showed no consistent differences in elimination. Likewise, Mazzucchelli and Guarneri (1965) found no difference in elimination rates between male alcoholics and controls, but Iber *et al.* (1969) reported a β-value of 0.049 in 30 alcoholics as compared with a β of 0.025 in 15 control subjects.

In the first section of this chapter, evidence for high rates of elimination in some alcoholics was presented, but it is not definitely known whether alcoholics as a group have a larger proportion of high elimination rates than the general population. Some studies have given evidence for induction of higher rates of alcohol elimination. In the study of the etiology of rum fits, the Lexington group (Isbell *et al.*, 1955; Wikler *et al.*, 1956) attempted to maintain a steady level of blood alcohol. After the critical period of establishing the suitable rate of intake for the various subjects, maintenance of a steady blood alcohol level required an increase of approximately 10% in the daily dosage, from 340 g (5.0 g/kg) initially to 380 g (5.5 g/kg) several weeks later. Mendelson and La Dou (1964) likewise found that their alcoholic subjects attained very high rates of alcohol intake, about 400 g daily, at the end of a 24-day period of heavy alcohol consumption.

The question whether high rates of alcohol elimination in alcoholics are inherent or acquired as a result of prolonged drinking may be approached by study of groups differing in age and duration of drinking. Nimura (1966) has presented data which show a tendency for rates of alcohol elimination to increase during the first 10 years of heavy drinking, but only 20 subjects were studied. A report published by Bonnichsen *et al.* (1968) and presented in Table 9–5 gives evidence in support of Nimura's finding. The great variability in the alcoholics is evident, as well as the normal elimination values of the young patients. A tentative conclusion is that some of the alcoholics acquire increased capacity to metabolize alcohol, or else that all alcoholics show this raised capacity in some phase of their drinking but lose it secondarily, for instance as a consequence of liver disease (see below, pp. 524–525). More extensive studies along these lines are indicated.

Some recent investigators have used measures of alcohol elimination which are not satisfactory for quantitative determination. Mendelson and Mello (1964), Mendelson *et al.* (1965c), and Mendelson *et al.* (1966) inferred an increased rate of alcohol metabolism after a period of high intake from measurement of $^{14}CO_2$ expired in the breath after injection of labeled ethanol. This change was attributed to induction of alcohol dehydrogenase activity by cortisol (Mendelson and Stein, 1966). Mendelson (1968) did not,

TABLE 9-5

RATE OF ALCOHOL ELIMINATION IN PATIENTS TREATED FOR ALCOHOLISM
COMPARED WITH THE RATES IN NORMAL CONTROLS
(Acc. to Bonnichsen et al., 1968)

| | Alcohol elimination (mg/kg/h) | | |
	Mean ± s.d.	Range	n
Controls	124 ± 19	99–160	24
Adult male alcoholic patients	153 ± 35	82–213	27
Young male alcoholic patients	127 ± 7	120–139	7
Female alcoholic patients	218 ± 33	180–250	4

The data have been recalculated from original values expressed in terms of g alcohol per hour eliminated by each subject. The values for the patients have been estimated on the basis of an assumed whole body water content of 60% in the males and 50% in the females: in the controls, alcohol elimination was measured directly on the basis of the duration of total elimination of the dose given.

however, find any difference between alcoholic and nonalcoholic male subjects in rate of output of $^{14}CO_2$ from labeled ethanol. In a discussion of the $^{14}CO_2$-excretion technique (Chapter 2, p. 46), we concluded that it does not give a trustworthy measure of alcohol metabolism. Other investigators, measuring LADH activity in biopsy specimens, have found lower enzyme activity in the livers of chronic alcoholics without diagnosed liver disease than in the livers of normal controls (Schwarzmann et al., 1962; Albertini et al., 1967; Ugarte et al., 1967). As discussed in Chapter 3, there is no direct relationship between LADH activity as determined in vitro and the rate of elimination of alcohol in the intact organism. Therefore, these findings do not contradict the high rates of alcohol metabolism which have been demonstrated in many alcoholics. Large concentrations of "atypical", highly active alcohol dehydrogenase have been reported to occur occasionally in the livers of humans and rhesus monkeys (cf. Chapter 3, p. 85) but rates of alcohol elimination were normal.

As pointed out by Forsander (1963), the question remains how the elevated rates of alcohol metabolism, in some individuals, can be maintained within the limits of energy expenditure of the liver. It is thus reasonable to consider alternative pathways, although most of what can be said is conjectural. Iber et al. (1969) found that the rate of alcohol elimination in a group of alcoholics differed from that of a group of controls not only in being higher, but also by fitting a logarithmic function better than a linear one. They suggest induction of a new enzyme for oxidizing ethanol. An increase in the activity of the hepatic microsomal ethanol oxidizing activity by 50–100 % in rats has been reported by Lieber and DeCarli (1968), but the quantitative role of this system remains obscure. Also, extrahepatic systems should be considered. For instance, ethanol might be oxidized only to acetaldehyde within the liver, and the acetaldehyde then oxidized further elsewhere, or else hydrogen from ethanol, bound to reduced compounds such as lactate, may be transported from the liver. This mechanism should be testable, but increased release of acetaldehyde is not likely, because the oxidation of acetaldehyde to acetate proceeds very rapidly in the liver, at least under normal conditions. An alternative possible mechanism for increased extrahepatic oxidation of ethanol is through activation of some peripheral system catalyzing oxidation of ethanol. This also should be testable.

Trémolières and associates in France have suggested that peroxidase systems (xanthine oxidase, amino acid oxidase, and catalase) may develop in the plasma as a consequence of heavy alcohol use. Such systems would function independently of oxidative phosphorylation, dissipating all the energy as heat. In this way, they would by-pass the normal regulation based on the energy requirement of the tissues. The French group has reported *in vitro* experiments in which uptake of ethanol occurred after addition of nucleotides and amino acids to plasma from alcoholics (Trémolières and Carré, 1960, 1961). They also reported elevation of the basal metabolic rate of some alcoholics after administration of ethanol (Cros and Trémolières, 1961; Trémolières and Carré, 1961). Studies of rat plasma (Trémolières and Carré, 1962) and liver homogenate (Griffaton and Lowy, 1964) showed similar induction of a coupled peroxide-ethanol oxidation after administration of heavy doses of ethanol. These and other studies have been reviewed and discussed by Trémolières and Lowy (1964), Lowy and Griffaton (1965), and Trémolières *et al.* (1967). They emphasize that the presumed breakdown of tissue nucleotides, caused by heavy intoxication, would provide the substrates for xanthine oxidase activity in the plasma. Much more substantial data are needed for proof of this interesting hypothesis. In no instance has the quantitative significance of raised plasma peroxide activity been demonstrated for the rate of alcohol elimination in a living human subject, and there is no information on the frequency of this type of physiological activity among alcoholics.

Some independently obtained data are relevant to the work of the French group briefly reviewed above. Tephly *et al.* (1965) have activated an alcohol-oxidating peroxidative system in mammalian erythrocytes *in vitro*. They pointed out that artificial induction of such systems might be expected to speed the rate of alcohol elimination, but that the rise in acetaldehyde production might cause problems because acetaldehyde is not oxidized by the erythrocytes. McGuire (1965) also described an *in vitro* system in which the peroxide for ethanol oxidation by catalase was derived from non-enzymic oxidation of cysteine. Fazekas *et al.* (1966) have demonstrated that alcohol administration causes a small, transient increase in catalase activity of the blood of rats. This response seems to depend on corticosteroids since it does not occur in adrenalectomized animals. According to Lecoq (1955), blood adenine normally rises in the initial phase of alcohol intoxication, whereas the level was within the normal range in 8 "habitual drinkers" and was lowered in tremulous, delirious and cirrhotic alcoholics. Hofmann and Kryspin-Exner (1966) found elevated catalase in the blood plasma of patients with delirium but not in alcoholics without delirium. Contrary to the assumption of Trémolières and associates, Klingman *et al.* in their studies of severe alcohol intoxication of dogs (Chapter 4, p. 190) found no increase in the nonprotein nitrogen of the blood.

(b) Animal studies

Pringsheim (1908) concluded that daily administration of large alcohol doses to rats and rabbits increased the rate of elimination. Subsequent studies reviewed by Elbel and Schleyer (1956) have given contradictory results, and data published later have been no more consistent. Troshina (1957) reported that administration of alcohol to rats in a dose of 3.55 g/kg daily for up to 6 months decreased the rate of elimination. Kinard and Hay (1960) administered alcohol 6 times weekly i.p. to female rats in doses beginning at 1 g/kg and rising to 4 g/kg toward the end of the experimental period of 10 to 12 weeks. Both *in vivo* and *in vitro* measurements showed no change in rate of alcohol oxidation. Drinking of 5, 10, or 20% ethanol as single fluid for 2 months did not alter rates of ethanol and acetaldehyde metabolism in rats (Majchrowicz *et al.*, 1968). Contrary to these findings, Ryan and Cornish (1966) have reported that prior treatment with ethanol induced a slight increase in the capacity of rat liver tissue to metabolize alcohol *in vitro*. Hawkins *et al.* (1966) found an increment of about 50% in the rate of fall of blood alcohol in male rats after alcohol intake of approximately 9 g/kg daily in the form of 4.5 g/kg by stomach tube and an approximately equal amount in a 12.5% v/v solution as the only source of fluid. In an experiment by Wallgren *et al.* (1967), administration of intoxicating doses of alcohol to rats every other day for 6 months increased the rate of alcohol elimination by 37%. Interpretation of the result is complicated by the fact that the animals were maintained on a deficient diet so that the incidence of liver fibrosis was high, although lower in the intoxication groups than in others.

Studies of liver ADH activity have also yielded inconsistent results. Prolonged administration of alcohol has caused at least transient and generally quite moderate increases in liver ADH activity of rats (Abe, 1961; Dajani *et al.*, 1963; Dajani *et al.*, 1965; Mendelson *et al.*, 1965b; Hawkins *et al.*, 1966; Khanna *et al.*, 1967; Albertini *et al.*, 1967) and mice (McClearn *et al.*, 1964; Mirone, 1965a, b; Schlesinger *et al.*, 1966). Mistilis and Birchall (1969) report increase in alcohol dehydrogenase of the stomach and small intestine as well as of the liver of rats, in an experiment involving alcohol feeding for two weeks. Decreased activity in rats has been found by Figueroa and Klotz (1964) and Morrison and Brock (1967b). No change in rats was found by Figueroa and Klotz (1962a), Greenberger *et al.* (1965) and Lieber and DeCarli (1968). In several studies, prolonged alcohol intake gave evidence of increasing liver metabolism. Abe (1961) and von Wartburg and Röthlisberger (1961) reported increased oxygen consumption by liver slices from rats given alcohol for prolonged periods. Von Wartburg and Röthlisberger (1961) found increased rates of production of $^{14}CO_2$ from labeled ethanol *in vivo* and by liver slices but Greenberger *et al.* (1965) found no change in intact rats. Meek *et al.* (1967) observed a very slight increase in excretion of $^{14}CO_2$ from labeled ethanol in rats, and Schlesinger *et al.* (1967) have reported a small but statistically significant rise for mice.

Several sources of variation in the experimental conditions may explain some of the discrepancies in findings. The dose–time relationship as well as the dietary conditions may be important. The methods for determination of LADH activity have not been standardized well enough to yield comparable results. Hawkins *et al.* (1966) suggest the possibility of sex difference, but this is not found in the subsequent study by Khanna *et al.* (1967), nor in the numerous studies on humans cited by Elbel and Schleyer (1956). Strain differences may be involved in the animal studies since Büttner (1965) found a sex difference in the LADH activity of Sprague–Dawley but not of Wistar rats. The use of different doses may have caused some differences, but as pointed out previously (Chapter 3, p. 100) the relationship between dosage and elimination rate is also a controversial topic. The main conclusion, however, when the results from studies with humans as well as animals are considered, is that liver alcohol dehydrogenase activity cannot consistently be induced by the substrate ethanol. Morrison and Brock (1967b) suggest that ethanol might not be the normal substrate of liver alcohol dehydrogenase. However, such an assumption is not necessary because many mammalian enzyme activities are not inducible by their substrates.

(c) Elimination of alcohol in liver disease

The rate of alcohol oxidation is decreased in liver fibrosis due to dietary deficiency (Mikata *et al.*, 1963). Reports on effects of liver damage caused by toxic agents are somewhat conflicting. Sirnes (1952) found that alcohol elimination rate was similar to that of controls in centrolobular necrosis caused by carbon tetrachloride (CCl_4), whereas alcohol elimination was markedly retarded in periportal necrosis caused by phosphorus. Campos *et al.* (1964) found significantly higher β-values for alcohol elimination rate in CCl_4-treated rats than in controls, but they had fewer animals than Sirnes and also reported the unusually low β-value of 0.157 mg/ml/h for the controls, compared with 0.354 in Sirnes' animals. Evans *et al.* (1963), in a study of the capacity of damaged perfused livers to remove alcohol from the perfusion fluid, showed a tendency for a lower rate but no significant effect of CCl_4 and a larger, significant drop in livers damaged by allyl alcohol. This greater effect of an agent affecting primarily periportal rather than centrolobular areas agrees with the finding by Sirnes (1952) but seems contrary to the report by Morrison and Brock (1967a) that LADH activity is higher in the centrolobular areas of rat livers. In dogs, pretreatment with CCl_4 has been reported to lower the elimination rate (Šlesingr, 1965). In rabbits, Fischer (1967) found a transient increase in alcohol elimination followed by a definite decrease about 20 h after injection of CCl_4.

Results are more consistent in studies of human alcoholics. Kulpe and Mallach (1961) found no difference in alcohol elimination rates between 15 cirrhotic patients and normals. According to Lieberman (1963) cirrhotic patients had lower rates of alcohol elimination than normal controls only when the disease was severe. This observation is supported by two comparisons between alcoholic cirrhotics and normal humans (Winkler *et al.*, 1966; Filip and Hoenigová, 1966) in which unusually low values were found in some of the cirrhotics, causing a lower average and greater variance in the patients than in controls. In a later study, Winkler *et al.* (1969) found similar distribution of values for hepatic ethanol elimination among 20 cirrhotic patients and 31 control subjects, but a slightly lower mean for the cirrhotics.

Fructose caused a smaller increase in ethanol elimination in the patients with liver disease. The cirrhosis was associated with alcoholism in only part of the patients. Clark and Senior (1968) found no difference in ethanol elimination in 5 patients with liver disease as compared with 4 control patients. Asada and Galambos (1963) found that biochemically and histochemically determined LADH activity was generally lower in biopsy specimens from cirrhotics than from normal controls. However, the level of activity did not correlate with the severity of the liver injury, and after relatively small doses alcohol elimination by the cirrhotic livers did not differ from the control level, nor was there any correlation between the biochemical findings and the rate of alcohol elimination. In two studies (Albertini et al., 1967; Ugarte et al., 1967), LADH activity was greatly decreased in alcoholics with fatty liver and cirrhosis of varying degrees of severity. Spanio and Carulli (1966) found lowered levels of LADH activity in alcoholic cirrhosis, whereas LADH activity was increased in cirrhosis not associated with alcoholism. Leevy (1967) has reported that both the rate of alcohol elimination and the LADH activity decrease with a progression from normal to fatty to cirrhotic livers. However, his data on alcohol elimination are inconclusive since he shows only blood alcohol levels obtained one hour after administration. We may conclude from data on alcohol-elimination rates that oxidation of ethanol is impaired only in severe liver disease. Thus alcohol elimination does not provide a useful measure for diagnosis of liver damage.

(2) Metabolic findings

An interesting and virtually unexplored question is whether prolonged intake of ethanol attenuates the striking suppression of hepatic carbon dioxide production and shift of the redox state in the negative direction that normally occur during oxidation of ethanol (Chapter 3). This possible mechanism for metabolic adaptation to alcohol has not been readily testable because there has been no measure of the redox state of the liver applicable to intact subjects. The addition of ethanol altered the lactate/pyruvate ratio in slices of liver from rats fed liquid diets with 35% of the calories as alcohol for 12 weeks, as much as in liver tissue from control rats (Wallgren, Ahlqvist, Nyholm and Salaspuro, unpublished). On the other hand, a changed response in terms of redox shift of mice maintained 6 months with 15% w/v alcohol as sole fluid, was suggested by the finding that added ethanol caused no change in liver lactate and pyruvate although α-glycerophosphate still was elevated (Ammon and Estler, 1967a, b).

Both the redox state (ratios lactate/pyruvate and β-hydroxybutyrate/ acetoacetate) and carbon dioxide production were much less affected by ethanol in perfused fatty livers from rats fed a high fat–low choline diet than in livers from normal controls (Salaspuro and Mäenpää, 1966). The changed response could not be produced by adaptation to fat only and thus seemed to be distinctive of choline deficiency. Salaspuro (1966) has used the rate of elimination of galactose known to be slowed by ethanol (Chapter 3, p. 114) as an *in vivo* test of effects of alcohol on the redox potential of the livers of rats. The galactose elimination rate is not affected by ethanol in animals with fatty livers caused by choline deficiency. This finding has been confirmed clinically by galactose tolerance tests combined with ethanol administration, in alcoholic patients whose livers were checked by biopsies (Salaspuro, 1967a-c). Experiments with comparison of perfused normal with choline-deficient fatty livers of rats likewise show that galactose elimination is inhibited in the controls but not in choline deficiency (Salaspuro and Salaspuro, 1968). Tygstrup and Lundquist (1962) found a relatively smaller effect of alcohol on galactose elimination capacity in cirrhotic patients than in controls. However, initial levels of galactose elimination are already lower in cirrhotics (Tygstrup and Lundquist, 1962; Tengström, 1966). This may imply a sustained decrease in the redox potential of cirrhotic livers, whereas in the studies of fatty livers cited above, the redox potential in control conditions has been approximately normal. A contradictory report by Leevy (1967) is that NADH was not affected by ethanol in normal human livers, but was raised in fatty and cirrhotic livers. This result is inconclusive because the NAD/NADH is not a good indicator of the redox state (Chapter 3, pp. 105–106) and the biopsy specimens presumably were not obtained by the freeze-stop technique.

These findings indicate that variable effects of ethanol on the redox potential can be expected in alcoholic patients because of variation in the pathological states of their livers. Consequently, any hepatic complications should be known when metabolic findings are interpreted. This applies also to the metabolism of monoamines and some amino acids because ethanol, through its effect on the redox state of the livers, increases formation of reduced metabolites from these compounds (Chapters 3 and 5). Olson *et al.* (1960) found that in a group of chronic alcoholics, excretion of 5-hydroxyindoleacetic acid (5-HIAA) was lowered, indicating depression of the metabolism of tryptophan to this product, a precursor of which is 5-hydroxytryptamine or serotonin. In four of the patients, the change persisted for four months. The kyrunenine pathway seemed to operate normally. Pasquariello et al. (1964) agreed essentially with Olson et al. (1960) but found that in alcoholics the excretion of xanthurenic acid following a tryptophan load was at the upper end of the normal distribution. As excretion of xanthurenic acid increases during pyridoxine (vitamin B_6) deficiency, the finding indicates incipient pyridoxine deficiency in the patients studied. Murphy et al. (1962) found no difference between 15 alcoholics during abstinence and 7 controls in 24-h urinary excretion of 5-HIAA. The apparent discrepancy from the results of Olson et al. (1960) may be due to differences in the hepatic conditions of the patients. Gabuzda and Davidson (1962) reported enhanced rates of tryptophan and nicotinic acid metabolism in alcoholic patients with cirrhosis of the liver, but without evidence of wasting.

Schenker et al. (1964, 1967) in experiments on man, and von Wartburg et al. (1961) with rats, have shown that ethanol causes a smaller rise in urinary excretion of monoamines in subjects who have consumed alcohol for long periods than in controls. The level of excretion in alcoholics was lowered during periods of abstinence (Schenker et al., 1964, 1967). Their data indicate a greater relative increase in tryptamine excretion after ethanol in the alcoholics, although the absolute amounts excreted were smaller than in the controls. The decreased excretion of epinephrine and norepinephrine may indicate a diminished stress response to alcohol. However, acute ethanol intoxication may affect excretion of other monoamines such as tryptamine in intact subjects by increasing release, by inhibiting monoamine oxidase, or perhaps through a change in metabolic pathways related to the redox state of the liver.

An important role has been attributed to acetaldehyde in the actions of ethanol, particularly in chronic alcoholism (Akabane, 1960; Freund and O'Hollaren, 1965; Truitt and Duritz, 1967a). This suggested role cannot be accepted until acetaldehyde has been shown to become elevated, at least in some conditions. Such elevation might be found in conditions when ethanol does not appreciably alter the redox state of the liver. The concentrations of the oxidized and reduced form of all substrates whose oxidation depends on NAD-linked dehydrogenases should vary with changes in the ratio NADH/NAD. The usual rise in the lactate/pyruvate ratio during oxidation of ethanol is mainly due to a decrease in the concentration of pyruvate. When the liver becomes resistant to this change, as in choline deficiency, the concentration of pyruvate does not decrease. If ethanol/ acetaldehyde form a redox-pair as do lactate/pyruvate, sorbitol/fructose, and others (Chapter 3, p. 106), acetaldehyde also should become elevated. As acetaldehyde is very potent pharmacologically and synergistic with ethanol, it may give rise to toxic symptoms. A preliminary communication (Truitt and Duritz, 1967b) indicates that in precirrhotic alcoholics, acetaldehyde is elevated during oxidation of ethanol. However, the result is not entirely conclusive since the analytical procedure may have given rise to spurious results (Truitt and Duritz, 1967a). In an experiment with rats in which the changes in redox level of the liver in response to ethanol were changed by manipulation of thyroid function, Forsander et al. (1969) found that the acetaldehyde concentration of peripheral blood did not at all correspond to that of the liver. Acetaldehyde in blood sampled from the hepatic vein was a good indicator of the concentration of acetaldehyde in the liver. However, acetaldehyde did not correlate with the redox state of the liver. The results of the experiment did not give any support for the hypothesis that acetaldehyde might become elevated in conditions where ethanol has little effect on the redox state of the liver. More studies are needed to definitely resolve this problem. Determination of acetaldehyde in biological samples is subject to errors (Truitt and Duritz, 1967a), and levels in the blood may not correlate satisfactorily with those in the liver. If these analytical problems are satisfactorily solved, interesting results concerning levels of acetaldehyde in different states of the liver should be obtainable. Lester (1960) and G. J. Martin (1965) have proposed that altered acetate metabolism may be involved in the development of alcoholism. Lester (1964), in a study of 28 alcoholics, failed to obtain support for the hypothesis from their acetylation capacity measured by rate of elimination of the antituberculosis drug isoniazid.

Although ethanol interferes with gluconeogenesis (Chapter 3), no marked or consistent abnormalities in glucose tolerance have been found in alcoholics (Voegtlin et al., 1943; Varela et al., 1953; Pelton et al., 1959; Dahl, 1964; Vel'shikayev, 1967). However, according to some reports alcoholics show a greater than normal frequency of diabetic types of blood glucose curves, especially in conjunction with liver disturbance and increasing age (Hed, 1958a, b; Lundquist, 1965; Molinier et al., 1966). On the other hand, Moynihan (1965) concluded that altered glucose tolerance was not related to liver damage. Some authors have proposed hypoglycemia as a predisposing factor in alcoholism (Tintera, 1966). Moynihan and Benjafield (1967) have reported that a large proportion of the fasting blood glucose values fall below the normal range in alcoholics admitted to hospital treatment, but instead of signifying a permanent disturbance this may have been an after-effect of drinking, since the blood glucose values were nearly normal after treatment. Wallgren *et al.* (1967) found abnormally low blood glucose two days after the last alcohol dose in some rats subjected to intoxication every other day for 6 months, but the group average did not differ significantly from that of the controls. Alcoholics (Molinier *et al.*, 1966) and even cirrhotic patients (Kulpe and Mallach, 1962) are still as capable of a hyperglycemic response to acute alcoholic intoxication as are normal controls. Hed *et al.* (1968) have in alcoholic patients encountered a diabetic type of glucose metabolism combined with hyperinsulinemia, as well as spontaneous hypoglycemia and hypersensitivity to insulin. Thus, clinical findings do not show any consistent abnormality in the glucose metabolism of alcoholics. Animal experiments give evidence for compensatory changes in the regulation of blood glucose and carbohydrate metabolism. In rats given 1.5 g alcohol/kg daily by intraperitoneal injection, blood glucose was significantly decreased after 1 week but not after 2 or 9 weeks (Akabane *et al.*, 1964). This result suggests a transient disturbance followed by a compensatory reaction. Ammon and Estler (1967b) found that in mice receiving 19 % v/v alcohol as sole fluid for 6 months, liver glycogen, lactate, and pyruvate were maintained at normal levels during oxidation of ethanol. Apparently, adaptive changes ensure a sufficient supply of pyruvate for normal formation of glycogen and regulation of blood glucose. Citterio *et al.* (1964) reported that the activity of aldolase, an enzyme which catalyzes the cleavage of fructose 1,6-diphosphate, increased in the plasma of alcoholics. A dose of 0.5 g alcohol per kg injected i.v. induced a more persistent increase of aldolase activity in alcoholics than in abstainers. Hofmann and Kryspin-Exner (1966) have reported determination of metabolites in the blood of alcoholics with and without delirium and studies *in vitro* of the metabolism in erythrocytes and plasma from the same patients. In comparison with controls, the alcoholics had elevated levels of several metabolites and particularly α-ketoglutarate. Incorporation of inorganic phosphate into phospholipoids and metabolites was increased particularly in the plasma, showing the largest increase in the patients with delirium. As the studies were concerned with the blood only, the significance of the findings is difficult to evaluate. The authors suggest that the increased incorporation of phosphate indicates a more rapid turnover of membrane components.

References p. 583

In ordinary clinical tests, acute ethanol intoxication has had little effect on liver function in normal subjects. Even less disturbance of liver function has been reported in alcoholics, but contrary findings have also been published. Mendelson *et al.* (1966) found that during a 4-day period of drinking in a controlled situation, serum glutamic oxalacetic transaminase (SGOT) increased in 4 controls while remaining unchanged in 4 healthy alcoholics. The observation that gastrointestinal trouble occurred in 3 of the controls but in none of the alcoholic subjects supported the interpretation that the alcoholics had developed tissue tolerance to the effects of alcohol. On the other hand, Bang *et al.* (1958) found rise in SGOT activity after acute alcohol intoxication in 27 out of 35 alcoholic patients, but no change in 12 healthy, nonalcoholic individuals. According to v. Oldershausen and Schweiger (1964), "habitual drinkers" show elevations of SGOT, SGPT, serum aldolase, and alkaline phosphatase. Lukasik *et al.* (1967a) found that of 27 patients of whom 12 were chronic alcoholics, only a few showed increased serum enzyme activities suggestive of liver damage after administration of ethanol. Among 110 alcoholics studied while in a treatment service, SGPT and serum γ-glutamyltranspeptidase were elevated in several cases, but the increased serum enzyme activity was not correlated with the physical state of the patients. The distribution of the values also showed considerable overlap with that of a control group. These findings fail to support the concept of a consistent toxic effect of alcohol on the liver, and also show that serum enzyme tests have little diagnostic value for detection of alcoholic liver disease (Lukasik *et al.*, 1967b). Weinstein *et al.* (1968) reported normal alkaline phosphatase but raised creatine phosphokinase and phosphohexose isomerase activity in male alcoholic subjects without known organic disease. Abbott *et al.* (1963) found increased SGOT activity in 74 out of 104 chronic alcoholics during acute alcoholic intoxication. In most of these studies, abnormalities were correlated with the extent of liver pathology. In the study of Abbott *et al.* (1963), a single dose of alcohol did not affect any of a number of tests for liver disease, including SGOT activity, in seven alcoholic patients who had recovered from acute alcoholic disease. The kind of tissue tolerance in alcoholics, suggested by Mendelson *et al.* (1966), apparently is often obscured by liver disease. Wendt *et al.* (1966) have reported that chronic alcoholics show increased resistance of myocardial functions to alcohol.

During oxidation of alcohol, the energy requirement of the liver is almost entirely fulfilled by mitochondrial oxidation of hydrogen derived from the cytoplasmic oxidation of ethanol and acetaldehyde (p. 481). Since this metabolic state prevails in many chronic alcoholics, the capacity of the liver mitochondria to handle normal substrates might conceivably become impaired. However, studies on liver mitochondria during prolonged alcohol intake so far have revealed only unspecific changes found in almost any kind of toxic insult on the liver, and are therefore discussed in the section on etiology of liver pathology (p. 556). Peripheral metabolic patterns should also be altered in alcoholism. Oxidation of ethanol results in a sustained production of acetate which is apparently oxidized in preference to other substrates since almost all ethanol is converted to water and carbon dioxide within a short span of time. Evidently, oxidation of this acetate in many alcoholics may fulfill nearly half of the energy demand over long periods of time. In the sense that utilization of acetate is a normal cellular process, this situation does not involve anything abnormal. However, the utilization of other substrates such as longer-chain fatty acids necessarily decreases. As deviant metabolic patterns might arise in this way, more attention should be paid to the role of ethanol-derived acetate in the peripheral metabolism of alcoholics, and to possible limitations in their capacity to utilize normal nutrients during the transition from drinking to abstinence. A recent study (Meek et al., 1967) on patterns of excretion of $^{14}CO_2$ from labeled acetate and glucose in rats given 5, 10, or 20% alcohol as sole fluid for 10 to 11 months did not, however, reveal any difference from water controls.

(3) Endocrine functions

Older work on endocrinological effects of prolonged alcohol consumption has been reviewed by Goldfarb and Berman (1949) who cite numerous proposals that alcoholism may be caused by endocrine abnormalities. Jellinek (1960) also reviews suggested relationships between endocrine disturbance and alcoholism. The few recent experimental studies of the effects of prolonged alcohol intake on endocrine functions deal mostly with the hypophyseal-adrenal system.

Measurements of urinary catecholamines have yielded contrary results in human alcoholics and in laboratory animals. Giacobini et al. (1960) did not find any difference between alcoholics and controls in 24-h excretion of catecholamines in the urine. Alcohol doses as high as 2.3 g/kg did not influence the excretion of epinephrine or norepinephrine. However, the condition of alcoholism in humans engenders stresses which might counteract any sedative effect of alcohol. Von Wartburg and Aebi (1960) maintained rats on 10% v/v alcohol as sole fluid. At days 52, 113, 116, 157, 171, 198 and 205 of the experiment, the 24-h excretion of catecholamines was determined in undisturbed condition and then after administration of alcohol by stomach tube in a dose of 1.5 ml/kg. In both conditions of measurement, the animals on the alcohol regimen excreted less epinephrine and norepinephrine than the controls. Histochemical examination revealed a decreased number of cell groups containing norepinephrine in the adrenal medullae of the animals receiving alcohol solution. Similar observations have been reported by von Wartburg et al. (1961). Since urinary excretion of epinephrine seems to be related to emotional reactions and that of norepinephrine to autonomic activation, the result may indicate a decrease in both emotional and autonomic responsiveness to environmental factors. Partial support for decreased responsiveness as a chronic effect of alcohol consumption was reported by Zarrow et al. (1962). They studied relative weights of a number of organs, including adrenals, hypophysis, thyroid, thymus, prostate, and testes, in rats receiving 12 g food a day and 10% alcohol as sole drinking fluid for 129–157 days. No change was found in endocrine functions, but the mean relative weights of the adrenals and testes were significantly smaller in the alcohol group than in the controls.

Adrenocortical function, which has attracted more interest than the medullar secretion, seems to show little effect of chronic alcohol intake in laboratory animals. According to Forbes and Duncan (1953), i.p. injections of intoxicating doses of alcohol to guinea pigs maintained on a diet deficient in vitamin C lowered ascorbic acid only slightly more than in control animals. Kalant and Czaja (1962) found that daily oral administration of 2.0 g alcohol/kg for 2 months had no significant effect on adrenal weights or content of ascorbic acid or cholesterol of rats. Andrzejewski (1961) administered to male rats for 10 weeks a daily alcohol dose of 2.8 or 3.5 g/kg. Deep depression of the adrenal cortical function was seen on the third day, followed by recovery to normal values at the termination of the experiment. Akabane et al. (1964) administered alcohol i.p. in a dose of 1.5 g/kg to rats for periods up to 9 weeks. Increased adrenal weight was found throughout, as well as histological signs of activation, whereas evidence of stress as revealed by adrenal cholesterol and ascorbic acid was more variable.

Studies of human alcoholics have been equally inconclusive. Dowden and Bradbury (1952), in a comparison of 99 alcoholics with 40 controls, found a similar eosinopenic response to administration of ACTH. Likewise, Mann

(1952) found that among 95 alcoholics, 59 had a normal eosinophil response and only 11 a subnormal response to ACTH. Since Owen (1954) found a normal eosinopenic response to ACTH in 14 of 27 alcoholic patients suffering from acute delirium tremens, disturbed adrenocortical function is not a necessary condition of delirium. However, subnormal eosinopenic response to ACTH was found in the other 13 patients. Kissin *et al.* (1959), who also found a high incidence of diminished eosinopenic response to ACTH in alcoholics, attributed it to the acute stress of the withdrawal state. Diminished conjugation of exogenous hydrocortisone, found in 6 out of 10 alcoholics, was attributed to changed liver function. These authors suggested that disturbed elimination of corticosteroids might lead to elevated plasma levels and secondarily to hypofunction of the adrenal cortex. However, Kissin *et al.* (1960) subsequently found that alcoholics and non-alcoholics reacted to administration of alcohol with similar elevation of the excretion of 17-hydroxycorticoids. The plasma levels were lower in the alcoholics, apparently because of their greater diuretic response to alcohol. Mendelson and Stein (1966) report that during a 4 day drinking period, serum cortisol was elevated in 4 normal subjects only when they developed signs of gastrointestinal trouble, whereas in 4 alcoholic subjects there was a sustained although rather moderate increase throughout the drinking period with a maximal value during withdrawal. The groups were similar in predrinking levels. Many alternative interpretations of this finding are discussed by the authors. Margraf *et al.* (1967) tentatively conclude from studies on patients that adrenocortical function in alcoholics is normal but that steroid metabolism is altered. Turner and Brum (1964), in a report of increased taurine excretion in alcoholics on admission to treatment, attributed this change to adrenocortical stimulation in the withdrawal phase.

An association between hypothyroidism and alcoholism has been proposed by Goldberg (1960), who presents some statistics in support of this notion. However, Selzer and Van Houten (1964) did not find any evidence of thyroid hypofunction in their study of 43 alcoholic patients. Similarly, Augustine (1967) did not detect any instance of decreased thyroid function in a series of 109 unselected alcoholic patients. These observations suggest that altered thyroid function is not a consequence of alcoholism. In agreement with the latter conclusion, Aschkenasy-Lelu and Guerin (1960) report that relative thyroid weights or iodine fixation were not altered in rats drinking 10% alcohol or red wine as sole fluid for 6 months. However, Murdock (1967) found increased uptake and excretion of radioiodine in the thyroid glands of rats which ingested 20% alcohol over periods of 2 to 3 weeks, with repeated supplemental injections of alcohol. The study was prompted by the observation that alcoholic patients on admission had elevated rates of turnover of iodine.

(4) Water and electrolyte balance

As discussed previously (Chapter 4, p. 166), one of the most marked effects of acute ethanol intoxication is diuresis caused by inhibition of secretion of antidiuretic hormone from the posterior lobe of the hypophysis. This effect persists during chronic administration, with an evident relationship between degree of intoxication and the magnitude of the diuretic response. Thus, fluid consumption has generally not been changed by voluntary intake of alcohol in free choice whereas the water intake is augmented by chronic administration of intoxicating doses of alcohol, as was first reported for chicks (Elhardt, 1930). Ogata (1963) showed that administration of approximately 2.8 g alcohol/kg 6 days per week progressively increased the diuretic response of rats up to 90 days after the beginning of the experiment. Neurohypophyseal content of antidiuretic hormone was not altered. Baïsset and Montastruc (1962) found that a daily alcohol dose (approximately 3 g/kg) increased the average daily water consumption by dogs from 88 to 338 ml after 10 days. This response was inhibited by posthypophysis extract. Intoxicating doses (4–6 g/kg) of alcohol, administered by stomach tube every other day, approximately doubled the average water intake of rats, both after 3 months and 6 months (Wallgren et al., 1967). The intoxication group was significantly higher in total body water volume, probably due to lower body weight and hence smaller fat content, but there were no major differences between the groups in plasma electrolytes. These animals were maintained on a deficient diet and at the start of the experiment were immature in a phase of rapid growth. One or both of these conditions was apparently necessary for their ethanol treatment to have a diuretic effect, because the same ethanol treatment had no effect on water consumption of adult rats fed a normal diet.

Beard et al. (1965) administered water or similar volumes of alcohol solutions to dogs in doses of 2, 3, or 4 g ethanol/kg daily. Body water compartments, sodium, potassium and chloride of blood plasma, erythrocytes and urine, and muscle water were determined weekly for 8 weeks. Alcohol increased water intake, urine output, the apparent volume of plasma and interstitial water, and total body water; these effects were large only with the higher doses of 3 and 4 g/kg. Neither weight of the animals nor distribution times of the various fluid spaces changed, thereby indicating a real increase in extracellular and decrease in intracellular volume of water. An increase in electrolyte retention was indicated by the fact that extracellular volume increased whereas electrolyte concentration was not significantly altered. Contrary to the general decrease in the intracellular volume, the water content of the skeletal muscles increased. A significant increase in this portion of the intracellular water volume was also found by Ogata and Saji (1966) after daily i.p. administration of alcohol to mice for 60 days. Dosage was not stated, and no significant change was observed in five other organs, including the brain. Karlsson *et al.* (1967) administered combinations of insulin and ethanol or epinephrine and ethanol to rats for two weeks. A histochemical study showed signs of activation of the hypothalamo-hypophyseal system, perhaps signifying release of antidiuretic hormone.

Studies of human alcoholics give further evidence for a diuretic effect of repeated intoxications. Ogata (1963) found that in a water diuresis test, the urine of 19 out of 33 alcoholics was abnormally high in volume and abnormally low in density. Alcohol (0.8 g/kg) caused a larger diuretic response in the alcoholics than in 15 nonalcoholic controls. Ogata (1963) concluded that chronic alcoholism enhances the known inhibitory effect of alcohol on secretion of antidiuretic hormone on the basis of the further finding that administration of antidiuretic hormone to the 19 alcoholics with abnormally high volume and abnormally low density of urine restored both measures to normal. This conclusion is supported by a study of 5 alcoholic patients without evidence of clinical complications, compared with 5 matched controls (Baïsset *et al.*, 1965). The subjects consumed 220 ml red wine twice daily (approximately 0.7 g alcohol/kg per day) with standardized meals and continuous access to drinking water. The alcoholics consumed more water and excreted more urine, which was lower in density and in sodium and potassium content. Injection of nicotine, which is known to release antidiuretic hormone from the posterior hypophysis, decreased urine flow of the controls more than of the alcoholics. Extract from the posterior hypophysis administered to the alcoholics brought their water consumption, urine volume, and excretion of sodium close to the normal level. In 6 alcoholics participating in an experiment which involved heavy drinking for 8 to 17 days, initial diuresis was observed which was not sustained (Ogata *et al.*, 1968). In all subjects, there was an increase of serum osmolality during

References p. 583

drinking. The increased concentration was correlated with but not explained by an increase in sodium. In several subjects, decreased hematocrit suggested increased blood volume. Urine concentration decreased.

There are some indications that the state of the liver may modify the effects of alcohol on water balance in alcoholics. Kissin et al. (1964) found that the diuretic response to alcohol was greater in a group of alcoholics who had recovered from acute episodes of drinking than in controls matched for age. The serum volumes were larger in the alcoholics than in the controls, but total quantity of electrolytes excreted as well as serum electrolyte levels were very similar in both groups. The authors suggest that the diuresis after alcohol in alcoholics is not primarily due to blocking of the secretion of antidiuretic hormone but instead represents a release of urine flow following water and salt retention caused by early liver disease. This interpretation was supported by their further finding that the diuretic response to alcohol was weak or absent in cirrhotics. A study by Sereny et al. (1966) gave evidence that liver disease affects the electrolyte and acid-base balance during alcohol withdrawal. Four alcoholic patients without liver disease gained weight with increases in plasma volume, sodium retention, and urine density. Their urine was more alkaline than that of control subjects. The findings were attributed to a rebound increase in the activity of antidiuretic hormone and also of aldosterone following prolonged suppression during chronic intoxication. In contrast, patients with liver disease lost body weight and sodium during withdrawal from alcohol; one cirrhotic patient lost both sodium and potassium. Beard and Knott (1968) found that 30 well-nourished, chronic alcoholics with abnormal liver function all were overhydrated on admission to hospital. Electrolyte concentrations were normal, and the total body water level returned to normal within four days, without specific therapy. These studies demonstrate that disturbance in secretion of anti-diuretic hormone is an important mechanism causing increased water flow in alcoholics, but that the condition of the liver influences the diuretic effect of alcohol.

The observation that liver disease modifies body water distribution and electrolyte patterns in alcoholics may partly explain why measurements of sodium and chloride in serum and urine from alcoholic subjects have given rather inconsistent results (Kennard et al., 1945; Silkworth and Texon, 1950; Martin et al., 1959; Roberts, 1963). Potassium in the serum as well as its excretion were decreased in at least some alcoholics (Boudin et al., 1961; Coirault and Laborit, 1956; Martin et al., 1959); the latter authors noted an increased concentration in the erythrocytes. Another difference between normal and alcoholic subjects in water and electrolyte metabolism is greater sensitivity of alcoholics to sodium depletion (Grayson *et al.*, 1963; Butcher, 1965). This was studied because of its importance in hemorrhagic shock.

One of the most important divalent cations is magnesium, depletion of which is known to cause hyperirritability (Bland, 1963). It is reasonable to expect chronic drinking to cause this condition, since acute alcoholic intoxication induces loss of magnesium (Chapter 4, p. 169). However, there is no convincing evidence for such an effect of chronic alcohol intake. Klingman *et al.* (1955) compared the effects of a diet deficient in magnesium with those of a normal diet in rats given 10% alcohol as the sole source of fluid. In both groups, susceptibility to seizures increased and was attributed to derangement of brain electrolytes. However, these changes seemed to be the result rather than cause of the seizures. Moses (1967) found no effect of ingestion of 15% ethanol as sole drink on magnesium and copper in the tissues of rats. In some studies, serum magnesium has been rather consistently lowered during withdrawal (Flink *et al.*, 1954; Sullivan *et al.*, 1963; Ogata *et al.*, 1968). Flink *et al.* (1954) and Suter and Klingman (1955) have reported beneficial effects of administration of magnesium sulfate during the withdrawal, but the severity of the withdrawal symptoms does not correlate with serum magnesium (Jankelson *et al.*, 1959; Mendelson *et al.*, 1959). Observations on red blood cells indicate more consistently lowered values for intracellular magnesium, which also is reported to show better correlation with the clinical withdrawal symptoms (Smith *et al.*, 1958; Smith and Hammarsten, 1959). According to Smith and Hammarsten (1959), 72 hours of therapy with intramuscular magnesium increased intracellular magnesium (measured in the red blood cells) together with clinical improvement. Contrary to these reports, McCollister *et al.* (1963) and Mendelson *et al.* (1965a) have demonstrated retention rather than depletion of magnesium in alcoholic patients during the withdrawal period. Martin and Bauer (1962) and Mendelson *et al.* (1965a) found that the magnesium exchangeable during 24 h is lowered in chronic intoxication or withdrawal, but 24-h exchangeable magnesium involves only a fraction of total body magnesium with unknown tissue location. Mendelson *et al.* (1965a) further found that serum magnesium was not altered during a 24-day period of heavy drinking, but fell abruptly 12 h following discontinuation of alcohol. This phenomenon may be caused by shifts of body magnesium between various tissue compartments. Further evidence against magnesium depletion as a cause of the withdrawal syndrome is that liver cirrhosis without withdrawal symptoms is associated with lowered magnesium and calcium (Bland, 1963, p. 259). Also, liver fibrosis has been found to correlate with lowered serum calcium in rats (Wallgren *et al.*, 1967). Recent experimental evidence (Saville and Lieber, 1965) indicates that magnesium deficiency in prolonged alcohol intake is due to nutritional deficiency rather than to a specific action of alcohol. Fankushen *et al.* (1964) and Durlach and Cachin (1967) also concluded that deficient nutrition and malabsorption are the principal causes of magnesium deficiency in chronic alcoholism.

The similar change in excretion of lactate and of magnesium mentioned in the discussion of acute effects of ethanol on electrolyte balance (Chapter 4, p. 169) is not a consistent effect of chronic alcohol intake. Sullivan *et al.* (1966) found a good correlation between change in lactate and magnesium excretion only when serum magnesium was normal. In alcoholic patients with low serum magnesium, alcohol ingestion was followed by increases in serum lactate and excretion of lactate but not in magnesium excretion. The observation that a group of alcoholics had less dense bones than a matched control group led Saville and Lieber (1965) to study bone density and muscle magnesium during chronic alcohol intake. They found a decrease in bone density, which was due to lower body weight of the alcohol-fed animals and not to increased magnesium loss. Muscle magnesium was not affected. Gottlieb *et al.* (1959) have reported that alcohol increases the magnesium requirement of rats.

Other electrolytes have also been measured in studies of effects of chronic alcohol intake. Serum zinc levels are lowered in severe alcoholic cirrhosis while urinary excretion of zinc is elevated (Vallee *et al.*, 1956; Vallee *et al.*, 1957). Sullivan and Lankford (1965) found a definite excess of zinc excretion in 42 out of 124 alcoholics without cirrhosis of the liver. The changes in excretion of zinc and magnesium are not correlated (Sullivan *et al.*, 1963). Alcohol apparently affects kidney mechanisms and also distribution between tissue compartments; furthermore, physicochemical effects of ethanol may alter the binding of electrolytes to tissue constituents. Since free bilirubin and its water-soluble conjugates inhibit liver alcohol dehydrogenase (Flitman and Worth, 1966), presumably by chelating the zinc atoms, the excessive bilirubin often found in late stages of cirrhosis might cause loss of zinc, but such effects would probably be important also in late stages of Laennec's cirrhosis in the absence of alcoholism. In rats, ingestion of 15% alcohol as sole drink caused loss of zinc in the feces but not in the urine; liver zinc increased (Moses, 1967). Zinc and manganese levels have been assumed to reflect the combined activities of the enzyme systems of which these metals constitute a functional part. Barak *et al.* (1967) claimed that an experiment on rats showed differing concentrations of these metals in serum and liver of rats with liver cirrhosis caused by alcohol and by choline deficiency. However, the results are inconclusive because the regimens were not adequate to induce cirrhosis, and the condition of the livers was not reported. Transient decrease in blood phosphates with spontaneous restoration of normal values has been reported by Stein *et al.* (1966) for alcoholic patients in an acute state.

Several conclusions can be drawn from the often conflicting findings. Chronic alcohol intake increases the flow of water through the body with little effect on electrolyte balance. This is at least partly due to inhibition of functioning and responsiveness of the system for secretion of antidiuretic hormone. These effects of alcohol are influenced by clinical complications, such as liver disease, and malabsorption, but we do not yet know the precise role of these factors. In any case, alcoholics are not nearly always dehydrated, as is often believed, and thus fluid and electrolytes should not be given indiscriminately to alcoholic patients.

D. Etiology of liver pathology

An overwhelming majority of the studies on organic complications of alcoholism deal with liver pathology. This undoubtedly is an example of fashion in research rather than a fair reflection of the significance of the topic in the general problem area of alcoholism. The massive research effort, however, has begun to pay off in some real understanding of the processes leading to liver disease in alcoholism. The combination of clinical studies with animal experimentation has contributed greatly to this achievement.

Instances of the role of the liver in metabolic alterations found in alcoholics have already been mentioned several times in prior sections of this chapter. Space precludes detailed presentation of the literature on liver pathology. Our account begins with reference to some important reviews, followed by a necessarily subjective attempt to summarize the experimental findings and their relationship to clinical knowledge. The review emphasizes the relationships among dietary regimen, alcohol toxicity, and gross liver pathology, because these have given encouraging prospects for clinical application. Biochemical and ultrastructural findings, discussed in the last part of this section, are the basis for our knowledge, as yet incomplete, about the cellular mechanisms by which alcohol contributes to liver disease. Comment on the prevalence of liver disease among alcoholics is given in Chapter 11, pp. 721–722.

(1) Prior reviews

The literature on alcoholic cirrhosis was extensively reviewed by Jolliffe and Jellinek (1942), who covered clinical, pathological, and experimental aspects. They concluded that the association between chronic alcoholism and cirrhosis of the liver was well established, that a direct causation through alcohol toxicity had been ruled out, and that none of the rival theories of indirect causation had been sufficiently documented to warrant acceptance.

Subsequent reviews are numerous. Edmondson *et al.* (1956) covered mainly clinical, statistical and pathological aspects. Mardones, Williams, and Phillips and Davidson discussed various aspects of alcoholic cirrhosis in a collection of papers on the liver edited by Miner (1954). Davidson discussed statistical-geographic aspects, Hartroft considered reproducibility of various types of human cirrhosis in animals, and Caroli and Ricordeau presented a classification of alcoholic cirrhosis with comments on diagnostics in Vol. 1 of *Progress in Liver Disease* edited by Popper and Schaffner (1961). In Vol. 2 (1965) of the same treatise, Lieber reviewed effects of alcohol on the liver, and Steiner, Jézéqúel, Phillips and Arakawa discussed some aspects of pathological alterations in the ultrastructure of the liver. The first volume of *Advances in Enzyme Regulation,* edited by Weber (1963), contains several chapters on various aspects of the biochemistry of the liver. A monumental treatise on the normal and pathological biology of the liver, edited by Rouiller (1963, 1964), is indispensable for anyone working on problems related to the liver but contains little information on alcoholic cirrhosis. Minor reviews include those by Waterlow and Bras (1957) on nutritional liver damage in man and by Patek (1963) on dietary factors in the pathogenesis and treatment of cirrhosis of the liver, and by Lieber and Rubin (1969) on alcoholic fatty liver. Klatskin (1959a, b; 1961a, b) reviewed animal experiments on the relation of alcohol to liver damage. Two extensive and relatively recent French reviews of etiology, pathology, clinical aspects, associated complications, experimental work, and therapy are the report *Cirrhose Alcoolique et Nutritionelle,* presented under multiple authorship at the 32nd French Congress of Medicine (1959), and that by

Etienne-Martin and Klepping (1960). Martini and Dölle (1965a, b) discussed classification of alcoholic cirrhosis. Recent papers that contain presentations of original material but also substantial review materials are those by Lieber (1967a, b), Leevy and ten Hove (1967), and Porta *et al.* (1967b). The latter includes a particularly important and illuminating discussion of experiments in this area. Green (1965), Wieser (1965) and Böhle *et al.* (1968) extensively covered clinical literature and discussed experimental evidence for the findings. A review on carbon tetrachloride hepatotoxicity by Recknagel (1967) is an important source of information on various aspects of liver metabolism and functioning, which are essential for understanding how a noxious agent might affect the liver and helpful for planning experiments in this area.

(2) The role of chronic alcohol intake

A prerequisite for comprehensive experimental study of a disease afflicting humans is that a similar condition can be induced in animals. Accordingly, the first part of this section begins with a discussion of equivalence of liver pathology in humans and experimental animals, followed by a review of the evidence for involvement of chronic alcohol intake in the etiology of liver pathology in both types of experimental subjects. In the third part of this section, we review recommendations, based on experimental findings in humans and laboratory animals, for prevention, therapy and diagnosis of liver pathology in alcoholics.

(a) Equivalence of liver lesions in animals and man

Hepatic pathology in human alcoholics varies greatly, but the majority of the cases appear to fall into the category of portal or Laennec's (fatty nutritional) type of cirrhosis. A history of alcoholism was found in 89% of 471 patients with Laennec's cirrhosis but in only 56% of 154 patients with postnecrotic cirrhosis (Garceau, 1964). In a material consisting of 1079 males and 269 females killed in accidents, Viel *et al.* (1968) found a strong correlation between evidence for alcoholism and presence of fatty liver and Laennec's cirrhosis. Laennec's cirrhosis is probably caused by intake of a diet lacking lipotropic factors, such as choline, methionine, and protein, which leads to fatty infiltration of the liver, followed by fibrosis and ultimately cirrhosis.

The fatty liver and cirrhosis produced in animals by dietary deficiency

References p. 583

lacks certain features common in cirrhosis of humans but is considered an acceptable "model" of Laennec's cirrhosis (Hartroft, 1961; Klatskin, 1961a). In rats the condition can be produced most easily when they are in a state of rapid growth, but even then, full development requires about 6 months. Dogs have also been successfully used, as well as rhesus monkeys (Wilgram, 1959). In a recent experiment with monkeys, alcohol administration failed to alter the development of the disease (Cueto et al., 1967). Mice easily develop fatty liver but not fibrosis. Guinea pigs may be more sensitive than rats to the effects of alcohol (Bourrinet, 1964) but have not been used for testing effects of alcohol on development of liver fibrosis. Rabbits have such a high incidence of spontaneous fibrosis that they are unsuitable for experiments in this area. They seem to differ from other animals studied, in that both acute and prolonged alcohol administration increases triglycerides in the blood but not in the liver (Bezman-Tarcher et al., 1966).

Alcoholics may suffer from diseases of the liver other than Laennec's cirrhosis. The symptoms and pathological alterations include sclerosing necrosis, fatty degeneration, enlargement of the liver, tenderness, jaundice, fever, portal hypertension, and postnecrotic cirrhosis, which occur in varying combinations. Sclerosing hyaline necrosis has been described as a separate entity (Edmondson et al., 1963). Other terms applied to some types in this heterogeneous group of disorders are "acute alcoholic hepatitis", "active" or "florid cirrhosis" and "toxic hepatitis". Necrosis apparently may proceed to cirrhosis without concomitant fatty infiltration in many such cases, but fatty degeneration often is an accompanying phenomenon (Baggenstoss, 1961; Green, 1965; Bertrand et al., 1966; Lee, 1966; Harinasuta et al., 1967).

"Alcoholic" hyaline bodies, first described by Mallory (1911), are a prominent distinctive feature of many of the conditions mentioned above, but are seen also in Laennec's cirrhosis of alcoholics. These hyaline bodies were considered specific for alcoholic conditions but have been demonstrated in clinical conditions not associated with alcoholism (Popper et al., 1960) and in livers of rats fed a choline-deficient diet but not receiving alcohol (Hartroft, 1961, 1964). Recently, however, Mallory-bodies have been produced in rats on regimens involving high alcohol intake (Porta et al., 1965, 1967b; Ahlqvist et al., 1968). The origin of Mallory-bodies is not clear, although they are most often assumed to be altered megamitochondria (Green, 1965; Phillips, 1967), a view supported by ultrastructural studies on rat livers (Minaker and Porta, 1967; Porta et al., 1967b; Hartroft and Porta, 1968), but contradicted by findings in biopsy specimens from alcoholic patients (Iseri and Gottlieb, 1968). In any case, production in the rat liver of Mallory-bodies and some other features similar to those seen in human alcoholic liver disease appears to extend the experimental models available for study in this area.

(b) Alcohol and the etiology of hepatic lesions

Jolliffe and Jellinek (1942) in their review, discussed the important finding by Connor and Chaikoff (1938), in dogs on a high-fat diet, that fatty liver could proceed to cirrhosis when alcohol was given in a dose of 3.6 g/kg daily. Daft *et al.* (1941) had produced fatty liver and fibrosis in rats on a low-fat low-protein diet with 20% alcohol as sole fluid. These studies laid the foundation for later work on the interaction between alcohol and nutritional factors in the production of cirrhosis. As nutritional cirrhosis is induced by a relative deficiency of protective factors, the etiological role of alcohol can be specified only by controlling the contribution of all calorigenic nutrients including alcohol. The long duration and large groups of animals required probably explain why there are few reports of adequately controlled studies of sufficient duration to produce cirrhotic lesions. Attempts at short-cuts are evident in this field of research.

The mode of alcohol administration is important both practically and theoretically. It is difficult to give alcohol in calorically important quantities as single daily doses because the repeated intoxication is poorly tolerated in prolonged experiments. Usually, investigators have given alcohol solutions as the only source of drinking fluid so that total intake can be made considerably larger than if single daily doses are administered. If the mechanism of action of alcohol is to be identified, it is necessary to differentiate between effects associated with elevated blood alcohol levels and effects induced by sustained metabolism during voluntary intake when substantial levels of blood alcohol are never built up. Jolliffe and Jellinek (1942) concluded that direct toxic effects of ethanol are probably not important, yet they repeatedly referred to an "association between inebriety and cirrhosis of the liver".

The importance of nutritional factors in the development of experimental alcoholic cirrhosis is well illustrated by the fact that little or no pathological change has been observed in the livers of animals fed normal laboratory rations and alcohol solutions as sole fluid (Klatskin *et al.*, 1951; Ralli *et al.*, 1959; Germer and Chol, 1959; Estable *et al.*, 1959; Dajani *et al.*, 1965; Jabbari *et al.*, 1965; Kaneko *et al.*, 1965; Saville and Lieber, 1965).

References p. 583

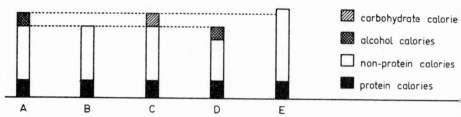

Fig. 9–2. Schematic representation of the distribution of dietary and alcohol calories in a feeding experiment (Klatskin *et al.*, 1954). Male rats were used and the duration was 6 months. The basal diet fed to group A contained 44.6% of the calories as fat and 45.9% as sucrose. The feeding conditions were as follows: A, basal diet + alcohol *ad lib.*; B, pair-fed diet only; C, pair-fed diet + sucrose supplement isocaloric with alcohol in A; D, pair-fed diet + alcohol, isocaloric with B through subtraction of sucrose; E, basal diet *ad lib.*

In experiments of long duration with rats receiving high-fat diets which were also slightly deficient in content of protective lipotropic agents, Lowry *et al.* (1942a), Best *et al.* (1949), and Klatskin *et al.* (1951) contributed evidence that alcohol acts primarily by decreasing the amount of the protective, lipotropic nutrients in relation to total calories. The results of Best *et al.* (1949) even suggested that this was the only mechanism by which alcohol induced liver pathology. However, a study by Klatskin *et al.* (1954) gives some indication that alcohol might increase the requirement for protective lipotropic nutrients. The design, shown in Fig. 9–2, is typical of the experimental designs used in this area of research. The sole drinking fluid was a 14.1% v/v alcohol solution throughout the 6-month experimental period. All aspects of the dietary intake were controlled and the amount of protein (12% in the basal diet) was kept similar in the 5 pair-fed groups (A–E) by adjusting carbohydrate in the diet. The aim was to test the effects

TABLE 9–6

RESULTS OF THE FEEDING EXPERIMENT ILLUSTRATED IN Fig. 9–2

Experimental groups	Number of rats	Number of survivors	Livers of survivors	
			Fat (%)	Number with fibrosis
A	15	10	7.6 ± 2.1	2
B	15	9	5.7 ± 2.1	1
C	15	12	16.6 ± 12.3	5
D	15	11	14.1 ± 8.2	6
E	25	21	11.1 ± 5.8	3/19

of the same quantity of alcohol at two levels of calorie intake. Fatty infiltration and fibrotic changes were found in most of the groups (Table 9–6). Sucrose in group C produced somewhat more lesions than alcohol in group A. The occurrence of marked changes in group D but not in group B suggests a specific effect of alcohol. However, since the amount and kind of dietary fat influences the development of fatty liver and fibrosis in choline deficiency, an alternative interpretation is that the high incidence of lesions in group D was due not to alcohol *per se*, but to its association with a high proportion of fat in the diet.

In a two-week experiment with weanling rats on a choline-deficient diet, Klatskin and Krehl (1954) showed more severe effects of ethanol than of isocaloric sucrose on development of kidney lesions, but it is doubtful whether this finding is relevant to the development of liver lesions in experiments of long duration. In three further reports on the relationship of alcohol to development of dietary cirrhosis (Wanscher, 1953; Daft, 1954; Germer and Chol, 1959) any specific action of alcohol is confounded with the effect of a decrease in protective food relative to total calories.

Ashworth (1947) concluded from an experiment of only two months' duration that liver lesions developed in spite of adequate nutrition because fatty liver was seen in rats fed high as well as low protein. Mallov (1955) administered to rats an alcohol-food mixture, with 22% of the calories as alcohol, given by stomach tube in two portions a day, the daily dose of alcohol being approximately 6 g/kg. Gross intoxication occurred, growth was suppressed, and fatty livers developed within 30 days.

These experiments pioneered later developments but lacked a number of controls needed for specifying the mode of action of ethanol. The conventional feeding techniques do not permit intake of alcohol in the large quantities relative to total calories which are actually consumed by human alcoholics. This difficulty has been solved by the introduction of new feeding techniques.

Lieber *et al.* (1963) and Lieber *et al.* (1965) have introduced the use of liquid diets in drinking tubes as the sole source of food and fluid. These diets, which incorporated pure amino acids instead of protein (16% of the calories), were quite expensive. In addition to the amino acids, the diet contained 43% of the calories as fat, 5% as sucrose, and 36% as ethanol. Later, a less expensive diet of casein supplemented with methionine and cystine, providing 18% of the calories as protein, has been used successfully (DeCarli and Lieber, 1966, 1967; Lieber, 1967a). The duration of the

References p. 583

experiments varied from a few days to 12 weeks. Experiments with controlled dietary intake combined with large amounts of alcohol have also been carried out on human volunteers, both alcoholic (Rubin and Lieber, 1967a, b; Lieber and Rubin, 1968) and normal subjects (Rubin and Lieber, 1968). In these experiments (Rubin and Lieber, 1967b; Rubin and Lieber, 1968) alcohol given for 8 to 18 days changed the fine structure of the liver, even when "excess" protein (25% of the calories) and low fat (25% of the calories) were given.

Lieber and associates have concluded that chronic ethanol administration can induce fatty liver both in rats and humans even when the diet contains ample amounts of protein and lipotropic factors. Since isocaloric replacement of the ethanol with sucrose and even with fat did not produce hepatic lesions, a specific toxic action was attributed to ethanol. The results obtained with rats fed liquid diets have been confirmed by Porta et al. (1965), who also reported development of mitochondrial alterations and Mallory-bodies, the latter within 12 weeks.

However, subsequent work makes it doubtful whether ethanol can properly be considered to be toxic to the liver. The question arises whether a diet can be termed adequate if it permits development of lesions when alcohol is given, since evidence is accumulating which shows that even large amounts of alcohol do not damage the liver if given in certain conditions of dietary intake. In a series of papers (Koch and Porta, 1968; Porta et al., 1968; Porta and Gomez-Dumm, 1968; Gomez-Dumm et al., 1968; Koch et al., 1968), reviewed and discussed by Hartroft and Porta (1968), a new approach has been described which is considered superior to the use of liquid diets. The technique consists of feeding solid diets in combination with an ethanol–sucrose solution as sole drinking fluid. This method takes advantage of the rats' preference for sweet solutions, well known from autoselection studies. Alcohol can then be fed in proportions up to half of the calories and the amount of protective food in the solid diet can be varied according to the requirement of the experiment. The technique is considered to simulate eating and drinking patterns of alcoholics better than the feeding of liquid diets. The results give strong support for the view that alcohol causes hepatic damage through the indirect mechanism of creating dietary imbalance. In some conditions in these experiments as well as in experiments with liquid diets (Koch et al., 1967), isocaloric sucrose caused more hepatic alterations than alcohol. This observation brings out an important aspect, illustrated by interactions between ethanol and fat discussed below, namely

ROLE OF CHRONIC ALCOHOL INTAKE

that not only the quantity of protective nutrients but also the quality of the purely calorigenic food components influence the final effect of ethanol. In particular, the amount and quality of dietary fat exert an influence.

Lieber and Spritz (1965) and Lieber et al. (1966a) showed by means of analysis of fatty acid composition that the excess fat accumulated in rat livers was of dietary origin. With a low-fat diet, much less lipid accumulated in the liver than with a high-fat diet, although the same quantity of alcohol was given. Similar findings have been reported by Hartman and DiLuzio (1968). In experiments of 3 weeks' duration, Jones (1965) and Jones and Greene (1966) found that alcohol caused no fat accumulation on a low-fat diet. The requirement for a high-fat diet, to cause fat accumulation in the liver, has been further confirmed by Porta et al. (1967b). Wallgren, Ahlqvist, Nyholm and Salaspuro (unpublished) found that in a 12-week experiment with rats, liquid diets containing 19% of the calories as casein and 36% as ethanol caused fatty infiltration, incipient fibrosis, glycogen depletion, mitochondrial alterations, and development of Mallory-bodies only when a large proportion of the calories (40%) was derived from fat. When sucrose replaced the fat, the high ethanol intake caused no pathological changes and even reduced the percentage of total lipids in the liver below that of the control animals. The findings in rats have partial support in observations on alcoholic patients (Lieber and Spritz, 1966; Lane and Lieber, 1966) in whom a greater degree of fatty degeneration was produced by alcohol with a high-fat diet than by alcohol with a low-fat diet. With a low-fat, nutritionally entirely inadequate diet which did not support growth, ethanol caused accumulation of triglycerides synthesized from endogenous fatty acids in the livers of rats (Lieber et al., 1966b).

Not only the amount but also the kind of dietary fat influence the final effect of association with ethanol. Medium-chain fatty acids such as octanoate cause less accumulation of triglycerides in the liver than normal dietary fatty acids which predominantly are long-chain, C_{16} and C_{18} fatty acids (Lieber and DeCarli, 1966). The reason seems to be primarily metabolic, particularly the tendency of the liver to utilize long-chain rather than medium-chain fatty acids for synthesis of triglycerides (Lieber et al., 1967; Zakim and Green, 1968). Chain-length thus is important, but degree of saturation of the fatty acids is not (Jones and Greene, 1966; Koch and Porta, 1967). Some possible mechanisms by which fat, ethanol, and protein might interact are discussed on p. 550.

The duration of the treatment has been excessively short in most of the experiments with liquid diets. Thompson *et al.* (1963) and Dajani *et al.* (1965) have found that the livers of guinea pigs and rats show transient fatty infiltration which subsequently disappears when ethanol is given with "adequate diets". Porta *et al.* (1968) demonstrated fat accumulation and some ultrastructural changes after 8 weeks in the livers of rats fed liquid diets with 25% of the calories as protein and 40% as ethanol, but after 16 weeks, the livers were indistinguishable from those of control animals. However, the histological and ultrastructural alterations found by Lane and Lieber (1966) in humans, and by Porta *et al.* (1965, 1967b) and Wallgren, Ahlqvist, Nyholm and Salaspuro (unpublished) in rats indicate incipient stages of conditions that probably would develop into more serious liver lesions. This conclusion is supported by observations by Hartroft and associates in the experiments cited above which involved administration of solid diets and sucrose–ethanol solutions for protracted periods.

The critical role of the rate of initial accumulation of liver fat in the growing rat for later development of lesions (Popper and Schaffner, 1961; Hartroft, 1964; Hoffbauer and Zaki, 1965), suggests that fatty infiltration of the liver may be aggravated by acute intoxication superimposed on a diet which otherwise promotes fatty degeneration of the liver. Wallgren *et al.* (1967) tested this hypothesis by giving the same amount of ethanol either as intoxicating doses every other day or as the sole fluid in dilute solutions to rats pair-fed isocaloric amounts of a high-fat, low-protein diet for 6 months. Fatty infiltration was very heavy in all groups including controls not receiving ethanol, but contrary to the hypothesis fibrosis and cirrhosis were clearly more severe in the controls and in the animals receiving dilute ethanol than in the intoxication group. A preliminary report by Lucas *et al.* (1968) shows similar results. The slower growth of the intoxication group may have contributed to the apparent protective effect of alcohol because development of fibrosis is faster when growth is rapid, a finding confirmed also in alcohol experiments (Porta and Gomez-Dumm, 1966). This finding demonstrates a difference between acute intoxication and chronic alcohol intake in effects on the liver, indicates the importance of nutritional and metabolic factors in the development of hepatic lesions during prolonged alcohol consumption, and provides evidence against a direct toxic action of ethanol. The finding is supported by Dajani and Kouyoumjian (1966), who showed that alcohol intoxication caused a much smaller percentage increase of liver triglycerides in rats chronically treated with alcohol than in normal controls. Further evidence against a direct toxic action of ethanol comes from an experiment by Schmäl *et al.* (1965) in which rats consumed extremely large quantities of alcohol daily for more than a year without any severe lesions in the liver. Alcohol does not show toxic effects on the fetal and immediate post-natal development of the liver in rats (Pilström and Kiessling, 1967). As full capacity to metabolize ethanol develops in the rat only about 18 days after birth (Chapter 3, pp. 86,96), this observation also gives indirect evidence for an important role of alcohol metabolism in the development of the liver lesions. However, Molimard (1958) has found that in adult rats, consumption of 10% alcohol or wine as the sole fluid does not interfere with regeneration of the liver tissue after partial hepatectomy although according to Räihä and Pikkarainen (personal communication) liver alcohol dehydrogenase activity is present in regenerating tissue.

(c) Prevention, therapy and diagnosis

The successful production of various types of liver lesions has enabled experiments on prevention and therapy. The results have also contributed information on the differences between various types of liver lesions.

We have already mentioned (Chapter 3, p. 119) that the rise in hepatic triglycerides caused by acute intoxication is prevented by ganglionic blocking agents and by various antioxidants but not by lipotropic agents. With oral administration, vitamin E is partially effective in acute intoxication whereas another antioxidant (G-50) is completely effective (Porta *et al.*, 1967b). Antioxidants given orally seem to be ineffective against fatty liver degeneration caused by nutritional deficiency during long-term intake of alcohol (Porta *et al.*, 1965, 1967b; Lieber and DeCarli, 1966; Lieber, 1967a). Lieber (1967b) reported that even with the more effective parenteral route of administration, vitamin E is inefficient in prolonged experiments. However, DiLuzio and Hartman (1967) and Hartman and DiLuzio (1968) have reported that intraperitoneal administration of the highly effective antioxidant *N,N'*-diphenyl-*p*-phenylenediamine partly prevents the rise in liver triglycerides in rats maintained for 3 weeks on a liquid diet with a large amount of ethanol. Therefore, preventive efficacy against long-term liver damage appears to be limited to certain efficient lipid soluble antioxidants, administered by the parenteral route. There is little information on the effect of ganglionic blocking agents during prolonged alcohol administration. Presumably, they counteract only the effects of acute intoxication which, as already mentioned, has not been found to aggravate fatty liver degeneration caused by nutritional deficiency. Ammon and Estler (1966) have

References p. 583

reported that administration of a β-sympathicolytic drug decreased liver fat in mice which had received 15% ethanol as sole fluid for 6 months.

The many experiments on the relationship between dietary regimens and development of liver lesions, reviewed in the preceding section, show efficient protection by certain nutrients. Lesions after prolonged alcohol intake have been prevented by diets supplemented with choline and methionine (Best et al., 1949; Wanscher, 1953; Klatskin et al., 1954; Germer and Chol, 1959). Mallov (1958) has reported a protective effect of high doses of choline or vitamin B_{12}. In diets containing 16% of the calories as protein and substantial amounts of fat, even large amounts of choline and methionine give only partial protection from the effects of alcohol (Lieber and DeCarli, 1966), but large amounts of protein had a fully protective effect in both rats and humans (Jabbari et al., 1965; Jabbari and Leevy, 1967; Leevy and ten Hove, 1967; Koch and Porta, 1968).

Prevention of liver lesions during prolonged alcohol intake depends not only on some specific protective nutrients but also on total dietary composition. There have been convincing demonstrations that the higher is the proportion of alcohol in the diet, the higher are the requirements for protein and lipotropic factors. The combination of alcohol with fat further raises the protein requirement. The mechanism of the interaction between ethanol and fat is not at all clear, but hepatic oxidation of lipid is decreased during metabolism of ethanol (Lieber, 1967a, b). Lundquist (see discussion of paper by Blomstrand, 1966) has pointed out that during ethanol oxidation, acetate derived from ethanol becomes quantitatively important in peripheral metabolism, and peripheral utilization of fatty acids should thereby decrease. With a high lipid intake, this may contribute further to the accumulation of excess fat in the liver. Also, when carbohydrate is given, there is no need to use protein for gluconeogenesis, whereas diets containing large proportions of fat increase the requirement for production of glucose from precursors such as amino acids. If, for instance, some amino acid in such situations is preferentially used for gluconeogenesis, protein synthesis may be inhibited because it is highly dependent on a good supply of all needed amino acids (Munro, 1968). By such a selective channelling of amino acids, the inhibitory effect of ethanol on glucoeneogenesis may enhance the protein requirement. In fact, liver lesions do not appear when fat is isocalorically substituted for alcohol in a high fat–high alcohol diet which contains normally adequate amounts of protein (Ahlqvist et al., 1968). In rats on a high-alcohol, high-carbohydrate diet, fat did not accumulate when very large amounts of vitamins, lipotropic factors, and minerals were given, although only 5.5% of the total calories were provided in the form of protein (Porta et al., 1967a).

French dietetic studies show a clear relationship between severe cirrhosis and a large proportion of calories derived from alcohol. Approximately 160 grams of alcohol (2.5 g/kg) daily seems to constitute an upper limit that cannot be exceeded without grave danger of hepatic lesions. This consumption level on the average corresponds to continuous oxidation of ethanol (Chapter 2, p. 48) and thus nearly complete subsistence of the liver on energy derived from the partial oxidation of ethanol. Daily consumption of 80 grams (approximately 1 g/kg) has been suggested as the maximum safe amount (Le Breton and Trémolières, 1955; Delore et al., 1959; Péquignot, 1963; sources cited by Schedifka, 1965, and by Lelbach, 1967). Bättig (1967) in Switzerland and Lelbach (1967) in Germany present estimates which agree with those of the French workers. Von Oldershausen (1964) also has assembled data which show the importance of both duration and amount of alcohol consumption. He suggests that liver damage is caused by a direct toxic action of alcohol, but the statistical and the experimental findings both support a nutritional-metabolic etiology of the hepatic lesions in alcoholism. Further evidence against a direct toxic action of alcohol is that in North America (Schmidt and Bronetto, 1962; de Lint and Bronetto, 1966) and Germany (Lelbach, 1967) no association was found between incidence of liver cirrhosis and type of alcoholic beverages consumed. With the possible exception of mitochondrial function (p. 557), a highly nutritious diet with ample protein appears to protect the liver even when maximal alcohol intake is maintained.

As in most pathological conditions, therapy of liver disease is more difficult than prevention. In animals, anabolic steroids had a lipotropic action during prolonged alcohol intake (Mallov, 1958; Jabbari et al., 1965; Leevy and Ten Hove, 1967) and experimentally, norethandrolone has been found beneficial also in humans (Jabbari et al., 1965), but they were not effective in a one-month clinical trial on human alcoholics (Fenster, 1966). Other agents reported to have some beneficial effect in animal experiments include ethyl-α-chlorophenobutyrate (Spritz and Lieber, 1966), a mixture of "essential" phospholipids (Samochowiec and Wójcicki, 1966; Wójcicki, 1967; Samochowiec et al., 1967b) and xanthinol-nicotinate (Brenner, 1967). In an important experiment on therapy, Takada et al. (1967) induced moderate to advanced cirrhosis in rats by a deficient diet. For three months these rats were given either a highly nutritious diet containing 36% of the calories as protein and 40% as fat, or the same diet with alcohol to furnish 36% of the calories. Although alcohol was not fed as an isocaloric substitute for other calorigenic food components, so that the diet of the alcohol animals contained only 23% of the calories as protein and 25% as fat, both clinical and biochemical measures showed great improvement in both groups of animals, with the same extent of regression of the cirrhosis. These observations have been extended by Porta *et al.* (1969). According to clinical findings, patients with Laennec's cirrhosis can improve despite continued intake of relatively large amounts of alcohol if a nutritious diet is provided (Erenoglu *et al.*, 1964; sources cited by Phillips and Davidson, 1954; by Lieber *et al.*, 1965; by Green, 1965; and by Porta *et al.*, 1967b).

Experimental efforts to improve diagnostic methods have been scarce in recent years. Ordinary clinical tests for liver function do not detect very sensitively pathological alterations in the livers of alcoholics, and differential diagnosis requires biopsy specimens which still give rise to some misclassifications (Garceau, 1964). Among commonly used tests, bromosulfophthalein clearance and serum protein fractionation seem to be the most sensitive indicators of damage (Lelbach, 1966a, b; Leevy and ten Hove, 1967; Harinasuta *et al.*, 1967). Lieberman and Childs (1967) have shown that bromosulfophthalein conjugation is somewhat impaired by ethanol. The test should thus not be performed while the patient is metabolizing alcohol. According to studies in alcoholics (Wilkinson *et al.*, 1968), the bromosulfophthalein storage capacity is selectively depressed in comparison with the maximum rate of excretion of the compound in bile. The serum γ-globulins are raised in cirrhosis, and special studies of this fraction have been reported (Waldenström *et al.*, 1964; Lee, 1965). An altered serum amino acid pattern resembling that seen in kwashiorkor has been reported for patients with alcoholic hepatitis (Ning *et al.*, 1967). Abnormally low protein-bound iodine in the serum of patients with alcoholic cirrhosis has been found to be associated with subnormal values for thyroxine-binding prealbumin (Agostoni *et al.*, 1968). Studies of release of tissue enzymes into the serum were already reviewed (p. 530) and did not appear as particularly useful diagnostically. However, alcohol dehydrogenase is released into the serum in patients with liver cell necrosis, and is an indicator of intrahepatic obstruction of the bile secretion (Merzey *et al.*, 1968). Spaventi *et al.* (1967) have shown that a new test of gammascintigraphy agreed rather well with other clinical tests but did not appear superior to them. The combined galactose-

ethanol elimination test described by Salaspuro (1967a–c, 1968) and discussed on p. 526 offers the prospect of real advance. This test seems more
sensitive than any in current use and appears to reveal a condition of known
etiology, *i.e.*, the fatty liver induced primarily by choline deficiency. Further
work for development of sensitive diagnostic methods is highly desirable
because fatty infiltration of the liver is easily reversed whereas cirrhosis is
an irreversible condition.

(3) Dynamics of the liver process

A large number of studies deal with the histopathology of cirrhotic livers.
There are also several reports on biochemical and ultrastructural findings
in cirrhosis. Longitudinal studies of the biochemical and morphological
alterations at various stages of their development are necessary for elucidation of the etiology of cirrhosis, but have remained rather few. The direct
biochemical and ultrastructural effects of alcohol, reviewed in the first part
of this section, must be distinguished from indirect actions such as infections,
reviewed in the second part. Further progress in this area of research is
necessary for development of a comprehensive theory of the cellular
mechanisms by which alcohol contributes to liver disease.

(a) Biochemical and ultrastructural findings

Biochemical alterations of cirrhotic livers in human alcoholics have been
identified by study of enzyme activities and of substrate utilization in biopsy
specimens (Frei *et al.*, 1959). Electrophoretic investigations of the protein
pattern of cirrhotic livers revealed alterations in the relative quantities of
various components but no abnormal protein moieties (Licht, 1963).
Activities of a number of enzymes, particularly dehydrogenases and trans-
aminases, have been measured in liver tissue from animals which have
received alcohol for periods of varying duration (Abe, 1961; Henley *et al.*,
1958; Figueroa and Klotz, 1962b, 1964; Kinard and Hay, 1960; Dajani *et
al.*, 1963; Von Oldershausen and Schweiger, 1964; Mirone, 1966a, b;
Schlesinger *et al.*, 1966; French, 1966a; Dajani and Kouyoumjian, 1966;
Marciniak *et al.*, 1968). The results are partly contradictory and therefore
difficult to interpret. Morrison and Brock (1967a, b) determined localization
of liver alcohol dehydrogenase within the liver lobules and found an activity
ratio of 5 to 3 between the centrilobular and periportal area. As a consequence
of prolonged alcohol consumption, total enzyme activity decreased without

References p. 583

change in its distribution. According to Samochowiec *et al.* (1967a), prolonged daily administration of 2.4 g alcohol/kg to rats alters the distribution of lysosomes and ATPase activity in the hepatocytes. Laasonen and Palkama (1967) have reported a decrease in histochemically demonstrable phosphorylase activity in liver, but not in muscle. Levels of histologically demonstrable glycogen are generally lowered when lesions become manifest. Contrary to this pathological effect of ethanol, however, Ammon and Estler (1967b) found no change in liver glycogen of mice that received 15% w/v alcohol as sole fluid for 6 months. Mirone (1965a, b) has shown by chemical means that combined NAD-NADH$_2$ decreases in mouse livers. The change could be prevented by *p*-aminobenzoate–ascorbate treatment and also by other vitamins. Chronic alcohol intake decreased ATP in the liver of mice, according to reports by Ammon and Estler (1967a, b), by French (1966b), whose method evidently did not measure total ATP actually present, and by Redetzki *et al.* (1966), who also found decreased NAD and increased lactate, with all of these effects being aggravated by deficient diets.

In studies of chronic effects of ethanol in rats, Klatskin and associates (Scheig *et al.*, 1966; Alexander *et al.*, 1966; Scheig and Klatskin, 1966) have shown some enhancement of fatty acid synthesis and decrease in triglyceride formation in adipose tissue, and also enhancement of fatty acid synthesis in cytoplasm from the liver. Sereny and Lowden (1967) found that with a high carbohydrate diet, alcohol appeared to decrease release of triglycerides from the liver, or formation of lipoproteins, with no effect on fatty acid metabolism. Interestingly, ethanol decreased the amount of depot fat.

The experiments reviewed in the prior subsection concerning prolonged feeding of ethanol with various dietary regimens did not establish clearly whether ethanol augments the need for lipotropic factors more than other calorie nutrients. Only a score of studies concern biochemical reactions directly involved in the action of lipotropic substances.

Choline deficiency impairs synthesis of phosphatidyl choline which is in the path of phospholipid synthesis (Haines, 1966), but inclusion of ethanol in a nutritious diet does not inhibit biosynthesis of phospholipids (Fallon *et al.*, 1965) and even increases the amount of phospholipid, particularly lyso-lecithin and phosphatidyl ethanolamine (French, 1966c).

Finkelstein and Kyle (1968) measured the effect of ethanol on the activities of four different enzymes involved in methionine metabolism in rat liver. They found that both acute and prolonged administration of ethanol increased the activity of methionine-activating enzyme, an effect which was not changed by feeding of methionine or choline. Prolonged ethanol feeding also increased the activity of cystathionase. Finkelstein and Kyle (1968) do not think that the induction of methionine-activating enzyme activity causes fatty infiltration but suggest that the change may render the liver more susceptible to methionine deficiency and to the action of ethanol. These observations do not as yet provide conclusive evidence that ethanol specifically augments the need for lipotropic agents or inhibits their action.

According to the hypothesis that lipid peroxidation contributes to the liver damage associated with intake of ethanol (Di Luzio and Hartman, 1967; Kalish and Di Luzio, 1966), peroxidation should decrease the amount of poly-unsaturated fatty acids (Recknagel, 1967). This assumption is refuted by observations of the fatty acid composition of lipids deposited in the liver (Chapter 3, p. 120; Scheig et al., 1966; Lieber and Spritz, 1966; Wallgren et al., 1967).

Although studies on protein synthesis in various conditions of prolonged ethanol intake would be very important, little work has been done along such lines. Albertini et al. (1969) report that in rat liver, synthesis of both RNA and ribosomal protein was slowed as a consequence of ingestion of 20% ethanol as sole fluid for 2 months.

Ultrastructural changes are nil, or very minute, after oral administration of single doses of alcohol whereas intraperitoneal administration of 5 g alcohol/kg to rats causes mitochondrial swelling and vesiculation of the endoplasmic reticulum (Chapter 3, p. 110). This mitochondrial swelling rapidly subsides. Apparently it differs markedly from the mitochondrial changes found during chronic intake of alcohol. Electron microscopical studies on biopsy and autopsy specimens have revealed fatty droplets and cysts, vesiculation of the endoplasmic reticulum with loss of rough, ribosome-carrying reticulum and increase in smooth reticulum, enlargement of the mitochondria and loss or relocation of their cristae, appearance of Mallory-bodies and fibrotic alterations, decrease in bile duct microvilli, disappearing spaces of Disse, and changes in the Golgi apparatus, in various stages of alcoholic liver disease (Flax and Tisdale, 1964; Svoboda and Manning, 1964; Albot and Parturier-Albot, 1966, 1967; Lane and Lieber, 1966; Hartroft and Porta, 1966; Edmondson et al., 1967; Porta et al., 1967b; Rubin and Lieber, 1967a, b; Klion and Schaffner, 1968) as well as in the livers of rats maintained on various diets (Porta et al., 1965, 1967b; Iseri et al., 1966; Thorpe and Shorey, 1966; Wallgren, Ahlqvist, Nyholm and Salaspuro, unpublished). All of these changes, however, occur also in other types of toxic and pathological insults to the liver (Boistesselin, 1966; Barka and Popper, 1967). Small changes may be within the rather wide range of variation in normal structure of hepatic tissue. For example, there are differences between mitochondria in the center and the periphery of a liver lobule (Hultquist, 1966), bizarrely shaped mitochondria may be present without any known reason, and the granular endoplasmic reticulum of cells in different locations varies in appearance (Iseri et al., 1966).

Although it is difficult to define precisely the nature of pathological effects on the mitochondria, the peculiar pattern of metabolism induced by ethanol, with marked suppression of the citric acid cycle and subsistence on oxidation of hydrogen produced extramitochondrially (Chapter 3, p. 108), suggests that degenerative and adaptive changes in mitochondrial function may develop. Indirect evidence for decreased efficacy of the citric acid cycle in the liver is provided by studies on substrate utilization of isolated mitochondria (Dajani and Orten, 1962; Dajani and Kouyoumjian, 1966). In particular, Kiessling and his associates have studied both structure and function of the mitochondria.

In human alcoholics, Kiessling et al. (1964) and Kiessling et al. (1965) have found a high positive correlation between abnormally large mitochondria and amount of alcohol consumption. In rats, ingestion of alcohol as the sole fluid, in a concentration of 15%, or 15 and 25% on alternating days, with ordinary stock rations, caused three types of changes; enlargement without structural changes, elongated, twisted mitochondria, and greatly enlarged, rounded mitochondria with disorganized cristae. The two latter types presumably represent pathological lesions. Brain mitochondria were not altered, and muscle mitochondria even showed more pronounced cristae (Kiessling and Tobé, 1964). Respiration with pyruvate, glutamate, or succinate as substrate decreased in liver mitochondria from male Wistar rats concomitant with the structural change (Kiessling and Tilander, 1961, 1963; Kiessling et al., 1963; Kiessling and Pilström, 1966a). Oxidation of α-glycerophosphate was enhanced. Neither of these changes occurred in female rats. This observation has been confirmed and studied in more detail by Kiessling (1968) who again found that in male rats, 15% alcohol as sole fluid in 200 days caused an increase in the size of the mitochondria and their oxidation of α-glycerophosphate. Kiessling (1968) suggests an induction of α-glycerophosphate oxidase activity as an adaptation to oxidation of the hydrogen derived from oxidation of ethanol in the cytoplasm. He suggests that the changes are not seen in females because their mitochondria at the outset have a higher capacity to oxidize α-glycerophosphate than those of the males. After the period on alcohol, the capacity of mitochondria from the males and the females to oxidize α-glycerophosphate are about similar. The appearance of lesions was slow and normalization of the mitochondria, after withdrawal of alcohol, took 4 months in male rats (Kiessling and Pilström, 1966b), a surprisingly slow rate as 10.3 days is the estimated half-life of mitochondria in the liver (Fletcher and Sanadi, 1961). With liquid diets containing high proportions of alcohol the appearance of incipient changes within a week indicates much more rapid effects (Porta et al., 1965, 1967b), but this rate is still much slower than in the reversible swelling caused by acute insults. Changes within one to three days, reported by Rubin and Lieber (1967a, b), were in alcoholics who had recovered from prior liver disease. The observations of Porta et al. (1965), including the formation of Mallory-bodies, have been confirmed in an experiment of 12 weeks' duration (Wallgren, Ahlqvist, Nyholm and Salaspuro, unpublished), with the exception that the mitochondria were enlarged, swollen, and fragmented with marked loss of cristae, instead of being prevalently bizarre in shape. In comparison with isocaloric sucrose, 40% of the calories in a liquid diet as ethanol fed for 4 weeks caused partial uncoupling of oxidative phosphorylation in liver mitochondria, reduced the mitochondrial protein fraction, and increased soluble and microsomal protein (Banks et al., 1969).

Particularly the observations of Kiessling suggest an effect of the metabolic pattern induced by ethanol rather than some direct physicochemical or toxic action of ethanol. This interpretation is further supported by the finding that the mitochondrial changes are aggravated by protein deprivation (Gomez-Dumm and Porta, 1966) and ameliorated or even prevented simply by decreasing the fat content and increasing the protein of the diet (Porta et al., 1967b). A particularly striking finding in an unpublished study by Wallgren, Ahlqvist, Nyholm and Salaspuro, was that 36% of the calories given as alcohol caused no changes in conjunction with carbohydrate, whereas both mitochondrial alterations and Mallory-bodies developed when the alcohol was given in conjunction with fat. Structurally normal mitochondria are not necessarily intact functionally, however, since Kiessling and Pilström (1967) found that supplementation of normal laboratory chow with an amino acid mixture, vitamins, and electrolytes prevented the structural changes but not the decrease in mitochondrial respiration. In the same study, choline and methionine also failed to prevent the changes in mitochondrial functioning. Kiessling and Lundquist (1966) and Lundquist *et al.* (1966) have reported that structural changes of the mitochondria are not accompanied by change in their lipid composition. According to Ihrig *et al.* (1969), fatty acid composition of the liver mitochondria of rats was significantly altered by ethanol feeding. Cholesterol and phospholipids were not changed, nor fatty acid composition of the microsomes. French (1968) found that mitochondria from the livers of rats given 30% ethanol for periods of 2 to 14 months had increased permeability to phenazine, giving evidence for damage to the mitochondrial membrane.

Failure to respond to ethanol by a shift in the redox state was already mentioned as a possibly distinctive feature of fatty livers caused by choline deficiency. Fatty livers induced by a high fat-high alcohol diet with ample protein show a normal increase in the ratio lactate/pyruvate during oxidation of ethanol (Wallgren, Ahlqvist, Nyholm and Salaspuro, *unpublished.*) French (1967) has pointed out that alcohol decreases phospholipids in choline deficiency but increases them with "adequate" nutrition.

(b) Contributory factors with indirect actions

Indirect factors affecting development of liver lesions include infections, both viral and bacterial, and also effects of endotoxins. Toxic effects of this type involve the reticuloendothelial system of the liver. This consists of phagocytic cells, such as the Kupffer cells, which clear foreign particles or solutes, including antigenic material, from the blood. Leevy *et al.* (1964) have obtained autoradiographic evidence that mesenchymal (reticuloendo-thelial) cell proliferation is correlated with presence of cirrhosis, necrosis or inflammatory changes in the livers of alcoholic patients and of protein-deficient rats fed alcohol. Wasz-Höckert *et al.* (1958, 1959) demonstrated persistent infection of the liver after inoculation with staphylococci in mice receiving 8% v/v ethanol as the sole drinking fluid. Forenbacher *et al.* (1961) have contributed evidence that alcohol may interfere with the defensive barrier of the portal circulation to bacteria and toxins. According to Broit-man *et al.* (1964), choline deficiency may somehow facilitate absorption of intraluminar endotoxins into the portal circulation, thus contributing to the development of fibrosis and cirrhosis.

In spite of this experimental evidence, clinical data do not indicate an important role of this type of indirect factor in the development of alcoholic liver disease. Garceau (1964) found that of 471 alcoholic patients with Laennec's cirrhosis, only 6% had evidence of prior (viral) hepatitis. Among 154 patients with postnecrotic or posthepatitic cirrhosis the corresponding proportion was 15%. Von Oldershausen (1964) also concluded that gastro-enteritis and infections are of minor etiologic importance. Neither Lelbach (1966a, b) nor Gigglberger (1968) found any correlation between the severity of alcoholic cirrhosis and previous illnesses involving the liver.

E. Pathology of other organs and tissues

Alcoholism has been linked with various diseases of the central nervous system, the cardiovascular system, and other organs and tissues. The present section summarizes clinical findings and reviews experimental studies of the etiology of these diseases. The findings may help to specify the changes caused by prolonged alcohol intake. In addition to this scientific importance the studies may have great clinical value for prevention, therapy and diagnosis. Large numbers of alcoholics are afflicted by these disorders, even though the majority of alcoholics show none of these types of physical pathology.

(1) The nervous system

Tolerance and physical dependence on alcohol are obviously based on organic changes although these have as yet to be defined. Pathological alterations are occasionally found in the nervous system of alcoholics, typically in association with the various psychoses of alcoholism. However, such pathological changes have not been found to be consistently associated with physical dependence or alcoholism. In contrast to the large amount of experimental data on liver pathology in prolonged alcohol intake, strikingly little experimental work has been devoted to the neurological complications of alcoholism.

Reviews by Jolliffe (1942) and Jolliffe et al. (1942) cover clinical, pathological and experimental studies, emphasizing etiology. Useful later reviews of pathological aspects include those by Courville and Myers (1954), Courville (1955), Edmondson et al. (1956), Tommasi (1957), Lapresle (1958), Hudolin (1967) and Colmant (1968). Victor and Adams (1953, 1961; French version by Adams and Victor, 1960) give excellent reviews and classification of the various disorders, discussing their symptomatology and attempting critical appraisal of etiology, largely on the basis of their own extensive clinical experience. Wieser (1965) has contributed a thorough review in German of psychiatric and neurologic complications in alcoholism. Janzen and Balzereit (1968) review clinical aspects of alcoholic polyneuropathy. The present section reviews the classifications and observations of neuropathy made in clinical and experimental studies, followed by the more direct measurements of central nervous system pathology by structural and biochemical studies.

(a) Classifications and observations

Various classifications have been made of the neurological disorders associated with chronic alcoholism. The terminology used by Lapresle (1958) and Victor and Adams (1961), which seems to fit the majority of current opinions, distinguishes polyneuropathy, amblyopia, pellagra, Wernicke's disease, Morel's cortical sclerosis, cerebellar degeneration, Marchiafava–Bignami's disease, central pontine myelinolysis, and disorders due to alcoholic cirrhosis. Lapresle (1958) makes a distinction between Wernicke's disease and Korsakoff's psychosis, but Victor and Adams (1961) equate these conditions, in accordance with the earlier observation by Jolliffe *et al.* (1942) that Korsakoff's psychosis is the behavioral counterpart of Wernicke's organic disease. In addition to the fairly well defined conditions enumerated above, atrophy of parts of the cerebral cortex, particularly of the frontal lobes, has been frequently described by pathologists (see *e.g.*, Pluvinage, 1954; Courville, 1955; Tumarkin *et al.*, 1955; Lynch and Hills, 1960; Hudolin, 1967). These may well be incipient stages of Wernicke's disease.

Strict adherence to the above classification is not possible, partly because in some cases there is no experimental material to review, and partly because in some experimental studies the disorder is not clearly diagnosed. This review is restricted to the development and symptoms of organ pathology and functional disturbances observed at the physiological level.

In alcoholic polyneuropathy, conduction in peripheral nerves is slowed in parallel with the severity of the clinical symptoms (Schubert, 1963; cited acc. to Jurko *et al.*, 1964; Juul-Jensen and Mayer, 1966). Jurko *et al.* (1964), Mawdsley and Mayer (1965), and Wanamaker and Skillman (1966) have even demonstrated abnormally slow conduction velocity in the peripheral nerves of chronic alcoholics without clinical diagnosis of peripheral motor neuropathy. Perfetti *et al.* (1967), in a study of patients with overt symptoms of polyneuropathy or other neurological disturbances, found that the large fibers of the ulnar nerve conducted at normal velocity whereas slowing was observed in small fibers. French workers have described in chronic alcoholics a differential chronaxie of motor nerve and muscle (*cf.* Chapter 6, p. 278).

The changes in this condition are useful for diagnosis and for follow-up studies (Lecoq, 1948, 1957; Martin, 1956; Béhague et al., 1959). Steinbach (1965) used electrophoresis of the cerebrospinal fluid for early detection of polyneuropathy. Marinacci (1961), Coërs and Hildebrand (1965), and Todesco and Merini (1966) report use of electromyography in diagnosis of polyneuropathy and describe histological alterations. As complete recovery is not possible if polyneuropathy advances beyond a certain point (Béhague et al., 1959; Fennelly et al., 1964), suggestions for improved diagnostic procedures are obviously important.

The association between chronic alcoholism and polyneuropathy has long been realized, as indicated in historical notes (Victor and Adams, 1961; Mawdsley and Mayer, 1965). The nutritional etiology has been appreciated much later. Thiamine deprivation is the primary feature, but associated deficiencies may also be prominent (Jolliffe, 1942). There is no evidence for a direct toxic effect of alcohol in this disease, which may develop and persist in the complete absence of alcohol. The fact that "advanced" neuropathy has persisted in spite of abstinence from alcohol and treatment with B-vitamin, which has been cited as showing a toxic effect of alcohol (Marinacci, 1961), only conforms with the known fact that the condition unfortunately becomes irreversible. Animal studies and clinical trials on this aspect of the disease have been reviewed by Jolliffe (1942) and Victor and Adams (1953, 1961). Later work (Fennelly et al., 1964) has confirmed the indirect role of alcohol.

A specific, more limited form of peripheral neuropathy is amblyopia, with its symptoms of dim vision. Victor (1963), in a critical examination of theories of causation, concluded that it is probably due to avitaminosis.

The encephalopathies include various degenerative brain diseases, such as Wernicke's disease, Morel's cortical sclerosis, cerebellar degeneration, Marchiafava–Bignami's disease, and central pontine myelinolysis.

Nizzoli et al. (1967) observe that the rare cerebellar degeneration seems always to be associated with cerebral lesions and suggest that it should be considered a mere extension of cerebral atrophy. Even the most conscientiously performed clinical studies on the causes of encephalopathies illustrate vividly the many complications that preclude control rigorous enough to match even modest experimental standards. Victor and Adams (1961) have obtained good evidence that Wernicke's disease is due to vitamin deficiencies. Lack of thiamine appears to be the primary factor involved. Shimojyo et al. (1967) concur with this view. In cerebellar degeneration, Marchiafava–

Bignami's disease, and central pontine myelinolysis, nutritional involvement seems possible, but its nature has not been defined, and direct toxic action of alcohol has not been excluded. Clinical evidence suggests that cerebellar ataxia is due to a direct toxic effect of alcohol (Dow and Moruzzi, 1958) but E. A. Martin (1965) cited evidence from experimental studies on rabbits that vitamin supplements can prevent appearance of cerebellar lesions. The greatest objection to the hypothesis of nutritional involvement is that cerebellar complications are extremely rare in nutritional disorders not associated with alcoholism. However, it seems quite possible that these diseases are etiologically similar and distinguished only by the different symptomatology caused by lesions affecting different parts of the brain.

(b) Direct measurements

Electroencephalographic studies of these disorders have been done with two objectives: to discover useful diagnostic aids and to distinguish abnormalities appearing as a consequence of excessive drinking from those which are prior and therefore prognostically significant features. Little and McAvoy (1952) concluded that the EEG's of alcoholics did not show more abnormalities than those of a control group. They also suggested that a low alpha index may indicate a predisposition for alcoholism, but this idea has not been tested by appropriate follow-up studies. Arentsen and Sindrup (1963) inferred prior differences in EEG by comparison between two groups of alcoholics. They suggested that predisposition for alcoholism may be associated with a primarily temporal localization of abnormal patterns, found in 14 alcoholics without other mental symptoms, but this characteristic also appeared to be a fairly common consequence of alcoholism, seen in 30 cases classified as mentally abnormal. Other studies (Funkhouser *et al.*, 1953; Bennet *et al.*, 1956; Delay *et al.*, 1957; Bennet *et al.*, 1960; Fau *et al.*, 1965; Igert *et al.*, 1965; Hiddema, 1965; Shimojyo *et al.*, 1967) indicate that abnormalities occur more frequently among alcoholics than in the general population. Admixture of theta activity and change in the distribution of alpha frequency seem to be the most frequent special characteristics. Lowered amplitude of the alpha waves (Giove, 1964; Hudolin, 1967; Hudolin and Gubarev, 1967) and decreased incidence of blocked alpha activity on photic stimulation (Delamonica *et al.*, 1966) have also been reported. According to Baskina (1966), alcoholics differ markedly from normal subjects in the acute effect of alcohol on the EEG. She further reported a persistent decrease in the activity of subcortical structures in alcoholics, suggesting a diminished vegetative activity. In contrast, however, Hudolin (1967) reports that rapid frequencies indicative of dominance of subcortical activities are relatively common. Some value for diagnosis of alcoholic encephalopathies is suggested, but so far, psychological and functional testing, sometimes in conjunction with pneumoencephalography, are indispensable for detecting central nervous disturbances. Hudolin (1967) provides evidence that gammaencephalography can be a useful diagnostic tool in cases of alcoholism.

Animal experiments are more difficult to carry out on these various brain lesions than in the study of peripheral neuropathy. There is no accepted model clearly relevant to the complex symptomatology of human subjects. This circumstance has impeded systematic experimental investigation. Studies on biochemical changes in cerebral tissue after prolonged intake represent an approach to the dynamics of the processes involved. However, these studies have been few and concerned with rather randomly selected aspects and generally indicate that alcohol causes only slight neurochemical changes. Fujita (1954) in experiments with rabbits and Kinard and Hay (1960) in experiments with rats reported lowered cholinesterase activity of the brain after both acute and chronic administration. The latter authors conclude that the change is not functionally significant. Moss et al. (1967) have reported that in rats, consumption of 15% ethanol as the sole fluid for 22 weeks led to a decrease in brain acetylcholine by nearly 40%, and that feeding of cysteine partly prevented the change. According to Abe (1961), the activities of succinic, lactic, glutamic, and malic dehydrogenases all increased in cerebral cortex. Marciniak et al. (1968), using dogs, likewise report increase in several enzyme activities in the brain. On the other hand, Kiessling and Tilander (1963) found no change in respiration and capacity of oxidative phosphorylation of cerebral mitochondria, with pyruvate and succinate as substrates, from rats receiving alcohol for prolonged periods. Hagen (1967) measured "free" and "bound" γ-aminobutyric acid (GABA) in the brains of male rats given 15% ethanol as sole fluid for 23 days. A weak, statistically insignificant lowering of bound GABA was found which seemed to be related to the blood alcohol level at termination of the experiment. In a study on humans which involved 11 chronic male alcoholics, Sutherland et al. (1960) reported elevation of blood levels of glutamic acid and glutamine and a slight change in cerebral metabolism of glutamic acid and glutamine, estimated from arterio–venous differences. After administration of 1 g alcohol/kg the cerebral metabolism of glutamic acid and glutamine

References p. 583

returned to normal whereas the level of glutamic acid in the blood increased significantly. Lack of nonalcoholic control subjects makes it difficult to assess whether there was a real difference between alcoholics and non-alcoholics. Cole *et al.* (1966) found that some patients with Wernicke's disease were highly refractory to thiamine therapy. This has been interpreted as being due to deficient synthesis of the apoenzyme of cocarboxylase (Leevy, 1968). Shimojyo *et al.* (1967) report increased cerebral blood flow, oxygen consumption and glucose uptake as well as increased cerebral vascular resistance in patients with Wernicke's disease. The lack of marked neurochemical alterations, in these studies of chronic alcohol effects on laboratory animals and human alcoholics, may be due to the effective protection of the brain from metabolic insult in a variety of conditions, or it may be a consequence of the paucity of intensive studies.

Two experimental-pathological studies on animals indicate severe pathology as a consequence of chronic alcohol administration. Scarlato and Menozzi (1959) gave rabbits daily intravenous injections of 1.5 ml of alcohol (approximately 0.6 g/kg) for 19 days. Histological examination of the brain was reported to reveal "the classical picture of chronic intoxication": lesions in glial elements, and to a lesser extent in nerve cells and axons, and proliferation of microglial elements. No change was found in peripheral nerve fibers. The result seems surprising in view of the rather moderate dosage, but rapid injection may temporarily have caused high concentrations of alcohol in the brain. In a study of dogs chronically intoxicated with alcohol, Sukhorukova and Yakobson (1965) found encephalopathy with demyelinization in the corpus callosum. Lesions were also found elsewhere and appeared more rapidly in vitamin deprivation. Hypoxia in localized areas through sludge formation and occlusion of small blood vessels has been suggested as a contributory factor in the development of lesions in the brain (Chapter 4, p. 161) and merits attention. Potentially, analysis of the conditions in which lesions arise and are reversed by neurochemical studies combined with neurophysiological and neuropathological investigation should lead to improvement of therapy in cases of diagnosed incipient neurological disorder in the alcoholic.

(2) The cardiovascular system

In spite of the high incidence of cardiovascular disease in modern civilization, there have been rather few studies of this type of pathology as a consequence of prolonged alcohol intake.

(a) The heart

Cardiomyopathy, defined as isolated non-coronary disease of the heart muscle, has for a long time been regarded as a consequence of alcoholism. Earlier literature was extensively reviewed by Jolliffe (1942). Concise accounts have been published by Heggtveit (1965), Heyden (1965), and Brandfonbrener (1967). A review by Hochrein and Schleicher (1965) mainly discusses acute effects of alcohol but also gives useful references to literature on chronic effects. Ferrans (1966) has contributed a thorough review of clinical and pathogenetic aspects of alcoholic cardiomyopathy.

Clinical studies on alcoholics (Abelmann *et al.*, 1954; Frederiksen and Hed, 1958; Evans, 1959; Cortis *et al.*, 1962; Brigden and Robinson, 1964) have shown that symptoms commonly encountered are mild tachycardia, extrasystoles, auricular fibrillation, conduction disturbances, and enlarged heart. As progression to irreversible damage is a grave risk, the value of early diagnosis has been stressed (Evans, 1959; Brigden and Robinson, 1964; Ferrans, 1966). Evans (1959) identified deformation of the T-wave of the electrocardiogram (ECG) as a distinctive feature. Other authors have also demonstrated that the deformed T-wave is a good diagnostic criterion of alcoholic cardiomyopathy (Cortis *et al.*, 1962; Levine *et al.*, 1965; Priest *et al.*, 1966). Priest *et al.* (1966) have used its remission as an indicator of recovery.

At the time of Jolliffe's (1942) review, most investigators assumed that cardiac myopathy of alcoholism was similar to the beri-beri heart of thiamine deficiency. Clear cases of beri-beri hearts are still encountered among alcoholic patients (Olson, 1964), but recent investigators have suggested a direct effect of alcohol. Thus, Evans (1959) and Brigden and Robinson (1964) in favor of this notion emphasized that apparently well-nourished alcoholics developed myopathy, which improved when they abstained from alcohol. This effect does not prove a direct action of alcohol because it might be attributable to a nutritional deficiency arising from the shift in dietary balance caused by alcohol. However, some recent histological and ultrastructural investigations give evidence for specific damage caused by alcohol, apart from nutritional effects. The observations on acute effects (Chapter 4, p. 158) indicate that repetitions of intoxication may have a cumulative effect. Evans (1959) emphasized that cardiomyopathy is usually limited to alcoholics who have been drinking large quantities of distilled spirits, but Brigden and Robinson (1964) reported cases among beer drinkers.

Evidence for a direct pathological effect of alcohol has been obtained mainly from histology and use of the electron microscope on autopsy and biopsy materials. Ferrans et al. (1965), in a study of autopsy samples of myocardium from patients who had died of this disease, reported accumulation of neutral lipids in the myocardial fibers and large decrease in histochemical staining for several mitochondrial oxidative enzymes. Observations with the electron microscope (Hibbs et al., 1965) confirmed the mitochondrial alterations and further showed swelling of the endoplasmic reticulum, degenerative changes of the myofibrils, and large numbers of lipid droplets. The samples were obtained 1–24 h after death, but the results have been confirmed on biopsy specimens (Alexander, 1966). Pintar et al. (1965), in a study of autopsy materials, concluded that vascular and cellular permeability increased, perhaps due to changes in electrolytes of the tissues. Wendt et al. (1965) and Regan et al. (1969) made similar conclusions on the basis of hemodynamic functions and myocardial metabolic parameters in alcoholics. Release of enzymes and zinc from the myocardium also increased after ingestion of alcohol by alcoholic subjects (Wendt et al., 1966), but the myocardial function was less affected by alcohol in the alcoholics than in normal controls.

Knott and Beard (1967) have reported that daily doses of alcohol (4 g/kg) markedly decreased tolerance of dogs to hemorrhages repeated once every week. The effect was ascribed to diminished myocardial efficiency. A direct effect of alcohol on the myocardium is also indicated by a careful study of pair-fed rats (Maines and Aldinger, 1967) in which ingestion of 25% v/v alcohol as the sole fluid progressively depressed myocardial contraction, decreased aortic blood pressure and heart rate, and induced cardiac arrhythmias. The changes became large after 20 weeks and could not be prevented by vitamin supplementation. A study in mice (Banner and Schenk, 1968) revealed hypertrophy of the heart, pathological structural alterations, and deteriorated cardiac function after 4 months on a liquid diet with 36% of the calories given as alcohol. Miller and Abelmann (1967) and Sohal and Burch (1969) report comparable observations. Catecholamine depletion is a mechanism which may cause the rise in lipoprotein lipase activity of the myocardium found in acute ethanol intoxication (Mallov and Cerra, 1967). In rabbit myocardium, Kikuchi and Kako (1969) found that alcohol given acutely caused an increase in the ratio α-glycerophosphate/dihydroxyacetone and an increase in triglyceride formation. Dogs accumulated triglycerides in the myocardium during prolonged feeding of ethanol (Marciniak et al., 1968). Thus, alteration of lipid metabolism and transport may be involved in myocardial disease as in the etiology of alcoholic liver disease, although the mechanism probably is different. A point to keep in mind is that in acutely ill alcoholics, a correlation between cardiac disturbances and hypokalemia has been found (Chapter 11, p. 748).

(b) The blood vessels

The relationship between alcoholism and arteriosclerosis has attracted some interest, partly because of a rather widespread belief that alcoholics are less afflicted than the general population by vascular and circulatory disease. Experiments on rats (Morgan *et al.*, 1957; Kritchevsky and Moyer, 1960; Paavilainen *et al.*, 1961), rabbits (Boyaner, 1969), dogs (Grande *et al.*, 1960) and chickens (Nikkilä and Ollila, 1959), with diets which included supplements of cholesterol and alcohol, all have shown that alcohol may elevate plasma cholesterol levels while neither protecting from nor promoting arteriosclerosis. Gottlieb *et al.* (1959) reported that alcohol enhanced arteriosclerosis, with some protective effect of magnesium, but the diet was low in protein and magnesium, and the large alcohol intakes, in a 20% solution as sole fluid, further reduced the proportion of protective nutrients in the diet.

These experiments are based on the tacit assumption that elevated cholesterol is an important cause of arteriosclerosis. The results give no evidence for a role of alcohol in the development of this disease. According to statistical data (Sullivan and Hatch, 1964; Hirst *et al.*, 1965; Nielsen and Kessing, 1965; Viel *et al.*, 1966; Sackett *et al.*, 1968) the incidence of sclerosis of the aorta and coronary arteries is not related to alcohol consumption, whereas a negative relation of this vascular disease with liver cirrhosis has been reported (Hirst *et al.*, 1965), but also denied (Nielsen and Kessing, 1965). These statistical studies have not been performed on a sufficiently large scale to yield conclusive results.

(c) Hematopoiesis

We have already mentioned (p. 494) that anemia is commonly associated with liver cirrhosis in alcoholism, apparently due to a disturbance of folate metabolism. Jarrold *et al.* (1967) report morphological changes in the bone marrow erythroids of alcoholic patients. The change correlated with dietary folate and serum folate levels. A vacuolization of the erythroids seemed to result from a direct action of alcohol. Direct action of alcohol has also been assumed to be the cause of decrease in the number of blood platelets

References p. 583

(thrombocytes) of alcoholic patients (Lindenbaum and Hargrove, 1968; Post and Desforges, 1968). Waters *et al.* (1966), in ferrokinetic and bone marrow studies of alcoholics who had neither liver cirrhosis nor anemia, found suppression of the hematopoiesis at the time of admission to the hospital, with improvement on withdrawal of alcohol. In an experimental study on dogs, Beard and Knott (1966) found that generalized suppression of reticulocytes in the bone marrow, during prolonged daily administration of alcohol, was paralleled by an anemia with a hematologic pattern different from those seen in any known nutritional deficiency. Therefore, both the clinical and the experimental study indicated that ethanol directly inhibits manufacture of red blood cells in the bone marrow. This effect of ethanol would be expected to induce anemia, but it is apparently limited to certain conditions because Knott and Beard (1967) found that alcohol did not depress the hematopoietic response in dogs subjected to repeated severe hemorrhages.

(3) Skeletal muscle

Hed and associates (Hed *et al.*, 1962; Ekbom *et al.*, 1964) have reported in chronic alcoholics an acute and a chronic muscular syndrome which is not associated with polyneuropathy. The acute syndrome, which develops after prolonged heavy drinking, is characterized by aching, tenderness, edema, and myoglobinuria. In the chronic syndrome, weakness of proximal limb and girdle muscles develops gradually. Even without these overt signs, both syndromes can be detected by electromyography and biopsy. Etiologically, these disorders are ascribed to large alcohol intake and may present a special case of toxic disintegration of muscle. Nutritional imbalance is also a possible causative influence.

Nygren (1966) found elevated serum creatine phosphokinase activities indicating muscular involvement, in 30 of 79 alcoholics. The occurrence of elevated serum creatine phosphokinase, in some patients without muscular complaints, was confirmed by Perkoff *et al.* (1967), who further reported decrease in the ability of the skeletal muscles to form lactic acid in response to insufficient blood supply during exercise. Lafair and Myerson (1968) similarly found elevated creatine phosphokinase in 36 out of 50 alcoholic patients of whom only 6 had overt symptoms of myopathy. Klinkerfuss *et al.* (1967) observed intracellular changes in histological and electron microscopical studies of biopsy specimens from skeletal muscles of patients with alcoholic myopathy. Douglas *et al.* (1966) presented a case report which included physiological and electron microscopic data. Perkoff *et al.* (1966) described a clear temporal relationship of the acute syndrome to excessive drinking, with recovery within two to four weeks. We have previously cited reports that chronic alcohol intake increases muscle water (p. 535). An editorial in the *New England Journal of Medicine* (*274*, 1326, 1966) has pointed out the possible relationship to the generalized muscular weakness found in alcohol withdrawal, and other aspects that require study.

(4) The gastrointestinal system

Alterations in gastrointestinal functions as a consequence of single alcohol doses were discussed on p. 183 (Chapter 4). A few experimental studies have shown pathological effects of chronic alcohol administration in laboratory animals. Figueroa and Klotz (1962b) found that diarrhea developed in young female rats receiving alcohol by intraperitoneal injection, 3 g/kg three times a week for 16 weeks. The effect may have been due both to irritant effects and to alterations in the composition of the microflora and microfauna of the gut. The importance of the irritating effect of alcohol has been variously judged (see *e.g.* Gillespie and Lucas, 1961; Bernard *et al.*, 1964). Gastritis developed in alcoholics toward the end of a 24-day period during which they ingested large amounts of alcohol (Mendelson and La Dou, 1964). A clinical study of digestive physiology of 471 skid row alcoholics indicated relatively mild disturbances, many of which were promptly cured during hospital treatment (Small *et al.*, 1959). Defective esophageal peristalsis was reported for chronic alcoholics suffering from neuropathy (Winship *et al.*, 1968). Alcohol does not increase development of stomach ulcers in rats (Schmidt and Klopfer, 1968).

Pancreatitis is fairly often associated with alcoholism, and as such is considered to be a distinct clinical entity. The incidence among various populations of alcoholics seems to be very variable (Chapter 11, p. 724). This condition as well as related experimental studies were the subject of an excellent recent review (Kalant, 1969). It has been suggested repeatedly that the pancreatitis may arise from a combination of increased secretion and obstruction of the pancreatic duct. We have already mentioned (Chapter 4, p. 186) that alcohol administered directly into the duodenum may cause congestion of the pancreatic duct, but relatively high local concentrations are required (Trémolières *et al.*, 1963; Ritter, 1965). When such congestion occurs and secretory activity continues, the accumulation of pancreatic juice apparently causes damage which if repeated may induce inflammatory and disruptive changes. Persistent vomiting, in response to the alcohol, might cause regurgitation of duodenal contents into the pancreatic duct, or might obstruct the duct (Myers and Keefer, 1934; cited acc. to Schapiro et al., 1966). In Chapter 4, p. 186, reference was given to experimental work with dogs and cats in which this mechanism has been shown to cause pancreatitis. Trémolières and Lowy (1964) have reported that the severity of the pancreatic lesions induced in experimental animals by repeated administration of alcohol is influenced by the dietary conditions.

In rats, drinking of 15% alcohol as the sole fluid has been reported to increase secretion of protease and lipase from the pancreas, without effect on amylase, and without development of pathologic lesions (Goslin et al., 1965). The effect was greater when the diet contained 18% casein rather than only 6%. Contrary to Goslin et al. (1965), Sarles and Figarella (1967) reported that 20% alcohol, given to rats as the sole fluid with a low protein diet (7% casein) for 110 days, decreased the pancreatic secretion of amylase, lipase, trypsinogen, and chymotrypsinogen. Ultrastructural alterations were also reported, such as cytoplasmic phospholipid inclusions, loss of zymogen granules, and mitochondrial changes (Tasso et al., 1967). In rats, ingestion of 20% ethanol as sole fluid caused decreased incorporation of $[1\text{-}^{14}C]$-leucine into pancreatic protein both in vivo and in vitro (Sardesai and Thal, 1967; Sardesai and Orten, 1968). Orrego-Matte et al. (1969) found that both acute and chronic administration of ethanol inhibited incorporation of labeled orthophosphate into phospholipids of the pancreas of rats. The effect was attributed to interference with secretory processes in the pancreas, possibly involving cholinergic vagal mechanisms. A report that ethanol pretreatment 12 hours before killing the rats inhibited subsequent active, Na^+-dependent uptake of amino acids by pancreatic tissue in vitro (Clayman et al., 1968) is difficult to interpret unless a persistent damaging effect on the membranes is assumed.

Zbinden and Pletscher (1958) have reported that in five of seven rabbits receiving daily doses of 48% alcohol by stomach tube for $10\frac{1}{2}$ weeks, the number of enterochromaffin cells and the amount of 5-hydroxytryptamine increased in the mucous membrane of pylorus, fundus, and duodenum. Atrophy and fibrosis of the membrane was seen in the two animals without an increase. The clinical opinion that alcoholism raises the incidence of gallstones has prompted an experimental study on rabbits (Borgman and

Haselden, 1967). A 15% ethanol solution as the sole fluid did not increase the formation of gallstones.

(5) Other disease processes

The evidence reviewed above shows that in many instances, prolonged alcohol intake definitely aggravates the progress of disease processes. In this section, we review experimental studies on conditions not falling within any of the categories already discussed.

Effects of alcohol on immune responses and resistance to infection have been studied only sporadically, although they are important both from a clinical and theoretical point of view. According to the review by Pickrell (1938), Robert Koch in 1885 demonstrated that ethanol decreased resistance of guinea pigs to cholera infection. Most of the subsequent studies date back to the beginning of this century and have been reviewed by Weeks (1938), who concludes that alcohol reduces resistance to infections. Pickrell (1940) subsequently investigated the effects of narcotizing doses of ethyl alcohol and of ether and avertin anesthesia on the susceptibility of rabbits to pneumococcal infection. Even in passively immunized animals, intoxication or anesthesia destroyed immunity by inhibiting the vascular inflammatory response, including leukocyte immigration, thus permitting undisturbed bacterial proliferation. Lushbaugh (1943) similarly reported that alcoholic stupor in non-immunized, passively immunized and actively immunized rabbits retarded the local inflammatory response against pneumococcal infection. Active immunization was the only condition which offered some protection during intoxication. These observations agree with the finding (Rubin, 1907; cited acc. to Edmondson et al., 1956) that as little as 0.2% alcohol in blood serum reduced by 44% the phagocytic action on cocci. Klepser and Nungester (1939) found that in rats intoxication prevented the chemotaxic response of leukocytes to pneumococci.

Weeks (1938) has cited other observations indicating that alcohol intoxication interferes with movements and functioning of phagocytes. In mice, intraperitoneal injection of 1 ml of 12% alcohol diminished the pulmonary clearance of staphylococci from 88 to 62% 4 h after deposition of the bacteria (Laurenzi et al., 1963). Later work (Green and Kass, 1965) indicates differences in the proportional effect of ethanol for different types of bacteria. Mobilization of phagocytes has been found to decrease in human subjects in vivo during a 1-h infusion of about 0.5 to 0.75 g alcohol per kg (Brayton *et al.*, 1965). However, the same investigators did not see impairment of phagocytosis and intracellular killing of staphylococci *in vitro* with 0.4% ethanol, which is close to the lethal concentration for humans *in vivo*. They concluded that defective diapedesis (passage of leukocytes between the endothelial cells) is the major deficiency in defenses of humans following alcohol ingestion. Results of a similar nature were obtained by Guarneri and Laurenzi (1968) who found that in mice inoculated with staphylococci through the lungs, alcohol interfered with the mobilization of alveolar phagocytes although it did not change the number and viability of alveolar phagocytes in uninfected controls.

Wasz-Höckert *et al.* (1958) tested effects of 8% v/v ethanol as the sole drinking fluid of mice inoculated with staphylococci. Although measurable quantities of alcohol were not detected in the blood, alcohol increased mortality. A more persistent liver infection was found in the animals receiving alcohol than in the controls, but there was no difference in bacterial counts taken from the spleen and kidney. Thus alcohol apparently impaired the resistance of the liver to infection, perhaps owing to a direct effect on liver metabolism. Alternatively, interference with the phagocytic function of the Kupffer cells may occur. Ali and Nolan (1967) have found that in rats, the reticulo-endothelial function, measured by determination of the clearance of micro-aggregated albumin from the blood, is depressed even at very low blood alcohol levels. Surprisingly, a correlation between the effect and the blood alcohol level was not found. Alcohol is considered as a factor aggravating tuberculosis, but Thomson *et al.* (1963) found that in guinea pigs, alcohol given in quantities sufficient to produce fatty liver did not worsen tuberculous infection.

Alcohol reduces resistance of mice to infection with dwarf tapeworm, but only after large doses and repeated infection (Larsh, 1945, 1946a, b, 1947). Alcohol does not reduce natural resistance to infection with *Trichinella spiralis* but causes a striking decrease in the immune response (Larsh and Kent, 1949). Alcohol in the drinking fluid of mice, substituted for glucose in an amount of one seventh of the calories, increased histopathological signs of trypanosomal infection in the heart within 49 days after inoculation but did not affect mortality (Miller and Abelman, 1967). Hahn (1961) could not verify an earlier report that alcohol ingestion causes Wasserman-positive serums indicating syphilis infection to give spurious negative reactions. Rogers (1946) found that alcohol modified the histologic changes in the liver caused by a second injection of serum in sensitized rabbits. The changed reaction was attributed to alterations in liver metabolism caused by alcohol. Specific lesions in the spleen were found after alcohol but not in control animals.

Alcohol given orally aggravates skin irritation caused by injection of bradykinin (Stüttgen and El Mahgoub, 1963). Barrière (1958) found that chronic ingestion of ethanol worsened skin lesions produced by potassium bichromate in guinea pigs. Although ethyl alcohol cannot possibly be an allergen, it has been reported as possibly being capable of provoking allergic reactions (Hicks, 1968). The mechanism of such an effect is entirely unknown.

Statistical findings suggest an increased incidence of certain types of cancer among alcoholics (Ledermann, 1952; Kamionkowski and Fleshler, 1965; Keller, 1967). In mice, rats, and hamsters, however, alcohol did not promote spread of cancer (Ketcham et al., 1963; Horie et al., 1965; Schmäl et al., 1965; Henefer, 1966). Alcohol may cause severe pain in patients with various types of tumors (Hall and Olson, 1955; Wanka, 1965; Brewin, 1966a, 1967). These reactions can be elicited with amounts of alcohol as small as 1 ml and have been attributed to sudden local congestion of blood vessels (Brewin, 1966b). In a mouse strain susceptible to development of liver cancer, drinking of dilute (0.5 or 5% v/v) alcohol as sole fluid by females during gestation or lactation was followed by decreased incidence of hepatomas in the offspring (Kahn, 1968).

Alcohol increases urinary excretion of coproporphyrins in humans (sources cited by Shanley et al., 1968), and may be an aggravating factor in porphyrinuria. Gajdos et al. (1965, 1966) have shown that in rats, alcohol raises the concentration of porphyrins in the liver and the red blood cells, a change attributed to deficient availability of ATP (Palma-Carlos and Palma-Carlos, 1968). Shanley et al. (1968) demonstrated that alcohol induced activity of the rate-controlling enzyme for biosynthesis of heme in the liver, δ-aminolaevinulate (ALA) synthetase. They suggested that the increase in ALA-synthetase activity caused the increased excretion of porphyrins, and that the induction of ALA-synthetase activity in turn is due to the rise in the ratio NADH/NAD caused by ethanol.

A relatively high incidence of iron storage disease has been noted in chronic alcoholics. MacDonald and Baumslag (1964) and MacDonald (1965) have emphasized the high content of iron in many alcoholic beverages and pointed out that conditions associated with alcoholism, such as deficient nutrition, enhance resorption of iron from the gut. Experimental results show both direct actions of ethanol on iron resorption, and interactions between ethanol and liver cirrhosis in their action on the uptake of iron from the gut.

Charlton *et al.* (1964) have shown experimentally that in humans, alcohol increases resorption of ferric iron administered as ferric chloride, with little effect on resorption of iron administered as hemoglobin or ascorbate in the ferrous form. The effect seemed to be due to the stimulating effect of alcohol on the gastric secretion of hydrochloric acid. In accordance with Charlton *et al.* (1964), Hoenig *et al.* (1968) did not find any effect of ethanol in 8 normal humans on resorption of ferrous iron, but in 16 cirrhotic patients, ethanol increased the uptake of iron as assessed from serum concentration. Ethanol thus seemed to potentiate the increased iron resorption found in liver cirrhosis. Oral administration of pancreatin prevented the rise in resorption, whereas pancreozymin diminished it. Sullivan and Herbert's (1964) finding, that in alcoholic patients during hospital treatment alcohol increased serum iron concentration and saturation of iron-binding protein, may thus have been related to liver disease of the patients. In an experiment with rats maintained for 21 days on 20% alcohol as sole fluid, total body uptake of ^{59}Fe ferrous citrate or ^{59}Fe ferric chloride was not changed, whereas a slight increase was found in absorption of ferric iron by isolated intestinal segments (Murray and Stein, 1965). Similarly, Tapper *et al.* (1968) and Hoszowska-Owczarek *et al.* (1967) reported that neither acute nor chronic administration of alcohol to rats increased the absorption of ferrous iron. Estler and Ammon (1967) found that in rats, administration of alcohol diminished the iron-binding capacity of the serum whereas the content of free iron was not affected in the spleen and the liver. Rogers and Gawienowski (1959) reported that the serum copper was elevated in a group of 49 alcoholics compared with 20 normal controls.

F. Summary

This chapter primarily reviews controlled experiments on biological processes and organ systems during prolonged exposure to ethanol. Some of the findings are compared with clinical information, particularly from controlled observations on chronic alcoholic patients. The literature is extensive, but the experimental work has been unsystematically scattered on a variety of topics. Clear goals and systematic studies are lacking in most research devoted to the "problem of alcoholism" since there is no satisfactory definition or description of this condition. A fruitful approach in biological research has been to identify limited problems associated with excessive drinking, such as the various diseases and organ pathologies known to be associated with chronic excessive drinking. However, it is difficult to mimic experimentally the wide range of conditions which characterize drinking by humans. Although cell and tissue cultures potentially could be valuable for acquisition of information concerning effects of prolonged exposure to ethanol, these techniques have been used little in alcohol research.

Among drugs used for their capacity of changing our state of mind, ethyl alcohol is unique in that it also is a source of readily available calories. The present authors are skeptical about etiological theories which attribute alcoholism to this singular quality of alcohol. Dependence on alcohol shows the general features of drug dependence, caused by the pharmacological effect on the central nervous system. However, the nutritional properties of alcoholic beverages contribute greatly to the physical complications of alcoholism.

Diffuse and pervasive imbalances in nutrition are caused by chronic alcohol intake. Nutritional balance studies on humans as well as laboratory animals show that calories from ethanol are fully utilizable in the metabolism, and substitute for calories from fat and carbohydrate. The utilization of ethanol is limited by the rate of its oxidation in the principal site of its metabolism, the liver. Usually, ethanol can provide no more than about one third to one half of the calories needed in moderate activity. In chronic animal experiments, alcohol solutions as sole fluid are well tolerated up to a concentration which forces the animal to restrict fluid intake in order to avoid accumulation of toxic amounts of ethanol. This concentration limit is about 10% v/v for the mouse and rat. Alcohol in quantities well tolerated if given diluted in the drinking water retards growth of animals if given as repeated intoxicating doses, but the mechanism for this detrimental pharmacological effect is poorly understood. Acute intoxication interferes with sexual functions, but prolonged intake of dilute ethanol has little influence on reproduction in animals. However, rat pups may starve when their mothers consume enough alcohol solution as sole fluid so that milk ejection in response to suckling stimuli is blocked through inhibition of oxytocin release.

Various types of evidence, including direct observation, dietary surveys, and buyers' surveillance, show that heavy drinkers for periods as long as many years may steadily consume alcohol to the limit of their ability to metabolize it. The rate of alcohol metabolism in many excessive drinkers exceeds the average human capacity of about 2–3 g/kg body weight/day by factors of 2–2.5 or even more, so that the total amount metabolized may rise above 400 g per day, corresponding to close to 3000 calories. Since no alcoholic beverage contains sufficient quantities of protective nutrients, continuous drinking thus may lead to serious nutritional imbalance, with restriction of the consumption of ordinary food in proportion to the amount of excess calories derived from ethanol. The economic difficulties and general neglect often associated with heavy drinking aggravate the poor nutritional condition. Particularly grave deficiencies have been described among wine drinkers with their steady pattern of drinking, whereas intermittent drinking provides periods of adequate nutrition between benders.

This nutritional imbalance appears to be the main cause of deficiency symptoms in alcoholism. Although ethanol may directly inhibit intestinal absorption of sugars and amino acids, and the gastrointestinal irritation and dysfunction prevalent during excessive drinking may cause temporary malabsorption, the nutritional effects of heavy drinking can evidently be compensated to a large extent by intake of high quality food. The effects of ethanol on uptake, metabolism, and excretion of most vitamins seem to be small or negligible. The metabolism of folic acid gives the clearest evidence for an inhibitory effect of ethanol, but even that is not entirely conclusive or consistent. On the other hand, ethanol spares thiamine which is required in carbohydrate but not in ethanol metabolism. Preponderance of dietary over more specific metabolic factors in nutritional disturbance of alcoholics is indicated by the usual occurrence of multiple deficiencies.

Within the central nervous system, increased tolerance and physical dependence are consequences of prolonged alcohol use, corresponding to the acute, pharmacological action of alcohol, causing a direct, physico-chemical change in the membranes of the nerve cells. Increased tolerance, manifested as decreased impairment with a given concentration of ethanol in the brain, has been demonstrated indirectly in humans, by comparisons between subjects with differing drinking habits, and directly in animal experiments. Signs of tolerance have been reported even during the course of single episodes of exposure to ethanol. The increase in dosage required to impair functions is generally no more than 30–50%, but neither the maximal degree nor the rate of disappearance of tolerance has been definitely established for any species. The relationship is uncertain between tolerance and physical dependence, which becomes manifest as an abstinence syndrome or withdrawal illness upon abrupt termination of alcohol administration.

Tolerance develops with dosages spaced so widely apart that the alcohol disappears entirely from the body between doses, whereas the withdrawal illness develops only after prolonged and heavy intoxication. A genuine alcohol abstinence syndrome has been convincingly demonstrated in experiments with human subjects, and also in monkeys, dogs, and mice. The basis of the increased tolerance and the withdrawal illness is not known. Alcohol's action on the neuronal membranes probably causes compensatory changes in their structure and function. Sudden withdrawal then gives rise to the often violent signs of hyperactivity and heightened excitability which gradually subside when normal membrane organization is restored. However, this description gives no direct information on the exact site of the changes or on the relative roles of alterations in synaptic processes compared with other aspects of membrane function. No histological changes are associated with the withdrawal illness. Even after fatal delirium tremens, autopsy has not revealed any characteristic pathological features. The symptoms of hangover include hyperexcitability and marked disturbances of central vegetative functions, which are characteristics of a mild withdrawal illness. In spite of the widespread occurrence of hangover and the great popular interest in this condition, it has been the subject of very few controlled studies.

Reactions of alcoholic subjects to acute intoxication provide important clues to the significance of alcohol for the drinker. Experimental findings suggest that "craving" cannot be induced by minute quantities of alcohol, because doses sufficient to cause subjective awareness of an effect were required to elicit desire for more alcohol. Physical dependence may contribute to sustained drinking, but its possible role in excessive drinking has not been evaluated. There is also evidence of improved performance in alcoholic subjects with no symptoms of withdrawal illness after doses of alcohol which in normal subjects would cause functional impairment. Feelings of elation or relief of tension often seem to be associated with the beginning of drinking whereas adverse effects become more predominant during prolonged drinking, but variable effects of alcohol on moods and emotions of alcoholics have been reported.

Increased rate of alcohol elimination has been suggested as a complementary or alternative explanation for increased tolerance. Studies in humans as well as animals fail to show any consistent effects of prolonged administration of ethanol on the rate of its elimination. Findings concerning

References p. 583

the activity of liver-alcohol dehydrogenase are variable but indicate that the enzyme is not strictly inducible by the substrate. However, very high rates of alcohol elimination, which have repeatedly been reported for some heavy drinkers, indicate either that some alcoholics have unusually high rates of alcohol elimination or that heavy drinkers acquire increased capacity to metabolize alcohol. Heavy drinking might increase metabolic capacity by development of an extrahepatic system for alcohol oxidation or by a manifold increase in the activity of the microsomal system which normally contributes only insignificantly to the oxidation of ethanol in the liver.

The rate of alcohol elimination decreases in severe liver disease associated with chronic alcoholism. Little is known about possible metabolic adaptations or derangements associated with chronic drinking. In fatty liver of nutritional etiology, the redox shift caused by alcohol is greatly attenuated. If ethanol/acetaldehyde form a redox pair similar to lactate/pyruvate and others, acetaldehyde might thereby become elevated to toxic levels. However, there is so far no reliable evidence that abnormally elevated acetaldehyde contributes to the complications of excessive drinking. The metabolic changes caused by ethanol may involve altered monoamine metabolism, but notwithstanding the biological reactivity of these physiologically important compounds, there is no information on changes during chronic alcohol intake. Although alcohol substitutes for other energy nutrients, particularly in the liver, little is known about possible derangements in the capacity to utilize other sources of energy, in the liver or in other organs. There is fairly good evidence from studies on humans as well as animals that adaptive changes compensate for the inhibitory action of alcohol on gluconeogenesis, but the nature of these changes has not been elucidated. Contrary to several proposals, the regulation of blood glucose is generally within normal limits in alcoholics.

Although endocrine causation of alcoholism has been suggested repeatedly, no endocrine disturbance is known to be consistently associated with alcoholism. There is some evidence from studies of catecholamine excretion that prolonged drinking decreases responsiveness to environmental stimuli. Findings concerning adrenocortical function are rather inconsistent but do not suggest abnormalities. The clinical finding that testicular size decreases and function is impaired in alcoholism has been confirmed in animal experiments. Increased turnover of iodine in the thyroid has been observed in alcoholic humans as well as in animals given alcohol for protracted periods.

The well-known diuretic action of acutely administered ethanol has caused the widespread belief that alcoholic patients are often dehydrated, but studies in patients as well as in animals have revealed complex changes in water and electrolyte balance. These changes are modified by liver disease. In animals and humans without liver disease, alcohol generally increases the water flow. Overhydration rather than water loss is the common finding. There is evidence for altered distribution of water within the organism, in particular increase in plasma and muscle water. Since electrolyte concentration generally stays within normal limits, some electrolyte retention seems to occur. Electrolyte depletion is sometimes caused by deficient intake and gastrointestinal disturbance, but there seem to be no consistent effects of ethanol leading to electrolyte loss. No consistent effects have been reported on the metabolism of trace elements such as zinc, copper and manganese.

Chronic, excessive drinking is often associated with pathology of the liver, pancreas, gastrointestinal tract, brain, and cardiac and skeletal muscles. Of these conditions, only the liver complications have attracted wide interest among experimental workers. The majority of the cases of liver cirrhosis among alcoholics are in the category of fatty nutritional or Laennec's cirrhosis. Other pathological alterations include postnecrotic cirrhosis, sclerosing necrosis, and sclerosing hyaline necrosis. Fatty degeneration is often characterized by enlargement of the liver, whereas hepatitis with jaundice and tenderness also occurs. These and other symptoms are found in varying combinations. A distinctive although not exclusive feature is occurrence of hyaline or Mallory bodies. Fatty liver has been produced in several species of laboratory animals by dietary means. Fibrotic alterations corresponding to human cirrhosis have been produced in conjunction with alcohol administration in rats and dogs. These findings have provided the basis for extensive experimental studies. Since long-term studies in the laboratory are laborious, different attempts at short-cuts have been frequent. The increase in liver triglyceride content in animals after acute alcohol intoxication has attracted particular interest as a possible model of the alcoholic fatty liver.

The results of the prolonged animal experiments show that alcohol acts primarily by shifting the balance between total calorie intake and protective nutrients in an unfavorable direction. The most important protective nutritional components are the lipotropic factors, including choline and methionine, which prevent fatty infiltration of the liver. The changes in liver

References p. 583

metabolism caused by alcohol, particularly the increase in α-glycerophosphate resulting from the redox shift, and the decrease in oxidation of fatty acids, also appear to favor formation and deposition of triglycerides. The effects of alcohol can be reproduced by feeding isocaloric amounts of sucrose, and they can be prevented by increased amounts of lipotropic factors and protein. A high proportion of fat in the diet aggravates the effects of alcohol. The fatty infiltration of acute intoxication is clearly different from that found in prolonged alcohol exposure, both in genesis and with respect to protective measures.

Epidemiological data also support the conclusion that the liver lesions are caused by a combination of nutritional and metabolic factors rather than by a direct "toxic" action. A close relationship is found between amount and duration of alcohol consumption and the appearance of liver lesions, but no relationship to specific beverage consumption or particular drinking patterns. Development of hepatic lesions is a risk with daily consumption of more than 80 grams of alcohol and is a grave danger when more than 160 grams of alcohol per day is consumed. Prevention should thus be based on restriction of drinking and provision of high quality food. Diagnostic procedures are not very satisfactory. Most liver-function tests may fail to show any alteration when biopsy reveals fatty degeneration and even fibrosis. Bromosulphthalein conjugation and analysis of serum proteins seem to be the most sensitive of ordinary clinical tests. A promising test is the measurement of combined galactose–ethanol elimination, based on the finding that ethanol in fatty liver fails to exert its usual inhibitory effect on galactose clearance.

Biochemical and ultrastructural studies of the liver in various stages of clinical and experimental alcoholic liver disease have revealed few specific changes. Swollen mitochondria with loss of cristae and proliferation of the smooth endoplasmic reticulum are among the typical changes, but are found also in other types of insult to the liver. Although alcohol decreases resistance to infections, clinical findings do not indicate that infectious diseases of the liver are important in the etiology of alcoholic liver disease.

Diseases of the nervous system associated with chronic excessive drinking include polyneuropathy, dim vision, and a number of encephalopathies, distinguished on the basis of overt symptomatology and pathological findings. For instance, Wernicke's disease is recognized as the physical counterpart of Korsakoff's psychosis. Polyneuropathy is due to nutritional deficiency, particularly lack of thiamine. Early diagnosis is difficult but is highly desirable since the degenerative changes affecting the peripheral nerves are irreversible. Slowed nerve conduction and changed electromyograms seem to be sensitive indicators of incipient stages of this disease. The encephalopathies are degenerative in character, but since the lesions affect different parts of the brain, the symptomatology is quite variable and often dramatic. The misleading impression of a number of different conditions has impeded experimental work in this area. The few experimental studies conform with the conclusion from clinical observations that nutritional deficiency is the most important causative factor. A large number of EEG studies have revealed various abnormalities, but almost nothing consistent enough to be of diagnostic value. Psychological and functional testing, sometimes combined with pneumoencephalography, are indispensable diagnostic aids. A few neurochemical studies have revealed altered enzyme activities and some metabolic changes, but do not as yet provide an organized body of information.

Isolated non-coronary disease of the heart muscle, or cardiomyopathy, is relatively common in alcoholic patients. Enlarged heart and deformation of the T-wave of the electrocardiogram are frequent occurrences. The disease seems to arise through a direct action of alcohol on the heart, resulting in fatty infiltration, pathological structural alterations, and deteriorated function. However, nutritional factors may also be involved to some extent. Other cardiovascular diseases do not seem to be typically associated with alcoholism. Arteriosclerosis is neither aggravated nor alleviated by alcohol. There are indications that alcohol causes anemia through a direct disturbance of blood-cell formation in the bone narrow. Considerable interest has been aroused by the recent clinical observation of a disease involving the skeletal muscles of alcoholics, with structural findings resembling those in cardiomyopathy, but experimental studies are lacking. Evidently, the condition deserves attention in the physical rehabilitation of alcoholic patients.

Alcohol is a gastric irritant in local concentrations exceeding about 5%. Gastritis, atrophies, and other changes are frequent concomitants of alcoholism, but these lesions are usually reversible. Pancreatitis is also considered as a disease associated with alcoholism. It has been attributed to obstruction of the pancreatic duct combined with increased pancreatic secretion, but the evidence is not conclusive. Extensive clinical evidence for an association of alcoholism with infectious diseases has been corroborated in numerous experimental studies. Alcoholism acts both by causing general neglect and deterioration, and by directly impairing the defense mechanism

References p. 583

of the body. Statistical data show increased incidence of certain types of cancer among alcoholics, but these findings have not been verified in experimental studies on animals.

REFERENCES

ABBOTT, R. R., CONBOY, J. L. AND REKATE, A. C. (1963). Liver function in alcoholism. *J. Michigan State Med. Soc.* 62, 990–996.

ABE, N. (1961). Dehydrogenase activity in alcohol-habituated rats. (Jap.) *Tohoku Med. J.* 64, 267–279. (Abstr. *Quart. J. Studies Alc.* 1964, 25, 581.)

ABELMANN, W. H., KOWALSKY, H. J. AND MCNEELEY, W. F. (1954). Circulation of the blood in alcoholic addicts. *Quart. J. Studies Alc.* 15, 1–8.

ADAMS, A. E. AND HUBACH, H. (1960). Hirnelektrische Korrelate der Wirkungen zentral dämpfender chemischer Substanzen im normalen EEG des Erwachsenen. *Deut. Z. Nervenheilk. 181*, 71–92.

ADAMS, R. D. AND VICTOR, M. (1960). Les maladies du système nerveux dues à l'alcoolisme. *Rev. Méd. Suisse Romande 80*, 857–877.

ADRIANI, J. AND MORTON, R. C. (1968). Drug dependence: important considerations from the anesthesiologist's viewpoint. *Anesthesia Analgesia 47*, 472–481.

AEBI, H. AND WARTBURG, J.-P. VON (1960). Vergleichende-biologische Aspekte der experimentellen Erforschung chronischer Alkoholwirkungen. *Bull. Schweiz. Akad. Med. Wiss. 16*, 25–35.

AGOSTONI, A., VERGANI, C., STABILINI, R. AND PETRELLA, A. (1968). Thyroxine-binding prealbumin in alcoholic cirrhosis. *Lancet 1*, 926–927.

AHLQUIST, R. P. AND DILLE, J. M. (1940). Reactions of alcohol tolerant rabbits to pentobarbital, evipal, ether, amidopyrine and metrazol. *J. Pharmacol. 70*, 301–308.

AHLQVIST, J., NYHOLM, M., SALASPURO, M. AND WALLGREN, H. (1968). Biochemical and morphological alterations in livers of rats fed high alcohol and high fat diets with ample protein and vitamin supply. *Acta Physiol. Scand. 74*, 15 A.

AKABANE, J. (1960). Pharmacological aspects of manifestation of the acute after-effects of alcoholic beverages: A role of acetaldehyde in alcoholism. *Med. J. Shinshu Univ. 5*, 113–122.

AKABANE, J., NAKANISHI, S., KOHEI, H., MATSUMURA, R. AND MARUYAMA, Y. (1964). Responses of the adrenal cortex to long-term administration of alcohol and acetaldehyde. *Med. J. Shinshu Univ. 9*, 59–69.

ALBERTINI, A., BONERA, E. AND RADAELI, E. (1967). Alcohol dehydrogenase in alcoholism. *Lancet 1*, 1061–1062.

ALBERTINI, A., FIACCAVENTO, S. AND BONERA, E. (1969). Turnover of liver ribosomes in ethanol intoxicated rats. *Fed. European Biochem. Soc., 6th Meeting, Madrid.* (Abstr. Commun. p. 193, 1969.)

ALBOT, G. AND PARTURIER-ALBOT, M. (1966). Lesions ultrastructurales du foie dans les hépatites alcooliques subaigües et dans les hépatites alcooliques cirrhogènes. *Semaine Hop. Paris 42*, 1757–1771.

ALBOT, G. AND PARTURIER-ALBOT, M. (1967). The toxic effect of alcohol on the human liver and its first ultrastructural manifestation. *Am. J. Gastroenterol. 48*, 319–327.

ALEXANDER, C. S. (1966). Idiopathic heart disease. 2. Electron microscopic examination of myocardial biopsy specimens in alcoholic heart disease. *Am. J. Med. 41*, 229 –234.

ALEXANDER, N. M., SCHEIG, R. AND KLATSKIN, G. (1966). Effects of prolonged ingestion of glucose or ethanol on fatty acid synthesis by mitochondria and cell sap of rat liver and adipose tissue. *J. Lipid Res. 7*, 197–203.

ALHA, A. R. (1951). Blood alcohol and clinical inebriation in Finnish men. *Ann. Acad. Sci. Fennicae*, Ser. A, 26, 1–92.

ALHA, A., HJELT, E. AND RAEKALLIO, J. (1957). Verenalkoholi ja alkoholin vaikutuksen alaisuus eri humalavaiheissa. *Alkoholipolitiikka 20*, 84–85.

ALI, M. B. AND NOLAN, J. P. (1967). Alcohol induced depression of reticuloendothelial function in the rat. *J. Lab. Clin. Med. 70*, 295–301.

ALLAN, F. D. AND SWINYARD, C. A. (1949). Evaluation of tissue tolerance to ethyl alcohol by alterations in electroshock seizure threshold in rats. *Anat. Record 103*, 419. (Abstr. *Quart. J. Studies Alc.* 1949, *10*, 351.)

ALLGÉN, L.-G. (1966). Some clinical biochemical methods used for the diagnosis of liver disease, especially in psychiatric cases (delirium tremens and after treatment with potentially hepatotoxic drugs). *Scand. J. Clin. Lab. Invest. 18*, Suppl. 92, 158–173.

ALLGÉN, L.-G., IZIKOWITZ, S., ORDELL, I.-B. AND SALUM, I. (1957). Klinisk-kemiska undersökningar vid delirium tremens och s.k. predelirium. *Nord. Med. 58*, 1921–1928.

ALLGÉN, L.-G., IZIKOWITZ, S., NAUCKHOFF, B., ORDELL, I.-B. AND SALUM, I. (1958). Serum diphosphopyridine nucleotide linked enzymes in delirium tremens and allied conditions. *Science 128*, 304–305.

AMMON, H. P. T. AND ESTLER, C.-J. (1966). Untersuchungen zur Pathogenese der Fettleber nach chronischer Alkoholverabreichung. *Arch. Exptl. Pathol. Pharmakol. 253*, 20.

AMMON, H. P. T. AND ESTLER, C.-J. (1967a). Influence of acute and chronic administration of alcohol on carbohydrate breakdown and energy metabolism in the liver. *Nature 216*, 158–159.

AMMON, H. P. T. AND ESTLER, C.-J. (1967b). Änderungen im Leberstoffwechsel nach akuter und chronischer Verabreichung von Alkohol. *Arch. Pharmakol. Exptl. Pathol. 257*, 260–261.

AMMON, H. P. T., ESTLER, C.-J. AND HEIM, F. (1965). Der Einfluss von Äthylalkohol auf den Kohlenhydrat- und Energiestoffwechsel des Gehirns weisser Mäuse. *Arch. Intern. Pharmacodyn. 154*, 108–121.

ANDRZEJEWSKI, S. (1961). Effect of prolonged feeding of ethyl alcohol to rats on adrenal cortex function. (Pol.) *Pol. Arch. Med. Wewnet. 31*, 137–146. (Abstr. *Quart. J. Studies Alc.* 1964, *25*, 162–163.)

Anonymous editorial (1961). Cause of hangover. *J. Am. Med. Assoc. 117*, 96.

ARENTSEN, K. AND SINDRUP, E. (1963). Electroencephalographic investigation of alcoholics. *Acta Psychiatrica Scand. 39*, 371–383.

ARIËNS, E. J., Ed. (1964). *Molecular Pharmacology. Mode of Action of Biologically Active Compounds.* Vol. 1. Academic Press, New York and London. 503 pp.

ARMSTRONG, R. W. AND GOULD, J. (1955). The nature and treatment of delirium tremens and allied conditions. *J. Mental Sci. 101*, 70–84.

ASADA, M. AND GALAMBOS, J. T. (1963). Liver disease, hepatic alcohol dehydrogenase activity, and alcohol metabolism in humans. *Gastroenterology 45*, 67–72.

ASCHAN, G., BERGSTEDT, M. AND GOLDBERG, L. (1964). Positional alcohol nystagmus in patients with unilateral and bilateral labyrinthine destructions. *Confinia Neurol. 24*, 80–102.

ASCHKENASY-LELU, P. (1957). Action du vin, de l'alcool et du jus de raisin sur la croissance pondérale du jeune rat male. *Compt. Rend. Acad. Sci., Paris 244*, 940–943.

ASCHKENASY-LELU, P. (1958). Effect of alcoholic beverages on reproduction of the rat. (Fr.) *Compt. Rend. Acad. Sci., Paris 246*, 1275–1277. (Abstr. *Quart. J. Studies Alc.* 1961, *22*, 660.)

ASCHKENASY-LELU, P. AND GUÉRIN, M. T. (1960). Action de boissons alcoolisées sur l'activité physiologique de la thyroide du rat. *Compt. Rend. Soc. Biol. 154*, 1409–1412.

ASHWORTH, C. T. (1947). Production of fatty infiltration of liver in rats in spite of adequate diet. *Proc. Soc. Exptl. Biol. Med. 66*, 382–385.

ATWATER, W. O. AND BENEDICT, F. G. (1902). An experimental inquiry regarding the nutritive value of alcohol. *Mem. Natl. Acad. Sci. 8*, 335–397. (Class. Abstr. No. 3946.)

AUGUSTINE, J. R. (1967). Laboratory studies in acute alcoholics. *Can. Med. Ass. J. 96* 1367–1370.

BAGGENSTOSS, A. H. (1961). The changing concepts of pathology in liver disease. *Am. J. Digest. Diseases 6*, 178–188.

BAÏSSET, A. AND MONTASTRUC, P. (1962). Effet de l'hormone antidiuretique sur le besoin d'alcool créé par l'habitude. *Compt. Rend. Soc. Biol., Paris 156*, 945–948.

BAÏSSET, A., MONTASTRUC, P. AND GARRIGUES, M. (1965). Recherches sur les interactions de l'alcool et de la sécrétion antidiurétique neurohypophysaire. Influence des préparations posthypophysaires sur la soif provoquée par l'ingestion d'alcool. *Pathologie-Biologie 13*, 241–251.

BAKUMENKO, M. S. (1957). The problem of prothrombin synthesis by the liver before and after administration of vitamin K_3 in patients with chronic alcoholism. (Russ.) *Terapevt. Arkh. 29*, 65–71. (Abstr. *Quart. J. Studies Alc.* 1959, *20*, 377.)

BANG, H. O. (1945). Determination of vitamin B_1 in the blood from healthy and diseased persons. *Acta Med. Scand. 122*, 38–59.

BANG, N. U., IVERSEN, K., JAGT, T. AND MADSEN, S. (1958). Serum glutamic oxalacetic transaminase activity in acute and chronic alcoholism. *J. Am. Med. Assoc. 168*, 156–160.

BANKS, W. L., JR., KLINE, E. S., BOND, J. S. AND HIGGINS, E. S. (1969). Metabolic alterations produced by chronic ethanol ingestion. *Federation Proc. 28*, No. 2, 626.

BANNER, A. A. AND SCHENK, E. A. (1968). Alcoholic cardiomyopathy: an experimental model. *Fed. Proc. 27*, No. 2, 556.

BARAK, A. J., BECKENHAUER, H. C. AND KERRIGAN, F. J. (1967). Zinc and manganese levels in serum and liver after alcohol feeding and development of fatty cirrhosis in rats. *Gut 8*, 454–457.

BARKA, T. AND POPPER, H. (1967). Liver enlargement and drug toxicity. *Medicine 46*, 103–117.

BARNES, E. W., COOKE, N. J., KING, A. J. AND PASSMORE, R. (1965). Observations on the metabolism of alcohol in man. *Brit. J. Nutr. 19*, 485–489.

BARRIÈRE, H. (1958). Experimental studies of cutaneous reactions in alcoholized guinea pigs. (Fr.) *Bull. Soc. Franc. Derm. Syph. 65*, 649–651. (Abstr. *Quart. J. Studies Alc.* 1961, *22*, 493–494.)

BARRY, H., III AND WALLGREN, H. (1968). A further note on preparing alcohol solutions. *Quart. J. Studies Alc. 29*, 176–178.

BASKINA, N. F. (1966). The study of impaired relations between cortical activity and certain vegetative functions in alcoholism, according to EEG, pneumographic and electrodermographic data. (Russ.) *Zh. Nevropat. 66*, 408–417. (Abstr. *Quart. J. Studies Alc.* 1967, *28*, 152–153.)

BÄTTIG, K. (1967). Alkoholismus: Epidemiologische Zusammenhänge und Folgen. *Naturw. Rundschau 20*, 200–204.

BEARD, J. D. AND KNOTT, D. H. (1966). Hematopoietic response to experimental chronic alcoholism. *Am. J. Med. Sci. 252*, 518–525.

BEARD, J. D. AND KNOTT, D. H. (1968). Fluid and electrolyte balance during acute withdrawal in chronic alcoholic patients. *J. Am. Med. Assoc. 204*, 135–139.

BEARD, J. D., BARLOW, G. AND OVERMAN, R. R. (1965). Body fluids and blood electrolytes in dogs subjected to chronic ethanol administration. *J. Pharmacol. Exptl. Therap. 148*, 348–355.

BÉHAGUE, P., SOULAS, B. AND CHAMPAILLET, MME. (1959). Les courbes d'excitabilité neuro-musculaire dans l'alcoolisme. Leur intérêt pour le dépistage et pour la surveillance de la désintoxication. *Rev. Neurol. Par. 101*, 184–188.

BENNETT, A. E., DOI, L. T. AND MOWERY, G. L. (1956). The value of electroencephalograhhy in alcoholism. *J. Nervous Mental Disease 124*, 27–32.

BENNETT, A. E., MOWERY, G. L. AND FORT, J. T. (1960). Brain damage from chronic alcopolism: the diagnosis of intermediate stage of alcoholic brain disease. *Am. J. Psychiat. 116*, 705–711.

BERNARD, A., DELATTRE, A. AND LAMELIN, P. (1964). Le mécanisme d'action de l'alcool sur la muqueuse gastrique: sa propriété hygroscopique et déshydratante. *Acta Gastroent. Belg.* 27, 129–147.

BERTINO, J. R., WARD, J., SARTORELLI, A. C. AND SILBER, R. (1965). An effect of ethanol on folate metabolism. *J. Clin. Invest.* 44, 1028.

BERTRAND, L., REYNOLDS, T.-B. AND MICHEL, H. (1966). La nécrose hyaline sclérosante du fois alcoolique. (Entité anatomoclinique et hémodynamique. Son potential cirrhogène.) *La Presse Médical* 74, 2837–2842.

BEST, C. H., HARTROFT, W. S., LUCAS, C. C. AND RIDOUT, J. H. (1949). Liver damage produced by feeding alcohol or sugar and its prevention by choline. *Brit. Med. J.* 2, 1001–1006.

BEZMAN-TARCHER, A., NESTEL, P. J., FELTS, J. M. AND HAVEL, R. J. (1966). Metabolism of hepatic and plasma triglycerides in rabbits given ethanol or ethionine. *J. Lipid Res.* 7, 248–257.

BJERRE, P. (1899). Über den Nährwert des Alkohols. *Skand. Arch. Physiol.* 9, 323–335.

BLAND, J. H. (1963). *Clinical metabolism of body water and electrolytes.* Saunders, Philadelphia and London. 623 pp.

BLIGNAUT, F. W. (1965). Alcohol and functional processes. *Commun. Univ. S. Afr.*, Series C. No. 55, 18 pp. (Abstr. *Quart. J. Studies Alc.* 1967, 28, 155.)

BLOMSTRAND, R. (1966). Lipid metabolism of the liver—in connection with carbohydrate and alcohol metabolism. *J. Clin. Lab. Invest.* 18, Suppl. 92, 62–75.

BÖHLE, E., ERB, W. AND SIEDE, W. (1968). Alkohol und Fettleber. *Der Internist 9*, 247–255.

BOISTESSELIN, R. DU (1966). Hepatotoxicity and the ultrastructure of the liver. In: *Experimental study of the effects of drugs on the liver.* S. J. ALCOCK, S. B. DE C. BAKER, A. I. SCOTT AND M. J. TUCKER, Eds., *Proc. European Soc. Study Drug Toxicity 7*, 65–82.

BONNICHSEN, R., DIMBERG, R., MAEHLY, A. AND ÅQVIST, S. (1968). Die Alkoholverbrennung bei Alkoholikern und bei übrigen Versuchspersonen. *Blutalkohol 5*, 301–317.

BORGMAN, R. F. AND HASELDEN, F. H. (1967). Experimental cholelithiasis and liver lipids in rabbits. Influence of ethanol. *Arch. Pathol.* 83, 411–414.

BORLONE, M., BASTIAS, H., PALESTINI, M. AND MARCONI, J. (1966). Effect of the acute and chronic administration of ethanol on the dorsomedial and other thalamic nuclei; preliminary report. (Span.) *Acta Psiquiat. Psicol. Amer. Lat. 12*, 241–250. (Abstr. *Quart. J. Studies Alc.* 1967, 28, 756.)

BOUDIN, G., LAURAS, A., LANIÉCE, M. AND KREBS, H. (1961). Le syndrome biologique du délirium tremens. *Presse Méd.* 68, 1469–1472, 1503–1506.

BOURRINET, P. (1964). Étude expérimentale de l'influence de l'alcoolisation aigüe et chronique sur l'activité des médicaments. *Revue Alcoolisme 10*, 186–198.

BOYANER, H. G. (1969). Influence of alcohol on coronary function in rabbits with atherosclerosis induced by cholesterol. *Nature 221*, 1066–1067.

BRANDFONBRENER, M. (1967). Editorial—Alcoholism and the heart. *J. Chronic. Diseases 20*, 345–349.

BRAYTON, R. G., STOKES, P. AND LOURIA, D. B. (1965). The effects of alcohol on host defences. *J. Clin. Invest.* 44, 1030–1031.

BRENNER, G. (1967). Untersuchungen über den Einfluss von 7-(2-Hydroxy-3-N-2-hydroxyäthyl-N-methylamino)-propyl-1,3-dimethylxanthin-pyridin-3-carboxylat auf die Lipidinfiltration der Rattenleber nach chronischer Tetrachlorkohlenstoff- und Alkoholintoxikation. *Arzneimittel-Forsch.* 17, 991–993.

BREWIN, T. B. (1966a). Alcohol shift and alcohol dysphagia in Hodgkin's disease, carcinoma of cervix and other neoplasms. *Brit. J. Cancer 20*, 688–702.

BREWIN, T. B. (1966b). Alcohol intolerance in neoplastic disease. *Brit. Med. J.* 2, 437–441.

REFERENCES

BREWIN, T. B. (1967). The incidence of alcohol intolerance in women with tumours of the uterus, ovary or breast. *Proc. Royal. Soc. Med. 60*, 1309.

BRIGDEN, W. AND ROBINSON, J. (1964). Alcoholic heart disease. *Brit. Med. J. 2*, 1283–1289.

BROITMAN, S. A., GOTTLIEB, L. S. AND ZAMCHECK, N. (1964). Influence of neomycin and ingested endotoxin in the pathogenesis of choline deficiency cirrhosis in the adult rat. *J. Exptl. Med. 119*, 633–642.

BSCHOR, F. (1951). Studien über den Ablauf der Alkoholintoxikation unter besonderer Berücksichtigung der pharmakopsychologischen Beziehungen in der Resorptionsphase bei Alkoholgewöhnten. *Deut. Z. Ges. Gerichtl. Med. 40*, 399–420. (Abstr. *Quart. J. Studies Alc.* 1952, *13*, 127.)

BSCHOR, F. (1952). Beobachtungen über ein funktionales Prinzip bei der psychomotorischen Leistungsminderung in den verschiedenen Phasen der akuten Alkoholintoxikation. *Deut. Z. Ges. Gerichtl. Med. 41*, 273–276. (Abstr. *Quart. J. Studies Alc.* 1953, *14*, 644.)

BUETOW, D. E. AND PADILLA, G. M. (1963). Growth of *Astasia longa* on ethanol. I. Effects of ethanol on generation time, population density and biochemical profile. *J. Protozool. 10*, 121–123.

BÜHRER, O. A. (1964). On 204 cases of delirium tremens. (Ger.) *Münch. Med. Wschr. 106*, 1016–1020. (Abstr. *Quart. J. Studies Alc.* 1966, *27*, 149.)

BUTCHER, H. R., JR. (1965). The pathophysiology of sodium depletion in man. *Surg. Clin. North Am. 45*, 345–363.

BUTLER, R. E. AND SARETT, H. P. (1948). The effect of isocaloric substitution of alcohol for dietary carbohydrate upon the excretion of B vitamins in man. *J. Nutr. 35*, 539–548.

BÜTTNER, H. (1965). Aldehyd- und Alkoholdehydrogenase-Aktivität in Leber und Niere der Ratte. *Biochem. Z. 341*, 300–314.

CAMPOS, I., SOLODKOWSKA, W., MUNOZ, E., SEGOVIA-RIQUELME, N., CEMBRANO, J. AND MARDONES, J. (1964). Ethanol metabolism in rats with experimental liver cirrhosis. I. Rate of combustion of labeled ethanol and rate of decrease of blood ethanol level. *Quart. J. Studies Alc. 25*, 417–422.

CARLSSON, C. AND HÄGGENDAL, J. (1967). Arterial noradrenaline levels after ethanol withdrawal. *Lancet 2*, 889.

CARPENTER, T. M. AND LEE, R. C. (1937). The effect of glucose on the metabolism of ethyl alcohol in man. *J. Pharmacol. 60*, 264–285.

CARRIE, J. R. G. (1965). Finger tremor in alcoholic patients. *J. Neurol. Neurosurg. Psychiat. 28*, 529–532.

CARROLL, J. R., ASHE, W. F. AND ROBERTS, L. B. (1964). Influence of the aftereffects of alcohol combined with hypoxia on psychomotor performance. *Aerospace Med. 35*, 990–993.

CASPERS, H. AND ABELE, G. (1956). Hirnelektrische Untersuchungen zur Frage der quantitativen Beziehungen zwischen Blutalkoholgehalt und Alkoholeffekt. *Deut. Z. Ges. Gerichtl. Med. 45*, 492–509.

CHARLTON, R. W., JACOBS, C., SEFTEL, H. AND BOTHWELL, T. H. (1964). Effect of alcohol on iron absorption. *Brit. Med. J. 2*, 1427–1429.

CHAUHAN, S. AND DONIACH, I. (1968). Effect of ethanol on growth rate in adult rats. *Nutr. Dieta 10*, 91–99.

CHEN, C.-S. (1968). Study of the alcohol-tolerance effect and an introduction of a new behavioural technique. *Psychopharmacologia 12*, 433–440.

CITTERIO, C., CUNEGO, A. AND GUIDI, M. (1964). Influence of ethyl alcohol on the aldolase activity of the plasma of abstainers and chronic alcoholics. (It.) *Arch. E. Maragliano Pathol. Clin. 20*, 305–311. (Abstr. *Quart. J. Studies Alc.* 1966, *27*, 548.)

CLARK, C. G. AND SENIOR, J. R. (1968). Ethanol clearance and oxidation of ethanol to carbon dioxide in persons with and without disease. *Gastroenterology 55*, 670–676.

CLAUSEN, S. W., BAUM, W. S., McCOORD, A. B., RYDEEN, J. O. AND BREESE, B. B. (1940). Mobilization of vitamin A from its stores in the tissues by ethyl alcohol. *Science 91*, 318–319.

CLAYMAN, S., SWAMINATHAN, C. V. AND SCHOLEFIELD, P. G. (1969). Transport and exchange diffusion of amino acids by *in vitro* preparations of pancreas from normal, tumor-bearing and alcohol-treated mice. *Biochem. Biophys. Res. Commun. 31*, 553–557.

CODA, G. (1961). Alcoholic mental confusion states; etiological and pathogenetic con siderations based on therapeutic experience. (It.) *Lavoro Neuropsichiat. 28*, 187–193. (Abstr. *Quart. J. Studies Alc.* 1965, *26*, 357–358.)

COËRS, C. AND HILDEBRAND, J. (1965). Latent neuropathy in diabetes and alcoholism: electromyographic and histological study. *Neurology 15*, 19–38.

COIRAULT, R. AND LABORIT, H. (1956). *Le delirium tremens*. Masson et Cie., Paris. 140 pp.

COLE, M., TURNER, A., FRANK, O., BAKER, H. AND LEEVY, C. M. (1966). Observations on thiamine metabolism in Wernicke's encephalopathy. *Am. J. Clin. Nutr. 18*, 303.

COLLIER, H. O. J. (1968). Supersensitivity and dependence. *Nature 200*, 228–231.

COLLINS, M. AND COHEN, G. (1968). Alcohol and formation of alkaloids in the brain. *Am. Chem. Soc. 15th Meeting*, Abstract No. 11337.

COLMANT, H. J. (1968). Patomorphologie des chronischen Alkoholismus. *Der Internist 9*, 256–260.

CONNOR, C. L. AND CHAIKOFF, I. L. (1938). Production of cirrhosis in fatty livers with alcohol. *Proc. Soc. Exptl. Biol. Med. 39*, 356–359.

CORTIS, B., GRANDE, A. AND TARQUINI, A. (1962). Alcoholic myocardiopathy. (It.) *Atti Soc. Ital. Cardiol. 2*, 208–209. (Abstr. *Quart. J. Studies Alc.* 1965, *26*, 159.)

COURVILLE, C. B. (1955). *Effects of alcohol on the nervous system of man.* San Lucas Press, Los Angeles. 102 pp.

COURVILLE, C. B. AND MYERS, R. O. (1954). Effects of extraneous poisons on the nervous system. II. The alcohols. *Bull. Los Angeles Neurol. Soc. 19*, 66–95.

CROS, J. AND TRÉMOLIÈRES, J. (1961). Influence de l'éthanol sur la thermolyse chez l'alcoolique chronique. *Rev. Alcool. 7*, 301–306.

CUETO, J., TAJEN, N., GILBERT, E. AND CURRIE, R. A. (1967). Experimental liver injury in the Rhesus monkey. I. Effect of cirrhogenic diet and ethanol. *Ann. Surg. 166*, 19–28.

CUTSHALL, B. J. (1965). The Saunders-Sutton syndrome: an analysis of delirium tremens. *Quart. J. Studies Alc. 26*, 423–448.

CUTTER, H. S. G. (1969). Alcohol, drinking patterns, and the psychological probability of success. *Behavioral Science 14*, 19–27.

DAFT, F. S. (1954). Experimental differentiation between liver necrosis and liver cirrhosis and some dietary factors affecting their development. *Ann. N. Y. Acad. Sci. 57*, 623–632.

DAFT, F. S., SEBRELL, W. H. AND LILLIE, R. D. (1941). Production and apparent prevention of a dietary liver cirrhosis in rats. *Proc. Soc. Exptl. Biol. Med. 48*, 228–229.

DAHL, S. (1964). Blutzuckeruntersuchungen bei erwachsenen Asthmapatienten im Vergleich mit Untersuchungen bei chronischen Alkoholikern. *Allergie und Asthma 10*, 205–218.

DAJANI, R. M. AND KOUYOUMJIAN, C. (1966). A study of some enzyme systems in livers of rats after prolonged ingestion of alcohol. *J. Nutr. 88*, 157–162.

DAJANI, R. M. AND ORTEN, J. M. (1962). Utilization of ethanol by way of the citric acid cycle in the rat. *J. Nutr. 76*, 135–142.

DAJANI, R. M., DANIELSKI, J. AND ORTEN, J. M. (1963). The utilization of ethanol. II. The alcohol-acetaldehyde dehydrogenase systems in the livers of alcohol-treated rats. *J. Nutr. 80*, 196–204.

DAJANI, R. M., GHANDUR-MNAYMNEH, L., HARRISON, M. AND NASSAR, T. (1965). The utilization of ethanol. III. Liver changes induced by alcohol. *J. Nutr.* 86, 29–36.

DALHAMN, T., HOLMA, B. AND TOMENIUS, L. (1967). *In vitro* studies of the ciliotoxic action of ethanol vapour in relation to its concentration in tracheal tissue. *Acta Pharmacol. Toxicol.* 25, 272–280.

DANIELS, D. H. AND OHLER, R. L. (1959). A study of delirium tremens with review of cases. *J. Maine Med. Assoc.* 50, 255–261.

DECARLI, L. M. AND LIEBER, C. S. (1966). Fatty liver after prolonged intake of ethanol with a nutritionally adequate liquid diet. *Federation Proc.* 25, No. 2, Pt. I, 304.

DECARLI, L. M. AND LIEBER, C. S. (1967). Fatty liver in the rat after prolonged intake of ethanol with a nutritionally adequate new liquid diet. *J. Nutr.* 91, 331–336.

DELAMONICA, E., MARSHALL, C. AND KURLAND, A. A. (1966). The alpha blocking response in chronic alcoholics. *Diseases Nervous System* 27, 451–454.

DELANEY, R. L., LANKFORD, H. G. AND SULLIVAN, J. F. (1966). Thiamine, magnesium and plasma lactate abnormalities in alcoholic patients. *Proc. Soc. Exptl. Biol. Med.* 123, 675–679.

DELAY, J., VERDEAUX, J. AND CHANOIT, P. (1957). The electroencephalograms of chronic alcoholics. Statistical study. *Ann. Med.-Psychol.* 115², 427–440. (Abstr. *Quart. J. Studies Alc.* 1960, 21, 157.)

DELORE, P., TOURNAIRE, J. AND GRIMALDI, MLLE (1959). Facteurs alimentaires et cirrhose alcoolique. In: *Cirrhose Alcoolique et Nutritionelle.* RAPPORTS PRÉSENTÉS AU 32 CONGRÈS FRANÇAIS DE MÉDÉCINE, Lausanne 1959. Masson & Cie, Paris. Pp. 235–259.

DENEAU, G., YANAGITA, T. AND SEEVERS, M. H. (1969). Self-administration of psycho-active substances by the monkey. A measure of psychological dependence. *Psychopharmacologia* 16, 30–48.

DENENBERG, V. H., PAWLOWSKI, A. A. AND ZARROW, M. X. (1961). Prolonged alcohol consumption in the rat. I. Acquisition and extinction of a bar-pressing response. *Quart. J. Studies Alc.* 22, 14–21.

DIETHELM, O. AND BARR, R. (1962a). Experimental study of amnesic periods in acute alcohol intoxication. *Psychiat. Neurol. (Basel)* 144, 5–14.

DIETHELM, O. AND BARR, R. (1962b). Psychotherapeutic interviews and alcohol intoxication. *Quart. J. Studies Alc.* 23, 243–251.

DI LUZIO, N. R. AND HARTMAN, A. D. (1967). Role of lipid peroxidation in the pathogenesis of the ethanol-induced fatty liver. *Federation Proc.* 26, No. 5, 1436–1442.

DOCTER, R. F. AND BERNAL, M. E. (1964). Immediate and prolonged psychophysiological effects of sustained alcohol intake in alcoholics. *Quart. J. Studies Alc.* 25, 438–449.

DOCTER, R. F., NAITOH, P. AND SMITH, J. C. (1966). Electroencephalographic changes and vigilance behavior during experimentally induced intoxication with alcoholic subjects. *Psychosom. Med.* 28, 605–615.

DOUGLAS, R. M., FEWINGS, J. D., CASLEY-SMITH, J. R. AND WEST, R. F. (1966). Recurrent rhabdomyolysis precipitated by alcohol: a case report with physiological and electron microscopic studies of skeletal muscle. *Australasian Ann. Med.* 15, 251–261.

DOW, R. S. AND MORUZZI, G. (1958). *The physiology and the pathology of the cerebellum.* Univ. of Minnesota Press, Minneapolis. 675 pp.

DOWDEN, C. W. AND BRADBURY, J. T. (1952). Eosinophil response to epinephrine and corticotropin. Studies in alcoholics and nonalcoholics. *J. Am. Med. Assoc.* 149, 725–728.

DUBE, B. AND KUMAR, S. (1962). Anemia in experimental cirrhosis of the rat. *Acta Haematol.* 28, 341–351.

DURLACH, J. AND CACHIN, M. (1967). Magnésium et alcoolisme chronique. *Rev. Alcoolisme* 13, 3–40.

EDDY, N. B., HALBACH, H., ISBELL, H. AND SEEVERS, M. H. (1965). Drug dependence: its significance and characteristics. *Bull. World Health Organ. 32*, 721–734.

EDMONDSON, H. A., HALL, E. M. AND MYERS, R. O. (1956). Pathology of alcoholism. In: *Alcoholism.* THOMPSON, G. N., Ed., Charles C. Thomas, Springfield, Ill. Pp. 233–290.

EDMONDSON, H. A., PETERS, R. L., REYNOLDS, T. B. AND KUZMA, O. T. (1963). Sclerosing hyaline necrosis of the liver in the chronic alcoholic. *Ann. Internal Med. 59*, 646–673.

EDMONDSON, H. A., PETERS, R. L., FRANKEL, H. H. AND BOROWSKY, S. (1967). The early stage of liver injury in the alcoholic. *Medicine 46*, 119–129.

EGGLETON, M. G. (1941). The effect of alcohol on the central nervous system. *Brit. J. Psychol. 32*, 52–61.

EICKHOLT, T. H., SCHILLACI, L. J. AND SEARCY, S. A. (1967). Possible ethanol-induced tolerance in rats. *J. Pharm. Sci. 56*, 275–277.

EKBOM, K., HED, R., KIRSTEIN, L. AND ASTROM, K.-E. (1964). Muscular affections in chronic alcoholism. *Arch. Neurol. 10*, 449–458.

ELBEL, H. AND SCHLEYER, F. (1956). *Blutalkohol. Die wissenschaftlichen Grundlagen der Beurteilung von Blutalkoholbefunden bei Strassenverkehrsdelikten.* 2nd ed., Georg Thieme, Stuttgart. 226 pp.

ELHARDT, W. E. (1930). Effect of ethyl alcohol on the growth of chicks. *Am. J. Physiol. 92*, 450–452.

ERENOGLU, E., EDREIRA, J. G. AND PATEK, A. J., JR. (1964). Observations on patients with Laennec's cirrhosis receiving alcohol while on controlled diets. *Ann. Internal Med. 60*, 814–823.

ESSIG, C. F. AND LAM, R. C. (1968). Convulsions and hallucinatory behavior following alcohol withdrawal in the dog. *Arch. Neurol. 18*, 626–632.

ESTABLE, J. J., GREZZI, J. W. AND BARAIBAR, B. (1959). Quantitative determination of collagen and liver lipids during chronic experimental intoxication with distilled alcoholic beverages. (Span.) *Anales Fac. Med. Montevideo 44*, 261–268. (Abstr. *Quart. J. Studies Alc.* 1960, *21*, 348–349.)

ESTLER, C.-J. AND AMMON, H. P. T. (1967). Der Einfluss des Äthylalkohols und eines β-Sympathicolyticums auf den Eisenhalt von Leber, Milz und Serum und die Eisenbindungskapazität des Serums. *Arzneimittel-Forsch. 17*, 69–70.

ÉTIENNE-MARTIN, P. AND KLEPPING, C. (1960). *Le foie alcoolique. De l'hépatite à la cirrhose alcoolique.* Masson & Cie., Paris. 161 pp.

EVANS, E. A., EISENLORD, G. AND HINE, C. H. (1963). Studies in detoxication by means of the isolated perfused liver. *Toxicol. Appl. Pharmacol. 5*, 129–141. (Abstr. *Quart. J. Studies Alc.* 1965, *26*, 341.)

EVANS, W. (1959). The electrocardiogram of alcoholic cardiomyopathy. *Brit. Heart J. 21*, 445–456.

FALLON, H. J., PESCH, L. A. AND KLATSKIN, G. (1965). Alterations in phospholipid metabolism induced by ethanol administration. *Biochim. Biophys. Acta 98*, 470–475.

FANKUSHEN, D., RASKIN, D., DIMICH, A. AND WALLACH, S. (1964). The significance of hypomagnesemia in alcoholic patients. *Am. J. Med. 37*, 802–812.

FAU, R., GARREL, S., GROSLAMBERT, R. AND PERRET, J. (1965). Étude électroencéphalographique comparative chez 3 types d'éthyliques. *Rev. Neurol. 113*, 332–336.

FAZEKAS, I. G., POSGAY, K. AND FAZEKAS, I. (1966). Einfluss von Äthylalkohol auf Katalase-Aktivität des Blutes von intakten und adrenalektomierten Ratten. *Enzymologia 30*, 116–126.

FENNELLY, J., FRANK, O., BAKER, H. AND LEEVY, C. M. (1964). Peripheral neuropathy of the alcoholic: I. Aetiological role of aneurin and other B-complex vitamins. *Brit. Med. J. 2*, 1290–1292.

FENSTER, L. F. (1966). The nonefficacy of short-term anabolic steroid therapy in alcoholic liver disease. *Ann. Internal Med.* 65, 738–744.

FERRANS, V. J. (1966). Alcoholic cardiomyopathy. *Am. J. Med. Sci.* 252, 89–104.

FERRANS, V. J., HIBBS, R. G., WEILBAECHER, D. G., BLACK, W. C., WALSH, J. J. AND BURCH, G. E. (1965). Alcoholic cardiomyopathy. A histochemical study. *Am. Heart J.* 69, 748–765.

FIGUEROA, R. B. AND KLOTZ, A. P. (1962a). Alterations of alcohol dehydrogenase and other hepatic enzymes following oral alcohol intoxication. *J. Clin. Nutr.* 11, 235–239.

FIGUEROA, R. B. AND KLOTZ, A. P. (1962b). Alterations of liver alcohol dehydrogenase and other hepatic enzymes in alcoholic cirrhosis. *Gastroenterology* 43, 10–12.

FIGUEROA, R. B. AND KLOTZ, A. P. (1964). The effect of whiskey and low-protein diets on hepatic enzymes in rats. *Am. J. Digest. Diseases* 9, 121–127.

FIGURELLI, F. A. (1958). Delirium tremens; reduction of mortality and morbidity with promazine. *J. Am. Med. Assoc.* 166, 747–750.

FILIP, J. AND HOENIGOVÁ, J. (1966). Rate of ethanol combustion, following intravenous administration, in cirrhotic patients. *Rev. Czech. Med.* 12, 82–91.

FINKELSTEIN, J. D. AND KYLE, W. E. (1968). Ethanol effects on methionine metabolism in rat liver. *Proc. Soc. Exptl. Biol. Med.* 129, 497–501.

FISCHER, H.-D. (1967). Zur Alkoholelimination bei Kaninchen nach CCl₄-Vergiftung. *Med. Pharmacol. Exptl.* 17, 60–64.

FLAX, M. H. AND TISDALE, W. A. (1964). An electron microscopic study of alcoholic hyalin. *Am. J. Pathol.* 44, 441–453.

FLEETWOOD, M. F. (1955). Biochemical experimental investigations of emotions and chronic alcoholism. In: *Etiology of chronic alcoholism.* O. DIETHELM, Ed., Charles C. Thomas, Springfield. Pp. 43–109.

FLETCHER, M. J. AND SANADI, D. R. (1961). Turnover of rat liver mitochondria. *Biochim. Biophys. Acta 51*, 356–360.

FLINK, E. B., STUTZMAN, F. L., ANDERSON, A. R., KONIG, T. AND FRASER, R. (1954). Magnesium deficiency after prolonged parenteral fluid administration and after chronic alcoholism complicated by delirium tremens. *J. Lab. Clin. Med.* 43, 169–183.

FLITMAN, R. AND WORTH, M. H. (1966). Inhibition of hepatic alcohol dehydrogenase by bilirubin. *J. Biol. Chem.* 241, 669–671.

FLYNN, P. A. (1958). *Water and electrolyte balance after alcohol ingestion.* Doctoral Diss., Yale University School of Medicine; New Haven. Typewr. 56 pp. (Abstr. *Quart. J. Studies Alc.* 1959, 20, 128–129.)

FORBES, J. C. AND DUNCAN, G. M. (1953). Effect of repeated alcohol administration on adrenal ascorbic acid and on development of scurvy in the guinea pig. *Quart. J. Studies Alc.* 14, 540–544.

FORENBACHER, S., CERLEK, S. AND MARZAN, B. (1961). The effect of protracted application of alcohol upon the liver of horses. *Acta Med. Iugoslav.* 15, 80–94. (Abstr. *Quart. J. Studies Alc.* 1964, 25, 371.)

FORSANDER, O. A. (1963). Influence of alcohol on the general metabolism of the body. In: *Alcohol and Civilization*, S. P. LUCIA, Ed., McGraw-Hill New York. Pp. 43–60.

FORSANDER, O. A. AND VARTIA, K. O. (1965). Hangover. *Alkoholpolitik 28*, 41–43.

FORSANDER, O. A., HILLBOM, M. E. AND LINDROS, K. O. (1969). Influence of thyroid function on the acetaldehyde level of blood and liver of intact rats during ethanol metabolism. *Acta Pharmacol. Toxicol.* 27, 410–416.

FRASER, H. F. (1957). Tolerance to and physical dependence on opiates, barbiturates and alcohol. *Ann. Rev. Med.* 8, 427–440.

FREDERIKSEN, P. AND HED, R. (1958). Clinical studies in chronic alcoholism. III. Cardiac changes in chronic alcoholism. An electrocardiographic study. *Acta Med. Scand. 162*, 203–209.

FREI, J., REYMOND, C., BOREL, C., BAER, A., RYSER, H., WILD, C. AND VANNOTTI, A. (1959). Exploration directe et indirecte de l'activité enzymatique du foie dans la cirrhose. In: *Cirrhose Alcoolique et Nutritionnelle*. RAPPORTS PRÉSENTÉS AU 32e CONGRÈS FRANÇAIS DE MÉDÉCINE, Lausanne, 1959. Masson & Cie., Paris. Pp. 319–343.

FRENCH, S. W. (1966a). Effect of chronic ethanol ingestion on liver enzyme changes induced by thiamine, riboflavin, pyridoxine, or choline deficiency. *J. Nutr. 88*, 291–302.

FRENCH, S. W. (1966b). Effect of acute and chronic ethanol ingestion on rat liver ATP. *Proc. Soc. Exptl. Biol. Med. 121*, 681–685.

FRENCH, S. W. (1966c). Chronic ethanol feeding and rat liver phospholipid content. *Federation Proc. 25*, No. 2, Pt. I, 479.

FRENCH, S. W. (1967). Effect of chronic ethanol feeding on rat liver phospholipid. *J. Nutr. 91*, 292–298.

FRENCH, S. W. (1968). Fragility of liver mitochondria in ethanol-fed rats. *Gastroenterology 54*, 1106–1114.

FRENCH, S. W. AND CASTAGNA, J. (1967). Some effects of chronic ethanol feeding on vitamin B_6 deficiency in the rat. *Lab. Invest. 16*, 526–531.

FREUND, G. (1969). Alcohol withdrawal syndrome in mice. *Arch. Neurol. 21*, 315–320.

FREUND, G. AND O'HOLLAREN, P. (1965). Acetaldehyde concentrations in alveolar air following a standard dose of ethanol in man. *J. Lipid Res. 6*, 471–477.

FUJITA, F. (1954). Experimental studies on habituation to alcohol. *Folia Pharmacol. Japon. 50*, 258–263. (Class. Abstr. No. 7654.)

FUNKHOUSER, J. B., NAGLER, B. AND WALKE, N. D. (1953). The electro-encephalogram of chronic alcoholism. *Southern Med. J. 46*, 423–428.

GABUZDA, G. J. AND DAVIDSON, C. S. (1962). Tryptophan and nicotinic acid metabolism in patients with cirrhosis of the liver. *Am. J. Clin. Nutr. 11*, 502–508.

GAJDOS, A., GAJDOS-TÖRÖK, M., PALMA-CARLOS, A. AND PALMA-CARLOS, L. (1965). Effet de l'intoxication aiguë du Rat blanc par l'éthanol sur le métabolisme des porphyrines et le taux hépatique de l'ATP, du DPN, du DPNH et des lipides. *Compt. Rend. Soc. Biol. 159*, 2185–2188.

GAJDOS, A., GAJDOS-TÖRÖK, M., PALMA-CARLOS, A. AND PALMA-CARLOS, L. (1966). Porphyria induced in rats by orotic acid and the effect of adenine-5'-monophosphoric acid. *Nature 211*, 974–975.

GARCEAU, A. J. and the Boston Inter-Hospital Liver Group (1964). The natural history of cirrhosis. II. The influence of alcohol and prior hepatitis on pathology and prognosis. *New Engl. J. Med. 271*, 1173–1179.

GEBAUER, H. (1959). On new experimental studies on the problem of vitamin deficiency damage. With a contribution on the effects of beer and beer extracts. (Ger.) *Pharmazie 14*, 224–228. (Abstr. *Quart. J. Studies Alc.* 1961, *22*, 152.)

GERMER, W. D. AND CHOL, H. (1959). Über die hepatische Fibrose bei der Ratte. *Z. Ges. Exptl. Med. 131*, 238–245.

GIACOBINI, E., IZIKOWITZ, S. AND WEGMANN, A. (1960). Urinary norepinephrine and epinephrine excretion in delirium tremens. *Arch. Gen. Psychiat. 3*, 289–296.

GIGGLBERGER, H. (1968). Zur Ätiologie der Leberzirrhose. *Acta Hepato-Splenologica 15*, 415–423.

GILLESPIE, R. J. G. AND LUCAS, C. C. (1961). Effect of single intoxicating doses of ethanol on the gastric and intestinal mucosa of rats. *Can. J. Biochem. Physiol. 39*, 237–241.

GIOVE, G. (1964). Clinical-electroencephalographic correlations in alcoholopathy. (It.) *Lavoro Neuropsichiat. 35*, 473–492. (Abstr. *Quart. J. Studies Alc.* 1966, *27*, 767.)

GOLDBERG, L. (1943). Quantitative studies on alcohol tolerance in man. *Acta Physiol. Scand. 5*, Suppl. 16, 128 pp.

GOLDBERG, L. (1963a). Effects and after-effects of alcohol, tranquillizers and fatigue on ocular phenomena. In: *Alcohol and road traffic*, Proc. 3rd Int. Conference, British Medical Association, London. Pp. 123–135.

GOLDBERG, L. (1963b). The metabolism of alcohol. In: *Alcohol and Civilization*, S. P. LUCIA, Ed., McGraw-Hill, New York. Pp. 23–42.

GOLDBERG, M. (1960). The occurrence and treatment of hypothyroidism among alcoholics. *J. Clin. Endocrinol. Metab. 20*, 609–621.

GOLDENBERG, M. A. AND KOROLENKO, T. P. (1963). Alcoholic "psychopathological" syndromes in experimental animals. (Russ.) *Zh. Nevropathol. 63*, 1861–1866. (Abstr. *Quart. J. Studies Alc.* 1966, *27*, 341–342.)

GOLDFARB, A. I. AND BERMAN, S. (1949). Alcoholism as a psychosomatic disorder. 1. Endocrine pathology of animals and man excessively exposed to alcohol; its possible relation to behavioral pathology. *Quart. J. Studies Alc. 10*, 415–429.

GOMEZ-DUMM, C. L. A. AND PORTA, E. A. (1966). Protein and hepatic injury associated with experimental chronic alcoholism. *Federation Proc. 25*, No. 2, Pt. I, 304.

GOMEZ-DUMM, C. L. A., PORTA, E. A., HARTROFT, W. S. AND KOCH, O. R. (1968). A new experimental approach in the study of chronic alcoholism. II. Effects of high alcohol intake in rats fed diets of various adequacies. *Lab. Invest. 18*, 365–378.

GOODHART, R. AND SINCLAIR, H. M. (1939). The amount of cocarboxylase (Vitamin B_1 diphosphate ester) in blood in health and disease. In: *III Congrès Neurologique International, Copenhague 1939. Comptes Rendus des Séances*, K. WINTHER, Ed., Munksgaard, Copenhague. Pp. 885–890.

GORZYM, H., JANISZEWSKI, L., NAREBSKI, J., OLEJARCZUK, G. AND SZAWLOWSKA, Z. (1957). Changes in the EEG and chronaxy of the vestibular system of rabbits under the influence of ethyl alcohol. (Pol.) *Acta Physiol. Polon. 8*, 339. (Abstr. *Quart. J. Studies Alc.* 1960, *21*, 147.)

GOSLIN, J., HONG, S. S., MAGEE, D. F. AND WHITE, T. T. (1965). Relationship between diet, ethyl alcohol consumption and some activities of the exocrine pancreas in rats. *Arch. Intern. Pharmacodyn. Therap. 157*, 462–469.

GOTTLIEB, L. S., BROITMAN, S. A., VITALE, J. J. AND ZAMCHECK, N. (1959). The influence of alcohol and dietary magnesium upon hypercholesterolemia and atherogenesis in the rat. *J. Lab. Clin. Med. 53*, 433–441.

GRANDE, F., HAY, L. J., HEUPEL, H. W. AND AMATUZIO, D. S. (1960). Effect of ethanol on serum cholesterol concentration in dog and man. *Circulation Res., N.Y. 8*, 810–819. (Abstr. *Quart. J. Studies Alc.* 1962, *23*, 329–330.)

GRAYSON, T. L., WHITE, J. E. AND MOYER, C. A. (1963). Oxygen consumptions; concentrations of inorganic ions in urine, serum and duodenal fluid, hematocrits, urinary excretions; pulse rates and blood pressure during duodenal depletions of sodium salts in normal and alcoholic man. *Ann. Surg. 158*, 840–858.

GREEN, G. M. AND KASS, E. H. (1965). The influence of bacterial species on pulmonary resistance to infection in mice subjected to hypoxia, cold stress, and ethanolic intoxication. *Brit. J. Exptl. Pathol. 46*, 360–366.

GREEN, J. R. (1965). Subclinical acute liver disease of the alcoholic. *Australasian Ann. Med. 14*, 111–124.

GREENBERGER, N. J., COHEN, R. N. AND ISSELBACHER, K. J. (1965). The effects of chronic ethanol administration on liver alcohol dehydrogenase activity in the rat. *Lab. Invest. 14*, 264–271.

GRIFFATON, G. AND LOWY, R. (1964). Oxydation de l'éthanol *in vitro* par un homogénat de foie de rat. *Compt. Rend. Soc. Biol. 158*, 998–1003.

GROSS, M. M. (1967). Management of acute alcohol withdrawal states. *Quart. J. Studies Alc. 28*, 655–666.

GROSS, M. M., HALPERT, E., SABOT, L. AND POLIZOS, P. J. (1963). Hearing disturbances and auditory hallucinations in the acute alcoholic psychoses. I. Tinnitus: incidence and significance. *J. Nervous Mental Disease 137*, 455–465. (Abstr. *Quart. J. Studies Alc.* 1965, *26*, 711.)

GROSS, M. M., TOBIN, M., KISSIN, B., HALPERT, E. AND SABOT, L. (1964). Evoked responses to clicks in delirium tremens: a preliminary report. *Ann. N.Y. Acad. Sci. 112*, 543–546.

GROSS, M. M., GOODENOUGH, D. R., TOBIN, M., HALPERT, E., LEPORE, D., PERLSTEIN, A., SIROTA, M., DiBIANCO, J., FULLER, R. AND KISHNER, I. (1966). Sleep disturbances and hallucinations in the acute alcoholic psychoses. *J. Nerv. Ment. Dis. 142*, 493–514.

GUARNERI, J. J. AND LAURENZI, G. A. (1968). Effect of ethanol on the mobilization of alveolar macrophages. *J. Lab. Clin. Med. 72*, 40–51.

HAGEN, D. (1967). GABA levels in rat brain after prolonged alcohol intake. *Quart. J. Studies Alc. 28*, 613–617.

HAHN, R. D. (1961). Wasserman-fast spinal fluid. *J. Am. Med. Assoc. 176*, 180. (Abstr. *Quart. J. Studies Alc.* 1962, *23*, 492.)

HAINES, D. S. M. (1966). The effects of choline deficiency and choline refeeding upon the metabolism of plasma and liver lipids. *Can. J. Biochem. 44*, 45–57.

HALL, C. A. AND OLSON, K. B. (1955). Alcohol-induced pain in Hodgkin's disease. *New Engl. J. Med. 253*, 608–609.

HALSTED, C. H., GRIGGS, R. C. AND HARRIS, J. W. (1967). The effect of alcoholism on the absorption of folic acid (H^3-PGA) evaluated by plasma levels and urine excretion. *J. Lab. Clin. Med. 69*, 116–131.

HANSON, F. B., SHOLES, F. N. AND HEYS, F. (1928). Alcohol and body weight in the albino rat. *Genetics 13*, 121–125.

HARINASUTA, U., CHOMET, B., ISHAK, K. AND ZIMMERMAN, H. J. (1967). Steatonecrosis —Mallory body type. *Medicine 46*, 141–162.

HARTMAN, A. D. AND DiLUZIO, N. R. (1968). Inhibition of the chronic ethanol-induced fatty liver by antioxidant administration. *Proc. Soc. Exptl. Biol. Med. 127*, 270–276.

HARTROFT, W. S. (1961). Experimental reproduction of human hepatic disease. In: *Progress in liver diseases*, H. POPPER AND F. SCHAFFNER, Eds. Grune & Stratton, New York. Vol. 1, pp. 68–85.

HARTROFT, W. S. (1964). Electron microscopy of liver and kidney cells in dietary deficiencies. *Ciba Found. Symp. Cellular Injury* 248–282. (Discussion 282–286.)

HARTROFT, W. S. (1967). Introductory remarks (Nutrition Soc. Symp., Alcohol, Metabolism and Liver Disease). *Federation Proc. 26*, No. 5, 1432–1435.

HARTROFT, W. S. AND PORTA, E. A. (1966). Experimental alcoholic hepatic injury. *Nutr. Rev. 24*, 97–101.

HARTROFT, W. S. AND PORTA, E. A. (1968). Alcohol, diet, and experimental hepatic injury. *Can. J. Physiol. Pharmacol. 46*, 463–473.

HASEBE, M. (1961). Klinische und experimentelle Studien über die chronische Alkoholvergiftung. (2. Mitteilung) Mit besonderer Rücksicht auf ihre Behandlung. *Yokohama Med. Bull. 12*, 218–227.

HATFIELD, G. K. (1966). Modification of drug action by repeated ethanol treatment in the rat. *Dissertation Abstr. 27*, 561-B.

HAWKINS, R. D., KALANT, H. AND KHANNA, J. M. (1966). Effects of chronic intake of ethanol on rate of ethanol metabolism. *Can. J. Physiol. Pharmacol. 44*, 241–257.

HED, R. (1958a). Clinical studies in chronic alcoholism. I. Incidence of diabetes mellitus in portal cirrhosis. *Acta Med. Scand. 162*, 189–194.

HED, R. (1958b). Clinical studies in chronic alcoholism. II. Carbohydrate metabolism in chronic alcoholism with particular reference to glucose and insulin tolerance. *Acta Med. Scand. 162*, 195–202.

HED, R., LUNDMARK, C., FAHLGREN, H. AND ORELL, S. (1962). Acute muscular syndrome in chronic alcoholism. *Acta Med. Scand. 171*, 585–599.

HED, R., NYGREN, A. AND SUNDBLAD, R. (1968). Insulin response in chronic alcoholism. *Lancet 1*, 145.

HEDENSTRÖM, I. VON AND SCHMIDT, O. (1951). Elektroencephalographische Untersuchungen nach Alkoholgabe. *Deut. Z. Ges. Gerichtl. Med. 40*, 234–251.

HEGGTVEIT, H. A. (1965). Alcohol and the heart. *Am. Heart J. 69*, 422–423.

HENEFER, E. P. (1966). Ethanol, 30 per cent, and hamster pouch carcinogenesis. *J. Dent. Res. 45*, 838–844. (Abstr. *Quart. J. Studies Alc.* 1968, *29*, 203–204.)

HENLEY, K. S., WIGGINS, H. S., HIRSCHOWITZ, B. I. AND POLLARD, H. M. (1958). The effect of oral ethanol on glutamic pyruvic and glutamic oxalacetic transaminase activity in the rat liver. *Quart. J. Studies Alc. 19*, 54–68.

HERBERT, V. R., ZALUSKY, R. AND DAVIDSON, C. S. (1963). Correlation of folate deficiency with alcoholism and associated macrocytosis, anemia, and liver disease. *Ann. Internal Med. 58*, 977–988.

HEYDEN, S. (1965). Alkohol und kardiovaskuläres System. *Münch. Med. Wochschr. 107*, 2488–2492.

HIBBS, R. G., FERRANS, V. J., BLACK, W. C., WEILBAECHER, D. G., WALSH, J. J. AND BURCH, G. E. (1965). Alcoholic cardiomyopathy. An electron microscopic study. *Am. Heart J. 69*, 766–779.

HICKS, R. (1968). Ethanol, a possible allergen. *Allergy 26*, 641–643.

HIDDEMA, E. (1965). Electroencephalographic findings in alcoholics. *Psychiat. Neurol. (Amsterdam) 68*, 355–359. (Abstr. *Quart. J. Studies Alc.* 1967, *28*, 365.)

HIESTAND, W. A., STEMLER, F. W. AND WIEBERS, J. E. (1952). The relationship of dilution of ethyl alcohol to intraperitoneal toxicity in mice. *Quart. J. Studies Alc. 13*, 361–364.

HIMWICH, H. E. (1956). Alcohol and brain physiology. In: *Alcoholism*, G. N. THOMPSON, Ed., Charles C. Thomas, Springfield, Ill. Pp. 291–408.

HIRST, A. E., HADLEY, G. G. AND GORE, I. (1965). The effect of chronic alcoholism and cirrhosis of the liver on atherosclerosis. *Am. J. Med. Sci. 249*, 143–149.

HOCHREIN, M. AND SCHLEICHER, I. (1965). Herz-Kreislaufbeeinflussung durch Alkohol. *Med. Klin. 60*, 41–46.

HOENIG, V., BRODANOVA, M. AND KORDAČ, V. (1968). Effect of ethanol on iron tolerance and endogenous serum iron in liver cirrhosis. *Scand. J. Gastroenterol. 3*, 334–338.

HOFFBAUER, F. W. AND ZAKI, F. G. (1965). Fatty cirrhosis in the rat. VII. Influence of different levels of dietary fat on early deposition of fat in liver. *Proc. Soc. Exptl. Biol. Med. 118*, 1130–1132.

HOFMANN, G. AND KRYSPIN-EXNER, K. (1966). Stoffwechseluntersuchungen bei Alkoholkranken. *Wiener Z. Nervenheilkunde 23*, 275–287.

HOGANS, A. F., MORENO, O. M. AND BRODIE, D. A. (1961). Effects of ethyl alcohol on EEG and avoidance behavior of chronic electrode monkeys. *Am. J. Physiol. 201*, 434–436.

HOLMBERG, G. AND MÅRTENS, S. (1955). Electroencephalographic changes in man correlated with blood alcohol concentration and some other conditions following standardized ingestion of alcohol. *Quart. J. Studies Alc. 16*, 411–424.

HOLT, L. E. AND SNYDERMAN, S. E. (1955). The influence of dietary fat on thiamine loss from the body. *J. Nutr. 56*, 495–500.

HORIE, A., KOHCHI, S. AND KURATSUNE, M. (1965). Carcinogenesis in the esophagus. II. Experimental production of esophageal cancer by administration of ethanolic solution of carcinogens. *Gann 56*, 429–441.

HOSZOWSKA-OWCZAREK, A., SAMOCHOWIEC, L. AND WÓJCICKI, J. (1967). Experimental investigations *in vitro* on the effect of chronic alcohol administration on iron absorption in the small intestine of rats. *Acta Physiol. Pol. 18*, 349–353.

HOUSSAY, B. A. (1955). *Human Physiology*. 2nd ed., McGraw-Hill, New York, London, Toronto. 1177 pp.

HUBACH, H. (1963). Veränderungen der Krampferregbarkeit unter Einwirkung von Medikamenten und während der Entziehung. *Fortschr. Psychiat. Neurol. 31*, 177–201.

HUDOLIN, V. (1967). Electroencephalographic characteristic in chronic alcoholism. *Alcoholism (Zagreb) 3*, Suppl. 1, 66 pp.

HUDOLIN, V. AND GUBAREV, N. (1967). The characteristics of the alpha rhythm in chronic alcoholics. *Brit. J. Addict. 62*, 55–60.

HULTQUIST, G. (1966). Microscopic appearance of the liver under physiological and pathological conditions. *Scand. J. Clin. Lab. Invest. 18*, Suppl. 92, 11–22.

IBER, F. L., CARULLI, N. AND KATER, R. M. H. (1969). The kinetics of alcohol removal from the blood of man: Comparison in recently drinking alcoholics and non-alcoholics. *Federation Proc. 28*, No. 2, 626.

IGERT, C., GESLAIN, P., GAULPIER, H., ERMINY, L. AND IGERT, B. (1965). Étude électro-clinique de 100 alcooliques chroniques traités en centre de rééducation. *Rev. Neurol. 113*, 336–339.

IHRIG, T. J., FRENCH, S. W. AND MORIN, R. J. (1969). Lipid composition of cellular membranes after ethanol feeding. *Federation Proc. 28*, No. 2, 626.

ISBELL, H., FRASER, H. F., WIKLER, A., BELLEVILLE, R. E. AND EISENMAN, A. J. (1955). An experimental study of the etiology of "rum fits" and delirium tremens. *Quart. J. Studies Alc. 16*, 1–33.

ISERI, O. A. AND GOTTLIEB, L. S. (1968). "Alcoholic hyalin" and enlarged mitochondria as distinct entities in alcoholic liver disease. *Fed. Proc. 27*, No. 2, 605.

ISERI, O. A., LIEBER, C. S. AND GOTTLIEB, L. S. (1966). The ultrastructure of fatty liver induced by prolonged ethanol ingestion. *Am. J. Pathol. 48*, 535–545.

JABBARI, M. AND LEEVY, C. M. (1967). Protein anabolism and fatty liver of the alcoholic. *Medicine 46*, 131–140.

JABBARI, M., BAKER, H. AND LEEVY, C. M. (1965). Factors influencing accumulation and removal of liver fat. *Am. J. Clin. Nutr. 16*, 382.

JANKELSON, O. M., VITALE, J. J. AND HEGSTED, D. M. (1959). Serum magnesium, cholesterol and lipoproteins in patients with atherosclerosis and alcoholism: some preliminary observations. *Am. J. Clin. Nutr. 7*, 23–29. (Abstr. *Quart. J. Studies Alc.* 1961, 22, 344–345.)

JANZEN, R. AND BALZEREIT, F. (1968). Polyneuropathie bei Alkoholabusus. *Der Internist 9*, 260–263.

JARROLD, T., WILL, J. J., DAVIES, A. R., DUFFEY, P. H. AND BRAMSCHREIBER, J. L. (1967). Bone marrow-erythroid morphology in alcoholic patients. *Am. J. Clin. Nutr. 20*, 716–722.

JELLINEK, E. M. (1955). Distribution of alcohol consumption and of calories derived from alcohol in various selected populations. *Proc. Nutr. Soc. 14*, 93–97.

JELLINEK, E. M. (1959). The withdrawal syndrome in alcoholism. *Can. Med. Assoc. J. 81*, 537–541.

JELLINEK, E. M. (1960). *The disease concept of alcoholism*. Hillhouse Press, New Haven, Connecticut. 246 pp.

JOHNSON, R. B. (1961). The alcohol withdrawal syndromes. *Quart. J. Studies Alc.*, Suppl. No. 1, 66–76.

JOKIVARTIO, E. AND OKKO, E. (1947). A study of the blood bilirubin, indican, and ketones, and of the vitamin B_1 content in the urine in chronic alcoholism, II. *Acta Psychiat. Neurol. Scand.*, Suppl. *47*, 208–218.

JOLLIFFE, N. (1942). Vitamin deficiencies in chronic alcoholism. In: *Alcohol addiction and chronic alcoholism*, E. M. JELLINEK, Ed., Yale University Press, New Haven. Pp. 173–240.

JOLLIFFE, N. AND JELLINEK, E. M. (1942). Cirrhosis of the liver. In: *Alcohol addiction and chronic alcoholism*, E. M. JELLINEK, Ed., Yale University Press, New Haven. Pp. 273–309.

JOLLIFFE, N., WORTIS, H. AND STEIN, M. H. (1942). Alcoholic encephalopathies and nutrition. In: *Alcohol addiction and chronic alcoholism*, E. M. JELLINEK, Ed., Yale University Press, New Haven. Pp. 241–272.

JONES, D. P. (1965). The importance of a high fat diet in the pathogenesis of alcoholic fatty liver. *Am. J. Clin. Nutr. 16*, 381–382.

JONES, D. P. AND GREENE, E. A. (1966). Influence of dietary fat on alcoholic fatty liver. *Am. J. Clin. Nutr. 18*, 350–357.

JURKO, M. F., CURRIER, R. D. AND FOSHEE, D. P. (1964). Peripheral nerve changes in chronic alcoholics: a study of conduction velocity in motor nerves. *J. Nervous Mental Disease 139*, 488–490.

JUUL-JENSEN, P. AND MAYER, R. F. (1966). Threshold stimulation for nerve conduction studies in man. *Arch. Neurol. (Chicago) 15*, 410–419.

KAHN, A. J. (1968). Effect of ethanol exposure during embryogenesis and the neonatal period on the incidence of hepatoma in C3H male mice. *Growth 32*, 311–316.

KALANT, H. (1969). Alcohol, pancreatic secretion, and pancreatitis. *Gastroenterology 56*, 380–384.

KALANT, H. AND CZAJA, C. (1962). The effect of repeated alcoholic intoxication on adrenal ascorbic acid and cholesterol in the rat. *Can. J. Biochem. 40*, 975–981.

KALANT, H. AND GROSE, W. (1967). Effects of ethanol and pentobarbital on release of acetylcholine from cerebral cortex slices. *J. Pharmacol. Exptl. Therap. 158*, 386–393.

KALANT, H. AND HAWKINS, R. D., Eds. (1969). *Experimental approaches to the study of drug dependence*. The Addiction Research Foundation, Toronto. 237 pp.

KALINOWSKY, L. (1942). Convulsions in non-epileptic patients on withdrawal of barbiturates, alcohol, and other drugs. *Arch. Neurol. Psychiat. 48*, 946–956.

KALISH, G. H. AND DI LUZIO, N. R. (1966). Peroxidation of liver lipids in the pathogenesis of the ethanol-induced fatty liver. *Science 152*, 1390–1392.

KAMIONKOWSKI, M. D. AND FLESHLER, B. (1965). The role of alcohol intake in esophageal carcinoma. *Am. J. Med. Sci. 249*, 696–700.

KANEKO, M., RAPPAPORT, A. M. AND LUCAS, C. C. (1965). The effects of continuous infusion of ethanol into the portal system of the rat. *Can. J. Physiol. Pharmacol. 43*, 421–429.

KARLSSON, L., HIRVONEN, J., SALORINNE, Y. AND VIRTANEN, K. (1967). Functional status of the hypothalamo-hypophyseal system after two weeks' administration of adrenalin and insulin in rats under continuous influence of ethanol. *Ann. Med. Exptl. Biol. Fenniae 45*, 72–75.

KARPMAN, B. (1957). *The Hangover*. Charles C. Thomas, Springfield, Ill. 531 pp.

KARVINEN, E., MIETTINEN, M. AND AHLMAN, K. (1962). Physical performance during hangover. *Quart. J. Studies Alc. 23*, 208–215.

KELLER, A. Z. (1967). Cirrhosis of the liver, alcoholism and heavy smoking associated with cancer of the mouth and pharynx. *Cancer, N.Y. 20*, 1015–1022. (Abstr. *Quart. J. Studies Alc.* 1968, *29*, 241.)

KENNARD, M. A., BUEDING, E. AND WORTIS, S. B. (1945). Some biochemical and electroencephalographic changes in delirium tremens. *Quart. J. Studies Alc. 6*, 4–14.

KENNEDY, A. AND FISH, F. J. (1959). Alcoholism, alcoholic addiction, and drug addiction. *Recent Progr. Psych.*, Vol. 3. G. W. T. H. FLEMING AND A. WALK, Eds., Churchill, London. Pp. 277–302.

KETCHAM, A. S., WEXLER, H. AND MANTEL, N. (1963). Effects of alcohol in mouse neoplasia. *Cancer Res. 23*, 667–670. (Abstr. *Quart. J. Studies Alc.* 1965, *26*, 134.)

KHANNA, J. M., KALANT, H. AND BUSTOS, G. (1967). Effects of chronic intake of ethanol on rate of ethanol metabolism. II. Influence of sex and of schedule of ethanol administration. *Can. J. Physiol. Pharmacol. 45*, 777–785.

KIESSLING, K.-H. (1968). Effect of alcohol on rat liver VI: A possible correlation between α-glycerophosphate oxidase activity and mitochondrial size in male and female rats fed alcohol. *Acta Pharmacol. Toxicol. 26*, 245–252.

KIESSLING, K.-H. AND LUNDQUIST, C.-G. (1966). The lipid composition of liver mitochondria from rats after prolonged ethanol treatment. *Scand. J. Clin. Lab. Invest. 18*, Suppl. 92, 80–81.

KIESSLING, K.-H. AND PILSTRÖM, L. (1966a). Effect of ethanol on rat liver. I. Enzymatic and histological studies of liver mitochondria. *Quart. J. Studies Alc. 27*, 189–200.

KIESSLING, K.-H. AND PILSTRÖM, L. (1966b). Effect of ethanol on rat liver. II. Number, size and appearance of mitochondria. *Acta Pharmacol. Toxicol. 24*, 103–111.

KIESSLING, K.-H. AND PILSTRÖM, L. (1967). Effect of ethanol on rat liver. 4. The influence of vitamins, electrolytes and amino acids on the structure and function of mitochondria from rats receiving ethanol. *Brit. J. Nutr. 21*, 547–556.

KIESSLING, K.-H. AND TILANDER, K. (1961). Biochemical changes in rat tissues after prolonged alcohol consumption. *Quart. J. Studies Alc. 22*, 535–543.

KIESSLING, K.-H. AND TILANDER, K. (1963). The effect of prolonged alcohol treatment on the respiration of liver and brain mitochondria from male and female rats. *Exptl. Cell Res. 30*, 476–480.

KIESSLING, K.-H. AND TOBÉ, U. (1964). Degeneration of liver mitochondria in rats after prolonged alcohol consumption. *Exptl. Cell Res. 33*, 350–354.

KIESSLING, K.-H., DEGERMAN, G. AND SKOGLUND, M. (1963). Influence of sex hormones upon disturbances caused by ethanol on mitochondrial oxidations in rats. *Acta Chem. Scand. 17*, 2513–2517.

KIESSLING, K.-H., LINDGREN, L., STRANDBERG, B. AND TOBÉ, U. (1964). Electron microscopic study of liver mitochondria from human alcoholics. *Acta Med. Scand. 176*, 595–598.

KIESSLING, K.-H., PILSTRÖM, L., STRANDBERG, B. AND LINDGREN, L. (1965). Ethanol and the human liver. Correlation between mitochondrial size and degree of ethanol abuse. *Acta Med. Scand. 178*, 533–535.

KIKUCHI, T. AND KAKO, K. J. (1969). The effect of ethanol on fatty acid esterification in the rabbit heart. *Federation Proc. 28*, No. 2, 451.

KINARD, F. W. AND HAY, M. G. (1960). Effect of ethanol administration on brain and liver enzyme activities. *Am. J. Physiol. 198*, 657–658.

KISSIN, B., SCHENKER, V. AND SCHENKER, A. (1959). The acute effects of ethyl alcohol and chlorpromazine on certain physiological functions in alcoholics. *Quart. J. Studies Alc. 20*, 480–492.

KISSIN, B., SCHENKER, V. AND SCHENKER, A. C. (1960). The acute effect of ethanol ingestion on plasma and urinary 17-hydroxycorticoids in alcoholic subjects. *Am. J. Med. Sci. 239*, 690–705.

KISSIN, B., SCHENKER, V. J. AND SCHENKER, A. C. (1964). Hyperdiuresis after ethanol in chronic alcoholics. *Am. J. Med. Sci. 248*, 660–669.

KLATSKIN, G. (1959a). Effect of alcohol on the liver. *J. Am. Med. Assoc. 170*, 1671–1676.

KLATSKIN, G. (1959b). Newer concepts of cirrhosis. *Arch. Internal Med. 104*, 899–902.

KLATSKIN, G. (1961a). Alcohol and its relation to liver damage. *Gastroenterology 41*, 443–451.

KLATSKIN, G. (1961b). Experimental studies on the role of alcohol in the pathogenesis of cirrhosis. *Am. J. Clin. Nutr. 9*, 439–442.

KLATSKIN, G. AND KREHL, W. A. (1954). The effect of alcohol on the choline requirement. II. Incidence of renal necrosis in weanling rats following short term ingestion of alcohol. *J. Exptl. Med. 100*, 615–627.

KLATSKIN, G., GEWIN, H. M. AND KREHL, W. A. (1951). Effects of prolonged alcohol ingestion on the liver of the rat under conditions of controlled adequate dietary intake. *Yale J. Biol. Med. 23*, 317–331.

KLATSKIN, G., KREHL, W. A. AND CONN, H. O. (1954). The effect of alcohol on the choline requirement. I. Changes in the rat's liver following prolonged ingestion of alcohol. *J. Exptl. Med. 100*, 605–614.

KLEPSER, R. G. AND NUNGESTER, W. J. (1939). Effect of alcohol upon chemotactic response of leucocytes. *J. Infect. Diseases 65*, 196–199.

KLINGMAN, W. O., SUTER, C., GREEN, R. AND ROBINSON, I. (1955). The role of alcoholism and magnesium deficiency in convulsions. *Trans. Am. Neurol. Assoc. 80*, 162–165.

KLINKERFUSS, G., BLEISCH, V., DIOSO, M. M. AND PERKOFF, G. T. (1967). A spectrum of myopathy associated with alcoholism. II. Light and electron microscopic observations. *Ann. Internal Med. 67*, 493–510.

KLION, F. M. AND SCHAFFNER, F. (1968). Ultrastructural studies in alcoholic liver disease. *Digestion 1*, 2–14.

KLIPSTEIN, F. A. AND LINDENBAUM, J. (1965). Folate deficiency in chronic liver disease. *Blood 25*, 443–456. (Abstr. *Quart. J. Studies Alc.* 1966, *27*, 769.)

KNOTT, D. H. AND BEARD, J. D. (1967). The effect of chronic ethanol administration on the response of the dog to repeated acute hemorrhage. *Am. J. Med. Sci. 254*, 178–188.

KOCH, O. R. AND PORTA, E. A. (1967). Saturated versus unsaturated fat in experimental chronic alcoholism. *Federation Proc. 26*, No. 2, 693.

KOCH, O. R. AND PORTA, E. A. (1968). A solid "super diet" for the prevention of hepatic fatty changes in rats consuming alcohol. *Fed. Proc. 27*, No. 2, 556 (1968).

KOCH, O. R., GOMEZ-DUMM, C. L. A., PORTA, E. A. AND HARTROFT, W. S. (1967). Effects of dietary protein on the liver in experimental chronic alcoholism. *Gastroenterology 52*, 319.

KOCH, O. R., PORTA, E. A. AND HARTROFT, W. S. (1968). A new experimental approach in the study of chronic alcoholism. III. Role of alcohol *versus* sucrose or fat-derived calories in hepatic damage. *Lab. Invest. 18*, 379–386.

KOKATA, S. AND FURUTOKU, S. (1956). Chronic alcohol intoxication. I. The influence of alcohol on growth. *Ionago Igaku Zasshi 7*, 484–492.

KONTTINEN, K., OURA, E. AND SUOMALAINEN, H. (1967a). Influence of short-term alcohol consumption on the excretion of some components of the vitamin-B group in the urine of rats. *Ann. Med. Exptl. Biol. Fenniae 45*, 63–67.

KONTTINEN, K., OURA, E. AND SUOMALAINEN, H. (1967b). Effect of long-continued alcohol consumption on the thiamine content of rat tissues. *Ann. Med. Exptl. Biol. Fenniae 45*, 68–71.

KRITCHEVSKY, D. AND MOYER, A. W. (1960). Effect of alcohol on experimental atherosclerosis in rabbits. *Naturwissenschaften 47*, 138.

KULPE, W. AND MALLACH, H. J. (1961). Zur Tauglichkeit der Alkoholbelastung als Leberfunktionsprüfung. *Z. Klin. Med. 156*, 432–444.

KULPE, W. AND MALLACH, H. J. (1962). Das Verhalten des Blutzuckerspiegels bei Lebercirrhosen unter Alkoholwirkung. *Z. Klin. Med. 157*, 55–60. (Abstr. *Rev. Alcoolisme* 1965, *11*, 225.)

LAASONEN, L. AND PALKAMA, A. (1967). Effect of alcohol on histochemically demonstrable liver and muscle phosphorylase activity in rats. *Ann. Med. Exptl. Biol. Fenniae 45*, 307–308.

LAFAIR, J. S. AND MYERSON, R. M. (1968). Alcoholic myopathy. *Arch. Int. Med. 122*, 417–422.

LAMBERT, R., BOURRAT, C., DESCOS, F. AND PASQUIER, J. (1965). Influence des boissons alcoolisées sur le taux de la polydipsie chez le rat porteur d'un diabète insipide expérimental. *Pathol. Biol. Semaine Hop. Paris 13*, 374–384. (Abstr. *Quart. J. Studies Alc.* 1967, *28*, 156.)

LANE, B. P. AND LIEBER, C. S. (1966). Ultrastructural alterations in human hepatocytes following ingestion of ethanol with adequate diets. *Am. J. Pathol. 49*, 593–603.

LAPRESLE, J. (1958). Les encephalopathies carentielles des alcooliques. *Pathol. Biol. Semaine Hop. Paris 34*, 1629–1637.

LARSH, J. E. (1945). Effect of alcohol on natural resistance to the dwarf tapeworm in mice. *J. Parasitol. 31*, 291–300. (Class. Abstr. No. 4295.)

LARSH, J. E. (1946a). A comparison of the percentage development of a mouse strain of *Hymenolepis* in alcoholic and non-alcoholic rats and mice. *J. Parasitol. 32*, 61–63. (Class. Abstr. No. 4401.)

LARSH, J. E. (1946b). The effect of alcohol on the development of acquired immunity to *Hymenolepis* in mice. *J. Parasitol. 32*, 72–78. (Class. Abstr. No. 4402.)

LARSH, J. E. (1947). The role of reduced food intake in alcoholic debilitation of mice infected with *Hymenolepis*. *J. Parasitol. 33*, 339–344. (Class. Abstr. No. 4799.)

LARSH, J. E. AND KENT, D. E. (1949). The effect of alcohol on natural and acquired immunity of mice to infection with *Trichinella spiralis*. *J. Parasitol. 35*, 45–53.

LAURENZI, G. A., GUARNERI, J. J., ENDRIGA, R. B. AND CAREY, J. P. (1963). Clearance of bacteria by the lower respiratory tract. *Science 142*, 1572–1573.

LEAKE, C. D. AND SILVERMAN, M. (1966). *Alcoholic beverages in clinical medicine*. The World Publ. Co., Cleveland. 160 pp.

LEBLANC, A. E., KALANT, H., GIBBINS, R. J. AND BERMAN, N. D. (1969). Acquisition and loss of tolerance to ethanol by the rat. *J. Pharmacol. Exptl. Therap. 168*, 244–250.

LE BRETON, E. AND TRÉMOLIÈRES, J. (1955). Part de l'alcool dans la dépence calorique. *Proc. Nutr. Soc. 14*, 97–102.

LECOQ, R. (1948). Modification des perturbations humorales et des chronaxies nerveuses sous l'effet de la cure de désintoxication alcoolique. *Compt. Rend. Soc. Biol. Paris 142*, 893–894.

LECOQ, R. (1955). La carance d'adénine dans les manifestations graves de l'alcoolisme chronique. *Compt. Rend. 241*, 825–826.

LECOQ, R. (1957). Les perturbations métaboliques de la "maladie alcoolique" et leurs rapports avec l'excitabilité neuro-musculaire et certaines manifestations d'hypertension artérielle, de glycosurie et d'albuminurie. *Rev. Alcoolisme 4*, 131–141.

LEDERMANN, S. (1952). Influence de la consommation de vins et d'alcools sur les cancers, la tuberculeuse pulmonaire et sur d'autres maladies. *Semaine Médicale 28*, 221–235.

LEE, F. I. (1965). Immunoglobulins in viral hepatitis and active alcoholic liver-disease. *Lancet 2*, 1043–1046.

LEE, F. I. (1966). Cirrhosis and hepatoma in alcoholics. *Gut 7*, 77–85.

LEE, M. AND LUCIA, S. P. (1965). Effect of ethanol on the mobilization of vitamin A in the dog and in the rat. *Quart. J. Studies Alc. 26*, 1–9.

LEE, P. K., CHO, M. H. AND DOBKIN, A. B. (1964). Effects of alcoholism, morphinism, and barbiturate resistance on induction and maintenance of general anaesthesia. *Can. Anaesth. Soc. J. 11*, 354–381.

LEEVY, C. M. (1967). Clinical diagnosis, evaluation and treatment of liver disease in alcoholics. *Federation Proc. 26*, No. 5, 1474–1481.

LEEVY, C. M. (1968). Cirrhosis in alcoholics. *Med. Clin. North Am. 52*, 1445–1455.

LEEVY, C. M. AND BAKER, H. (1963). Metabolic and nutritional effects of alcoholism. *Arch. Environ. Health 7*, 453–459.

LEEVY, C. M. AND BAKER, H. (1968). Vitamins and alcoholism: Introduction. *Am. J. Clin. Nutr. 21*, 1325–1328.

LEEVY, C. M. AND TENHOVE, W. (1967). Pathogenesis and sequelae of liver disease in alcoholic man. In: *Biochemical factors in alcoholism*, R. P. MAICKEL, Ed., Pergamon Press, Oxford-London etc. Pp. 151–165.

LEEVY, C. M., TENHOVE, W. AND HOWARD, M. (1964). Mesenchymal cell proliferation in liver disease of the alcoholic. *J. Am. Med. Assoc. 187*, 598–600.

LEEVY, C. M., BAKER, E., TENHOVE, W., FRANK, O. AND CHERRICK, G. R. (1965). B-complex vitamins in malnourished alcoholics. *Am. J. Clin. Nutr. 16*, 339–346.

LEHMANN, H. (1955). Delirium tremens og andre akutte alkoholpsykoser. *Tidskr. for den Norske Laegeforen. 75*, 796–798.

LELBACH, W. K. (1966a). Leberschäden bei chronischem Alkoholismus. I. Klinische Ergebnisse. *Acta Hepato-Splenol. 13*, 321–334.

LELBACH, W. K. (1966b). Leberschäden bei chronischem Alkoholismus. II. Klinisch-chemische Ergebnisse. *Acta Hepato-Splenol. 13*, 334–349.

LELBACH, W. K. (1967). Leberschäden bei chronischem Alkoholismus. III. Bioptisch-histologische Ergebnisse. *Acta Hepato-Splenol. 14*, 9–39.

LELOIR, L. F. AND MUÑOZ, J. M. (1938). Ethyl alcohol metabolism in animal tissues. *Biochem. J. 31*, 299–307.

LESTER, D. (1960). A biological approach to the etiology of alcoholism. *Quart. J. Studies Alc. 21*, 701–703.

LESTER, D. (1964). The acetylation of isoniazid in alcoholics. *Quart. J. Studies Alc. 25*, 541–543.

LESTER, D., BUCCINO, R. AND BIZZOCCO, D. (1960). The vitamin C status of alcoholics. *J. Nutr. 70*, 278–282. (Abstr. *Quart. J. Studies Alc.* 1961, *22*, 151.)

LEUNG, K. C., STONE, G. S. AND HINE, C. H. (1966). Some effects of alcohol and reduced temperature on the performance of rats. *Proc. Western Pharmacol. Soc. 9*, 60–61.

LEVEDAHL, B. H. AND WILSON, B. W. (1965). Succinate utilization by Euglena: comparison of growth on low levels of succinate, acetate and alcohol. *Exptl. Cell Res. 39*, 242–248.

LEVINE, H. D., PIEMME, T. E. AND AMER, K. E. (1965). A brisk electrocardiogram observed in chronic alcoholics. *Am. Heart J. 69*, 140–142. (Abstr. *Quart. J. Studies Alc.* 1965, *26*, 723.)

LÉVY, J. (1935a). Contribution à l'étude de l'accoutumance expérimentale aux poisons. I. Alcoolisme expérimental. *Bull. Soc. Chim. Biol. 17*, 13–26.

LÉVY, J. (1935b). Contribution à l'étude de l'accoutumance expérimentale aux poisons. II. Alcoolisme expérimental. Fixation d'alcool sur les tissus de l'organisme accoutumé à cette substance. *Bull. Soc. Chim. Biol. 17*, 27–46.

LÉVY, J. (1935c). Contribution à l'étude de l'accoutumance expérimentale aux poisons. III. Alcoolisme expérimental. L'accoutumance à l'alcool peut-elle être considérée comme une consequence de hyposensibilité cellulaire? *Bull. Soc. Chim. Biol. 17*, 47–59.

LICHT, W. (1963). Die Eiweisszusammensetzung der gesunden und cirrhotischen menschlichen Leber. Elektrophoretische und immunelektrophoretische Untersuchungen. *Hoppe-Seyler's Z. Physiol. Chem. 334*, 275–278.

LIEBER, C. S. (1967a). Alcoholic fatty liver, hyperlipemia and hyperuricemia. In: *Biochemical factors in alcoholism*, R. P. MAICKEL, Ed., Pergamon Press, Oxford-London etc. Pp. 167–183.

LIEBER, C. S. (1967b). Chronic alcoholic hepatic injury in experimental animals and man: biochemical pathways and nutritional factors. *Federation Proc. 26*, No. 5, 1443–1448.

LIEBER, C. S. AND DECARLI, L. M. (1966). Study of agents for the prevention of the fatty liver produced by prolonged alcohol intake. *Gastroenterology 50*, 316–322.

LIEBER, C. S. AND DECARLI, L. M. (1968). Ethanol oxidation by hepatic microsomes: Adaptive increase after ethanol feeding. *Science 162*, 917–918.

LIEBER, C. S. AND RUBIN, E. (1968). Alcoholic fatty liver in man on a high protein and low fat diet. *Am. J. Med. 44*, 200–206.

LIEBER, C. S. AND RUBIN, E. (1969). Alcoholic fatty liver. *New Engl. J. Med. 280*, 705–708.

LIEBER, C. S. AND SPRITZ, N. (1965). Ethanol-induced fatty liver on fat-free and fat-containing diets: role of dietary, adipose, and endogenously synthesized fatty acids. *J. Clin. Invest. 44*, 1069–1070.

LIEBER, C. S. AND SPRITZ, N. (1966). Effects of prolonged ethanol intake in man: role of dietary, adipose, and endogenously synthesized fatty acids in the pathogenesis of the alcoholic fatty liver. *J. Clin. Invest. 45*, 1400–1411.

LIEBER, C. S., JONES, D. P., MENDELSON, J. AND DECARLI, L. M. (1963). Fatty liver, hyperlipemia and hyperuricemia produced by prolonged alcohol consumption, despite adequate dietary intake. *Trans. Assoc. Am. Physicians 76*, 289–300.

LIEBER, C. S., JONES, D. P. AND DECARLI, L. M. (1965). Effects of prolonged ethanol intake: production of fatty liver despite adequate diets. *J. Clin. Invest. 44*, 1009–1021.

LIEBER, C. S., SPRITZ, N. AND DECARLI, L. M. (1966a). Role of dietary, adipose, and endogenously synthesized fatty acids in the pathogenesis of the alcoholic fatty liver. *J. Clin. Invest. 45*, 51–62.

LIEBER, C. S., SPRITZ, N. AND DECARLI, L. M. (1966b). Hepatic effects of ethanol given with deficient diets. *Am. J. Clin. Nutr. 18*, 309.

LIEBER, C. S., LEFÈVRE, A., SPRITZ, N., FEINMAN, L. AND DECARLI, L. M. (1967). Difference in hepatic metabolism of long- and medium-chain fatty acids: the role of fatty acid chain length in the production of the alcoholic fatty liver. *J. Clin. Invest. 46*, 1451–1460.

LIEBERMAN, A. H. AND CHILDS, A. W. (1967). Effect of ethanol on hepatic metabolism of sulfobromophthalein. *Am. J. Physiol. 213*, 353–357.

LIEBERMAN, F. L. (1963). The effect of liver disease on the rate of ethanol metabolism in man. *Gastroenterology 44*, 261–266. (Abstr. *Quart. J. Studies Alc.* 1965, *26*, 337.)

LINDENBAUM, J. AND HARGROVE, B. L. (1968). Thrombocytopenia in alcoholism. *Ann. Intern. Med. 68*, 526–532 (1968).

LINT, J. DE (1968). Alcohol use in Canadian society. *Addictions 15*, 14–28.

LINT, J. DE AND BRONETTO, J. (1966). A brief note on distilled spirits consumption and liver cirrhosis mortality. *Alkoholpolitik 29*, 96.

LINT, J. DE AND SCHMIDT, W. (1965). Maximum individual alcohol consumption. *Quart. J. Studies Alc. 26*, 670–673.

LITTLE, S. C. AND MCAVOY, M. (1952). Electroencephalographic studies in alcoholism. *Quart. J. Studies Alc. 13*, 9–15.

LOLLI, G. (1946). The hang-over in relation to the theory and treatment of alcohol addiction. *Quart. J. Studies Alc. 7*, 193–213.

LOWRY, J. V., ASHBURN, L. L., DAFT, F. S. AND SEBRELL, W. H. (1942a). Effect of alcohol in experimental liver cirrhosis. *Quart. J. Studies Alc. 3*, 168–175.

LOWRY, J. V., SEBRELL, W. H., DAFT, F. S. AND ASHBURN, L. L. (1942b). Polyneuropathy in thiamine deficient rats delayed by alcohol or whisky. *J. Nutr. 24*, 73–83. (Abstr. *Quart. J. Studies Alc.* 1942, *3*, 677.)

LOWY, R. AND GRIFFATON, G. (1965). Métabolisme et toxicité cellulaires de l'alcool éthylique. *Biol. Méd. 54*, 279–302.

LUCAS, C. C., RIDOUT, J. H. AND LUMCHICK, G. L. (1968). Dietary proteins and chronic intoxication with ethanol. *Can. J. Physiol. Pharmacol. 46*, 475–485.

LUKASIK, S., WRABEC, K., HRYNKIEWICZ, L. AND SZYDLIK, H. (1967a). An attempt to evaluate the effect of acute ethanol intoxication on the liver function on the basis of some enzyme tests. *Alcoholism (Zagreb) 3*, 130–134.

LUKASIK, S., WRABEC, K., HRYNKIEWICZ, L. AND SZYDLIK, H. (1967b). Evaluation of the liver function in chronic alcoholism on the basis of some enzyme tests. *Alcoholism (Zagreb)* 3, 153–157.

LUNDGREN, N. (1947). Alkohol och tungt kroppsarbete. Konditionsförändringar efter vanligt förekommande spritbruk. *Tirfing 41*, 9–13.

LUNDQUIST, C.-G., KIESSLING, K.-H. AND PILSTRÖM, L. (1966). Effect of ethanol on rat liver. III. Lipid composition of liver mitochondria from rats after prolonged alcohol consumption. *Acta Chem. Scand. 20*, 2751–2754.

LUNDQUIST, F., TYGSTRUP, N., WINKLER, K., MELLEMGAARD, K. AND MUNCK-PETERSEN, S. (1962). Ethanol metabolism and production of free acetate in the human liver. *J. Clin. Invest. 41*, 955–961.

LUNDQUIST, G. (1959). Delirium tremens. *Acta Psychiat. Scand. 36*, 443–466.

LUNDQUIST, G., NETTELBLADT, E. AND REICHARD, H. (1959). Delirium tremens och akut leverskada. (Delirium tremens and acute liver damage.) *Nord. Med. 61*, 433–436.

LUNDQUIST, G. A. R. (1965). Glucose tolerance in alcoholism. *Brit. J. Addict. 61*, 51–55.

LUSHBAUGH, C. C. (1943). The effect of alcoholic intoxication upon acquired resistance to pneumococcal infection in rabbits. *J. Immunol. 46*, 151–159. (Abstr. *Quart. J. Studies Alc.* 1943, *4*, 110.)

LYNCH, M. J. G. AND HILLS, P. (1960). Brain lesions in chronic alcoholism. *Arch. Pathol. 69*, 342–353.

MACDONALD, R. A. (1965). Hemochromatosis and cirrhosis in different geographic areas. *Am. J. Med. Sci. 249*, 36–46.

MACDONALD, R. A. AND BAUMSLAG, N. (1964). Iron in alcoholic beverages. Possible significance for hemochromatosis. *Am. J. Med. Sci. 247*, 649–654.

MACDOWELL, E. C. (1922). Alcoholism and the growth of white rats. *Genetics 7*, 427–445.

MAINES, J. E., III AND ALDINGER, E. A. (1967). Myocardial depression accompanying chronic consumption of alcohol. *Am. Heart J. 73*, 55–63.

MAJCHROWICZ, E., LIPTON, M. A., MEEK, J. L. AND HALL, L. (1968). Effects of chronic alcohol consumption on the clearance of acutely administered ethanol and acetaldehyde from blood in rats. *Quart. J. Studies Alc. 29*, 553–557.

MALLORY, F. B. (1911). Cirrhosis of the liver. Five different types of lesions from which it may arise. *Johns Hopkins Hosp. Bull. 22*, 69–75.

MALLOV, S. (1955). Effect of chronic ethanol intoxication on liver lipid content of rats. *Proc. Soc. Exptl. Biol., N.Y. 88*, 246–249.

MALLOV, S. (1958). Effect of sex hormones on ethanol induced fatty infiltration of liver in rats. *Proc. Soc. Exptl. Biol., N.Y. 97*, 226–229.

MALLOV, S. AND CERRA, F. (1967). Effect of ethanol intoxication and catecholamines on cardiac lipoprotein lipase activity in rats. *J. Pharmacol. Exptl. Therap. 156*, 426–444.

MALMÉJAC, J. AND PLANE, P. (1956). Étude expérimentale sur l'influence nerveuse générale de faibles doses d'alcool. *Bull. Acad. Natl. Méd. 140*, 38–42.

MANN, N. M. (1952). Hypoadrenalism and the alcoholic. *Quart. J. Studies Alc. 13*, 201–203.

MARCINIAK, M., GUDBJARNASON, S. AND BRUCE, T. A. (1968). The effect of chronic alcohol administration on enzyme profile and glyceride content of heart muscle, brain and liver. *Proc. Soc. Exptl. Biol. Med. 128*, 1021–1025.

MARCONI, J., FINK, K. AND MOYA, L. (1967). Experimental study on alcoholics with an "Inability to stop". *Brit. J. Psychiat. 113*, 543–545.

MARGRAF, H. W., MOYER, C. A., ASHFORD, L. E. AND LAVALLE, L. W. (1967). Adrenocortical function in alcoholics. *J. Surg. Res. 7*, 55–62.

MARINACCI, A. A. (1956). Electroencephalography in alcoholism. In: *Alcoholism.* G. N. THOMPSON, Ed., Charles C. Thomas, Springfield, Ill. Pp. 484–536.

MARINACCI, A. A. (1961). Alcoholic neuropathy: its characteristic picture and variants viewed in the light of electromyography. *Bull. Los Angeles Neurol. Soc. 26*, 132–142. (Abstr. *Quart. J. Studies Alc.* 1964, *25*, 181–182.)

MARTIN, E. A. (1965). Alcoholic cerebellar degeneration; a report of 3 cases. *J. Irish Med. Assoc. 56*, 172–175.

MARTIN, G. J. (1965). A concept of the etiology of alcoholism. *Exptl. Med. Surg. 23*, 315–319.

MARTIN, H. E. AND BAUER, F. K. (1962). Magnesium 28 studies in the cirrhotic and alcoholic. *Proc. Roy. Soc. Med. 55*, 912–914.

MARTIN, H. E., McCUSKEY, C. AND TUPIKOVA, N. (1959). Electrolyte disturbance in acute alcoholism. *Am. J. Clin. Nutr. 7*, 191–196.

MARTIN, R. (1956). Étude de l'excitabilité neuro-musculaire chez l'alcoolique chronique; ses variations en fonction de la fatigue. *Arch. Maladies Profess. Med. Trav. Securité Sociale 17*, 473–477.

MARTINI, G. A. AND DÖLLE, W. (1965a). Krankheitsbilder bei Leberschädigung durch Alkohol. *Deut. Med. Wochschr. 90*, 793–799.

MARTINI, G. A. AND DÖLLE, W. (1965b). Clinical features associated with liver damage due to alcohol. *Ger. Med. Monthly 10*, 483–489.

MAWDSLEY, C. AND MAYER, R. F. (1965). Nerve conduction in alcoholic polyneuropathy. *Brain 88*, 335–356.

MAYFIELD, D. G. (1968a). Psychopharmacology of alcohol. I. Affective change with intoxication, drinking behavior and affective state. *J. Nerv. Mental Dis. 146*, 314–321.

MAYFIELD, D. G. (1968b). Psychopharmacology of alcohol. II. Affective tolerance in alcohol intoxication. *J. Nerv. Mental Dis. 146*, 322–327.

MAYFIELD, D. AND ALLEN, D. (1967). Alcohol and affect: A psychopharmacological study. *Am. J. Psychiat. 123*, 1346–1351.

MAYNERT, E. W. AND KLINGMAN, G. I. (1960). Acute tolerance to intravenous anesthetics in dogs. *J. Pharmacol. 128*, 192–200.

MAZZUCCHELLI, B. AND GUARNERI, A. (1965). L'assorbimento e l'eliminazione dell'alcool etilico nei soggetti normali e negli alcoolisti cronici senza danno somatici. *Minerva Medicolegale 84*, 5–14.

McCLEARN, G. E., BENNETT, E. L., HEBERT, M., KAKIHANA, R. AND SCHLESINGER, K. (1964). Alcohol dehydrogenase activity and previous ethanol consumption in mice. *Nature 203*, 793–794.

McCOLLISTER, R. J., FLINK, E. B. AND LEWIS, M. D. (1963). Urinary excretion of magnesium in man following ingestion of ethanol. *Am. J. Clin. Nutr. 12*, 415–420.

McGUIRE, J. (1965). Coupled aldehyde dehydrogenase and catalase in mitochondrial extracts. *Arch. Biochem. Biophys. 110*, 104–108.

McGUIRE, M. T., STEIN, S. AND MENDELSON, J. H. (1966). Comparative psychosocial studies of alcoholic and nonalcoholic subjects undergoing experimentally induced ethanol intoxication. *Psychosomat. Med. 28*, 13–26.

McLAUGHLIN, J., MARLIAC, J.-P., VERRETT, M. J., MUTCHLER, M. K. AND FITZHUGH, O. G. (1964). Toxicity of fourteen volatile chemicals as measured by the chick embryo method. *Am. Ind. Hyg. Assoc. 25*, 282–284.

McNAMEE, H. B., MELLO, N. K. AND MENDELSON, J. H. (1968). Experimental analysis of drinking patterns of alcoholics: Concurrent psychiatric observations. *Am. J. Psychiat. 124*, 1063–1069.

McQUARRIE, D. G. AND FINGL, E. (1958). Effects of single doses and chronic administration of ethanol on experimental seizures in mice. *J. Pharmacol. Exptl. Therap. 124*, 264–271.

MEEK, J. L., MAJCHROWICZ, E. AND LIPTON, M. A. (1967). Rates of $C^{14}O_2$ production from labeled ethanol, acetate and glucose in alcohol drinking and non-drinking rats. *Proc. Soc. Exptl. Biol. Med. 126*, 379–383.

MELLANBY, E. (1919). Alcohol: its absorption into and disappearance from the blood under different conditions. *National Research Council, Special Report Series*, No. 31, London. 48 pp.

MELLO, N. K. (1968). Some aspects of the behavioral pharmacology of alcohol. In: *Psychopharmacology: A review of progress 1957–1967*, D. H. EFRON, Ed., Public Health Service Publication No. 1836, Washington D.C. Pp. 787–809.

MENAKER, T. (1967). Anxiety about drinking in alcoholics. *J. Abn. Psychol. 72*, 43–49.

MENDELSON, J. H., Spec. Ed. (1964). Experimentally induced chronic intoxication and withdrawal in alcoholics. *Quart. J. Studies Alc.*, Suppl. No. 2, 129 pp.

MENDELSON, J. H. (1968). Ethanol-1-C^{14} metabolism in alcoholics and nonalcoholics. *Science 159*, 319–320.

MENDELSON, J. H. AND LA DOU, J. (1964). Experimentally induced chronic intoxication and withdrawal in alcoholics. Pt. 2. Psychophysiological findings. *Quart. J. Studies Alc.*, Suppl. No. 2, 14–39.

MENDELSON, J. H. AND MELLO, N. K. (1964). Metabolism of C-14 alcohol and behavioral adaptation of alcoholics during experimentally induced intoxication. *Trans. Am. Neurol. Assoc. 89*, 133–135.

MENDELSON, J. H. AND STEIN, S. (1966). Serum cortisol levels in alcoholic and nonalcoholic subjects during experimentally induced ethanol intoxication. *Psychosomat. Med. 28*, 616–626.

MENDELSON, J., WEXLER, D., KUBZANSKY, P., LEIDERMAN, P. H. AND SOLOMON, P. (1959). Serum magnesium in delirium tremens and alcoholic hallucinosis. *J. Nervous Mental Disease 128*, 352–357.

MENDELSON, J. H., LA DOU, J. AND SOLOMON, P. (1964). Experimentally induced chronic intoxication and withdrawal in alcoholics. Pt. 3. Psychiatric findings. *Quart. J. Studies Alc.*, Suppl. No. 2, 40–52.

MENDELSON, J. H., BARNES, B., MAYMAN, C. AND VICTOR, M. (1965a). The determination of exchangeable magnesium in alcoholic patients. *Metabolism 14*, 88–98.

MENDELSON, J. H., MELLO, N. K., CORBETT, C. AND BALLARD, R. (1965b). Puromycin inhibition of ethanol ingestion and liver alcohol dehydrogenase activity in the rat. *J. Psychiat. Res. 3*, 133–143.

MENDELSON, J. H., STEIN, S. AND MELLO, N. K. (1965c). Effects of experimentally induced intoxication on metabolism of ethanol-1-C^{14} in alcoholic subjects. *Metabolism 14*, 1255–1266.

MENDELSON, J. H., STEIN, S. AND McGUIRE, M. T. (1966). Comparative psychophysiological studies of alcoholic and nonalcoholic subjects undergoing experimentally induced ethanol intoxication. *Psychosomat. Med. 28*, 1–12.

MERRY, J. (1966). The "Loss of control" myth. *Lancet 1*, 1257–1258.

MERZEY, E., CHERRICK, G. R. AND HOLT, P. R. (1968). Serum alcohol dehydrogenase, an indicator of intrahepatic cholestasis. *New Engl. J. Med. 279*, 241–248.

MIKATA, A., DIMAKULANGAN, A. A. AND HARTROFT, W. S. (1963). Metabolism of ethanol in rats with cirrhosis. *Gastroenterology 44*, 159–167.

MILLER, H. AND ABELMANN, W. H. (1967). Effects of dietary ethanol upon experimental trypanosomal *(T. cruzi)* myocarditis. *Proc. Soc. Exptl. Biol. Med. 126*, 193–198.

MINAKER, E. AND PORTA, E. A. (1967). Tinctorial affinities of experimentally produced Mallory bodies in epon-embedded hepatic tissues of rats. *J. Microscopie 6*, 41–52.

MINER, R. W., Ed. (1954). Nutritional factors and liver diseases. *Ann. N.Y. Acad. Sci. 57*, 915–962.

MIRONE, L. (1952). The effect of ethyl alcohol on growth, fecundity and voluntary consumption of alcohol by mice. *Quart. J. Studies Alc. 13*, 365–369.

MIRONE, L. (1965a). Effect of prolonged ethanol intake on body weight, liver weight and liver nitrogen, glycogen, ADH, NAD and NADH of mice. *Life Sci. 4*, 1195–1200.

MIRONE, L. (1965b). Effect of ethanol on growth and liver components in mice. *Life Sci. 4*, 1823–1830.

MIRONE, L. (1966a). Effect of vitamins in single dose on liver of mice on prolonged ethanol intake. *Life Sci. 5*, 317–324.

MIRONE, L. (1966b). Effect of ethanol in single dose on liver of ethanol-treated and nontreated mice. *Am. J. Physiol. 210*, 390–394.

MIRSKY, I. A., PIKER, P., ROSENBAUM, M. AND LEDERER, H. (1941). "Adaptation" of the central nervous system to varying concentrations of alcohol in the blood. *Quart. J. Studies Alc. 2*, 35–45.

MISTILIS, S. P. AND BIRCHALL, A. (1969). Induction of alcohol dehydrogenase in the rat. *Nature 223*, 199–200.

MITCHELL, H. H. AND CURZON, E. G. (1940). The food value of ethyl alcohol. *Quart. J. Studies Alc. 1*, 227–245.

MIZOI, Y., KIMURA, A., OHGA, N. AND ISHIDO, T. (1963). Electromyographic studies for diagnosis of mild drunkenness. (Jap.) *Japan. J. Leg. Med. 17*, 1–8. (Abstr. *Quart. J. Studies Alc.* 1964, *25*, 759.)

MOLIMARD, R. (1958). Study of compensatory hepatic hypertrophy after partial hepatectomy in rats receiving an alcoholic drink over a prolonged period. (Fr.) *Compt. Rend. Soc. Biol. 152*, 1643–1646. (Abstr. *Quart. J. Studies Alc.* 1961, *22*, 493.)

MOLINIER, A., MAUGARD, A. AND TCHOURUMOFF, N. (1966). Étude des variations de la glycémie chez les alcooliques. *Semaine Hop. Paris 42*, 1569–1578.

MORGAN, A. F., BRINNER, L., PLAA, C. B. AND STONE, M. M. (1957). Utilization of calories from alcohol and wines and their effects on cholesterol metabolism. *Am. J. Physiol. 189*, 290–296.

MORRISON, G. R. AND BROCK, F. E. (1967a). Quantitative measurement of alcohol dehydrogenase in the lobule of normal livers. *J. Lab. Clin. Med. 70*, 116–120.

MORRISON, G. R. AND BROCK, F. E. (1967b). Quantitative measurement of alcohol dehydrogenase activity within the liver lobule of rats after prolonged ethanol ingestion. *J. Nutr. 92*, 286–292.

MOSES, H. A. (1967). Some biochemical effects of ethanol on the rat. *J. Nat. Med. Assoc. 59*, 35–37.

MOSKOWITZ, H. AND WAPNER, M. (1964). Studies on the acquisition of behavioral tolerance to alcohol. *Quart. J. Studies Alc. 25*, 619–626.

MOSS, J. N., SMYTH, R. D., BECK, H. AND MARTIN, G. J. (1967). Ethanol impact on brain acetylcholine and its modification by cysteine. *Arch. Intern. Pharmacodyn. 168*, 235–238.

MOYNIHAN, N. H. (1965). Alcohol and blood-sugar. *Alcoholism (Zagreb) 1*, 180–187.

MOYNIHAN, N. H. AND BENJAFIELD, J. C. (1967). Alcohol and blood sugar. *Practitioner 198*, 552–559.

MUNRO, H. N. (1968). Role of amino acid supply in regulating ribosome function. *Federation Proc. 27*, No. 5, 1231–1237.

MURDOCK, H. R. (1967). Thyroidal effect of alcohol. *Quart. J. Studies Alc. 28*, 419–423.

MURPHY, G. E., GUZE, S. B. AND KING, L. J. (1962). Urinary excretion of 5-HIAA in chronic alcoholism. *J. Am. Med. Assoc. 182*, 565. (Abstr. *Rev. Alcoolisme* 1967, *13*, 160.)

MURRAY, M. R. (1965). Nervous tissues *in vitro*. In: *Cells and tissues in culture*, E. N. WILLMER, Ed., Vol. 2, Academic Press, New York and London. Pp. 373–455.

MURRAY, J. AND STEIN, N. (1965). Effect of ethanol on absorption of iron in rats. *Proc. Soc. Exptl. Biol. Med. 120*, 816–819.

NEVILLE, J. N., EAGLES, J. A., SAMSON, G. AND OLSON, R. E. (1968). Nutritional state of alcoholics. *Am. J. Clin. Nutr. 21*, 1329–1340.

NEWELL, G. W., SHELLENBERGER, T. E. AND REINKE, D. R. (1964). Chronic effects of alcohol, muscatel, and sherry on the growth and performance of male rats. *Toxicol. Appl. Pharmacol. 6*, 696–700.

NEWMAN, H. W. (1941). Acquired tolerance to ethyl alcohol. *Quart. J. Studies Alc. 2*, 453–463.

NEWMAN, H. AND CARD, J. (1937). Duration of acquired tolerance to ethyl alcohol. *J. Pharmacol. Exptl. Therap. 59*, 249–252.

NEWMAN, H. W. AND LEHMAN, A. J. (1938). Nature of acquired tolerance to alcohol. *J. Pharmacol. Exptl. Therap. 62*, 301–306.

NEWMAN, H. W., WILSON, R. H. L. AND NEWMAN, E. J. (1952). Direct determination of maximal daily metabolism of alcohol. *Science 116*, 328–329.

NICHOLS, M. M. (1967). Acute alcohol withdrawal syndrome in a newborn. *Am. J. Diseases Children 113*, 714–715.

NIELSEN, B. L. AND KESSING, S. V. (1965). Hepatic cirrhosis and atherosclerotic heart disease. *Geriatrics 20*, 374–378.

NIELSEN, J. (1965). Delirium tremens in Copenhagen. *Acta Psychiat. Scand. 41*, Suppl. 187, 92 pp.

NIKKILÄ, E. A. AND OLLILA, O. (1959). Effect of alcohol ingestion on experimental chicken atherosclerosis. *Circulation Res. 7*, 588–594.

NIMURA, T. (1966). The metabolism of alcohol in chronic alcoholism. *Japan. J. Studies Alc. 1*, 100–112.

NING, M., LOWENSTEIN, L. M. AND DAVIDSON, C. S. (1967). Serum amino acid concentrations in alcoholic hepatitis. *J. Lab. Clin. Med. 70*, 554–562.

NIZZOLI, V., FAGGIOLI, L. AND FERRAZZI, D. (1967). Atrofie cerebellari dell'alcoolismo cronico. *Riv. Neurobiol. 13*, 847–858.

NYGREN, A. (1966). Serum creatine phosphokinase activity in chronic alcoholism, in connection with acute alcohol intoxication. *Acta Med. Scand. 179*, 623–630.

OGATA, M. (1963). Clinical and experimental studies on water metabolism in alcoholism. *Quart. J. Studies Alc. 24*, 398–411.

OGATA, M., MENDELSON, J. H. AND MELLO, N. K. (1968). Electrolytes and osmolality in alcoholics during experimentally induced intoxication. *Psychosom. Med. 30*, 463–488.

OGATA, S. AND SAJI, H. (1966). Distribution of alcohol in various internal organs of alcoholic habit and non-habit mice. *Japan. J. Studies Alc. 1*, 118–130.

OGATA, S., HOSOI, T., SAJI, H., INUKAI, M., MORITA, K., MORITA, M. AND OUTA, H. (1966). Studies on acute alcohol intoxication. Especially concerning its relation to the carbohydrate metabolism. *Japan. J. Studies Alc. 1*, 67–79.

OLDERHAUSEN, H.-F. VON (1964). Über die Pathogenese alkoholischer Leberschäden. *Deut. Med. Wochschr. 89*, 867–874.

OLDERSHAUSEN, H.-F. VON AND SCHWEIGER, M. (1964). Über Veränderungen von Enzymaktivitäten im Serum und Lebergewebe nach Einwirkung von Äthylalkohol sowie Verabreichung von anabolen Steroiden und einigen anderen Medikamenten. *Verhandl. Deut. Ges. Inn. Med. 70*, 645–654.

OLSON, R. E. (1964). Nutrition and alcoholism. In: *Modern nutrition in health and disease*. M. G. WOHL AND P. S. GOODHART, Eds. 3rd ed., Henry Kimpton, London. Pp. 779–795.

OLSON, R. E., GURSEY, D. AND VESTER, J. W. (1960). Evidence for a defect in tryptophan metabolism in chronic alcoholism. *New Engl. J. Med. 263*, 1169–1174.

ORREGO-MATTE, H., NAVIA, E., FERES, A. AND COSTAMAILLERE, L. (1969). Ethanol ingestion and incorporation of ^{32}P into phospholipids of pancreas in the rat. *Gastroenterology* 56, 280–285.

ORTEN, J. M., SHRIVASTAVA, K. C. AND SHIH, M. (1967). Hematuria following administration of ethanol. *Science 157*, 72–73.

OURA, E., KONTTINEN, K. AND SUOMALAINEN, H. (1963). The influence of alcohol intake on vitamin excretion in the rat. *Acta Physiol. Scand. 59*, suppl. 213, 119.

OWEN, M. (1954). A study of the rationale of the treatment of delirium tremens with adrenocorticotropic hormone. I. The eosinophil response of patients with delirium tremens, after a test with ACTH. II. Clinical correlations to responsiveness to ACTH in delirium tremens. *Quart. J. Studies Alc. 15*, 384–386 and 387–401.

PAAVILAINEN, TERHO, PAAVILAINEN, TIMO AND NÄÄTÄNEN, E. (1961). Effect of ethyl alcohol on the development of experimentally induced arteriosclerosis in rats. *Ann. Med. Exptl. Biol. Fenniae 39*, 110–114.

PACE, D. M. AND FROST, B. L. (1948). The effects of ethyl alcohol on growth and respiration in *Pelomyxa carolinensis* and upon conjugation in *Paramecium caudatum. Anat. Record 101*, 730. (Class. Abstr. 5186.)

PALMA-CARLOS, A. G. AND PALMA-CARLOS, M. L. (1968). Ethyl alcohol and porphyrin metabolism. *Lancet 1*, 867.

PARKER, R. C., MORGAN, J. F. AND MORTON, H. J. (1950). Nutrition of animal cells in tissue culture. III. Effect of ethyl alcohol on cell survival and multiplication. *J. Cellular Comp. Physiol. 36*, 411–420. (Class. Abstr. No. 5709.)

PASQUARIELLO, G., QUADRI, A. AND TENCONI, L. T. (1964). Tryptophan-nicotinic acid metabolism in chronic alcoholics. *Acta Vitaminol. 1*, 3–6.

PATEK, A. J. (1963). Dietary factors in the pathogenesis and treatment of cirrhosis of the liver. *Med. Clin. N. Am. 47*, 753–763.

PAWAN, G. L. S. (1968). Physical excercise and alcohol metabolism in man. *Nature 218*, 966–967.

PELAEZ, E., SEGOVIA, M. N. AND MARDONES, R. J. (1949). The effect of *ad libitum* consumption of alcohol on the growth of the white rat. (Sp.) *Boll. Soc. Biol., Santiago 6*, 58–60. (Abstr. *Quart. J. Studies Alc.* 1949, *12*, 521–522.)

PELTON, R. B., WILLIAMS, R. J. AND ROGERS, L. L. (1959). Metabolic characteristics of alcoholics. I. Response to glucose stress. *Quart. J. Studies Alc. 20*, 28–32.

PÉQUIGNOT, F. G. (1963). Les enquêtes par interrogatoires permettent-elles de déterminer la fréquence de l'étiologie alcoolique des cirrhoses du foie? *Bull. Acad. Natl. Méd. 147*, 90–100.

PERFETTI, C. C., MILONE, F. F. AND PACCHIANI, A. (1967). Studio di valori di dispersione della velocitá di conduzione (VDC) delle fibre motorie negli alcoolisti. *Riv. Neurol. 37*, 453–461.

PERGOLA, F. AND CACHIN, M. (1957). Involvement of the liver in nervous complications of alcoholism. (Fr.) *Semaine Hop. 33*, 3161–3167. (Abstr. *Quart. J. Studies Alc.* 1960, *21*, 158.)

PERKOFF, G. T., HARDY, P. AND VELEZ-GARCIA, E. (1966). Acute muscular syndrome in chronic alcoholism. *New Engl. J. Med. 274*, 1277–1285.

PERKOFF, G. T., DIOSO, M. M., BLEISCH, V. AND KLINKERFUSS, G. (1967). A spectrum of myopathy associated with alcoholism. I. Clinical and laboratory features. *Ann. Internal Med. 67*, 481–492.

PHILLIPS, G. B. AND DAVIDSON, C. S. (1954). Nutritional aspects of cirrhosis in alcoholism – effect of a purified diet supplemented with choline. *Ann. N.Y. Acad. Sci. 57*, 812–830.

PHILLIPS, M. J. (1967). Electron microscopy of the liver. *Postgrad. Med. 41*, 3–14.

PICKRELL, K. L. (1938). The effect of alcoholic intoxication and other anesthesia on resistance to pneumococcal infection. *Bull. Johns Hopkins Hosp. 63*, 238–260.

PICRKELL, K. L. (1940). The effect of alcoholic intoxication, avertin and ether anesthesia on resistance to pneumococcal infection. *Current Res. Anesthesia Analgesia 19*, 272–278.

PIKER, P. (1937). On the relationship of the sudden withdrawal of alcohol to delirium tremens. *Am. J. Psychiat. 93*, 1387–1390.

PILSTRÖM, L. AND KIESSLING, K.-H. (1967). Effect of ethanol on the growth and on the liver and mitochondrial functions of offspring of rats. *Acta Pharmacol. Toxicol. 25*, 225–232.

PINTAR, K., WOLANSKYJ, B. M. AND GUBBAY, E. R. (1965). Alcoholic cardiomyopathy. *Can. Med. Assoc. J. 93*, 103–107.

PLUVINAGE, R. (1954). Les atrophies cérébrales des alcooliques. *Bull. Soc. Méd. Hop., Paris 70*, 524–526.

PLUVINAGE, R. AND LELUS, R. (1962). Chronic alcoholism and pyridoxine deficiency. (Fr.) *Bull. Soc. Méd. Hop., Paris 113*, 1030–1036. (Abstr. *Quart. J. Studies Alc.* 1964, *25*, 782).

POLLACK, D. (1966). Coping and avoidance in inebriated alcoholics and normals. *J. Abn. Psychol. 71*, 417–419.

POPPER, H. AND SCHAFFNER, F., Eds. (1961). *Progress in liver diseases.* Vol. 1, Grune and Stratton, New York and London, 363 pp.

POPPER, H. AND SCHAFFNER, F., Eds. (1965). *Progress in liver diseases.* Vol. 2. Grune and Stratton, New York and London, 554 pp.

POPPER, H., RUBIN, E., KRUS, S. AND SCHAFFNER, F. (1960). Postnecrotic cirrhosis in alcoholics. *Gastroenterology 39*, 669–689.

PORTA, E. A. AND GOMEZ-DUMM, C. L. A. (1966). Food patterns, spontaneous alcoholic intake and hepatic damage. *Federation Proc. 25*, No. 2, Pt. I, 304.

PORTA, E. A. AND GOMEZ-DUMM, C. L. A. (1968). A new experimental approach in the study of chronic alcoholism. I. Effects of high alcohol intake in rats fed a commercial laboratory diet. *Lab. Invest. 18*, 352–364.

PORTA, E. A., HARTROFT, W. S. AND IGLESIA, F. A. DE LA (1965). Hepatic changes associated with chronic alcoholism in rats. *Lab. Invest. 14*, 1437–1455.

PORTA, E. A., HARTROFT, W. S., GOMEZ-DUMM, C. L. A. AND KOCH, O. R. (1967a). Dietary factors in the progression and regression of hepatic alteration associated with experimental chronic alcoholism. *Federation Proc. 26*, No. 5, 1449–1457.

PORTA, E. A., HARTROFT, W. S. AND IGLESIA, F. A. DE LA (1967b). Structural and ultrastructural hepatic lesions associated with acute and chronic alcoholism in man and experimental animals. In: *Biochemical factors in alcoholism*, R. P. MAICKEL, Ed., Pergamon Press, Oxford etc. Pp. 201–238.

PORTA, E. A., KOCH, O. R., GOMEZ-DUMM, C. L. A. AND HARTROFT, W. S. (1968). Effects of dietary protein on the liver of rats in experimental chronic alcoholism. *J. Nutr. 94*, 437–446.

PORTA, E. A., KOCH, O. R. AND HARTROFT, W. S. (1969). Recovery of chronic hepatic lesions in rats fed alcohol and a solid "super diet". *Federation Proc. 28*, No. 2, 626.

POST, R. M. AND DESFORGES, J. F. (1968). Thrombocytopenia and alcoholism. *Ann. Int. Med. 68*, 1230–1236.

PRIEST, R. G., BINNS, J. K. AND KITCHIN, A. H. (1966). Electrocardiogram in alcoholism and accompanying physical disease. *Brit. Med. J. No. 5501*, 1453–1454.

PRINGSHEIM, J. (1908). Chemische Untersuchungen über das Wesen der Alkoholtoleranz. *Biochem. Z. 12*, 143–192.

RALLI, E. P., DUMM, M. E. AND LAKEN, B. (1959). The effects in rats of vitamin B_{12}, with and without ethyl alcohol, on nitrogen balance, serum albumin, liver nitrogen and fat. *J. Nutr. 67*, 41–57.

RANG, H. P. (1960). Unspecific drug action. The effects of a homologous series of primary alcohols. *Brit. J. Pharmacol. 15*, 185–200.

RAPPORTS PRÉSENTÉS AU XXXII CONGRÈS FRANÇAIS DE MÉDECINE. (1959). *Cirrhose alcoolique et nutritionnelle.* Lausanne 1959. Masson & Cie., Paris. Pp. 1–346.

RAUSCHKE, J. (1954). Tests of performance during rising and falling blood alcohol levels under special conditions. (Ger.) *Deut. Z. Ges. Gerichtl. Med. 43*, 27–37. (Abstr. *Quart. J. Studies Alc.* 1956, *17*, 685.)

RECKNAGEL, R. (1967). Carbon tetrachloride toxicity. *Pharmacol. Rev. 19*, 145–208.

REDETZKI, H. M., LEWIS, C. AND WELSCH, R. A. (1966). Influence of dietary deficiencies on cellular concentrations of coenzymes and substrates during chronic intake of ethanol. *Federation Proc. 25*, No. 2, Part I, 657.

REGAN, T. J., LEVINSON, G. E., OLDEWURTEL, H. A., FRANK, M. J., WEISSE, A. B. AND MOSCHOS, C. B. (1969). Ventricular function in noncardiacs with alcoholic fatty liver: Role of ethanol in the production of cardiomyopathy. *J. Clin. Invest. 48*, 397–407.

RICHTER, C. P. (1926). A study of the effect of moderate doses of alcohol on the growth and behavior of the rat. *J. Exptl. Zool. 44*, 397–418.

RICHTER, C. P. (1941). Alcohol as a food. *Quart. J. Studies Alc. 1*, 650–662.

RICHTER, C. P. (1953). Alcohol, beer and wine as foods. *Quart. J. Studies Alc. 14*, 525–539.

RITTER, U. (1965). Zur Alkoholpankreatitis. *Deut. Med. Wochschr. 90*, 382–386.

ROBERTS, K. E. (1963). Mechanism of dehydration following alcohol ingestion. *Arch. Internal Med. 112*, 154–157.

ROGERS, L. L. AND GAWIENOWSKI, A. M. (1959). Metabolic characteristics of alcoholics. II. Serum copper concentrations in alcoholics. *Quart. J. Studies Alc. 20*, 33–37.

ROGERS, W. N. (1946). Changes in liver and spleen of normal and allergic rabbits after intraparenchymal injections of serum, and the modifications induced by oral administration of alcohol. *Quart. J. Studies Alc. 7*, 325–340.

ROSENBAUM, M. (1942). Adaptation of the central nervous system to varying concentrations of alcohol in the blood. *Arch. Neurol. Psychiat., Chicago 48*, 1010–1012.

ROUILLER, C., Ed. (1963). *The liver. Morphology, biochemistry, physiology,* Vol. I. Academic Press, New York and London. 683 pp.

ROUILLER, C., Ed. (1964). *The liver. Morphology, biochemistry, physiology,* Vol. II. Academic Press, New York. 674 pp.

RUBIN, E. AND LIEBER, C. S. (1967a). Early fine structural changes in the human liver induced by alcohol. *Gastroenterology 52*, 1–13.

RUBIN, E. AND LIEBER, C. S. (1967b). Experimental alcoholic hepatic injury in man; ultrastructural changes. *Federation Proc. 26*, No. 5, 1458–1467.

RUBIN, E. AND LIEBER, C. S. (1968). Alcohol-induced hepatic injury in nonalcoholic volunteers. *New Engl. J. Med. 278*, 869–876.

RUTTER, L. (1966). Transaminase deficiency in alcoholics and cases of peptic ulcer. *Nature 210*, 538.

RYAN, R. C. AND CORNISH, H. H. (1966). Alcohol metabolism in methanol- and ethanol-pretreated rats. *Toxicol. Appl. Pharmacol. 8*, 352–353.

SABOT, L. M., GROSS, M. M. AND HALPERT, E. (1968). A study of acute alcoholic psychoses in women. *Brit. J. Addiction 63*, 29–49.

SACKETT, D. L., GIBSON, R. W., BROSS, I. D. J. AND PICKREN, J. W. (1968). Relation between aortic atherosclerosis and cigarettes and alcohol. *New Engl. J. Med. 279*, 1413–1420.

SADOUN, R., LOLLI, G. AND SILVERMAN, M. (1965). *Drinking in French culture.* College & University Press, New Haven, Conn. 133 pp.

SALASPURO, M. P. (1966). Ethanol inhibition of galactose oxidation as related to the redox state of the fatty liver. *Scand. J. Clin. Lab. Invest. 18*, Suppl. 92, 145–147.

SALASPURO, M. P. (1967a). Method for the early diagnosis of fatty liver in human alcoholics. *Scand. J. Clin. Lab. Invest. 19*, Suppl. 95, 90.

SALASPURO, M. P. (1967b). Early diagnosis of fatty liver. *Alkoholpolitik 30*, 149–151.

SALASPURO, M. P. (1967c). Application of the galactose tolerance test for the early diagnosis of fatty liver in human alcoholics. *Scand. J. Clin. Lab. Invest. 20*, 274–280.

SALASPURO, M. P. (1968). *Studies on the influence of ethanol on the metabolism of the normal and pathological liver. I. Liver perfusion experiments with normal, fatty and cirrhotic rat livers. II. Application of the galactose tolerance test for the early diagnosis of fatty liver in human alcoholics.* Thesis, Alko Offset, Helsinki. 50 pp.

SALASPURO, M. P. AND MÄENPÄÄ, P. H. (1966). Influence of ethanol on the metabolism of perfused normal, fatty and cirrhotic rat livers. *Biochem. J. 100*, 768–774.

SALASPURO, M. P. AND SALASPURO, A. E. (1968). The effect of ethanol on galactose elimination in rats with normal and choline-deficient fatty livers. *Scand. J. Clin. Lab. Invest. 22*, 49–53.

SAMOCHOWIEC, L. AND WÓJCICKI, J. (1966). Therapieversuch bei chronischer Alkoholintoxikation weisser Ratten. *Med. Pharmacol. Exptl. 15*, 530–538.

SAMOCHOWIEC, L., STEPLEWSKI, Z. AND WÓJCICKI, J. (1967a). Cytochemical studies on the liver and kidney of rats after chronic intoxication with ethyl alcohol and simultaneous medication with essential phospholipids. (Ger.) *Acta Biol. Med. Ger. 18*, 625–632.

SAMOCHOWIEC, L., WÓJCICKI, J. AND DOMINICZAK, K. (1967b). Der Einfluss der "essentiellen" Phospholipide auf Leberveränderungen nach chronischer Äthylalkohol- und Allylisosulfocyanat-Intoxikation bei weisser Ratten. *Arzneimittel-Forsch. 17*, 1374–1376.

SARAVAY, S. M. AND PARDES, H. (1967). Auditory elementary hallucinations in alcohol withdrawal psychosis. *Arch. Gen. Psychiat. 16*, 652–658.

SARDESAI, V. M. AND ORTEN, J. M. (1968). Effect of prolonged alcohol consumption in rats on pancreatic protein synthesis. *J. Nutr. 96*, 241–246.

SARDESAI, V. M. AND THAL, A. P. (1967). Effect of ethanol on pancreatic protein synthesis. *Federation Proc. 26*, 693.

SARLES, H. AND FIGARELLA, C. (1967). Étude de l'action de l'éthanol et des graisses alimentaires sur le pancréas du rat. I. Variations des enzymes pancréatiques (lipase, amylase, chymotrypsinogène, trypsinogène). *Pathol. Biol. Semaine Hop. 15*, 725–732.

SAUTET, J., DESANTI, E., PAYAN, H., ALDIGHIERI, J., GAY, R., ARNAUD, G., DELUY, M., CASTELLI, P., CASTELLI, C. AND RAMPAL, C. (1960). Contribution to the experimental study of the action of various wines and alcohols in the white mouse; weight, mortality, basal metabolism, muscular contraction, anatomopathology. (Fr.) *Rev. Pathol. Gen. 60*, 1623–1673. (Abstr. *Quart. J. Studies Alc.* 1963, *24*, 543.)

SAVILLE, P. D. AND LIEBER, C. S. (1965). Effect of alcohol on growth, bone density and muscle magnesium in the rat. *J. Nutr. 87*, 477–484.

SCARLATO, G. AND MENOZZI, C. (1959). Effect of meprobamate on experimental chronic alcohol intoxication: a histological and histochemical study of the nervous system. (It.) *Sistema Nervoso 11*, 165–174. (Abstr. *Quart. J. Studies Alc.* 1961, *22*, 148–149.)

SCHAPIRO, H., WRUBLE, L. D. AND BRITT, L. G. (1966). The possible mechanism of alcohol in the production of acute pancreatitis. *Surgery 60*, 1108–1111.

SCHEDIFKA, R. (1965). Klinisch-chemische Leberuntersuchungen an Alkoholikern. *Med. Welt 5*, 246–250.

SCHEIG, R. AND KLATSKIN, G. (1966). Effects of ethanol and hormones on lipogenesis from glucose in adipose tissue. *Federation Proc. 25*, No. 2, Pt. I, 366.

SCHEIG, R., ALEXANDER, N. M. AND KLATSKIN, G. (1966). Effects of prolonged ingestion of glucose or ethanol on tissue lipid composition and lipid biosynthesis in rat. *J. Lipid Res. 7*, 188–196.

SCHENKER, V. J., KISSIN, B., MAYNARD, L. S. AND SCHENKER, A. C. (1964). *The effect of ethanol on amine metabolism in alcoholism.* Mimeographed lecture. 27th International Congress on Alcohol and Alcoholism, Frankfurt, Germany.

SCHENKER, V. J., KISSIN, B., MAYNARD, L. S. AND SCHENKER, A. C. (1967). The effects of ethanol on amine metabolism in alcoholism. In: *Biochemical factors in alcoholism*, R. P. MAICKEL, Ed., Pergamon Press, Oxford etc. Pp. 39–52.

SCHLESINGER, K., BENNETT, E. L., HEBERT, M. AND McCLEARN, G. E. (1966). Effects of alcohol consumption on the activity of liver enzymes in C57BL/Crgl mice. *Nature* 209, 488–489.

SCHLESINGER, K., BENNETT, E. L. AND HEBERT, M. (1967). Effects of genotype and prior consumption of alcohol on rates of ethanol-1-^{14}C metabolism in mice. *Quart. J. Studies Alc. 28*, 231–235.

SCHMÄL, D., THOMAS, C., SATTLER, W. AND SCHELD, G. F. (1965). Experimentelle Untersuchungen zur Syncarcinogenese. 3. Mitteilung. Versuche zur Krebserzeugung bei Ratten bei gleichzeitiger Gabe von Diäthylnitrosamin und Tetrachlorkohlenstoff bzw. Äthylalkohol; zugleich ein experimenteller Beitrag zur Frage der "Alkoholcirrhose". *Z. Krebsforsch. 66*, 526–532.

SCHMIDT, K. M. AND KLOPFER, F. D. (1968). Ethanol and stomach ulcers: absence of influence in the albino rat. *Quart. J. Studies Alc. 29*, 558–565.

SCHMIDT, W. AND BRONETTO, J. (1962). Death from liver cirrhosis and specific alcoholic beverage consumption. *Am. J. Public Health 52*, 1473–1482.

SCHUBERT, H. A. (1963). A study of motor nerve conduction: determination of velocity. *Southern Med. J. 56*, 666–668.

SCHUELER, F. W. (1960). *Chemobiodynamics and drug design.* McGraw-Hill, New York. 638 pp.

SCHWARZMANN, V., JULIEN, C., BORENSTEIN, P., ÉTÉVÉ, J. AND BERTHAUX, N. (1962). L'alcooldéshydrogénase hépatique chez les alcooliques. *Rev. Franc. Études Clin. Biol. 7*, 762–765.

SEEVERS, M. H. AND DENEAU, G. A. (1963). Physiological aspects of tolerance and physical dependence. In: *Physiological pharmacology*, Vol. 1, W. S. ROOT AND F. G. HOFMANN, Eds., Academic Press, New York and London. Pp. 565–640.

SELZER, M. L. AND VAN HOUTEN, W. H. (1964). Normal thyroid function in chronic alcoholism. *J. Clin. Endocrinol. Metab. 24*, 380–382.

SERENY, G. AND LOWDEN, J. A. (1967). Mechanism of production of fatty liver by 10 days of ethanol ingestion. *Federation Proc. 26*, 693.

SERENY, G., RAPOPORT, A. AND HUSDAN, H. (1966). The effect of alcohol withdrawal on electrolyte and acid-base balance. *Metabolism Clin. Exptl. 15*, 896–904.

SHANLEY, B. G., ZAIL, S. S. AND JOUBERT, S. M. (1968). Effect of ethanol on liver δ-aminolaevulinate synthetase in rats. *Lancet 1*, 70–71.

SHIMOJYO, S., SCHEINBERG, P. AND REINMUTH, O. (1967). Cerebral blood flow and metabolism in the Wernicke-Korsakoff syndrome. *J. Clin. Invest. 46*, 849–854. (Abstr. *Quart. J. Studies Alc. 1968, 29*, 748–749.)

SILKWORTH, W. D. AND TEXON, M. (1950). Chloride levels in the blood of alcoholic patients in relation to the phenomena of craving. *Quart. J. Studies Alc. 11*, 381–384.

SINCLAIR, H. M. (1939). The causes of deficiency of vitamin B$_1$ and its relation to the nervous system. In: *III Congrès Néurologique International, Copenhague 1939. Comptes Rendus des Séances.* Munksgaard, Copenhague. Pp. 885–890.

SINCLAIR, H. M. (1955). Vitamin deficiencies in alcoholism. *Proc. Nutr. Soc. 14*, 107–115.

SIRNES, T. B. (1952). The blood alcohol curve in zonal necrosis of the liver. *Quart. J. Studies Alc. 13*, 189–195.

ŠLESINGR, L. (1965). Belastung der Leber gesunder und kranker Hunde mit Äthylalkohol im Vergleich mit der Exkretion des Bromosulphaleins und Bilirubine. *Arch. Exptl. Veterinärmed. 19*, 609–613.

SMALL, M., LONGARINI, A. AND ZAMSCHECK, N. (1959). Disturbances of digestive physiology following acute drinking episodes in "skid-row" alcoholics. *Am. J. Med. 27*, 575–585. (Abstr. *Quart. J. Studies Alc.* 1961, *22*, 348.)

SMITH, W. O. AND HAMMARSTEN, J. F. (1959). Intracellular magnesium in delirium tremens and uremia. *Am. J. Med. Sci. 237*, 413–417.

SMITH, W. O., WARREN, R. J. AND HAMMARSTEN, J. F. (1958). Intracellular magnesium in delirium tremens and uremia. *Clin. Res. 6*, 408.

SOHAL, R. S. AND BURCH, G. E. (1969). Effects of alcohol ingestion on the intercalated disc in the mouse heart. *Experientia 25*, 279–280.

SPANIO, L. AND CARULLI, N. (1966). Comportamento dell'alcooldeidrogenasi (ADH) epatica in soggetti portatori di epatopatie cirrogene. *Acta Vitaminol. 20* (Fasc. 2–3), 53–57.

SPAVENTI, S., HUDOLIN, V., RUDAR, M., GABELIC, I. AND METZGER, B. (1967). Damage to the liver of alcoholics in gamma-scintigraphic pictures. *Brit. J. Addict. 62*, 61–69.

SPEIDEL, C. C. (1937). Changes in nerve fibers during alcoholic intoxication and recovery. *Sci. Monthly 44*, 178–185. (Class. Abstr. No. 2291.)

SPRITZ, N. AND LIEBER, C. S. (1966). Decrease of ethanol-induced fatty liver by ethyl α-p-chlorophenoxyisobutyrate. *Proc. Soc. Exptl. Biol. Med. 121*, 147–149.

STEIN, J. H., SMITH, W. O. AND GINN, W. E. (1966). Hypophosphatemia in acute alcoholism. *Am. J. Med. Sci. 252*, 78–83.

STEINBACH, M. (1965). Liquorelektrophoretische Untersuchungen bei Alkohol-Polyneuropathie. *Arch. Psychiat. Nervenkrankh. 207*, 168–173.

STÜTTGEN, B. J. AND EL MAHGOUB, M. (1963). Die Hautreaktionen auf Bradykinin und ihre Beeinflussung durch Alkohol. *Dermatol. Wochschr. 148*, 89–95.

SUKHORUKOVA, L. I. AND YAKOBSON, I. S. (1965). Changes in central nervous system of dogs in chronic alcohol intoxication; a morphological and histochemical study. (Rus.) *Zh. Nevropatol. i Psikhiatr. 65*, 423–430.

SULLIVAN, J. F. AND HATCH, L. K. (1964). Alcoholism and vascular disease. *Geriatrics 19*, 442–446.

SULLIVAN, J. F. AND LANKFORD, H. G. (1965). Zinc metabolism and chronic alcoholism. *Am. J. Clin. Nutr. 17*, 57–63.

SULLIVAN, J. F., LANKFORD, H. G., SWARTZ, M. J. AND FARRELL, C. (1963). Magnesium metabolism in alcoholism. *Am. J. Clin. Nutr. 13*, 297–303.

SULLIVAN, J. F., LANKFORD, H. G. and ROBERTSON, P. (1966). Renal excretion of lactate and magnesium in alcoholism. *Am. J. Clin. Nutr. 18*, 231–236.

SULLIVAN, L. W. AND HERBERT, V. (1964). Suppression of hematopoiesis by ethanol. *J. Clin. Invest. 43*, 2048–2062.

SUOMALAINEN, H. (1963). The influence of alcohol consumption on vitamin deficiencies. *Alkoholikysymys 31*, 110–118. (English abstract.)

SUTER, C. AND KLINGMAN, W. O. (1955). Neurologic manifestations of magnesium depletion states. *Neurology 5*, 691–699.

SUTHERLAND, V. C., BURBRIDGE, T. N., ADAMS, J. E. AND SIMON, A. (1960). Cerebral metabolism in problem drinkers under the influence of alcohol and chlorpromazine hydrochloride. *J. Appl. Physiol. 15*, 189–196.

SVOBODA, D. J. AND MANNING, R. T. (1964). Chronic alcoholism with fatty metamorphosis of the liver: Mitochondrial alterations in hepatic cells. *Am. J. Pathol. 44*, 645–662.

TAKADA, A., PORTA, E. A. AND HARTROFT, W. S. (1967). Regression of dietary cirrhosis in rats fed alcohol and a "super diet". Evidence of the non-hepatotoxic nature of ethanol. *Am. J. Clin. Nutr. 20*, 213–225.

TAKALA, M., SIRO, E. AND TOIVAINEN, Y. (1958). Intellectual functions and dexterity during hangover. Experiments after intoxication with brandy and with beer. *Quart. J. Studies Alc. 19*, 1–29.

TAKEMORI, A. E. (1961). Cellular adaptation to morphine in rats. *Science 133*, 1018–1019.

TALLAND, G. A., MENDELSON, J. H. AND RYACK, P. (1964a). Experimentally induced chronic intoxication and withdrawal in alcoholics. Pt. 4. Tests of motor skills. *Quart. J. Studies Alc.* Suppl. No. 2, 53–73.

TALLAND, G. A., MENDELSON, J. H. AND RYACK, P. (1964b). Experimentally induced chronic intoxication and withdrawal in alcoholics. Part 5. Tests of attention. *Quart. J. Studies Alc. Suppl. No. 2*, 74–86.

TAMERIN, J. S. AND MENDELSON, J. H. (1969). The psychodynamics of chronic inebriation: Observations of alcoholics during the process of drinking in an experimental group setting. *Amer. J. Psychiat. 125*, 886–899.

TAPPER, E. J., BUSHI, S., RUPPERT, R. D. AND GREENBERGER, N. J. (1968). Effect of acute and chronic ethanol treatment on the absorption of iron in rats. *Am. J. Med. Sci. 255*, 46–52.

TASSO, F., CLOP, J., SARLES, H. AND PICARD, D. (1967). Étude de l'action de l'éthanol et des graisses alimentaires sur le pancréas du rat. II. Étude ultrastructurale. *Pathol. Biol. Semaine Hop. 15*, 733–745.

TENGSTRÖM, B. (1966). An intravenous galactose tolerance test with an enzymatic determination of galactose. A comparison with other diagnostic aids in hepatobiliary disease. *Scand. J. Clin. Lab. Invest. 18*, Suppl. 92, 132–141.

TEPHLY, T. R., ATKINS, M., MANNERING, G. J. AND PARKS, R. E. (1965). Activation of a catalase peroxidative pathway for the oxidation of alcohols in mammalian erythrocytes. *Biochem. Pharmacol. 14*, 435–444.

THIESSEN, D. D., WHITWORTH, N. S. AND RODGERS, D. A. (1966). Reproductive variables and alcohol consumption of the C57BL/Crgl female mouse. *Quart. J. Studies Alc. 27*, 591–595.

THOMPSON, J. R., TAKIMURA, Y. AND SHER, B. C. (1963). Stress in experimental tuberculosis: alcohol. *Am. Rev. Respirat. Diseases 88*, 89–91. (Abstr. *Quart. J. Studies Alc.* 1965, *26*, 331–332.)

THORÉN, L. (1963). The use of carbohydrate and alcohol in parenteral nutrition. *Nutr. Dieta 5*, No. 3–4, 305–333.

THORÉN, L. (1964). Parenteral nutrition with carbohydrate and alcohol. *Acta Chir. Scand.*, Suppl. 325, 75–93.

THORPE, M. E. C. AND SHOREY, C. D. (1966). Long-term alcohol administration. Its effects on the ultrastructure and lipid content of the rat liver cell. *Am. J. Pathol. 48*, 557–568.

TINTERA, J. W. (1966). Stabilizing homeostasis in the recovered alcoholic through endocrine therapy: Evaluation of the hypoglycemia factor. *J. Am. Geriat. Soc. 14*, 126–150.

TODESCO, C. V. AND MERINI, A. (1966). L'indagine elettromiografica nella diagnosi di neuropatia latente nell'etilismo cronico. *G. Psichiat. Neuropat. 94*, 1123–1128.

TOMASULO, P. A., KATER, R. M. H. AND IBER, F. L. (1968). Impairment of thiamine absorption in alcoholism. *Am. J. Clin. Nutr. 21*, 1341–1344.

TOMMASI, M. (1957). Les encéphalopathies des alcooliques. Essai de classification anatomopathologique et pathogénique. Imprimérie de Trévoux, Lyon. 159 pp. (Abstr. *Quart. J. Studies Alc.* 1959, *20*, 677.)

TRÉMOLIÈRES, J. AND CARRÉ, L. (1960). Mise en évidence de systèmes peroxydasiques, oxydant l'alcool chez l'alcoolique. *Compt. Rend. 251*, 2785–2787.

TRÉMOLIÈRES, J. AND CARRÉ, L. (1961). Études sur les modalités d'oxydation de l'alcool chez l'homme normal et alcoolique. *Rev. Alcoolisme 7*, 202–227.

TRÉMOLIÈRES, J. AND CARRÉ, L. (1962). Induction d'un système peroxydasique oxydant l'éthanol par injection d'éthanol au rat à des doses toxiques. *Compt. Rend. Soc. Biol.* *156*, 458–461.

TRÉMOLIÈRES, J. AND LOWY, R. (1964). Résultats de recherches récentes sur les mécanismes biochimiques de la toxicité de l'alcool éthylique. *Ann. Biol. Clin. 22*, 1023–1033.

TRÉMOLIÈRES, J., CARRÉ, L., SCHEGGIA, E., POTET, F. AND MARTIN, E. (1963). Pancreatites necrosantes et hémorrhagiques par administration d'éthanol à doses toxiques et répétées au rat. *Compt. Rend. Soc. Biol. 157*, 1189–1190.

TRÉMOLIÈRES, J., LOWY, R. AND GRIFFATON, G. (1967). Physiologie de l'oxydation et de l'utilisation de l'éthanol à doses normales et toxiques. *Ann. Nutr. Aliment. 21*, No. 4, 69–103.

TRIPP, C. A., FLUCKIGER, F. A. AND WEINBERG, G. H. (1959). Effects of alcohol on the graphomotor performances of normals and chronic alcoholics. *Percept. Motor Skills 9*, 227–236.

TROSHINA, A. E. (1957). On the mechanism of habituation of the organism to alcohol. *Sb. Tr. Ryazansk. Med. Inst. 4*, 1–9. (Abstr. *Quart. J. Studies Alc. 1959, 20*, 783).

TROWELL, O. A. (1965). Lymphocytes. In: *Cells and tissues in culture*, Vol. 2, E. N. WILLMER, Ed. Academic Press, London and New York. Pp. 95–172.

TRUITT, E. B. AND DURITZ, G. (1967a). The role of acetaldehyde in the actions of ethanol. In: *Biochemical factors in alcoholism*, R. P. MAICKEL, Ed., Pergamon Press, Oxford. Pp. 61–69.

TRUITT, E. B. AND DURITZ, G. (1967b). Discussion, paper by Leevy (1967) In: *Federation Proc. 26*, No. 5, 1481.

TUMARKIN, B., WILSON, J. D. AND SNYDER, G. (1955). Cerebral atrophy due to alcoholism in young adults. *U.S. Armed Forces Med. J. 6*, 67–74.

TURNER, F. P. AND BRUM, V. C. (1964). The urinary excretion of free taurine in acute and chronic disease, following surgical trauma, and in patients with acute alcoholism. *J. Surg. Res. 4*, 423–431.

TYGSTRUP, N. AND LUNDQUIST, F. (1962). The effect of ethanol on galactose elimination in man. *J. Lab. Clin. Med. 59*, 102–109.

TYGSTRUP, N., WINKLER, K. AND LUNDQUIST, F. (1965). The mechanism of the fructose effect on the ethanol metabolism of the human liver. *J. Clin. Invest. 44*, 817–830.

UGARTE, G., PINO, M. E. AND INSUNZA, I. (1967). Hepatic alcohol dehydrogenase in alcoholic addicts with and without hepatic damage. *Am. J. Digest. Diseases 12*, 589–592.

UNGLEY, C. C. (1938). Some deficiencies of nutrition and their relation to disease. *Lancet 1*, 981–987.

VALLEE, B. L., WACKER, W. E. C., BARTHOLOMAY, A. F. AND ROBIN, E. D. (1956). Zinc metabolism in hepatic dysfunction. I. Serum zinc concentrations in Laënnec's cirrhosis and their validation by sequential analysis. *New Engl. J. Med. 255*, 403–408.

VALLEE, B. L., WACKER, W. E. C., BARTHOLOMAY, A. F. AND HOCH, F. L. (1957). Zinc metabolism in hepatic dysfunction. II. Correlation of metabolic patterns with biochemical findings. *New Engl. J. Med. 257*, 1055–1065.

VANDERPOOL, J. A. (1969). Alcoholism and the self-concept. *Quart. J. Studies Alc. 30*, 59–77.

VARELA, A., PENNA, A., ALCAINO, G., JOHNSON, E. AND MARDONES, R. J. (1953). Sugar, pyruvate and acetaldehyde levels in the blood of alcohol addicts after ingestion of dextrose. *Quart. J. Studies Alc. 14*, 174–180.

VARTIA, O. K., FORSANDER, O. A. AND KRUSIUS, F.-E. (1960). Blood sugar values in hangover. *Quart. J. Studies Alc. 21*, 597–604.

VEL'SHIKAYEV, R. KH. (1967). On the dynamics of carbohydrate metabolism in the alcohol abstinence syndrome. (Rus.) *Zh. Nevropat. i Psikhiatr. 67*, 262–268. (Abstr. *Quart. J. Studies Alc.* 1967, *28*, 566.)

VICTOR, M. (1963). Tobacco-alcohol amblyopia. A critique of current concepts of this disorder, with special reference to the role of nutritional deficiency in its causation. *Arch. Ophthalmol. (Chicago) 70*, 313–318.

VICTOR, M. AND ADAMS, R. D. (1953). The effect of alcohol on the nervous system. *Res. Publ. Assoc. Res. Nervous Mental Disease 32*, 526–573.

VICTOR, M. AND ADAMS, R. D. (1961). On the etiology of the alcoholic neurologic diseases. With special reference to the role of nutrition. *Am. J. Clin. Nutr. 9*, 379–397.

VICTOR, M. AND HOPE, J. M. (1958). The phenomenon of auditory hallucinations in chronic alcoholism. A critical evaluation of the status of alcoholic hallucinosis. *J. Nervous Mental Disease 126*, 451–481.

VIEL, B., DONOSO, S., SALCEDO, D., ROJAS, P., VARELA, A. AND ALESSANDRI, R. (1966). Alcoholism and socioeconomic status, hepatic damage, and arteriosclerosis. *Arch. Internal Med. 117*, 84–91.

VIEL, B., DONOSO, S., SALCEDO, D. AND VARELA, A. (1968). Alcoholic drinking habit and hepatic damage. *J. Chronic Dis. 21*, 157–166.

VOEGTLIN, W. L., O'HOLLAREN, P. AND O'HOLLAREN, N. (1943). The glucose tolerance of alcohol addicts. A study of 303 cases. *Quart. J. Studies Alc. 4*, 163–182.

VOLLMER, H. (1932). Untersuchungen über oxydative Giftung und Entgiftung in Abhängigkeit von der Gewöhnung. *Arch. Exptl. Pathol. Pharmacol. 166*, 405–431.

WALDENSTRÖM, J., WINBLAD, S., HÄLLÉN, J., LIUNGMAN, S. AND PERSSON, B. (1964). Hypergammaglobulinämie und Ausfall verschiedener serologischer Reaktionen bei alkoholischer und kryptogenetischer Leberzirrhose. *Acta Hepato-Splenol. 11*, 347–355.

WALLGREN, H. AND FORSANDER, O. (1963). Effect of adaptation to alcohol and of age on voluntary consumption of alcohol by rats. *Brit. J. Nutr. 17*, 453–457.

WALLGREN, H. AND LINDBOHM, R. (1961). Adaptation to ethanol in rats with special reference to brain tissue respiration. *Biochem. Pharmacol. 8*, 423–424.

WALLGREN, H. AND SAVOLAINEN, S. (1962). The effect of ethyl alcohol on a conditioned avoidance response in rats. *Acta Pharmacol. Toxicol. 19*, 59–67.

WALLGREN, H. AHLQVIST, J., ÅHMAN, K. AND SUOMALAINEN, H. (1967). Repeated alcoholic intoxication compared with continued consumption of dilute ethanol in experiments with rats on a marginal diet. *Brit. J. Nutr. 21*, 643–660.

WANAMAKER, W. M. AND SKILLMAN, T. G. (1966). Motor nerve conduction in alcoholics. *Quart. J. Studies Alc. 27*, 16–22.

WANKA, J. (1965). Alcohol-induced pain associated with adenocarcinoma of the bronchus. *Brit. Med. J. 2*, 88–89.

WANSCHER, O. (1953). Experimental portal cirrhosis. Pathogenesis and relation to administration of alcohol. *Acta Pathol. Microbiol. Scand. 32*, 348–354.

WARTBURG, J.-P. VON AND AEBI, H. (1960). Der Einfluss langdauernder Aethylalkohol-Belastung auf die Katecholaminausscheidung im Harn der Ratte. *Helv. Physiol. Pharmacol. Acta 18*, C95–C97.

WARTBURG, J.-P. VON AND RÖTHLISBERGER, M. (1961). Enzymatic changes in the liver after prolonged administration of ethanol and methanol to rats. (Ger.) *Helv. Physiol. Pharmacol. Acta 19*, 30–41. (Abstr. *Quart. J. Studies Alc.* 1963, *24*, 145–146.)

WARTBURG, J.-P. VON, BERLI, W. AND AEBI, H. (1961). Der Einfluss langdauernder Äthylalkoholbelastung auf die Katecholaminausscheidung im Harn der Ratte. *Helv. Med. Acta 28*, 89–98.

WASZ-HÖCKERT, O., KOSUNEN, T. AND KOHONEN, J. (1958). Effect of ethyl alcohol on the susceptibility of mice to staphylococcal infection. 1. *Ann. Med. Exptl. Biol. Fenniae* *36*, 360–365.

WASZ-HÖCKERT, O., KOSUNEN, T. AND KOHONEN, J. (1959). Effect of ethyl alcohol on the susceptibility of mice to staphylococcal infection. 2. *Ann. Med. Exptl. Biol. Fenniae* *37*, 121–127.

WATERLOW, J. C. AND BRAS, G. (1957). Nutritional liver damage in man. *Brit. Med. Bull.* *13*, 107–112.

WATERS, A. H., MORLEY, A. A. AND RANKIN, J. C. (1966). Effect of alcohol on haemopoiesis. *Brit. Med. J.* 2, 1565–1568.

WEBER, C., Ed. (1963). *Advances in enzyme regulation.* Vol. 1. Pergamon Press, Oxford. 420 pp.

WEEKS, C. C. (1938). *Alcohol and human life,* 2nd ed., Lewis, London. 454 pp.

WEEKS, J. R. (1964). Experimental narcotic addiction. *Sci. Am. 210*, 46–52.

WEINSTEIN, H. G., BREEN, M. AND FREEMAN, S. (1968). Enzyme activity and blood alcohol levels in human alcoholic subjects. *Fed. Proc. 27*, No. 2, 556.

WEISS, A. D., VICTOR, M., MENDELSON, J. H. AND LA DOU, J. (1964a). Experimentally induced chronic intoxication and withdrawal in alcoholics. Pt. 6. Critical flicker fusion studies. *Quart. J. Studies Alc.,* Suppl. No. 2, 87–95.

WEISS, A. D., VICTOR, M., MENDELSON, J. H. AND LA DOU, J. (1964b). Experimentally induced chronic intoxication and withdrawal in alcoholics. Pt. 7. Electroencephalographic findings. *Quart. J. Studies Alc.,* Suppl. No. 2, 96–99.

WENDT, V. E., WU, C., BALCON, R., DOTY, G. AND BING, R. J. (1965). Hemodynamic and metabolic effects of chronic alcoholism in man. *Am. J. Cardiol. 15*, 175–184.

WENDT, V. E., AJLUNI, R., BRUCE, T. A., PRASAD, A. S. AND BING, R. J. (1966). Acute effects of alcohol on the human myocardium. *Am. J. Cardiol. 17*, 804–812.

WESTERFELD, W. W. AND DOISY, E. A. (1945). Alcohol metabolism as related to the production of thiamine deficiency. *J. Nutr. 30*, 127–136.

WIESER, S. (1965). Alkoholismus II: Psychiatrische und neurologische Komplikationen. *Fortschr. Neurol. Psychiat. 33*, 349–409.

WIKLER, A., PESCOR, F. T., FRASER, H. F. AND ISBELL, H. (1956). Electroencephalographic changes associated with chronic alcoholic intoxication and the alcohol abstinence syndrome. *Am. J. Psychiat. 113*, 106–114.

WILGRAM, G. F. (1959). Experimental Laennec type of cirrhosis in monkeys. *Ann. Internal Med. 51*, 1134–1158.

WILKINSON, A. W. (1955). Alcohol in intravenous feeding. *Proc. Nutr. Soc. 14*, 124–129.

WILKINSON, P., BREEN, K. J. AND RANKIN, J. G. (1968). Bromsulphthalein metabolism in acute alcoholic liver disease. *Gut 9*, 707–711.

WINKLER, K., LUNDQUIST, F. AND TYGSTRUP, N. (1966). The metabolism of ethanol in normal man and in patients with cirrhosis of the liver. *Scand. J. Clin. Lab. Invest. 18*, Suppl. 92, 78.

WINKLER, K., LUNDQUIST, F. AND TYGSTRUP, N. (1969). The hepatic metabolism of ethanol in patients with cirrhosis of the liver. *Scand. J. Clin. Lab. Invest. 23*, 59–69.

WINSHIP, D. H., CAFLISCH, C. R., ZBORALSKE, F. F. AND HOGAN, W. J. (1968). Deterioration of esophageal peristalsis in patients with alcoholic neuropathy. *Gastroenterology 55*, 173–178.

WÓJCICKI, J. (1967). The influence of the liver hydrolysate and essential phospholipids on the development of changes in blood serum and in the liver caused by protracted administration of ethyl alcohol to white rats. (Pol.) *Dissertationes Pharm. 19*, 1–8.

YAMASHITA, M. (1962). Histopathological studies of the brain tissues of four patients of alcohol delirium. In: *Third World Congress of Psychiatry Proc.,* Vol. I, Toronto/Montreal. Univ. of Toronto Press and McGill University Press. Pp. 396–398. (Abstr. *Quart. J. Studies Alc.* 1965, *26*, 356.)

ZAHORSKA, A., BERGER, S. AND KRUS, S. (1955). Studies on vitamin A in liver disease. II. Relationship of vitamin A content of the liver to damage caused by ethyl alcohol. (Pol.) *Polski Tygod. Lekar. 10*, 99–101. (Abstr. *Quart. J. Studies Alc.* 1958, *19*, 167.)

ZAKIM, D. AND GREEN, J. (1968). Relation of ethanol inhibition of hepatic fatty acid oxidation to ethanol-induced fatty liver. *Proc. Soc. Exptl. Biol. Med. 127*, 138–142.

ZARROW, M. X., PAWLOWSKI, A. A. AND DENENBERG, V. H. (1962). Electroshock convulsion threshold and organ weights in rats after alcohol consumption. *Am. J. Physiol. 203*, 197–200.

ZBINDEN, G. AND PLETSCHER, A. (1958). Experimental studies on the 5-hydroxytryptamine content and the enterochromaffin cell count of the gastrointestinal tract after chronic stimulation with ethyl alcohol. (Ger.) *Schweiz. Z. Allgem. Pathol. Bakteriol. 21*, 1137–1144. (Abstr. *Quart. J. Studies Alc.* 1961, *22*, 150.)

Volume II, Part D

Applications to Clinical and Other Topics

Chapter 10

Drug Actions in Relation to Alcohol Effects

The widespread use of alcoholic beverages makes it important to know which medication can lead to undesirable joint effects, and which agents may have clinical value by antagonizing effects of alcohol. From a theoretical point of view, data in this field may contribute to our understanding of the mechanisms by which alcohol and other drugs exert their action. However, so far studies of drug effects in relation to those of alcohol have been on an empiricial level and have contributed little to real explanations of the basic phenomena involved.

As the possible ways of interaction between drugs and their implications are numerous, rather diverse subjects are included in this chapter. The questions will be dealt with in the following order: (a) drug effects during conditions of acute ethanol administration; (b) general comparisons between ethanol and other drugs; (c) drug effects in conditions of prolonged or "chronic" alcohol intake; (d) mechanism of action of drugs creating aversive reactions to ethanol; (e) substances in alcoholic beverages other than ethanol, including other alcohols, and their possible significance in giving rise to differences in the pharmacological effects of various beverages.

The review will again be restricted to the relevant experimental work. Thus the abundant clinical evidence for enhancement of alcohol-induced depression by general anesthetics, barbiturates, and narcotic analgesics will not be reviewed here. Among prior reviews which give partial coverage of the topics which are discussed here, the following may be mentioned. Elbel and Schleyer (1956) discuss mainly effects on blood alcohol, but also briefly review especially European work on other aspects of joint drug-alcohol actions. Göres (1964) deals particularly with drugs acting as antagonists of

References p. 695

[621]

alcohol in acute intoxication, and drugs enhancing the effects of alcohol. Three recent reviews of joint alcohol-drug effects (Soehring and Schüppel, 1966, 1967; Stolman, 1967; Koppanyi and Maengwyn-Davies, 1968) are based on only a minor proportion of the relevant literature. Zipf and Hamacher (1967) review the topic with particular reference to problems of traffic safety. A broad presentation of pharmacological aspects is due to Forney and Hughes (1968).

A. Joint action of drugs and acutely administered alcohol

Present knowledge of the systems involved is too superficial and fragmentary to permit a theoretically and logically consistent way of exposition. For instance, attempts to correlate chemical structure with drug action have so far been largely unsuccessful because the possible sites of interaction are so diverse and in many cases also unknown. Since published investigations also generally have been limited in scope and not systematically performed, a detailed review and discussion will not be attempted. We have composed a table (Table 10–1) in which the conditions and principal results of experiments in the field have been summarized, with the hope that this will provide a useful summary of the conclusions that can be made. In preparing the table, the 1965 edition of Goodman and Gilman's *The Pharmacological Basis of Therapeutics* has been used as a guide for classification of the drugs. The drugs have been named according to Marler's (1967) pharmacological dictionary. The present section of this chapter will supplement Table 10–1 with general comments and with some additional specific information.

Because of the variation and ambiguities in terminology for drug interactions, this section begins with specification of the terminology used by the present reviewers. Further, some general methodological problems are briefly discussed. One drug may theoretically alter the effect of another by direct molecular interaction, by interaction at a site of action in a biological system, or by action on another site in the same system. However, as a rule, there is little information about the specific mechanisms in cases where such interactions seem to be involved. A drug may also modify the action of another by altering its effective concentration at the site of action, through change in absorption from the gut or penetration into the cells, or through change in rate of metabolism or of excretion. Evidence for this type of interaction is reviewed separately. The present section is concluded

TABLE 10–1
SUMMARY OF JOINT ACTIONS OF ACUTELY ADMINISTERED ETHYL ALCOHOL WITH OTHER DRUGS

Drug	Species	Measure	Finding	Comment	Authors
GENERAL ANESTHETICS					
Ether	Rabbit, guinea pig, mouse	Duration of anesthesia	Synergism	—	Frommel and Seydoux (1964)
	Mouse	Duration of anesthesia	Synergism	—	Bourrinet (1964); Quevauviller and Bourrinet (1964)
HYPNOTICS AND SEDATIVES					
Long-acting barbiturates					
Barbital	Humans: healthy adults	Ring test	No significant effect, subjective feelings of fatigue enhanced	3/4 l 8.8% wine, 500 mg drug	Elbel (1938)
	Humans: 7 male, 1 female student	Simple psychomotor tests, behavior	Synergism	500 mg drug, alc. variable dosage, immediately or with appr. 2 or 12 h delay. Even after 12 h some severe reactions	Osterhaus (1964)
	Dog	Onset and duration of anesthesia	Antagonism first: subsequent synergism	Onset delayed but duration markedly prolonged	Ramsey and Haag (1946)
Diallylbarbituric acid	Mouse	Time for induction of anesthesia	Synergism	—	Sandberg (1951)
+ pyramidon	Humans: healthy adults	Psychomotor performance	Synergism	1/4 l cognac, 30 mg diallylbarbiturate + 220 mg pyramidon	Peter (1939)
Phenobarbital	Humans: healthy adults	Psychomotor performance	Synergism	1/4 l cognac, 300 mg drug	Peter (1939)

TABLE 10–1 (continued)

Drug	Species	Measure	Finding	Comment	Authors
Phenobarbital (cont.)	Humans: 8 male students	Reaction time, typing	Synergism (potentiation ?)	Alc. 60 or 30 ml, drug 65 mg. Alc. alone increased errors, drug slowed but decreased errors	Joyce et al. (1959)
	Rabbit	Duration of anesthesia	Synergism (potentiation ?)	—	Dille and Ahlquist (1937)
	Rabbit	Mortality	Synergism	The rabbits under urethan anesthesia	Aston and Cullumbine (1959)
	Guinea pig	Duration of anesthesia	Synergism	—	Frommel et al. (1963b)
	Mouse, guinea pig, rabbit	Duration of anesthesia	Synergism	—	Frommel and Seydoux (1964)
	Rat	Mortality	Synergism	—	Jetter and McLean (1943)
	Mouse	Duration of anesthesia	Synergism, additive	Careful statistical evaluation, theoretical discussion	Gruber (1955)
	Mouse	Mortality	Synergism	Max. mortality when adm. 2 h before alc.	Aston and Cullumbine (1959)
Short- and medium-acting barbiturates					
Amobarbital	Rat	Blood alcohol producing respiratory failure	Not modified	Drug given in "non-toxic" dose	Haggard et al. (1940)
	Rat	Chronaxies	Not modified	Combination antabuse–alcohol–drug was depressant	Lecoq et al. (1964a)
	Mouse	Time for induction of anesthesia	Synergism	—	Sandberg (1951)

TABLE 10–1 (*continued*)

Drug	Species	Measure	Finding	Comment	Authors
Amobarbital (*cont.*)	Mouse	Duration of anesthesia, mortality	Synergism, additive	Careful statistical evaluation	Fearn and Hodges (1953)
Butabarbital	Humans: healthy adults	Psychomotor performance	Synergism	200 mg drug, after 2 h 1/2 l beer	Doenicke (1962)
	Rat	Duration of anesthesia	Synergism (potentiation?)	—	Olszycka (1936)
	Mouse	Duration of anesthesia	Synergism (potentiation?)	—	Olszycka (1935)
Cyclobarbital	Mouse	Time for induction of anesthesia	Synergism	—	Sandberg (1951)
Hexethal	Rabbit	Respiratory rate and volume	No change	—	Raspopova and Zaikonnokova (1955)
Pentobarbital	Rabbit	Duration of anesthesia	Synergism (potentiation?)	—	Dille and Ahlquist (1937)
	Mouse, rabbit	Mortality, duration of anesthesia	Synergism (nearly additive)	—	Ramsey and Haag (1946)
	Rat	Shock avoidance ("anxiety"), correct escape response ("discrimination"), ability to respond	Synergism, potentiation of effect on first two measures, additive effect on responses	Effect one of general depression, not of anxiety reduction	Kopmann and Hughes (1959) Hughes and Rountree (1961)
	Mouse	Mortality	Synergism, additive	—	Graham (1960)
	Mouse, rat	Duration of anesthesia, anticonvulsive action	Synergism	—	Bourrinet (1964); Quevauviller and Bourrinet (1964)
Secobarbital	Humans: 4 healthy adult males	Performance in driving simulator (AAA Driver-Trainer)	Synergism (at least additive) with higher dose of drug	Blood alc. level 0.1%, drug 25 or 50 mg	Loomis (1963)
	Dog	Overt symptomatology	Synergism	—	Melville et al. (1966)

References p. 695

TABLE 10–1 (*continued*)

Drug	Species	Measure	Finding	Comment	Authors
Secobarbital (*cont.*)	Mouse	Duration of anesthesia	Synergism, additive	Careful statistical evaluation, theoretical discussion	Gruber (1955)
	Mouse	Mortality	Synergism, additive	—	Archer (1956)
	Mouse	Mortality	Synergism, less than additive	LD_{50} of alcohol reduced, max. mortality when drug adm. simult. with alc.	Aston and Cullumbine (1959)
Ultrashort-acting barbiturates					
Hexobarbital	Rabbit, guinea pig, mouse	Duration of anesthesia	Synergism	—	Frommel and Seydoux (1964)
	Mouse	Time for induction of anesthesia	Synergism	—	Sandberg (1951)
	Mouse	Mortality	Synergism, additive	Extensive study with review of literature	Eerola (1961)
	Mouse	Sleeping time	Synergism	—	Aston and Stolman (1966)
Thiopental	Dog	Minimal anesthetic dose, dur. of anesthesia, lethal dose	Synergism, nearly additive	—	Ramsay and Haag (1946)
	Dog, rabbit, mouse	Duration of anesthesia	Synergism	—	Smith and Loomis (1951)
	Rabbit	Respiratory rate and volume	No change	—	Raspopova and Zaikonnikova (1955)
	Rat, mouse	Duration of anesthesia, anticonvulsive action	Synergism	—	Bourrinet (1964); Quevauviller and Bourrinet (1964)
	Mouse	Time for induction of anesthesia	Synergism	—	Sandberg (1951)

TABLE 10–1 (continued)

Drug	Species	Measure	Finding	Comment	Authors
Thiopental (cont.)	Mouse	Reaction time (hot-plate technique)	No significant change	—	Smith and Loomis (1951)
	Mouse	Mortality	Synergism, additive	See above under hexobarbital	Eerola (1961)
Thialbarbital	Mouse	Time for induction of anesthesia	Synergism	—	Sandberg (1951)
Miscellaneous hypnotics					
Chloral hydrate	Dog	Ataxia, sleep	Tendency to synergism	—	Kaplan et al. (1969)
	Rat	Chronaxies	Synergism	—	Lecoq et al. (1963)
	Rat	Chronaxies	Synergism	Enhanced depressant action of antabuse–alcohol combination	Lecoq et al. (1963)
	Mouse	Righting reflex	Synergism	—	Gessner and Cabana (1964)
	Mouse	Sleeping time	Synergism, potentiation	—	Kaplan et al. (1969)
Paraldehyde	Mouse	Mortality	Synergism, less than additive	—	Weatherby and Clements (1960)
	Mouse	Mortality	Synergism, additive	—	Kaye and Haag (1964)
Urethan	Rabbit	Respiratory frequency and volume	Synergistic depression	—	Raspopova and Zaikonnikova (1955)
	Guinea pig, rabbit	Duration of anesthesia, lethal dose (rabbit)	Synergism	—	Bourrinet (1964); Quevauviller and Bourrinet (1964)
Bromine	Rat	Blood alcohol concentration required to produce respiratory failure	Not modified	—	Haggard et al. (1940)

References p. 695

TABLE 10–1 *(continued)*

Drug	Species	Measure	Finding	Comment	Authors
Bromine (cont.)	Rat	Chronaxies	Synergism	—	Lecoq et al. (1963)
	Rat	Chronaxies	Synergism	Antabuse–alcohol reaction not modified	Lecoq et al. (1963)
Methyprylone	Humans: 24 subjects	Observer's rating	No change	—	Hoffer (1958)
Methylpentynol	Rat	Chronaxies	Synergism	—	Lecoq et al. (1962)
	Mouse	Strength of pull	Synergism, potentiation	—	Bourrinet, (1964); Quevauviller and Bourrinet (1964)
Glutethimide	Dog	Overt symptomatology	Synergism	—	Melville et al. (1966)
	Mouse	Mortality	Drug enhances effect of large alc. doses, counteracts small doses	—	Glass and Mallach (1966)
Thalidomide	Mouse	Mortality	Synergism	—	Somers (1960)
Clomethiazole	Mouse	Duration of anesthesia	Synergism, additive	—	Ross (cited acc. to Svedin, 1966)
Phenethyl alcohol	Mouse	Tilting plane test	Synergism, additive	—	Wallgren et al. (1963)
Meprobamate	Humans: 50 healthy adults	Driving simulator	No sign. alteration	800 mg 30 min to 1 h before tests, 20 g alc. as whisky	Marquis et al. (1957)
	Humans: 22 healthy adults	8 psychomotor and psychological tests	In 3 tests, significant synergism in depression of function	Drug 400 mg 4 times daily for 7 days prior to test, blood alc. 0.05%	Zirkle et al. (1960)
	Humans: 4 young adults	Reaction time	No sign. change	One dose 1 h before alc., blood alc. 0.13–0.16%	Burger (1961)

TABLE 10–1 (continued)

Drug	Species	Measure	Finding	Comment	Authors
Meprobamate (cont.)	Humans: healthy adult males	Positional alcohol nystagmus (PAN I and PAN II); roving ocular movements (ROM); standing steadiness; feeling of drowsiness	Antagonistic effect on PAN I and II, increase in ROM and subjective feeling of drowsiness, decreased standing steadiness	400 + 400 mg at 4 h intervals prior to testing	Goldberg (1961)
	Humans: 4 healthy adults	Driving simulator (AAA Driver-Trainer)	Synergism with large dose	200 or 800 mg of drug 2 h before alc.	Loomis (1963)
	Humans: 8 young adults	Mental performance with delayed auditory feedback inducing anxiety	Non-significant tendency to synergism	4×400 mg at fixed intervals, last 1 h before 0.5 g alc./kg	Forney and Hughes (1965)
	Humans: 20 adults	Driving test	Alcohol effect not altered	—	Kielholz et al. (1967)
	Dog	Overt symptomatology, minimal dose for appearance	Synergism, additive	—	Forney et al. (1963a)
	Rat	Shock avoidance ("anxiety"), correct escape response ("discrimination"), ability to respond	Synergism, effect on all measures potentiated	—	Kopmann and Hughes (1959)
	Rat	ibid.	Alc. antagonizes anxiety-reducing action, increases errors	Dose of alc. 0.5 g/kg, drug given acutely	Hughes and Rountree (1961)
	Rat	Chronaxies	Synergism	Increased depressant action of antabuse–alcohol combination	Lecoq et al. (1964b)

References p. 695

TABLE 10–1 (continued)

Drug	Species	Measure	Finding	Comment	Authors
Meprobamate (cont.)	Mouse	Suspension on cord	Synergism, potentiation	—	Bourrinet (1964); Quevauviller and Bourrinet (1964)
Antihistaminic sedatives					
Buclizine	Humans: adult, healthy subjects	Positional alcohol nystagmus (PAN I and PAN II); roving ocular movements (ROM); standing steadiness; feeling of drowsiness	Antagonistic depression of PAN I and II, synergistic increase of ROM and drowsiness, decrease in standing steadiness	10 + 10 mg with 4-h interval before alcohol	Goldberg (1961)
Hydroxyzine	Humans: adult, healthy males	See above, buclizine	See above, buclizine	25 + 25 mg with 4-h interval before alcohol	Goldberg (1961)
	Mouse	Mortality	Synergism, additive	—	Eerola (1963)
Tripelennamine, chlorocyclizine, meclizine, promethazine	Humans, 36 subjects, 87 tests	Alcohol gaze nystagmus (AGN), positional alcohol nystagmus (PAN I and PAN II)	Tripelennamine no effect, all others diminished PAN II, promethazine diminished PAN I slightly, intensified AGN	Tripelennamine light sedative without effect on motion sickness. Antiemetic effect of drugs influences PAN	Aschan et al. (1957)
Clemizole, diphenhydramine, tripelennamine	Humans: 16 students	Delayed auditory feedback system for measuring mental performance in condition of self-induced anxiety	Diphenhydramine potentiated alc. in 2 out of 9 tests	Drug adm. four times at intervals prior to alc. (0.53 g/kg) and tests	Hughes and Forney (1964a)
Dimenhydrinate	Humans: four young adults	Sensory and motor coordination	Synergism, appr. additive	—	Tang and Rosenstein (1967)
Benactyzine	Mouse	Sleeping time	Synergism	—	Holten and Larsen (1956)

TABLE 10–1 (continued)

Drug	Species	Measure	Finding	Comment	Authors
LOCAL ANESTHETICS					
Cocaine-HCl	Rabbit	Corneal anesthesia	Synergism, potentiation	Increased capillary permeability and increased sensitivity of nerve cells	Quevauviller and Bourrinet (1962); Bourrinet (1964)
Procaine-HCl	Guinea pig	Cutaneous anesthesia	Synergism, potentiation	As cocaine	Quevauviller and Bourrinet (1962); Bourrinet (1964)
ANALGESICS					
Morphine	Dog	Overt symptomatology, minimal dose for appearance	Synergism	Alc. 1 g/kg	Forney et al. (1963a)
	Rabbit, guinea pig, mouse	Duration of anesthesia	Synergism	—	Frommel and Seydoux (1964)
	Guinea pig	Duration of anesthesia	Synergism	—	Frommel et al. (1963b)
	Rat	Alcohol concentration causing respiratory failure	Synergism	—	Haggard et al. (1940)
	Rat	Pain threshold	Synergism	Only brief summary statement	Bourrinet (1964)
	Mouse	Mortality	Synergism	Authors claim potentiation, but data rather suggest summation	Eerola et al. (1955)
Methadone	Mouse	Mortality	Synergism, additive	—	Eerola (1961)
	Mouse	Mortality	Synergism, additive	—	Wagner and Wagner (1958)
d-Propoxyphene	Dog	Overt symptomatology, minimal dose for appearance	Synergism, potentiation	Alc. 1 g/kg	Forney et al. (1963a)

TABLE 10–1 (continued)

Drug	Species	Measure	Finding	Comment	Authors
Pethidine	Rat	Pain threshold	Synergism	Only brief summary statement	Bourrinet (1964)
Dextromoramide	Rat	Pain threshold	Synergism	As pethidine	Bourrinet (1964)
Codeine	Dog	Overt symptomatology, minimal dose for appearance	Effect not modified	Alc. 1 g/kg	Forney et al. (1964a)
"Extracts" of valerian, opium	Rat	Chronaxies	Antagonistic action	No detailed description	Lecoq et al. (1963)
Benzacine and two closely related derivatives	Mouse	Sleeping time	Insign. tendency to prolongation	—	Dandiya and Rungta (1964)
ANTIPYRETICS					
Acetylsalicylic acid Aminophenazone	Humans: healthy adults	Ring test	Performance not modified	3/4 l of 8.8% wine, 1 g of ac., 0.6 g of am. Subjective feeling of drowsiness increased	Elbel (1938)
Acetylsalicylic acid, phenazone, phenacetin, acetanilide	Rat	Alcohol concn. causing respiratory failure	Effect not modified	—	Haggard et al. (1940)
Acetanilide	Rabbit, mouse	Mortality	Synergism, additive	—	Higgins and McGuigan (1933)
Phenylbutazone	Rat	Chronaxies	Not modified	Depressant action of alcohol–antabuse combination enchanced	Lecoq et al. (1964a)

TABLE 10–1 (continued)

Drug	Species	Measure	Finding	Comment	Authors
TRANQUILIZERS AND ALLIED DRUGS					
Chlorpromazine	Humans: adult, healthy subjects	Psychomotor performance, including AAA Driver-Trainer	Synergism	Drug 200 mg/day for a week, alcohol to produce blood level of 0.05%	Zirkle et al. (1959)
	Humans: adult healthy subjects	Positional alcohol nystagmus (PAN I and PAN II); roving ocular movements (ROM); standing steadiness; feeling of drowsiness	Antagonistic depression of PAN I and II, synergistic increase of ROM and drowsiness, decrease in standing steadiness	10 + 10 mg with 4-h interval before alcohol	Goldberg (1961)
	Humans: 4 healthy adult males	Performance in driving simulator (AAA Driver-Trainer)	Synergism 6 h after drug adm.	No change 2 h after drug adm. Drug 25 mg in single dose 2 or 6 h before test, blood alc. 0.1%	Loomis (1963)
	Dog	Overt symptomatology, minimal dose for appearance	Synergism, potentiation	Simultaneous adm.	Forney et al. (1963a)
	Guinea pig, rabbit	Duration of anesthesia	Synergism	Simultaneous adm.	Frommel and Seydoux (1964)
	Guinea pig	Duration of anesthesia	Not affected in animals weighing less than 800 g; in larger animals, sleep shortened	—	Frommel et al. (1963b)
	Rat	Chronaxies	Not modified	No change in antabuse-alcohol reaction	Lecoq et al. (1964b)

TABLE 10–1 (continued)

Drug	Species	Measure	Finding	Comment	Authors
Chlorpromazine (cont.)	Rat	Overt symptomatology, duration of anesthesia, mortality	Synergism	Drug 10 mg/kg 15 min before varying doses of alc.	Courvoisier et al. (1953)
	Rat	Shock avoidance ("anxiety"), correct escape response ("discrimination"), response to stimuli	Synergism, potentiation on all measures	Simultaneous adm.	Kopmann and Hughes (1959)
	Rat	Shock avoidance ("anxiety"), correct escape response ("discrimination")	Alcohol synergistically prolonged anxiety reduction without effect on errors	Alc. 0.5 g/kg, drug given simultaneously	Hughes and Rountree (1961)
	Rat	Chronaxies	Synergism	Simultaneous adm.	Lecoq et al. (1962)
	Rat	Chronaxies	Not modified	Enchanced depressant action of antabuse–alcohol combination	Lecoq et al. (1964b)
	Mouse	Duration of anesthesia	Synergism	Simultaneous adm.	Brodie et al. (1955)
	Mouse	Sleeping time	Synergism	—	Brodie and Shore (1957)
	Mouse	Duration of anesthesia	Synergism	Adm. of alc. at varying intervals after drug: duration of effect longer with larger dose. After successive adm. of drug, synergism decreased	Kopf (1957)
	Mouse	Mortality	Synergism, additive	—	Eerola (1963)

TABLE 10–1 (continued)

Drug	Species	Measure	Finding	Comment	Authors
Chlorpromazine (cont.)	Mouse	Sleeping time	Synergism	—	Aston and Cullumbine (1960)
Promazine, pecazine	Mouse	Loss of righting reflex	Synergism	—	Herr et al. (1961)
	Humans: 4 young adults	Reaction time to light and sound	Effect not modified	Drug 1 h before alc., blood alc. 0.13–0.16%	Burger (1961)
Promazine	Mouse	Mortality	Synergism, additive	—	Eerola (1963)
Pecazine	Mouse	Duration of anesthesia	Synergism	Duration of effect about 10 h with 10 mg drug/kg. Repeated adm. of drug and alc. diminished synergism	Kopf (1957)
Promethazine	Mouse	Mortality	Synergism, additive	—	Eerola (1963)
Fluphenazine	Humans: adult, healthy males	Psychomotor performance, projection test of social behavioral reaction	Synergism up to 8 h after adm. of drug	Drug followed at various intervals by half a liter of beer	Doenicke and Sigmund (1964)
Levomepromazine	Rat	Chronaxies	Not modified	No change in antabuse–alcohol reactions	Lecoq et al. (1964b)
Methdilazine Prothipendyl	Mouse	Sleeping time	Synergism	—	Lish et al. (1960)
	Humans: 4 young adults	Reaction time, speech and movement	Synergism in action on speech and movement, reaction time variable effect	Drug 1 h before alc., blood alc. 0.13–0.16%	Burger (1961)
Thioridazine	Rat	Chronaxies	Not modified	Increased depressant action of alcohol–antabuse combination	Lecoq et al. (1964b)
Trifluoperazine	Rat	Chronaxies	Not modified	No change in antabuse–alcohol reaction	Lecoq et al. (1964b)

TABLE 10-1 (continued)

Drug	Species	Measure	Finding	Comment	Authors
Trifluoperazine (cont.)	Rat	Chronaxies	Not modified	No change in antabuse–alcohol reaction	Lecoq et al. (1964b)
Azacyclonol	Mouse	Sleeping time	Not modified	—	Aston and Cullumbine (1960)
Benzquinamide	Humans: 8 male, 8 female, healthy adult subjects	Delayed auditory feedback system for measuring mental performance in condition of self-induced anxiety	Effect not modified	Drug 25 mg at onset of drinking, alc. appr. 0.5 g/kg body weight	Hughes et al. (1963b)
	Rat	Shock avoidance ("anxiety"), correct escape response ("discrimination")	Synergism in relief of anxiety, antagonism of errors	Effect persisted after alc. disappeared from blood	Forney and Hughes (1963)
Chlorprothixene	Rat	Chronaxies	Not modified	No change in antabuse–alcohol reaction	Lecoq et al. (1964b)
	Mouse	Righting reflex	Synergism, potentiation	—	Herr et al. (1961)
SKF-183A	Mouse	Sleeping time	Synergism	—	Aston and Cullumbine (1960)
Butyrophenone	Mouse	Suspension on cord	Synergism, potentiation	—	Bourrinet (1964); Quevauviller and Bourrinet (1964)
Chlordiazepoxide	Humans: 6 adult subjects	Evaluation of behavior in drinking situation by two observers	No change	4 double-blind expts. over 6 weeks, placebo or therap. dose 3 times a day, 6 oz. of whisky in the evening	Hoffer (1962)

TABLE 10–1 (*continued*)

Drug	Species	Measure	Finding	Comment	Authors
Chlordiazepoxide (cont.)	Humans: adult	EEG: positional alcohol nystagmus (PAN I and PAN II); roving ocular movements (ROM); standing steadiness; feeling of drowsiness	Antagonistic depression of PAN I and PAN II, synergistic increase of ROM and decrease in standing steadiness	Only general summary statement, no detailed information. EEG shifted in direction of sleep pattern.	Goldberg (1963)
	Humans: 12 male, 6 female students	Attentive motor performance with pursuit meter; mental performance with delayed auditory feedback inducing anxiety	Over-all interaction not significant although in some measures alc. synergistically increased drug effect	Drug adm. in 3 daily doses 2 days prior to testing and on morning test, alc. to give appr. 0.05 % blood level	Hughes et al. (1965)
	Humans: 20 adult subjects per treatment	Driving test	Alcohol effect not altered	—	Kielholz et al. (1967)
	Rat	Shock avoidance ("anxiety"), correct escape response ("discrimination")	Tranquilizing effect of drug antagonized by alc.	Alc. 0.5 g/kg; effect persisted after alc. disappeared from blood	Hughes et al. (1963a)
	Guinea pig	Duration of anesthesia	Not changed	—	Frommel et al. (1963b)
	Guinea pig, mouse	Duration of anesthesia	Weak synergism	—	Frommel and Seydoux (1964)
	Mouse	Loss of righting reflex	Weak synergism	—	Zbinden et al. (1961)
Diazepam	Humans: 20 healthy males	Psychological and psychomotor tests	Slight, statistically significant synergistic effect on psychomotor performance	Tests on every 4th day of medication, 1.25 h after 35 g of alc. as vodka, double blind study	Lawton and Cahn (1963)

References p. 695

TABLE 10–1 (*continued*)

Drug	Species	Measure	Finding	Comment	Authors
Diazepam (*cont.*)	Humans: 12 male, 6 female students	See above, chlordiazepoxide, same authors	Synergistic increase in impairment significant in 2 tests of 9 of mental and 2 of 4 of motor performance	See above, chlordiazepoxide, same authors	Hughes *et al.* (1965)
Phenaglycodol	Humans: healthy adult males	Positional alcohol nystagmus (PAN I and II); roving ocular movements (ROM); standing steadiness	Antagonistic effect on PAN I and II, increase in ROM and subjective feeling of drowsiness	300 + 300 mg with 4-h interval before alc.	Goldberg (1961)
	Dog	Overt symptomatology, minimal dose for appearance	Synergism, additive	—	Forney *et al.* (1963a)
	Rat	Shock avoidance ("anxiety"), correct escape response ("discrimination"), ability to respond	On first measure, synergistic additive action, on both others potentiation	—	Kopmann and Hughes (1959)
Mephenoxalone	Humans: 25 male, 14 female healthy, adult subjects	Psychomotor tests, self-report inventory	No significant alteration of impairment in any of 7 tests	Drug 400 mg 4 times daily 7 days prior to test, 35 g alc. as 100-proof vodka	Muller *et al.* (1964)
ANTIDEPRESSANTS AND ALLIED DRUGS					
Reserpine	Humans: 4 young adults	Reaction time to light and sound	Synergism, potentiation	Drug 1 h before alc. giving 0.13–0.16% blood alc.	Burger (1961)
	Dog	Overt symptomatology, minimal dose for appearance	Synergism, potentiation	—	Forney *et al.* (1963a)

TABLE 10–1 (*continued*)

Drug	Species	Measure	Finding	Comment	Authors
Reserpine (*cont.*)	Rat	Shock avoidance ("anxiety"), correct escape responses ("discrimination"), ability to respond	Synergism, additive	Simultaneous adm.	Kopmann and Hughes (1959)
	Rat	Shock avoidance ("anxiety"), correct escape responses ("discrimination")	Alcohol antagonizes anxiety-reducing action, synergistically increased errors	Dose of alc. 0.5 g/kg, drug given acutely	Hughes and Rountree (1961)
	Rat	Chronaxies	Synergism	Enhanced depressant action of alcohol–antabuse combination	Lecoq et al. (1964b)
	Mouse	Duration of anesthesia	Synergism	Simultaneous adm.	Brodie et al. (1955)
	Mouse	Duration of anesthesia	Synergism	5 mg/kg 1 h before alc.	Brodie and Shore (1957)
	Mouse	Sleeping time	Synergism	Drug 1 h prior to alc.	Aston and Cullumbine (1960)
	Mouse	Suspension on cord	Synergism (additive)	—	Bourrinet (1964); Quevauviller and Bourrinet (1964)
Reserpine; res. + imipramine	Rat	Duration of anesthesia	Synergism	Effect of res. nearly completely antagonized by pretreatment with imipramine	Sulser and Watts (1960; cited by Holtz and Westerman, 1965)
Reserpine; res. after pretreatment with imipramine or desipramine	Mouse	Duration of anesthesia	Synergism	Pretreatment with imipramine and desipramine antagonized effect of reserpine–alc. combination	Sulser et al. (1962)
Nialamide	Humans: 5 male, 5 female healthy adults	Personality, cognitive, and psychomotor tests	No change	Intoxication "seemed" more marked when drug given with alc.	Caird et al. (1960)

TABLE 10–1 (*continued*)

Drug	Species	Measure	Finding	Comment	Authors
Nialamide (*cont.*)					
Imipramine	Rat	Chronaxies	Not modified	No effect on antabuse–alcohol combination	Lecoq *et al.* (1964c)
	Cats	Circulatory effects	Not changed	Cats under anesthesia	Theobald *et al.* (1964)
	Cat, rat, mouse	Mortality (mouse); anesthetic potency	Synergism	—	Theobald and Stenger (1962)
	Rat	Chronaxies	Not changed	No effect on antabuse–alcohol combination	Lecoq *et al.* (1964c)
	Mouse	Righting reflex	Synergism	—	Herr *et al.* (1961)
	Mouse	Mortality; anesthetic potency; suspension on cord	Synergism	—	Theobald *et al.* (1964)
Desipramine	Mouse	Mortality; anesthetic potency; suspension on cord	Synergism	—	Theobald *et al.* (1964)
Opipramol	Mouse	Mortality; anesthetic potency; suspension on cord	Synergism	—	Theobald *et al.* (1964)
Amitriptyline	Humans: 21 young healthy adults	Driving simulator	Synergism	—	Landauer *et al.* (1969)
	Mouse	Righting reflex	Synergism	—	Herr *et al.* (1961)
	Rat	Toxicity	Not changed	Subchronic adm. of drug	Meyers *et al.* (1966)
	Mouse	Sleeping time	Synergism	—	Milner (1967)
	Mouse	Confinement motor activity	Synergism	—	Milner (1968a)
Amitriptyline, nortriptyline	Mouse	Mortality	Synergism	—	Milner (1968b)
Tranylcypromine	Rabbit	CNS depression	Synergism	—	Redetzki (1967)
	Rat, mouse	Motor activity	Antagonism	—	Redetzki (1967)
	Mouse	Toxicity	Not modified	—	Redetzki (1967)

TABLE 10–1 (continued)

Drug	Species	Measure	Finding	Comment	Authors
Tetrabenazines (7 derivatives)	Mouse	Spontaneous locomotion, duration of anesthesia	All compounds synergistic	Synergism independent of effect on cerebral 5-HT	Pletscher et al. (1962)
5-Hydroxytryptamine	Rat, mouse	Mortality; duration of anesthesia	Synergism	Potentiation in rat	Tammisto (1968)
	Mouse	Sleeping time	Synergistic	—	Aston and Cullumbine (1960)
5-HT; dopamine; tryptamine; tyramine	Mouse	Mortality; duration of anesthesia	Synergism, strongest with 5-HT, weakest with tyramine	Amines ineffective when adm. 30 min before alc.; synergism when adm. 30 min after alc.	Rosenfeld (1960)
PSYCHOTOMIMETICS					
LSD	Rabbit	Depression of cortical EEG	Antagonism	—	Greenberg (1967)
	Mouse	Sleeping time	Not changed	Synergism of reserpine with alc. antagonized by LSD	Brodie and Shore (1957)
	Rat	Chronaxies	Not modified	Enhanced depressant action of antabuse–alc. combination	Lecoq et al. (1964c)
LSD + reserpine or 5-HT	Mouse	Sleeping time	Antagonized synergism of reserpine and 5-HT with alc.	Synergism of chlorpromazine, meprobamate and SKF 183-A not antagonized	Aston and Cullumbine (1960)
Psilocybin	Rat	Chronaxies	Not modified	Enhanced depressant action of antabuse–alc. combination	Lecoq et al. (1964c)

TABLE 10–1 (continued)

Drug	Species	Measure	Finding	Comment	Authors
CNS-STIMULANTS					
Amphetamine	Humans: 6 adult, healthy males	Balance, hand steadiness, fusion, EEG	Slight and variable effects	Authors conclude that drug lacks practical value as antagonist of alc.	Newman and Newman (1956)
	Humans: 2 adult, healthy males	Driving simulator	Complete antagonism of 0.5 g alc./kg, incomplete antagonism of 1 g alc./kg	No effect on balance or self-criticism	Rutenfranz and Jansen (1959)
	Humans: healthy adults	Driving simulator + distracting stimuli	Drug antagonized alc. up to blood alc. of 0.06%	—	Jansen (1960)
	Humans: 8 healthy male students	Mental performance in situation of delayed auditory feed-back inducing anxiety	No clear evidence of modification	Tendency for antagonism? Dose of alc. 0.52 g/kg	Hughes and Forney (1964b)
	Humans: 25 healthy, young adults	12 tests for personality, mental, and psycho-physical performance	No sign. interaction with psycho-motor tests. Drug antagonized alc. in 3 tests of mental performance, alc. drug in 1 test	Alc. 1.2 g/kg, drug 25 mg, double-blind study	Wilson et al. (1966)
	Dog	Operant response duration	Drug and alc. synergistically increased number of responses	—	Weiss and Laties (1964)

TABLE 10–1 (continued)

Drug	Species	Measure	Finding	Comment	Authors
Amphetamine (cont.)	Rabbit	Duration of anesthesia	Antagonism in onset and duration of anesthesia, synergism in mortality	Drug did not protect against alc., but alc. offered some protection against toxic doses of drug	Reifenstein (1941)
	Rabbit	Depression of cortical EEG	Antagonism	—	Greenberg (1967)
	Rabbit, guinea pig, mouse	General activity	Alc. antagonized excitatory action of drug	—	Frommel and Seydoux (1964)
	Rat	Conc. of alc. causing respiratory failure	Not modified	—	Haggard et al. (1940)
	Rat	Performance in tilted plane test	Antagonism after 2 g alc./kg i.p.	No effect after 3 g alc./kg	Wallgren and Tirri (1963)
	Rat	Chronaxies	Antagonism	Depressant action of antabuse–alc. combination not modified	Lecoq et al. (1964c)
Caffeine	Mouse	Duration of anesthesia	Weak antagonism	—	Rosenfeld (1960)
	Humans: 6 adult, healthy males	Balance, hand steadiness, fusion, EEG	Slight and variable effects	Authors conclude that drug lacks practical value as antagonist of alc.	Newman and Newman (1956)
	Humans: 2 adult, healthy males	Driving simulator	Some antagonism (less than amphetamine)	No effect on balance or self-criticism	Rutenfranz and Jansen (1959); Jansen (1960)
	Humans: 4 male, 4 female young, healthy adults	Mental performance under delayed auditory feedback inducing anxiety	In 2 of 9 tests, drug significantly (0.5% level) antagonized alc.	—	Forney and Hughes (1965)
	Rat	Conc. of alc. causing respiratory failure	Not modified	—	Haggard et al. (1940)

TABLE 10–1 (continued)

Drug	Species	Measure	Finding	Comment	Authors
Caffeine (cont.)	Rat	Conditioned and unconditioned shock avoidance involving discrimination	Synergism	Drug potentiated depressant action of alc.	Hughes and Forney (1961)
Nortriptyline	Humans: 8 male, 8 female young, healthy adults	Mental performance under delayed auditory feedback inducing anxiety	Tendency towards antagonism, but not significant on any of nine tests	—	Hughes and Forney (1963)
Pentetrazole	Humans: 2 chronic alcoholics	Overt symptomatology	Antagonism	Return of consciousness and responsiveness in alc.-induced coma	Rosenbaum (1942)
	Dog	Respiratory failure induced by alc.	Antagonism	Spontaneous breathing resumed after drug	McCrea and Taylor (1940)
	Rabbit	Dose of drug causing convulsions	Antagonism	Convulsions after 25 mg in controls, after 60 mg with 3.15 g alc./kg	Bourrinet (1964)
Picrotoxin	Rabbit	Duration of anesthesia caused by alc.-pentobarbital combination	Weak antagonism	—	Ramsey and Haag (1946)
Nikethamide	Mouse, guinea pig, rabbit	General activity	Antagonism	—	Frommel and Seydoux (1964)
Strychnine	Cat, dog, rabbit, frog	Respiration; drowsiness, ataxia and narcosis; spinal reflexes; muscle relaxation and postural reflexes; rate of recovery from effects of alc.	Slight antagonism on "higher" functions	Drug does not protect from respiratory paralysis, but alc. protects against lethal dose of drug	Gold and Travell (1934a, b)
	Rat	Conc. of alc. causing resp. failure	Not modified	—	Haggard et al. (1940)

TABLE 10–1 (continued)

Drug	Species	Measure	Finding	Comment	Authors
Doxapram-HCl	Dog, rabbit, rat	CNS-depression	Antagonism	—	DaVanzo et al. (1964)
SYMPATHOMIMETICS AND SYMPATHOLYTICS: RELATED AGENTS					
Epinephrine	Rabbit	Overt symptoms of depression	Transient synergism	With dose of epinephrine used, 50 μg/kg i.v., transient change in distribution of alc. with overshoot in brain	Hulpieu and Cole (1946)
	Rat	Sleeping time	Synergism	—	Milošević (1956)
	Rat	Tilted-plane test	Sign. antagonism 15 min after simultaneous injection	Dose of drug 1 mg/kg i.p., alc. 2 g/kg i.p.	Wallgren and Tirri (1963)
Epinephrine, ephedrine, ergotamine, yohimbine	Rabbit (?)	Vasopressive response	Not modified	No exptl. details given	Bourrinet (1964)
Desmethyl carnitine, dimethyl-amino-ethanol	Rabbit	Depression of cortical EEG	Antagonism	Behavioral intoxication was not modified in spite of antagonistic action on EEG	Greenberg (1967)
PARASYMPATHOMIMETICS AND PARASYMPATHOLYTICS					
Acetylcholine	Cat, rabbit, frog	Depressor effect in intact cat; motility of isolated rabbit intestine; contraction of normal and eserinized frog m. rectus abdominis	Synergism in all preparations	Authors concluded that effect of alc. is partly due to inhibition of acetylcholine esterase	Ettinger et al. (1941)

TABLE 10–1 (continued)

Drug	Species	Measure	Finding	Comment	Authors
Acetylcholine (cont.)	Rabbit	Carotid pressure, bronchoconstriction	Antagonism of bronchial constriction	Hypotensive action on carotis not changed	Bourrinet (1964)
Acetylcholine; carbachol	Frog	Contraction of m. rectus abdominis	Synergism in both normal and eserinized preparation	—	Sachdev et al. (1963); Sachdev et al. (1964)
Acetylcholine, acetylcholine with physostigmine, decamethonium, hexamethonium	Rat	Respiratory response to electrical stimulation of isolated cerebral cortex tissue	Not changed	—	Wallgren (1961)
Pralidoxime dodecyl iodide, cetyltrimethyl-ammonium bromide, atropine	Rat	Respiratory response to electrical stimulation of isolated cerebral cortex tissue	Synergism, appr. additive	Alc. effect not enhanced by surface tension lowering, nonionized detergent Triton X-100	Wallgren (1961)
Pralidoxime dodecyl iodide	Rat	Tilted-plane test	Synergism, potentiation	"Potentiation" probably due to enhanced abs. of drug at simultaneous adm. i.p. of alc.	Wallgren (1961)
Carbachol, neostigmine	Rat	Maze performance, motor coordination	Synergism, less marked with neostigmine	—	MacLeod (1952)
Atropine, scopolamine	Mouse	Mortality	Synergism, additive	—	Eerola (1961)
Pilocarpine	Mouse	Duration of anesthesia	Synergism after prior adm. of atropine methyl bromide	—	Proctor et al. (1966)
Methacholine	Mouse	Duration of anesthesia	Not changed	—	Proctor et al. (1966)

TABLE 10–1 (continued)

Drug	Species	Measure	Finding	Comment	Authors
CARDIOVASCULAR DRUGS					
Digitaline	Guinea pig	Lethal dose of drug, slow infusion	Not modified	—	Bourrinet (1964)
Ouabain	Rat	Respiratory response of cerebral tissue to electrical stimulation *in vitro*	Not modified	Alc. and drug both depressed response	Wallgren (1963)
DIURETICS					
Ethacrynic acid	Mouse, dog	Mortality of mice, venous blood alc. of dogs	Increased mortality, higher blood alc.	Weak inhibition of liver alc. dehydrogenase; alc. may enhance diuretic action	Dixon and Rall (1965)
CHEMOTHERAPEUTICS					
Isoniazid	Mouse	Mortality	Synergism in LD_{50}; small doses of either drug antagonize toxicity of other	Small doses of alc. protect completely from LD_{50} of drug	Glass et al. (1964)
	Mouse	Mortality	Previous finding repeated	Drug adm. on 8 consecutive days prior to test	Glass and Mallach (1965)
Quinine	Dog, cat, rabbit, rat	Duration of anesthesia	Synergism when drug adm. 30–60 min before alc.	At simultaneous adm. effect not altered	Orahovats et al. (1957)
NON-THERAPEUTIC AGENTS					
L-Asparagine	Mouse	Mortality, duration of anesthesia, immobility time	Mortality not changed, synergism with other measures	—	Forney et al. (1963)

References p. 695

TABLE 10–1 (continued)

Drug	Species	Measure	Finding	Comment	Authors
γ-Aminobutyric acid	Mouse	Mortality, duration of anesthesia	Mortality not changed, antagonism of anesthesia	—	Rosenfeld (1960)
Glutamine	Rat	Tilted-plane test	Variable response, generally antagonism	Rats fasted overnight	Sammalisto (1962)
Dimethylsulfoxide	Humans: young, healthy adults	Conduction velocity, ulnar nerve	Synergism	—	Mayer et al. (1966)
	Mouse	Mortality	Synergism, nearly additive	With alc. LD_{50} and drug LD_{50}, some antagonism of alc. toxicity	Mallach and Etzler (1965)
Malonate	Rat	Respiratory response of cerebral tissue to electrical stimulation in vitro	Not modified	Both alc. and malonate depress response	Wallgren (1960a)
Maleate	Rat	Test for motor co-ordination	Antagonistic	Drug 75 mg daily for 6 days prior to test	MacLeod (1952)
	Rat	Tilted-plane test	Not modified	Procedure of MacLeod repeated	Wallgren (unpubl.)
Fluorocitrate	Rat	Tilted-plane test	Synergism	Effect may be related to anticholine-esterase activity of drug	Wallgren (unpubl.)
Sodium azide	Rat	Respiratory response of cerebral cortex to K^+-stimulation in vitro	Drug antagonistic in 5 μM conc., additively synergistic in 1 mM conc.	—	Fischer (1957)
Dinitrophenol	Rat	Blood alc. conc. causing respiratory failure	Not modified	"Non-toxic" dose of drug	Haggard et al. (1940)

TABLE 10–1 (continued)

Drug	Species	Measure	Finding	Comment	Authors
Carbon monoxide	Humans: 11 patients with chronic producer gas intoxication; 7 simultaneous controls and 49 subjects studied previously	Psychomotor performance	Alcohol effect not modified	Clinical data (Mallach and Rössler, 1961) suggest synergism in CO-poisoning	Bjerver and Goldberg (1948)
	Mouse	CO-hemoglobin levels at death	Lower during alc. intoxication	Result may be related to efficiency of respiration	Mallach and Rössler (1961)
Carbon tetrachloride, trichloroethylene, perchloroethylene, 1,1-trichloroethylene	Rat	Toxicity to liver assessed from serum enzymes (SGOT, SGPT, SICD)	Alc. enhanced enzyme activities after carbon tetrachloride and trichloroethylene	Alc. 5 g/kg, exposure to vapors 2 h, blood samples 24 or 48 h	Cornish and Adefuin (1966)
Monofluoroethanol, monochloroethanol	Monkey, rat	Mortality	Antagonism of drug effect by alc.	—	Peterson et al. (1968)

with general comments on the experimental findings summarized in Table 10–1.

(1) A note on terminology and methodology

In summarizing the interactions of ethanol with other drugs, we have preferred current British terminology as adopted for instance by Macgregor (1965) to that proposed by Goodman and Gilman (1965). According to this, drug interactions can be antagonistic, inapparent, or synergistic. These terms, especially the last of them, require further qualification.

The term "antagonistic" is self-explanatory. One manifestation of antagonism is the case of equal and opposite actions which cancel each other out, as found in Rutenfranz and Jansen's (1959) and Jansen's (1960) experiments on effects of amphetamine and alcohol on performance in a driving simulator (Table 10–1). Macgregor (1965) exemplifies such cases as inapparent interaction, but the joint drug action differs from the effect of either drug alone. Two drugs may also affect an organism or a preparation in a manner that looks superficially similar, but have a joint action which does not differ from that of one agent given singly. Obviously then, only the effect of that agent becomes manifest which at that particular concentration has a greater effect. We may then assume that the two agents affect different rate-limiting processes in an entirely independent manner, or in other words, neither of them influences the biological action of the other.

"Synergism" is here used to indicate joint actions in the same direction, as the Greek roots of the word suggest. Synergism can be "additive" in the case when the combined action is equal to the sum of the separate actions of the drugs in the doses employed. It can also be less than additive, or more than additive. In the latter case, the action will be indicated as "potentiation". A distinction between additive and summated effects will not be adopted here.

As pointed out in the introductory remarks of this section, one drug can affect the action of another in various ways. Also, many conditions affect the joint actions found. These possibilities obscure the nature of interactions in the intact organism. When joint actions of drugs are tested, a number of variables should be controlled, including age, sex, time of day, nutritional state, external temperature, dosage, route and mode of administration, the time of administration of one agent in relation to the other, and use of isolated or grouped individuals. If one wants precise information concerning the nature of possible interactions, observations on the intact organism usually have to be supplemented with data on effects in organ preparations and even subcellular fractions. Isolated preparations have the advantage that the nature of interactions can be relatively easily determined, but the disadvantage that the findings do not always correspond to joint effects in the intact organism. For evaluation of the practical aspects of joint actions, therefore, experiments with intact organisms are obviously necessary, although they do not specify the mechanism for synergism or antagonism. Experiments with one or a few species naturally preclude generalization, and predictions from animals to man cannot be safely made.

Determination of the quantitative relationships in joint drug actions is especially difficult when measuring actions of small dosages on various psychophysiological parameters. One source of complications is that a drug combination can give rise to entirely new reaction patterns not obtained at any dosage level with the drugs administered singly. When the interaction occurs primarily in the central nervous system, it is easy to picture how such novel patterns might arise. If for instance one of the drugs at a certain dose level depresses inhibitory pathways and the other is given in a dose which slightly lowers thresholds in excitatory systems, the joint result may be one of excitation and hyperactivity not obtained with either of the drugs alone at any dose level. Some instances of deviating patterns of action have been reported for instance by Hughes, Forney, and their associates in studies on the joint action of alcohol and various tranquilizers. Thus, joint action of one tranquilizer with alcohol cannot be used to predict that of another.

Further, when a battery of tests is used, the characteristic effect of one of the drugs may be modified in some of the tests, whereas no significant interaction is apparent in others. The use of several tests should thus give a more reliable picture of the over-all interaction than is possible with a single test. A case in point is the study by Wilson et al. (1966) on the joint action of 1.2 g ethanol/kg plus 15 mg amphetamine in human subjects. Twelve tests for personality, mental capability, and psychophysical perform-ance were employed in a double-blind design with appropriate controls. Amphetamine counteracted alcohol in three tests of mental performance, whereas it decreased test-retest reliability in the Wonderlic personnel test, an effect which was significantly counteracted by alcohol.

Carpenter and Varley (1963) deal with problems in experimental design for psychological testing of joint drug actions and suggest some mathematical and statistical approaches to analysis of interactions. They also point out that the normal use of psychotherapeutic agents is often chronic, so that prolonged observation is necessary for a realistic view of the interaction with alcohol. In the comments in Table 10–1 concerning experiments with human subjects, particular attention has been paid to whether drugs have been administered in one "acute" dose or in a more chronic fashion.

(2) Modification of absorption and penetration

According to Siegmund (1938), Rinkel and Myerson (1941), and Koda (1966), epinephrine and related sympathomimetic drugs (amphetamine, paredrine, and atropine) delay absorption of orally administered ethanol in humans. Epinephrine has the most marked effect but does not change the distribution of ethanol administered i.v. In a study by Wilson *et al.* (1966) a dose of 15 mg amphetamine was not found to modify the blood alcohol curve in human subjects. Elbel and Schleyer (1956) concluded in their review that the absorption of alcohol in man or animals is not influenced by barbiturates in therapeutic doses, whereas alcohol absorption may be somewhat slowed by doses of barbiturate sufficient to cause narcosis. Various antipyretics and non-narcotic analgesics generally appear to have no effect, but some (quinine, acetylsalisylic acid in rats), have been found to delay absorption. Caffeine does not influence the blood alcohol curve. The absorption of ethanol was slowed in humans under treatment with nialamide, chlorpromazine, and haloperidol, whereas imipramine and diazepam had no effect (Casier *et al.*, 1966). Contrariwise, Sutherland *et al.* (1960) found chlorpromazine to speed the absorption of alcohol in problem drinkers. In dogs, chlorpromazine given acutely did not modify the absorption of ethanol (Seidel *et al.*, 1964a). According to sources cited by Elbel and Schleyer (1956), the rate of alcohol absorption can be increased by cholinergic agents that stimulate gastrointestinal motility. In rabbits, dimethyl-aminoethanol and desmethylcarnitine do not alter the distribution of ethanol (Greenberg, 1967).

Magnussen and Frey (1967) and Magnussen (1968) have reported that in rats, alcohol given orally in a concentration of 2.5 to 10% w/v or present in the blood in a concentration of 0.15% enhances the absorption of pentobarbital and phenobarbital, apparently through an increase in splanchnic blood flow since absorption through isolated intestine was not affected. Seidel (1967) found that in mice, ethanol administered orally in a dose of 3 g/kg increased the concentration of pentobarbital but not of barbital or thiopental in the blood and tissues.

In some cases, various diffusional barriers, at sites of intestinal absorption or at the tissue or organ level, clearly modify joint actions. Many pharmaceutical preparations include alcohol as a solvent and vehicle for therapeutic agents. In the same capacity, alcohol may also enhance the effect of certain noxious agents. Alha (1950) has described clinical cases of joint alcohol-carbon tetrachloride poisoning in which alcohol appeared to act by promoting intestinal absorption of the carbon tetrachloride. This finding has apparently not been verified experimentally. A different assumption is necessary to explain the finding of Kutob and Plaa (1962) that sleeping time induced by chloroform was prolonged in mice that had been given alcohol in a dose of 5 g/kg 12 or 48 h before the chloroform. They attributed the effect to retention of chloroform in liver lipids accumulated as a result of ethanol intoxication.

Although synergism between acetylcholine and alcohol is seen in preparations of peripheral organs (*cf. e.g.* Ettinger *et al.*, 1941; Chapter 5, p. 222), actions of ethanol in isolated cerebral tissue are modified only by lipid soluble analogues of acetylcholine, apparently on account of their ability to penetrate into the tissue (Wallgren, 1961). Of this group of agents, pyridinealdoximedodecyl iodide (pralidoxime, PAD) is additively synergistic with alcohol *in vitro* but potentiates the effect of alcohol *in vivo* (Wallgren, 1961). On the basis of indirect evidence, alcohol appeared to act as a vehicle promoting absorption of PAD after intraperitoneal administration, and also perhaps promoting permeation through the blood–brain barrier. Thus the finding *in vitro*, rather than the one *in vivo*, seemed to correspond to the actual quantitative relationship of the effects of the two drugs at the site of action. Rosenfeld's (1960) findings suggest that alcohol may facilitate penetration of monoamines through the blood-brain barrier, as suggested by Estler and Ammon (1965) for noradrenaline.

Barbiturates are generally assumed to enhance the effects of alcohol by sensitizing central neurons, but a contributing factor may also be that alcohol facilitates their penetration into the brain. Dille *et al.* (1935) have found that when barbiturates are injected in the carotid arteries of dogs in alcoholic solutions (50% methyl alcohol), the levels of barbiturate in the brain tissue rise considerably higher than after injection in aqueous solution. It is not known whether this would be true also after normal systemic dilution of the alcohol, as suggested by Miller (1952). In kidney slices and erythrocytes, no marked effect on alcohol after barbiturate uptake was found by Greiser and Soehring (1967) who claimed that 0.4% ethanol diminished uptake of pentobarbital in a low concentration and enhanced uptake in a high concentration. Both of these effects accounted for only a small, energy-dependent fraction of the total barbiturate uptake.

Studies have also been reported with some other compounds less commonly tested for interactions with ethanol. According to Kudsk (1965), ethanol reduces the pulmonary absorption of mercury from contaminated air. Levy *et al.* (1966) have reported that the non-ionic surfactant polysorbate 80 does not change the absorption of alcohol in goldfish, a finding which is not surprising considering how easily ethanol penetrates tissues.

(3) Modification of metabolism or excretion

Theoretically, there are several possibilities for metabolic interactions of ethanol with drugs. The substrate specificity of liver alcohol dehydrogenase is relatively low, and competitive inhibition may be expected between ethanol and other substrates of LADH. Drugs may also be direct inhibitors of LADH. The LADH-catalyzed reaction in the cytoplasm is absolutely dominant in the removal of ethanol and evidently is not substrate-inducible (Chapter 9, p. 524), but some microsomal oxidation of ethanol also occurs. In the present section of this chapter, we review some data on direct metabolic interaction between ethanol and drugs resulting from acute rather than chronic administration of ethanol and other drugs. Examples of competitive interactions will be provided particularly in section D 2 of this chapter which deals with other alcohols. Since changes in microsomal enzyme activities generally can be expected only after repeated drug administration, this aspect is discussed in section C in which relationships between ethanol and drugs in chronic use are reviewed.

There are a number of observations on levels of alcohol in blood, and in some cases also in tissues, made at a sufficient time interval after administration of alcohol to indicate effects of other drugs on alcohol concentrations independent of absorption changes. Elbel and Schleyer (1956) cite many instances when drugs have not been observed to modify blood alcohol levels. Several other studies have led to similar conclusions. According to Bonnichsen *et al.* (1968), a combination of butethal and aprobarbital does not affect elimination of alcohol in humans. In dogs, barbital does not influence blood alcohol (Ramsey and Haag, 1946). Phenobarbital does not alter the rate of alcohol elimination in rabbits (Dille and Ahlquist, 1937) or guinea pigs (Frommel *et al.*, 1963a). Brain and blood alcohol levels in rats are unaffected by butabarbital (Olszycka, 1936).

In humans, no effect on blood alcohol levels has been detected for chlordiazepoxide (Hughes *et al.*, 1965; Bonnichsen *et al.*, 1968), benzquinamide (Khan *et al.*, 1964), clomethiazole and chlorprotixen (Bonnichsen *et al.*, 1968), amphetamine (Rutenfranz and Jansen, 1959), nialamide, imipramine, haloperidol, and diazepam (Casier *et al.*, 1966; Hughes *et al.*, 1965), and carbon monoxide (Bjerver and Goldberg, 1948).

In dogs, pentylenetetrazol fails to alter the rate of alcohol elimination (McCrea and Taylor, 1940). Seidel and Soehring (1965) have reported that 41 commonly used therapeutic agents, including barbiturates, tranquilizers and related drugs, antidepressants, central stimulants, analgesics, and a few chemotherapeutics, all lack influence on the rate of alcohol elimination in dogs. Dixon and Rall (1965) found that in dogs, ethacrynic acid slightly slowed the rate of elimination, a finding reported for pheniprazine by Smith *et al.* (1961).

Blood alcohol in guinea pigs is unaffected by morphine (Frommel *et al.*, 1963a). In rats, rate of alcohol elimination is not influenced by hydroxyzine, meprobamate, chlordiazepoxide, reserpine, benzquinamide (Khan *et al.*, 1964), iproniazid (Smith *et al.*, 1961), amphetamine (Wallgren and Tirri, 1963), glutamine (Sammalisto, 1962), and fluorocitrate (Wallgren, *unpubl.*). In the mouse, Rosenfeld (1960) found brain and blood alcohol levels to be unaffected by the primary aromatic monoamines 5–hydroxytryptamine, dopamine, tryptamine, and tyramine.

Species differences may occur. Khan *et al.* (1964) found that the metabolism of alcohol in mice was slowed by benzquinamide whereas it was unaffected in man and rat. According to Redetzki (1967), the monoamine oxidase inhibitor trancylpromine decreased the rate of alcohol elimination in mice but not in rabbits. Species differences may in part explain conflicting observations with respect to chlorpromazine. In rabbits and rats (Schleyer and Janitzki, 1963), rabbits (Mathieu *et al.*, 1964) and dogs (Smith *et al.*, 1961) single doses have been found to slow alcohol elimination. Tipton *et al.* (1961) reported a similar effect of daily injection of chlorpromazine to rabbits for a week. On the other hand, experiments with dogs (Seidel *et al.*, 1964a; Seidel and Soehring, 1965), rats (Khan *et al.*, 1964), mice (Brodie *et al.*, 1955) and humans (Casier *et al.*, 1966) have failed to show an effect of chlorpromazine. Thus consistent results have been obtained with rabbits only.

References p. 695

A few experimenters have demonstrated direct inhibition of liver alcohol dehydrogenase (LADH) by common therapeutic agents. Dixon and Rall (1965) found ethacrynic acid to be a weak inhibitor of the enzyme. Pyrazole and pyrazolone drugs such as phenylbutazone inhibit the LADH reaction in both directions. This inhibition can be reversed by NAD and NADH. Pyrazole and some of its derivatives are among the most effective inhibitors of LADH tested so far. Experiments have been performed with animals *in vivo* (Goldberg and Rydberg, 1969; Rydberg, 1969; Lester and Benson, 1969; Watkins *et al.*, 1969) and shown a dose-dependent slowing of the rate of ethanol elimination. Lelbach (1969) induced hepatic lesions in rats by combined prolonged administration of ethanol and pyrazole in doses sufficient to cause partial inhibition of LADH. Since the evidence reviewed in Chapter 9, section D suggests metabolic interactions and nutritional imbalance as predominant etiological factors in liver damage associated with chronic alcohol consumption, the result seems paradoxical. A direct action of pyrazole, perhaps synergistic with ethanol, is indicated. *In vitro* inhibition of liver ADH has been found with psychopharmacological agents such as pheniprazine (JB 516) and 1–amphetamine (Sankar *et al.*, 1961; Smith *et al.*, 1961). Khouw *et al.* (1963) demonstrated that chlorpromazine inhibited horse and rabbit LADH in an unspecific way. A report by Japanese workers that thiamine tetrahydrofurfuryl disulfide inhibits yeast ADH prompted Berndt and Kutschke (1967) to study its effect on alcohol elimination in humans, with negative result. Evidently, direct inhibition of LADH activity by drugs is relatively rare. In an abstract, DaVanzo *et al.* (1964) communicate the rather unique finding that both LADH activity and the rate of alcohol elimination in rats are markedly raised by doxapram hydrochloride. The finding has apparently not been reported in detail.

The depressant action of chloral hydrate is in part due to its metabolite trichloroethanol. Alcohol has been found to enhance the conversion of chloral hydrate to this metabolite (Gessner and Cabana, 1967a). According to Kaplan *et al.* (1969), ethanol and chloral hydrate mutually inhibited each other's metabolism in mice. In dogs, chloral hydrate did not affect the metabolism of ethanol, but ethanol caused increase in the concentrations of both chloral hydrate and its metabolite trichloroethanol. This apparent species difference may in part have been due to the larger dose used in mice. Gessner and Cabana (1967b) have shown that the greater hypnotic effect of chloral alcoholate than of chloral hydrate arises through splitting of the alcoholate into chloral hydrate and ethanol. Creaven and Roach (1969) report that chloral hydrate in doses of 200 and 400 mg/kg causes marked increase in blood acetaldehyde of mice during the first hour after injection of ethanol, and also changes the elimination of ethanol from a linear to a logarithmic time course.

The smooth endoplasmic reticulum of the liver cells contains a number of oxidative, NADP-dependent enzyme systems which participate in the metabolism of a variety of drugs. These systems are connected with an electron transport chain terminating in a heme protein, cytochrome P-450. One of these enzymes metabolizes ethanol, according to observations in microsomes from pig and rat livers (Chapter 3, p. 90), but its quantitative role is not known. In any case, the existence of this enzyme system has aroused interest in possible changes in these systems as a consequence of administration of ethanol or other drugs. Lind and Parkes (1967) assumed that such interactions explained their finding that SKF 525A, an inhibitor of these enzymes, slightly prolonged ethanol-induced sleeping time in mice whereas pretreatment with the enzyme inductors chlorpromazine, pento-barbital, and amitriptyline (but not imipramine) shortened the sleeping time. However, the rationale of the experiments was the controversial claim that in mice, ethanol elimination would be higher during the first half hour after administration than later (Marshall and Owens, 1955; Forney et al., 1962), a finding not confirmed by Kinard (1963). Since Lind and Parkes (1967) worked within the time span required for absorption and distribution of alcohol, and very small changes in the drug level in the brain affect sleeping time markedly, their interesting conclusion as yet can be accepted only with reservation.

Some older work on barbiturate elimination does not suggest any effect of ethanol in animals (Dille and Ahlquist, 1937; Ramsey and Haag, 1946; Kato and Chiesara, 1962) or humans (Graham, 1960). However, Schüppel et al. (1967) have published a preliminary report according to which ethanol slows the elimination of pentobarbital in rats. Rubin and Lieber (1968b) found that ethanol inhibited the aerobic microsomal enzymes metabolizing pentobarbital, aniline, and benzpyrene, whereas the anaerobic nitroreductase system was not affected. Part of the synergism in joint action of pentobarbital and alcohol was attributed to this effect. Schüppel et al. (1967) also reported that ethanol inhibited the hydroxylation of acetanilide in rat liver tissue. Schüppel (1968) observed increased amounts of acetanilide glucuronate in rat liver after administration of ethanol, and assumed that the reason was inhibition of the oxidative degradation. In later experiments Jofre de Breyer

References p. 695

and Soehring (1968) found that in rat liver slices, small and moderate concentrations of ethanol (17 μM and 17 mM) did not suppress hydroxylation but rather enhanced glucuronate-conjugation. With 85 mM ethanol (approximately 0.4%), hydroxylation was inhibited whereas conjugation still was enhanced. Evidently, interactions between ethanol and other drugs in the microsomal enzyme systems require much more study.

The studies reviewed in the prior section show that alcohol-drug interactions are not infrequently modified by changes in absorption and penetration, whereas the present section indicates that direct metabolic interactions are rare. Most cases of joint actions seem to arise through interactions at the target sites, but more studies are needed of possible effects of ethanol on drug metabolism.

(4) Further comments

Even a cursory examination of Table 10–1 shows that the majority of the studies deal with interactions between alcohol and other drugs acting primarily on the central nervous system. This orientation is a natural consequence of the predominantly central actions of ethanol. In some cases, placement of a drug in a particular group in the table has been decided primarily on the basis of the assumed dominant site of interaction rather than the drug's structural and pharmacological relationships to other drugs. Thus, amphetamine has been placed with the central nervous stimulants although it is structurally related to norepinephrine and has sympathomimetic actions. The aromatic monoamines, also structurally related to epinephrine, have been placed with the antidepressants because drugs such as reserpine may act through effects on the binding of monoamines.

Some reports of joint effects of alcohol and other drugs give only brief summary statements concerning technique and results, thus precluding critical appraisal (Quevauviller and Bourrinet, 1964; Bourrinet, 1964; Frommel and Seydoux, 1964; Lecoq et al., 1962; 1963; 1964a, b, c). However, most of the studies cited in Table 10–1 appear to have been carefully conducted and adequately reported. A problem which has attracted rather extensive investigation is whether the synergism of alcohol with other central nervous depressants is additive or potentiating. Theoretical discussions are included in the papers by Gruber (1955) and Eerola (1961). Potentiation has been observed almost exclusively with hypnotic agents and tranquilizers, and then usually in measures of behavioral performance but not in lethal effects. When definite conclusions have been possible, the synergism has usually been additive or slightly less than additive rather than showing effects of potentiation. In some instances, potentiation has been assumed on an entirely erroneous basis. For example Olszycka (1935, 1936) used an index of potentiation defined as the duration of anesthesia ("sleeping time") caused by alcohol and butabarbital jointly divided by the sum of the sleeping times found after administration of each drug alone. This index is based on the invalid assumption that sleeping time is related to potency in an arithmetic rather than logarithmic or other function. With this index, her own results lead to the obviously spurious conclusion that 0.8 g of alcohol/kg "potentiates" by 8–27 times the effect of 2.4 g/kg of the same drug. Lind and Parkes (1967) likewise have shown that in mice, increase of the alcohol dose given i.p. from 5 to 6 g/kg increases the sleeping time from 10 to 65 min. A better basis for comparison could be obtained by administering alcohol and the other drug tested separately in doses twice as large as those used in the joint testing. The index of potentiation then could be the sleeping time after joint administration divided by the mean sleeping time after the double doses of both drugs separately. Eerola *et al.* (1955) incorrectly assumed that morphine potentiated the effect of alcohol on the basis of statistical treatment of mortality rates at various dosage levels, because they were not aware that the slope of the dose–response relationship is much steeper for alcohol than for morphine. Eerola (1961) with the use of another statistical method which is widely employed in this kind of pharmacological work, convincingly demonstrated that the synergism between alcohol and morphine is slightly less than additive.

Although the quantitative nature of synergistic action is often difficult to measure, the potencies of related drugs can be compared more easily. Sandberg (1951) concluded that barbiturates potentiated alcohol to varying degrees in the following order of decreasing potency: hexobarbital, amobarbital, diallylbarbituric acid, thialbarbital, thiopental, and cyclobarbital. However, the differences among these barbiturates in potency may have been due in part to variations in the duration of action, which naturally influences the results when drugs are given at a constant time in relation to alcohol administration. Aston and Cullumbine (1959) found maximum mortality when secobarbital was administered simultaneously with the alcohol whereas the maximal effect with the slow-acting phenobarbital was obtained when the drug was administered 2 h before alcohol.

In the case of drugs which are metabolized extremely rapidly, the time relation is particularly important, as exemplified by Rosenfeld's (1960) experiments with aromatic monoamines (Table 10–1, antidepressants and allied drugs). For paraldehyde, Weatherby and Clements (1960) reported maximal effect of simultaneous administration intraperitoneally whereas Kaye and Haag (1964) with the oral route of administration found the largest effect when paraldehyde was given 3–6 h after alcohol. Etzler, Joswig and Mallach (1966) showed that with simultaneous administration small doses of dimethyl sulfoxide somewhat diminished the toxicity of alcohol to mice, whereas administration one hour apart enhanced the toxicity irrespective of the order in which the drugs were given. Several experimenters have studied the possibility of synergistic cardiovascular effects of anesthetic agents and alcohol. These problems are of obvious clinical interest, owing to the numerous instances when alcohol intoxication leads to an accident followed by surgery. Ganz (1963) demonstrated that myocardial oxygen consumption of dogs anesthetized with thiopental increased during alcohol infusion whereas stroke volume and cardiac output decreased. Similar results were obtained by Willard and Horvath (1964) with dogs under pentobarbital anesthesia. The observation of decreased myocardial efficiency has been substantiated in later studies on dogs under pentobarbital (Degerli and Webb, 1963; Webb and Degerli, 1965; Valicenti and Newman, 1968) in which stroke work and systemic pressure increased and myocardial function deteriorated after doses of alcohol as small as 0.5 g/kg. When alcohol in a total dose of appr. 1.5 g/kg was slowly infused into anesthetized dogs over a period of 2 h, diminished efficiency was evident already at 15 min and persisted for 5 h (Regan et al., 1966). Significant elevations of coronary sinus potassium, phosphate, and transaminase suggested direct myocardial injury. Triglyceride content of the myocardium increased from 0.38 to 1.25 mg/g wet weight. The authors point out that sympathetic stimulation may be involved since infusion of catecholamines provoked similar effects. The results also showed the importance of the joint action of the anesthetics used and the ethanol administered. Even a low dose of alcohol can have a deleterious effect on the heart in combination with anesthesia. Variable responses to alcohol have been reported under other conditions of anesthesia or shock. Knott et al. (1963) did not see any deleterious effect of ethanol (3 g/kg by stomach tube) on the response to a moderate hemorrhagic stress induced in anesthetized dogs. However, in other experiments with dogs (Gettler and Albritten, 1963), acute hemorrhage comprising 33% of the blood volume caused 30% mortality of animals receiving alcohol in addition to anesthesia compared to no deaths in anesthetized controls. This toxic effect was partly due to lowered arterial pressure, and also acidosis resulting from hypoventilation. Webb *et al.* (1966) in experiments with anesthetized dogs, found that ouabain and cortisol aided effectively in restoration and maintenance of myocardial function when doses of up to 1.5 g alcohol/kg were given. Paradise and Stoelting (1965) have on the other hand reported that when ventricular tachycardia had been induced in dogs under pentobarbital anesthesia by administration of acetyl strophantidin, alcohol restored normal sinus rhythm. Also Madan and Gupta (1967) have shown that experimentally induced cardiac arrhythmias are attenuated by ethanol.

An occasional side effect particularly of unbuffered salicylates is erosion of the gastric mucosa with bleeding. According to Bouchier and Williams (1969), simultaneous ingestion of buffered sodium acetylsalicylate and alcohol, the latter in a dose of approximately 0.6 g/kg, did not cause gastric bleeding in healthy humans. Goulston and Cooke (1968) found that a slightly larger dose of alcohol (0.7 g/kg) significantly increased the fecal blood loss caused by unbuffered acetylsalicylate.

The interactions between alcohol and monoamines, acetylcholine and related compounds functioning as transmitter substances at synaptic junctions, were already discussed (Chapter 5, p. 238–242) because they may provide valuable clues to the sites of alcohol action. These agents act synergistically with a number of general anesthetics as well as with alcohol; for example curarizing agents are synergistic with ether (Naess, 1950; Secher, 1951) and barbiturates (Goodman and Gilman, 1965), and pentobarbital, ether and halothane are synergistic with 5-hydroxytryptamine (Tammisto, 1965).

Antagonism of the effects of ethanol is almost exclusively a property of central nervous system stimulants. In some cases as with caffeine, the effect evidently is weak enough to be questionable. In a critical review, Menninger-Lerchenthal (1960) stated that central stimulants mitigate the effects of alcohol only when intoxication is not too severe. Wallgren and Tirri (1963) suggested that the central activating effect of amphetamine antagonizes depression of the brain-stem midbrain reticular formation, but only at low concentrations of alcohol whose effects become irreversible at higher concentrations. A possible exception is pentylenetetrazol, which according to McCrea and Taylor (1940) induced spontaneous breathing in dogs after respiratory failure had been induced with alcohol. No effect was seen on rate of alcohol elimination or duration of coma. Rosenbaum (1942) carried out similar experiments on two alcoholics. After a large dose of alcohol, inducing coma, 9 ml of 10% pentylenetetrazol restored consciousness and responsiveness in spite of blood alcohol levels above 0.4%. Picrotoxin, as a powerful central stimulant, might have similar effects. However, the convulsant property of these drugs probably has been the main factor precluding their use in treatment of alcohol poisoning.

Table 10–1 does not include several investigations on joint actions of drugs with alcohol which were cited in the review by Elbel and Schleyer (1956). Some reports also cited by Dille and Ahlquist (1937) indicated that barbiturates antagonized the effects of alcohol, but later investigators have almost unanimously agreed that the joint action is synergistic. Elbel and Schleyer also cite a weak synergism between alcohol and nicotine. Other drugs reported to act synergistically with alcohol, which thus cannot be used to mitigate intoxication, were some antipyretics and non-narcotic analgesics, especially pyrazolon-derivatives which now are known to inhibit liver alcohol dehydrogenase. The central nervous system stimulant nikethamide was reported to be an effective antagonist, with a prompt arousing effect in alcohol intoxication. The antagonistic effect of caffeine was found to be weak, directed only on selected aspects of functioning, and on the whole without practical significance. These conclusions are similar to those given above and in Table 10–1.

The interactions between alcohol and other agents affecting water and ion excretion seem to be quite complex. Alcohol inhibits production of antidiuretic hormone (Chapter 4, p. 166); caffeine has the opposite effect, but through a direct effect on the kidney, its net effect like that of alcohol is a rise in urine flow. Alcohol and caffeine together cause a large increase in urine flow in intact dogs; after hypophysectomy, the response to caffeine is increased whereas that to caffeine and alcohol given together is smaller than in the intact animal (Heidenreich, 1957). Alcohol reduces chloride excretion (Chapter 4, p. 168) whereas caffeine and nicotine alone both have the opposite effect. The effect of alcohol is not altered by joint administration with caffeine (Heidenreich, 1957) but is antagonized by nicotine (Bisset and Walker, 1957).

Most of the findings summarized in Table 10–1 were obtained from laboratory animals, and as already mentioned this information can be accepted only with reservations as valid for humans. However, a substantial number of studies on humans have been carried out with hypnotics, tranquilizers, and central stimulants. At least in their broad features, the data

TABLE 10–2

AGREEMENT OF EXPERIMENTS ON HUMANS AND ANIMALS IN SHOWING ANTAG-
ONISM, ADDITIVE SYNERGISM OR POTENTIATING SYNERGISM BETWEEN ETHYL
ALCOHOL AND OTHER DRUGS

The figures have been compiled from Table 10–1

Drug category		Total number of studies	Number of studies showing		
			Antago-nism	Synergism	Potentiation
General anesthetics	Humans	—	—	—	—
	Animals	2	—	2	—
Hypnotics and	Humans	19	—	10	1+2?
sedatives	Animals	64	1	50	4+4?
Local anesthetics	Humans	—	—	—	—
	Animals	2	—	—	2
Analgesics	Humans	—	—	—	—
	Animals	14	1	10	1
Antipyretics	Humans	1	—	—	—
	Animals	3	—	1	—
Tranquilizers	Humans	15	—	9	—
	Animals	35	2	21	4
Antidepressants	Humans	3	—	1	1
	Animals	30	1	23	1
Psychotomimetics	Humans	—	—	—	—
	Animals	5	1	—	—
CNS-stimulants	Humans	10	5	—	—
	Animals	17	11	3	—
Sympathomimetics	Humans	—	—	—	—
and -lytics	Animals	5	2	2	—
Parasympathomimetics	Humans	—	—	—	—
and -lytics	Animals	13	1	6	1
Miscellaneous	Humans	2	—	1	—
agents	Animals	19	4	10	—
Sum	Humans	50	5	20	2+2?
	Animals	209	24	128	13+4?

on animals and humans agree very well for these groups of drugs (Table
10–2). The implications of experimental work on these drugs for clinical
treatment of alcoholics are discussed further in the section on treatment
of acute alcohol intoxication in Chapter 11 on pages 739–748.

B. Comparison between ethanol and other drugs

The material in Table 10-1 indicates actions synergistic with ethanol for such diverse types of agents that they cannot possibly all act by closely similar mechanisms. One striking feature, however, is that among the various agents without a primarily central action, synergism with alcohol is usually exhibited by drugs known to act primarily by depressing excitable membranes.

The two types of drugs to which alcohol is regarded as most closely related pharmacologically are the general anesthetics and the hypnotics and sedatives, particularly the barbiturates. In comparison with ethyl alcohol, volatile anesthetics and barbiturates act on membrane conductance of excitable cells and on the excitation cycle in approximately the same manner, but apparently with a more selective action on impulse transmission (Goodman and Gilman, 1965; for action of alcohol, see Chapter 5, pp. 218–221). The barbiturates seem to have a complex type of biochemical action affecting metabolic reactions and excitable membranes simultaneously, whereas ethyl alcohol seems more exclusively to disturb membrane function by a physico-chemical mode of action.

Electrophysiological observations on integrative functions have demonstrated resemblance in the actions of ether, barbiturates, and alcohol, but some differences have been detected. The barbiturates have a very selective action on the brain stem reticular formation and also on inhibitory systems (Killam, 1962; Brazier, 1963). Although alcohol also acts selectively on these structures, the degree of specificity seems to be considerably smaller. In unpublished work in Domino's laboratory (*personal communication*), a direct comparison has shown that phenobarbital acts much more selectively on inhibitory pathways. Electroencephalographic investigations have revealed differences among alcohol, barbiturates and ether, especially in their effects on the distribution of fast and slow activity (Horsey and Akert, 1953; Wikler, 1957). A study of evoked potentials showed progressive slowing with increasing doses of ethanol and urethan, whereas pentobarbital and chloralose in low doses caused excitation (Nakai, 1964; Nakai and Takaori, 1965). However, the slight stimulating effect of ethanol reported by Hadji-Dimo et al. (1968) suggests that the difference may be one in quantity rather than in type of effect. Alcohol and barbiturates are rather similar in their effects on optokinetic fusion (Blomberg and Wassén, 1962). In general anesthetic action, the principal difference is that the safety margin between the dose causing surgical anesthesia and that causing respiratory failure is much narrower for alcohol than for gaseous, volatile, and barbiturate anesthetics.

The little information there is on cross-tolerance and cross-dependence (pp. 669–672; Seevers and Deneau, 1963) and on EEG-changes in withdrawal (Chapter 9, p. 507) gives further evidence of rather close similarity among ether, barbiturates, and alcohol. Other drugs which clinically resemble ethanol are all hypnotics and sedatives. These include chloral hydrate, paraldehyde, meprobamate, chlordiazepoxide, glutethimide, and methyprylon (Seevers and Deneau, 1963). Hubach (1963) also comments on the similarity between the actions of paraldehyde and ethanol. Clinical experience indicates that clomethiazole may be added to this group.

A few studies of laboratory animals, while showing similar effects of alcohol and barbiturates, have also provided information on differential effects of these drugs under the same experimental conditions. Barry and Miller (1962), in an approach–avoidance conflict test (Chapter 7, p. 360) found a much stronger fear-reducing effect of amobarbital (20 mg/kg i.p.) than of alcohol (1.2 g/kg i.p.). In a test of the effects of these drugs on a lever-pressing rather than running response, Barry et al. (1962) again found a fear-reducing effect of amobarbital whereas alcohol had a strong, generalized depressant effect. Barry and Buckley (1966) suggested that these differential findings might indicate for alcohol, but not the barbiturate, a much greater detrimental effect on a lever-pressing than on a locomotor response, perhaps due to the higher degree of motor coordination needed for lever pressing. In another experiment, the two drugs differed in the pattern of their disinhibitory effect when a previously learned food-approach response was inhibited by frustrating non-reward. Barry (1967) pointed out that amobarbital had the same effect as weak hunger, apparently alleviating the avoidance-producing effect of frustration while reducing the intensity of the approach response, whereas alcohol failed to alter the response pattern characteristic with intense hunger. Some other studies on barbiturates suggest differences from alcohol, although lacking a comparison between the two drugs under the same experimental conditions. Low doses of barbiturates have stimulant effects under a wide variety of conditions (Watzman et al., 1968) whereas such effects with alcohol seem to be small and difficult to elicit (Chapter 6). Schmidt et al. (1967) have reported a series of experiments showing that barbiturates increase water consumption of rats, whereas such effects of alcohol do not occur consistently.

References p. 695

In spite of the extensive use of alcohol and barbiturates for various purposes in contemporary civilization, experiments on humans have generally not included both types of drug in the same test situation. When several drugs have been compared, experimenters have apparently selected one or the other but not both of these similar drugs. However, a study by Frankenhaeuser and Post (1966), on effects of 3 mg/kg pentobarbital on 30 humans, may be compared with other studies, including one from the same laboratory (Ekman *et al.*, 1963), on effects of alcohol. Both drugs impair objective performance of various tasks requiring speed and skill, with less detrimental effect on subjectively estimated performance. In accordance with the consensus of findings for alcohol reviewed in Chapter 6, pentobarbital had a smaller detrimental effect on choice reaction time than on simple reaction time. However, a difference from alcohol is that pentobarbital appears to have a more depressive effect on subjective mood (decreasing alertness, increasing sleepiness) whereas small alcohol doses cause the subjects to feel preponderantly more talkative, elated, happy, and hazy (Ekman *et al.*, 1963). Also, pentobarbital slightly decreases heart rate, contrary to reports reviewed in Chapter 4 and 7 that alcohol increases heart rate.

In comparisons between drugs, an important question is whether the recipient perceives their effects as similar or dissimilar. In recent years, objective techniques have been developed for answering this question with the use of rats trained to make differential responses depending on whether they are in the drug or nondrug condition. Similarity or dissimilarity of this drug to a new drug is measured by whether the animal chooses the drug or nondrug response in a test under the new drug. In spite of large differences in various aspects of experimental procedure, alcohol has consistently been perceived as similar to pentobarbital (Overton, 1966; Kubena and Barry, 1969). Other hypnotic drugs have also been perceived as similar to these, including phenobarbital, ethyl carbamate, meprobamate and chloral hydrate. With the use of various doses, to identify the minimal dose sufficient to produce a perceived effect, Kubena and Barry (1969) found that the dose eliciting a 50% probability of the drug response was 0.6 g/kg i.p. for alcohol and 6.0 mg/kg for pentobarbital. The narcotic analgesics of the opiate group are pharmacologically rather distant from alcohol (Seevers and Deneau, 1963). With respect to the tranquilizers, the intensive studies on chlorpromazine, reviewed by Bradley (1963), show great differences from alcohol in the actions on the central nervous system, both biochemically and electrophysiologically. In general behavioral effects, also, these types of drugs are usually clearly differentiated from ethanol, except at doses high enough to cause a severe, generalized depression of performance. With the technique for measuring perceived similarity between effects of different drugs, 1.2 g/kg alcohol was perceived as different from 2 mg/kg chlorpromazine (Kubena and Barry, 1969). An interesting demonstration of this dissimilarity is the finding by St-Laurent and Olds (1967) that chlorpromazine suppresses self-stimulation of the brain in rats very readily whereas alcohol does not.

C. Chronic alcohol administration and drug effects

Alcohol administered chronically has pharmacological effects not found with acute use. Differences can thus be expected also in joint effects of alcohol and other drugs. Changed metabolic interactions between ethanol and other drugs represent a special type of alteration which will be discussed separately. Chronic use of one drug may lead to decreased sensitivity to another drug at the site of its action, manifested as an increase in the tissue level of the second drug required for an effect of a certain magnitude. This phenomenon is referred to as *cross-tolerance*. A special instance of cross-tolerance, when the second drug has the ability to prevent or diminish the withdrawal symptoms arising from discontinuation of a prior drug producing physical dependence, is referred to as *cross-dependence*. Chronic administration of a drug may also increase rather than decrease sensitivity to another drug.

There are obvious clinical implications of cross-tolerance. Information on cross-tolerance and particularly cross-dependence is also valuable for establishing whether drugs act by similar mechanisms, and is thus helpful for the development of theories concerning the mechanisms of drug action. Therefore, we have been astonished to find very little experimental work on such relations of alcohol to other drugs.

(1) Changes in capacity to metabolize drugs

A number of drugs unspecifically induce activity of the hepatic microsomal enzyme systems which metabolize drugs (for review, see Conney, 1965). As ethanol is metabolized mainly by the cytoplasmic liver alcohol dehydrogenase, an enzyme which is not substrate-inducible, it has generally been assumed that chronic use of alcohol would not alter drug metabolism. Experimental results in agreement with this view have been reviewed by Remmer (1961)

References p. 695

and reported by Kato and Vassanelli (1962). The proliferation of the smooth endoplasmic reticulum (ER) of the liver cells which is caused by high intake of ethanol particularly in connection with certain dietary deficiencies (Chapter 9), has led some investigators to assume that the activity of drug-metabolizing enzymes also might increase. Rubin et al. (1968) indeed showed increase in the activities of aniline hydroxylase and cytochrome P450 in rat liver when large amounts of ethanol were fed. These changes were enhanced by a deficient diet (Rubin and Lieber, 1968a). Rubin and Lieber (1968b) also report increased activity of liver pentobarbital and benzpyrene hydroxylases of rats, and of pentobarbital hydroxylase in humans.

The implications of these findings are discussed in review articles by Rubin and Lieber (1968c) and Lieber and Rubin (1968). They also suggest that adaptive changes in microsomal oxidation of ethanol might occur. Fischer and Oelssner (1960) and Fischer (1962) have indeed found that 5 days pretreatment with hexobarbital increases the rate of alcohol elimination in rabbits and mice by 30% without change in the activities of LADH or hepatic catalase. In rats, pretreatment with phenobarbital had similar effects (Spector and Reinhard, 1966). Wooles (1968) found that in rats repeated administration of chlorocyclizine led to lowered blood alcohol levels after administration of ethanol by gavage. However, the result was not necessarily caused by increased rate of metabolism because total time of elimination was not shortened. Klaassen (1969) failed to find increased rates of ethanol elimination in rats after administration of phenobarbital, chlorcyclizine, chlordane, and 3-methylcholanthrene sufficiently many times to induce microsomal drug-oxidizing activity in the livers of the rats.

Evidently, much more data are needed before it can be judged whether quantitatively significant changes in the rates of drug metabolism occur in human alcoholics, and what conditions are necessary for such changes. It should also be noted that parallel structural and biochemical studies are necessary because hypertrophy of the smooth ER can occur without increase in the activities of the drug-metabolizing enzymes. Occurrence in rats of hypertrophic smooth ER with lowered enzyme activities has indeed been reported (Hutterer et al., 1968). All these findings are of great interest and may explain why, as pointed out in Chapter 9, alcoholics seem to pass through a phase of increased ability to metabolize ethanol. The data reviewed above suggest that when alcoholics have unusually high rates of alcohol elimination, they should also have a heightened capacity to metabolize other drugs. This phase should coincide with hypertrophy of the smooth

ER in the liver cells and with hepatic fatty infiltration. It may lead over to a state with grave liver damage and secondary loss of the heightened microsomal enzyme activities.

(2) Cross-tolerance to general anesthetics and barbiturates

It is a common clinical impression that heavy drinkers tolerate doses of hypnotics and sedatives that in normal subjects would be unduly depressant (Seevers and Deneau, 1963). Conversely, unusually high tolerance to ethyl alcohol in subjects dependent on pentobarbital and secobarbital has been reported by Fraser et al. (1957). However, although the tolerance to anesthesia of alcoholics belongs to the phenomena which are "generally known", good clinical documentation is scanty. Alcoholics who used isopropyl alcohol or methyl alcohol in addition to ethyl alcohol seemed to have greater tolerance to each of these alcohols (Mendelson et al., 1957). Bourne (1960) reports 12 cases of unsatisfactory dental anesthesias in patients accustomed to alcohol. Induction was with cyclopropane and maintenance with nitrous oxide and oxygen. Anesthesiologists such as Bloomquist (1959) often state that alcoholics show stormy inductions, increased resistance, and other abnormal reactions to anesthesia. In a particularly illuminating discussion of the phenomenon from the anesthesiologist's point of view, Adriani and Morton (1968) state that alcoholics often show tolerance to chloral hydrate, paraldehyde, tribromethanol, ether, vinyl ether, nitrous oxide, cyclopropane, halothane, methoxyflurane, and in some cases to barbiturates. In spite of the wide recognition of the phenomenon, few controlled studies of its nature and extent have been reported. One source of variability in the clinical impressions presumably is the state of the alcoholics. Systematic reporting of clinical findings requires that withdrawal illness is recognized as a source of agitation, and that careful assessment is made of the general physical state of the patient as well as of indications of alcohol tolerance.

Contrary to the common clinical impressions, Shagass and Jones (1957), in measurements of the threshold doses of amobarbital required to induce certain changes in speech and EEG of nonalcoholic and alcoholic humans, failed to detect any signs of cross-tolerance. They suggested that alcoholics may require large doses of sedatives as a consequence of their underlying state of anxiety rather than because of cross-tolerance.

The development of cross-tolerance has been demonstrated in an experiment on rabbits reported by Ahlquist and Dille (1940). Tolerance to alcohol was induced by intraperitoneal injection of 1.5 g alcohol/kg daily for 15 to 25 days. Two days after the last dose of alcohol, a time lapse sufficient to allow elimination of ethanol but not long enough to diminish tolerance, resistance to the depressant effects of pentobarbital, hexobarbital, and diethyl ether clearly increased as indicated by the duration of anesthesia. The response to amidopyrine and pentylenetetrazol was not measurably changed. Since the rabbits showed no withdrawal symptoms, tolerance apparently developed earlier than the increased excitability characterizing a withdrawal state (Chapter 9, p. 503).

Hatfield (1966) demonstrated that female (but not male) rats, tolerant to alcohol after daily i.p. injection of 2.5 g/kg, also showed increased tolerance to hexobarbital, meprobamate, pentobarbital, and zoxazolamine, but not to barbital and phenobarbital. In a well controlled study, Scheinin (*personal communication*) showed that when specific tolerance to orally administered ethanol had been established in male rats, their tolerance was markedly heightened to diethyl ether, thiopental and halothane. Their tolerance to propanidid had somewhat increased but the response was highly variable. Tolerance was indicated by a more rapid restoration of reflexes, after administration for a uniform duration of 2 to 3 min, in the case of the gaseous and volatile anesthetics, or after i.v. injection of propanidid or thiopental. Also, animals habituated to halothane and thiopental exhibited tolerance to ethyl alcohol.

Consistent evidence for cross-tolerance has not been found in other studies. The main reason seems to be various flaws in the experimental design rather than elusiveness of the phenomenon. Abreu and Emerson (1939) injected mice i.p. with alcohol every day in doses which increased weekly in steps of 1.5 g/kg, from 1.5 to 9 g/kg. Their induction time for diethyl ether anesthesia, compared with that of control animals, was found to increase during the first 3 weeks, but then to decrease again. However, mortality was high, apparently owing to interior hemorrhages and other damage resulting from the daily injections. Bourrinet (1964) administered alcohol to rats 5 times a week for 5 months in a dose of 3.95 g/kg p.o. The anticonvulsant action of phenobarbital decreased, but duration of thiopental anesthesia was unchanged. Similar treatment even prolonged pentobarbital anesthesia in mice, and prolonged urethan anesthesia in guinea pigs. It is striking that the rather unique antiepileptic action of phenobarbital gave signs of cross-tolerance whereas the anesthetic effect shared by barbiturates, alcohol and urethan did not. This was probably due to effects of the withdrawal syndrome as indicated by Bourrinet's (1964) finding that the rats after 3 months' daily administration of alcohol showed lowered convulsion thresholds for electroshock as well as for pentylenetetrazol. Ahlquist and Dille (1940) found the opposite effect of 15–25 days of alcohol administration, *i.e.*, increased tolerance to anesthetics and unchanged response to convulsants. The difference may have been caused at least in part by their much shorter duration of treatment with ethanol.

As we have seen (Chapter 9, p. 522) it is doubtful whether consumption of dilute alcohol solutions as the sole source of fluid induces tolerance to alcohol in experimental animals. Lee *et al.* (1964) used this method of administering alcohol to rats. Ethanol tolerance was not independently verified, and induction and maintenance of anesthesia were measured by removing the animals for observation of recovery immediately when they collapsed instead of using a uniform time of exposure to the anesthetic. Tolerance to diethyl ether, methoxyflurane, and methoxital also did not increase significantly, but a tendency in this direction caused increased variance.

In guinea pigs given 5, 10, and 15% alcohol as their sole fluid for consecutive two-week periods, tolerance to pentobarbital, hexobarbital, and methitural increased in weekly determinations of induction and maintenance time (Frahm *et al.*, 1962). Control measurements 14 days after the end of the alcohol administration showed that the increase in tolerance had disappeared. However, the development of tolerance to alcohol was not established, and data on water consumption of the animals suggest that dehydration may have occurred and acted as an unspecific stressor. Soehring and Schüppel (1966) cite unpublished thesis work that has shown cross-tolerance to local anesthetics, reserpine, and barbiturates, but no experimental details are given. The increased resistance to pentobarbital claimed by Frahm *et al.* (1962) prompted a study by Seidel *et al.* (1964b) on possible changes in drug distribution in guinea pigs given 5% alcohol as their sole drinking fluid for a week. Pentobarbital in serum and brain was measured at 30, 55, and 110 min after injection i.p. In comparison with the controls, the brains of the animals that had received alcohol were found to contain significantly less pentobarbital at 55 min whereas their serum levels were higher at 30 min.

In general, cross-tolerance to general anesthetics and barbiturates as a result of prolonged alcohol consumption is only partially confirmed by experimental findings. When due attention has been paid to the experimental procedures and to the development of tolerance to alcohol, cross-tolerance to anesthetics has been demonstrated. Very few experiments have been adequately controlled, and this is a topic in which more research is especially needed.

Experimental data are even more scanty on cross-dependence than on cross-tolerance. The syndrome caused by abrupt withdrawal of barbiturates is clinically very similar to the withdrawal illness in alcoholics (Kielholz and Battegay, 1967). According to Hubach (1963), symptoms of paraldehyde withdrawal can be controlled by administration of alcohol just as paraldehyde can be used to mitigate signs of alcohol withdrawal. Clinical experience in treatment of the alcohol withdrawal state with medication naturally has given relevant information which is briefly reviewed in Chapter 11 on pp. 745–748.

An important study on cross-dependence is that by Fraser et al. (1957) who tested alcohol as a substitute for barbiturates in human subjects. Ten subjects previously dependent on morphine but in good physical health, 8 of whom were at the time dependent on barbiturates, participated in the experiment. After withdrawal of the opiates, continuous intoxication with pentobarbital and secobarbital was maintained for 22 or 44 days, followed by substitution of alcohol for barbiturates for 14 days, after which alcohol was abruptly withdrawn. Alcohol significantly although not entirely miti- gated the symptoms of barbiturate withdrawal, and when alcohol was subsequently withdrawn, only 3 of 9 patients who completed the experiment had convulsions or delirium or both. The authors concluded that alcohol is a partial substitute for barbiturates. Experiments such as this on cross- dependence are important but involve a number of complex legal, moral, and humanitarian problems. Recent developments in induction of alcohol dependence in animals (Chapter 9, pp. 508–509) should make possible systematic experimentation on mechanisms involved and on substitution and other forms of therapy.

(3) Interactions with other agents

Chronic alcohol consumption increased sensitivity to morphine according to an experiment by Venho et al. (1955). Doses of morphine producing 5% and 10% mortality in control mice killed 71% and 78% of the mice that had consumed alcohol as the sole source of fluid for three and a half months, ending with 10% concentration of alcohol for the last one and a half months. Takemori (1962), demonstrating a smaller depressant effect of morphine on the respiratory response in vitro to potassium stimulation of cerebral cortex tissue from rats in which tolerance to morphine had been induced *in vivo*, found that the potassium-stimulated respiration was as greatly depressed by ethanol in tissue from animals of the control group as the experimental group. Furthermore, nalorphine but not ethanol prevented the depressant action of morphine in the tissue. Smith *et al.* (1966), in a study of lens opacity in the eye caused by morphine and related drugs, found that ethanol blocked the development of tolerance to this response.

Very little experimental evidence is available about various psychotherapeutic agents although so many of them have been used in clinical trials as adjuncts in the management of alcoholics. According to Kopf (1957), in experiments on mice, repeated administration of alcohol reduced the synergism with chlorpromazine and mepazine, and repeated administration of the tranquilizers similarly diminished the synergism with an acute dose of alcohol. On the other hand, Bourrinet (1964) found that chronic administration of alcohol to mice did not alter the effect of chlorpromazine or meprobamate. Tirri (1966) has found no increase in resistance to ethanol among mice tolerant to promazine. According to observations in rats (Watts *et al.*, 1967), various side effects of desmethyl-imipramine were enhanced by alcohol when both drugs were administered chronically.

Bourrinet (1964) summarized briefly a number of observations on effects of drugs in animals subjected to chronic administration of alcohol. The effect of the local anesthetics cocaine and procaine hydrochloride was enhanced in guinea pigs. This is contrary to a report by Balodis (1933). The procaine esterase activity of the serum was lowered. In rabbits and guinea pigs, sensitivity to acetylcholine increased and choline esterase activity of the serum decreased. The activity of atropine was also slightly enhanced. Sensitivity to sympathomimetic and sympatholytic agents was unchanged in rabbits. Digitaline toxicity was found slightly increased. In rats given ethanol chronically, the effect on heart muscle contractility of strophanthin increased and that of epinephrine and acetylcholine decreased (Wójcicki, 1967). The change in heart rate caused by strophanthin was unaffected, whereas the reaction to epinephrine increased, and that to acetylcholine decreased. Kahil *et al.* (1964) have reported that tolbutamide causes sustained hypoglycemia in dogs receiving alcohol chronically. According to Riedler (1966), alcohol enhances the decrease in the activity of some blood clotting factors caused by prolonged treatment with anticoagulants, particularly if the patient has liver damage or some cardiovascular insufficiency.

References p. 695

With present knowledge, meaningful comparisons between drug effects cannot be carried far. However, such comparisons should be valuable in developing more comprehensive theories of drug action, and in helping to guide work on less intensively studied drugs with the aid of information gathered with better known compounds. From a practical point of view, however, when trying to make predictions it is important to realize the many ways in which drug interactions can arise, in many cases with different drug effects after chronic intake.

D. Drugs with special relationships to ethanol

Two types of compounds are included in this section. First we discuss the aversively protective drugs, which give rise to unpleasant symptoms only when alcohol is simultaneously present in the body. They are important not only because of their extensive clinical use, described in Chapter 11, as an aid to therapy of alcoholics, but also as tools in the study of the effect of alcohol. Secondly, we discuss the non-ethyl alcohols, with their various degree of structural and pharmacological similarity to ethanol. The purposes of this book require an examination of experimental studies on these drugs with special relationships to ethanol. On the other hand, a detailed, thorough account of all features of these drugs is not undertaken as it would be beyond the scope of the book.

(1) The aversively protective drugs

Various compounds, including substances occurring naturally as in the fungus *Coprinus atramentarius* are known to sensitize to the effects of ethanol. Such sensitizing has been described in workers exposed to carbon disulfide (Haas and Heim, 1912; cited acc. to Perman, 1962), or cyanamide (Koelsch, 1914). In 1937, Williams reported sensitization to alcohol after exposure to tetramethylthiuram disulfide and tetraethylthiuram monosulfide, and also suggested the use of these compounds to cure alcoholism. Only considerably later, tetraethylthiuram disulfide (disulfiram) was put to clinical trial by a group of Danish workers (Hald *et al.*, 1948; Asmussen *et al.*, 1948) and also studied in animals (Larsen, 1948). Under the trade name of Antabuse, the compound was proposed for use in the treatment of chronic alcoholism.

In the present section, a summary is given of experimental work on the mechanism of action of this group of compounds, without attempting a detailed review. Extensive presentations of the literature are found in the papers by Himwich (1956), Casier and Polet (1958), and Perman (1962) who deal primarily with disulfiram, and in a book by Royer (1963) on the anti-alcoholic effect of the antidiabetic sulfonyl urea drugs. An excellent review by Weissman and Koe (1969) gives a particularly valuable presentation of biochemical aspects of the disulfiram-alcohol reaction. Royer (1963), Büttner (1960, 1961), Göres (1964), and Zipf and Hamacher (1967) mention a number of other compounds with effects of this type, but only a few have become widely used clinically. In addition to disulfiram, citrated calcium carbimide (CCC) appears to be the most commonly used of these drugs. Boyd (1960) screened 71 common therapeutic agents for disulfiram-like activity but found indications of sensitization with one compound only, tolazoline hydrochloride.

The symptoms of the alcohol–disulfiram reaction include flushing of face and legs, conjunctival vasodilation, anxiety, nausea, a decrease in arterial blood pressure, and increase in heart and respiratory rate. There may subsequently be slowing of the heart rate accompanied by respiratory difficulties, and consequently a serious fall in blood pressure. A study of EEG and circulatory function has confirmed that the disturbances are primarily vasomotor.

Hald and Jacobsen (1948) ascribed the pharmacological action of the alcohol-disulfiram combination to acetaldehyde which was found to increase, supposedly because of inhibition of its further metabolism. Later work has generally confirmed an elevation of acetaldehyde both in humans and in animals (MacLeod, 1950; Newman and Petzold, 1951; Hine *et al.*, 1952; Raby, 1954; Polet, 1956; Casier and Polet, 1958; Akabane and Ikomi, 1958). However, this increase is generally small, and discrepant findings, showing no elevation of acetaldehyde, have also been reported (*cf.* Perman, 1962; Göres, 1964). The high values found in early work may have been due to the low specificity of the methods used. More precise methods have been developed, based on enzymic analysis (Wagner, 1957a; Lundquist, 1958) or assay of radioactivity (Casier and Polet, 1958). With a specific gas chromatographic method, Duritz and Truitt (1964) and Truitt and Duritz (1967) showed that the rise in acetaldehyde in rats and rabbits was substantial, approximately 5-fold. In animals treated with disulfiram prior to administration of ethanol in doses of 2 or 4 g/kg, the acetaldehyde level during oxidation of ethanol was 12–20 μg/ml (0.27–0.44 mM) compared to 2–4 μg/ml (0.045–

0.09 mM) in controls. According to Casier and Polet (1958), disulfiram slows the oxidation of ethanol as well as of acetaldehyde.

Although the rise in acetaldehyde seems well established, it can hardly explain all the symptoms seen in the reaction. As pointed out by Hine *et al.* (1952), acetaldehyde acts predominantly as a sympathomimetic, and thus in part causes changes in circulation opposite to those typical of the alcohol–disulfiram reaction. Also, acetaldehyde alone (Perman, 1962) or with disulfiram (Casier and Merlevede, 1962, 1963) does not give rise to the characteristic symptoms. These findings also argue against Perman's (1962) suggestion that a metabolite of acetaldehyde is the cause of the reaction.

Wagner (1957b) suggested that a rise in pyruvate and other metabolites might explain the reaction, but at least one of the possible metabolites, acetoin, is not formed in sufficient quantity to play a role (Hassinen, 1963). From experiments with mitochondria and other cellular subfractions, Hassinen (1967) has concluded that interference with mitochondrial hydrogen oxidation might explain the effect, but his observations cannot account for the fact that the reaction occurs only when ethanol and disulfiram are present simultaneously. Furthermore, disulfiram does not modify the effect of ethanol on the ratio NADH/NAD found during oxidation of ethanol in rats (Büttner *et al.*, 1961). The metabolism of disulfiram (for references to original work, see Merlevede and Casier, 1961) has generally been regarded as being associated with inhibition of –SH enzymes. Strömme (1963, 1965a, b) found that ethanol depressed glucuronate formation from the diethylthiocarbamate formed from disulfiram, but Merlevede and Casier (1961) have demonstrated that diethylthiocarbamate in conjunction with alcohol does not give rise to the symptoms of the disulfiram-alcohol reaction.

Casier and Merlevede (1962) have suggested that the reaction might be due to a quaternary ammonium base formed through reaction between ethanol and disulfiram. They reported that in dogs a compound of this nature, readily formed from disulfiram in ethanol, gave rise to the characteristic symptoms of the disulfiram-alcohol reaction. Considering the synergism of ethanol with quaternary ammonium compounds (p. 661), this is quite an attractive hypothesis but as yet there has been no observation of the postulated compound in the organism during the disulfiram-alcohol reaction. Deitrich and Hellerman (1963), in an extensive study of inhibitors of acetaldehyde dehydrogenase, found that disulfiram inhibits the enzyme by competition with NAD. They suggest that accumulation of other aldehydes than acetaldehyde, formed for instance through the action of monoamine oxidase on biogenic amines, may explain the reaction. This possibility is discussed also by Truitt and Duritz (1967). In agreement with this notion, Feldstein and Williamson (1968) found that formation of 5-hydroxy-indoleacetaldehyde increased in liver homogenate of rats after pretreatment with ethanol and disulfiram. Walsh and Truitt (1968) found that ethanol and disulfiram jointly caused a rise in plasma catecholamines which seemed to be caused by acetaldehyde. Following the observation that disulfiram inhibits dopamine-β-hydroxylase, causing a decrease in norepinephrine and an increase in dopamine levels in the hearts and spleens of cats and rats, Nakano et al. (1969) studied cardiovascular responses to sympathetic stimulation of dogs and guinea pigs treated with disulfiram, as well as responses in the animals after administration of ethanol. Particularly after the joint disulfiram–alcohol treatment, both reflex responses and contractile force of the myocardium were strongly deteriorated. It thus seems that changes in monoamine metabolism and levels are important factors in the ethanol–disulfiram reaction.

In addition to the work on the mechanism of the sensitizing effect of disulfiram cited above, a few pharmacological observations may be mentioned. According to Gruber et al. (1954), disulfiram prolongs ethanol-induced anesthesia in rats, mice and rabbits; Korablev (1959) found that in mice, disulfiram increases mortality caused by alcohol. Zappi and Millifiorini (1955) have found amphetamine to antagonize coma induced by the disulfiram–alcohol combination in rabbits.

The reaction to alcohol produced after medication with the oral anti-diabetics of the sulfonyl urea group, such as tolbutamide, carbutamide, and chlorpropamide, very much resembles the disulfiram–alcohol reaction. It has also been attributed to elevated acetaldehyde or slowing of the metabolism of both alcohol and acetaldehyde (Czyzyk and Mohnike, 1957; Büttner and Portwich, 1960; Büttner, 1961; Larsen and Madsen, 1962). Japanese workers have shown in rats that the rise in acetaldehyde caused by tolbutamide and alcohol is rather moderate. The rate of ethanol elimination was not altered, and only minor changes were found in the carbohydrate metabolism of the perfused liver (Nakanishi, 1963a, b; Akabane et al., 1963). A significant role of acetaldehyde has been questioned as in the case of disulfiram (Fitzgerald et al., 1962; Truitt et al., 1962). Royer (1963), in an extensive investigation that involved clinical observation, experiments utilizing self-selection of alcohol in rats, and measurements of cardiovascular response in rabbits, concluded that the slowing of alcohol and acetaldehyde

References p. 695

metabolism accompanies but does not cause the adverse reaction. The author obtained indirect evidence for an antioxidant effect of disulfiram and of some metabolites formed from the sulfonyl urea compounds, and he further suggested that the reaction might be partly due to increased release of 5-hydroxytryptamine and decreased rate of its oxidation. Podgainy and Bressler (1968) have reported that liver aldehyde dehydrogenase is directly inhibited by chlorpropamide and tolbutamide, and that chlorpropamide by itself increases the formation of reduced metabolites of 5-hydroxytryptamine. The latter effect was enhanced by ethanol.

Calcium cyanamide in its citrated form (CCC, Temposil) was proposed for clinical use by Ferguson (1956), Armstrong and Kerr (1956), Bell (1956) and Armstrong (1957). Elevation of acetaldehyde and similar symptomatology (Warson and Ferguson, 1955; Goldberg, 1960) indicate that the reaction is very similar to that caused by disulfiram and alcohol. Interference with the oxidation of ethanol-derived acetaldehyde into acetate has been accepted as the cause of the reaction (Armstrong, 1957), but there is no exact information on the actual mechanism involved. Deitrich and Worth (1968) report formation of a metabolite with the character of a carboxylic acid.

The antioxidant n-butyraldoxime causes a reaction to alcohol resembling the Antabuse–alcohol reaction although it is milder (Lewis and Schwartz, 1956). Also in this case, the symptoms were attributed to elevated acetaldehyde. The compound decreases voluntary intake of alcohol in mice (Koe and Tenen, 1969) and rats (Forsander, 1970). According to Koe and Tenen (1969), n-butyraldoxime in $vitro$ inhibits LADH but not liver aldehyde dehydrogenase of mice. Administration to intact mice, however, decreased activity of both enzymes and slowed elimination of ethanol. When small doses of the compound were given on a continuous basis, only acetaldehyde dehydrogenase was inhibited, and blood aldehyde levels became elevated after administration of ethanol. Forsander (1970) found in acute experiments on rats that n-butyraldoxime was a competitive inhibitor of LADH and prevented the redox shift normally occurring during metabolism of ethanol.

Metronidazole (Flagyl), a drug used as trichomonacide, was accidentally found to have a relatively weak sensitizing effect to alcohol. Its therapeutic use is discussed in Chapter 11, p. 763. In rats, the drug has been found to cause a reduction in voluntary intake of alcohol (Campbell et al., 1967). Part of its effect might be linked to its inhibitory effect on alcohol dehydrogenase, reported by Manthei (1962) and Manthei et al. (1963) (cited acc. to Lehman et al., 1966). Fried and Fried (1966) found that metronidazole had an appreciable effect on the horse liver enzyme in a concentration as low as 0.25 mM, and that it also inhibited xanthine oxidase. Edwards and Price (1967a, b) demonstrated that approximately 5–6 mM concentrations of the drug are required for 50 % inhibition of both ordinary and atypical human LADH. Montanini et al. (1966) report slowing by metronidazole of alcohol elimination in humans after a dose of 0.5 g alcohol per kg.

The alcohol-sensitizing effect of the fungus *Coprinus atramentarius* was first described by Fischer (1945). Experimental investigations (List and Reith, 1960; Barkman and Perman, 1963; Genest et al., 1968) have demonstrated the similarity to the disulfiram-alcohol reaction. Simandl and Franc (1956) have reported that they were able to isolate and identify disulfiram by means of paper chromatography in fungi collected from their sites of growing. On the other hand, Wier and Tyler (1960) could not detect disulfiram in fungus grown on artificial medium. List and Reith (1960) repeated the isolation and fractionation procedure of Simandl and Franc (1956) but were also unable to find disulfiram in the fungus. These authors concluded that the effect must be due to some other compound.

Crude animal charcoal gives rise to sensitization to alcohol in humans, dogs (Clark and Hulpieu, 1958; Poiré et al., 1965), rats and rabbits (Lamarche and Royer, 1965) much in the same manner as disulfiram and CCC. According to these authors, the reaction is not obtained with animal charcoal extracted by acid or with vegetable charcoal. With respect to other agents that have corresponding actions, the present authors have not seen any experimental studies.

(2) Other alcohols

In this review we do not attempt to give an exhaustive account of the enormous literature on the non-ethyl alcohols. The following discussion points out some important aspects of their interactions with ethanol and provides some references. Relatively recent reviews are those by Sollman (1957) and by Mardones (1963).

Ethanol belongs to the aliphatic alcohols whose chemistry was briefly discussed in Chapter 2 (pp. 19–21). They have been discussed in this book as substrates for liver alcohol dehydrogenase (Chapter 3, p. 83), and as depressants in biological systems (Chapter 5, pp. 245–247). Among the polyhydric alcohols (alcohols with more than one –OH group), only diols (with two hydroxyls per molecule) can be pharmacologically active. Ethylene glycol is approximately as toxic as ethanol whereas propylene glycol is much less toxic. These differences are attributable to metabolites and to the diols as such. The anesthetic potency of the diols is apparently very low. Among polyhydric alcohols with three or more hydroxyls are several intermediary metabolites and nutrients such as glycerol and the sugar alcohols.

As was already pointed out (Chapter 5, p. 245), there is a close relationship between the biological activity of the aliphatic alcohols and their molecular size and shape and physical properties. This relationship has furnished a major portion of the empirical basis for various physicochemical hypotheses of the mechanism of narcocis. A close relationship between the chemical potential of alcohols and their depressant action on biological functions is generally obtained with rather simple test systems, such as cells or isolated tissues or organs. In the intact mammalian organism, however, the effects of the alcohols are influenced by systemic factors which modify their absorption, distribution, metabolism, and elimination. Primary alcohols all have a high affinity to liver alcohol dehydrogenase and are oxidized to the corresponding aldehydes which are rapidly oxidized further. Secondary alcohols are converted to ketones and further oxidized, but also conjugated with glucuronic acid to a much larger extent than are the primary alcohols. The ketones may contribute to the toxicity, as in the case of isopropyl alcohol. The tertiary alcohols are not oxidized at all. Their elimination involves primarily conjugation with glucuronic acid and elimination in unchanged form (Williams, 1959). Experiments have also clearly brought out the long duration of action of the tertiary alcohols, of which tertiary amyl alcohol has been used as a hypnotic. If these relationships are taken into account, results of *in vivo* experiments show reasonable agreement with the activities observed in simpler systems (Welch and Slocum, 1943; Wallgren, 1960b; Lindbohm and Wallgren, 1962; MacGregor *et al.*, 1964).

Generally, the toxicity of aliphatic alcohols is proportional to their depressant action, thus leaving approximately the same margin of safety between anesthetic and lethal doses. Methanol is an exception to this rule. Many cases of serious poisoning have been caused by the acidosis it produces and by its toxic action on the retina and optic nerve in humans. The literature on methanol poisoning was reviewed by Røe (1946); a critical review and discussion of biochemical aspects of methanol poisoning is by Cooper and Kini (1962). The toxic effects of methanol arise through formation of metabolites, primarily formaldehyde and formic acid. This process is slowed by ethanol as shown by Røe (1950), because both methanol and ethanol are substrates for human LADH. The higher affinity of ethanol than methanol for LADH provides the basis for the well-known effectiveness of ethanol as an antidote to methanol poisoning. Rietbrock and Säger (1967) have pointed out the value of supplementing ethanol with folic acid in the treatment of methanol poisoning, in order to facilitate the metabolism of the formic acid formed. In mice, methanol seems to be metabolized chiefly by a catalase–peroxide system inhibited by acetanilide (Hassan *et al.*, 1967), and acetanilide also had some value in mice as an antidote to methanol (Hassan *et al.*, 1969).

A few experiments have provided information on toxicity of other aliphatic alcohols. Ethylene glycol is oxidized to oxalic acid which is deposited as insoluble salts in the kidney tubules and thereby causes renal failure. By competitition for the LADH, ethanol prevents this process in rats (Debray *et al.*, 1965) and humans (Wacker *et al.*, 1965). Allyl alcohol is much more toxic than its saturated analogue, propyl alcohol. Hepatic portal necrosis is a characteristic feature of allyl alcohol poisoning. In a study on toxicity of allyl alcohol, Kodama and Hine (1958) pointed out that at toxic levels, this alcohol essentially lacks hypnotic action in rats. The dosages used were 60 and 120 mg/kg, and the LD_{50} was about 100 mg/kg. Corresponding doses of propyl alcohol would indeed hardly result in any measurable hypnotic effect in the rat.

Comparisons of ethanol with other closely related alcohols provide an opportunity for varying the metabolic impact and duration of action while holding constant essential features of the pharmacological effects of ethyl alcohol. In spite of the value of this technique, there have been few such comparisons, and in particular there is apparently no experimental evidence concerning effects of chronic ingestion of higher alcohols. Mendelson *et al.* (1957) have given an interesting account of 9 alcoholics who regularly consumed other compounds, including methanol or isopropyl alcohol or both. Surprisingly, their physical state was not very poor. Mendelson *et al.* (1957) also reviewed statistical, toxicological, and psychiatric aspects of non-ethyl alcoholism. Gadsden *et al.* (1958) described a group of 50 patients who had been habitually consuming "scrap iron", a mixture containing 20–40% ethyl alcohol, 15–25% isopropyl alcohol, and some naphtalene. More than half of these patients had an acute brain syndrome identical with delirium tremens. The authors suggested that chronic drinking of "scrap" will produce effects which are similar to those of alcoholism, but more severe and within a shorter period.

References p. 695

E. Components of alcoholic beverages

Many drinkers believe that there are differences in both the intoxication and the hangover resulting from different alcoholic beverages. Human suggestibility is at least part of the reason for these often very emphatic descriptions of peculiar experiences. The literature is also replete with claims that "impurities" of beverages rather than ethyl alcohol may be the cause of various pathological changes associated with heavy drinking. Many beverages indeed contain a great number of substances in addition to the two main constituents of alcoholic beverages, ethanol and water. Any major differences between beverages should of course be attributable to such additional compounds, often called congeners. The latter term carries the connotion of close relationship and is therefore not very appropriate, because of the great chemical variation among the compounds in beverages.

Beverage composition was briefly reviewed in Chapter 2 (pp. 22–25). Chapter 9 (pp. 480–495), contains comments on the nutritional value of alcoholic beverages. The present section discusses evidence for or against any major pharmacological effect of various substances in alcoholic beverages. A review of studies on effects and after-effects in conditions of acute administration is followed by a review of studies on chronic use.

(1) Acute effects

Measurements of the quantities of various minor constituents in alcoholic beverages indicate that they usually should lack appreciable pharmacological action. Their main importance lies in the contribution to the characteristic appearance and flavor of the beverages. The most active compounds pharmacologically are the aldehydes, methanol, and the fusel alcohols. Of these, aldehydes never occur in sufficient amounts to produce detectable effects. McKennis and Haag (1959) discuss possible pharmacological actions of whisky congeners and point out the lack of scientific studies on this topic. Haag et al. (1959) prepared various fractions of compounds present in whisky (Bourbon) and determined their LD_{50} in rats. The most toxic compound was furfural with an LD_{50} of 135 mg/kg body weight. The largest amount of furfural found by Snell (1958) in any whisky was 9 mg/l. Thus 4 l (approx. one gallon) of Bourbon whisky would be needed to provide the median lethal dose of furfural for one rat weighing 250 grams.

Methanol is formed from pectin in fermentation of fruit. About 0.05–

0.20 g/l occurs in various wines and liqueurs. Exceptionally high levels are found in certain plum spirits (slivowicz) which may contain up to 4 g/l (Amerine, 1954). The quantities of methanol that produce blindness in humans may be as low as 12 g, but cases are known when ingestion of 72 g has not had any serious consequences (Goodman and Gilman, 1965). It is clearly not possible to ingest any alcoholic beverage in sufficient quantities to accumulate toxic amounts of methanol.

The fusel alcohols consist of various aliphatic alcohols formed during fermentation, such as isobutyl, isoamyl, optically active amyl alcohol, some n-butyl and n-propyl alcohol, and also some aromatic alcohols. Their high pharmacological efficacy was referred to in the preceding section. However, all fusel alcohols are rapidly metabolized, and usually the amounts present are minute. Of commercially available beverages, Bourbon whisky, some malt whiskeys, and Dutch gin (genever) have the highest content of fusel. Bourbon may contain about 2 g of amyl alcohol and 0.6 g of butanol per liter. This may account for no more than about one tenth of the inebriating effect. Genever contains 0.45–1.00 g amyl alcohol and 0.20–0.40 g butanol per liter, amounts which may have some pharmacological effect.

A recently identified fusel component is phenethyl alcohol, demonstrated in beer (Sihto et al., 1964), wines (Äyräpää, 1962), and cider (Kieser et al., 1964). Its pharmacological potency in mice is about twice that of ethanol (Wallgren et al., 1963). The amounts in beverages are far too small to modify their effects.

A few studies have been reported on effects of ethanol-free concentrates of compounds from beverages, or beverages with raised content of "congeners". Damrau and Liddy (1960, 1962), who prepared congeners without ethanol, reported that the congeners of Bourbon whisky caused symptoms of hangover in humans whereas corresponding quantities of vodka congeners or vodka had no such effect. However, the quantities consumed of compounds other than ethyl alcohol were much larger than those ingested in normal drinking. According to Murphree and Price (1965) and Murphree et al. (1966), Bourbon and vodka given to humans in doses equivalent to 0.8 ml of ethanol/kg had similar effects on EEG and nystagmus. After disappearance of the blood alcohol, however, Bourbon caused somewhat more EEG signs of drowsiness (Murphree et al., 1967). Nystagmus was more frequent and prolonged only when the amount of Bourbon congeners was raised 32 times and the preparation given in a dose of 0.2 g ethanol/kg, comparing one quarter of the ethanol with 8 times more congeners than the original beverage (Murphree *et al.*, 1966, 1967). The results do not convincingly support Damrau and Liddy's (1962) conclusion that "pure" beverages such as vodka are less likely to produce after-effects. Indeed, there are areas of the world where severe hangovers from vodka are sadly common. The main cause of the hangover undoubtedly is ethanol and detectable differences in after-effects as a result of differences in alcoholic beverages can be expected only after very heavy drinking.

Acute toxicity of various beverages has been rather little studied but the results support the conclusion that compounds other than ethanol have little effect. Haggard *et al.* (1943) performed an extensive study on rats, testing altogether 64 different distilled spirits, including 31 brands of whisky, 10 neutral spirits, applejack, etc. The blood alcohol level at which respiratory arrest ensued was similar in all cases. Estable *et al.* (1955) in Uruguay compared the toxicity of pure alcohol, various local distilled beverages, cognac, and whisky in one species of fish, and in mice, guinea pigs, and dogs. The effects of all solutions and beverages were proportional to their content of ethanol. In a review of alcohol poisoning, Edmondson *et al.* (1956) concluded that toxic effects of other compounds in beverages are insignificant and that even when denatured industrial alcohols are ingested, ethanol poisoning occurs before a poisonous dose of denaturant has been taken. Di Luzio (1962) reported the same rise in liver triglycerides in rats after a dose of 6 g ethanol/kg whether given as a pure solution or in six different commercial beverages.

A variety of physiological functions have shown no more than modest evidence for differential effects of various beverages. Haggard *et al.* (1941) found that the diuretic effect in man of solutions of pure ethanol, gin, whisky, port, and sherry was related only to the amount of ethyl alcohol ingested. Lolli *et al.* (1964), in a comparison between red wine and dry Martini cocktails, both given to human subjects in doses of 0.4 g/kg of ethanol on empty stomachs, reported slight differences in the proportion of subjects with altered electroencephalograms and in the distribution of minus and plus deviations in electromyograms. Webb and Degerli (1965) reported that bonded Bourbon and laboratory alcohol caused similar changes in the blood circulation of dogs. Ogden and Southard (1946) found that the stimulant effect on gastric secretion of acid in human subjects was less steep and more sustained with white wine than with a 14% ethanol solution. Experiments with de-alcoholized wine indicated that the other compounds in the wine caused the difference. Vogel (1966) and Vogel *et al.* (1967)

have reported that beer increases urine flow in rats less than pure ethanol solution, wine or brandy. This difference can be expected as the diuretic effect is related to the rate of rise in blood alcohol. Contrariwise, beer increased lymph production in rats more than pure ethanol or the beverages studied, and retained this property also after removal of the alcohol. The beer used thus seemed to contain some pressurizing compound.

Serianni *et al.* (1955) tested liver function in human subjects by measuring secretion of hippuric acid after administration of sodium benzoate. They concluded that the excretion of hippuric acid was decreased by aqueous solution of ethanol but not by wine. However, only 4 subjects were used and the results were quite variable.

Carpenter (1957) and Greenberg and Carpenter (1957) compared the effects of 12% alcohol solution and American Burgundy wine in doses of 50 and 350 ml on skin conductance and galvanic skin response in human subjects. The conductance level was differently affected, a result which was attributed to the unpleasant reactions to the pure alcohol solution. This observation gives useful emphasis to the obvious fact that the palatability of the beverages, the subjective reactions to them, and the other circumstances of the experiment have to be taken into account in any comparison of effects of different alcoholic beverages on performance of human subjects.

Brewed and distilled beverages have been compared in their effects on psychophysical performance and some physiological parameters in human subjects in Sweden by Goldberg (1952, 1958) and in Finland by Alha (1953) and Pihkanen and associates (Pihkanen, 1957a, b; Takala *et al.*, 1957). Goldberg administered variable doses, whereas the Finnish investigators kept the quantity of alcohol identical. In all these studies, blood alcohol was repeatedly determined. A general result, including Goldberg's experiments with alcohol solutions as dilute as beer, was a more rapid rise in blood alcohol and a higher peak concentration with the distilled than with the brewed beverage. Performance was more rapidly and strongly affected by the distilled beverages. Thus not only the dilution but also the various other compounds present affect the absorption of alcohol from the gastrointestinal tract, presumably by affecting its motility. An unexplained difference is that Goldberg (1952) found the blood alcohol curves after beer to run their entire course at a lower level than after ingestion of spirits, whereas in the experiments of Alha (1953) and of Takala *et al.* (1957), the curves joined each other after about two hours. In this way, Goldberg's experiments suggest that alcohol from beer would be eliminated more rapidly than alcohol from distilled beverages, whereas in the Finnish investigations a difference was seen only in the absorption phase. Although Takala *et al.* (1957) make an effort to attribute the "nastier" inebriation after brandy than after beer to other factors, their results seem largely explainable by the difference in the rate of rise in blood alcohol. In a later study, Takala *et al.* (1958) compared the effects of brandy (1.42 g alcohol/ kg) and beer (1.34 g/kg) on intellectual performance and manual dexterity. Performance was decreased by both beverages with no significant difference in their effects. Ten hours after consumption, following an overnight rest, there was a tendency for greater impairment of intellectual capacities after beer than after brandy. The authors suggested that the difference may have been due to more fatigue and poorer concentration after the beer, perhaps because of the large amount of fluid ingested. Gardiner and Stewart (1968) studied blood alcohol and blood glucose of human subjects after administration of high-extract or low-extract ale, sherry, whisky, or whisky with ginger ale, to human subjects fed or fasted for 6 hours. The dose of alcohol was 0.5 g/kg. No differences in blood alcohol were detected in the fasting condition, whereas the delay in absorption of alcohol caused by food was particularly marked after ingestion of whisky. Blood glucose was significantly increased only by ale in the fasting condition.

A potential hazard is the immense variety of new therapeutic agents which may cause unexpected reactions. Thus medication with a monoamine oxidase inhibitor has caused toxic reactions after consumption of tyramine in cheese of a particular brand (Horwitz *et al.*, 1964). Certain types of wine also contain considerable amounts of tyramine and may become sources of similar symptoms. Marquardt *et al.* (1963) have reported that some German beers and wines contain amounts of histamine which might contribute to their effects. Individual allergic reactions to compounds in beverages may of course occur, but we may conclude from the scarcity of reliable reports that such reactions are probably rare. Genuine differences appear to exist in gastrointestinal reactions to combinations of particular foods and beverages, but remain unexplained.

(2) Chronic effects

There is little evidence for any major differences in the actions of various beverages chronically administered to laboratory animals. A study by Ariyama and Takahasi (1929) indicates less adverse effects of pure alcohol than of cognac on growth of young rats. However, there were only 3 animals in one group and 4 in the other; furthermore, unbelievably high dosages were reported. Aschkenasy-Lelu (1955) reported significantly slower growth rate and increased mortality in rats drinking red wine compared with 10% ethanol as sole fluid for 2 to 6 months. Similarly, Morgan *et al.* (1957) found that growth of rats drinking red wine lagged behind that of animals drinking rosé wine or aqueous solutions of pure ethanol, but only in proportion to a decrease in calorie intake. Sautet *et al.* (1960) found slight differences in mortality of mice given alcohol solutions and different types of wine. Newell *et al.* (1964) measured growth, and also performance in simple psychomotor tests, in rats given cheap or expensive sherry, cheap or expensive muscatel, or solutions of pure alcohol. No differential effects were detected in any measures, including tissue pathology.

Some experimenters have claimed to show differential effects of different beverages. Estable *et al.* (1959) compared growth of rats whose sole fluid consisted of 10% ethyl alcohol, two local distilled beverages, or brandy diluted to 10% alcohol content. The four solutions had somewhat differential effects, with brandy retarding weight gain most severely but also decreasing total caloric intake. No differential effects were found in quantitative determinations of liver fat and collagen, and in histological examination. The authors concluded that alterations in the liver compared with water-fed controls should be attributed to ethyl alcohol. Figueroa and Klotz (1964), in an experiment of six weeks' duration on rats, reported slight differences between an ethanol solution and whisky in their effects on hepatic enzyme activities, but histological examinations revealed no difference.

Kiessling and Pilström (1968) compared effects of alcoholic beverages on the livers of growing male rats, taking biopsy specimens for electron microscopy and biochemical determinations at 150 and 270 days of the experiment. Water controls were compared with animals given pure ethanol, cognac, whisky or vermouth at 15% v/v alcohol concentration, and white and red wine with an alcohol concentration of 12% v/v. The validity of the conclusions is somewhat impaired by the fact that food was given *ad libitum* without control of the amounts eaten. The growth was not changed by red wine and decreased 6% with white wine, 14% with ethanol and cognac, and 20% with whisky and vermouth. The size of the mitochondria increased significantly with ethanol and all the beverages except white wine within 150 days. After 270 days, the effect of cognac and red wine was not significant, and some regression of mitochondrial size was seen also in the groups

References p. 695

receiving vermouth and red wine. Wine drinking increased the capacity of the mitochondria to oxidize α–glycerophosphate whereas vermouth and whisky significantly increased the aerobic glycolysis of liver homogenate. All the beverages decreased the activity of isocitric dehydrogenase whereas pure ethanol did not. Particularly the observation mentioned last suggests an effect of beverage components other than ethyl alcohol, but the significance of the findings is difficult to judge. Clinical-statistical data (Chapter 9, p. 551) do not support a relationship between specific beverage consumption and the development of liver lesions in human alcoholics. It is worth emphasizing that according to clinical-statistical data, alcohol ingested in beer is as damaging for the liver as alcohol from any other source (Lelbach, 1967; Frank et al., 1967). Lelbach (1967) cites a number of claims according to which various impurities in beverages, as for instance the tannins and organic acids of wines or the fusel oils of whiskies produced in pot-stills, would be responsible in part or wholly for the liver damage caused by alcoholism. However, Lelbach's own clinical–statistical evidence contradicts this view which appears rather naive because of the massive body of data (Chapter 9) that show the role of ethyl alcohol in the pathogenesis of liver disease in alcoholism.

Another implausible suggestion, apparently in the service of certain commercial interests, is that greater liver damage would be caused by hybrid wines, made of grapes from crossing between European and American stock, than by "thoroughbred" European wines. Kliewe and associates (Kliewe, 1961; Kliewe et al., 1961a, b; Kliewe et al., 1961c) studied damage caused in the rat liver by combinations of allyl alcohol, ethanol, and various wines. They first concluded that hybrid wines caused more damage, but later reported that no reliable differences could be established (Kliewe and Anabtawi, 1964). Similar failures to establish differential effects among wines have been reported by Leuschner and Leuschner (1967) on basis of data on pharmacological effects and liver alterations in rats. Both groups of investigators reported somewhat less changes with pure alcohol than with the wines. Schlierf et al. (1964) reported that wine had less effect than solutions of pure ethanol in raising the level of ketone bodies in the blood of human subjects.

Definite conclusions are difficult because of the failure to control calorie intake and the effect of palatability in most of the studies cited in the three preceding paragraphs. When calorie consumption has been measured, however, the growth of animals has corresponded to the calorie intake irrespective of the beverage consumed, as in the experiments of Morgan *et al.* (1957) and Estable *et al.* (1959) cited above. The only commonly used beverage definitely known to contain a deleterious added substance is absinthe, a liqueur that contains extract of wormwood. A terpene in this extract, thujone, gives rise to a special type of dependence characterized by distinct psychic disturbances and convulsions. Since discovery of the cause of the symptoms, the thujone has been removed from the extract in the manufacture of absinthe. According to Lelbach (1967), this has been required by law in Germany since 1923. As vermouths contain small amounts of wormwood extract, a special toxic effect has been attributed to them. However, Holtz (1960) has pointed out that the amount of thujone in vermouth wine is only 0.015–0.045 mg per liter. A dose of 0.8 mg/kg body weight is required to induce convulsions in a mouse. As thujone does not accumulate in the body, an effect of this compound in vermouth is clearly impossible.

There are instances when compounds added to beverages for technical reasons have caused damage. A recent epidemiological outbreak of myo-cardiac disease among heavy beer drinkers in the Quebec area in Canada was evidently due to cobalt added to the beer to improve its foaming properties. Various aspects of this even fatal disease are discussed in several publications (Alexander, 1968; Anonymous, 1968; Sullivan *et al.*, 1968; Bonenfant *et al.*, 1969; Morin *et al.*, 1969).

As the decisive property of alcoholic beverages is their content of ethyl alcohol, there is an obvious relationship among the concentration, the mode of drinking, and the ensuing action. Average rates of alcohol elimination in humans require an intake of more than 6–8 grams of alcohol per h for accumulation of alcohol in the body. Such intake is possible with any alcoholic beverage, beer, cider, natural wine, fortified wine, or spirits. However, the high dilution of beers and ordinary ciders places them in a special category with which deep intoxication cannot be achieved rapidly. In this respect, wines may be considered intermediate. It is difficult to judge other beverages in this respect, because the customary ways of drinking them vary so much. The effect of whisky diluted to form a long drink presumably differs from the effect of straight whisky.

Chapter 2 and 4 give many examples indicating that the pharmacological effects depend on the rate of rise of blood and tissue alcohol in addition to the maximal level reached. Jellinek (1960) has rather extensively discussed the possibility of a pharmacological component in the etiology of alcoholism.

If his concept of vulnerability is valid, it seems very likely that repeated drinking in a fashion that rapidly induces intoxication would promote development of alcoholism. Concentrated beverages thus would be potentially more dangerous than the dilute ones. Wallgren (1960c) compared statistics on the choice of beverage with estimates of the frequency of alcoholism in various countries. The data suggested that in countries where a large proportion of alcohol was consumed as spirits, there was also a high frequency of alcoholism in relation to the amount of alcohol consumed. However, the conclusiveness of this finding is limited by the fact that mortality in liver cirrhosis, which is the basis for the WHO estimate of alcoholism used in this study, is not correlated with specific beverage consumption (Chapter 9, p. 551). There is no doubt that a realistic appreciation of the hazards involved in the use of various beverages would be very valuable for an effective educational program and for developing policies aiming at prevention of alcoholism. No laboratory experiment can simulate actual drinking patterns and food habits among human beings in their usual environment. The only method for obtaining the necessary information is the difficult task to collect detailed data on actual drinking patterns, consumption, and harmful effects caused by alcohol in selected geographical areas. As we still have very incomplete data concerning the most important component of alcoholic beverages, ethyl alcohol itself, it does not appear advisable to emphasize laboratory experimentation on comparisons between beverages. However, psychological experiments on reactions of humans to properties of the beverages might have special practical interest.

Quite contrary conclusions about wine are offered by Lucia (1963), who expresses the opinion that various compounds lend unique therapeutic properties to wine. These assertions are mostly based on anecdotal accounts of human use rather than on experiments.

F. Summary

Joint action of alcohol and other drugs is of interest both for medical practice and pharmacological theory. The interactions may depend on whether the drugs are administered acutely or chronically. Cross-tolerance and cross-dependence may reveal pharmacological kinship between drugs and become apparent in drug therapy of withdrawal illness. Unpleasant reactions to some compounds when given jointly with alcohol have been used in aversion therapy for alcoholics. The presence of many compounds other than ethanol and water in alcoholic beverages may contribute to their actions.

The joint actions of acutely administered drugs and alcohol are affected in a very complex manner by many factors. There is lack of uniformity in both procedures and conceptual bases of the large number of experiments on these interactions. The present chapter summarizes the data in tabular form, indicating whether the reported joint action is antagonistic or synergistic. We have distinguished between additive or nearly additive synergism, meaning that the joint action is close to or identical with the sum of the separate actions, and potentiation, which indicates a joint action considerably more powerful than the sum of the separate actions. Synergism with alcohol has been found with a number of agents having a depressant action on the CNS, including general anesthetics, hypnotics and sedatives, and narcotic analgesics, and less consistently with tranquilizing drugs. Other types of drug synergistic with alcohol are antidepressant psychotherapeutics and natural transmitter substances and related compounds, both cholinergic and adrenergic. A clinically important observation is that alcohol and surgical anesthetics have a joint synergistic action, not only on the CNS but also on the heart. The synergism is usually additive; potentiation is quite rare and has in some instances been reported on the basis of evidence which is open to alternative interpretations. Antagonism of effects of alcohol is also rare and almost entirely restricted to stimulants of the CNS. Unfortunately for therapy of alcohol poisoning, the most efficient antagonists of alcohol, such as pentylenetetrazol, also have strong convulsant properties. Experiments with human subjects and with laboratory animals show a high degree of agreement in the type of joint actions found.

Alcohol is widely used as a solvent and vehicle for other drugs in pharmaceutical preparations. In some cases, alcohol promotes absorption by causing an increase in splanchnic blood flow. It facilitates absorption of several compounds by enhancing penetration through the wall of the gastrointestinal tract. After systemic dilution, the concentrations of alcohol in blood and other body fluids are so small that corresponding actions at other barriers to diffusion of drugs hardly can be expected. However, there is evidence that ethanol may facilitate penetration through the blood-brain barrier of monoamines and their metabolites as well as of compounds related to acetylcholine. Drugs do not generally affect absorption and distribution of ethanol except for those which modify gastrointestinal motility and splanchnic blood flow, thereby changing the rate of uptake of ethanol from the gut.

References p. 695

Only a few of the many drugs tested have any effect on the metabolism of ethanol. Similarly, ethanol modifies the metabolism of very few other drugs. An important reason for this general lack of metabolic interaction is that ethanol is oxidized mainly by a cytoplasmic NAD-dependent dehydrogenase system, but most other drugs by microsomal enzymes of various types which include NADP-dependent oxidases. Among compounds which inhibit liver alcohol dehydrogenase are pyrazole and pyrazolon derivatives, ethacrynic acid, pheniprazine, 1-amphetamine, and butyraldoxime. Some of these compounds are efficient inhibitors of alcohol elimination also *in vivo*. Ethanol may exert an inhibitory action on NAD-dependent systems metabolizing other drugs through its effect on the redox state, provided that the drug-metabolizing system is so active that the effect becomes apparent. Little is known about such interactions, except for the competition between ethanol and other alcohols. Recent studies indicate that prolonged administration of ethanol activates the microsomal alcohol oxidase and also other microsomal drug-metabolizing systems.

The greatest similarity in action is found among alcohol, general anesthetics, and the barbiturates. All these agents interfere with mechanisms linked with the generation of action potentials, but the barbiturates apparently also affect metabolic reactions of the nerve cells in a more complex manner than do alcohol and the general anesthetics. Similarities are seen in the behavioral effects of these drugs, in the drug action perceived by experimental animals, and in effect on the EEG. Differences are evident particularly in the degree of selectivity exerted on various aspects of CNS functioning; the selectivity appears to be particularly low for alcohol. Such differences presumably account for the differences in the patterns of over-all reactions to these various drugs. Both on the cellular and integrative level, narcotic analgesics and major tranquilizers such as the phenothiazine derivatives differ markedly from alcohol in their actions. A suggestive finding is that among agents with predominantly peripheral actions, those known to act on synaptic function by altering membrane permeability are most often synergistic with ethanol.

Chronic alcoholics are generally thought to be quite resistant to anesthesia, but there is little solid evidence for this postulated cross-tolerance. Documented clinical cases are astonishingly few. A source of discrepancies is the variable clinical state of alcoholic patients. Several reported experimental studies contain flaws in the design which render the results inconclusive. A score of well conducted animal experiments show heightened tolerance to general anesthetics and sedatives in animals tolerant to alcohol, and increased tolerance to alcohol in animals with raised resistance to other drugs. Alcohol was found to be a partial substitute for barbiturates in the only experimental study on cross-dependence, which was performed in humans. Experience with treatment of alcohol withdrawal illness shows that several other hypnotics and sedatives can be used for control of this illness, thus giving evidence for cross-dependence. These include chloral hydrate, paraldehyde, meprobamate, glutethimide, clomethiazole, chlordiazepoxide, and methyprylon. Information is scanty concerning changes in action of other groups of therapeutic agents after prolonged alcohol consumption.

Several compounds cause unpleasant reactions to alcohol in doses which by themselves have no detectable pharmacological effects. The first recognized reactions of this type were caused by occupational exposure to chemicals such as carbon disulfide, cyanamide, and tetra-alkylthiuram sulfides. The compounds with this alcohol-sensitizing action are many, and they include a few therapeutic agents such as oral antidiabetics of the sulfonylurea type, and even components of natural products, as the fungus *Coprinus atramentarius*. This property has been exploited for aversion therapy of alcoholism. The agents most commonly used for this purpose are tetraethylthiuram disulfide (disulfiram, Antabuse), and citrated calcium cyanamide (CCC, Temposil). There is no definite explanation of the mechanism for the flushing, nausea, decrease in arterial blood pressure, and anxiety characteristic of the joint action of these drugs with alcohol. These symptoms have often been ascribed to rise in acetaldehyde concentration caused by metabolic inhibition, on the basis of observations that both ethanol and acetaldehyde oxidation are inhibited and levels of acetaldehyde are raised. However, administration of acetaldehyde causes some opposite symptoms such as raised blood pressure. Since several of these compounds or their metabolites are antioxidants, their interactions with alcohol may be caused by disturbance of monoamine balance through a combination of direct enzymatic inhibition and competitive metabolic effects involving acetaldehyde and monoamines.

Although ethanol and all the other aliphatic monohydric alcohols are pharmacologically closely related to each other, there are important metabolic differences. In contrast to the primary and secondary alcohols, the tertiary ones are not oxidized and therefore lack the metabolic impact of ethanol and are eliminated much more slowly. Few experimenters have taken advantage of this opportunity to study the pharmacological actions of

References p. 695

alcohols separately from their metabolic actions. Instances of special toxicity of alcohols include toxic actions of metabolic products of methanol and ethylene glycol. Ethanol is a useful antidote in poisoning by these alcohols because it slows formation of the toxic products by a competitive metabolic action. Alcohols with three or more hydroxyls are generally not toxic; these include normal metabolic intermediates and nutrients such as glycerol and the sugar alcohols.

Various "higher" alcohols of larger molecular size than ethanol are among the components of fusel oil. Differential effects of alcoholic beverages are often attributed to these and other minor constituents. Subjective reactions may be strongly influenced by flavor and aroma, but neither acute nor chronic experiments give evidence for any major differences in the pharmacological action of different beverages. Analytical data also indicate that although many components of beverages are biologically active, the quantities are far too small to be significant. In some instances added compounds have caused dangerous effects, such as those caused by thujone from wormwood extract, formerly used in the manufacture of absinthe, and some recent outbreaks of myocardial disease among people consuming large quantities of particular brands of beer, due to added cobalt. However, the pharmacologically most important characteristic of alcoholic beverages generally seems to be their degree of dilution. The apparent reason is that many of the effects of alcohol depend not only on the concentration achieved in the organism, but also on the rate of rise of the concentration. Reports of less violent intoxication after beer than after brandy or vodka in similar quantities seem to be mainly explainable by this effect of slower rise in blood alcohol. On the other hand, reports of more severe fatigue and drowsiness in the hangover phase after beer than distilled beverages may be due to components derived from hops.

Among the most compelling evidence that beverage composition has little significance in chronic use is the epidemiological finding that the development of liver disease among heavy drinkers is correlated with duration and amount of consumption but not with the specific beverage consumed. The extent to which pharmacological properties of beverages contribute to development of dependence on alcohol is unknown. For elucidation of this problem, it would be valuable to acquire data on actual drinking patterns, consumption rates, and signs of dependence associated with the use of various types of beverages. One of the obstacles for such studies is the lack of objective, quantitative measures of dependence.

REFERENCES

ABREU, B. E. AND EMERSON, G. A. (1939). Susceptibility to ether anesthesia of mice habituated to alcohol, morphine or cocaine. *Anesthesia Analgesia 18*, 294–300.

ADRIANI, J. AND MORTON, R. C. (1968). Drug dependence: important considerations from the anesthesiologist's viewpoint. *Anesthesia Analgesia 47*, 472–481.

AHLQUIST, R. P. AND DILLE, J. M. (1940). Reactions of alcohol tolerant rabbits to pentobarbital, evipal, ether, amidopyrine and metrazol. *J. Pharmacol. Exptl. Therap. 70*, 301–308.

AKABANE, J. AND IKOMI, F. (1958). Effects of disulfiram (tetraethylthiuramdisulfide) and its related compounds on the metabolism of alcohol. *Med. J. Shinshu Univ. 3*, 345–351.

AKABANE, J., NAKANISHI, S., KOHEI, H., MATSUMURA, R. AND OGATA, H. (1963). Effect of sulfonylurea derivative on the metabolism of alcohol. Experiments with isolated perfused liver. *Med. J. Shinshu Univ. 8*, 71–79.

ALEXANDER, C. S. (1968). The concept of alcoholic myocardiopathy. *Med. Clin. North America 52*, 1183–1192.

ALHA, A. (1950). Carbon tetrachloride mass poisoning. *Ann. Med. Intern. Fenn. 39*, Suppl. 8, 1–32.

ALHA, A. (1953). Stenograferingsförmågan vid tilltagande och avtagande berusning med brännvin och öl. (Shorthand skill during the rising and declining stages of intoxication.) *Alkoholpolitik 16*, 66–77 (Eng. sum. pp. 91–92).

AMERINE, M. A. (1954). Composition of wines. I. Organic constituents. *Advan. Food Res. 5*, 353–510.

ANONYMOUS (1968). Epidemic cardiac failure in beer drinkers. *Nutr. Rev. 26*, 173–175.

ARCHER, J. D. (1956). An experimental study of the lethal synergism between secobarbital and alcohol. *Texas Rept. Biol. Med. 14*, 1–5.

ARIYAMA, H. AND TAKAHASI, K. (1929). Über den relativen Nährwert der Kohlenhydrate und verwandten Substanzen. *Biochem. Z. 216*, 269–277.

ARMSTRONG, J. D. (1957). The protective drugs in the treatment of alcoholism. *Can. Med. Assoc. J. 77*, 228–232.

ARMSTRONG, J. D. AND KERR, H. T. (1956). A new protective drug in the treatment of alcoholism. (Preliminary trial of citrated calcium carbimide.) *Can. Med. Assoc. J. 74*, 795–797.

ASCHAN, G., BERGSTEDT, M. AND GOLDBERG, L. (1957). The effect of some antihistaminic drugs on positional alcohol nystagmus. *Acta Oto-Laryngol.*, Suppl. 140, 79–90. (Abstr. *Quart. J. Studies Alc.* 1960, *21*, 347.)

ASCHKENASY-LELU, P. (1955). Action d'une ingestion modérée et prolongée d'alcool ou de vin sur la croissance et le poids relatif des organes du rat mâle. *J. Physiol. Paris 47*, 78–80.

ASMUSSEN, E., HALD, J., JACOBSEN, E. AND JØRGENSEN, G. (1948). Studies on the effect of tetraethylthiuramdisulphide (Antabuse) and alcohol on respiration and circulation in normal human subjects. *Acta Pharmacol. Toxicol. 4*, 297–304.

ASTON, R. AND CULLUMBINE, H. (1959). Studies on the nature of the joint action of ethanol and barbiturates. *Toxicol. Appl. Pharmacol. 1*, 65–72. (Abstr. *Quart. J. Studies Alc.* 1961, *22*, 335.)

ASTON, R. AND CULLUMBINE, H. (1960). The effects of combinations of ataraxics with hypnotics, LSD and iproniazid in the mouse. *Arch. Intern. Pharmacodyn. 126*, 219–227.

ASTON, R. AND STOLMAN, S. (1966). Influence of route and concentration of ethanol upon central depressant effect in the mouse. *Proc. Soc. Exptl. Biol. Med. 123*, 496–498.

ÄYRÄPÄÄ, T. (1962). Phenethyl alcohol in wines. *Nature 194*, 472–473.

BALODIS, K. (1933). Weitere Versuche über Aufhebung örtlicher Anesthesie durch Gewöhnung an Alkohol. *Naunyn Schmiedeberg Arch. Pharm. Exptl. Pathol. 173*, 589–594.

BARKMAN, R. AND PERMAN, E. S. (1963). Supersensitivity to ethanol in rabbits treated with *Coprinus atramentarius*. *Acta Pharmacol. Toxicol. 20*, 43–46.

BARRY, H., III (1967). Effects of drive strength on extinction and spontaneous recovery. *J. Exptl. Psychol. 73*, 419–421.

BARRY, H., III AND BUCKLEY, J. P. (1966). Drug effects on animal performance and the stress syndrome. *J. Pharm. Sci. 55*, 1159–1183.

BARRY, H., III AND MILLER, N. E. (1962). Effects of drugs on approach-avoidance conflict tested repeatedly by means of a "telescope alley". *J. Comp. Physiol. Psychol. 55*, 201–210.

BARRY, H., III, WAGNER, A. R. AND MILLER, N. E. (1962). Effects of alcohol and amobarbital on performance inhibited by experimental extinction. *J. Comp. Physiol. Psychol. 55*, 464–468.

BELL, R. G. (1956). Clinical trial of citrated calcium carbimide. *Can. Med. Assoc. J. 74*, 797–798.

BERNDT, H. AND KUTSCHKE, I. (1967). Der Einfluss von Thiamintetrahydrofurfuryldisulfid (TTFD) auf den Alkoholabbau. *Klin. Wochschr. 45*, 685–686.

BISSET, G. W. AND WALKER, J. M. (1957). The effects of nicotine, Hexamethonium and ethanol on the secretion of the antidiuretic and oxytocic hormones of the rat. *Brit. J. Pharmacol. 12*, 461–467.

BJERVER, K. AND GOLDBERG, L. (1948). Alcohol tolerance in individuals with chronic producer-gas intoxication. *Quart. J. Studies Alc. 9*, 329–352.

BLOMBERG, L.-H. AND WASSÉN, A. (1962). The effect of small doses of alcohol on the "optokinetic fusion limit". *Acta Physiol. Scand. 54*, 193–199.

BLOOMQUIST, E. R. (1959). Addiction, addicting drugs, and the anesthesiologist. *J. Am. Med. Assoc. 171*, 518–523.

BONENFANT, J.-L., AUGER, C., MILLER, G., CHENARD, J. AND ROY, P.-E. (1969). Quebec beer-drinker's myocardosis: pathological aspects. *Ann. N.Y. Acad. Sci. 156*, 577–582.

BONNICHSEN, R., DIMBERG, R., MAEHLY, A. AND ÅQVIST, S. (1968). Die Alkoholverbrennung bei Alkoholikern und bei übrigen Versuchspersonen. *Blutalkohol 5*, 301–317.

BOUCHIER, I. A. D. AND WILLIAMS, H. S. (1969). Determination of faecal blood-loss after combined alcohol and sodium-acetylsalicylate intake. *Lancet 1*, 178–180.

BOURNE, J. G. (1960). *Nitrous oxide in dentistry*. Lloyd Luke, London.

BOURRINET, P. (1964). Étude expérimentale de l'influence de l'alcoolisation aiguë et chronique sur l'activité des médicaments. *Rev. Alcoolisme 10*, 186–198.

BOYD, E. M. (1960). A search for drugs with disulfiram-like activity. *Quart. J. Studies Alc. 21*, 23–25.

BRADLEY, P. B. (1963). Phenothiazine derivatives. In: *Physiological pharmacology*, ROOT, W. S. AND HOFMANN, F. G., Eds., Academic Press, New York; Vol. 1, Pp. 417–477.

BRAZIER, M. A. B. (1963). Effects upon physiological systems. *a*. The electrophysiological effects of barbiturates on the brain. In: *Physiological pharmacology*, ROOT, W. S. AND HOFMANN, F. G., Eds., Academic Press, New York; Vol. 1. Pp. 219–238.

BRODIE, B. B. AND SHORE, P. A. (1957). A concept for a role of serotonin and norepinephrine as chemical mediators in the brain. *Ann. N.Y. Acad. Sci. 66*, 631–642.

BRODIE, B. B., SHORE, P. A. AND SILVER, S. L. (1955). Potentiating action of chlorpromazine and reserpine. *Nature 175*, 1133–1134.

BURGER, E. (1961). Einfluss von Tranquillizer-Substanzen auf die Alkoholwirkung. *Hefte z. Unfallheilk. 66*, 99–102. (Abstr. *Quart. J. Studies Alc.* 1962, *23*, 656.)

BÜTTNER, H. (1960). Arzneimittel und Alkohol. *Therapie der Gegenwart 99*, 384–386.

BÜTTNER, H. (1961). Äthanolunverträglichkeit beim Menschen nach Sulfonylharnstoffen. *Deut. Archiv Klin. Med. 207*, 1–18.

BÜTTNER, H. AND PORTWICH, F. (1960). Wirkungen des N-(4-Methylbenzolsulfonyl)-N'-butyl-harnstoffs (D 869) auf den Stoffwechsel des Äthanols. *Arch. Exptl. Pathol. Pharmakol. 238*, 45–46.

BÜTTNER, H., PORTWICH, F. AND ENGELHARDT, K. (1961). Der DPN⁺- und DPN-H-Gehalt der Rattenleber während des Abbaues von Äthanol und seine Beeinflussung durch Sulfonylharnstoff und Disulfiram. *Arch. Exptl. Pathol. Pharmakol. 240*, 573–583.

CAIRD, W. K., SLOANE, R. B. AND INGLIS, J. (1960). The effects of nialamide and ethyl alcohol on some personality, cognitive and psychomotor variables in normal volunteers. *J. Neuropsychiat. 2*, 31–34. (Abstr. *Quart. J. Studies Alc.* 1962, *23*, 337.)

CAMPBELL, B., TAYLOR, J. A. T. AND HASLETT, W. L. (1967). Anti-alcohol properties of metronidazole in rats. *Proc. Soc. Exptl. Biol. Med. 124*, 191–195.

CARPENTER, J. A. (1957). Effects of alcoholic beverages on skin conductance. *Quart. J. Studies Alc. 18*, 1–18.

CARPENTER, J. A. AND VARLEY, M. (1963). The joint action of tranquillizers and alcohol on driving. In: *Alcohol and Road Traffic*, J. D. J. HAVARD, Ed., Proc. Intern. Conf., 3rd, London 1962, Brit. Med. Assoc. Publ. Pp. 156–161.

CASIER, H. AND MERLEVEDE, E. (1962). On the mechanism of the disulfiram-ethanol intoxication symptoms. *Arch. Intern. Pharmacodyn. 139*, 165–176.

CASIER, H. AND MERLEVEDE, E. (1963). Mechanism of the disulfiram-ethanol intoxication symptoms. *Brit. J. Addict. 59*, 105.

CASIER, H. AND POLET, H. (1958). Influence du disulfiram (Antabus) sur le métabolisme de l'alcool éthylique marqué chez la souris. *Arch. Intern. Pharmacodyn. 113*, 439–496.

CASIER, H., DANECHMAND, L., DESCHAEPDRYVER, A., HERMANS, W. AND PIETTE, Y. (1966). Blood alcohol levels and psychotropic drugs. *Arzneimittel-Forsch. 16*, 1505–1506.

CLARK, W. C. AND HULPIEU, H. R. (1958). The disulfiram-like activity of animal charcoal. *J. Pharmacol. Exptl. Therap. 123*, 74–80. (Abstr. *Quart. J. Studies Alc.* 1959, *20*, 140.)

CONNEY, A. H. (1965). Enzyme induction and drug toxicity. In: *Drugs and enzymes*, PROC. INTERN. PHARMACOL. MEETING, 2ND, PRAGUE 1963, BRODIE, B. B. AND GILLETTE, J. R., Eds., Pergamon, Oxford; Vol. 4. Pp. 277–297.

COOPER, J. R. AND KINI, M. M. (1962). Biochemical aspects of methanol poisoning. *Biochem. Pharmacol. 11*, 405–416.

CORNISH, H. H. AND ADEFUIN, J. (1966). Ethanol potentiation of halogenated aliphatic solvent toxicity. *Am. Ind. Hyg. Assoc. J. 27*, 57–61.

COURVOISIER, S., FOURNEL, J., DUCROT, R., KOLSKY, M. AND KOETSCHET, P. (1953). Propriétés pharmacodynamiques du chlorhydrate de chloro-3-(diméthyl-amino-3'-propyl)-10 phénothiazine (4.560 R.P.). Étude expérimentale d'un nouveau corps utilisé dans l'anesthésie potentialisée et dans l'hibernation artificielle. *Arch. Intern. Pharmacodyn. 92*, 305–361.

CREAVEN, P. J. AND ROACH, M. K. (1969). The effect of chloral hydrate on the metabolism of ethanol in mice. *J. Pharm. Pharmacol. 21*, 332–333.

CZYZYK, A. AND MOHNIKE, G. (1957). Über die Beeinflussung der Alkoholtoleranz durch blutzuckersenkende Harnstoffderivate. *Deut. Med. Wochschr. 82*, 1585–1586.

DAMRAU, F. AND LIDDY, E. (1960). Hangovers and whisky congeners. Comparison of whisky with vodka. *J. Nat. Med. Assoc. 52*, 262–265.

DAMRAU, F. AND LIDDY, E. (1962). The use of vodka in geriatrics. *Ind. Med. Surg. 31*, 463–464.

DANDIYA, P. C. AND RUNGTA, S. S. (1964). Studies on central nervous system depressants (VI). Central nervous system actions of three esters of benzilic acid. *Arch. Intern. Pharmacodyn. 149*, 493–506.

DAVANZO, J. P., RUCKART, R., KANG, L. AND DAUGHERTY, M. (1964). Biochemical studies with doxapram HCl. *Federation Proc. 23*, No. 2, Part I, 386.

DEBRAY, C., VAILLE, C., MARTIN, E., SOUCHARD, M. AND ROZE, C. (1965). Influence de l'éthanol sur la lithiase renale expérimentale a l'éthylene-glycol chez le rat. *Presse Méd. 73*, 1559–1561. (Abstr. *Quart. J. Studies Alc.* 1966, *27*, 744.)

DEGERLI, I. U. AND WEBB, W. R. (1963). Alcohol, cardiac function and coronary flow. *Surg. Forum 14*, 252–254.

DEITRICH, R. A. AND HELLERMAN, L. (1963). Diphosphopyridine nucleotide-linked aldehyde dehydrogenase. II. Inhibitors. *J. Biol. Chem. 238*, 1683–1689.

DEITRICH, R. A. AND WORTH, W. S. (1968). Metabolism of cyanamide in relation to its use in alcoholism and other diseases. *Federation Proc. 27*, No. 2, 237.

DILLE, J. M. AND AHLQUIST, R. P. (1937). The synergism of ethyl alcohol and sodium pentobarbital. *J. Pharmacol. Exptl. Therap. 61*, 385–392.

DILLE, J. M., LINEGAR, C. R. AND KOPPANYI, T. (1935). Studies on barbiturates. XII. Factors governing the distribution of barbiturates. *J. Pharmacol. Exptl. Therap. 55*, 46–61.

DiLUZIO, N. R. (1962). Comparative study of the effect of alcoholic beverages on the development of the acute ethanol-induced fatty liver. *Quart. J. Studies Alc. 23*, 556–561.

DIXON, R. L. AND RALL, D. P. (1965). Enhancement of ethanol toxicity by ethacrynic acid. *Proc. Soc. Exptl. Biol. Med. 118*, 970–973.

DOENICKE, A. (1962). Beeinträchtung der Verkehrssicherheit durch Barbiturat-Medikation und durch die Kombination Barbiturat/Alkohol. *Arzneimittel-Forsch. 11*, 1050.

DOENICKE, A. AND SIGMUND, W. (1964). Prüfung der Verkehrssicherheit nach Verabreichung von Fluphenazindihydrochlorid und Alkohol. *Arzneimittel-Forsch. 14*, 907–911.

DURITZ, G. AND TRUITT, E. B., JR. (1964). A rapid method for the simultaneous determination of acetaldehyde and ethanol in blood using gas chromatography. *Quart. J. Studies Alc. 25*, 498–510.

EDMONDSON, H. A., HALL, E. M. AND MYERS, R. O. (1956). Pathology of alcoholism. In: *Alcoholism*, G. N. THOMPSON, Ed., Charles C. Thomas, Springfield, Ill. Pp. 233–290.

EDWARDS, J. A. AND PRICE, J. (1967a). Metronidazole and human alcohol dehydrogenase. *Nature 214*, 190–191.

EDWARDS, J. A. AND PRICE, J. (1967b). Metronidazole and atypical human alcohol dehydrogenase. *Biochem. Pharmacol. 16*, 2026–2027.

EEROLA, R. (1961). The effect of ethanol on the toxicity of hexobarbital, thiopental, morphine, atropine and scopolamine. An experimental study on mice. *Ann. Med. Exptl. Biol. Fenniae, Helsinki 39*, Suppl. 3, 70 pp.

EEROLA, R. (1963). The effect of ethanol on the toxicity of promazine, chlorpromazine, promethazine and hydroxyzine; an experimental study on mice. *Acta Anaesthesiol. Scand. 7*, 7–95. (Abstr. *Quart. J. Studies Alc.* 1965, *26*, 135.)

EEROLA, R., VENHO, I., VARTIAINEN, O. AND VENHO, E. V. (1955). Acute alcoholic poisoning and morphine. An experimental study of the synergism of morphine and ethyl alcohol in mice. *Ann. Med. Exptl. Biol. Fenniae, Helsinki 33*, 253–261.

EKMAN, G., FRANKENHAEUSER, M., GOLDBERG, L., BJERVER, K., JÄRPE, G. AND MYRSTEN, A.-L. (1963). Effects of alcohol intake on subjective and objective variables over a five-hour period. *Psychopharmacologia 4*, 28–38.

ELBEL, H. (1938). Neues zur Blutalkoholfrage. *Deut. Z. Ges. Gerichtl. Med. 30*, 218–226.

ELBEL, H. AND SCHLEYER, F. (1956). *Blutalkohol. Die wissenschaftlichen Grundlagen der Beurteilung von Blutalkoholbefunden bei Strassenverkehrsdelikten*. 2nd ed., Georg Thieme, Stuttgart; 226 pp.

ESTABLE, J. J., GREZZI, J. W. AND RODRIGUEZ, J. V. (1955). Comparative toxicity of alcohol and various national distilled alcoholic beverages for fish kept in aquariums. *Arch. Soc. Biol. Montevideo 21*, 43–47.

ESTABLE, J. J., GREZZI, J. W. AND BARAIBAR, B. (1959). Determinación cuantitativa del colageno y los lipidos hepáticos en el curso de la intoxicación crónica experimental con bebidas alcohólicas destiladas. *Anales Fac. Med. Montevideo 44*, 261–268.

ESTLER, C.-J. AND AMMON, H. P. T. (1965). Phosphorylaseaktivität und Glykogengehalt des Gehirns unter dem Einfluss von Äthanol und Adrenalin. *J. Neurochem. 12*, 871–876.

ETTINGER, G. H., BROWN, A. B. AND MEGILL, A. H. (1941). Potentiation of acetylcholine by alcohol and ether. *J. Pharmacol. Exptl. Therap. 73*, 119–126.

ETZLER, K., JOSWIG, E. H. AND MALLACH, H. J. (1966). Weitere Ergebnisse über die gemeinsame Wirkung von Alkohol und Dimethylsulfoxyd im Tierversuch. *Arzneimittel-Forsch. 16*, 1228–1232.

FEARN, H. J. AND HODGES, J. R. (1953). Synergic effects of amylobarbitone sodium and ethanol. *J. Pharm. Pharmacol. 5*, 1041–1044.

FELDSTEIN, A. AND WILLIAMSON, O. (1968). The effect of ethanol and disulfiram on serotonin-^{14}C metabolism in rat liver homogenates. *Life Sciences 7*, 777–783.

FERGUSON, J. K. W. (1956). A new drug for the treatment of alcoholism. *Can. Med. Assoc. J. 74*, 793–795.

FIGUEROA, R. B. AND KLOTZ, A. P. (1964). The effect of whiskey and low-protein diets on hepatic enzymes in rats. *Am. J. Digest. Diseases 9*, 121–127. (Abstr. *Quart. J. Studies Alc.* 1965, *26*, 132.)

FISCHER, E. (1957). The counteraction of weak concentrations of azide on the depressing effect of alcohol on the oxygen consumption of brain slices. In: *Alcoholism*, HIMWICH, H. E., Ed., Publ. No. 47, Am. Assoc. Advan. Sci., Washington, D.C. Pp. 19–27.

FISCHER, H.-D. (1962). Der Einfluss von Barbituraten auf die Entgiftungsgeschwindigkeit des Äthanols. *Biochem. Pharmacol. 11*, 307–314.

FISCHER, H.-D. AND OELSSNER, W. (1960). Der Einfluss von Hexobarbital und Phenobarbital auf die Alkoholelimination bei Kaninchen. *Med. Exptl. 3*, 213–218.

FISCHER, I. (1945). Säregen svampförgiftning. *Svenska Läkartidn. 42*, 2513–2515.

FITZGERALD, M. G., GADDIE, R., MALINS, J. M. AND O'SULLIVAN, D. J. (1962). Alcohol sensitivity in diabetics receiving chlorpropamide. *Diabetes 11*, 40–43. (Abstr. *Quart. J. Studies Alc.* 1962, *23*, 657.)

FORNEY, R. B. AND HUGHES, F. W. (1963). Behavioral effects on the rat of benzquinamide and benzquinamide-alcohol combinations. *Arch. Int. Pharmacodyn. 142*, 237–242.

FORNEY, R. B. AND HUGHES, F. W. (1965). Effect of caffeine and alcohol on performance under stress of audiofeedback. *Quart. J. Studies Alc. 26*, 206–212.

FORNEY, R. B. AND HUGHES, F. W. (1968). *Combined effects of alcohol and other drugs.* Thomas, Springfield, Illinois. 124 pp.

FORNEY, R. B., HUGHES, F. W., HULPIEU, H. R. AND CLARK, W. C. (1962). Rapid early metabolism of ethanol in the mouse. *Toxicol. Appl. Pharmacol. 4*, 253–256.

FORNEY, R. B., HUGHES, F. W. AND HULPIEU, H. R. (1963a). Potentiation of ethanol-induced depression in dogs by representative ataractic and analgesic drugs. *Quart. J. Studies Alc. 24*, 1–8.

FORNEY, R. B., HUGHES, F. W., RICHARDS, A. B. AND GATES, P. W. (1963b). Toxicity and depressant action of ethanol and hexobarbital after pretreatment with asparagine. *Toxicol. Appl. Pharmacol. 5*, 790–793.

FORSANDER, O. A. (1970). Influence of ethanol and butyraldoxime on liver metabolism. *Biochem. Pharmacol. 19*, 2131–2136.

FRAHM, M., LÖBKENS, K. AND SOEHRING, K. (1962). The influence of subchronic administration of alcohol on barbiturate narcosis in guinea pigs. (Ger.) *Arzneimittel-Forsch. 12*, 1055–1056. (Abstr. *Quart. J. Studies Alc.* 1964, *25*, 581–582.)

FRANK, H., HEIL, W. AND LEODOLTER, I. (1967). Leber und Bierkonsum. Vergleichende Untersuchungen an 450 Arbeitern. *Münch. Med. Wochschr. 109*, 892–897.

FRANKENHAEUSER, M. AND POST, B. (1966). Objective and subjective performance as influenced by drug-induced variations in activation level. *Scand. J. Psychol.* 7, 168–178.

FRASER, H. F., WIKLER, A., ISBELL, H. AND JOHNSON, N. K. (1957). Partial equivalence of chronic alcohol and barbiturate intoxications. *Quart. J. Studies Alc. 18*, 541–551.

FRIED, R. AND FRIED, L. W. (1966). The effect of Flagyl on xanthine oxidase and alcohol dehydrogenase. *Biochem. Pharmacol. 15*, 1890–1894.

FROMMEL, E. AND SEYDOUX, J. (1964). De l'effet de l'éthanol sur l'encéphale. Bilan des tests dits de neuropharmacologie chez l'animal. *Helv. Physiol. Pharmacol. Acta 22*, 34–38.

FROMMEL, E., SEYDOUX, J. AND FASEL, M. (1963a). Do morphine and phenobarbital modify induced blood alcohol levels in the guinea pig? (Fr.) *Experientia 19*, 602–603. (Abstr. *Quart. J. Studies Alc.* 1965, *26*, 702.)

FROMMEL, E., SEYDOUX, J. AND LEDEBUR, I. VON (1963b). Which is the antidote for the psychomotor excitation of the alcoholic? Phenobarbital, morphine, Librium or chlorpromazine? Experimental study. (Fr.) *Compt. Rend. Soc. Biol. 157*, 526–529. (Abstr. *Quart. J. Studies Alc.* 1965, *26*, 702.)

GADSDEN, R. H., MELLETTE, R. R. AND MILLER, W. C. (1958). Scrap iron intoxication. *J. Am. Med. Assoc. 168*, 1220–1224. (Abstr. *Quart. J. Studies Alc.* 1959, *20*, 797.)

GANZ, V. (1963). The acute effect of alcohol on the circulation and on the oxygen metabolism of the heart. *Am. Heart J. 66*, 494–497.

GARDINER, R. J. AND STEWART, H. B. (1968). Blood alcohol and glucose changes after ingestion of ale, wine and spirit. *Quart. J. Studies Alc. 29*, 313–322.

GENEST, K., COLDWELL, B. B. AND HUGHES, D. W. (1968). Potentiation of ethanol by *Coprinus atramentarius* in mice. *J. Pharm. Pharmacol. 20*, 102–106.

GESSNER, P. K. AND CABANA, B. E. (1964). The effect of ethanol on chloral hydrate hypnosis in mice. *Fed. Proc. 23*, No. 2, Part I, 348.

GESSNER, P. K. AND CABANA, B. E. (1967a). Chloral alcoholate: reevaluation of its role in the interaction between the hypnotic effects of chloral hydrate and ethanol. *J. Pharmacol. Exptl. Ther. 156*, 602–605.

GESSNER, P. K. AND CABANA, B. E. (1967b). The effect of ethanol on the kinetics of chloral hydrate metabolism in mice. *Fed. Proc. 26*, 568.

GETTLER, D. T. AND ALLBRITTEN, F. F., JR. (1963). Effect of alcohol intoxication on the respiratory exchange and mortality rate associated with acute hemorrhage in anesthetized dogs. *Ann. Surg. 158*, No. 2, 151–158.

GLASS, F. AND MALLACH, J. (1965). Tierexperimentelle Untersuchungen über die Alkoholwirkung nach längerer Belastung mit Isonicotinsäurehydrazid. *Arzneimittel-Forsch. 15*, 1069–1070.

GLASS, F. AND MALLACH, H. J. (1966). Beobachtungen und Untersuchungen über die gemeinsame Wirkung von Alkohol und alpha-phenyl-alpha-aethylglutarsäureimid (Glutethimid). *Arzneimittel-Forsch. 16*, 528–532.

GLASS, F., GOSSOW, H. AND MALLACH, H. J. (1964). Beobachtungen und Untersuchungen über die gemeinsame Wirkung von Alkohol und Isonicotinsäurehydrazid. *Arzneimittel-Forsch. 14*, 1203–1207.

GOLD, H. AND TRAVELL, J. (1934a). Ethyl alcohol and strychnine antagonism. *J. Pharmacol. Exptl. Therap. 52*, 30–53.

GOLD, H. AND TRAVELL, J. (1934b). Strychnine in poisoning by alcohol. *J. Pharmacol. Exptl. Therap. 52*, 345–354.

GOLDBERG, L. (1952). Verkan på den mänskliga organismen av maltdrycker med olika alkoholhalt. *Svenska Statens Offentliga Utredningar, 44*. 134 pp.

GOLDBERG, L. (1958). Verkan på organismen av olika slag av viner. *Alkoholfrågan 52*, 354–363.

GOLDBERG, L. (1960). Teoretisk alkoholforskning. In: *Karolinska Medikokirurgiska Institutets Historia*, Stockholm; Vol. 3. Pp. 281–308.

GOLDBERG, L. (1961). Alcohol, tranquilizers and hangover. *Quart. J. Studies Alc.*, Suppl. No. 1, 37–56.

GOLDBERG, L. (1963). Effects and after-effects of alcohol, tranquillizers and fatigue on ocular phenomena. In: *Alcohol and Road Traffic*, J. D. J. HAVARD, Ed., Proc. Intern. Conf., 3rd, London 1962, Brit. Med. Assoc. Publ., London. Pp. 123–135.

GOLDBERG, L. AND RYDBERG, U. (1969). Inhibition of ethanol metabolism *in vivo* by administration of pyrazole. *Biochem. Pharmacol. 18*, 1749–1762.

GOODMAN, L. S. AND GILMAN, A., Eds. (1965). *The pharmacological basis of therapeutics*, 3rd ed., Macmillan, New York; Collier-Macmillan, London and Toronto. xviii + 1785 pp.

GÖRES, E. (1964). Einige pharmakologische Probleme der Äthanolwirkung. 1. Teil, *Pharmazie 19*, 433–447. 2. Teil, *idem*, 489–507.

GOULSTON, K. AND COOKE, A. R. (1968). Alcohol, aspirin, and gastrointestinal bleeding. *Brit. Med. J. 14*, 664–665.

GRAHAM, J. D. P. (1960). Ethanol and the absorption of barbiturate. *Toxicol. Appl. Pharmacol. 2*, 14–22.

GREENBERG, L. A. AND CARPENTER, J. A. (1957). The effect of alcoholic beverages on skin conductance and emotional tension. I. Wine, whisky and alcohol. *Quart. J. Studies Alc. 18*, 190–204.

GREENBERG, R. E. (1967). Prevention of alcohol-induced cortical depression with stimulants and tertiary amines. *Quart. J. Studies Alc. 28*, 1–10.

GREISER, E. AND SOEHRING, K. (1967). Der Transport von Pentobarbital durch biologische Membranen und seine Beeinflussung durch Äthanol. *Arzneimittel-Forsch. 17*, 207–214.

GRUBER, C. M. (1955). A theoretical consideration of additive and potentiated effects between drugs, with a practical example using alcohol and barbiturates. *Arch. Intern. Pharmacodyn. 102*, 17–32.

GRUBER, C. M., LASCHICHENKO, Z. AND SOO LEE, K. (1954). The effect of orally administered Antabuse on the sleeping time of mice, rats, and rabbits given barbiturates, ether, chloroform, urethane, chloral hydrate, alcohol, or acetaldehyde by injection. *Arch. Intern. Pharmacodyn. 97*, 79–97. (Abstr. *Quart. J. Studies Alc.* 1957, *18*, 137.)

HAAG, H. B., FINNEGAN, J. K., LARSON, P. S. AND SMITH, R. B. (1959). Studies on the acute toxicity and irritating properties of the congeners in whisky. *Toxicol. Appl. Pharmacol. 1*, 618–627. (Abstr. *Quart. J. Studies Alc.* 1962, *23*, 362–363.)

HADJI-DIMO, A. A., EKBERG, R. AND INGVAR, D. H. (1968). Effects of ethanol on EEG and cortical blood flow in the cat. *Quart. J. Studies Alc. 29*, 828–838.

HAGGARD, H. W., GREENBERG, L. A., RAKIETEN, N. AND COHEN, L. H. (1940). Studies on absorption, distribution and elimination of alcohol. VII. The influence of inhalation of oxygen and carbon dioxide and certain drugs on the concentration of alcohol in the blood causing respiratory failure. *J. Pharmacol. Exptl. Therap. 69*, 266–271. (Abstr. *Quart. J. Studies Alc.* 1940, *1*, 389.)

HAGGARD, H. W., GREENBERG, L. A. AND CARROLL, R. P. (1941). Studies in the absorption, distribution and elimination of alcohol. VIII. The diuresis from alcohol and its influence on the elimination of alcohol in the urine. *J. Pharmacol. Exptl. Therap. 71*, 349–357.

HAGGARD, H. W., GREENBERG, L. A. AND COHEN, L. H. (1943). The influence of the congeners of distilled spirits upon the physiological action of alcohol. *Quart. J. Studies Alc. 4*, 3–56.

HALD, J. AND JACOBSEN, E. (1948). The formation of acetaldehyde in the organism after ingestion of Antabuse (tetraethylthiuramdisulphide) and alcohol. *Acta Pharmacol. Toxicol. 4*, 305–310.

HALD, J., JACOBSEN, E. AND LARSEN, V. (1948). The sensitizing effect of tetraethylthiuram-disulphide (Antabuse) to ethyl alcohol. *Acta Pharmacol. Toxicol. 4*, 285–296.

HASSAN, A., ELGHAMRY, M. I. AND ABDEL-HAMID, F. M. (1967). Acetanilide as a potent inhibitor of methanol metabolism in mice. *Can. J. Physiol. Pharmacol. 45*, 291–298.

HASSAN, A., MONROE, R. J. AND GUTHRIE, F. E. (1969). A possible antidote for methanol poisoning in mice. *Can. J. Physiol. Pharmacol. 47*, 107–109.

HASSINEN, I. (1963). Acetoin as a metabolite of ethanol. *Acta Physiol. Scand. 57*, 135–143.

HASSINEN, I. (1967). Hydrogen transfer into mitochondria in the metabolism of ethanol II. Effect of disulfiram on the hydrogen and energy transfer. *Ann. Med. Exptl. Biol. Fenniae (Helsinki) 45*, 46–56.

HATFIELD, G. K. (1966). Modification of drug action by repeated ethanol treatment in the rat. *Dissertation Abstr. 27*, 561-B.

HEIDENREICH, O. (1957). Die diuretische Wirkung von Coffein und Alkohol bei normalen und hypophysektomierten Hunden. *Arzneimittel-Forsch. 7*, 439–442.

HERR, F., STEWART, J. AND CHAREST, M.-P. (1961). Tranquilizers and antidepressants: a pharmacological comparison. *Arch. Intern. Pharmacodyn. 134*, 328–342.

HIGGINS, J. A. AND MCGUIGAN, H. A. (1933). The influence of caffeine on the effects of acetanilid. *J. Pharmacol. Exptl. Therap. 49*, 466–478.

HIMWICH, H. E. (1956). Alcohol and brain physiology. In: *Alcoholism*, G. N. THOMPSON, Ed., Charles C. Thomas, Springfield, Ill. Pp. 291–408.

HINE, C. H., BURBRIDGE, T. N., MACKLIN, E. A., ANDERSON, H. H. AND SIMON, A. (1952). Some aspects of the human pharmacology of tetraethylthiuramdisulphide (Antabus)-alcohol reactions. *J. Clin. Invest. 31*, 317–325.

HOFFER, A. (1958). Lack of potentiation of alcoholic excitement by methyprylon (Noludar). *Can. Med. Assoc. J. 79*, 191–217. (Abstr. *Quart. J. Studies Alc.* 1960, *21*, 350.)

HOFFER, A. (1962). Lack of potentiation by chlordiazepoxide (Librium) of depression or excitation due to alcohol. *Can. Med. Assoc. J. 87*, 920–921. (Abstr. *Quart. J. Studies Alc.* 1963, *24*, 739.)

HOLTEN, C. H. AND LARSEN, V. (1956). The potentiating effect of benactyzine derivatives and some other compounds on evipal anaesthesia in mice. *Acta Pharmacol. Toxicol. 12*, 346–363.

HOLTZ, P. (1960). Thujongehalt im Wermutwein? *Deut. Wein-Zt. 96*, 674–676.

HOLTZ, P. AND WESTERMANN, E. (1965). Psychic energizers and antidepressant drugs. In: *Physiological pharmacology*, W. S. ROOT AND F. G. HOFMANN, Eds., Academic Press, New York and London, Vol. II. Pp. 201–254.

HORSEY, W. J. AND AKERT, K. (1953). The influence of ethyl alcohol on the spontaneous electrical activity of the cerebral cortex and subcortical structures of the cat. *Quart. J. Studies Alc. 14*, 363–377.

HORWITZ, D., LOEWENBERG, W., ENGELMAN, K. AND SJOERDSMA, A. (1964). Monoamine oxidase inhibitors, tyramine, and cheese. *J. Am. Med. Assoc. 188*, 1108–1110.

HUBACH, H. (1963). Veränderungen der Krampferregbarkeit unter Einwirkung von Medikamenten und während der Entziehung. *Fortschr. Psychiat. Neurol. 31*, 177–201.

HUGHES, F. W. AND FORNEY, R. B. (1961). Alcohol and caffeine in choice-discrimination tests in rats. *Proc. Soc. Exptl. Biol. Med. 108*, 157–159. (Abstr. *Quart. J. Studies Alc. 24*, 341.)

HUGHES, F. W. AND FORNEY, R. B. (1963). Delayed audiofeedback (DAF) for induction of anxiety. Effect of nortriptyline, ethanol, or nortriptyline-ethanol combinations on performance with DAF. *J. Am. Med. Assoc. 185*, 556–558.

HUGHES, F. W. AND FORNEY, R. B. (1964a). Comparative effect of three antihistaminics and ethanol on mental and motor performance. *Clin. Pharmacol. Therap. 5*, 414–421.

HUGHES, F. W. AND FORNEY, R. B. (1964b). Dextro-amphetamine, ethanol and dextro-amphetamine-ethanol combinations on performance of human subjects stressed with delayed auditory feedback (DAF). *Psychopharmacologia 6*, 234–238.

HUGHES, F. W. AND ROUNTREE, C. B. (1961). Influence of alcohol-tranquilizer combinations on choice-discrimation in rats. *Arch. Intern. Pharmacodyn. 133*, 418–432.

HUGHES, F. W., ROUNTREE, C. B. AND FORNEY, R. B. (1963a). Suppression of learned avoidance and discriminative responses in the rat by chlordiazepoxide (Librium) and ethanol-chlordiazepoxide combinations. *J. Genet. Psychol. 103*, 139–145.

HUGHES, F. W., FORNEY, R. B. AND GATES, P. W. (1963b). Performance in human subjects under delayed auditory feedback after alcohol, a tranquilizer (benzquinamide) or benzquinamide–alcohol combination. *J. Psychol. 55*, 25–32.

HUGHES, F. W., FORNEY, R. B. AND RICHARDS, A. B. (1965). Comparative effect in human subjects of chlordiazepoxide, diazepam, and placebo on mental and physical performance. *Clin. Pharmacol. Therap. 6*, 139–145.

HULPIEU, H. R. AND COLE, V. V. (1946). Potentiation of the depressant action of alcohol by adrenalin. *Quart. J. Studies Alc. 7*, 89–97.

HUTTERER, F., SCHAFFNER, F., KLION, F. M. AND POPPER, H. (1968). Hypertrophic, hypoactive smooth endoplasmic reticulum: a sensitive indicator of hepatotoxicity exemplified by dieldrin. *Science 161*, 1017–1019.

JANSEN, G. (1960). Experimentelle Untersuchungen in Form von pharmakologischen Arbeitsversuchen. *Med. Exptl. 2*, 209–216.

JELLINEK, E. M. (1960). *The disease concept of alcoholism*. Hillhouse Press, New Haven, Conn. 246 pp.

JETTER, W. W. AND MCLEAN, R. (1943). Poisoning by the synergistic effect of pheno-barbital and ethyl alcohol. An experimental study. *Arch. Pathol. 36*, 112–122.

JOFRE DE BREYER, I. J. AND SOEHRING, K. (1968). Wirkungen von Aethanol auf den Acetanilid-Stoffwechsel in Rattenleberschnitten. *Arzneimittel-Forsch 18*, 604–605.

JOYCE, C. R. B., EDGECOMBE, P. C. E., KENNARD, D. A., WEATHERALL, M. AND WOODS, D. P. (1959). Potentiation by phenobarbitone of effects of ethyl alcohol on human behaviour. *J. Mental Sci. 105*, 51–60.

KAHIL, M. E., CASHAW, J., SIMONS, E. L. AND BROWN, H. (1964). Alcohol and the tol-butamide response in the dog. *J. Lab. Clin. Med. 64*, 808–814.

KAPLAN, H. L., JAIN, N. C., FORNEY, R. B. AND RICHARDS, A. B. (1969). Chloral hydrate-ethanol interactions in the mouse and dog. *Toxicol. Appl. Pharmacol. 14*, 127–137.

KATO, R. AND CHIESARA, E. (1962). Increase of pentobarbitone metabolism induced in rats pretreated with some centrally acting compounds. *Brit. J. Pharmacol. 18*, 29–38.

KATO, R. AND VASSANELLI, P. (1962). Induction of increased meprobamate metabolism in rats pretreated with some neurotropic agents. *Biochem. Pharmacol. 11*, 779–794.

KAYE, S. AND HAAG, H. B. (1964). Study of death due to combined action of alcohol and paraldehyde in man. *Toxicol. Appl. Pharmacol. 6*, 316–320.

KHAN, A. U., FORNEY, R. B. AND HUGHES, F. W. (1964). Effect of tranquilizers on the metabolism of ethanol. *Arch. Intern. Pharmacodyn. 150*, 171–176.

KHOUW, L. B., BURBRIDGE, T. N. AND SUTHERLAND, V. C. (1963). The inhibition of alcohol dehydrogenase. I. Kinetic studies. *Biochim. Biophys. Acta 73*, 173–185.

KIELHOLZ, P. AND BATTEGAY, R. (1967). Vergleichende Untersuchungen über die Genese und den Verlauf der Drogenabhängigkeit und des Alkoholismus. *Schw. Med. Wochschr. 97*, 893–898, 944–949.

KIELHOLZ, P., GOLDBERG, L., IM OBERSTEG, J., POELDINGER, W., RAMSEYER, A. AND SCHMID, P. (1967). Strassenverkehr, Tranquilizer und Alkohol. *Deutsche Med. Wochschr. 92*, 1525–1531.

KIESER, M. E., POLLARD, A., STEVENS, P. M. AND TUCKNOTT, O. G. (1964). Determination of 2-phenylethanol in cider. *Nature 204*, 887.

KIESSLING, K.-H. AND PILSTRÖM, L. (1968). Effect of ethanol on rat liver. V. Morphological and functional changes after prolonged consumption of various alcoholic beverages. *Quart. J. Studies Alc. 29*, 819–827.

KILLAM, E. K. (1962). Drug action on the brain-stem reticular formation. *Pharmacol. Rev. 14*, 175–223.

KINARD, F. W. (1963). Changes in the rate of metabolism following administration of ethanol in the mouse. *Nature 200*, 852–854.

KLAASSEN, C. D. (1969). Ethanol metabolism in rats after microsomal metabolizing enzyme induction. *Proc. Soc. Exptl. Biol. Med. 132*, 1099–1102.

KLIEWE, H. (1961). Über Unterschiede verschiedener Weinsorten in medizinischer Sicht. *Wein-Wiss. Beil. Fachz. Deut. Weinbau 16*, 177–196.

KLIEWE, H. AND ANABTAWI, A. (1964). Ein Vergleich von Hybridenweinen mit Weinen von europäischer Edelreben. *Wein-Wiss. Beil. Fachz. Deut. Weinbau 19*, 113–126.

KLIEWE, H., GILLISSEN, G. AND WIENER, K. (1961a). Die Wirkung von Hybridenwein auf die Leber. *Experientia 17*, 42.

KLIEWE, H., GILLISSEN, G. AND WIENER, K. (1961b). Vergleichende Untersuchungen über biologische Wirkungen von Hybridenwein. *Med. Exptl. 4*, 227–233.

KLIEWE, H., GILLISSEN, G. AND NESSLING, W. (1961c). Die Serum-Glutamat-Pyruvat-Transaminase als Indikator für Leberschäden nach Gaben aethanolhaltiger Flüssigkeiten. *Medizin und Ernährung*, No. 6, 127–130.

KNOTT, D. H., BARLOW, G. AND BEARD, J. D. (1963). Effects of alcohol ingestion on the production of and response to experimental hemorrhagic stress. *New Engl. J. Med. 269*, 292–295. (Abstr. *Quart. J. Studies Alc.* 1965, *26*, 329–330.)

KODA, H. (1966). Influence of adrenalin on blood alcohol level. *Jap. J. Studies Alc. 1*, 212–225.

KODAMA, J. K. AND HINE, C. H. (1958). Pharmacodynamic aspects of allyl alcohol toxicity. *J. Pharmacol. Exptl. Therap. 124*, 97–107.

KOE, B. K. AND TENEN, S. S. (1969). Blockade of ethanol metabolism and reduced alcohol selection in C57BL mice by butyraldoxime. *Federation Proc. 28*, No. 2, 546.

KOELSCH, F. (1914). Über neuartige gewerbliche Erkrankungen in Kalkstickstoffbetrieben. *Münch. Med. Wochschr. 61*, 1869–1870.

KOPF, R. (1957). Zur Frage der Alkoholpotenzierung durch Phenothiazine. *Arch. Intern. Pharmacodyn. 110*, 56–64.

KOPMANN, E. AND HUGHES, F. W. (1959). Potentiating effect of alcohol on tranquilizers and other central depressants. *A.M.A. Arch. Gen. Psychiat. 1*, 7–11.

KOPPANYI, T. AND MAENGWYN-DAVIES, G. D. (1968). Drugs used in alcohol research and treatment. In: *Topics in medicinal chemistry*, J. L. RABINOWITZ AND R. M. MYERSON, Eds. Vol. 2. Pp. 155–183.

KORABLEV, M. V. (1959). Effect of polysulfides of the thiuram group on the course and outcome of alcohol intoxication. (Russ.) *Farmakol. i Toksikol. 22*, 259–261. (Abstr. *Quart. J. Studies Alc.* 1961, *22*, 149.)

KUBENA, R. K. AND BARRY, H., III. (1969). Generalization by rats of alcohol and atropine stimulus characteristics to other drugs. *Psychopharmacologia 15*, 196–206.

KUDSK, F. N. (1965). The influence of ethyl alcohol on the absorption of mercury vapours from the lungs in man. *Acta Pharmacol. Toxicol. 23*, 263–274.

KUTOB, S. D. AND PLAA, G. L. (1962). The effect of acute ethanol intoxication on chloroform-induced liver damage. *J. Pharmacol. Exptl. Therap. 135*, 245–251. (Abstr. *Quart. J. Studies Alc.* 1965, *26*, 131.)

LAMARCHE, M. AND ROYER, R. (1965). Etude expérimentale de l'activité antialcool du charbon animal. *Med. Pharmacol. Exptl. 12*, 15–20.

LANDAUER, A. A., MILNER, G. AND PATMAN, J. (1969). Alcohol and amitriptyline effect on skills related to driving behavior. *Science 163*, 1467–1468.

LARSEN, J. A. AND MADSEN, J. (1962). Inhibition of ethanol metabolism by oral anti-diabetics. *Proc. Soc. Exptl. Biol. Med. 109*, 120–122.

LARSEN, V. (1948). The effect on experimental animals of Antabuse (tetraethylthiuramdi-sulphide) in combination with alcohol. *Acta Pharmacol. Toxicol. 4*, 321–332.

LAWTON, M. P. AND CAHN, B. J. (1963). The effects of diazepam (Valium) and alcohol on psychomotor performance. *J. Nervous Mental Disease 136*, 550–554. (Abstr. *Quart. J. Studies Alc.* 1965, *26*, 707.)

LECOQ, R., CHAUCHARD, P. AND MAZOUÉ, H. (1962). Étude chronaximétrique du comportement expérimental de quelques psycholeptiques sur les effets de l'alcool (avec et sans action associée du disulfirame). *Compt. Rend. 254*, 941–943.

LECOQ, R., CHAUCHARD, P. AND MAZOUÉ, H. (1963). Étude chronaximétrique expérimentale de l'action de quelques sédatifs mineraux ou végétaux et des effets associés de l'alcool éthylique, avec ou sans disulfirame. *Compt. Rend. 257*, 1403–1405.

LECOQ, R., CHAUCHARD, P. AND MAZOUÉ, H. (1964a). Étude chronaximétrique expérimentale de quelques agents psychotropes et de leur action sur les effets nerveux de l'alcool éthylique. I. Sédatifs, analgésiques et hypnotiques. *Therapie 19*, 967–974.

LECOQ, R., CHAUCHARD, P. AND MAZOUÉ, H. (1964b). Étude chronaximétrique expérimentale de quelques agents isotropes et de leur action sur les effets nerveux de l'alcool éthylique II. Neuroleptiques, tranquillisants et orthoneurotiques. *Therapie 19*, 975–981.

LECOQ, R., CHAUCHARD, P. AND MAZOUÉ, H. (1964c). Étude chronaximétrique expérimentale de quelques agents psychotropes et de leur action sur les effets nerveux de l'alcool éthylique. III. Psychotoniques et psychodysleptiques. *Therapie 19*, 983–989.

LEE, P. K., CHO, M. H. AND DOBKIN, A. B. (1964). Effects of alcoholism, morphinism, and barbiturate resistance on induction and maintenance of general anaesthesia. *Can. Anaesthetists' Soc. J. 11*, 354–381.

LEHMANN, H. E., BAN, T. A. AND NALTCHAYAN, E. (1966). Metronidazole in the treatment of the alcoholic. *Psychiat. Neurol. (Basel) 152*, 395–401.

LELBACH, W. K. (1967). Zur leberschädigenden Wirkung verschiedener Alkoholika. *Deut. Med. Wochschr. 92*, 233–238.

LELBACH, W. K. (1969). Liver cell necrosis in rats after prolonged ethanol ingestion under the influence of an alcoholdehydrogenase inhibitor. *Experientia 25*, 816–818.

LESTER, D. AND BENSON, G. D. (1969). Pyrazole inhibition of *in vivo* alcohol oxidation. *Federation Proc. 28*, No. 2, 546.

LEUSCHNER, F. AND LEUSCHNER, A. (1967). Vergleichende tierexperimentelle Untersuchungen mit Weinen aus Hybriden- und Europäerreben. *Arzneimittel-Forsch. 17*, 59–65.

LEVY, G., MILLER, K. E. AND REUNING, R. H. (1966). Effect of complex formation on drug absorption. 3. Concentration- and drug-dependent effect of a nonionic surfactant. *J. Pharm. Sci. 53*, 394–398.

LEWIS, W. AND SCHWARTZ, L. (1956). An occupational agent (*n*-butyraldoxime) causing reaction to alcohol. *Med. Ann. District Columbia 25*, 485–490.

LIEBER, C. S. AND RUBIN, E. (1968). Ethanol – a hepatotoxic drug. *Gastroenterology 54*, 642–646.

LIND, N. AND PARKES, M. W. (1967). Effects of inhibition and induction of the liver microsomal enzyme system on the narcotic activity of ethanol in mice. *J. Pharm. Pharmacol. 19*, 56–57.

LINDBOHM, R. AND WALLGREN, H. (1962). Changes in respiration of rat brain cortex slices induced by some aliphatic alcohols. *Acta Pharmacol. Toxicol. 19*, 53–58.

LISH, P. M., ALBERT, J. R., PETERS, E. L. AND ALLEN, L. E. (1960). Pharmacology of methdilazine (Tacaryl^R). *Arch. Intern. Pharmacodyn. 129*, 77–107.

LIST, P. H. AND REITH, H. (1960). Der Faltentintling, *Coprinus atramentarius Bull.*, und seine dem Tetraäthylthiuramdisulfid ähnliche Wirkung. *Arzneimittel-Forsch. 10*, 34–40.

LOLLI, G., NENCINI, R. AND MISITI, R. (1964). Effects of two alcoholic beverages on the electroencephalographic and electromyographic tracings of healthy men. *Quart. J. Studies Alc. 25*, 451–458.

LOOMIS, T. A. (1963). Effects of alcohol on persons using tranquillizers. In: *Alcohol and Road Traffic*, J. D. J. HAVARD, Ed., Proc. Intern. Conf., 3rd, London 1962. Brit. Med. Assoc. Publ., London. Pp. 119–122.

LUCIA, S. P. (1963). *A history of wine as therapy*. Lippincott, Philadelphia and Montreal, 234 pp.

LUNDQUIST, F. (1958). Enzymic determination of acetaldehyde in blood. *Biochem. J. 68*, 172–177.

MCCREA, F. D. AND TAYLOR, H. M. (1940). The use of pentamethylenetetrazol (Metrazol) as a respiratory stimulant in acute alcoholic depression. *J. Pharmacol. Exptl. Therap. 68*, 41–44.

MACGREGOR, A. G. (1965). Review of points at which drugs can interact. *Proc. Roy. Soc. Med. 58*, 943–946.

MACGREGOR, D. C., SCHÖNBAUM, E. AND BIGELOW, W. G. (1964). Acute toxicity studies on ethanol, propanol and butanol. *Can. J. Physiol. Pharmacol. 42*, 689–696.

MCKENNIS, H., JR. AND HAAG, H. B. (1959). On the congeners of whiskey. *J. Am. Geriat. Soc. 7*, 848–858.

MACLEOD, L. D. (1950). Acetaldehyde in relation to intoxication by ethyl alcohol. *Quart. J. Studies Alc. 11*, 385–390.

MACLEOD, L. D. (1952). Monthly Bulletin research report, 1950. *Brit. J. Addict. 49*, 60–69.

MADAN, B. R. AND GUPTA, R. S. (1967). Effect of ethanol in experimental auricular and ventricular arrhythmias. *Japan. J. Pharmacol. 17*, 683–684.

MAGNUSSEN, M. P. (1968). The effect of ethanol on the gastrointestinal absorption of drugs in the rat. *Acta Pharmacol. Toxicol. 26*, 130–144.

MAGNUSSEN, M. P. AND FREY, H.-H. (1967). Einfluss von Alkohol auf die Resorption zentral depressiver Pharmaka aus dem Magen. *Arch. Pharmakol. Exptl. Pathol. 257*, 39.

MALLACH, H. J. AND ETZLER, K. (1965). Tierexperimentelle Untersuchungen über die gemeinsame Wirkung von Dimethylsulfoxid und Aethylalkohol. *Arzneimittel-Forsch. 15*, 1305–1308.

MALLACH, H. J. AND RÖSSLER, P. (1961). Beobachtungen und Untersuchungen über die gemeinsame Wirkung von Alkohol und Kohlenmonoxyd. *Arzneimittel-Forsch. 11*, 1004–1008.

MARDONES, J. (1963). The alcohols. In: *Physiological pharmacology*, W. S. ROOT AND F. G. HOFMANN, Eds., Academic Press, New York; Vol. 1. Pp. 99–183.

MARLER, E. E. J. (1967). *Pharmacological and chemical synonyms*. Excerpta Medica Foundation, Amsterdam, etc. Fourth ed. 349 pp.

MARQUARDT, P., SCHMIDT, H. AND SPÄTH, M. (1963). Histamin in alkoholhaltigen Getränken. *Arzneimittel-Forsch. 13*, 1100–1102.

MARQUIS, D. G., KELLY, E. L., MILLER, J. G., GERARD, R. W. AND RAPOPORT, A. (1957). Experimental studies of behavioral effects of meprobamate on normal subjects. *Ann. N.Y. Acad. Sci. 67*, 701–711.

MARSHALL, E. K. AND OWENS, A. H. (1955). Rate of metabolism of ethanol in the mouse. *Proc. Soc. Exptl. Biol. Med. 89*, 571–573.

MATHIEU, P., SERUSCLAT, F. AND REVOL, L. (1964). Influence de la chlorpromazine sur le taux sanguin d'alcool chez le lapin. *Bull. Trav. Soc. Pharm. Lyon 2*, 79–84.

MAYER, K., MARTIN, H. AND MALLACH, H. J. (1966). Motorische Nervenleitgeschwindigkeit unter dem Einfluss von Alkohol und Dimethylsulfoxyd. *Arzneimittel-Forsch. 16*, 1226–1228.

MELVILLE, K. I., JORON, G. E. AND DOUGLAS, D. (1966). Toxic and depressant effects of alcohol given orally in combination with glutethimide or secobarbital. *Toxicol. Appl. Pharmacol. 9*, 363–375.

MENDELSON, J., WEXLER, D., LEIDERMAN, P. H. AND SOLOMON, P. (1957). A study of addiction to nonethyl alcohols and other poisonous compounds. *Quart. J. Studies Alc. 18*, 561–580.

MENNINGER-LERCHENTHAL, E. (1960). Kritik der Alkoholernüchterungsversuche. *Wien. Klin. Wochschr. 72*, 419–422.

MERLEVEDE, E. AND CASIER, H. (1961). Teneur en sulfure de carbone de l'air expiré chez des personnes normales ou sous l'influence de l'alcool éthylique au cours du traitement par l'Antabuse (disulfiram) et le diéthyldithiocarbamate de soude. *Arch. Intern. Pharmacodyn. 132*, 427–453.

MEYERS, D. B., KANYUCK, D. O. AND ANDERSON, R. C. (1966). Effect of chronic nortriptyline pretreatment on the acute toxicity of various medicinal agents in rats. *J. Pharm. Sci. 55*, 1317–1318.

MILLER, M. M. (1952). Combined use of ethyl alcohol and amobarbital (Amytal^R) sodium for ambulatory narcoanalysis. *Arch. Neurol. Psychiat. 67*, 620–624.

MILNER, G. (1967). Amitriptyline-potentiation of alcohol. *Lancet 1*, 222–223.

MILNER, G. (1968a). Modified confinement motor activity test for use in mice. *J. Pharm. Sci. 57*, 1900–1902.

MILNER, G. (1968b). Cumulative lethal dose of alcohol in mice given amitriptyline. *J. Pharm. Sci. 57*, 2005–2006.

MILOSEVIĆ, M. P. (1956). The action of sympathomimetic amines on intravenous anesthesia in rats. *Arch. Intern. Pharmacodyn. 106*, 437–446.

MONTANINI, R., GIOVANUCCI, M. AND PALTRINIERI, E. (1966). Modificazione dei tassi alcolemici da administrazione di metronidazolo. *G. Psichiat. Neuropat. 94*, 889–896.

MORGAN, A. F., BRINNER, L., PLAA, C. B. AND STONE, M. M. (1957). Utilization of calories from alcohol and wines and their effects on cholesterol metabolism. *Am. J. Physiol. 189*, 290–296. (Abstr. *Quart. J. Studies Alc.* 1959, *20*, 126.)

MORIN, Y., TÊTU, A. AND MERCIER, G. (1969). Québec beer-drinkers' cardiomyopathy: clinical and hemodynamic aspects. *Ann. N.Y. Acad. Sci. 156*, 566–576.

MULLER, B. P., TARPEY, R. D., GIORGI, A. P., MIRONE, L. AND ROUKE, F. L. (1964). Effects of alcohol and mephenoxalone on psycho-physiological test performance. *Diseases Nervous System 25*, 373–375.

MURPHREE, H. B. AND PRICE, L. M. (1965). EEG effects of bourbon and vodka. *Federation Proc. 24*, 517.

MURPHREE, H. B., PRICE, L. M. AND GREENBERG, L. A. (1966). Effect of congeners in alcoholic beverages on the incidence of nystagmus. *Quart. J. Studies Alc. 27*, 201–213.

MURPHREE, H. B., GREENBERG, L. A. AND CARROLL, R. B. (1967). Neuropharmacological effects of substances other than ethanol in alcoholic beverages. *Fed. Proc. 26*, No. 5, 1468–1473.

NAESS, K. A. (1950). A comparison of the effect of ether and curare on the neuro-muscular transmission, investigated by means of prostigmine. *Acta Physiol. Scand. 20*, 117–124.

NAKAI, Y. (1964). Effects of intravenous infusion of central depressants on the evoked potentials of the auditory cortex in the cats. *Japan. J. Pharmacol. 14*, 235–255.

NAKAI, Y. AND TAKAORI, S. (1965). Effects of central depressants on the cortical auditory responses evoked by repetitive click stimuli in the cat. *Japan. J. Pharmacol. 15*, 165–175.

NAKANISHI, S. (1963a). Effect of oral hypoglycemic agents on alcohol metabolism in normal and alloxan-diabetic rabbits. I. Experiments with non-diabetic rabbits. *Med. J. Shinshu Univ. 8*, 81–99.

NAKANISHI, S. (1963b). Effect of oral hypoglycemic agents on alcohol metabolism in normal and alloxan-diabetic rabbits. II. Experiments with alloxan-diabetic rabbits. *Med. J. Shinshu Univ. 8*, 101–118.

NAKANO, J., HOLLOWAY, J. E. AND SCHACKFORD, J. S. (1969). Effects of disulfiram on the cardiovascular responses to ethanol in dogs and guinea pigs. *Toxicol. Appl. Pharmacol. 14*, 439–446.

NEWELL, G. W., SHELLENBERGER, T. E. AND REINKE, D. R. (1964). Chronic effects of alcohol, muscatel, and sherry on the growth and performance of male rats. *Toxicol. Appl. Pharmacol. 6*, 696–700.

NEWMAN, H. W. AND NEWMAN, E. J. (1956). Failure of Dexedrine and caffeine as practical antagonists of the depressant effect of ethyl alcohol in man. *Quart. J. Studies Alc. 17*, 406–410.

NEWMAN, H. W. AND PETZOLD, H. V. (1951). The effect of tetraethylthiuram disulfide on the metabolism of ethyl alcohol. *Quart. J. Studies Alc. 12*, 40–45.

OGDEN, E. AND SOUTHARD, F. D. (1946). The influence of wine on gastric acidity. *Federation Proc. 5*, 77.

OLSZYCKA, L. (1935). Étude quantitative des phénomenènes de synergie. Potentialisation de l'action hypnotique chez la souris. *Compt. Rend. 201*, 796–797.

OLSZYCKA, L. (1936). Étude quantitative des phénomènes de synergie. Contribution à l'étude du mécanisme des phénomènes de potentialisation de l'action hypnotique chez le rat. *Compt. Rend. 202*, 1107–1109.

ORAHOVATS, P. D., LEHMAN, E. G. AND CHAPIN, E. W. (1957). Potentiating effects of quinine. I. Analgesics and hypnotics. *Arch. Intern. Pharmacodyn. 110*, 245–258.

OSTERHAUS, E. (1964). Untersuchungen über das Verhalten nach Einnahme von Natriumbarbital, nachträglicher Alkoholzufuhr und Ausscheidung der zugeführten Barbitursäure. *Med. Welt 44*, 2363–2368.

OVERTON, D. A. (1966). State-dependent learning produced by depressant and atropine-like drugs. *Psychopharmacologia 10*, 6–31.

PARADISE, R. R. AND STOELTING, V. (1965). Conversion of acetyl strophanthidin-induced ventricular tachycardia to sinus rhythm by ethyl alcohol. *Arch. Int. Pharmacodyn. 157*, 312–321.

PERMAN, E. S. (1962). Studies on the Antabuse-alcohol reaction in rabbits. *Acta Physiol. Scand. 55*, Suppl. 190. 46 pp.

PETER, H. (1939). Alkohol und Sedativa. *Deut. Z. Ges. Gerichtl. Med. 31*, 113–514.

PETERSON, D. I., PETERSON, J. E. AND HARDINGE, M. G. (1968). Protection by ethanol against the toxic effects of monofluoroethanol and monochloroethanol. *J. Pharm. Pharmacol. 20*, 465–468.

PIHKANEN, T. A. (1957a). Neurological and physiological studies on distilled and brewed beverages. *Ann. Med. Exptl. Biol. Fenniae, Helsinki 35*, Suppl. 9. 152 pp.

PIKHANEN, T. A. (1957b). On static atactic functional disorders caused by alcohol. A comparison of different beverages. *Quart. J. Studies Alc. 18*, 183–189.

PLETSCHER, A., BESENDORF, H., STEINER, F. A. AND GEY, K. F. (1962). The effect of 2-hydroxy-benzoquinolizines on cerebral 5-hydroxytryptamine, spontaneous locomotor activity, and ethanol hypnosis in mice. *Med. Exptl. 7*, 15–20.

PODGAINY, H. AND BRESSLER, R. (1968). Biochemical basis of the sulfonyl-urea-induced Antabuse syndrome. *Diabetes 17*, 679–683.

POIRÉ, R., ROYER, P., VANET, G. AND LINARD, C. (1965). Étude électrographique (technique polygraphique) de la réaction charbon animal non purifié-alcool. *Rev. Neurol. 113*, 318–322.

POLET, H. (1956). Influence of disulfiram (Antabuse, TETD) on the metabolism of radio-active $CH_3C^{14}H_2OH$ and acetaldehyde in mice. *Arch. Intern. Pharmacodyn. 107*, 109–111.

PROCTOR, C. D., DENEFIELD, B. A., ASHLEY, L. G. AND POTTS, J. L. (1966). Extension of ethyl alcohol action by pilocarpine. *Brain Res. 3*, 217–220.

QUEVAUVILLER, A. AND BOURRINET, P. (1962). Influence of acute and chronic alcoholism on the activity of local anesthetics in the rabbit and guinea pig. (Fr.) *Thérapie 17*, 1219–1223. (Abstr. *Quart. J. Studies Alc.* 1964, *25*, 368.)

QUEVAUVILLER, A. AND BOURRINET, P. (1964). Étude chez l'animal de l'influence de l'alcoolisation aiguë et chronique sur l'activité de quelques anesthésiques généraux et neuro-sédatifs. *Anesthésie Analgésie Réanimation 21*, 431–439.

RABY, K. (1954). Relation of blood acetaldehyde level to clinical symptoms in disulfiram-alcohol reaction. *Quart. J. Studies Alc. 15*, 21–32.

RAMSEY, H. AND HAAG, H. B. (1946). The synergism between the barbiturates and ethyl alcohol. *J. Pharmacol. Exptl. Therap. 88*, 313–322.

RASPOPOVA, T. V. AND ZAIKONNIKOVA, I. V. (1955). Effects of alcohol on respiration after giving morphine, urethan, or barbiturates. *Farmakol. i Toksikol. 18*, No. 6, 27–29. (Abstr. *Chem. Abstr.* 1956, *50*, 6686 b.)

REDETZKI, H. M. (1967). The interactions of monoamine oxidase inhibitors (MAOI) with alcohol. Biochemical and pharmacological analysis. *Fed. Proc. 26*, 616.

REGAN, T. J., KOROXENIDIS, G., MOSCHOS, C. B., OLDEWURTEL, H. A., LEHAN, P. H. AND HELLEMS, H. K. (1966). The acute metabolic and hemodynamic responses of the left ventricle to ethanol. *J. Clin. Invest. 45*, 270–280.

REIFENSTEIN, E. C., JR. (1941). Amphetamine sulfate–ethyl alcohol antagonism in the rabbit. *J. Lab. Clin. Med. 27*, 131–139.

REMMER, H. (1961). Drugs as activators of drug enzymes. *Biochem. Pharmacol. 8*, 138.

RIEDLER, G. (1966). Einfluss des Alkohols auf die Antikoagulantientherapie. *Thromb. Diath. Haemorrhag. 16*, 613–635.

RIETBROCK, N. AND SÄGER, U. (1967). Einfluss intermittierender Äthanolgaben auf den Methanolumsatz im Hunde. *Arch. Pharmakol. Exptl. Pathol. 257*, 57.

RINKEL, M. AND MYERSON, A. (1941). Pharmacological studies in experimental alcoholism. I. The effect of sympathomimetic substances on the blood-alcohol level in man. *J. Pharmacol. Exptl. Therap. 71*, 75–86.

RØE, O. (1946). Methanol poisoning. Its clinical course, pathogenesis and treatment. *Acta Med. Scand. 126*, Suppl. 182, 1–253.

RØE, O. (1950). The roles of alkaline salts and ethyl alcohol in the treatment of methanol poisoning. *Quart. J. Studies Alc. 11*, 107–112.

ROSENBAUM, M. (1942). Adaptation of the central nervous system to varying concentrations of alcohol in the blood. *Arch. Neurol. Psychiat. 48*, 1010–1012.

ROSENFELD, G. (1960). Potentiation of the narcotic action and acute toxicity of alcohol by primary aromatic monoamines. *Quart. J. Studies Alc. 21*, 584–596.

ROYER, R. (1963). *La réaction antialcool des sulfamides hypoglycémiants.* Doin, Deren & Co., Paris. 115 pp.

RUBIN, E. AND LIEBER, C. S. (1968a). Increase of hepatic drug metabolizing enzymes induced by ethanol. *Fed. Proc. 27*, No. 2, 605.

RUBIN, E. AND LIEBER, C. S. (1968b). Hepatic microsomal enzymes in man and rat: induction and inhibition by ethanol. *Science 162*, 690–691.

RUBIN, E. AND LIEBER, C. S. (1968c). Alcohol, other drugs, and the liver. *Ann. Internal Med. 69*, 1063–1067.

RUBIN, E., HUTTERER, F. AND LIEBER, C. S. (1968). Ethanol increases hepatic smooth endoplasmic reticulum and drug-metabolizing enzymes. *Science 159*, 1469–1470.

RUTENFRANZ, J. AND JANSEN, G. (1959). On compensation of the alcohol effect by caffeine and Pervitin in a psychomotor performance. (Ger.) *Intern. Z. Angew. Physiol. 18*, 62–81. (Abstr. *Quart. J. Studies Alc.* 1962, *23*, 337.)

RYDBERG, U. S. (1969). Inhibition of ethanol metabolism *in vivo* by 4-iodo-pyrazole. *Biochem. Pharmacol. 18*, 2424–2428.

SACHDEV, K. S., PANJWANI, M. H. AND JOSEPH, A. D. (1963). Potentiation of the response to acetylcholine on the frog's rectus abdominis by ethyl alcohol. *Arch. Intern. Pharmacodyn. 145*, 36–43.

SACHDEV, K. S., RANA, P. K., DAVE, K. C. AND JOSEPH, A. D. (1964). A study of the mechanism of action of the potentiation by aliphatic alcohols of the acetylcholine response on the frog's rectus abdominis. *Arch. Intern. Pharmacodyn. 152*, 408–415.

SAMMALISTO, L. (1962). Effect of glutamine on intoxication by ethyl alcohol. *Nature 195*, 185.

SANDBERG, F. (1951). A quantitative study on the alcohol-barbiturate synergism. *Acta Physiol. Scand. 22*, 311–325.

SANKAR, D. V. S., GOLD, E., SANKAR, B. AND McRORIE, N. (1961). Effect of psycho-pharmacological agents on DPN-dependent enzymes. *Fed. Proc. 20*, 394.

SAUTET, J., DESANTI, E., PAYAN, H., ALDIGHIERI, J., GAY, R., ARNAUD, G., DELUY, M., CASTELLI, P., CASTELLI, C. AND RAMPAL, C. (1960). Contribution to the experimental study of the action of various wines and alcohols in the white mouse; weight, mortality, basal metabolism, muscular contraction, anatomopathology. (Fr.) *Rev. Pathol. Gen. Physiol. Clin. 60*, 1623–1673. (Abstr. *Quart. J. Studies Alc.* 1963, *24*, 543.)

SCHLEYER, F. AND JANITZKI, U. (1963). Studies on the effect of Megaphen on the blood alcohol level. (Ger.) *Arch. Intern. Pharmacodyn. 141*, 254–261. (Abstr. *Quart. J. Studies Alc.* 1964, *25*, 758.)

SCHLIERF, G., GUNNING, B., UZAWA, H. AND KINSELL, L. W. (1964). The effects of calorically equivalent amounts of ethanol and dry wine on plasma lipids, ketones and blood sugar in diabetics and nondiabetic subjects. *Am. J. Clin. Nutr. 15*, 85–89.

SCHMIDT, H., JR., KLEINMAN, K. M. AND DOUTHITT, T. C. (1967). Enhancement of the drinking response to phenobarbital after a previous course of barbiturates. *Physiol. Behav. 2*, 265–271.

SCHÜPPEL, R. (1968). Untersuchungen zur Spezifität äthanolbedingter Arzneistoffwechsel-störungen. *Arch. Exptl. Pathol. Pharmakol. 260*, 197–198.

SCHÜPPEL, R., DE BREYER, I. J., STRELLER, J. AND SOEHRING, K. (1967). Weitere Unter-suchungen zum Arzneistoffwechsel der Ratte unter Äthanolbelastung. *Arch. Exptl. Pathol. Pharmakol. 257*, 329–330.

SECHER, O. (1951). The peripheral action of ether estimated on isolated nerve-muscle preparation. II. Synergism of ether and curarizing substances. *Acta Pharmacol. Toxicol. 7*, 83–93.

SEEVERS, M. H. AND DENEAU, G. A. (1963). Physiological aspects of tolerance and physical dependence. In: *Physiological pharmacology*, W. S. ROOT AND F. G. HOFMANN., Eds., Academic Press, New York and London; Vol. 1. Pp. 565–640.

SEIDEL, G. (1967). Verteilung von Pentobarbital, Barbital und Thiopental unter Äthanol. *Arch. Exptl. Pathol. Pharmakol. 257*, 221–229.

SEIDEL, G. AND SOEHRING, K. (1965). Zur Frage der Änderung der Blutalkoholwerte durch Medikamente. *Arzneimittel-Forsch. 15*, 472–473.

SEIDEL, G., STRELLER, I. AND SOEHRING, K. (1964a). Zur Frage der Beeinflussung des Alkohol-Gehaltes im Blut durch Chlorpromazin. *Arzneimittel-Forsch. 14*, 412–415.

SEIDEL, G., STRELLER, I. AND SOEHRING, K. (1964b). Der Einfluss subchronischer Alkohol-gaben auf die Pentobarbitalaufnahme des Meerschweinchengehirns. *Arch. Exptl. Pathol. Pharmakol. 247*, 312.

SERIANNI, E., LOLLI, G. AND VENTURINI, M. (1955). The effects of solid food and alcoholic beverages, especially wine, on the excretion of hippuric acid. *Quart. J. Studies Alc. 16*, 67–85.

SHAGASS, C. AND JONES, A. L. (1957). A neurophysiological study of psychiatric patients with alcoholism. *Quart. J. Studies Alc. 18*, 171–182.

SIEGMUND, B. (1938). Resorptionshemmung bei alimentärer Alkolämie durch Adrenalin. *Klin. Wochschr. 17*, 1842.

SIHTO, E., NYKÄNEN, L. AND SUOMALAINEN, H. (1964). Gas chromatography of the aroma compounds of alcoholic beverages. *Qualitas Plant. Mater. Vegetabiles 11*, 211–228.

SIMANDL, J. AND FRANC, J. (1956). Isolace tetraethylthiuramdisulfidu z hníku inkoustového *(Coprinus atramentarius)*. *Chem. Listy 50*, 1862–1863.

SMITH, A. A., KARMIN, M. AND GAVITT, J. (1966). Blocking effect of puromycin, ethanol, and chloroform on the development of tolerance to an opiate. *Biochem. Pharmacol. 15*, 1877–1879.

SMITH, J. W. AND LOOMIS, T. A. (1951). The potentiating effect of alcohol on thiopental induced sleep. *Proc. Soc. Exptl. Biol. Med. 78*, 827–829.

SMITH, M. E., EVANS, R. L. NEWMAN, E. J. AND NEWMAN, H. W. (1961). Psychotherapeutic agents and ethyl alcohol. *Quart J. Studies Alc. 22*, 241–249.

SNELL, C. A. (1958). The congener content of alcoholic beverages. *Quart. J. Studies Alc. 19*, 69–71.

SOEHRING, K. AND SCHÜPPEL, R. (1966). Wechselwirkungen zwischen Alkohol und Arzneimitteln. *Deut. Med. Wochschr. 91*, 1892–1896.

SOEHRING, K. AND SCHÜPPEL, R. (1967). Interaction between alcohol and drugs. *German Medical Monthly 12*, 87–90.

SOLLMANN, T. (1957). *A manual of pharmacology and its application to therapeutics and toxicology.* Saunders, Philadelphia and London; 8th ed. 1525 pp.

SOMERS, G. F. (1960). Pharmacological properties of thalidomide (α-phthalimido gluta-rimide), a new sedative hypnotic drug. *Brit. J. Pharmacol. 13*, 111–116.

SPECTOR, E. AND REINHARD, J. F. (1966). *Accelerated metabolism of ethanol in the rat.* American Pharmaceutical Assoc. Meeting, Dallas, Texas. Academy of Pharmaceutical Sciences—Pharmacology and Biochemistry. Abstr. No. 31, p. 66.

ST-LAURENT, J. AND OLDS, J. (1967). Alcohol and brain centers of positive reinforcement. In: *Alcoholism, behavioral research, therapeutic approaches,* R. Fox, Ed. Springer, New York. Pp. 80–101.

STOLMAN, A. (1967). Combined action of drugs with toxicological implications.—Part I. *Progr. Chem. Toxicol. 3*, 305–361.

STRÖMME, J. H. (1963). Inhibition of hexokinase by disulfiram and diethylthiocarbamate. *Biochem. Pharmacol. 12*, 157–166.

STRÖMME, J. H. (1965a). Interactions of disulfiram and diethyldithiocarbamate with serum proteins studied by means of a gel-filtration technique. *Biochem. Pharmacol. 14*, 381–392.

STRÖMME, J. H. (1965b). Metabolism of disulfiram and diethylthiocarbamate in rats with demonstration of an *in vivo* ethanol-induced inhibition of the glucuronic acid conjuga-tion of the thiol. *Biochem. Pharmacol. 14*, 393–410.

SULLIVAN, J., PARKER, M. AND CARSON, S. B. (1968). Tissue cobalt content in "beer drinkers' myocardiopathy". *J. Lab. Clin. Med. 71*, 893–896.

SULSER, F., WATTS, J. AND BRODIE, B. B. (1962). On the mechanism of antidepressant action of imipraminelike drugs. *Ann. N.Y. Acad. Sci. 96*, 279–288.

SUTHERLAND, V. C., BURBRIDGE, T. N., ADAMS, J. E. AND SIMON, A. (1960). Cerebral metabolism in problem drinkers under the influence of alcohol and chlorpromazine hydrochloride. *J. Appl. Physiol. 15*, 189–196.

SVEDIN, C.-O. (1966). Tissue distribution of chlormethiazole and compatibility with ethanol and certain drugs. *Acta Psychiat. Scand. 42*, Suppl. 192, 27–34.

TAKALA, M., PIHKANEN, T. A. AND MARKKANEN, T. (1957). The effects of distilled and brewed beverages. A physiological, neurological, and psychological study. *Finnish Found. Alc. Studies*, Publ. No. *4*, 1957. 195 pp.

TAKALA, M., SIRO, E. AND TOIVAINEN, Y. (1958). Intellectual functions and dexterity during hangover. Experiments after intoxication with brandy and with beer. *Quart. J. Studies Alc. 19*, 1–29.

TAKEMORI, A. E. (1962). Studies on morphine-adapted cerebral cortical slices of rats. *Fed. Proc. 21*, 2, 117.

TAMMISTO, T. (1965). The acute toxicity of 5-hydroxytryptamine in anesthetized rats. *Ann. Med. Exptl. Biol. Fenniae (Helsinki) 43*, Suppl. No. 7, 49 pp.

TAMMISTO, T. (1968). Increased toxicity of 5-hydroxytryptamine by ethanol in rats and mice. *Ann. Med. Exptl. Biol. Fenniae (Helsinki) 46*, 382–384.

TANG, P. C. AND ROSENSTEIN, R. (1967). Influence of alcohol and dramamine, alone and in combination, on psychomotor performance. *Aerospace Med. 38*, 818–821.

THEOBALD, W. AND STENGER, E. G. (1962). Reciprocal potentiation between alcohol and psychotropic drugs. (Ger.) *Arzneimittel-Forsch. 12*, 531–533. (Abstr. *Quart. J. Studies Alc.* 1964, *25*, 368.)

THEOBALD, W., BÜCH, O., KUNZ, H. A., MORPURGO, C., STENGER, E. G. AND WILHELMI, G. (1964). Vergleichende pharmakologische Untersuchungen mit Tofranil, Pertofran and Insidon. *Arch. Int. Pharmacodyn. 148*, 560–596.

TIPTON, D. L., SUTHERLAND, V. C., BURBRIDGE, T. N. AND SIMON, A. (1961). Effect of chloropromazine on blood level of alcohol in rabbits. *Am. J. Physiol. 200*, 1007–1010.

TIRRI, R. (1966). Induced tolerance to promazine in mice as a physiological adaptation. *Ann. Acad. Sci. Fennicae*, A IV, No. *103*. 54 pp.

TRUITT, E. B., JR. AND DURITZ, G. (1967). The role of acetaldehyde in the actions of ethanol. In: *Biochemical factors in alcoholism*, R. P. MAICKEL, Ed., Pergamon Press, Oxford etc. Pp. 61–69.

TRUITT, E. B., JR., DURITZ, G., MORGAN, A. M. AND PROUTY, R. W. (1962). Disulfiramlike actions produced by hypoglycemic sulfonylurea compounds. *Quart. J. Studies Alc. 23*, 197–207.

VALICENTI, J. F. AND NEWMAN, W. H. (1968). Cardiac size, contractile force and wall tension following ethanol, pentobarbital and ouabain. *Federation Proc. 27*, No. 2, 658.

VENHO, I., EEROLA, R., VENHO, E. V. AND VARTIAINEN, O. (1955). Sensitisation to morphine by experimentally induced alcoholism in white mice. *Ann. Med. Exptl. Biol. Fenniae (Helsinki) 33*, 249–252.

VOGEL, G. (1966). Über eine bisher unbekannte Wirkung von Bier—Steigerung der Produktion von Lymphe. *Brauwissenschaft 19*, 307–310.

VOGEL, G., LEHMANN, G., MEYERING, E. AND WENDT, B. (1967). Tierexperimentelle Untersuchungen zur lymphagogen, diuretischen und chloretischen Wirkung verschiedener Alkoholica. *Arzneimittel-Forsch. 16*, 673–677.

WACKER, W. E. C., HAYNES, H., DRUYAN, R., FISHER, W. AND COLEMAN, J. E. (1965). Treatment of ethylene glycol poisoning with ethyl alcohol. *J. Am. Med. Assoc. 194*, 1231–1233. (Abstr. *Quart. J. Studies Alc.* 1966, *27*, 554.)

WAGNER, H.-J. (1957a). Effect of drugs on the acetaldehyde concentration in the blood after alcohol administration; enzymatic determination of acetaldehyde. (Ger.) *Deut. Z. Ges. Gerichtl. Med. 46*, 70–78. (Abstr. *Quart. J. Studies Alc.* 1959, *20*, 675.)

WAGNER, H.-J. (1957b). Effects of various drugs followed by alcohol on the intermediary metabolism. (Ger.) *Deut. Z. Ges. Gerichtl. Med. 46*, 575–582. (Abstr. *Quart. J. Studies Alc.* 1959, *20*, 675.)

WAGNER, K. AND WAGNER, H.-J. (1958). *Nil nocere!* Die Gefahren einer medikamentösen Behandlung von alkoholbeeinflussten Unfallverletzten mit Barbituraten, Morphin und Polamidon. *Münch. Med. Wochschr. 100*, 1923–1925.

WALLGREN, H. (1960a). Comparison of the effect of ethanol and malonate on the respiration of rat brain cortex slices. *Acta Physiol. Scand. 49*, 216–223.

WALLGREN, H. (1960b). Relative intoxicating effects on rats of ethyl, propyl and butyl alcohols. *Acta Pharmacol. Toxicol. 16*, 217–222.

WALLGREN, H. (1960c). Alcoholism and alcohol consumption. *Alkoholpolitik 23*, 177–179; Ref. p. 149.

WALLGREN, H. (1961). Effects of acetylcholine analogues and ethanol on the respiration of brain cortex tissue *in vitro. Biochem. Pharmacol. 6*, 195–204.

WALLGREN, H. (1963). Ouabain-induced depression of the respiration of electrically stimulated brain slices in presence and absence of ethanol. *Ann. Med. Exptl. Biol. Fenniae (Helsinki) 41*, 166–173.

WALLGREN, H. AND TIRRI, R. (1963). Studies on the mechanism of stress-induced reduction of alcohol intoxication in rats. *Acta Pharmacol. Toxicol. 20*, 27–38.

WALLGREN, H., SAMMALISTO, L. AND SUOMALAINEN, H. (1963). Physiological effect of phenethyl alcohol. *J. Inst. Brewing 69*, 418–420.

WALSH, M. J. AND TRUITT, E. B., JR. (1968). Release of 7-H^3-norepinephrine in plasma and urine by acetaldehyde and ethanol in cats and rabbits. *Fed. Proc. 27*, No. 2, 601.

WARSON, M. D. AND FERGUSON, J. K. W. (1955). Effects of cyanamide and ethanol on bleeding, weight and blood acetaldehyde in mice and rats. *Quart. J. Studies Alc. 16*, 607–613.

WATKINS, W. D., GOODMAN, J. I., AND TEPHLY, T. R. (1969). Effect of pyrazole on methanol and ethanol oxidation. *Federation Proc. 28*, No. 2, 546.

WATTS, J. S., CASSIDY, P., BYRON, W., REILLY, J. AND KROP, S. (1967). Ethanol augmentation of desmethylimipramine effects in the rat. *Toxicol. Appl. Pharmacol. 11*, 372–377.

WATZMAN, N., BARRY, H., III, KINNARD, W. J., JR. AND BUCKLEY, J. P. (1968). Some conditions under which pentobarbital stimulates spontaneous motor activity of mice. *J. Pharmaceut. Sci. 57*, 1572–1576.

WEATHERBY, J. H. AND CLEMENTS, E. L. (1960). Concerning the synergism between paraldehyde and ethyl alcohol. *Quart. J. Studies Alc. 21*, 394–399.

WEBB, W. R. AND DEGERLI, I. U. (1965). Ethyl alcohol and the cardiovascular system. Effects on coronary blood flow. *J. Am. Med. Assoc. 191*, 1055–1058.

WEBB, W. R., DEGERLI, I. U., COOK, W. A. AND UNAL, M. O. (1966). Alcohol, digitalis and cortisol, and myocardial capacity in dogs. *Ann. Surg. 163*, 811–817.

WEISS, B. AND LATIES, V. G. (1964). Effects of amphetamine, chlorpromazine, pentobarbital, and ethanol on operant response duration. *J. Pharmacol. Exptl. Therap. 144*, 17–23.

WEISSMAN, A. AND KOE, B. K. (1969). Drugs and deterrence of alcohol consumption. In: *Annual Reports in Medicinal Chemistry, 1968*, C. K. CAIN, Ed., Academic Press, New York. Pp. 246–258.

WELCH, H. AND SLOCUM, G. G. (1943). Relation of length of carbon chain to the primary and functional toxicity of alcohols. *J. Lab. Clin. Med. 28*, 1440–1445.

WIER, J. K. AND TYLER, V. E. (1960). An investigation of Coprinus atramentarius for the presence of disulfiram. *J. Am. Pharm. Assoc. Sci. Ed. 49*, 426–429.

WIKLER, A. (1957). *The relation of psychiatry to pharmacology.* Williams & Wilkins, Baltimore. 322 pp.

WILLARD, P. W. AND HORVATH, S. M. (1964). Coronary circulation during and following ethyl alcohol infusion. *Arch. Int. Pharmacodyn. 148*, 181–185.

WILLIAMS, E. E. (1937). Effects of alcohol on workers with carbon disulfide. *J. Am. Med. Assoc. 109*, 1472–1473.

WILLIAMS, R. T. (1959). *Detoxication mechanisms. The metabolism and detoxication of drugs, toxic substances and other organic compounds.* Chapman and Hall, London; 2nd ed. 796 pp.

WILSON, L., TAYLOR, J. D., NASH, C. W. AND CAMERON, D. F. (1966). The combined effects of ethanol and amphetamine sulfate on performance of human subjects. *Can. Med. Assoc. J. 94*, 478–484.

WÓJCICKI, J. (1967). The influence of protracted experimental alcoholism on the reactivity of the isolated heart of rat to strophanthin and poisons of the vegetative system. *Diss. Pharm. Pharmacol. 19*, 9–14. (Polish with English summary.)

WOOLES, W. R. (1968). Prevention of the acute ethanol-induced fatty liver by antihistamines and stimulants of hepatic microsomal enzyme activity. *Toxicol. Appl. Pharmacol. 12*, 186–193.

ZAPPI, F. AND MILLIFIORINI, M. (1955). Treatment of the Antabus–alcohol complications with betaphenylisopropylamine. Experimental contribution. (It.) *Riv. Neurol. 25*, 725–732. (Abstr. *Quart. J. Studies Alc.* 1957, *17*, 694.)

ZBINDEN, G., BAGDON, R. E., KEITH, E. F., PHILLIPS, R. D. AND RANDALL, L. O. (1961). Experimental and clinical toxicology of chlordiazepoxide (Librium^R). *Toxicol. Appl. Pharmacol. 3*, 619–637.

ZIPF, H. AND HAMACHER, J. (1967). Kombinationseffekte. 4. Mitteilung: Verkehrsmedizinische Probleme des Kombinationseffektes. *Arzneimittel-Forsch. 17*, 70–79.

ZIRKLE, G. A., KING, P. D., MCATEE, O. B. AND VAN DYKE, R. (1959). Effects of chlorpromazine and alcohol on coordination and judgment. *J. Am. Med. Assoc. 171*, 1496–1499.

ZIRKLE, G. A., MCATEE, O. B., KING, P. D. AND VAN DYKE, R. (1960). Meprobamate and small amounts of alcohol. Effects on human ability, coordination, and judgment. *J. Am. Med. Assoc. 173*, 1823–1825.

Chapter 11

Understanding and Treatment of Alcoholics

The present chapter examines the disorder called alcoholism. The material is divided into four principal topics: characteristics of alcoholics, etiology of alcoholism, treatment of acute intoxication, and therapy of chronic alcoholics. The prior chapters of this book, reviewing research on the acute and chronic effects of alcohol, are expected to provide valuable background material for understanding and treatment of prolonged, excessive consumption of alcoholic beverages. In particular, Chapter 9 reviews experimental studies and clinical observations of physiological effects of chronic alcohol consumption in humans and laboratory animals. The present chapter on alcoholism is unfortunately limited to humans, because of the inability thus far of experimenters to induce voluntary, chronic, excessive alcohol consumption in laboratory animals (Chapter 8, p. 419). In common with Chapter 9, the present chapter reviews a number of non-experimental, clinical studies. Inclusion of such observational, uncontrolled data is justified, in both chapters, both by the scarcity of experimental studies and by the great social and scientific value of increasing our knowledge on this topic. In addition to the pressing practical need for improving understanding and therapy of alcoholics, scientific knowledge about any chemical substance should include the cumulative effects of chronic consumption of excessive quantities.

The present chapter does not attempt a complete coverage of the voluminous literature on alcoholism, and the emphasis is on review and evaluation of controlled, experimental studies on alcoholics. Most of the information is obtained from articles in professional journals. General reviews of scientific knowledge about alcoholism were by Bowman and

References p. 779

Jellinek (1941) and Wieser (1962, 1965, 1966), but most reviews have been limited to particular portions of the topic, such as etiology or therapy. Several books have appeared in recent years, containing articles on various aspects of alcoholism; a number of good articles, although in some cases published previously, are found in the books edited by Thompson (1956) and Fox (1967a). Most other books on the general topic of alcoholism are limited to a superficial and opinionated account, with little presentation or evaluation of scientific evidence for the conclusions.

A. Characteristics of alcoholics

One of the problems in describing alcoholism is that it is not a single distinct disorder. Therefore, it is important to attempt a definition of alcoholism. Description of its typical symptoms and course may help further to define this disorder. This information is necessarily based mainly on clinical observations, rather than controlled experiments.

(1) Definitions and types of alcoholics

Some temperance workers have placed the label "alcoholic" upon the individual who becomes intoxicated only on a few special occasions or even upon some people who never become intoxicated and whose alcohol consumption is moderate and controlled in terms of their social customs. However, in scientific usage of the term, there is a high degree of agreement about the kinds of behavior which constitute alcoholism, as pointed out by Bowman and Jellinek (1941). Definitions of alcoholism are ably discussed by these authors and subsequently by Keller (1960). A more recent definition is given by Keller and McCormick (1968). In spite of the general consensus among scientists about the basic characteristics of the alcoholic, there has been lively controversy over the definition, as exemplified in an article by Seeley (1959b) which quotes and severely criticizes a definition formulated by an Expert Committee on Mental Health of the World Health Organization.

The definitions generally include three criteria, all of which must be present for the person to be regarded as an alcoholic:

(a) Large quantity of alcohol consumed over a period of years.

(b) Abnormal, chronic loss of control over drinking, shown by inability to refrain or inability to stop.

(c) The drinking causes chronic damage to physical health or social standing.

The most objective, easily observable of these criteria is the chronically large quantity of alcohol consumption. Lereboullet *et al.* (1966) reported on the daily alcohol consumption of a group of hospitalized alcoholics compared with a group of nonalcoholic patients. The percentage of cases reporting consumption within specified ranges of daily intake is shown in Fig. 11–1. There is considerable overlap between the highest consumption

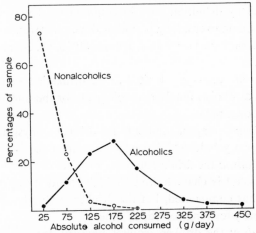

Fig. 11–1. Distribution of alcohol consumption among a sample of 737 nonalcoholic and 2720 alcoholic subjects in France. The values have been calculated from Table 3–1 in a study by Lereboullet *et al.* (1966).

by nonalcoholics and the lowest consumption by alcoholics. On the other hand, the majority of alcoholics definitely drink an abnormally high amount and many exceed the average metabolic capacity of approx. 175 g/day (2.4 g/kg/day) for nonalcoholic people (Chapter 2, Table 2–7). Therefore, this report adds to the evidence given in Chapter 9 (p. 490) for increased capacity to metabolize alcohol.

As a result of lack of knowledge about etiology of alcoholism, these criteria all concern drinking behavior and pathological effects of alcohol rather than the motives or abnormalities which give rise to the disorder. Behavior and pathological outcomes are influenced by social norms, and accordingly these criteria for alcoholism are limited to the human species and depend on the cultural setting. The social customs partly determine what constitutes a large quantity of consumption and an abnormal loss of control. The effects of the drinker's behavior on his social standing depend primarily on the community's attitudes about excessive drinking. Since alcoholics may include many types of people, who drink excessively for diverse reasons, alcoholism should not be described as a single disease (Farnsworth, 1968). The widely popularized description of alcoholism as a disease (Jellinek, 1960) thus is misleading, although it has had the useful function of emphasizing that it is a medical problem, requiring treatment, rather than a moral problem, requiring punishment or deterrence.

All alcoholics by definition have in common the behavior of excessive alcohol consumption over a long period of time. However, some differences in drinking patterns have been noted. Jellinek (1960, pp. 36–39) distinguished among 5 types.

Alpha alcoholism: damage is limited to the drinker's social standing. The dependence on alcohol is purely psychological, for the purpose of relieving bodily or emotional pain.

Beta alcoholism: damage is limited to the drinker's physical health. There is no physical or psychological dependence on alcohol.

Gamma alcoholism: the drinker acquires physical dependence on alcohol. Craving for alcohol is characterized by inability to stop (loss of control) after drinking has commenced, but the drinker is able to abstain ("go on the water wagon") for long periods of time.

Delta alcoholism: the drinker acquires physical dependence on alcohol, but the craving is characterized by inability to abstain rather than loss of control.

Epsilon alcoholism: an intermittent form of alcoholism in which the loss of control occurs at periodic intervals. The periodic drinking bouts are sometimes described as expressions of dipsomania.

Alpha, gamma, and epsilon alcoholism are more prevalent in Northern Europe and North America, beta and delta alcoholism are prevalent in wine-drinking countries such as France and Italy (Jellinek, 1960).

These 5 types are described in the context of a highly inclusive definition of alcoholism as "any drinking that leads to any damage". If loss of control over drinking is required as a criterion of alcoholism, the alpha and beta types might be defined as forms of excessive drinking without alcoholism. In many cases, they may represent early stages prior to the development of addictive drinking. Uncontrolled craving seems necessary to motivate consumption of damaging amounts of liquor for a prolonged period, although in many cases the craving may be concealed from self-awareness and from others.

The two principal types of craving for alcohol, represented by gamma and delta alcoholism, have been distinguished by Marconi (1959) in a comparison of drinkers who are unable to stop (intermittent alcoholism) with drinkers who are unable to abstain (continuous or inveterate alcoholism). The inability to stop results in compulsive, excessive drinking, once a small amount of alcohol has been consumed. The inability to abstain is strongest several hours after the last drink, presumably due to withdrawal symptoms, but the craving is relieved by moderate quantities of alcohol. Studies of personality characteristics of alcoholics indicate that more severe pathology is associated with inability to stop drinking characteristic of gamma alcoholics. Korman (1960), with an extensive questionnaire given to 61 alcoholic patients, reported that those who developed preoccupation with alcohol more rapidly tended to drink less frequently, but expressed stronger need for alcohol and more severe general pathology. Walton (1968) found that the gamma type alcoholics exhibited more severe anxiety and aggression directed against themselves. However, the steady drinking associated with delta alcoholism may give rise to more severe physical pathology.

Other classifications of alcoholics have been proposed. Blane (1968) has described alcoholics as dependent, mixed, or counterdependent on the basis of their general responses to other people. Fleeson and Gildea (1942) distinguished endogenous alcoholics, presumably with a constitutional predilection to addiction, from exogenous alcoholics, whose excessive drinking was induced by external influences. A similar, more recent classification (Sugerman et al., 1965) is between essential and reactive alcoholics. Statistical analyses of characteristics of alcoholics have resulted in the identification of several different patterns of personality type and drinking behavior (Schaefer, 1954; Horn and Wanberg, 1969; Partington and Johnson, 1969). In many patients, the alcoholism has obscured concomitant psychiatric diseases, such as schizophrenia, depression or psychopathic personality. Studies of sex differences indicate that female alcoholics are characterized by a higher incidence of depression (Winokur and Clayton, 1968) and by more rapid development of alcoholism, with more severe physical and emotional pathology (Hirsh, 1956). These important variations indicate that published reports on alcoholics should include detailed descriptions of their characteristics with regard to drinking pattern and other psychiatric diseases.

References p. 779

(2) Stages of alcoholism

The slow progression of alcoholism over a number of years provides valuable information about the development of this disorder. Jellinek (1952) has identified 4 typical stages of events and symptoms, based on questionnaire answers from approximately 2000 alcoholics. An independent study of 252 alcoholics in Wisconsin (Trice and Wahl, 1958) showed a closely similar sequence of symptoms. Both samples were limited to North America and are descriptive only of gamma alcoholics. According to the studies by Glatt (1961), Park (1962) and Kiviranta (1969) these stages, listed below, apply also to gamma alcoholics in England and Finland.

(a) Prealcoholic phase, in which there is a gradual change from occasional to constant drinking for relief of emotional or physical distress. An increase in tolerance for alcohol also is usually observable during this stage.

(b) Prodromal phase, marked by the occurrence of amnesia in the subsequent sober condition concerning some events while intoxicated. These episodes are commonly called blackouts and also are more technically named alcoholic palimpsests. Moderate alcohol doses, far short of an anesthetic or stuporous effect, may be sufficient to cause such blackouts, in drinkers whose general tolerance to alcohol is elevated. Goodwin et al. (1969a, b) have discussed variations found among alcoholics in occurrence and other characteristics of the blackouts. This "dissociation" of the intoxicated condition from sobriety (Storm and Smart, 1965) may have the useful function of separating the normal, sober life from the pathological needs and behavior aroused by intoxication, but it also helps to release the drinking situation from the constraints of sober judgment and custom. Other symptoms include avid drinking and an increased but secretive preoccupation with alcohol.

(c) Crucial phase, in which the drinker loses control. Each drinking episode begins a chain reaction which is felt as a physical demand for alcohol. The individual is still able to abstain, and the occasions of excessive drinking are typically separated by periods of total abstinence. The manifestly abnormal and pathological behavior toward alcohol becomes accompanied by guilt, fear, aggression, rationalizations and social isolation. This is the first stage in which the drinker fulfills all the criteria for alcoholism, defined above. The alcoholic at this stage usually begins to drink regularly in the mornings ("matutinal" drinking), and the excessive drinking typically causes neglect of proper nutrition and the initial occurrence of hospitalization.

(d) Chronic phase, characterized by the onset of prolonged intoxications, commonly called benders. The alcoholic suffers marked social, moral and physical deterioration. Withdrawal symptoms are severe, and the tolerance for alcohol, which is increased above normal levels at an earlier stage, commonly becomes reduced to normal or below.

The specification of the stages should not give the impression of a steady, inevitable progression. Most excessive drinkers struggle valiantly to maintain a healthy life and normal adjustment, as is indicated by the typically slow progression of the disorder. For example, the solitary drinking characteristic of alcoholics, is due to the addictive need for alcohol rather than a preference for drinking alone. Alcoholics generally seek drinking companions (Selzer *et al.*, 1963). Even in the absence of clinical treatment, remission of alcoholism occurs in a substantial proportion of cases (Lemere, 1953; Schmidt, 1968). Most of the medical complications of alcoholism are reversible short of extreme pathology. Hospitalized alcoholics show marked and rapid improvement of intellectual function (Jonsson *et al.*, 1962) and of sensori-motor performance (Goldstein *et al.*, 1968a). The progression toward severe pathology can be halted or reversed more easily at the earlier than at the later stages. Such variations increase the difficulty of classifying individuals as alcoholic or nonalcoholic.

(3) Illnesses associated with heavy drinking

Physical complications are found in only a minority of alcoholics, but the presence of certain types of physical damage in conjunction with prolonged, heavy drinking provides one of the most reliable criteria for alcoholism. Other illnesses associated with alcoholism include a wide variety of types of physical pathology, mental disorder and disruption of social behavior.

Cirrhosis of the liver is one of the best known consequences of heavy drinking. This disease is found in some moderate drinkers and even abstainers, but alcoholism greatly increases the risk. Samochowiec *et al.* (1967) state that the incidence of cirrhosis is 6 times higher in alcoholics than in those who are not habitual drinkers. Liver cirrhosis was found in 39 (12%) of 320 alcoholic patients (Lelbach, 1966b) and in 20% of 3000 randomly selected alcoholic patients (Leevy and TenHove, 1967). Since cirrhosis is an irreversible end stage of a progressing disease, incipient liver disease must occur in a fairly large proportion of alcoholics. The small percentage of the population who are alcoholics accounts for a high proportion of liver cirrhosis cases. According to estimations by Lelbach (1966a), alcoholism contributes to cirrhosis as follows: North and South America in 25–87% of the cases, France in 65–83%, Switzerland in 49–88%, England in 4.2–55% and Germany in 5.7–46%. Alcoholics comprise 63% of the male deaths and 22% of the female deaths from liver cirrhosis (Brenner, 1959).

The importance of liver cirrhosis as a criterion for alcoholism is emphasized by the widespread use of the Jellinek Estimation Formula (World Health Organization, 1951) for prevalence of alcoholism, based on the annual incidence of deaths from liver cirrhosis. However, this physical complication characterizes only a minority of alcoholics. According to the usual estimates, 25% of alcoholics suffer from physical complications; autopsy data indicate that only 9% of these (2.25% of all alcoholics) had liver cirrhosis, which was the cause of only 8% of the deaths of cirrhotic alcoholics (representing 0.2% of all the alcoholics alive at the time). The value of this formula depends on comparability and stability of the percentage estimations, but these values may be expected to differ in various cultural settings and to change during a span of years. For example, a pattern of steady, excessive drinking, by the delta type of alcoholic, would be more likely to produce damage than an equivalent amount of gamma type drinking. This may partly account for national variations in the incidence of liver cirrhosis, particularly relationships between type of beverage and liver cirrhosis reported by Wallgren (1960). Regardless of drinking pattern, a general improvement in diet would be expected to decrease the incidence of liver cirrhosis. These and other aspects of the Jellinek Estimation Formula have been criticized severely (Seeley, 1959a; Brenner, 1959; Jellinek, 1959). Therefore, this formula fails to provide a valid and reliable measure of national differences and of changes in the prevalence of alcoholism, although the formula includes adjustments for some sources of variations in the data on deaths due to liver cirrhosis.

Alcoholic polyneuropathy is less common than liver cirrhosis. According to Jolliffe (1942), polyneuropathy occurred in 20% of alcoholic patients in the U.S.A. and in 15–20% of the patients in Europe. The incidence was probably for populations of severe alcoholics and thus higher than for alcoholics in general. Janzen and Balzereit (1968) during 12 years detected 80 cases, comprising 0.3% of 25 000 patients.

The encephalopathies include various degenerative brain diseases, such as Wernicke's disease, Morel's cortical sclerosis, cerebellar degeneration, Marchiafava–Bignami's disease, and central pontine myelinolysis. Many of these disorders have attracted wide attention because of their dramatic symptomatology, but the incidence of full-blown syndromes is usually low. Lereboullet and Pluvinage (1956) diagnosed cerebral atrophy in 6% of 1500 alcoholics. Smith-Moorhouse (1963), with a highly selected sample of patients, reported central nervous system involvement in 77% of 43 patients regarded as belonging to Jellinek's (1952) most severe category of alcoholics. Hudolin (1967) found pathologic disturbances of the EEG in 18% of 391 alcoholic patients. Marchiafava–Bignami's disease is extremely rare, first described in Italy. Victor and Adams (1961) mention a few cases from the U.S.A. Cerebellar degeneration also is very rare. According to E. A. Martin (1965) about 110 cases have been reported in the literature. Allsop and Turner (1966) describe 9 cases and Mouren et al. (1965) 10 cases. However, a recent study of oculomotor reactions in alcoholics (Gabersek, 1965) indicates that signs of cerebellar involvement are more frequent than the literature generally suggests. Both an acute and a chronic muscular syndrome have been reported in chronic alcoholics. Although the syndrome has been described quite recently (Chapter 9, p. 568), it may be fairly common among alcoholics. Nygren (1966) found elevated serum creatine phosphokinase activities indicating muscular involvement, in 30 of 79 alcoholics.

Studies of performance requiring nervous system control of motor responses have indicated pathological effects of prolonged, excessive alcohol consumption. The use of a technique for measuring finger tremor (Carrie, 1965) revealed consistently greater amplitude of tremors in alcoholic patients than in nonalcoholic controls. A study of reaction times (Talland, 1963) showed slower performance by alcoholics than by normals.

In spite of the direct irritating action of alcohol, gastrointestinal disturbances are not consistently found in alcoholics. Mackay (1966), in a review, stated that fatty infiltration of the salivary glands, esophagic rupture, and gastritis (but not peptic ulcer) are common pathological findings. A clinical study of digestive physiology of 471 skid row alcoholics indicated relatively mild disturbances, many of which were promptly cured during hospital treatment (Small et al., 1959). According to a brief report (Cathell, 1954), the development of alcoholism was accompanied in a number of cases by relief of gastric ulcers or of other digestive disturbances. This almost unique report of a beneficial effect of alcoholism presumably represents the

References p. 779

substitution of one pathological condition for another, but it might also indicate an incentive for excessive drinking.

Mackay (1966) mentioned pancreatitis, but the incidence of this disease among alcoholics seems to vary greatly among different countries. Ritter (1965) concluded that alcohol is not a major cause of pancreatitis but some studies have shown a high incidence among alcoholics. Sobel and Waye (1963), in a study of cirrhotic patients, found 3 times higher incidence of pancreatitis among those who were alcoholics than in the nonalcoholic patients. Schapiro et al. (1966), in a review, concluded than there is an association between alcoholism and pancreatitis.

The pathological condition of alcoholism is associated with other types of physical pathology. Statistical findings suggest an increased incidence of certain types of cancer among alcoholics (Ledermann, 1952; Kamionkowski and Fleshler, 1965; Keller, 1967). The mechanism for this association is unknown; Chapter 9 (p. 573) reviews experimental findings that alcohol did not promote spread of cancer in mice, rats and hamsters. Barchha et al. (1968) found that in a series of general hospital ward patients, alcoholics were overrepresented, particularly among those with certain diseases. Increased mortality rates of alcoholics from various causes have been reported by Babigian and Odoroff (1969) and by Schmidt and de Lint (1969).

Other types of physical pathology associated with alcoholism seem to be attributable to deterioration in self-control and in social standing. Fox (1966) reported that alcoholic patients have a high incidence of cuts and bruises, including head injuries and rib fractures. Even severe injuries were typically untreated during a long period of time before hospitalization. The same author observed also that alcoholics are generally heavy smokers and highly susceptible to acute lung infections. Dreher and Fraser (1967, 1968) found heavier smoking by alcoholics than by the general population. Nolan (1965) reported on characteristics of 124 cases classified as alcoholics among 900 consecutive admissions to a general hospital. The majority of the alcoholics had delayed inordinately in seeking medical attention, and multiple illnesses were typical. One primary diagnosis with a greatly elevated incidence among the alcoholics was acute pneumonia. Tuberculosis is another pulmonary infectious disease with a much higher incidence among alcoholics than in the general population (Pincock, 1964). In France, occurrence of pneumonia and lung tuberculosis is strongly associated with heavy drinking (Ledermann, 1952, 1964).

These indications of general neglect and carelessness may be related to evidence for social pathology of alcoholics. Several studies of alcoholics have shown abnormally high incidences of marital separation and divorce (Straus and Bacon, 1951; Scott, 1958; Bailey *et al.*, 1965). Social isolation, measured by several criteria, was higher in a group of previously undiagnosed alcoholics than in a comparison group (Singer *et al.*, 1964). More profound mental pathology, associated with alcoholism, is seen in the high incidence among alcoholics of other mental illnesses, in particular depression, schizophrenia and psychopathic personality. A self-destructive tendency is evident in reports that the incidence of suicide is much higher among alcoholics than the general population (Lemere, 1953; Cassidy *et al.*, 1957; Robins *et al.*, 1959; Kessel and Grossman, 1961; Palola *et al.*, 1962; Pokorny, 1964; Stenbäck and Blumenthal, 1964; Stenbäck *et al.*, 1965; Kendell and Staton, 1966; Pitts and Winokur, 1966; Murphy and Robins, 1967). Alcoholics also have an elevated incidence of other types of fatal accident (B. Brenner, 1967) and of highway accidents and fatalities (Schmidt and Smart, 1959; Selzer and Weiss, 1966; Waller and Turkel, 1966; Selzer *et al.*, 1967; Waller, 1967, 1968a, b; U.S. Deartment of Transportation, 1968; Selzer, 1969). Various types of crime also are associated with alcoholism (Ahto, 1951; Guze *et al.*, 1962). In a review of studies on a widely used personality questionnaire (MMPI), Dahlstrom and Welsh (1960) concluded that alcoholics show a strong psychopathic trend.

In general, a wide variety of physical, social and psychiatric illnesses are associated with chronic heavy drinking. Nearly all of the evidence is based on clinical observations rather than on controlled experiments. The mechanisms for development of the illness can be inferred in some cases, but in others, especially psychiatric illnesses, it is uncertain whether the symptom was due to the excessive drinking or was a pre-existing tendency and perhaps even one of the causes of alcoholism. These possibilities are discussed in the next section, on etiology of alcoholism.

B. Etiology of alcoholism

Some of the conditions associated with development of alcoholism have been identified earlier in this book. The preceding section indicates that an uncontrollable craving for liquor generally develops only after heavy drinking for a period of years. The research reviewed in Chapter 8 leads to the conclusion that laboratory animals under almost all circumstances avoid inebriation or prolonged, excessive drinking. Thus some social or physiological characteristics of humanity appear to be another prerequisite for alcoholism. Various theories of the etiology of alcoholism have been proposed in the attempt to identify the conditions which cause some human drinkers to become alcoholics while others maintain control of their drinking. Unfortunately, the scientific evidence in support of these theories is generally meager and inconclusive. The scarcity of well-established facts about the etiology of alcoholism has permitted the survival thus far of diverse, conflicting theories.

The present section is divided into three parts. The first reviews theories of constitutional vulnerability to alcoholism. The second reviews characteristics of personality or childhood development believed to increase susceptibility to alcoholism. The third reviews protective factors, both constitutional and personality attributes, which prevent the development of alcoholism. An excellent, critical evaluation by Jellinek (1960) provides a strong background for the present brief review.

(1) Constitutional predisposition

Etiological theories based on constitutional susceptibility generally portray an abnormal type of person who is pathologically affected by alcohol. Although both factors seem necessary for an adequate explanation of alcoholism, usually one or the other factor is emphasized. At one extreme is a theory of pathological alcohol effects without explaining why only some drinkers become alcoholics. At the other extreme is a description of a physical abnormality related to alcoholism without explaining why alcoholism is a specific effect of the physical condition.

(a) Pathological effects of alcohol

The characteristic slow development of alcoholism suggests the possibility that the intoxication itself may be the origin of a vicious spiral toward more and more craving, excessive drinking, and pathology. This conception of drinking as the etiological factor was prevalent several decades ago (e.g., Emerson, 1934). More recent investigations, reviewed in Chapter 9, have established that prolonged, heavy drinking may cause tolerance, physiological dependence and withdrawal symptoms. Dole and Nyswander (1967), in a discussion of dependence on heroin, argue that drug dependence develops because of a change in the response of the nervous system to the drug.

Jellinek (1960, pp. 33–155) summarizes various theories which attribute alcoholism to effects of pathological conditions, such as brain damage, dietary deficiency, liver cirrhosis, endocrinological abnormalities or allergic reactions, which are assumed to be directly or indirectly induced by prolonged, heavy drinking. These theories, if proven, can satisfactorily account for the fact that the alcoholic's consumption of liquor arouses the craving for still more alcohol, leading to a vicious spiral in the intensification of the disease. However, the physiological pathology appears to develop only at an advanced stage of alcoholism, after a long period of the excessive drinking which according to these theories is a consequence of the physiological changes. The uncontrollable craving for alcohol generally occurs long before the excessive drinker loses control over any other facilities. Jellinek (1960, p. 90) points out that if brain damage is the cause of alcoholism, the symptom is implausibly limited and specific in its manifestation. The same criticism seems to apply to the other theories which attribute alcoholism to the physiological pathologies induced by the alcohol itself. If the physiological pathology which causes alcoholism is reversible, physical treatment should drastically reduce the craving for alcohol. However, vitamin supplements have been found ineffective as means of reducing the alcoholic's craving for alcohol (Smith et al., 1951). Chapter 8 reviews evidence that dietary deficiencies and cirrhosis of the liver can increase the voluntary consumption of alcohol by laboratory animals, but there is no evidence for the development or intensification of addictive craving in these animals. G. J. Martin (1965) has proposed that acetaldehyde formed from ethanol would prevent formation of acetylcholine through a reaction with –SH groups blocking the formation of acetyl-CoA, and thus also acetylations. He further proposes that this effect would induce the withdrawal syndrome and thus explain continuation of drinking. However, work on the acetylcholine system, reviewed in Chapter 5 (p. 221) has not revealed any major alterations caused by alcohol. Reports by Martin and associates (Martin et al., 1966; Smyth et al., 1967; Moss et al., 1967) give some support in that chronic ingestion by rats of alcohol solutions as their sole source of fluid caused significant decrease in the concentration of acetyl-CoA in their brains. Considering the hypothesis, the experiments have the serious flaw that no evidence is presented that the rats showed any sign of a withdrawal syndrome or "craving"; indeed, their amount of alcohol consumption cannot be expected to result in physical dependence.

(b) Prior abnormalities related to alcohol effects

Even if a specific physiological change caused by alcohol were demonstrated to induce craving for alcohol, it would be an incomplete explanation for alcoholism because it is evident that many people who experience repeated, heavy intoxication do not become alcoholics. Addictive drinking seems to develop only in some drinkers and only after drinking for many months or years. Therefore, most of the recent etiological theories of alcoholism have specified predisposing characteristics prior to the initial experience with alcohol. Such theories are compatible with the hypothesis that the physical changes caused by alcohol induce the craving for further alcohol, and indeed the predisposing characteristic according to some theorists consists of a heightened susceptibility to the physical changes caused by alcohol.

The inebriety sought by alcoholics seems to indicate a desire for pharmacological rather than nutritional effects. Nevertheless, several etiological theories are based on the nutritive characteristics of alcohol as a food rather than its pharmacological actions as a drug. R. J. Williams (1947, 1959) assumes that susceptibility to alcoholism is caused by a "genetotrophic" need for certain dietary substances in larger amounts than are provided by a normal diet. Alcohol temporarily alleviates the symptoms of dietary deficiency, but does not provide the needed substances, and the caloric intake in the form of liquor causes the drinker to consume less of the needed food. Thus the alcoholic's large alcohol consumption aggravates the dietary deficiency which induces the craving for yet more liquor. Williams' hypothesis has been severely criticized both on the grounds of insufficient evidence (*e.g.*, Popham, 1953) and for theoretical reasons (*e.g.*, Lester, 1960). The hypothesis remains unproven. Roach and Williams (1966) have presented a modified hypothesis, assuming impaired glucose metabolism in the brain as an etiological factor, but the evidence is not presented in full, and the formulation is highly speculative and in part contradictory to known facts about the role of alcohol in cerebral metabolism (Chapter 5, p. 227).

Other theorists have proposed various mechanisms by which the action of alcohol as a food may cause the development of alcoholism in individuals who are susceptible because of a physiological deficiency. Mardones (1951) has suggested thiamine deficiency as the predisposing factor. Lester (1960) has speculated that susceptible individuals may be those who synthesize a hypothetical two-carbon metabolic intermediate more efficiently from alcohol than from acetate or other normal nutrients. Randolph (1956) and

Karolus (1961) have suggested that alcohol addiction results from a sensitive, "allergic" reaction to alcohol or to other components of alcoholic beverages. Most of these theories assume that alcohol immediately relieves the adverse symptoms of the susceptible drinker, followed by intensification of the symptoms and craving for more alcohol. Contrary to this assumption, humans and other animals generally learn to consume foods which are beneficial and to avoid harmful diets. It seems implausible that the nutritional deficiency would induce a specific craving for a detrimental food. Also, any hypothesis that ascribes alcoholism to the properties of alcohol as a nutrient also implies some unique metabolic pathways for alcohol. Nothing of the kind is known: the only intermediate formed from alcohol which is not normal for the organism is acetaldehyde. The acetate derived from ethanol *via* acetaldehyde enters the common acetate pool and passes over acetyl-CoA into reactions shared by acetate from any other precurser. There is nothing "mystical" in the metabolism of alcohol.

Lovell and Tintera (Tintera and Lovell, 1949; Lovell, 1951; Lovell and Tintera, 1951; Tintera, 1966) have suggested that adrenocortical or combined pituitary–adrenocortical deficiency is a primary factor in alcoholism, and that hypoglycemia caused by adrenal dysfunction would result in unpleasant emotional symptoms constituting an important stimulus to addictive drinking. Alcohol is suggested to bring temporary relief by raising the blood sugar level, but afterward the chronic hypoglycemia is intensified so that the drinker becomes dependent on increasing amounts of alcohol to obtain relief. The evidence on adrenocortical function and on glucose metabolism in alcoholics, reviewed in Chapter 9 on pp. 529 and 533, does not support the argument. This hypothesis of adrenocortical insufficiency implies that the deficiency either arises as a result of drinking or is present as a predisposing trait which is aggravated by the drinking. Similarly, disturbed thyroid function has been suggested as a cause of alcoholism. In a very speculative paper, Gross (1945) suggested hyperthyroidism as a factor promoting alcoholism. We have already seen (Chapter 8, p. 454) that Richter has made the contrary suggestion that hyperthyroidism should decrease voluntary intake of alcohol. Goldberg (1960) proposes an association between hypothyroidism and alcoholism and presents some supporting statistics. However, there is no clear evidence from autoselection studies for a relationship between thyroid function and intake of alcohol. Selzer and Van Houten (1964) studied thyroid function in 43 and Augustine (1967) in 109 alcoholic patients; in no case was hypofunction observed. This is good

References p. 779

evidence that lowered thyroid function plays no role in the genesis of alcoholism. Other theorists have identified susceptibility to alcoholism with other endocrinological abnormalities which are generally less clearly defined. Fleetwood and Diethelm (1951) reported that alcoholics secrete elevated amounts of a hormone which induces the emotion of resentment. Smith (1949) and Tintera (1956) stated that alcoholics are deficient in adrenocortical and gonadal secretions. Hoffer and Osmond (1959) suggested that alcoholics suffer from abnormally strong feelings of tension, indicated by a high rate of metabolism of adrenochrome.

All of these theories assume that the designated physiological deficit is an antecedent of alcoholism, but none of them is supported by adequate evidence that the physiological deficiencies precede the onset of excessive drinking. The physical measurements have been made on people under treatment for alcoholism, so that their pathological conditions may well be consequences rather than antecedents of the excessive drinking. Further evidence contrary to these proposed physio-pathological etiologies is that none of the proposed traits is common to all alcoholics. In general, none of the proposed physiological deficits has been convincingly established or generally accepted as cause of alcoholism. Most of the theories are reviewed and cogently criticized by Jellinek (1960, pp. 82–110). Criticism of some of these theories has been made by Wexberg (1950), Keller (1951), Lester and Greenberg (1952), Mann (1952), Robinson and Voegtlin (1952), Greenberg and Lester (1957), Lester (1966), and an editorial in the *Can. Med. Assoc. J.* (1967).

(c) Unexplained relationships to alcoholism

Efforts to establish a constitutional, hereditary predisposition to alcoholism have not been well substantiated. Nordmo (1959) reported a higher incidence of blood group A among 939 alcoholics than 4774 control persons in Colorado, but Achté (1958) found no difference in blood groups between 212 alcoholics and 1383 controls in Finland. An over-representation of deficiencies in color vision among alcoholics (Cruz-Coke, 1965; Cruz-Coke and Valera, 1966) has been challenged (Gorrell *et al.*, 1967) and is at least partly explainable by evidence that the excessive drinking impairs performance in tests of color vision (Fialkow *et al.*, 1966). Lisker *et al.* (1968) have reported evidence that the elevated incidence of color blindness among alcoholics is due to liver disease rather than heavy drinking or a genetic defect in color vision. Sheldon and Stevens (1942, p. 313) reported a preponderance of muscular, "mesomorphic" body types among a sample of alcoholics, but Tintera and Lovell (1949) supported their conception of endocrinological deficiency by characterizing many young, male alcoholics as slender with a soft, smooth, womanly body. Damon (1963) critically reviews prior studies on the relationship between constitution and alcoholism and presents his own, carefully evaluated data on three ethnic groups, with almost entirely negative results.

Most of the proposed physical characteristics do not appear to be plausible as causes of the craving for alcohol or inability to control consumption. Even if alcoholism were shown convincingly to be related to a constitutional factor such as blood type, color blindness or body build, a more probable cause of the alcoholism would be some other variable, such as ethnic group membership or motivational condition, which was also related to the constitutional factor. The highly complex picture of human alcoholism makes it extremely unlikely that a simple one-to-one relationship could be found between a metabolic or somatic peculiarity and alcoholic disease.

A more direct test for a hereditary predisposition toward alcohol has been made in a comparison of 198 monozygotic with 641 dizygotic pairs of twins in Finland (Partanen *et al.*, 1966). Measures of alcoholism (arrests for drunkenness and presence of addictive symptoms) showed rather low correlations between the pairs of twins and no reliably higher correlation for the monozygotic than dizygotic pairs. Abstention from alcohol and heavy use of alcohol showed similar correlations for the dizygotic pairs but much higher correlations for the monozygotic pairs. These data provide evidence against the existence of a strong genetic predisposition toward alcoholism, especially in comparison with the evidence for a genetic predisposition toward abstention or heavy drinking. However, a study reported by Kaij (1960) of 174 pairs of twins in South Sweden, with one member of each pair registered on account of alcohol abuse, shows somewhat higher concordance with respect to chronic alcoholism for the monozygotic than for the dizygotic pairs.

Another method of investigating general hereditary influences on predisposition to alcoholism is by a study of children of alcoholics, reared by foster parents who are not alcoholics. Roe (1945) reported no excessive drinking during adulthood among 27 individuals of alcoholic parentage and 22 of normal parentage, placed in foster homes in early childhood. The 20–30% incidence of alcoholism, to be expected in people with alcoholic parentage, thus seems to be due to the effects of the childhood environment rather than to a hereditary predisposition.

References p. 779

(2) Personality predisposition

The great diversity among alcoholics applies to personality as well as physiological characteristics. No single trait or type of background is found in most alcoholics. However, a number of studies and clinical observations have given evidence that certain pathological conditions in early childhood are associated with alcoholism. The most convincing evidence is based on objective features of the childhood family environment, especially in studies of young boys followed by identification of which ones subsequently became alcoholics. Some studies of adult alcoholics have provided information about personality characteristics which are presumed to antedate the development of alcoholism and thus may be etiological factors.

(a) Childhood pathology of alcoholics

In a follow-up study over a period of many years, information about childhood conditions and behavior may be correlated with subsequent drinking of alcoholic beverages. The childhood circumstances are thereby measured prior to the knowledge of which children later became alcoholics. Research of this type is unfortunately a rarity because several decades must elapse between the initial measurements in early childhood and the manifestation of addictive drinking. However, three such studies all indicate pathological family environment and antisocial, unrestrained behavior as etiological factors.

McCord et al. (1959, 1960) conducted a long-term observation on a sample of 650 boys in the United States. At 30 years of age, the cases still being traced included 29 with evidence of alcoholism, who were compared with 158 nonalcoholics. Several measures of the childhood family background were related to the subsequent manifestation of alcoholism. The 29 alcoholics included 31% of the 26 sons of criminal fathers, but only 12% of the 151 sons of noncriminal fathers. The alcoholics included only 10% of the 62 boys who had been highly restricted and overprotected during childhood, compared with 19% of the 117 normally or subnormally restricted boys. The alcoholics included only 6% of the 50 boys who had displayed strong inferiority feelings, compared with 19% of the 135 boys who had been classified as moderately or very self-confident.

Robins (1966) and Robins et al. (1962) reported on a study of 524 patients of both sexes at a child guidance clinic in the United States and a matched comparison group of 100 normal children; follow-up data were collected on all available cases 30 years later. Alcoholism was manifested in 15% of 503 former patients, but in only 2% of 99 comparison cases, although the proportion of heavy drinkers was similar (22% of the patients and 18% of the comparison cases). Examination of the childhood environment of the clinic patients showed that alcoholism subsequently developed in 49% of the patients whose parents were classified as inadequate, 34% of those whose parents were mixed or somewhat inadequate, and only 14% of those whose parents (or only parent) were adequate. This classification of parental adequacy was based on various observable criteria, of which antisocial behavior of the father, especially as indicated by arrests for criminal activities, was most strongly associated with subsequent alcoholism. The categories of paternal antisocial behavior included excessive drinking, which was more weakly associated with later alcoholism than were the other types of antisocial behavior. An environmental rather than hereditary basis for this predisposition to alcoholism is indicated by the fact that alcoholism did not develop in any of the eight cases with an antisocial father when the child was brought up exclusively by an adequate mother or adequate foster parents. Antisocial behavior of the child was strongly related to later alcoholism, shown by the incidence of alcoholism in 45% of 105 clinic patients with a juvenile court record, 25% of 57 patients without a court record but showing other evidence of antisocial behavior, and only 15% of 59 patients without evidence of antisocial behavior. Various neurotic symptoms, investigated in the clinic patients, were not related to the subsequent development of alcoholism. All of these childhood characteristics related to alcoholism had little effect on the proportion of heavy drinkers and generally had little effect on the proportion of cases with a complete absence of excessive drinking. Therefore, these antecedents seem to predispose the individual to the development of chronic, problem drinking rather than merely the heavy use of alcohol. Jones (1968) tested childhood personality characteristics in 66 boys. The six cases who subsequently became problem drinkers had been undercontrolled, impulsive, and rebellious during childhood.

The study by McCord et al. (1959, 1960) included evidence that the constitutional abnormalities of nutritional deficiency and glandular disorder did not predispose the boys to the development of alcoholism. Subsequently, alcoholism was found in none of the 21 boys with hyperthyroidism, diabetes mellitus or other glandular disorders, whereas 17% of the 166 boys without such disorders became alcoholic.

Certain types of objective information about the childhood family environment can usually be obtained accurately by retrospectively questioning alcoholics or their relatives. Chen and Cobb (1960) reviewed several studies showing an elevated incidence of parental death, separation or divorce during the childhood of the alcoholic. Subsequent studies have generally supported the conclusion of an elevated incidence of early parental loss among alcoholics (Hilgard and Newman, 1963; Dennehy, 1966; Oltman and Friedman, 1967). Differences from the control groups were generally small; in all samples only a minority of the alcoholic patients had suffered parental loss. Therefore, this event cannot account for most cases of alcoholism, but it suggests a type of childhood environment which may predispose the individual to becoming an alcoholic. In reviews of studies of ordinal positions, Sampson (1965) and Barry *et al.* (1969) concluded that later and last birth positions were over-represented in samples of alcoholics from large families. The relationship of this birth order difference to large family size was shown especially clearly in a sample of 600 alcoholics in Austria (Navratil, 1959). A similar distribution of birth positions among schizophrenics (Barry and Barry, 1967) was attributed to the parental deprivations and rejections often experienced by later children in large families. This seems consistent with a suggestion by de Lint (1964) that the over-representation of later birth positions among alcoholics is due to the effects of the elevated incidence of early parental deprivation among these children. A finding by Martensen-Larsen (1957), perhaps suggestive of a tendency for alienation of the alcoholic from his parents, was that in contrast to the over-representation of last birth position among alcoholics, their mothers and to a lesser extent their fathers were more often first than last born. Their wives also were more often first than last born.

Most retrospective studies of the early childhood of alcoholics have failed to present a clear or consistent description of the etiological factors. In clinical case histories of male alcoholics by Knight (1938) and Wall and Allen (1944), the mother was generally overprotective and over-indulgent, shielding her son from a severe father, so that the boy developed passive, childish, feminine wishes conflicting with the masculine strivings inculcated by his father and by the cultural norms. Wood and Duffy (1966), in a study of 69 alcoholic women, reported that most of them described their mothers as dominant in the household and emotionally distant, whereas their fathers were warmer, but alcoholic and unable to protect them from the dominant mother. In such accounts, a nonalcoholic group is lacking and also the description of the alcoholic's parents and early life is subject to failures of memory and purposeful distortions. Erroneous reports might be especially prone to occur in a sample of alcoholics. Therefore, retrospective studies should be received with skepticism.

(b) Traits of alcoholics

Prolonged, excessive drinking gives rise to various types of pathological behavior, as described earlier in this chapter. However, some investigators have assumed that certain personality traits, found to be more prevalent among alcoholics than among normal people, are stable behavior patterns which existed prior to the development of alcoholism. Such traits should be considered as possible predisposing factors toward alcoholism.

Ability to cope with the perceived environment has been measured by three tests in which the observer is asked to overcome conflicting visual relationships. Two of these require the vestibular sense of gravity as the cue for placing oneself vertically (body-adjustment) and placing a rod vertically (rod-and-frame). The third test requires the observer to identify obscured objects in a picture (embedded figures). Alcoholics have been shown to perform these tasks more poorly than normals and nonalcoholic psychiatric patients (Witkin et al., 1959). This deficiency in performance of the alcoholics was interpreted as an expression of perceptual dependence, related to the orally fixated, dependent personality which is emphasized in psychoanalytic theories of alcoholism. Further studies gave evidence that this deficiency in the performance of alcoholics is highly stable, regardless of whether the alcoholic is currently under the influence of liquor (Karp et al., 1965b), regardless of how many or few years of excessive drinking have preceded the test (Karp and Konstadt, 1965) and regardless of whether the alcoholic has achieved sobriety (Karp et al., 1965a). Reilly and Sugerman (1967), in a study of individual differences among a group of alcoholic patients, related perceptual dependence to other personality functions. Patients who performed more poorly in the embedded figures test tended to express more submissiveness and less independence in a sentence-completion test.

Perceptual dependence is related to other pathological conditions in addition to alcoholism. Perceptual dependence is greater in older people, both alcoholic and nonalcoholic (Karp and Konstadt, 1965). Members of Alcoholics Anonymous, whether currently drinking or abstaining from alcohol, are superior to patients in an alcoholism clinic (Karp et al., 1965a).

References p. 779

Bailey *et al.* (1961), with the use of the rod-and-frame test alone, found greater perceptual dependence in alcoholics than in normals and schizophrenics, but the highest degree of perceptual dependence was found in cases with chronic brain syndrome, with or without involvement of alcoholism. They concluded that brain damage produced by excessive drinking is the probable cause of the perceptual dependence found in alcoholics. These studies show that perceptual dependence is not specific to alcoholism but also give further evidence for a strong association of perceptual dependence to alcoholism. Jacobson (1968), in demonstrating that the immediately preceding experience altered field dependence, also found an unusually high degree of perceptual dependence in alcoholics. Goldstein *et al.* (1968b) questioned the validity of the rod-and-frame test because it showed little correlation with other measures of dependency in a sample of 30 alcoholics, but most of the pertinent correlations were positive and a more suitable validity test would have been a comparison of alcoholics with nonalcoholics.

The recurrence of excessive drinking by alcoholics, despite repeated experiences of unpleasant and self-destructive consequences, provides the basis for a theory that alcoholics are deficient in the ability to form an association between their drinking behavior and its aversive effects. As a result of this deficiency in alcoholics, the drastic but delayed aversive effects of alcohol might be weaker than the immediate anxiety reduction or other pleasurable effects which motivate the drinking. Deficient avoidance learning by alcoholics was found in one study (Parke and Walters, 1966) but not in another (Franks and Mantell, 1966). In a conflict situation, established by training a rewarded response which was then punished by painful electric shocks, the alcoholics usually continued to make the punished response and failed to perceive the relationship between their response and the punishment (Vogel-Sprott, 1967). The alcoholics also learned the original rewarded response more slowly (Vogel-Sprott and Banks, 1965). These findings are consistent with an earlier, independent report that alcoholics failed to adapt to a repeatedly presented light or tone (Imber *et al.*, 1961). They found that the galvanic skin response evoked by these stimuli was generally as high on trials 8–10 as on the first 3 presentations.

A greater deficit in acquisition of the association was found among the alcoholics with a greater degree of pathology measured by personality tests (Vogel-Sprott and Banks, 1965; Imber *et al.*, 1961). Another type of difference among alcoholics was reported in earlier studies by Vogel. Alcoholics classified as introverted on the basis of a personality questionnaire were more likely to be steady, solitary drinkers (delta type), whereas extraverted alcoholics tended to be periodic, spree drinkers (gamma type), with a higher incidence of blackouts (Vogel, 1961a). A galvanic skin response to an originally neutral stimulus, paired with a loud buzzer, was learned more rapidly and persisted during more unreinforced trials by the introverted, delta type of alcoholics (Vogel, 1960, 1961b).

Adherents of Sigmund Freud's psychoanalytic theory have formulated an etiological theory relating pathology in early childhood development to traits of adult alcoholics (Fenichel, 1945). The theoretical formulations have also been summarized by Menninger (1938), Bowman and Jellinek (1941), Lorand (1945) and Lisansky (1960). A later critique, including a large bibliography, has been written by Blum (1966). Alcoholics are described as being fixated at the infantile, oral stage of personality development, associated with craving for a passive, dependent role. The conflict of this tendency with harsh reality gives rise to denial, fantasies of omnipotence, and intense anger directed especially against oneself as manifested by the self-destructive behavior of excessive drinking. Menninger (1938) characterized alcoholism as a form of suicidal behavior.

This theoretical formulation is consistent with the emphasis on conflict between dependence and independence motives (Blane, 1968) based on clinical impressions. Some research findings provide evidence for or against specific predictions from psychoanalytic theory. McCord et al. (1959, 1960) reported that 3 out of 10 boys with suicidal inclinations (30%) subsequently became alcoholic compared with 14% of the 139 others. A higher incidence of oral-passive tendency among 30 alcoholics than 30 matched controls (Wolowitz, 1964) was inferred from responses to a questionnaire of oral trait scales and also from preference on the part of alcoholics for sweeter, softer and liquid forms of food (Wolowitz, 1964; Wolowitz and Barker, 1969). This claim that alcoholics show preference for sweets appears contrary to reports of a negative correlation between consumption of alcohol and consumption of sugar and sweets in humans (Bresard and Chabert, 1963; Chabert et al., 1964; Bresard, 1965; Partanen et al., 1966) and in rats (Chapter 8, p. 442). Strong homosexual drives, repressed from conscious awareness, have been attributed to male alcoholics (Lorand, 1945). Contrary to the suggestion of repression of this tendency is a report by McCord et al. (1959, 1960), that two out of six homosexual boys (33%) became alcoholic compared with 16% of 166 normally masculine boys and only one (4%) of 24

References p. 779

feminine boys. Gibbins and Walters (1960) reported that male alcoholics were intermediate between male homosexuals and normal men in their reactions to verbal and pictorial symbols of male and female sexuality. This finding is consistent with Menninger's (1938) suggestion of inadequate development of mature sexuality in alcoholics.

(3) Factors preventing alcoholism

The development of alcoholism in some rather than all drinkers might be due not only to greater susceptibility in some people but also to protective factors, impeding or preventing the development of this disorder in others. Since a high degree of tolerance to alcohol seems to be found in alcoholics even at an early stage, it seems likely that people with unusually low tolerance for this drug are prevented from heavy drinking by a higher degree of avoidance of the unpleasant effects of intoxication. Forsander (1962) has proposed a protective mechanism of this kind, based on observations of variations among animals in rate of alcohol metabolism. If alcoholism in humans should be found to be related to constitutional factors, such a protective mechanism in some people seems to be a likelier mechanism than the widespread assumption that some people suffer from an extraordinarily high degree of susceptibility to alcoholism.

With regard to personality as well as constitutional variations, more attention should be directed to protective factors which prevent the individual from developing alcoholism. A stable, loving childhood environment provides the basis for a mature, healthy personality, effectively prevented from developing alcoholism. All studies showing that pathology of childhood environment or adult personality is related to alcoholism thereby imply the converse relationship of mental health to the absence of alcoholism. An extensive study of intellectually gifted children showed that they tended to be physically and emotionally as well as mentally superior. Responses to follow-up questionnaires indicated low incidence of problem drinking more than 30 years later (Terman and Oden, 1959) and more than 40 years later (Oden, 1968).

Some of the sociological and cultural variations in the incidence of alcoholism seem to be most plausibly attributable to differences in the effectiveness of social controls, preventing the development of this disorder. Barry (1968) has suggested that in comparisons among various nationality and ethnic groups of contemporary civilization, the unusually low alcoholism rates found in some groups, such as Jewish, Italian and Chinese people, are due primarily to more effective social restraints against excessive drinking. A further protective mechanism may be the relatively high degree of satisfaction of dependency needs in these societies. A study of more than 100 preliterate societies (Bacon *et al.*, 1965) showed that low frequency of drunkenness was associated with high satisfaction of dependency needs. Similarly, the lower incidence of alcoholism among women than men in the United States (Lisansky, 1957), and the smaller amount of alcohol consumption by women than men in all known preliterate societies where a sex difference is reported (Child *et al.*, 1965), is attributable to the protectively deterrent effects of greater social disapproval and more effective social controls, and also to the greater satisfaction of dependency needs in women (Barry, 1968).

These sociological and cultural differences in alcoholism rates can be viewed also in terms of the increased susceptibility under one condition. For example, higher prevalence of alcoholism in urban locations (Keller and Efron, 1955, 1956) implies a protective effect of the rural or small-town environment. Theories of the etiology of alcoholism have led to an emphasis on the conditions related to high alcoholism rates. However, consideration of the alternative conditions related to low alcoholism rates is needed for a comprehensive understanding of etiology and also is an aid in the development of methods for preventing and controlling this disorder.

C. Treatment of acute intoxication

Scientific and clinical knowledge about acute and chronic effects of alcohol, reviewed in the present chapter and in the prior ones, may be expected to contribute useful ideas for therapy of illnesses caused by excessive drinking. Two types of acute intoxication are distinguished: acute alcohol poisoning and the condition of the alcoholic who is acutely ill after a period of excessive drinking. Both cases require immediate treatment of the toxic effects of alcohol, but the acutely ill alcoholic often suffers from additional pathological developments due to his years or at least months of heavy consumption.

(1) Acute alcohol poisoning

There have been and will continue to be many instances of voluntary consumption of a lethal dose of ethanol, both by alcoholics and by normal drinkers. The concentration of alcohol in the blood required for the drinker to "pass out" is generally more than 50% of the concentration that can cause death, and the margin of difference may have already been ingested at the time further consumption is prevented by unconsciousness. Chapter 2 (pp. 58–60) discusses some factors which affect the lethal dose of alcohol in humans and other species. Observations on physiological mechanisms for alcohol poisoning are summarized in Chapter 4 (pp. 188–191).

Clinically, the usual symptoms of alcohol poisoning are stupor or coma, lowered body temperature, cold and clammy skin, slow and noisy respiration, and accelerated heart rate. Metabolic acidosis is usually marked and aggravated by poor ventilation. Although these signs are well known, diagnostic errors are not rare. To avoid such errors, concentration of alcohol in body fluids or in expired air should be determined. Death is usually attributable to respiratory failure, due to a direct, depressant action of alcohol on the brain center which regulates respiration. However, in some cases hypotension and circulatory failure cause death which is typically delayed a number of hours after the blood alcohol concentration has begun to decline below the maximal level (*cf.* Chapter 4, p. 189).

There has been remarkably little progress in methods of therapy beyond those described in the excellent review by Newman (1941). Treatment has been limited to measures for alleviating the symptoms, because of insufficient knowledge of the mechanisms for resistance to and recovery from alcohol poisoning. The research reviewed in Chapter 5 (p. 227) and Chapter 10 (p. 661) suggests no techniques by which the depressant action of ethanol on the nerve cells might be counteracted directly. Therapy of acute alcohol poisoning has concentrated on two methods: attempts to speed the rate of elimination of alcohol, and supportive treatment with centrally stimulating drugs (analeptics) or other agents that might antagonize the effects of alcohol.

(a) Speeding the rate of elimination

There have been many attempts to develop treatments which accelerate the elimination of alcohol. The discussion of ethanol metabolism in Chapter 3 (p. 78) concluded that the principal route of elimination is by oxidation in the liver. There does not appear to be any plausible mechanism by which a drug or food could raise the rate of this process above the normal maximum in well-nourished individuals. For example, diuretics and respiratory stimulants contribute so little to the removal of alcohol that they have no practical value. Experiments with sugars, proteins, and various other substances, reviewed in Chapter 3, have led to the conclusion (p. 101) that, with the possible exception of fructose, they have no effect in well-nourished animals and increase ethanol elimination in fasted animals only by counteracting the effect of dietary deficiency on rate of liver metabolism. A combined glucose–insulin treatment was formerly advocated by many therapists as a means of speeding elimination of alcohol. The effectiveness of this treatment has not been proven, and in addition it is contraindicated because victims of alcohol poisoning often are hypoglycemic. Some clinicians have reported that more rapid sobering and alcohol elimination occurred after administration of triiodothyronine (Rawson *et al.*, 1957; Goldberg *et al.*, 1960) or after massive doses of vitamins, especially B_1, B_6 and B_{12} injected parenterally. However, experimenters have generally found no effect of these treatments on rate of alcohol elimination (Chapter 3, p. 103).

Various other methods of increasing alcohol excretion have been tried. Gastric lavage to remove unabsorbed alcohol may be helpful, if the therapist takes care to maintain free respiratory passage and to prevent transfer of fluid with high alcohol content from the stomach to the intestines. Koppanyi *et al.* (1961) successfully speeded removal of alcohol by massive intravenous infusion of physiological salt solution. Such fluid input must be balanced by urine flow in order to forestall pulmonary and cerebral edema and heart failure. There are clinical reports of successful treatment of ethanol poisoning by the use of an artificial kidney for hemodialysis, thereby speeding removal of substances in the blood (Wieth and Jørgensen, 1961; Perey *et al.*, 1965). In experiments on the effect of hemodialysis in dogs, after alcohol doses which are ordinarily lethal, Marc-Aurele and Schreiner (1960) reported 4-fold increase in the rate of alcohol elimination, and Koppanyi *et al.* (1961) found that the blood alcohol was lowered from 0.52% to 0.175% in 3 hours. Peritoneal dialysis, which has been used for treating methanol poisoning according to a review by Riccitelli (1967), is an alternative method of speeding ethanol elimination when facilities are not available for hemodialysis.

(b) Supportive treatment

The data summarized in Chapter 10 show that the action of alcohol is potentiated by sedative and hypnotic drugs. Therefore, depressant drugs should be avoided in cases of alcohol poisoning, whereas analeptics may be used in an effort to counteract the depressant effects of alcohol. Caffeine, ephedrine, nikethamide, picrotoxin, pentylenetetrazol, and amphetamine have all been recommended. McCrea and Taylor (1940) reported that after administration of sufficient alcohol to cause respiratory failure in dogs, pentylenetetrazol induced spontaneous breathing without altering rate of alcohol elimination or duration of coma. Similarly, Rosenbaum (1942), in an experiment on two alcoholics, found that 9 ml of 10% pentylenetetrazol restored consciousness and responsiveness after the subjects had been given enough alcohol to induce coma with blood alcohol levels above 0.4%. Picrotoxin, another powerful central stimulant, might also be expected to have therapeutic effects. However, the convulsant action of these drugs constitutes a serious disadvantage and has probably prevented their widespread use in treatment of alcohol poisoning.

Other analeptic drugs have generally not been effective in counteracting severe intoxication. Haggard *et al.* (1940), in an experiment on rats, found no effect of "non-toxic" doses of caffeine, dinitrophenol, strychnine, and amphetamine, and also of the antipyretics acetanilide, phenacetin, antipyrine, and aspirin, when the concentration of alcohol in the blood was sufficient to cause respiratory failure. According to Newman and Newman (1956), Dexedrine (D-amphetamine) and caffeine in therapeutic doses have so little effect in antagonizing even moderate doses of alcohol in humans that they lack practical value. Menninger-Lerchenthal (1960) and Wallgren and Tirri (1963) concluded that the central activating effect of amphetamine is insufficient to counteract the depressant action of severe alcohol intoxication. According to a brief report by DaVanzo *et al.* (1964), doxapram–HCl counteracts the depressant action of ethanol, but the authors gave no detailed information. A report that nalorphine counteracts the slowing of respiration caused by alcohol in rabbits (Frommel *et al.*, 1963) suggests a species difference since Goodman and Gilman (1965) state that nalorphine has no such action in humans.

Because of the lack of specific drugs for counteracting alcohol poisoning, treatment primarily consists of procedures for maintaining respiratory and cardiovascular functions and keeping the victim warm. For stimulation of respiration, carbon dioxide, as the most effective physiological activator of the respiratory center, has been used rather extensively (Newman, 1941). It has a stimulant effect on the respiratory center even in alcoholic coma (Haggard *et al.*, 1940). Artificial hyperventilation without administration of carbon dioxide (*cf.* Gervais, 1963) may be even more beneficial because it is more efficient in combating acidosis. Infusion of bicarbonate, and recently also intravenous administration of trihydroxymethylaminomethane (Gervais, 1963), have been used as specific treatments for acidosis. Hypertonic glucose may help to counteract the cerebral edema associated with hypotension and circulatory failure. While blood alcohol levels are rising, epinephrine tends to aggravate alcohol intoxication, probably by changes in the blood distribution which cause the concentration of alcohol in the brain to increase (Hulpieu and Cole, 1946). However, in rats epinephrine briefly counteracts the behavioral depression caused by moderate doses of alcohol (Wallgren and Tirri, 1963). In delayed collapse due to lowered blood pressure and circulatory failure, vasopressive amines such as epinephrine should be used (Gervais, 1963). Blood transfusions may also be necessary to raise the blood pressure. Massive doses of multiple vitamins have been reported to be beneficial (Pullar-Strecker, 1953; Cohen, 1961), but no mechanisms are apparent for therapeutic effects except in cases of gross malnutrition. Pyridoxine has been specifically recommended (Gould, 1953, cited acc. to Elbel and Schleyer, 1956; Teijeira and Martinez-Lage, 1961). However, in experiments with human subjects (Small *et al.*, 1955; review by Elbel and Schleyer, 1956), with dogs (Newman and Smith, 1959) and with rats (Wallgren, unpublished), pyridoxine did not modify intoxication or hasten recovery in a consistent, predictable manner. Vanha-Perttula (1960) has reported that 100 mg of ascorbic acid diminishes the eosinopenic response of humans to alcohol.

Several experiments show that ethanol is less toxic at high than at low blood glucose levels (Haggard and Greenberg, 1937; Tennent, 1941; Heim *et al.*, 1952; Hiestand *et al.*, 1953). Elevated blood glucose levels also diminish the effects of moderate levels of ethanol intoxication (Kanitz, 1936; Newman and Abramson, 1942; Mouriquand *et al.*, 1946; Sammalisto, 1962). Insulin, which lowers blood glucose, enhances the disturbance of motor incoordination (Sammalisto, 1962) and lowers the fatal dose of alcohol in rabbits (Barta, 1963). These effects of insulin may be due partly to direct synergism with alcohol, because insulin enhances the effects of ganglionic blocking agents in the cat's superior cervical ganglion (Minker and Koltai, 1965). Recent clinical reports on treatment of alcohol poisoning (Roche *et al.*, 1963; Vinke, 1964) emphasize the value of glucose infusions and warn against the use of insulin which may cause dangerous decrease of the blood glucose in the victims who in any case after prolonged drinking tend to be hypoglycemic (Chapter 3, p. 111).

Children seem to be more sensitive to alcohol than adults. One explanation might be that they are sensitive to the hypoglycemic effect of alcohol. A recent report by Szamosi (1967) gives support to the view that children are more prone to the effects of alcohol than grown people, since all cases with blood alcohol above 0.2% were unconscious. However, of 181 cases, only one was slightly hypoglycemic; all others had blood glucose within or slightly above the normal range. In spite of this, glucose infusion was found to be the most efficient therapy for restoration of consciousness and psycho-motor control. The reason for this counteraction by glucose of the depressant action of alcohol remains unexplained.

(2) The acutely ill alcoholic

In most cases of acute intoxication which require medical treatment, the patient is a chronic alcoholic who suffers from acute complications which arise directly from his drinking. If he is in a drunken coma, he must first be treated for acute alcohol poisoning by the methods summarized in the preceding discussion. After the intoxication has subsided, a number of complications requiring treatment may become apparent. The withdrawal state is the only one of these which is specifically and directly caused by the ingestion of excessive amounts of alcohol. A variety of additional complications, such as psychoses, gastric distress, acute liver disease, infections, muscular and myocardial afflictions, and excessive fluid and electrolyte loss, may have complex origins in such pathological conditions as injuries, poor nutrition, diarrhea, vomiting, and excessive perspiration, associated with the alcoholism. The patient should be carefully checked for all of these ailments. In any case, treatment for the first few days is essentially a medical problem.

Much of the material reviewed in prior chapters of this book contributes to an understanding of the condition of the acutely ill alcoholic, but there has been hardly any acceptable experimental investigation aimed directly at this particular condition. Animal experimentation on this topic has been prevented by the fact that until quite recently, it has not been possible to induce in any infrahuman species a condition analogous to that of the chronic alcoholic. Essig and Lam (1968) have now described in dogs tremulousness, convulsions, hallucinatory behavior, and even death following withdrawal of alcohol. There is an overwhelmingly extensive clinical literature on chronic alcoholism, but the multiplicity of histories and complications in alcoholic patients precludes the replication of uniform cases necessary for a conclusive, controlled study. The large variety of available drugs and methods of modern medicine adds to the problem, because no consensus has been developed concerning the best treatment procedures.

Drug treatment in alcohol withdrawal has largely progressed by trial and error because there is no firm empirical basis for a more sophisticated approach. Victor (1966, 1968) has contributed thoughtful and critical discussions of the therapy of the alcohol withdrawal syndrome. He emphasizes that one principal shortcoming in much of the clinical literature is failure to define the nature and severity of the condition that has been treated. Henry and Mann (1965) have written an excellent general review of diagnosis and treatment of various manifestations of delirium. A brief but balanced and good discussion of the treatment of the alcohol withdrawal state is found in Goodman and Gilman (1965). It is extremely difficult to perform truly controlled evaluation of medicinal treatment. The many problems and pitfalls in procedures and statistical design are well discussed by Benor and Ditman (1966, 1967). With the present multitude of treatments, even the most carefully performed double-blind study comparing drug with placebo is not entirely satisfactory, because an important consideration is the value of one drug in comparison with others. Selection of drugs must be based not only on their efficacy in controlling the withdrawal symptoms but also on side effects and on tendency to prolong dependence. It is desirable to match the drug's potency to the severity of the patient's symptoms. Therefore, valuable information is provided by comparative evaluation of different drugs, as reported by Sereny and Kalant (1965), Harfst *et al.* (1967), Golbert *et al.* (1967), Motto (1968) and Kaim *et al.* (1969).

Since the alcohol withdrawal illness is a real dependence syndrome, one method of treatment has been to use agents capable of substituting for alcohol. The results of the few studies on cross-dependence cited in Chapter 10 (p. 672) are supported by the clinical experience that general depressants, hypnotics, and sedatives are effective. These agents should be administered only after the alcohol has been eliminated, in order to prevent dangerous combined actions. Alcohol itself may of course be used, but in addition to the obvious disadvantage that dependence is prolonged, a steady level is difficult to maintain. Paraldehyde, chloral hydrate, various barbiturates, and among newer agents meprobamate and gluthetimide have all been used, but there is no consensus on which is preferable. Paraldehyde, one of the earliest drugs used in the management of withdrawal illness, is still considered by some experienced clinicians to be the best (Victor, 1966, 1968; Gross, 1967). As a rationale for paraldehyde treatment, Gross (1967) stressed that it effectively controls the disturbance of delta sleep caused by intoxication (cf. Chapter 9, p. 507). Pentobarbital with its well-known anticonvulsant properties effectively combats the withdrawal symptoms in dogs (Essig et al., 1969).

Encouraging results have been reported with a new hypnotic, clomethiazole (chlormethiazole, hemineurin), which Laborit and Coirault (1957) introduced as a treatment for delirium. Its use has been widespread in Europe, and it has also been tested in America. The proceedings of a symposium (Frisch, 1966) contain a comprehensive review of metabolic, pharmacological, toxicological, and clinical information on this rapidly acting hypnotic and anticonvulsant which is structurally related to thiamine (vitamin B_1). According to some accounts (e.g., Amler and Bergener, 1965; Huhn and Böcker, 1966) clomethiazole is the drug of choice in the treatment of alcohol withdrawal illness. Glatt (1966), in a comparison of this drug with glutethimide and methyprylone, found clomethiazole particularly satisfactory for control of delirium tremens. He stressed that the treatment should not be greatly prolonged in view of the risk of new dependence. In another controlled trial, Harfst et al. (1967) found that clomethiazole did not offer any particular advantage over amobarbital in producing sedation, relieving disturbances of sleep, or reducing excessive pulse rate, blood pressure, palmar sweat, and tremor. However, most of the clinical experiences seem so promising that more data should be gathered, particularly on side effects of clomethiazole compared with other sedative drugs.

One striking feature of the trials with drugs capable of substituting for alcohol is that such diverse chemical structures are effective. This suggests that alcohol acts in a rather unspecific manner, so that it may be very difficult to discover a drug which checks the withdrawal symptoms without the drawbacks of causing excessive sedation and prolonging dependence. The situation may be changed when more concrete and detailed knowledge is obtained about how alcohol alters the functioning of the central nervous system.

Another method of treating the alcohol withdrawal illness has been with the use of centrally acting drugs known to control excitement and tension without the sedative or hypnotic actions which are synergistic with the effect of alcohol. This method of drug therapy has been very actively developed in recent years with the advent of many new agents. Illustrative statistical information on the variety of drugs used for treatment of the acute withdrawal state of alcoholism has been compiled by the present authors from the print-outs of references on therapy of alcoholics, stored on magnetic tape and made available by the National Clearinghouse for Mental Health Information, U.S.A. National Institute of Mental Health. Of 181 titles published between 1957 and 1965, 137 mention the use of a total of 59 tranquilizing, hallucinogenic, sedative, and even antidepressant drugs. The drugs most frequently used were chlorpromazine (21 citations), promazine (17), reserpine (15), chlordiazepoxide (14), and meprobamate (13). 5 citations mention aversive drugs, 12 are on drug treatment without specifying the name of the drug, 7 deal with the use of vitamins or enzyme cofactors, and 2 mention magnesium. Some reports claim that combinations, such as chlorpromazine with disulfiram, or an antidepressant with a sedative, are more efficient than single drugs in controlling agitation and restlessness.

Benor and Ditman (1966, 1967) considered the benzodiazepines (chlordiazepoxide and diazepam) to be the most satisfactory agents, followed by the phenothiazine drugs, such as chlorpromazine. The phenothiazines were also recommended by Henry and Mann (1965) and by McNichol et al. (1967). These drugs seem to control the agitation of the withdrawal state by a fairly localized action which differs from the action of the sedatives. Thorough examination of data on drug treatment in the withdrawal state may provide some useful clues to the neural mechanisms involved.

Some drugs have been used primarily as supportive measures rather than for specific antagonism of the withdrawal symptoms. In the field of endocrine treatment, administration of adrenocortical hormones was enthusiastically recommended around 1950 (Tintera and Lovell, 1949; Smith, 1950; Izikowitz et al., 1952). However, other workers (Smith and Brown, 1952; Cummins and Friend, 1954; Owen, 1954) shortly thereafter presented evidence that adrenocortical hormones are valuable for supportive treatment but have no outstanding therapeutic value. Similar experiences have been reported more recently by McNichol et al. (1967). When a highly agitated patient reaches a state of adrenal exhaustion, adrenocortical hormones may be helpful, but this treatment should probably be rather brief. Further investigations are needed on the role of endocrine disturbance in the condition of the acutely ill alcoholic.

Water, electrolytes, vitamins and glucose have been given rather indiscriminately without consistent evidence for specific value in combating postalcoholic psychomotor agitation. However, this fluid and nutrition therapy provides helpful, supportive treatment when judiciously used in relation to the variable condition of the patient. Endocrine disturbance due to alcoholism has generally been located in the supra-optical–posthypophyseal system (Chapter 9, p. 533). Baïsset *et al.* (1965) have reported preliminary trials on control of thirst and water balance in alcoholics by means of posthypophyseal extract. Knott *et al.* (1967) emphasize that, contrary to general beliefs, overhydration is common in the withdrawal state. Use of the diuretic compound furosemide in treatment of alcohol withdrawal is described by Knott and Beard (1969). Vetter *et al.* (1967) recently found a rather consistent correlation between presence of cardiac arrhythmias and subnormal blood potassium in acute alcoholic withdrawal. The cardiac abnormality usually could be corrected by administration of potassium. Vetter *et al.* (1967), in a discussion of fluid–glucose–ion therapy, noted that a patient's condition may deteriorate if he is given only glucose in water without ions. The glucose must also be accompanied by sufficient thiamine to avoid neural complications caused by nutritional deficiency. It is possible that thiamine further improves functioning of the central nervous system by a more direct mechanism than the metabolic and nutritional effects.

With the exception of some specific types of malnutrition, which respond very rapidly to the appropriate treatment, other nutritional therapy is purely supportive, contributing to the slow process of rehabilitation rather than alleviating acute alcoholic sickness. However, Williams (1968) found an amino acid mixture to aid in overcoming the agitation of the withdrawal state. In another study, Corley and Hoff (1968) found no effect of adding a protein supplement to a regimen which included a nutritious diet. The result of Williams (1968) may simply indicate that good nutrition helps, but does not necessarily prove that a particular kind of protein supplementation provides any advantage over that of a nutritious food generally.

D. Therapy of chronic alcoholism

The methods of treatment reviewed in the preceding section have the limited goal of relieving the physical symptoms associated with intoxication, withdrawal illness, and the various types of damage resulting from prolonged, excessive alcohol consumption. The long-term goal of therapy is to help the patient to break the habit of excessive drinking after the immediate physical problem has subsided, or preferably before it has occurred. Successful achievement of this goal has the important effect of preventing the further development of physical and mental deterioration associated with chronic alcoholism. Since the damage caused by excessive drinking generally seems to be reversible until it has progressed to an extreme degree, any improvements in effectiveness of therapy will provide tremendous benefit to the chronic alcoholics and to society.

Many different methods of therapy have been applied to chronic alcoholics. Reviews by Bowman and Jellinek (1941), Voegtlin and Lemere (1942) and Gibbins (1953) include the full range of therapeutic methods which have been reported. Reviews of more limited types of therapy are by Quinn (1967) on aversion therapy, Benor and Ditman (1966, 1967) on the use of tranquilizing drugs, and Hill and Blane (1967) on methods of psychotherapy. The 49 studies reviewed in the latter article are summarized in a separate document, deposited with the ADI Auxiliary Publications Project, a photoprint or microfilm of which is available as specified in the article (footnote 13, p. 100).

Brief accounts of various methods of therapy are given in an article by Ruth Fox (1967b), in many of the chapters in a book edited by Fox (1967a) and in a book edited by Catanzaro (1968). In spite of the importance of alcoholism as a public health problem and the large number of patients being treated for this condition, only one book (Blum and Blum, 1967) is devoted to a description of methods of therapy. Its account is rather superficial but also sophisticated and suitable both as a physician's reference book and for enlightening the general public.

The large amount of literature on therapy of alcoholics provides very little conclusive proof of therapeutic effectiveness. The shortcomings of the studies have been emphasized especially in the reviews by Voegtlin and Lemere (1942) and by Hill and Blane (1967). In the present section of this chapter, the evaluation of methods of therapy begins with a discussion of the general problems in conducting therapy and evaluating its success. A controversial question, related to theories of the etiology of alcoholism, is whether the ultimate goal of therapy must be permanent abstinence. The increasing number of reports of controlled drinking by former alcoholics are discussed here. The next topic of this section is a review and evaluation of physical methods conducted in a single session or a brief series of sessions, designed to train the patient to avoid alcohol by associating liquor with an unpleasant stimulus ("aversion treatment") or by the dramatic experience of the hallucinogenic drug LSD. This is followed by a review of chronic, physical treatments, including aversively protective drugs and various substitute drugs or supportive treatments. The following topic, psychotherapy, comprises a wide range of individual and group treatments, some brief and others chronic. Individual treatment includes such diverse techniques as psychoanalysis and training aversion for alcohol by hypnotic suggestion. Group treatment includes therapy led by a psychiatrist and the generally anti-clinical fellowship of Alcoholics Anonymous. The concluding section of this chapter, a review of factors which affect therapeutic success, is intended to integrate findings from studies with the various methods of therapy.

(1) General problems

Research on therapy requires both effective treatment methods and accurate measurements of their success. Unfortunately, such research has been severely hampered by obstacles against conducting and evaluating therapy for chronic alcoholics. Even the ultimate goal of treatment is disputed. Most therapists try to induce abstinence from liquor, which is an immediate requirement for all alcoholics and a permanent necessity for most. However, a complete cure of all aspects of the alcoholic craving would require the ability to consume liquor in a controlled manner. Fierce controversy has been aroused by reports of controlled drinking by former alcoholics.

(a) Conducting and evaluating therapy

Several characteristics of most alcoholics frustrate the therapist's efforts. Any type of addictive craving, once established, is very difficult to cure. The alcoholic's prepotent and thoroughly learned habit of getting drunk is facilitated by the fact that liquor is readily available to most adults and is customarily consumed in many social situations. The pharmacological effects of the alcohol itself tend to reduce restraints and inhibitions, so that intoxication is a tendency in every drinking situation.

Certain typical traits of alcoholics, described in earlier sections of this chapter, add to the obstacles against successful therapy. Passivity, dependence and immaturity are combined with a suspicious and resistant attitude toward authority figures, including physicians. A strong tendency for alcoholics to deny their problem generally prevents them from accepting treatment until their physical and social condition has deteriorated to a degree which impedes therapeutic efforts. Among alcoholics who do submit to treatment, therapeutic efforts tend to aggravate the conflicts and anxieties which in the past motivated the excessive drinking. The relapses and failures may be especially frustrating to the therapist because of the exaggerated optimism and show of high resolve characteristic of the alcoholic during the intervals between drinking bouts and especially at the outset of therapy. Therefore, most physicians and hospitals have been reluctant to accept alcoholics. The large number of alcoholics contributes to this tendency to reject them, because a doctor or hospital who welcomes them risks being deluged with cases of this type, most of them returning again and again after relapses. However, the high prevalence of this destructive condition also means that even a small improvement in the effectiveness of therapy would contribute great benefit to society. This enhances the value of efforts by various individuals and organizations to develop and apply superior methods of therapy for chronic alcoholics.

A crucial requirement of research on treatment methods is accurate measurement of therapeutic effectiveness. This can best be evaluated by comparison with an untreated control group, but treatment facilities are reluctant to deny help to potential patients and usually cannot prevent them from seeking help elsewhere. Precise evaluation of a particular treatment method is possible only in isolation, without any additional treatment, but most programs include a wide variety of therapeutic activities, including medical treatment, institutional support, and the expressed concern and sympathy of one or more therapists, in addition to whatever specialized techniques may be the focus of research attention.

Most studies of therapy effectiveness have been completely lacking in untreated control groups, although the proportion of patients who recover without special therapy would be expected to vary considerably among samples of alcoholics with different characteristics. Some data indicate recovery by many alcoholics without special therapeutic efforts. Lemere (1953) obtained from his patients life histories of 500 deceased, alcoholic relatives, most of whom had not received professional treatment. Although severe, unremitted cases were prevalent in this sample, drawn mostly from an earlier generation, 21% were reported to have stopped or moderated

References p. 779

their drinking. Kendell and Staton (1966) reported on 66 alcoholics referred to the Outpatient Department of a hospital, who either refused treatment or were not given treatment because of poor prospects of success. In spite of these unfavorable characteristics, 21 % of the patients were abstinent or drank in a controlled manner for at least a year at the time of follow-up. However, most of them had received therapy from other sources. Many reports of therapeutic methods show no convincing benefit in comparison with these outcomes reported for untreated alcoholics. Bowman and Jellinek (1941), in their review of various types of psychotherapy, concluded that 25–30 % of patients generally were found to attain two or more years of abstinence. In most of the studies reviewed recently by Hill and Blane (1967), less than half of the patients achieved a less stringent criterion of either abstinence or improvement.

Dramatically high rates of cure or improvement have been reported in some of the studies reviewed by Hill and Blane (1967), but none of these included an equivalent control group of cases who were untreated or treated by a different, less effective method. Systematic comparisons of different types of therapy (Ends and Page, 1957, 1959; Wallerstein, 1956, 1957) showed only moderate differences among them in effectiveness. Methodological deficiencies, emphasized by Hill and Blane (1967), severely limit the conclusions that can be drawn from most of the studies.

Reports of percentage of therapeutic success should include all cases introduced to the treatment rather than only those who completed treatment and were available in the follow-up. This is an important methodological consideration, especially because therapists and clinics generally lose contact with a large proportion of their alcoholic patients. In a study by Gerard and Saenger (1966, pp. 104–105), the clinics lost contact with 25 % of the cases and thus obtained no follow-up information from them. These were characterized predominantly by low social stability at intake and by low extent of contact with the clinic. Since these two attributes are associated with lower percentage of recovery, the missing cases were probably predominantly non-abstinent and unimproved.

Although the value of research on efficacy of therapy depends largely on the accuracy of the follow-up information, in most studies it is collected hastily and incompletely, sometimes only by a mailed questionnaire. Follow-up information obtained from the patient should be verified if possible by independent reports, especially because alcoholics are notoriously untrustworthy and often eager to give an impression of being cured. In particular, reports of "improvement" should be regarded with skepticism, especially if a sample shows a large percentage of cases in this category compared with the percentage who are reported to be abstinent. However, encouraging evidence for potential reliability of those measures is given in a report by Gerard and Saenger (1966) on information obtained from the family or alcoholism agency to verify the classification based on a follow-up interview with the alcoholic. Discrepant information was obtained on only 2% of 125 alcoholics who claimed abstinence and on only 6% of 34 alcoholics who claimed controlled drinking.

(b) Is permanent abstinence necessary?

The first purpose of therapy is to require or help the patient to abstain from alcohol. Chafetz (1965) has reviewed a number of studies indicating that the abstinence enforced by prolonged imprisonment or hospitalization may have therapeutic efficacy. Abstinence also is the objective of most of the specific treatment methods reviewed later in this chapter. In studies of therapeutic success, the most valid criterion has been abstinence for a prolonged period of a year or more. Studies by Bolman (1965) and Pattison (1966) show clearly that improvement is associated with complete abstinence from alcohol. The category of "improved" in the follow-up information is likely to signify a resumption of addictive drinking which has not yet renewed the physical pathology which required treatment originally. This indicates the desirability of an adequately lengthy follow-up period.

Permanent abstinence is necessary according to some of the theories of the etiology of alcoholism, reviewed earlier in this chapter. Such theories include abnormal biochemical susceptibility to alcohol, such as an allergy or the genetotrophic theory of Williams (1959), and the development of irreversible biochemical or other physiological changes as a result of exposure to alcohol. The permanent inability of alcoholics to control their drinking is a widely publicized doctrine of most Alcoholics Anonymous members. The evidence reviewed earlier in the present chapter and in Chapter 9 indicates no biochemical basis for addictive drinking, either before or after introduction to alcohol beyond the habituation and threat of withdrawal symptoms at rather advanced stages of drinking. The loss of control over drinking appears to be a behavior pattern which becomes strongly established as a habit. The alcoholic by definition has become incapable of moderate, controlled drinking. Each episode of intoxication strengthens the habit of excessive drinking and further weakens the control over this behavior, because of the emotional needs served by intoxication and the weakening of inhibitions and restraints under the influence of alcohol. This mechanism of learning seems sufficient to explain why most alcoholics are permanently unable to drink in a controlled manner. It is also difficult for alcoholics to abstain, but any habitual pattern of excessive response is easier to avoid than to stop once begun. Thus abstinence is an obvious necessity as a first step in the treatment of alcoholism, and most therapists strongly recommended it to their patients as a permanent change in behavior.

In spite of the almost universal therapeutic goal of permanent abstinence, a substantial number of alcoholics have been reported to acquire a pattern of moderate, controlled drinking. Shea (1954), in a description of a single case who resumed moderate drinking after five years' abstinence, emphasized that it was an unusual instance. Lemere (1953), in a survey of 500 alcoholics, most of them untreated, found that 14 of them (3%) decreased the quantity consumed and degree of intoxication to the level of normal drinking. Subsequent to these accounts, four reports by therapists have claimed controlled drinking by a total of 33 (10%) out of 344 alcoholics (Selzer and Holloway, 1957; Davies, 1962; Kendell, 1965; Bailey and Stewart, 1967). In a study of eight outpatient clinics (Gerard and Saenger, 1966), 41 (5%) out of 797 cases were reported to be controlled drinkers at the time of follow-up. Reinert and Bowen (1968) and Räkköläinen and Turunen (1969) have described ten more such cases (4%) among a total of 227 alcoholics. The reports of controlled drinking by former alcoholics have aroused lively discussion (Tiebout et al., 1963; Bolman, 1965; Pattison, 1966). The occurrence of this behavior seems well established. Arguments that they had not been truly addictive drinkers, or that their subsequent drinking was not truly controlled, may be valid for some but not all of these cases.

Gerard and Saenger (1966), in a comparison of the patients who were controlled drinkers with those who were abstinent at follow-up, found no significant difference in most attributes, but the clinic contact and the percentage of patients treated with tranquilizers had been reliably less for the controlled drinkers. This suggests a higher degree of self-reliance among the patients who became controlled drinkers. Advancing age also may enable controlled drinking, perhaps due to alleviation of some of the conflicts and anxieties which motivate excessive drinking. The study by Lemere (1953) indicates abatement of the drinking problem in some aged alcoholics. Drew (1968) has reviewed both sociological and clinical evidence for spontaneous decrease in the incidence of heavy or uncontrolled drinking in elderly people.

Alcoholism may be regarded as an expression of pathological characteristics which are not removed by abstinence. Gerard *et al.* (1962) reported severe character disorders remaining in many alcoholic patients after they had become abstinent. Conversely, relief of the conflicts and anxieties which motivate alcoholism should enable the patient to drink in a controlled manner. Addictive drinkers are more differentiated from normal, controlled drinkers than from abstainers (Barry, 1968). The ultimate goal of research on therapy should be the development of methods which enable controlled drinking rather than permanent abstinence. However, this research is impeded by the fact that it would be dangerous to require or urge abstinent alcoholics to attempt controlled drinking. Therapeutic efforts begin with enforcing or inducing complete abstinence. Patients are almost invariably told that they must remain permanently abstinent. Studies of the circumstances under which controlled drinking can be resumed must rely on accounts of patients who on their own initiative decide to try controlled drinking after a period of abstinence. No responsible therapist would encourage patients to try this experiment on themselves.

(2) Brief physical interventions

All methods of treating chronic alcoholics must attempt to produce a difficult and far-reaching change in the patient's behavior throughout the rest of his life. However, therapists are understandably attracted to techniques which offer the hope of permanent therapeutic effects resulting from only one or a few sessions. The incentive for developing and using brief methods of therapy is intensified by the shortage of therapists and treatment facilities for the large number of alcoholics.

Two principal types of brief physical intervention have been used extensively for treatment of alcoholics. One is aversion training, also called conditioning or counter conditioning. This is an attempt to induce a lasting aversion for alcohol by one or a few sessions in which the sight and taste of alcohol is closely associated with an intensely unpleasant experience induced by a physical or chemical agent such as an emetic drug, painful electric shock, or paralysis of breathing. The second type of brief physical intervention is the use of LSD (lysergic acid diethylamide-25) to induce an intense hallucinogenic experience which results in alteration of the emotions and motivations underlying the excessive drinking. The severity and danger of both of these types of physical intervention preclude frequent repetitions of the treatment.

(a) Aversion training

Franks (1958) and Quinn (1967) have contributed extensive reviews and evaluations of aversion therapy, although much of the material on learning theory, presented by both authors, has not yet been effectively applied to the problems of alcoholism. Blum and Blum (1967) give practical details of the various specific treatment methods but also emphasize the limitations and dangers of this type of therapy. Characteristics of the most commonly used drugs (apomorphine, emetine, disulfiram, calcium carbimide) are summarized briefly by LaVerne (1962).

Aversion therapy consists of training the patient to associate the sight, smell, and taste of an alcoholic beverage with an unpleasant reaction caused by a drug, painful electric shock, or other physical treatment. The appetitive approach response to alcohol is punished by the immediately following aversive reaction, and the patient is expected to transfer the resulting avoidance from the clinical situation to all other occasions when he has an opportunity to drink. The treatment is commonly referred to as conditioning, but a more accurate description would be counter conditioning of the appetitive, approach response which the alcoholic has previously learned toward liquor.

The drugs which have been used in aversion therapy generally produce nausea and vomiting as their principal symptoms. This effect may be especially compatible with counter conditioning of the craving for alcohol because excessive intake of liquor also causes nausea and vomiting. In effect the counter conditioning sessions cause this response to be generalized from a high dose of alcohol to the conditioned stimuli of the sight and taste of liquor. This connection with the natural effect of alcohol may account for the fact that the conditioning, accomplished in only a few sessions, may persist as a stable reaction for a long time. The emetic agents used most frequently for therapy are apomorphine, emetine, and calcium carbimide. Techniques and results in the use of emetine on several thousand alcoholic patients are described in a series of papers (Lemere et al., 1942; Voegtlin and Broz, 1949; Lemere and O'Hollaren, 1950; Lemere and Voegtlin, 1950), and by a separate therapist on several hundred patients (Thimann, 1949a, b). In both series of patients, prolonged abstinence was reported for less than half of those introduced to the treatment, a recovery rate which does not appear to be definitely superior over that obtained with other methods of therapy. Claims by the authors of higher recovery rates were based on the inappropriate devices of excluding the patients unavailable for follow-up and including patients who relapsed and were treated again a long interval after their original treatment.

Aversion therapy was compared with other treatment methods in one of the few studies with adequate controls, including random selection of patients for the different treatments and careful collection of follow-up information (Wallerstein, 1956, 1957). The aversion therapy procedures are specified by Hammersley (1957). In the follow-up survey, only 24% of the 50 patients given this treatment were classified as improved. This percentage was lower than for any of the other therapy methods. A highly compliant and cooperative spirit may be necessary for patients to complete and benefit from this punishing form of treatment. Among the 50 patients, a group of 15 classified as aggressive responded unfavorably to this treatment; only one of these 15 (7%) maintained a regular follow-up contact with the hospital.

The emetic drugs have potentially severe side effects in addition to inducing nausea and vomiting, and descriptions of emetine therapy have included precautions and warnings (Lemere et al., 1942; Thimann, 1949b). Since these drugs should be avoided by patients with heart disease or other pathological physical conditions, their use is limited to physically healthy subjects, who unfortunately are not prevalent among alcoholics. A more general limitation to the effectiveness of this therapy is that the counter conditioning occurs only in a particular situation, usually alone with a clinician. It seems unlikely that the vomiting or other aversive reaction to alcohol would occur dependably when the patient undertakes to drink in his usual social situation, especially if the beverage is different from the one used in the counter conditioning. Administration of aversion therapy to alcoholics in a group might be expected to help the counter conditioning transfer to the typical drinking situation and also provide social facilitation of the aversion training. According to a report on 20 patients (Miller et al., 1960), group therapy of this type was unusually successful. Other variations in procedures might be expected to have important effects, because the aversion therapy represents only one component of the interaction between patient and therapist. In the emetine treatment program for several thousand patients, the aversion therapy was supplemented in many cases by psychotherapy

References p. 779

while the patient was narcotized with thiopental (Lemere and O'Hollaren, 1950) in order to relieve the nervous and emotional tension which motivated drinking.

A serious disadvantage of aversion therapy with emetic drugs is the difficulty of controlling the timing of onset of the symptoms. Effective conditioning depends on the presentation of the unconditioned stimulus of nausea and vomiting, after rather than before the unconditioned stimulus (exposure to alcohol) but with a time interval as short as possible, preferably one second or less. There is a variable delay from the intake of the emetic drug to the onset of the symptoms, and many therapists have presented the alcohol only after the initial symptoms of nausea. It would probably be preferable to instruct the subject to sip liquor continuously, beginning immediately after the drug is taken, to insure optimal association between the drinking and the symptoms.

Disulfiram is a drug which causes vomiting and other unpleasant physical reactions only in combination with alcohol. Therefore, the use of this drug in aversion therapy ensures that the counter conditioning is associated with the immediately preceding response of drinking. However, the dangerous severity of the reaction is a strong deterrent to the use of disulfiram as the counter conditioning agent (Blum and Blum, 1967). A recently introduced counter conditioning agent is painful electric shock. This permits precise control of the timing and also of the severity of the unconditioned stimulus. It can be applied to all alcoholics regardless of their physical condition, and the sessions can be briefer and more precisely controlled. However, the emotional and muscular reactions to electric shock seem very different from the effects of alcohol overdose, so that the counter conditioning with electric shock seems likely to be more difficult to establish and less stable. Therapeutic efficiency is unimpressive according to several studies (McGuire and Vallance, 1964; Hsu, 1965; Blake, 1965, 1967) especially if one takes into account the cases who failed to complete treatment (Hsu, 1965) and those who relapsed and received further therapy (Blake, 1965, 1967).

Another type of unconditioned stimulus for aversion therapy is intravenous injection of succinylcholine, which paralyzes the muscles and thus suppresses breathing for about one minute. This reaction of apnea occurs rapidly and predictably and thus is easy to control, but it seems greatly different from the unconditioned aversive responses to alcohol overdose and thus difficult to establish as an anticipatory, conditioned stimulus to alcohol. This treatment does not seem to have much therapeutic efficacy, according to reports on the same patients (Sanderson *et al.*, 1963; Madill *et al.*, 1966; Laverty, 1966), and a separate study (Farrar *et al.*, 1968).

A feature which all the methods of aversion therapy have in common is that they counteract only the symptom of excessive drinking without directly affecting the motivations which impel this pathological behavior. Since these methods can function only to support or strengthen the patient's own desire to stop drinking, they can only be effective with those who already are trying to resist their craving for alcohol. It seems likely that the greatest therapeutic effect of counter conditioning is to help prevent the patient from making the initial decisions in the chain of actions which lead to the resumption of drinking. Thus, for example, it may help the patient to avoid going to the bar or joining in a drinking group rather than specifically inhibiting the drinking when he has decided to do it or producing the aversive reaction when he actually resumes drinking. Since the counter conditioning is generally not specifically directed against the initial actions of the sequence, its effect seems to be primarily supportive in conjunction with other therapy and with the patient's desire to stop drinking. The necessary cooperation of the patient may be aided by the elaborate procedures, symbolizing an earnest effort to help. The self-destructive motive of many alcoholics, associated with a need for punishment, may enhance the therapeutic value of this punishing procedure (Wallerstein, 1956, 1957).

(b) LSD treatment

The hallucinogenic drug lysergic acid diethylamide-25 (LSD), given in minute doses, often results in an intense perceptual and emotional experience. This has been used in an effort to disrupt the pathological pattern associated with uncontrolled drinking. A possibly important therapeutic aspect of this treatment is its dramatic chemical intervention which may express the physician's concern for the patient without the disadvantage of the severe punishment of aversion therapy. In spite of this drug's recent introduction and widespread illegal misuse, it has been tested extensively as an aid to therapy for various psychopathological conditions, and a substantial number of studies have appeared in a short time. Alcoholism appears to be one of the principal types of psychopathology for which therapeutic effects of LSD have been claimed. Ditman (1967) has given a concise review of some of the studies on LSD therapy in alcoholics. Highly critical evaluations of research methods have been made by Smart and Storm (1964) and by Smart *et al.* (1966, 1967b). Accounts by Hoffer and Osmond (1967, 1968)

References p. 779

and by Godfrey (1968) include a defense of the therapeutic efficacy of this drug. A book edited by Abramson (1967) contains many reports and discussions of the use of LSD for therapy of alcoholics, but most of the accounts of therapeutic results have been published in more detail elsewhere, either earlier or subsequently.

Most of the reports of therapeutic efficacy of LSD have lacked a control group to determine the effects obtained without this treatment. In several cases, the patients have been described as having an unusually poor prognosis so that even a low percentage of improvement is impressive. Smith (1958) reported improvement in 50% of 24 especially difficult cases at an average of one year after a single LSD session. Improvement in more than half of the cases treated with LSD was claimed by Chwelos et al. (1959), MacLean et al. (1961) and Jensen (1962). This last study (Jensen, 1962) reported equivalent improvement in only 23% of comparison patients not treated with LSD, but there was no indication of random, non-biased assignment of the patients to the different treatment conditions. O'Reilly and Funk (1964) reported abstinence by 38% of 68 alcoholics at an average of 14 months after an LSD session.

Some vivid descriptions but no statistical analyses are given in reports of the use of LSD treatment on a large number of alcoholic patients (Kurland et al., 1967a, b). Surveys of the attitudes of alcoholics about an LSD session give evidence for beneficial effects (Ditman et al., 1962; Sarett et al., 1966).

Hoffer and Osmond (1967, 1968) have described procedures for LSD treatment, emphasizing the desirability that the LSD session be an integral part of the psychotherapeutic procedure, conducted in an informal, attractive setting with an experienced, friendly therapist who is not concurrently under the influence of LSD. They characterize LSD as the most effective of available treatments for alcoholics, with the exception of those cases, comprising about one-third of alcoholics, in whose blood the presence of malvaria allegedly indicates a basic psychotic illness. However, the evidence has not been given in detail nor verified by independent investigators. Attempts have been made by others to relate improvement after LSD treatment to diagnostic characteristics of the patient (Chwelos et al., 1959) or to his response to LSD (O'Reilly and Funk, 1964) but without any well defined differentiation between those who improved and those who failed to improve.

These reports by various therapists give considerable evidence for therapeutic efficacy of LSD, but most of the studies suffer from methodological faults which are pointed out by Smart and Storm (1964). Smart *et al.* (1966, 1967b) reiterated the requirements for a controlled experiment and reported on such a study comparing the effects of three treatment conditions (LSD, ephedrine, control). They found improvement in all three groups with no significant difference among them. The small number of 10 patients in each group may have been an important factor in this negative result, because the data suggested more gain by both the LSD and ephedrine than by the control group and also slight superiority of the LSD over ephedrine treatment. Their procedures have been criticized for failing to provide optimal conditions for LSD therapy (MacLean and Wilby, 1967; Fadiman, 1967; Hoffer and Osmond, 1968). A rejoinder has been made by Smart *et al.* (1967a). A negative report on therapeutic efficacy of LSD on female alcoholics (Van Dusen *et al.*, 1967) was characterized by an unusually high degree of average improvement in all the patients. Johnson (1969), in a study of 95 alcoholics, divided into groups with and without LSD therapy, likewise reported improvement by all groups and no statistically significant differences among the groups, but no details of the data were given. Controlled experiments by Hollister *et al.* (1969) on 72 alcoholics and by Ludwig *et al.* (1969) on 176 alcoholics give evidence for greater improvement during the first few months after the LSD than control therapy, but subsequently this difference disappeared.

The LSD treatment has almost always been given in conjunction with psychotherapy, and even more than other types of treatment, the effects of LSD are difficult to dissociate from the accompanying psychotherapy and other experiences. Treatment with this highly dangerous drug must be limited to one or a few sessions and thus may help to initiate recovery but cannot sustain it throughout the long time necessary.

(3) Chronic physical aids to therapy

The necessity for a long-lasting change in alcoholics gives compelling logic to a corresponding chronic application of therapeutic procedures. The physical methods may be divided into two principal types. One is the chronic administration of aversively protective drugs; the second is the use of substitute or supportive treatments, including tranquilizing or antidepressant drugs, and nutritional or other rehabilitative treatment. Such methods are insufficient by themselves and thus must be used as portions of a total treatment program. However, the chronic application of physical aids to therapy has the important value of demonstrating a long-term concern for the patient, and the treatment procedures facilitate recurrent communication between therapist and patient.

(a) Aversively protective drugs

An important potential benefit of hospitalization for the alcoholic is the enforcement of abstinence (Chafetz, 1965). The aversively protective drugs provide the opportunity for enforcing abstinence during outpatient treatment. Because of ethical and practical considerations, this chemical enforcement of abstinence depends on the voluntary cooperation of the patient in swallowing the pill every day. Many alcoholics have the necessary rational desire to abstain and thus are eligible for this method of protection from the sudden, overpowering craving and the impulsive decision to drink which afflict most alcoholics.

Chapter 10 (pp. 674–679) includes a discussion of the physiological mechanisms for the interactions of the aversively protective drugs with ethanol. Articles by Ruth Fox (1958, 1968) give clinical advice and information based on her use of disulfiram (Antabuse) on more than 2000 alcoholics. Even without alcohol consumption, heavy doses of disulfiram may have severe side effects, notably depression, lethargy and headaches, but lower doses can apparently minimize such symptoms.

Research reports suggest that disulfiram has a high degree of therapeutic efficacy. A controlled comparison of four treatment methods (Wallerstein, 1956, 1957) included 47 patients treated with disulfiram. A higher proportion of these completed the inpatient treatment (83%) and were classified as improved after two years (53%) than with any of the other three treatment methods. Details of the disulfiram treatment, and references to prior clinical reports, are given by Winship (1957). In a study of treatment in several outpatient clinics, Gerard and Saenger (1966, p. 140) found a higher percentage of improvement in 50 patients given disulfiram than in 495 patients whose treatment did not include disulfiram. This study did not include a control for the possibility that the drug might have been prescribed or accepted in cases with better prognosis, but several other drug treatments (including vitamins, barbiturates, tranquilizers) were associated with lower percentages of improvement. Disulfiram was associated with substantially increased percentages of improvement only in patients who maintained more than minimal contact with the clinic, indicating the apparent necessity for continuing, supportive contact by the therapist in order to obtain the maximum benefit from this treatment. Hoff (1961) reported evidence that the superior outcome for 1020 alcoholics given disulfiram compared to 484 patients without this treatment was mostly attributable to a lower incidence of prematurely leaving the hospital and thus breaking off treatment by the patients treated with disulfiram. Armstrong (1957) and Levy et al. (1967) compared clinical effects and uses of disulfiram with a similar but shorter-acting and less toxic compound, citrated calcium carbimide (CCC).

In contrast to the undeniable potency of disulfiram as an aversively protective drug, the interaction of metronidazole (Flagyl) with alcohol apparently is difficult to detect, and there have been many claims and denials concerning the therapeutic potency of metronidazole. Lal (1969) has reviewed a number of the studies. The initial, enthusiastic report of therapeutic efficacy lacked control groups (Taylor, 1964; Friedland and Vaisberg, 1968), and controlled studies have given only slight evidence for superiority of the metronidazole over a placebo condition (Elosuo, 1966; Lehmann and Ban, 1967). Several studies with double-blind procedures have shown no superiority in outcome for alcoholic patients given metronidazole rather than placebo (Linton and Hain, 1967; Egan and Goetz, 1968; Penick et al., 1969) or chlordiazepoxide (Gallant et al., 1968). Other studies without the rigorous double-blind control for subjective expectations of therapist or patient likewise showed no therapeutic effect of metronidazole at all (Goodwin, 1967) or in comparison with an alternative therapeutic procedure (Merry and Whitehead, 1968; Lal, 1969).

Contrary to these negative reports, an impressive positive report is by Kissin and Platz (1968), in a double-blind study of 125 patients given metronidazole compared with 94 given placebo. The drug increased both the percentage of rapid dropouts and the percentage improvement after six months. Many of the patients receiving metronidazole reported that liquor tasted unpleasant or caused slight nausea. Even some of the reports of no therapeutic efficacy of metronidazole, such as Penick et al. (1969), have given evidence that the drug enhances the aversiveness of the response to alcohol in some cases. In an experiment on the patients, given a drink once after ten days of metronidazole and once after ten days of placebo, with a randomized sequence and double-blind procedure, Gelder and Edwards (1968) found that the metronidazole condition caused the prospect of a second drink to be rated less pleasant in taste and more dangerous. These results are consistent with a report that chronic metronidazole administration in rats decreased the spontaneous choice of an alcohol solution (Chapter 8,

References p. 779

p. 452). In general, any aversively protective effect of metronidazole appears to be weak in relation to the intensity of the alcoholic's craving, but the short treatment period of several months or less, in most of these studies, may have contributed to the failures to find therapeutic effects. Even a weak treatment may be helpful if given for a prolonged time to a wide range of patients.

(b) Substitute and supportive treatments

In general, a wide variety of substitute drugs for chronic alcoholics are prescribed in different treatment facilities and sometimes in the same clinic. The diversity of therapeutic agents indicates that none of them is highly satisfactory, and the controlled experiments thus far have failed to identify any substitute drug or combination of drugs as the optimal treatment for alcoholics.

Substitute drugs with cross-dependence, such as paraldehyde or barbiturates, have saved the lives of many acutely ill alcoholics (p. 745) but are not often used as chronic substitutes for alcohol because high doses are equally incapacitating and dangerous and may result in withdrawal symptoms which are even more severe and dangerous. Hope for a useful substitute treatment has been aroused by the recent introduction of various types of tranquilizing drugs, notably chlorpromazine and other phenothiazines, meprobamate, and chlordiazepoxide. These drugs have been proven effective in various psychiatric illnesses, including acute alcoholic illness (p. 747) but not for the chronic alcoholic. Benor and Ditman (1966, 1967), in a review of studies on various tranquilizers, concluded that they gave little or no evidence for therapeutic value. Gerard and Saenger (1966) reported a much lower percentage of improvement among 289 patients given tranquilizers than among 256 patients not given this type of treatment. However, there is some evidence for therapeutic effects of chlordiazepoxide (Hoff, 1961; Ditman, 1961; Kissin and Gross, 1968; Kissin and Platz, 1968).

Since depression is a characteristic of many alcoholics, antidepressant or stimulant drugs might be expected to have therapeutic effects. Chafetz (1967) claimed good results with imipramine and with amitriptyline hydrochloride in alcoholics. However, these and other antidepressants gave no evidence for therapeutic effects in several double-blind studies on alcoholics (Ditman, 1961; Kissin and Gross, 1968). Kissin and Platz (1968) reported preliminary evidence for beneficial effects of imipramine combined with chlordiazepoxide but not of imipramine alone. According to Miller (1942) the use of amphetamine as a substitute drug decreased the percentage of rearrests during a period of 4–14 months, but the "control" group, not given amphetamine, differed from the experimental group in important additional respects.

Enthusiastic claims for therapeutic benefit of massive nutritional supplements have been reported in an abstract by O'Malley *et al.* (1951) and in a brief article by Butler (1967). According to some theories of the etiology of alcoholism, reviewed earlier in this chapter (p. 727), adequate nutrition should cure the craving for alcohol. However, there is very little experimental evidence for such a simple cure of alcoholism. Hoff and Forbes (1955) reported improvement after a year or more of outpatient treatment in 79% of 50 patients given massive vitamin supplements compared with 70% of a comparison group. This difference was small and short of statistical significance, in spite of the observation of a greater sense of well-being among the patients given vitamin supplements. Although there is little evidence that the addictive craving for alcohol is caused by dietary deficiency or cured by vitamin supplements, studies reviewed in Chapter 9 (pp. 492–495) show that chronic, excessive drinking often leads to nutritional deficiencies which contribute to the symptoms of acute alcoholic illness and may also aggravate the craving for alcohol. The necessity of nutritional supplements is generally recognized in the treatment of this condition (p. 748). It should be obvious that continuation of an adequate diet is essential for long-term rehabilitation of the alcoholic, but most therapeutic programs include no special dietary provisions in spite of the alcoholic's long-established habit of existing on an inadequate diet. The beneficial effects of an enriched diet have probably been underestimated because of the difficulty of inducing outpatient alcoholics to adhere to the diet (Hoff, 1961), especially if they resume drinking. Butler (1967) described the use of a permanently implanted stomach fistula for administering the food supplements to the outpatient.

(4) Psychotherapy

Alcoholism is primarily a psychiatric disorder, and the principal goal of therapy is to alter the self-destructive loss of control over alcohol intake. In most treatment programs, psychotherapy rather than physical therapy is the principal method. All types of contact and communication with the patient, by physicians and all staff members of the clinic or hospital, and by other patients, are potentially psychotherapeutic.

In spite of the importance of psychotherapeutic methods in the treatment of alcoholism, there is little information on the efficacy of the various techniques. A thorough review of the earlier literature by Voegtlin and Lemere (1942) emphasized the lack of quantitative reports of therapeutic success. Many subsequent descriptions of therapeutic methods have claimed a specific percentage of success, but a review by Hill and Blane (1967) pointed out that with few exceptions the experimental design and follow-up data were seriously defective. The present review divides the psychotherapeutic techniques into two principal categories: individual and group treatment. Since the available data provide little basis for evaluation or comparison of different treatments, this account will describe briefly some of the more popular or promising techniques.

(a) Individual treatment

Much of the effectiveness of psychotherapy depends on the therapist's expression of sympathetic interest in the patient. Several studies have demonstrated the efficacy of certain procedures in establishing treatment relations with alcoholics. Psychotherapeutic interview with acutely ill alcoholics, shortly after their admission to the emergency ward, greatly increased the probability of subsequent clinic visits by two samples of 100 alcoholics each (Chafetz et al., 1962, 1964). Koumans and Muller (1965), in a study of 100 acutely ill alcoholics who were hospitalized as soon as they initially came to the clinic, reported that a personal letter from the clinic to a randomly selected sample of 50 cases elicited a much higher probability of subsequent contact with the clinic than by the other 50 patients.

Most of the specific techniques of skillful, successful therapists have not been subjected to experimental test. Therefore, a finding of special interest is a report on attributes of the psychiatrist's voice (Milmore et al., 1967). The degree of success of 9 physicians in causing alcoholics seen at the hospital emergency service to go to the clinic was correlated with a low degree of anger and a high degree of anxiety in the voices of the therapists, rated on a later occasion. Kindliness and sympathetic concern were presumably the characteristics conveyed in the voices which evoked a favorable response from the alcoholics.

Hypnotic suggestion is a psychotherapeutic method which generally is limited to relief of symptoms and accomplished in a brief time. Abrams (1964) reviewed studies of the use of hypnotic suggestion for establishing a conditioned aversion to liquor. Most alcoholics appear to be susceptible to hypnosis, but reports of therapeutic efficacy are conflicting. A different application of hypnotherapy was a case report by Kraft and Al-Issa (1967). The patient allegedly drank excessively as a reaction to his disruptive anxiety and stuttering in social situations. A gradual procedure of "desensitization", by learning to relax while imagining social situations under the influence of hypnosis, cured all the symptoms including the excessive drinking.

When patients at the same treatment facility are given different forms of therapy, the effects of the procedures are likely to be distorted by subjective expectations and comparisons on the part of both therapists and patients. Therefore, the excellent scientific method of assigning patients randomly to different treatment procedures does not necessarily yield a valid measurement of their effects. Bruun (1963) reported on an experimental design which overcame this drawback by comparison between two clinics, one which included a new, intense psychotherapeutic program whereas the other was limited to the traditional methods. An essential feature of this design was random assignment of each patient to one of the clinics. A follow-up classification as cured and changed was given for 15% of the 203 patients more than two years after the new psychotherapeutic program compared to 9% of the 100 patients after the traditional program. This advantage of the more intense therapeutic effort was short of statistical significance. The same experimental design could and should be used for comparing other therapeutic techniques.

Whereas most types of therapy are designed to counteract the symptoms, such as craving for alcohol or the behavior of drinking, psychoanalysis and other forms of deep psychotherapy attempt to cure the mental illness itself by exposing to conscious knowledge the conflicts and anxieties which motivate the craving for intoxication. Unfortunately the comprehensive goal of psychoanalysis engenders special obstacles against achieving it. Analysis of the repressed desires and conflicts generally requires many hours of therapy, during which intense anxiety may be aroused. These difficulties are especially severe in the case of most alcoholics. Only a small minority of alcoholics can undertake this expensive and lengthy procedure, and the patient tends to alleviate the anxieties aroused in the analysis by the well-established refuge of intoxication. Psychoanalysis is feasible only if alcohol is inaccessible, as in a hospital, or after the patient has established a stable habit of abstinence. Only alcoholics with a relatively high degree of emotional stability should attempt this difficult and potentially dangerous therapeutic program. The review by Voegtlin and Lemere (1942) included a thorough survey of reports on psychoanalytic treatment of alcoholics, leading to the conclusion that the results were not encouraging. It may be indicative that a later review of psychoanalytic views of alcoholism (Blum, 1966) was devoted primarily to etiology rather than therapy of alcoholism. Her brief sections on psychoanalytic therapy emphasized modifications to adapt the classical methods to the special need of alcoholics for gratification of their intense, conflicted dependency wishes. Experimental verification of psycho-analytic success is made difficult both by the limited number of patients treated and by the duration and complexity of the therapeutic procedures.

(b) Group treatment

Many of the same methods used in individual therapy can be applied to the treatment of alcoholics in groups. This gives the practical advantage of multiplying the number of patients treated and the more fundamental advantage that it is more similar to common drinking situations, than is the confrontation of a single patient with a psychiatrist. The intense de-pendency needs of alcoholics, which can block the achievement of insight in individual psychotherapy, appear to make these patients particularly susceptible to the social facilitation of contact with other alcoholics in a group therapy situation. In a brief survey of treatment methods, Feldman (1956) commented that the experience of being with other alcoholics helps the patient to accept treatment in a group. Some of the papers already cited also give evidence for beneficial effects of group psychotherapy for alcoholics. In his review of hypnotic therapy, Abrams (1964) commented that the conditioned aversive response is strengthened by the similar reaction of the others when the training is in a group. Aversive conditioning with emetine was also reported to be more effective in a group setting (Miller *et al.*, 1960).

Specific types of group therapy have been described by Fox (1962) and Weiner (1965). In a well-controlled experimental comparison of different treatment methods for alcoholics, Wallerstein (1956, 1957) included group hypnotherapy, described by Friend (1957), and milieu therapy, described by Perlswig (1957). Both forms of psychotherapy resulted in a lower percent-age of patients who completed treatment than aversion therapy with chronic disulfiram treatment.

Another systematic, well designed comparison of different types of therapy has been reported by Ends and Page (1957). They randomly assigned 63 alcoholics to four different group therapy procedures. The follow-up data, obtained 18 months after the 5-week therapeutic procedure, showed a higher percentage of cases classified as greatly improved after client-centered or analytic therapy than after the learning-theory or control procedure. A more realistic self-understanding appeared to result from the client-centered than from the analytic therapy. In a later study, Ends and Page (1959) reported evidence that doubling the number of client-centered group psychotherapy sessions in the same six-week period enhances the beneficial effect.

Many variations are possible in group psychotherapy procedures. Narrol (1967) reported on a system whereby hospitalized alcoholics earned various privileges and recreational facilities only by performance of tasks and duties. Although the reinforcements for responsible behavior were applied individually, a considerable degree of group cohesion apparently resulted. Outpatient treatment is another setting in which group psychotherapy can be beneficial. Gerard and Saenger (1966) reported evidence that group therapy might be especially effective as a means of inducing non-hospitalized alcoholics to continue treatment.

One of the most effective and well-known forms of group psychotherapy for alcoholics is the fellowship of Alcoholics Anonymous, which is conducted entirely outside a clinic or hospital setting. This worldwide organization has probably helped a larger number of alcoholics, than all of the medical facilities combined. Alcoholics Anonymous has aroused great interest, and among the many informative and perceptive discussions are articles by Gibbins (1953), Rosenman (1955), Stewart (1955), Trice (1958), Ripley and Jackson (1959), McMillan (1967), and Reader (1967). One of the prevalent characteristics of alcoholics is denial of their drinking problem. Alcoholics Anonymous explicitly combats this tendency by assisting every member to admit frankly that he is an alcoholic. The difficulty and necessity of this self-admission may account for some of the associated doctrines of most members. "Hitting bottom" is often regarded as a prerequisite for membership. Not only is lifetime abstinence from alcohol believed necessary, but a constitutional, biochemical etiology of alcoholism is widely accepted. Alcoholism is a lifetime condition, and membership in Alcoholics Anonymous is limited to those who have realized and confessed that they are alcoholics. This high degree of group cohesiveness is offset by a loose organizational structure which may be regarded as a concession to the alcoholic's characteristic resentment of authority. Other features of the program further express and alleviate the alcoholic's conflicts about dependence and hostility motives.

References p. 779

Research on the therapeutic efficacy of Alcoholics Anonymous is very difficult because of the loose structure of the organization and the need to protect the anonymity of the members. A questionnaire completed by 306 members in London demonstrated the relatively high degree of social stability of alcoholics in this program; the groups consisted of a majority of faithful, long-abstinent members with a smaller number of transients (Edwards *et al.*, 1967). The same conclusion may be drawn from a report by Bailey and Leach (1965) on 1,058 members in New York City.

(5) Factors affecting therapeutic success

The diversity among alcoholics has been emphasized in earlier portions of this chapter and in Chapter 9. Various characteristics of alcoholics might be expected to influence the probability of favorable response to therapy, and a number of the studies of treatment of chronic alcoholics included data on different therapeutic outcomes for patients who differed in various characteristics. Different therapeutic methods should be preferable for different types of alcoholics, but unfortunately very little experimental evidence has been reported on this important topic.

Any pathological condition should be treated as early as possible. Therapy at an early stage enhances both the probability and the completeness of beneficial effect, in accordance with the principle that prevention is easier than cure. This principle applies especially to the pathological effects of chronic alcoholism. Several studies have indicated the advantage of receiving therapy at an early stage, before severe, irreversible impairment of the alcoholic's social and physical condition. Pfeffer and Berger (1957) reported that 92% of 78 voluntary patients, who underwent treatment as an alternative to dismissal from the steady job they held at the time, showed definite improvement. The majority of them were described as continuously abstinent for at least a year. This much higher percentage of success than with most samples of alcoholics was attributed to the earlier stage of their condition and the incentive of holding their job. Studies of more typical samples of alcoholics, with lower percentages of therapeutic success, have also given evidence for better response to therapy by those with lesser degrees of pathology. Kissin and Platz (1968), in a study of 407 patients given various types of therapy, found that a successful outcome was consistently associated with greater job stability. Other measures of social stability, including marital, high-status occupation, and college education, were related less consistently to therapeutic success. Voegtlin and Broz (1949), in an analysis of data on more than one thousand patients, reported that a stable employment record prior to treatment was highly related to increased probability of a successful outcome. Other measures of social stability, such as stable marriage and good financial status, were also related to successful therapy. Similar measures of social stability were likewise related to therapeutic success according to reports by Gerard and Saenger (1966) on several hundred patients, by Mindlin (1959) on 233 patients, Kendell and Staton (1966) on 66 patients, and by Perlswig (1957) on 42 patients given "milieu" therapy. Successful outcome was also associated with relatively superior intellectual and emotional functioning in the study by Mindlin (1959) and in studies by Tillotson and Fleming (1937) on 120 patients and by Rossi *et al.* (1963) on 149 patients. The same characteristics might explain the high degree of success reported for therapy of Catholic priests (Hoffer and Osmond, 1968).

Contrary to the advantages of early treatment and relatively mild pathology, some of the research findings give evidence that prolonged, frightening experience with excessive drinking may be a necessary prelude to therapeutic success. Denial is characteristic of many alcoholics until the physical and social damage have progressed to an extreme, often irreversible degree. Moore and Murphy (1961), in a study of 100 patients, reported that the degree of diminution of this denial as a result of psychotherapy was positively related to improvement. Many members of Alcoholics Anonymous have been able to admit their dangerous condition and maintain sobriety only after "hitting bottom". Voegtlin and Broz (1949) and Wolff and Holland (1964) found a higher percentage of abstinence among patients who were older. Therapeutic success was also related positively to a longer duration of excessive drinking and to the finding of enlarged liver but was related negatively to the more extreme pathology of delirium tremens. Rathod *et al.* (1966) also found that therapeutic success was positively related both to higher age and to longer duration of excessive drinking in 84 patients. A tendency for superior outcome of therapy in older alcoholic patients was also found by Kissin and Platz (1968), by Wolff and Holland (1964) in a study of 93 patients, and by Winship (1957) in a study of 47 patients given disulfiram treatment. The advantages of therapy at an earlier stage may explain the contrary finding of superior therapeutic outcome in younger patients after a shorter duration of excessive drinking, reported by Tillotson and Fleming (1937), and also by Fox and Smith (1959) on 272

References p. 779

patients. Conflicting relationships of age to therapeutic success were likewise reported in earlier studies reviewed by Bowman and Jellinek (1941).

The greater severity of symptoms believed to be characteristic of female alcoholics might impair their likelihood of therapeutic success due to the greater pathology or might improve their prognosis due to a reduced tendency to deny their dangerous condition. Both opposite effects are reported in the review by Bowman and Jellinek (1941) and in subsequent studies. Superior therapeutic outcome was reported for women by Voegtlin and Broz (1949) and by Fox and Smith (1959) but for men by Pemberton (1967) in a comparison of 50 males with 50 females.

Some other studies give further evidence that ordinarily adverse characteristics may be positively related to therapeutic success. Blane and Meyers (1963) reported that therapy was continued for five or more interviews by a much higher percentage of overtly dependent than counter-dependent alcoholics. The overtly dependent type was characterized by poorer adjustment and less maturity in most respects. Similarly, Tarnower and Toole (1968) reported that continuation in treatment for more than 10 years was characteristic of passive-dependent types of alcoholics. Measures of improvement, rather than mere persistence in therapy, have also indicated better therapeutic outcome for alcoholics who are more passive, psychologically or socially isolated, and emotionally disturbed (Muzekari, 1965; Pokorny et al., 1968). Four different treatment methods reported in a monograph by Wallerstein (1957) all resulted in higher percentages of improvement among passive-dependent alcoholics than among most of the other types. Machover and Puzzo (1959) reported that 23 remitted alcoholics showed a more feminine identification, especially with their mother, more severe ambivalent and obsessive compulsive symptoms, and overcontrol in comparison with 23 drinking alcoholics, but these findings would have been more convincing if the personality measures had been obtained prior to treatment instead of after the period of differential abstinence. Blane and Meyers (1964) attributed a finding of better therapeutic success with patients from lower socio-economic class to the beneficial effect of greater overt dependence aroused by the large difference in social status between the patient and therapist.

The studies reviewed above give little information on the type of treatment most suitable for particular types of alcoholics, although most therapists would agree that different types of alcoholic should be treated differently. Blane and Meyers (1963) and Blane (1968) suggested that a therapeutic emphasis on sympathy, support and permissiveness may be particularly suitable for the overtly dependent type of alcoholic, whereas more authoritarianism might help to induce counter-dependent alcoholics to enter treatment and overcome their characteristic denial of the drinking problem. Trice (1957) stated that the affiliative, extroverted drinker is more receptive to Alcoholics Anonymous than is the withdrawn, socially isolated drinker, whereas Vogel (1960, 1961b) reported that aversive conditioning is more effective for the introverted, solitary drinker. The systematic comparison of several therapeutic methods by Wallerstein (1956, 1957) gave evidence that some treatment techniques are most beneficial for certain types of patient. Disulfiram therapy, which required that the patient continue taking the pill daily after discharge from the hospital, was most successful with patients who had a stable home (Winship, 1957); hypnotherapy was most successful with the patients who experienced the deepest hypnotic trances (Friend, 1957); the unpleasant, punishing aversive conditioning was least successful with the passive-aggressive patients (Hammersley, 1957).

E. Summary

Much of the available knowledge about alcoholism is based on clinical observations and sociological statistics. Controlled experimentation on this topic is severely limited by inability to induce voluntary, chronic consumption of intoxicating alcohol doses in laboratory animals. Useful information on alcoholism is contributed by studies of other aspects of alcohol actions, especially effects of prolonged intake reviewed in Chapter 9.

Various definitions of alcoholism have been proposed. Some are highly inclusive, such as "any drinking that leads to any damage". However, most definitions require the development of severe, long-standing pathology associated with alcohol, indicated by presence of each of the following three characteristics: (a) large quantity of alcohol consumption over a period of years; (b) abnormal, chronic loss of control over drinking shown by inability to refrain or inability to stop; (c) chronic damage to physical health or social standing as a result of drinking. Each of these criteria depends largely on cultural standards and social settings. The most objective of these criteria is the quantity of alcohol consumption, but considerable overlap has been found between alcoholics and nonalcoholics in this respect. Alcoholism is a complex, variable disorder which cannot readily be classified as a single, coherent disease. The importance of physical dependence on alcohol in maintaining the loss of control over drinking is a controversial issue. Different types of alcoholic have been identified, in particular spree drinkers (gamma alcoholics) who are unable to stop drinking, and steady, excessive drinkers (delta alcoholics), who are unable to abstain. Many alcoholics also suffer from schizophrenia, depression, psychophatic personality, and other psychiatric disorders. Such characteristics of alcoholics should be measured and reported in experimental and clinical studies.

Four stages in the typical development of gamma alcoholism have been identified: (a) prealcoholic, with onset of constant drinking and increase in tolerance for alcohol; (b) prodromal, marked by occurrence of "blackouts" (alcoholic palimpsests) and avid drinking; (c) crucial, in which the drinker loses control and usually begins to drink regularly in the mornings; (d) chronic, characterized by onset of "benders" (prolonged intoxications) and often physical pathology, aggravated by reduction in tolerance for alcohol and occurrence of severe withdrawal symptoms. At the later stages, many alcoholics suffer deterioration in self-respect and social standing, and this social pathology contributes to a greatly elevated incidence of suicide, homicide, other forms of violence and crime, and also various types of injury and illness. The high proportion of the liver activity devoted to metabolism of alcohol gives rise to nutritional deficiencies which are aggravated by the inadequate dietary intake almost always associated with excessive drinking. Physical pathologies which may develop in the last stage of alcoholism, caused at least partly by the nutritional deficiency, include polyneuropathy, Wernicke's disease and cirrhosis of the liver. However, the typical progression of alcoholism can be halted at any stage, and the pathological effects short of extreme deterioration are generally reversible. Even among alcoholics who reach the final, chronic stage, only a minority develop extreme forms of physical pathology. Estimates of the number of alcoholics in a population are generally based on the number of deaths attributed to cirrhosis of the liver, although only a minority of such cases are alcoholics and only a small minority of alcoholics are killed by this disease. These estimates of the prevalence of alcoholism, emphasizing the criterion of physical damage, are subject to bias from factors which influence the incidence of deaths attributed to liver cirrhosis, either among alcoholics or among nonalcoholics.

There have been various attempts to identify an etiological factor giving rise to alcoholism. Some theories have been based on physical dependence on alcohol without adequate explanation why alcoholism develops only in some drinkers. Constitutional factors, proposed to explain why some individuals become alcoholics, have not been closely related to the actions of alcohol. Theories which have been proposed include an unusual predisposition to physical dependence on alcohol, nutritional deficiency or allergy to alcohol which induces craving for liquor, various metabolic or endocrinological disorders, or unspecified genetic abnormality. No physical or metabolic abnormalities have been found prevalent in alcoholics, other than consequences of their prolonged, excessive drinking. There is little evidence for a specific hereditary predisposition to alcoholism.

Some etiological theories have been based on a predisposing personality or childhood environment. A high proportion of young boys who subsequently became alcoholic manifested antisocial, unrestrained behavior and were reared in a pathological family environment, in particular with a criminal father. Retrospective information on adult alcoholics indicates a high incidence of early parental deprivation or rejection, with an over-representation of cases in the second half of large families. However, most retrospective studies have failed to obtain reliable comparisons between alcoholics and nonalcoholics with respect to early experiences or characteristics. Personality traits, found to be associated with alcoholism according to several studies, include greater perceptual dependence and deficiency in ability to learn to avoid unpleasant consequences, but the existence of these characteristics prior to the excessive drinking has not been demonstrated. According to the psychoanalytic theory of Sigmund Freud and his followers, the alcoholic is fixated at the infantile, oral stage of personality development, characterized by craving for a passive, dependent role. The conflict with harsh reality gives rise to denial, fantasies of omnipotence, and intense anger, especially directed against oneself and expressed in the self-destructive behavior of excessive drinking. This conception is supported by clinical impressions of intense conflict between dependence and independence strivings in many alcoholics, and by some research findings in particular showing a close relationship of alcoholism to suicide. Although various personality factors appear to be related to alcoholism, the diversity among alcoholics severely limits the generality of etiological theories based on personality. There is no single trait or type of background common to a majority among the alcoholics.

Each characteristic associated with alcoholism implies the existence of the opposite characteristic which may protect the individual from developing this disorder. A probable mechanism for a relationship between consti-

References p. 779

tutional variations and alcoholism is that aversion or low tolerance for intoxication prevents some people from developing alcoholism. A large group of intellectually gifted children had an unusually low incidence of problem drinking more than 40 years later. Relatively low incidence of alcoholism in some cultural groups, such as Jews and Italians, and among some categories of people, such as women, may be attributed to more effective social control and less arousal of the pathological motives for excessive drinking. The development of methods for preventing and controlling this disorder may be aided by emphasis on the factors associated with absence rather than presence of alcoholism.

Direct alcohol poisoning is rare except in alcoholics, because most people cannot drink an acutely toxic quantity before emesis or unconsciousness intervenes, but when this condition occurs it is dangerous. Various treatments have been recommended and usually several are applied simultaneously. Because of lack of specific knowledge, these are all essentially symptomatic. Many drugs have been reported to hasten alcohol elimination but such effects have not been scientifically validated. Various centrally stimulating drugs have been suggested for combating depression due to alcohol poisoning, but none has been found to show outstanding value. Because of the highly generalized actions of alcohol, the acutely toxic effects cannot be counteracted by neutralizing its interaction with specific receptor sites in the central nervous system. The most essential therapeutic procedures consist of maintaining the respiratory and cardiovascular functions and keeping the victim warm. Hypertonic glucose is useful to counteract the cerebral edema and hypoglycemia which are concomitants of acute alcohol poisoning.

The withdrawal syndrome in the acutely ill alcoholic can be very severe and even fatal. Treatment is with a variety of different drugs including tranquilizers and substitutes for alcohol such as paraldehyde. No single agent or combination of agents has been identified as the treatment of choice. The potency of the drug should be matched to the severity of the illness. Attention should be given to fluid and electrolyte balance. Alcoholics may suffer from fluid loss but contrary to common belief they are frequently overhydrated. Subnormal potassium and magnesium are the most usual electrolyte disturbances. This is also the time to begin remedying the nutritional deficiency which often aggravates the acute illness. Massive vitamin supplements are often given but do not produce any dramatic short-term therapeutic effect. A balanced nutritional regimen may be more beneficial.

Most experiments on therapeutic methods for chronic alcoholics have failed to test the effect of a single, specified method in comparison with a control treatment. Follow-up information is often incomplete and unreliable, obtained on only a portion of the sample and at a short time after the therapeutic procedures. Abstinence or improvement after therapy has generally been claimed for less than 50% of the cases except in a few studies of special types of patients without a control treatment. Thus therapeutic efficacy is rather low, especially as a substantial proportion of alcoholics (approximately 20%) apparently recover without known therapeutic intervention.

In spite of the almost universal therapeutic goal of permanent abstinence, a number of reports show that a substantial proportion of alcoholics, ranging from 3% to 10%, acquired moderate, controlled drinking. This behavior pattern appears to be associated with advancing age and a self-reliant personality. An intervening period of abstinence may be necessary for the establishment of controlled drinking subsequent to alcoholism. Research on this outcome is impeded by the fact that no responsible therapist would encourage patients to try this experiment on themselves.

Brief, physical intervention appears to have rather slight efficacy for changing the habitual, long-established drinking behavior of the alcoholic. The technique of aversion training, for associating the sight, smell and taste of liquor with an unpleasant consequence, has most often been used with emetic drugs which induce nausea and vomiting, such as emetine, apomorphine or citrated calcium carbimide (CCC). Painful electric shock, and succinylcholine for inducing apnea, have the advantage of permitting precise timing of the aversive reaction, but they seem to have less therapeutic efficacy, perhaps because their effects are dissimilar to the natural occurrence of the emetic response to intoxicating doses of alcohol. Various reports give evidence that the recently introduced use of LSD has some therapeutic efficacy, but this claim has been disputed.

Chronic physical assistance to therapy is provided by the use of a drug which prevents consumption of liquor because of an aversive effect in combination with alcohol. Several studies indicate superior effectiveness of disulfiram treatment with evidence that its advantage depends on its effect in encouraging continued contact with the therapist. CCC has similar effects but shorter-acting and less toxic. Metronidazole gives evidence for weakly aversive effects in combination with alcohol and according to some studies has substantial therapeutic efficacy, but this claim has been denied

References p. 779

by a number of investigators. Another type of chronic physical aid to therapy is by substitute or supporting treatments. Research reports give no consistent evidence for therapeutic effectiveness of any tranquilizer, antidepressant or stimulant, but some studies indicate a small beneficial effect of chlordiazepoxide. Nutritional supplements might be expected to have beneficial long-term effect, but this has not been convincingly demonstrated, probably because this form of treatment has seldom been attempted or studied in chronic alcoholics.

Psychotherapy includes various forms of contact with the alcoholic by a number of different people. Even seemingly minor expression of interest and concern may have substantial beneficial effect. Success with alcoholics has been claimed for various forms of individual psychotherapy, including hypnotic suggestion. Psychoanalysis has the ambitious goal of curing the pathological motives for the excessive drinking, but this intensive form of individual therapy has seldom been successful with alcoholics, presumably because the anxiety aroused by the self-exposure is excessive and readily alleviated by drinking. Research reports indicate therapeutic efficacy of various forms of group psychotherapy. The fellowship of Alcoholics Anonymous appears to express and alleviate the alcoholic's intense, conflicted motives concerning dependence and hostility. This group treatment has been successfully applied to many alcoholics but is inaccessible to most research on therapeutic outcome.

Several studies have given evidence that some treatment techniques are more beneficial for certain types of patient, but most of the reports on differences among alcoholics do not include comparisons of different therapeutic methods. An early stage or relatively mild degree of the pathology is a favorable prognosis for treatment of alcoholism, as of other disorders. On the other hand, superior outcome in some studies was characteristic of older patients, with enlarged liver, and after longer durations of drinking, presumably because "hitting bottom" is necessary for some alcoholics to overcome their characteristic denial. Superior therapeutic outcome has also been found related to other ordinarily unfavorable characteristics, including passive-dependent personality, greater psychological or social isolation, and more severe emotional disturbance.

REFERENCES

ABRAMS, S. (1964). An evaluation of hypnosis in the treatment of alcoholics. *Am. J. Psychiat. 120*, 1160–1165.

ABRAMSON, H. A. (1967). *The use of LSD in psychotherapy and alcoholism.* Bobbs-Merrill Co. Indianapolis, 697 pp.

ACHTÉ, K. (1958). Korreloituvatko ABO-veriryhmät ja alkoholismi? (Do ABO blood groups correlate with alcoholism?). *Duodecim 74*, 20–22.

AHTO, A. (1951). Dangerous and habitual criminals. *Acta Psychiat. Neurol. Scand.*, Suppl. *69*, 7–157.

ALLSOP, J. AND TURNER, B. (1966). Cerebellar degeneration associated with chronic alcoholism. *J. Neurol. Sci. 3*, 238–258.

AMLER, G. AND BERGENER, M. (1965). Elektroencephalographische Veränderungen bei der Behandlung des Delirium tremens mit Chlormethiazol und ihre Interpretation. *Arzneimittel-Forsch. 15*, 837–840.

ARMSTRONG, J. D. (1957). The protective drugs in the treatment of alcoholism. *Can. Med. Assoc. J. 77*, 228–232.

AUGUSTINE, J. R. (1967). Laboratory studies in acute alcoholics. *Can. Med. Assoc. J. 96*, 1367–1370.

BABIGIAN, H. M. AND ODOROFF, C. L. (1969). The mortality experience of a population with psychiatric illness. *Am. J. Psychiat. 126*, 470–480.

BACON, M. K., BARRY, H. III, AND CHILD, I. L. (1965). A cross-cultural study of drinking. II. Relations to other features of culture. *Quart. J. Studies Alc.*, Suppl. 3, 29–48.

BAILEY, M. B. AND LEACH, B. (1965). *Alcoholics Anonymous pathway to recovery: A study of 1,058 members of the AA fellowship in New York City.* National Council on Alcoholism, New York. iii + 58 pp.

BAILEY, M. B. AND STEWART, J. (1967). Normal drinking by persons reporting previous problem drinking. *Quart. J. Studies Alc. 28*, 305–315.

BAILEY, M. B., HABERMAN, P. W. AND ALKSNE, H. (1965). The epidemiology of alcoholism in an urban residential area. *Quart. J. Studies Alc. 26*, 19–40.

BAILEY, W., HUSTMYER, F. AND KRISTOFFERSON, A. (1961). Alcoholism, brain damage and perceptual dependence. *Quart. J. Studies Alc. 22*, 387–393.

BAÏSSET, A., MONTASTRUC, P. AND GARRIGUES, M. (1965). Recherches sur les interactions de l'alcool et de la sécrétion antidiurétique neurohypophysaire. Influence des préparations post-hypophysaires sur la soif provoquée par l'ingestion d'alcool. *Pathol. Biol. Semaine Hop. 13*, 241–251.

BARCHHA, R., STEWART, M. A. AND GUZE, S. B. (1968). The prevalence of alcoholism among general hospital ward patients. *Am. J. Psychiat. 125*, 681–684.

BARRY, H., III (1968). Sociocultural aspects of alcohol addiction. In: *The addictive states*, A. WIKLER, Ed., Association for Research in Nervous and Mental Disease, Research Publications Vol. 46, Williams & Wilkins, Baltimore. Pp. 455–471.

BARRY, H., III AND BARRY, H. JR. (1967). Birth order, family size, and schizophrenia. *Arch. Gen. Psychiat. 17*, 435–440.

BARRY, H., JR., BARRY, H., III AND BLANE, H. T. (1969). Birth order of delinquent boys with alcohol involvement. *Quart. J. Studies Alc. 30*, 408–413.

BARTA, L. (1963). Kohlenhydratstoffwechseluntersuchungen bei Alkoholvergiftung. *Deut. Z. Verdauungs-Stoffwechselkrankh. 23*, 320–325.

BENOR, D. AND DITMAN, K. S. (1966). Tranquilizers in the management of alcoholics: A review of the literature to 1964. Part I. *J. New Drugs 6*, 319–337.

BENOR, D. AND DITMAN, K. S. (1967). Tranquilizers in the management of alcoholics: A review of the literature to 1964. Part II. *J. Clin. Pharmacol. 7*, 17–25.

BLAKE, B. G. (1965). The application of behaviour therapy to the treatment of alcoholism. *Beh. Res. Therapy 3*, 75–85.

BLAKE, B. G. (1967). A follow-up of alcoholics treated by behaviour therapy. *Beh. Res. Therapy 5*, 89–94.

BLANE, H. T. (1968). *The personality of the alcoholic: Guises of dependency.* Harper & Row, New York. 175 pp.

BLANE, H. T. AND MEYERS, W. R. (1963). Behavioral dependence and length of stay in psychotherapy among alcoholics. *Quart. J. Studies Alc. 24*, 503–510.

BLANE, H. T. AND MEYERS, W. R. (1964). Social class and establishment of treatment relations by alcoholics. *J. Clin. Psychol. 20*, 287–290.

BLUM, E. M. (1966). Psychoanalytic views of alcoholism. A review. *Quart. J. Studies Alc. 27*, 259–299.

BLUM, E. M. AND BLUM, R. H. (1967). *Alcoholism: Modern psychological approaches to treatment.* Joey-Bass, San Francisco, Calif. 373 pp.

BOLMAN, W. M. (1965). Abstinence versus permissiveness in the psychotherapy of alcoholism. *Arch. Gen. Psychiat. 12*, 456–463.

BOWMAN, K. M. AND JELLINEK, E. M. (1941). Alcohol addiction and its treatment. *Quart. J. Studies Alc. 2*, 98–176.

BRENNER, B. (1959). Estimating the prevalence of alcoholism: Toward a modification of the Jellinek Formula. *Quart. J. Studies Alc. 20*, 255–260.

BRENNER, B. (1967). Alcoholism and fatal accidents. *Quart. J. Studies Alc. 28*, 517–528.

BRESARD, M. (1965). La relation entre la consommation d'alcool et celle du sucre. *Bull. Inst. Nat. Hyg. 20*, 601–606.

BRESARD, Mme AND CHABERT, Mlle (1963). Note sur la relation entre la consommation d'alcool et celle du sucre. *Bull. Inst. Nat. Hyg. 18*, 639–650.

BRUUN, K. (1963). Outcome of different types of treatment of alcoholics. *Quart. J. Studies Alc. 24*, 280–288.

BUTLER, F. S. (1967). Alcoholism: Control of the uncontrolled alcoholic. *J. Am. Geriatrics Soc. 15*, 848–851.

CARRIE, J. R. G. (1965). Finger tremor in alcoholic patients. *J. Neurol. Neurosurg. Psychiat. 28*, 529–532.

CASSIDY, W. L., FLANAGAN, N. B., SPELLMAN, M. AND COHEN, M. E. (1957). Clinical observations in manic-depressive disease. A quantitative study of one hundred manic-depressive patients and fifty medically sick controls. *J. Am. Med. Assoc. 164*, 1535–1546.

CATANZARO, R. J. (1968). *Alcoholism: The total treatment approach.* C. C. Thomas, Springfield, Ill. 508 pp.

CATHELL, J. L. (1954). The occurrence of certain psychosomatic conditions during different phases of the alcoholic's life. *North Carolina Med. J. 15*, 503–505.

CHABERT, Mlle, MEDA, Mme, POMEAU, Mlle AND DURIEU, Mme (1964). La relation entre la consommation d'alcool et celle du sucre. *Bull. Inst. Nat. Hyg. 19*, 111–128.

CHAFETZ, M. E. (1965). Is compulsory treatment of the alcoholic effective? *Northwest Med. 64*, 932–937.

CHAFETZ, M. E. (1967). Alcoholism prevention and reality. *Quart. J. Studies Alc. 29*, 345–348.

CHAFETZ, M. E., BLANE, H. T., ABRAM, H. S., GOLNER, J., LACY, E., MCCOURT, W. F., CLARK, E. AND MEYERS, W. (1962). Establishing treatment relations with alcoholics. *J. Nervous Mental Disease 134*, 395–409.

CHAFETZ, M. E., BLANE, H. T., ABRAM, H. S., CLARK, E., GOLNER, J. H., HASTIE, E. L. AND MCCOURT, W. F. (1964). Establishing treatment relations with alcoholics: A supplementary report. *J. Nervous Mental Disease 138*, 390–393.

CHEN, E. AND COBB, S. (1960). Family structure in relation to health and disease. *J. Chronic Diseases 12*, 544–567.

CHILD, I. L., BARRY, H., III AND BACON, M. K. (1965). A cross-cultural study of drinking. III. Sex differences. *Quart. J. Studies Alc.*, Suppl. 3, 49–61.

CHWELOS, N., BLEWETT, D. B., SMITH, C. M. AND HOFFER, A. (1959). Use of *d*-lysergic acid diethylamide in the treatment of alcoholism. *Quart. J. Studies Alc. 20*, 577–590.

COHEN, S. (1961). Treatment of acute alcoholism. *Can. Med. Assoc. J. 84*, 950–952.

CORLEY, K. C. AND HOFF, E. C. (1968). Protein supplementation during the initial hospitalization of alcoholics. *Quart. J. Studies Alc. 29*, 931–938.

CRUZ-COKE, R. (1965). Colour-blindness and cirrhosis of the liver. *Lancet 1*, 1131–1133.

CRUZ-COKE, R. AND VALERA, A. (1966). Inheritance of alcoholism. Its association with colour-blindness. *Lancet 2*, 1282–1284.

CUMMINS, J. F. AND FRIEND, D. G. (1954). Use of chlorpromazine in chronic alcoholics. *Am. J. Med. Sci. 227*, 561–564.

DAHLSTROM, W. G. AND WELSH, G. S. (1960). *An MMPI handbook: A guide to use in clinical practice and research.* Univ. of Minnesota Press, Minneapolis. xviii + 559 pp.

DAMON, A. (1963). Constitution and alcohol consumption: physique. *J. Chronic Diseases 16*, 1237–1250.

DAVANZO, J. P., RUCKART, R., KANG, L. AND DAUGHERTY, M. (1964). Biochemical studies with doxapram HCl. *Federation Proc. 23*, No. 2, Part I, 386.

DAVIES, D. L. (1962). Normal drinking in recovered alcohol addicts. *Quart. J. Studies Alc. 23*, 94–104.

DENNEHY, C. M. (1966). Childhood bereavement and psychiatric illness. *Brit. J. Psychiat. 112*, 1049–1069.

DITMAN, K. S. (1961). Evaluation of drugs in the treatment of alcoholics. *Quart. J. Studies Alc.*, Suppl. No. 1, 107–116.

DITMAN, K. S. (1967). The use of LSD in the treatment of the alcoholic. In: *Alcoholism: Behavioral research, therapeutic approaches.* R. Fox, Ed., Springer, New York. Pp. 256–271.

DITMAN, K. S., HAYMAN, M. AND WHITTLESEY, J. R. B. (1962). Nature and frequency of claims following LSD. *J. Nervous Mental Dis. 134*, 346–352.

DOLE, V. P. AND NYSWANDER, M. E. (1967). Heroin addiction—a metabolic disease. *Arch. Internal Med. 120*, 19–24.

DREHER, K. F. AND FRASER, J. G. (1967). Smoking habits of alcoholic out-patients. I. *Intern. J. Addictions 2*, 259–270.

DREHER, K. F. AND FRASER, J. G. (1968). Smoking habits of alcoholic out-patients. II. *Intern. J. Addictions 3*, 65–80.

DREW, L. R. H. (1968). Alcoholism as a self-limiting disease. *Quart. J. Studies Alc. 29*, 956–967.

Editorial (1967). Pathophysiological factors in the etiology of alcoholism. *Can. Med. Assoc. J. 97*, 542–544.

EDWARDS, G., HENSMAN, C., HAWKER, A. AND WILLIAMSON, V. (1967). Alcoholics Anonymous: The anatomy of a self help group. *Social Psychiat. 1*, 195–204.

EGAN, W. P. AND GOETZ, R. (1968). Effect of metronidazole on drinking by alcoholics. *Quart. J. Studies Alc. 29*, 899–902.

ELBEL, H. AND SCHLEYER, F. (1956). *Blutalkohol. Die wissenschaftlichen Grundlagen der Beurteilung von Blutalkoholbefunden bei Strassenverkehrsdelikten.* 2nd ed., Georg Thieme, Stuttgart. 226 pp.

ELOSUO, R. (1966). Metronidatsoli alkoholismin hoidossa (Metronidazole in the treatment of alcoholism). *Suom. Lääkärilehti 21*, 2178–2181.

EMERSON, H. (1934). *Alcohol: Its effects on man.* Appleton-Century, New York. 114 pp.

ENDS, E. J. AND PAGE, C. W. (1957). A study of three types of group psychotherapy with hospitalized male inebriates. *Quart. J. Studies Alc. 18*, 263–277.

ENDS, E. J. AND PAGE, C. W. (1959). Group psychotherapy and concomitant psychological change. *Psychological Monographs 73*, 31 pp.

ESSIG, C. F. AND LAM, R. C. (1968). Convulsions and hallucinatory behavior following alcohol withdrawal in the dog. *Arch. Neurol. 18*, 626–632.

ESSIG, C. F., JONES, B. E. AND LAM, R. C. (1969). The effect of pentobarbital on alcohol withdrawal in dogs. *Arch. Neurol. 20*, 554–558.

FADIMAN, J. (1967). Treatment of alcoholism with lysergide. Comment on the article by Smart et al. *Quart. J. Studies Alc. 28*, 146–147.

FARNSWORTH, D. L. (1968). Medical perspectives on alcoholism and around-the-clock psychiatric services. *Am. J. Psychiat. 124*, 1659–1663.

FARRAR, C. H., POWELL, B. J. AND MARTIN, L. K. (1968). Punishment of alcohol consumption by apneic paralysis. *Behav. Res. Therapy 6*, 13–16.

FELDMAN, D. J. (1956). The treatment of chronic alcoholism: A survey of current methods. *Ann. Int. Med. 44*, 78–87.

FENICHEL, O. (1945). *The psychoanalytic theory of neurosis.* W. W. Norton Co., New York. x + 703 pp.

FIALKOW, P. J., THULINE, H. C. AND FENSTER, L. F. (1966). Lack of association between cirrhosis and the common types of color blindness. *New Engl. J. Med. 275*, 584–587.

FLEESON, W. AND GILDEA, E. F. (1942). A study of the personalities of 289 abnormal drinkers. *Quart. J. Studies Alc. 3*, 409–432.

FLEETWOOD, M. F. AND DIETHELM, O. A. (1951). Emotions and biochemical findings in alcoholism. *Am. J. Psychiat. 108*, 433–438.

FORSANDER, O. A. (1962). Metabolic tolerance to alcohol as a possible limiting factor in its consumption. *Quart. J. Studies Alc. 23*, 480–482.

FOX, R. (1958). Antabuse as an adjunct to psychotherapy in alcoholism. *New York State J. Med. 58*, 1540–1544.

FOX, R. (1962). Group psychotherapy with alcoholics. *Int. J. Group Psychother. 12*, 56–63.

FOX, R. (1967a). *Alcoholism—Behavioral research, therapeutic approaches.* Springer, New York. 340 pp.

FOX, R. (1967b). A multidisciplinary approach to the treatment of alcoholism. *Am. J. Psychiat. 123*, 769–778.

FOX, R. (1968). Disulfiram (Antabuse) as an adjunct in the treatment of alcoholism. In: *Alcoholism—Behavioral research, therapeutic approaches.* R. Fox, Ed., Springer, New York. Pp. 242–255.

FOX, V. (1966). Treatment of the non-neurologic complications of alcoholism. *Modern Treatment 3*, 502–508.

FOX, V. AND SMITH, M. A. (1959). Evaluation of a chemopsychotherapeutic program for the rehabilitation of alcoholics: Observations over a two-year period. *Quart. J. Studies Alc. 20*, 767–780.

FRANKS, C. M. (1958). Alcohol, alcoholism and conditioning: A review of the literature and some theoretical considerations. *J. Ment. Sci. 104*, 14–33.

FRANKS, C. M. AND MANTELL, D. (1966). Introversion-extraversion and the verbal conditioning and generalization of meaning responses to nonsense syllables in normal and alcoholic subjects. *Brit. J. Soc. Clin. Psychol. 5*, 299–305.

FRIEDLAND, P. AND VAISBERG, M. (1968). The use of metronidazole in the treatment of alcoholism (A further study). *Diseases Nervous System 29*, 326–327.

FRIEND, M. B. (1957). Group hypnotherapy treatment. In: *Hospital treatment of alcoholism. A comparative, experimental study.* R. S. WALLERSTEIN, Ed., *Menninger Clinic Monogr. Series 11*, 77–120.

FRISCH, E. P. (1966). Chlormethiazole (Heminevrin[R], distraneurin[R]. Proceedings of a symposium arranged by ASTRA, Hankø, Norway, July 11–13, 1965. *Acta Psychiat. Scand. 42*, Suppl. 192, 233 pp.

FROMMEL, E., V. LEDEBUR, I., JOYE, E., DUDA, M. AND SEYDOUX, J. (1963). The antidotal action of nalorphine in combatting alcohol induced bradypnea in the rabbit. *Med. Exptl. 9*, 38–40.

GABERSEK, V. (1965). Les temps de réactions oculomotrices chez des alcooliques après une cure de désintoxication. *Rev. Neurol. 113*, 293–297.

GALLANT, D. M., BISHOP, M. P., CAMP, E. AND TISDALE, C. (1968). A six-month controlled evaluation of metronidazole (Flagyl) in chronic alcoholic patients. *Current Therapeutic Res. 10*, 82–87.

GELDER, M. G. AND EDWARDS, G. (1968). Metronidazole in the treatment of alcohol addiction. A controlled trial. *Brit. J. Psychiat. 114*, 473–475.

GERARD, D. L. AND SAENGER, G. (1966). *Out-patient treatment of alcoholism: A study of outcome and its determinants.* Brookside Monogr. No. 4, Alcoholism and Drug Addiction Research Foundation of Ontario, Toronto, 249 pp.

GERARD, D. L., SAENGER, G. AND WILE, R. (1962). The abstinent alcoholic. *Arch. Gen. Psychiat. 6*, 83–95.

GERVAIS, P. (1963). Les troubles des intoxications alcooliques massives; traitements nouveaux. *Ann. Méd. Légale Criminol. Police Sci. Toxicol. 43*, 164–170.

GIBBINS, R. J. (1953). *Chronic alcoholism and alcohol addiction. A survey of current literature.* Brookside Monogr. No. 1, Alcoholism Research Foundation, Toronto. 57 pp.

GIBBINS, R. J. AND WALTERS, R. H. (1960). Three preliminary studies of a psychoanalytic theory of alcohol addiction. *Quart. J. Studies Alc. 21*, 618–641.

GLATT, M. M. (1961). Drinking habits of English (middle class) alcoholics. *Acta Psychiat. Scand. 37*, 88–113.

GLATT, M. M. (1966). Controlled trials of non-barbiturate hypnotics and tranquillizers. With special reference to their use in alcoholics. *Psychiat. Neurol. 152*, 28–42.

GODFREY, K. E. (1968). LSD therapy. In: *Alcoholism: The total treatment approach.* R. J. CATANZARO, Ed., C. C. Thomas, Springfield, Ill. Pp. 237–252.

GOLBERT, T. M., SANZ, C. J., ROSE, H. D. AND LEITSCHUH, T. H. (1967). Comparative evaluation of treatments of alcohol withdrawal syndromes. *J. Am. Med. Ass. 201*, 99–102.

GOLDBERG, M. (1960). The occurrence and treatment of hypothyroidism among alcoholics. *J. Clin. Endocrinol. Metab. 20*, 609–621.

GOLDBERG, M., HEHIR, R. AND HUROWITZ, M. (1960). Intravenous tri-iodothyronine in acute alcoholic intoxication. *New Engl. J. Med. 263*, 1336–1339.

GOLDSTEIN, G., CHOTLOS, J. W., McCARTHY, R. J. AND NEURINGER, C. (1968a). Recovery from gait instability in alcoholics. *Quart. J. Studies Alc. 29*, 38–43.

GOLDSTEIN, G., NEURINGER, C., REIFF, C. AND SHELLY, C. H. (1968b). Generalizability of field dependency in alcoholics. *J. Consulting Clin. Psychology 32*, 560–564.

GOODMAN, L. S. AND GILMAN, A. Eds., (1965). *The pharmacological basis of therapeutics.* 3rd ed. Macmillan, New York, Collier-Macmillan, London and Toronto. 1785 pp.

GOODWIN, D. W. (1967). Metronidazole in the treatment of alcoholism: A negative report. *Am. J. Psychiat. 123*, 1276–1278.

GOODWIN, D. W., CRANE, J. B. AND GUZE, S. B. (1969a). Alcoholic "blackouts": A review and clinical study of 100 alcoholics. *Am. J. Psychiat. 126*, 191–198.

GOODWIN, D. W., CRANE, J. B. AND GUZE, S. B. (1969b). Phenomenological aspects of the alcoholic "blackout". *Brit. J. Psychiat. 115*, 1033–1038.

GORRELL, G. J., THULINE, H. C. AND CRUZ-COKE, R. (1967). Inheritance of alcoholism. *Lancet 1*, 274–275.

GREENBERG, L. A. AND LESTER, D. (1957). Vitamin deficiency and the etiology of alcoholism. In: *Alcoholism*. H. E. HIMWICH, Ed., AAAS Publ. No. 47, Washington. Pp. 67–71.

GROSS, M. (1945). The relation of the pituitary gland to some symptoms of alcoholic intoxication and chronic alcoholism. *Quart. J. Studies Alc. 6*, 25–35.

GROSS, M. M. (1967). Management of acute alcohol withdrawal states. *Quart. J. Studies Alc. 28*, 655–666.

GUZE, S. B., TUASON, V. B., GATFIELD, P. D., STEWART, M. A. AND PICKEN, B. (1962). Psychiatric illness and crime with particular reference to alcoholism: A study of 223 criminals. *J. Nerv. Ment. Dis. 134*, 512–521.

HAGGARD, H. W. AND GREENBERG, L. A. (1937). The effect of alcohol as influenced by blood sugar. *Science 85*, 608–609.

HAGGARD, H. W., GREENBERG, L. A., RAKIETEN, N. AND COHEN, I. H. (1940). Studies on the absorption, distribution and elimination of alcohol. VII. The influence of inhalation of oxygen and carbon dioxide and certain drugs on the concentration of alcohol in the blood causing respiratory failure. *J. Pharmacol. Exptl. Therap. 69*, 266–271.

HAMMERSLEY, D. W. (1957). Conditioned-reflex treatment. In: *Hospital treatment of alcoholism—A comparative, experimental study*. R. S. WALLERSTEIN, Ed., *Menninger Clinic Monogr. Series 11*, 53–76.

HARFST, M. J., GREENE, J. C. AND LASSALLE, F. G. (1967). Controlled trial comparing amobarbital and clomethiazole in alcohol withdrawal symptoms. *Quart. J. Studies Alc. 28*, 641–648.

HEIM, F., LANZ, W., GRIES, G. AND AMELUNG, D. (1952). Über den Einfluss von Monosacchariden auf den Alkoholabbau und die Alkoholtoleranz. *Arch. Exptl. Pathol. Pharmakol. 214*, 280–291.

HENRY, D. W. AND MANN, A. M. (1965). Diagnosis and treatment of delirium. *Can. Med. Assoc. J. 93*, 1156–1166.

HIESTAND, W. A., STEMLER, F. W., WIEBERS, J. E. AND ROCKHOLD, W. T. (1953). Alcohol toxicity as related to (alloxan) diabetes, insulin, epinephrine and glucose in mice. *Federation Proc. 12*, 67.

HILGARD, J. R. AND NEWMAN, M. F. (1963). Parental loss by death in childhood as an etiological factor among schizophrenic alcoholic patients compared with a non-patient community sample. *J. Nerv. Ment. Dis. 137*, 14–28.

HILL, M. J. AND BLANE, H. T. (1967). Evaluation of psychotherapy with alcoholics. A critical review. *Quart. J. Studies Alc. 28*, 76–104.

HIRSH, J. (1956). Public health and social aspects of alcoholism. In: *Alcoholism*, G. N. THOMPSON, Ed., Charles C. Thomas, Springfield, pp. 3–102.

HOFF, E. C. (1961). The use of pharmacological adjuncts in the psychotherapy of alcoholics. *Quart. J. Studies Alc.* Suppl. 1, 138–150.

HOFF, E. C. AND FORBES, J. C. (1955). Some effects of alcohol on metabolic mechanisms with applications to therapy of alcoholics. In: *Origins of resistance to toxic agents*, M. G. SEVAG, R. D. REID AND O. E. REYNOLDS, Eds., Academic Press, New York. Pp. 184–193.

HOFFER, A. AND OSMOND, H. (1959). Concerning an etiological factor in alcoholism. The possible role of adrenochrome metabolism. *Quart. J. Studies Alc. 20*, 750–756.

HOFFER, A. AND OSMOND, H. (1967). *The hallucinogens*. Academic Press, New York. 626 pp.

HOFFER, A. AND OSMOND, H. (1968). *New hope for alcoholics*. University Books, Hyde Park, N.Y.

HOLLISTER, L. E., SHELTON, J. AND KRIEGER, G. (1969). A controlled comparison of lysergic acid diethylamide (LSD) and dextroamphetamine in alcoholics. *Am. J. Psychiat. 125*, 1352–1357.

HORN, J. L. AND WANBERG, K. W. (1969). Symptom patterns related to excessive use of alcohol. *Quart. J. Studies Alc. 30*, 35–58.

HSU, J. J. (1965). Electroconditioning therapy of alcoholics: A preliminary report. *Quart. J. Studies Alc. 26*, 449–459.

HUDOLIN, V. (1967). Electroencephalographic characteristic in chronic alcoholism. *Alcoholism (Zagreb) 3*, Suppl. 1, 66 pp.

HUHN, A. AND BÖCKER, F. (1966). Effect of chlormethiazole upon the clinical course of alcoholic delirium. *Acta Psychiat. Scand. 42*, Suppl. 192, 145–151.

HULPIEU, H. R. AND COLE, V. V. (1946). Potentiation of the depressant action of alcohol by adrenalin. *Quart. J. Studies Alc. 7*, 89–97.

IMBER, S. D., NASH, E. H., NEUSTADT, J. O. AND STONE, A. R. (1961). Non-adaptation of alcoholics to sensory stimuli. *Psychol. Rep. 9*, 264.

IZIKOWITZ, S., MÅRTENS, S. AND DAHLBOM, L. (1952). On the cortisone treatment of alcoholism. *Acta Psychiat. Neurol. Scand.*, Suppl. 80, 175–180.

JACOBSON, G. R. (1968). Reduction of field dependence in chronic alcoholic patients. *J. Abn. Psychol. 73*, 547–549.

JANZEN, R. AND BALZEREIT, F. (1968). Polyneuropathie bei Alkoholabusus. *Der Internist 9*, 260–263.

JELLINEK, E. M. (1952). Phases of alcohol addiction. *Quart. J. Studies Alc. 13*, 673–684.

JELLINEK, E. M. (1959). Estimating the prevalence of alcoholism: Modified values in the Jellinek formula and an alternative approach. *Quart. J. Studies Alc. 20*, 261–269.

JELLINEK, E. M. (1960). *The disease concept of alcoholism.* Hillhouse Press, New Haven. 246 pp.

JENSEN, S. E. (1962). A treatment program for alcoholics in a mental hospital. *Quart. J. Studies Alc. 23*, 315–320.

JOHNSON, F. G. (1969). LSD in the treatment of alcoholism. *Am. J. Psychiat. 126*, 481–487.

JOLLIFFE, N. (1942). Vitamin deficiencies in chronic alcoholism. In: *Alcohol addiction and chronic alcoholism*, E. M. JELLINEK, Ed., Yale University Press, New Haven. Pp. 173–240.

JONES, M. C. (1968). Personality correlates and antecedents of drinking patterns in adult males. *J. Consult. Clin. Psychol. 32*, 2–12.

JONSSON, C.-O., CRONHOLM, B. AND IZIKOWITZ, S. (1962). Intellectual changes in alcoholics. Psychometric studies on mental sequels of prolonged intensive abuse of alcohol. *Quart. J. Studies Alc. 23*, 221–242.

KAIJ, L. (1960). *Alcoholism in twins. Studies on the etiology and sequels of abuse of alcohol* Almqvist and Wiksell, Lund. 144 pp.

KAIM, S. C., KLETT, C. J. AND ROTHFELD, B. (1969). Treatment of the acute alcohol withdrawal state: A comparison of four drugs. *Am. J. Psychiat. 125*, 1640–1646.

KAMIONKOWSKI, M. D. AND FLESHLER, B. (1965). The role of alcohol intake in esophageal carcinoma. *Am. J. Med. Sci. 249*, 696–700.

KANITZ, H. R. (1936). Über die Wirkung des Insulins auf den Verlauf der alimentär-hyperglykämischen und alimentärhyperalkoholämischen Kurve. *Arch. Exptl. Pathol. Pharmakol. 83*, 380–386.

KAROLUS, H. E. (1961). Alcoholism and food allergy. *Ill. Med. J. 119*, 151–152.

KARP, S. A. AND KONSTADT, N. L. (1965). Alcoholism and psychological differentiation: Long-range effect of heavy drinking on field dependence. *J. Nerv. Ment. Dis. 140*, 412–416.

KARP, S. A., WITKIN, H. A. AND GOODENOUGH, D. R. (1965a). Alcoholism and psychological differentiation: Effect of achievement of sobriety on field dependence. *Quart. J. Studies Alc. 26*, 580–585.

KARP, S. A., WITKIN, H. A. AND GOODENOUGH, D. R. (1965b). Alcoholism and psychological differentiation: Effect of alcohol on field dependence. *J. Abnorm. Psych. 70*, 262–265.

KELLER, A. Z. (1967). Cirrhosis of the liver, alcoholism and heavy smoking associated with cancer of the mouth and pharynx. *Cancer* N.Y. *20*, 1015–1022. (Abstr. *Quart. J. Studies Alc.* 1968, *29*, 241.)

KELLER, M. (1951). (Book Review) *Quart. J. Studies Alc. 12*, 543–548.

KELLER, M. (1960). Definition of alcoholism. *Quart. J. Studies Alc. 21*, 125–134.

KELLER, M. AND EFRON, V. (1955). The prevalence of alcoholism. *Quart. J. Studies Alc. 16*, 619–644.

KELLER, M. AND EFRON, V. (1956). Alcoholism in the big cities of the United States. *Quart. J. Studies Alc. 17*, 63–72.

KELLER, M. AND McCORMICK, M. (1968). *A dictionary of words about alcohol.* Rutgers Center of Alcohol Studies, New Brunswick, N.J. xxviii + 236 pp.

KENDELL, R. E. (1965). Normal drinking by former alcohol addicts. *Quart. J. Studies Alc. 26*, 247–257.

KENDELL, R. E. AND STATON, M. C. (1966). The fate of untreated alcoholics. *Quart. J. Studies Alc. 27*, 30–41.

KESSEL, N. AND GROSSMAN, G. (1961). Suicide in alcoholics. *British Med. J. 2*, 1671–1672.

KISSIN, B. AND GROSS, M. M. (1968). Drug therapy in alcoholism. *Am. J. Psychiat. 125*, 31–41.

KISSIN, B. AND PLATZ, A. (1968). The use of drugs in the long term rehabilitation of chronic alcoholics. In: *Psychopharmacology: A review of progress 1957–1967*, D. E. EFRON, Ed., Public Health Service Pub. No. 1836, Washington. Pp. 835–851.

KIVIRANTA, P. (1969). *Alcoholism syndrome in Finland. A comparative analysis of members of the AA movement, outpatients of A clinics and inmates of the institutions for the care of alcoholics.* Finnish Foundation for Alcohol Studies, Helsinki. 137 pp.

KNIGHT, R. P. (1938). The psychoanalytic treatment in a sanatorium of chronic addition to alcohol. *J. Am. Med. Assoc. 111*, 1443–1448.

KNOTT, D. H. AND BEARD, J. D. (1969). A diuretic approach to acute withdrawal from alcohol. *Southern Med. J. 62*, 485–489.

KNOTT, D. H., BEARD, J. D. AND WALLACE, J. A. (1967). Acute withdrawal from alcohol. *Postgraduate Medicine 42*, A-109–A-115.

KOPPANYI, T., CANARY, J. J. AND MAENGWYN-DAVIES, G. D. (1961). Problems in acute alcohol poisoning. *Quart. J. Studies Alc.* Suppl. No. 1, 24–36.

KORMAN, M. (1960). Two MMPI scales for alcoholism: What do they measure? *J. Clin. Psychol. 16*, 296–298.

KOUMANS, A. J. R. AND MULLER, J. J. (1965). Use of letters to increase motivation for treatment in alcoholics. *Psychol. Reports 16*, 1152.

KRAFT, T. AND AL-ISSA, I. (1967). Alcoholism treated by desensitization: a case report. *Behav. Res. Therapy 5*, 69–70.

KURLAND, A. A., SAVAGE, C., SHAFFER, J. W. AND UNGER, S. (1967a). The therapeutic potential of LSD in medicine. In: *LSD, man and society*, R. C. DE BOLD AND R. C. LEAF, Eds. Wesleyan Univ. Press, Middletown, Conn. Pp. 20–35.

KURLAND, A. A., UNGER, S., SHAFFER, J. W. AND SAVAGE, C. (1967b). Psychedelic therapy utilizing LSD in the treatment of the alcoholic patient: A preliminary report. *Am. J. Psychiat. 123*, 1202–1209.

LABORIT, H. AND COIRAULT, R. (1957). L'utilisation en clinique médicale et psychiatrique de l'action hypogène d'un dérivé du noyau thiazolique de la vitamine B 1: le S.C.T.Z. *Semaine Méd., Paris 33*, 1704–1708.

LAL, S. (1969). Metronidazole in the treatment of alcoholism. A clinical trial and review of the literature. *Quart. J. Studies Alc. 30*, 140–151.

LAVERNE, A. A. (1962). Compendium of neuropsychopharmacology: Preparations used in treatment of alcoholism. *J. Neuropsychiat. 4*, 127–133.

LAVERTY, S. G. (1966). Aversion therapies in the treatment of alcoholism. *Psychosom. Med. 28*, 651–666.

LEDERMANN, S. (1952). Influence de la consommation de vins et d'alcools sur les cancers, la tuberculeuse pulmonaire et sur d'autres maladies. *Semaine Méd. 28*, 221–235.

LEDERMANN, S. (1964). *Alcool, alcoolisme, alcoolisation. Mortalité, morbidité, accidents du travail.* Institut national d'études demographiques. Travaux et Documents No. 41. Presses Universitaires de France, Paris. 613 pp.

LEEVY, C. M. AND TENHOVE, W. (1967). Pathogenesis and sequelae of liver disease in alcoholic man. In: *Biochemical factors in alcoholism*, R. P. MAICKEL, Ed., Pergamon Press, Oxford-London etc. Pp. 151–165.

LEHMANN, H. E. AND BAN, T. A. (1967). Chemical reduction of the compulsion to drink with metronidazole: A new treatment modality in the therapeutic program of the alcoholic. *Current Therap. Res. 9*, 419–428.

LELBACH, W. K. (1966a). Leberschäden bei chronischem Alkoholismus. I. Klinische Ergebnisse. *Acta Hepato-Splenol. 13*, 321–334.

LELBACH, W. K. (1966b). Leberschäden bei chronischem Alcoholismus. II. Klinisch-chemische Ergebnisse. *Acta Hepato-Splenol. 13*, 334–349.

LEMERE, F. (1953). What happens to alcoholics. *Amer. J. Psychiat. 109*, 674–676.

LEMERE, F. AND O'HOLLAREN, P. (1950). Thiopental U.S.P. (pentothal) treatment of alcoholism. *Arch. Neurol. Psychiat. 63*, 579–585.

LEMERE, F. AND VOEGTLIN, W. L. (1950). Evaluation of the aversion treatment of alcoholism. *Quart. J. Studies Alc. 11*, 199–204.

LEMERE, F., VOEGTLIN, W. L., BROZ, W. R., O'HOLLAREN, P. AND TUPPER, W. E. (1942). Conditioned reflex treatment of chronic alcoholism: VII. Technic. *Dis. Nervous System 3*, 243–247.

LEREBOULLET, J. AND PLUVINAGE, R. (1956). L'atrophie cérébrale des alcooliques; ces conséquences médico-sociales. *Bull. Acad. Nat. Med. 140*, 398–401.

LEREBOULLET, J., AMSTRUTZ, C. F. AND FABRA, I. (1966). Enquête hospitalière sur l'alcoolisme dans le départment de la Seine. Ses facteurs individuels et sociaux. *Rev. Alcool. 12*, 249–298.

LESTER, D. (1960). A biological approach to the etiology of alcoholism. *Quart. J. Studies Alc. 21*, 701–703.

LESTER, D. (1966). Self-selection of alcohol by animals, human variation, and the etiology of alcoholism. A critical review. *Quart. J. Studies Alc. 27*, 395–438.

LESTER, D. AND GREENBERG, L. A. (1952). Alcoholism, 1941–1951: A survey of activities in research, education and therapy. III. The status of physiological knowledge. *Quart. J. Studies Alc. 13*, 444–452.

LEVY, M. S., LIVINGSTONE, B. L. AND COLLINS, D. M. (1967). A clinical comparison of disulfiram and calcium carbimide. *Am. J. Psychiat. 123*, 1018–1022.

LINT, J. E. E. DE (1964). Alcoholism, birth rank and parental deprivation. *Am. J. Psychiat. 120*, 1062–1065.

LINTON, P. H. AND HAIN, J. D. (1967). Metronidazole in the treatment of alcoholism. *Quart. J. Studies Alc. 28*, 544–546.

LISANSKY, E. S. (1957). Alcoholism in women: Social and psychological concomitants. I. Social history data. *Quart. J. Studies Alc. 18*, 588–623.

LISANSKY, E. S. (1960). The etiology of alcoholism: The role of psychological predisposition. *Quart. J. Studies Alc. 21*, 314–343.

LISKER, R., TRUJEQUE, M., BARRERA, A. AND VILLALOBOS, J. DE J. (1968). Cirrosis del hígado y ceguera al color. (Liver cirrhosis and color blindness.) *Acta Cient. Venezolana 19*, 202–205.

LORAND, S. (1945). A survey of psychoanalytical literature on problems of alcohol: Bibliography. *Yearbook Psychoanal. 1*, 359–370.

LOVELL, H. W. (1951). *Hope and help for the alcoholic.* Doubleday, Garden City, N.Y. 215 pp.

LOVELL, H. W. AND TINTERA, J. W. (1951). Hypoadrenocorticism in alcoholism and drug addiction. *Geriatrics 6*, 1–11.

LUDWIG, A., LEVINE, J., STARK, L. AND LAZAR, R. (1969). A clinical study of LSD treatment in alcoholism. *Am. J. Psychiat. 126*, 59–69.

MACHOVER, S. AND PUZZO, F. S. (1959). Clinical and objective studies of personality variables in alcoholism. II. Clinical study of personality correlates of remission from active alcoholism. *Quart. J. Studies Alc. 20*, 520–527.

MACKAY, I. R. (1966). The effects of alcohol on the gastro-intestinal tract. *Med. J. Australia 2*, 372–376.

MACLEAN, J. R. AND WILBY, W. E. (1967). Treatment of alcoholism with lysergide. Comment on the article by SMART *et al.*, with special reference to issues of responsibility in research reporting. *Quart. J. Studies Alc. 28*, 140–146.

MACLEAN, J. R., MACDONALD, D. C., BYRNE, U. P. AND HUBBARD, A. M. (1961). The use of LSD-25 in the treatment of alcoholism and other psychiatric problems. *Quart. J. Studies Alc. 22*, 34–45.

MADILL, M.-F., CAMBELL, D., LAVERTY, S. G., SANDERSON, R. E. AND VANDEWATER, S. L. (1966). Aversion treatment of alcoholics by succinylcholine-induced apneic paralysis. *Quart. J. Studies Alc. 27*, 483–509.

MANN, N. M. (1952). Hypoadrenalism and the alcoholic. Preliminary report. *Quart. J. Studies Alc. 13*, 201–203.

MARC-AURELE, J. AND SCHREINER, G. E. (1960). The dialysance of ethanol and methanol: a proposed method for the treatment of massive intoxication by ethyl or methyl alcohol. *J. Clin. Invest. 39*, 802–807. (Abstr. *Quart. J. Studies Alc.* 1962, *23*, 347.)

MARCONI, J. T. (1959). The concept of alcoholism. *Quart. J. Studies Alc. 20*, 216–235.

MARDONES, J. (1951). On the relationship between deficiency of B vitamins and alcohol intake in rats. *Quart. J. Studies Alc. 12*, 563–575.

MARTENSEN-LARSEN, O. (1957). The family constellation analysis and alcoholism. *Acta Genet. 7*, 441–444.

MARTIN, E. A. (1965). Alcoholic cerebellar degeneration. A report of 3 cases. *J. Irish Med. Assoc. 56*, 172–175.

MARTIN, G. J. (1965). A concept of the etiology of alcoholism. *Exptl. Med. Surg. 23*, 315–319.

MARTIN, G. J., MOSS, J. N., SMYTH, R. D. AND BECK, H. (1966). The effect of cysteine in modifying the action of ethanol given chronically in rats. *Life Sci. 5*, 2357–2362.

MCCORD, W., MCCORD, J. AND GUDEMAN, J. (1959). Some current theories of alcoholism: A longitudinal evaluation. *Quart. J. Studies Alc. 20*, 727–749.

MCCORD, W., MCCORD, J. AND GUDEMAN, J. (1960). *Origins of alcoholism.* Stanford University Press, Stanford, Calif. 193 pp.

MCCREA, F. D. AND TAYLOR, H. M. (1940). The use of pentamethylenetetrazol (Metrazol) as a respiratory stimulant in acute alcoholic depression. *J. Pharmacol. Exptl. Therap. 68*, 41–44.

MCGUIRE, R. J. AND VALLANCE, M. (1964). Aversion therapy by electric shock: A simple technique. *Brit. Med. J. 1*, 151–153.

MCMILLAN, J. J. (1967). Some essentials in the rehabilitation of the addictive personality. In: *Alcoholism*, R. FOX, Ed., Springer, New York. Pp. 24–35.

MCNICHOL, R. W., CIRKSENA, W. J., PAYNE, J. T. AND GLASGOW, M. C. (1967). Management of withdrawal from alcohol (including Delirium tremens). *Southern Med. J. 60*, 7–12.

MENNINGER, K. (1938). *Man against himself.* Harcourt, Brace, New York. 485 pp.

MENNINGER-LERCHENTHAL, E. (1960). Kritik der Alkoholernüchterungsversuche. *Wien. Klin. Wochschr. 72,* 419–422.

MERRY, J. AND WHITEHEAD, A. (1968). Metronidazole and alcoholism. *Brit. J. Psychiat. 114,* 859–861.

MILLER, E. C., DVORAK, B. A. AND TURNER, D. W. (1960). A method of creating aversion to alcohol by reflex conditioning in a group setting. *Quart. J. Studies Alc. 21,* 424–431.

MILLER, M. M. (1942). Ambulatory treatment of chronic alcoholism. *J. Am. Med. Assoc. 120,* 271–275.

MILMORE, S., ROSENTHAL, R., BLANE, H. T., CHAFETZ, M. E. AND WOLF, I. (1967). The doctor's voice: Postdictor of successful referral of alcoholic patients. *J. Abn. Psychol. 72,* 78–84.

MINDLIN, D. F. (1959). The characteristics of alcoholics as related to prediction of therapeutic outcome. *Quart. J. Studies Alc. 20,* 604–619.

MINKER, E. AND KOLTAI, M. (1965). Effect of insulin on synaptic transmission in cat's superior cervical ganglion. *Naturwissenschaften 52,* 189–190.

MOORE, R. A. AND MURPHY, T. C. (1961). Denial of alcoholism as an obstacle to recovery. *Quart. J. Studies Alc. 22,* 597–609.

MOSS, J. N., SMYTH, R. D., BECK, H. AND MARTIN, G. J. (1967). Ethanol impact on brain acetylcholine and its modification by cysteine. *Arch. Intern. Pharmacodyn. 168,* 235–238.

MOTTO, J. A. (1968). Acute alcohol-withdrawal syndromes; a controlled study of phenothiazine effectiveness. *Quart. J. Studies Alc. 29,* 917–930.

MOUREN, P., TATOSSIAN, A., SERRATRICE, G., VIGOROUX, R.-A., BLUMEN, G. AND LAVIEILLE J. (1965). Late cerebellar atrophy, predominantly vermian; role of chronic alcoholism; concerning 10 personal observations. (Fr.) *Marseille Méd. 102,* 91–102. (Abstr. *Quart. J. Studies Alc. 1966, 27,* 767.)

MOURIQUAND, G., COISNARD, J. AND EDEL, V. (1946). Recherches biocliniques sur le vin: vin et indice chronologique vestibulaire. *Presse Méd. 54,* 725. (Abstr. *Quart. J. Studies Alc. 1947, 8,* 122.)

MURPHY, G. E. AND ROBINS, E. (1967). Social factors in suicide. *J. Am. Med. Assoc. 199,* 303–308.

MUZEKARI, H. (1965). The MMPI in predicting treatment outcome in alcoholism. *J. Consulting Psychol. 29,* 281.

NARROL, H. G. (1967). Experimental application of reinforcement principles to the analysis and treatment of hospitalized alcoholics. *Quart. J. Studies Alc. 28,* 105–115.

NAVRATIL, L. (1959). On the etiology of alcoholism. *Quart. J. Studies Alc. 20,* 236–244.

NEWMAN, H. W. (1941). *Acute alcohol intoxication. A critical review.* Stanford University Press, Stanford, Calif., 207 pp.

NEWMAN, H. AND ABRAMSON, M. (1942). Absorption of various alcoholic beverages. *Science 96,* 43–44.

NEWMAN, H. W. AND NEWMAN, E. J. (1956). Failure of Dexedrine and caffeine as practical antagonists of the depressant effect of ethyl alcohol in man. *Quart. J. Studies Alc. 17,* 406–410.

NEWMAN, H. AND SMITH, M. E. (1959). Effect of pyridoxine in acute alcoholic intoxication. *Proc. Soc. Exptl. Biol. Med. 100,* 258–259.

NOLAN, J. P. (1965). Alcohol as a factor in the illness of university service patients. *Am. J. Med. Sci. 249,* 135–142.

NORDMO, S. H. (1959). Blood groups in schizophrenia, alcoholism and mental deficiency. *Am. J. Psychiat. 116,* 460–461.

NYGREN, A. (1966). Serum creatine phosphokinase activity in chronic alcoholism, in connection with acute alcohol intoxication. *Acta Med. Scand. 179,* 623–630.

ODEN, M. H. (1968). The fulfillment of promise: 40-year follow-up of the Terman gifted group. *Genetic Psychology Monographs 77*, 3–93.

OLTMAN, J. E. AND FRIEDMAN, S. (1967). Parental deprivation in psychiatric conditions, III (In personality disorders and other conditions). *Diseases Nervous System 28*, 298–303.

O'MALLEY, E., HEGGIE, V., TRULSON, M., FLEMING, R. AND STARE, F. J. (1951). Nutrition and alcoholism. *Fed. Proc. 10*, 390.

O'REILLY, P. O. AND FUNK, A. (1964). LSD in chronic alcoholism. *Can. Psychiat. Assoc. J. 9*, 258–261.

OWEN, M. (1954). A study of the rationale of the treatment of delirium tremens with adrenocorticotropic hormone. I. The eosinophil response of patients with delirium tremens, after a test with ACTH. II. Clinical correlations to responsiveness to ACTH in delirium tremens. *Quart. J. Studies Alc. 15*, 384–386 and 387–401.

PALOLA, E. G., DORPAT, T. L. AND LARSON, W. R. (1962). Alcoholism and suicidal behavior. In: *Society, culture, and drinking patterns*. D. J. PITTMAN AND C. R. SNYDER, Eds., Wiley, New York. Pp. 511–534.

PARK, P. (1962). Drinking experiences of 806 Finnish alcoholics in comparison with similar experiences of 192 English alcoholics. *Acta Psychiat. Scand. 38*, 227–246.

PARKE, R. D. AND WALTERS, R. H. (1966). Alcoholism, avoidance learning and emotional responsiveness. *Brit. J. Soc. Clin. Psychol. 5*, 276–289.

PARTANEN, J., BRUUN, K. AND MARKKANEN, T. (1966). Inheritance of drinking behavior: A study on intelligence, personality and use of alcohol of adult twins. *Alcohol Research in the Northern countries*. Vol. 14, The Finnish Foundation for Alcohol Studies, Helsinki. 159 pp.

PARTINGTON, J. T. AND JOHNSON, F. G. (1969). Personality types among alcoholics. *Quart. J. Studies Alc. 30*, 21–34.

PATTISON, E. M. (1966). A critique of alcoholism treatment concepts: With special reference to abstinence. *Quart. J. Studies Alc. 27*, 49–71.

PEMBERTON, D. A. (1967). A comparison of the outcome of treatment in female and male alcoholics. *Brit. J. Psychiat. 113*, 367–373.

PENICK, S. B., CARRIER, R. N. AND SHELDON, J. B. (1969). Metronidazole in the treatment of alcoholism. *Am. J. Psychiat. 125*, 1063–1066.

PEREY, B. J., HELLE, S. J. AND MacLEAN, L. D. (1965). Acute alcoholic poisoning; a complication of gastric hypothermia. *Can. J. Surg. 8*, 194–196.

PERLSWIG, E. A. (1957). Milieu therapy. In: *Hospital treatment of alcoholism—A comparative, experimental study*. WALLERSTEIN, R. S., Ed. Menninger Clinic Monogr. Series *11*, 121–146.

PFEFFER, A. Z. AND BERGER, S. (1957). A follow-up study of treated alcoholics. *Quart. J. Studies Alc. 18*, 624–648.

PINCOCK, T. A. (1964). Alcoholism in tuberculous patients. *Can. Med. Assoc. J. 91*, 851–854.

PITTS, F. N., JR. AND WINOKUR, G. (1966). Affective disorder-VII: Alcoholism and affective disorder. *J. Psychiat. Res. 4*, 37–50.

POKORNY, A. D. (1964). Suicide rates in various psychiatric disorders. *J. Nervous Mental Disease 139*, 499–506.

POKORNY, A. D., MILLER, B. A. AND CLEVELAND, S. E. (1968). Response to treatment of alcoholism. A follow-up study. *Quart. J. Studies Alc. 29*, 364–381.

POPHAM, R. E. (1953). A critique of the genetotrophic theory of the etiology of alcoholism. *Quart. J. Studies Alc. 14*, 228–237.

PULLAR-STRECKER, H. (1953). Intravenous detoxication of drunkenness. *Brit. Med. J. 1*, 935. (Abstr. *Quart. J. Studies Alc.* 1953, *14*, 663.)

QUINN, J. T. (1967). Learning theory in the management of alcoholism. *Papers Psychology 1*, 1–9.

RÄKKÖLÄINEN, V. AND TURUNEN, S. (1969). From unrestrained to moderate drinking. *Acta Psychiat. Scand. 45*, 47–52.

RANDOLPH, T. G. (1956). The descriptive features of food addiction: Addictive eating and drinking. *Quart. J. Studies Alc. 17*, 198–224.

RATHOD, N. H., GREGORY, E., BLOWS, D. AND THOMAS, G. H. (1966). A two-year follow-up study of alcoholic patients. *Brit. J. Psychiat. 112*, 683–692.

RAWSON, R. W., KOCH, H. AND FLACH, F. F. (1957). The thyroid hormones and their relationships to mental health. In: *Hormones, brain function and behavior*, H. HOAGLAND, Ed., Academic Press, New York. Pp. 221–242.

READER, D. H. (1967). Alcoholism and excessive drinking: A sociological review. *Psychologia Africana*, Monogr. Suppl. *3*, 69 pp.

REILLY, D. H. AND SUGERMAN, A. A. (1967). Conceptual complexity and psychological differentiation in alcoholics. *J. Nervous Mental Disease 144*, 14–17.

REINERT, R. E. AND BOWEN, W. T. (1968). Social drinking following treatment for alcoholism. *Bull. Menninger Clinic 32*, 280–290.

RICCITELLI, M. L. (1967). Treatment of alcoholism—modern concepts. *J. Am. Geriat. Soc. 15*, 523–534.

RIPLEY, H. S. AND JACKSON, J. K. (1959). Therapeutic factors in Alcoholics Anonymous. *Am. J. Psychiat. 116*, 44–50.

RITTER, U. (1965). Zur Alkoholpankreatitis. *Deut. Med. Wochschr. 90*, 382–386.

ROACH, M. K. AND WILLIAMS, R. J. (1966). Impaired and inadequate glucose metabolism in the brain as an underlying cause of alcoholism—an hypothesis. *Proc. Nat. Acad. Sci. U.S. 56*, 566–571.

ROBINS, E., MURPHY, G. E., WILKINSON, R. H., GASSNER, S. AND KAYES, J. (1959). Some clinical considerations in the prevention of suicide based on a study of 134 successful suicides. *Am. J. Public Health 49*, 888–899.

ROBINS, L. N. (1966). *Deviant children grown up: A sociological and psychiatric study of sociopathic personality*. Williams and Wilkins, Baltimore. xiv + 351 pp.

ROBINS, L. N., BATES, W. M. AND O'NEAL, P. (1962). Adult drinking patterns of former problem children. In: *Society, culture, and drinking patterns*. D. J. PITTMAN AND C. R. SNYDER, Eds., Wiley, New York. Pp. 395–412.

ROBINSON, M. W. AND VOEGTLIN, W. L. (1952). Investigations of an allergic factor in alcohol addiction. *Quart. J. Studies Alc. 13*, 196–200.

ROCHE, L., VEDRINNE, J. AND DUSSERT, D. (1963). Coma hypoglycémique et intoxication éthylique aiguë. Intérêt du dosage de la glycémie au cours des coma alcooliques. *Ann. Méd. Légale Criminol. Police Sci. Toxicol. 43*, 236–241.

ROE, A. (1945). Children of alcoholic parents raised in foster homes. In: *Alcohol, science and society*, Yale Summer School of Alcohol Studies, New Haven, Conn. Pp. 115–127.

ROSENBAUM, M. (1942). Adaptation of the central nervous system to varying concentrations of alcohol in the blood. *A.M.A. Arch. Neurol. Psychiat. 48*, 1010–1012.

ROSENMAN, S. (1955). Pacts, possessions, and the alcoholic. *Am. Imago 12*, 241–274.

ROSSI, J. J., STACH, A. AND BRADLEY, N. J. (1963). Effects of treatment of male alcoholics in a mental hospital. *Quart. J. Studies Alc. 24*, 91–108.

SAMMALISTO, L. (1962). Blood sugar and alcohol intoxication in the rat. *Acta Physiol. Scand. 55*, 313–318.

SAMOCHOWIEC, L., STEPLEWSKI, Z. AND WOJCICKI, J. (1967). Cytochemical studies on the liver and kidney of rats after chronic intoxication with ethyl alcohol and simultaneous medication with essential phospholipids. Ger. *Acta Biol. Med. Ger. 18*, 625–632.

SAMPSON, E. E. (1965). The study of ordinal position: Antecedents and outcomes. In: *Progress in experimental personality research*, B. A. MAHER, Ed., Academic Press, New York, Vol. 2. Pp. 175–228.

SANDERSON, R. E., CAMPBELL, D. AND LAVERTY, S. G. (1963). An investigation of a new aversive conditioning treatment for alcoholism. *Quart. J. Studies Alc. 24*, 261–275.

SARETT, M., CHEEK, F. AND OSMOND, H. (1966). Reports of wives of alcoholics of effects of LSD-25 treatment of their husbands. *Arch. Gen. Psychiat. 14*, 171–178.

SCHAEFER, E. S. (1954). Personality structure of alcoholics in outpatient psychotherapy. *Quart. J. Studies Alc. 15*, 304–319.

SCHAPIRO, H., WRUBLE, L. D. AND BRITT, L. G. (1966). The possible mechanism of alcohol in the production of acute pancreatitis. *Surgery 60*, 1108–1111.

SCHMIDT, W. (1968). The prevalence of alcoholism and drug addiction in Canada. *Addictions 15*, 1–13, 29–36.

SCHMIDT, W. AND LINT, J. DE (1969). Mortality experiences of male and female alcoholic patients. *Quart. J. Studies Alc. 30*, 112–118.

SCHMIDT, W. S. AND SMART, R. G. (1959). Alcoholics, drinking and traffic accidents. *Quart. J. Studies Alc. 20*, 631–644.

SCOTT, E. M. (1958). Psychosexuality of the alcoholic. *Psychol. Rep. 4*, 599–602.

SEELEY, J. R. (1959a). Estimating the prevalence of alcoholism: A critical analysis of the Jellinek formula. *Quart. J. Studies Alc. 20*, 245–254.

SEELEY, J. R. (1959b). The W.H.O. definition of alcoholism. *Quart. J. Studies Alc. 20*, 352–356.

SELZER, M. L. (1969). Alcoholism, mental illness, and stress in 96 drivers causing fatal accidents. *Behavioral Sci. 14*, 1–10.

SELZER, M. L. AND HOLLOWAY, W. H. (1957). A follow-up of alcoholics committed to a state hospital. *Quart. J. Studies Alc. 18*, 98–120.

SELZER, M. L. AND VAN HOUTEN, W. H. (1964). Normal thyroid function in chronic alcoholism. *J. Clin. Endocrinol. Metab. 24*, 380–382.

SELZER, M. L. AND WEISS, S. (1966). Alcoholism and traffic fatalities: Study in futility. *Am. J. Psychiat. 122*, 762–767.

SELZER, M. L., PAYNE, C. E., GIFFORD, J. D. AND KELLY, W. L. (1963). Alcoholism, mental illness and the "drunk driver". *Am. J. Psychiat. 120*, 326–331.

SELZER, M. L., PAYNE, C. E., WESTERVELT, F. H. AND QUINN, J. (1967). Automobile accidents as an expression of psychopathology in an alcoholic population. *Quart. J. Studies Alc. 28*, 505–516.

SERENY, G. AND KALANT, H. (1965). Comparative clinical evaluation of chlordiazepoxide and promazine in treatment of alcohol-withdrawal syndrome. *Brit. Med. J. 1*, 92–97. (Abstr. *Quart. J. Studies Alc.* 1965, *26*, 540.)

SHEA, J. E. (1954). Psychoanalytic therapy and alcoholism. *Quart. J. Studies Alc. 15*, 595–605.

SHELDON, W. H. AND STEVENS, S. S. (1942). *The varieties of temperament: A psychology of constitutional differences.* Harper, New York. 520 pp.

SINGER, E., BLANE, H. T. AND KASSCHAU, R. (1964). Alcoholism and social isolation. *J. Abn. Soc. Psychol. 69*, 681–685.

SMALL, M. D., ZAMCHECK, N., VITALE, J. J., LONGARINI, A. AND FISHER, B. (1955). The effect of pyridoxine hydrochloride in acute alcoholic intoxication. *J. Lab. Clin. Med. 46*, 12–20.

SMALL, M., LONGARINI, A. AND ZAMCHECK, N. (1959). Disturbances of digestive physiology following acute drinking episodes in "skid-row" alcoholics. *Am. J. Med. 27*, 575–585. (Abstr. *Quart. J. Studies Alc.* 1961, *22*, 348.)

SMART, R. G. AND STORM, T. (1964). The efficacy of LSD in the treatment of alcoholism. *Quart. J. Studies Alc. 25*, 333–338.

SMART, R. G., STORM, T., BAKER, E. F. W. AND SOLURSH, L. (1966). A controlled study of lysergide in the treatment of alcoholism. I. The effects on drinking behavior. *Quart. J. Studies Alc. 27*, 469–482.

SMART, R. G., STORM, T., BAKER, E. F. W. AND SOLURSH, L. (1967a). A controlled study of lysergide. Response by the authors. *Quart. J. Studies Alc. 28*, 351–353.

SMART, R. G., STORM, T., BAKER, E. F. W. AND SOLURSH, L. (1967b). *Lysergic acid diethylamide (LSD) in the treatment of alcoholism: An investigation of its effects on drinking behavior, personality structure, and social functioning.* Univ. of Toronto Press, Toronto. 152 pp.

SMITH, C. M. (1958). A new adjunct to the treatment of alcoholism: The hallucinogenic drugs. *Quart. J. Studies Alc. 19*, 406–417.

SMITH, J. A. AND BROWN, W. T. (1952). Treatment in alcoholism. *Am. J. Psychiat. 109*, 279–282.

SMITH, J. A., DARDIN, P. A. AND BROWN, W. T. (1951). The treatment of alcoholism by nutritional supplement. *Quart. J. Studies Alc. 12*, 381–385.

SMITH, J. J. (1949). A medical approach to problem drinking. Preliminary report. *Quart. J. Studies Alc. 10*, 251–257.

SMITH, J. J. (1950). The endocrine basis of hormonal therapy of alcoholism. *N.Y. State J. Med. 50*, 1704–1706, 1711–1715.

SMITH-MOORHOUSE, P. M. (1963). The physical complications of alcoholism. *Brit. J. Addict. 59*, 137–146.

SMYTH, R. D., MOSS, J., BECK, H. AND MARTIN, G. J. (1967). Brain coenzyme activity in rats chronically ingesting ethanol. *Am. J. Pharm. 139*, 239–244.

SOBEL, H. J. AND WAYE, J. D. (1963). Pancreatic changes in various types of cirrhosis in alcoholics. *Gastroenterology 45*, 341–344.

STENBÄCK, A. AND BLUMENTHAL, M. (1964). Relationship of alcoholism, hypochondria, and attempted suicide. *Acta Psychiat. Scand. 40*, 133–140.

STENBÄCK, A., ACHTÉ, K. A. AND RIMÓN, R. H. (1965). Physical disease, hypochondria, and alcohol addiction in suicides committed by mental hospital patients. *Brit. J. Psychiat. 111*, 933–937.

STEWART, D. A. (1955). The dynamics of fellowship as illustrated in Alcoholics Anonymous. *Quart. J. Studies Alc. 16*, 251–262.

STORM, T. AND SMART, R. G. (1965). Dissociation: A possible explanation of some features of alcoholism, and implication for its treatment. *Quart. J. Studies Alc. 26*, 111–115.

STRAUS, R. AND BACON, S. D. (1951). Alcoholism and social stability. A study of occupational integration in 2,023 male clinic patients. *Quart. J. Studies Alc. 12*, 231–260.

SUGERMAN, A. A., REILLY, D. AND ALBAHARY, R. S. (1965). Social competence and essential-reactive distinction in alcoholism. *Arch. Gen. Psychiat. 12*, 552–556.

SZAMOSI, J. (1967). Alkoholvergiftungen im Kindesalter. *Z. Kinderheilk. 99*, 356–365.

TALLAND, G. A. (1963). Alcoholism and reaction time. *Quart. J. Studies Alc. 24*, 610–621.

TARNOWER, S. M. AND TOOLE, H. M. (1968). Evaluation of patients in alcoholism clinic for more than 10 years. *Diseases Nervous System 29*, 28–31.

TAYLOR, J. A. T. (1964). Metronidazole—a new agent for combined somatic and psychic therapy of alcoholism. *Bull. Los Angeles Neurol. Soc. 29*, 158–162.

TEIJEIRA, J. AND MARTINEZ-LAGE, J. M. (1961). Antagonismo entre piridoxina y disulfuro de piridoxina y alcohol etílico. *Rev. Espan. Fisiol. 17*, 11–25. (Abstr. *Quart. J. Studies Alc.* 1962, *23*, 490.)

TENNENT, D. M. (1941). Factors influencing effects of alcohol on blood sugar and liver glycogen. *Quart. J. Studies Alc. 2*, 263–270.

TERMAN, L. M. AND ODEN, M. H. (1959). *Genetic studies of genius.* Vol. 5. *The gifted group at mid-life.* Stanford University Press, Stanford. 187 pp.

THIMANN, J. (1949a). Conditioned-reflex treatment of alcoholism. I. Its rationale and technic. *New Engl. J. Med. 241*, 368–370.

THIMANN, J. (1949b). Conditioned reflex treatment of alcoholism. II. The risks of its application, its indications, contraindications and psychotherapeutic aspects. *New Engl. J. Med. 241*, 406–410.

THOMPSON, G. N. (1956). *Alcoholism.* Charles C. Thomas, Springfield, Ill. 548 pp.

TIEBOUT, H. M., WILLIAMS, L., SELZER, M. L., BLOCK, M. A., FOX, R., ZWERLING, I., ARMSTRONG, J. D. AND ESSER, P. H. (1963). Normal drinking in recovered alcohol addicts: Comment on the article by D. L. DAVIES. *Quart. J. Studies Alc. 24*, 109–121.

TILLOTSON, K. J. AND FLEMING, R. (1937). Personality and sociologic factors in the prognosis and treatment of chronic alcoholism. *New Engl. J. Med. 217*, 611–615.

TINTERA, J. W. (1956). Office rehabilitation of the alcoholic. *N.Y. State J. Med. 56*, 3896–3902.

TINTERA, J. W. (1966). Stabilizing homeostasis in the recovered alcoholic through endocrine therapy: Evaluation of the hypoglycemia factor. *J. Am. Geriat. Soc. 14*, 126–150.

TINTERA, J. W. AND LOVELL, H. W. (1949). Endocrine treatment of alcoholism. *Geriatrics 4*, 274–280.

TRICE, H. M. (1957). A study of the process of affiliation with Alcoholics Anonymous. *Quart. J. Studies Alc. 18*, 39–54.

TRICE, H. M. (1958). Alcoholics Anonymous. *Ann. Am. Acad. Pol. Social Sci. 315*, 108–116.

TRICE, H. M. AND WAHL, J. R. (1958). A rank order analysis of the symptoms of alcoholism. *Quart. J. Studies Alc. 19*, 636–648.

U.S. Department of Transportation (1968). *Alcohol and highway safety.* Washington, D.C. iv + 123 pp.

VAN DUSEN, W., WILSON, W., MINERS, W. AND HOOK, H. (1967). Treatment of alcoholism with lysergide. *Quart. J. Studies Alc. 28*, 295–304.

VANHA-PERTTULA, T. P. J. (1960). The influence of vitamin C on eosinophil response to acute alcohol intoxication in rats. *Acta Endocrinol. 35*, 585–593.

VETTER, W. R., COHN, L. H. AND REICHGOTT, M. (1967). Hypokalemia and electrocardiographic abnormalities during acute alcohol withdrawal. *Arch. Internal Med. 120*, 536–541.

VICTOR, M. (1966). Treatment of alcoholic intoxication and the withdrawal syndrome. A critical analysis of the use of drugs and other forms of therapy. *Psychosomat. Med. 28*, 636–650.

VICTOR, M. (1968). The use of drugs in the treatment of the alcohol withdrawal syndrome. In: *Psychopharmacology: A review of progress 1957–1967.* D. H. EFRON, Ed., Public Health Service Publication No. 1836, Washington, D.C. Pp. 829–834.

VICTOR, M. AND ADAMS, R. D. (1961). On the etiology of the alcoholic neurologic diseases. With special reference to the role of nutrition. *Am. J. Clin. Nutr. 9*, 379–397.

VINKE, B. (1964). Hypoglycaemic coma and hyperkalaemic acidosis due to alcohol intoxication. *Trop. Geograph. Med. 16*, 115–119.

VOEGTLIN, W. L. AND BROZ, W. R. (1949). The conditioned reflex treatment of chronic alcoholism. X. An analysis of 3125 admissions over a period of ten and a half years. *Ann. Intern. Med. 30*, 580–597.

VOEGTLIN, W. L. AND LEMERE, F. (1942). The treatment of alcohol addiction: A review of the literature. *Quart. J. Studies Alc. 2*, 717–798.

VOGEL, M. D. (1960). The relation of personality factors to GSR conditioning of alcoholics: An exploratory study. *Canad. J. Psychol. 14*, 275–280.

VOGEL, M. D. (1961a). The relationship of personality factors to drinking patterns of alcoholics: An exploratory study. *Quart. J. Studies Alc. 22*, 394–400.

VOGEL, M. D. (1961b). The relationship of GSR conditioning to drinking patterns of alcoholics. *Quart. J. Studies Alc. 22*, 401–410.

VOGEL-SPROTT, M. D. (1967). Individual differences in the suppressing effect of punishment on a rewarded response in alcoholics and nonalcoholics. *Quart. J. Studies Alc. 28*, 33–42.

VOGEL-SPROTT, M. D. AND BANKS, R. K. (1965). The effect of delayed punishment on an immediately rewarded response in alcoholics and nonalcoholics. *Behav. Res. Ther. 3,* 69–73.

WALL, J. H. AND ALLEN, E. B. (1944). Results of hospital treatment of alcoholism. *Am. J. Psychiat. 100,* 474–479.

WALLER, J. A. (1967). Identification of problem drinking among drunken drivers. *J. Am. Med. Assoc. 200,* 114–120.

WALLER, J. A. (1968a). Patterns of traffic accidents and violations related to drinking and to some medical conditions. *Quart. J. Studies Alc.* Suppl. 4, 118–137.

WALLER, J. A. (1968b). Holiday drinking and highway fatalities. *J. Am. Med. Assoc. 206,* 2693–2697.

WALLER, J. A. AND TURKEL, H. W. (1966). Alcoholism and traffic deaths. *New Engl. J. Med. 275,* 532–536.

WALLERSTEIN, R. S. (1956). Comparative study of treatment methods for chronic alcoholism: The alcoholism research project at Winter VA Hospital. *Amer. J. Psychiat. 113,* 228–233.

WALLERSTEIN, R. S. (1957). *Hospital treatment of alcoholism. A comparative, experimental study.* Menninger Clinic Monograph Series No. 11, Basic Books, New York. 212 pp.

WALLGREN, H. (1960). Alcoholism and alcohol consumption. *Alkoholpolitik 23,* 177–179, ref. p. 149.

WALLGREN, H. AND TIRRI, R. (1963). Studies on the mechanism of stress-induced reduction of alcohol intoxication in rats. *Acta Pharmacol. Toxicol. 20,* 27–38.

WALTON, H. J. (1968). Personality as a determinant of the form of alcoholism. *Brit. J. Psychiat. 114,* 761–766.

WEINER, H. B. (1965). Treating the alcoholic with psychodrama. *Group Psychother. 18,* 27–49.

WEXBERG, L. E. (1950). A critique of physiopathological theories of the etiology of alcoholism. *Quart. J. Studies Alc. 11,* 113–118.

WIESER, S. (1962). Alkoholismus (1940–1959). I. Teil: Dokumentation, Begriffe und Definitionen, Stoffwechsel. Ätiologie. *Fortschr. Neurol. Psychiat. 30,* 169–228.

WIESER, S. (1965). Alkoholismus II. Psychiatrische und neurologische Komplikationen. *Fortschr. Neurol. Psychiat. 33,* 349–409.

WIESER, S. (1966). Alkoholismus III. Katamnesen und Prognose. *Fortschr. Neurol. Psychiat. 34,* 565–588.

WIETH, J. O. AND JØRGENSEN, H. E. (1961). Treatment of methanol and ethanol poisoning with hemodialysis. *Danish Med. Bull. 8,* 103–106.

WILLIAMS, A. F. (1968). Psychological needs and social drinking among college students. *Quart. J. Studies Alc. 29,* 355–363.

WILLIAMS, H. M. (1968). An improved detoxication regimen. In: *Alcoholism: The total treatment approach,* R. J. CATANZARO, Ed., Charles C. Thomas, Springfield, Ill. Pp. 409–422.

WILLIAMS, R. J. (1947). The etiology of alcoholism: A working hypothesis involving the interplay of hereditary and environmental factors. *Quart. J. Studies Alc. 7,* 567–587.

WILLIAMS, R. J. (1959). *Alcoholism: The nutritional approach.* Univ. of Texas Press, Austin. x + 118 pp.

WINOKUR, G. AND CLAYTON. P. J. (1968). Family history studies. IV. Comparison of male and female alcoholics. *Quart. J. Studies Alc. 29,* 885–891.

WINSHIP, G. M. (1957). Antabuse treatment. In: *Hospital treatment of alcoholism—A comparative, experimental study.* WALLERSTEIN, R. S., Ed., Menninger Clinic Monogr. Series 11, 23–51.

WITKIN, H. A., KARP, S. A. AND GOODENOUGH, D. R. (1959). Dependence in alcoholics. *Quart. J. Studies Alc. 20*, 493–504.

WOLFF, S. AND HOLLAND, L. (1964). A questionnaire follow-up of alcoholic patients. *Quart. J. Studies Alc. 25*, 108–118.

WOLOWITZ, H. M. (1964). Food preferences as an index of orality. *J. Abn. Soc. Psychol. 69*, 650–654.

WOLOWITZ, H. M. AND BARKER, M. J. (1969). Alcoholism and oral passivity. *Quart. J. Studies Alc. 30*, 592–597.

WOOD, H. P. AND DUFFY, E. L. (1966). Psychological factors in alcoholic women. *Am. J. Psychiat. 123*, 341–345.

World Health Organization (1951). Expert committee on mental health: Report of the first session of the alcoholism subcommittee. Geneva: *WHO Technical report series* No. 42, 24 pp.

Chapter 12

Conclusions

The prior chapters of the book have reviewed particular aspects of the actions of ethyl alcohol on living organs and organisms. These aspects are interrelated, but in each chapter material from other chapters has been presented only in the context of the special topic covered. Evaluations of prior research, recommendations for future research, and conclusions have been stated only in the context of the topic of the particular chapter. Accordingly, the present chapter of general conclusions is needed to provide an integrated account, covering all aspects of alcohol effects.

A. Implications of research findings

This first section of the concluding chapter attempts to show a general, unified picture of what ethanol really does. A pattern of interrelated effects is identified. The implications of the research findings can conveniently be divided into acute effects of ethanol, based mostly on the data reviewed in Chapters 3–7, and chronic effects and clinical aspects, based mostly on the data reviewed in Chapters 8–11. However, our conclusions represent an attempt to integrate all the aspects of ethanol effects. For example, the first section which follows includes material from Chapter 10 on acute interactions of alcohol with other drugs and from Chapter 9 on the acute tolerance which develops during a single drinking episode.

(1) Acute effects of ethanol

Ethyl alcohol is a widely used beverage primarily because of its effects on the central nervous system. Most studies of nerve conduction and transmission, EEG records, and behavioral performance indicate stimulant actions of low doses and depressant actions of high doses. A selective depression of inhibitory functions, at doses with little effect on excitatory functions,

References p. 839

[797]

can cause an apparent stimulant action, accompanied by disorganization, at doses above those with direct stimulant effects. Since the various inter-related functions differ in their thresholds for these opposite effects, an intoxicating dose of alcohol gives rise to a complex combination of sedation, disorganization, disinhibition, and stimulation.

The effects of any drug should be regarded in relation to other drugs. The central actions of alcohol are closely similar to those of barbiturates, other hypnotics, and general anesthetic agents. The onset and duration of action are almost identical for alcohol and for the short-acting barbiturates, such as pentobarbital and amobarbital. The synergistic actions of alcohol and barbiturates, which have been demonstrated in many experiments, are further indicated by the unhappily frequent occurrence of accidental death in humans as a result of taking an ordinarily sublethal number of sleeping pills at the same time as drinking an ordinarily sublethal amount of liquor. However, certain unique characteristics of alcohol result in some important differences. One of the distinctive features of ethanol is its simple molecular structure, consisting of two carbon atoms and a single hydroxyl group, and composed entirely of carbon, hydrogen, and oxygen, which are the three elements basic to organic compounds. The small molecule is readily absorbed into the body by any route and rapidly penetrates into all body compartments, being distributed according to their water content. Therefore, ethanol is not blocked by the blood-brain barrier which protects the central nervous system from many drugs. Alcohol is probably the weakest psychotropic drug with respect to effect per quantity in g/kg. Substantial effects on behavioral performance generally require an alcohol dose of approximately 1 g/kg (1000 mg/kg). This is approximately 100 times the corresponding effective dose of pentobarbital or amobarbital. At the opposite extreme, strong mental effects in humans can be caused by LSD-25 with a dose of 1 μg/kg, approximately one-millionth the usual effective dose of alcohol.

Alcohol readily penetrates the central nervous system and acts primarily upon it, but without as strong preponderance of neural over other physiological actions as is found in other drugs with primarily central action. Among drugs used primarily because of their capacity to change the mood and state of mind, ethanol is unique in that it is also a food. In humans, the normal rate of ethanol metabolism supplies about half the energy needed in moderate activity. This feature causes complex metabolic changes, and the nutritional consequence is a change in the normal balance between intake of calories and of protective nutrients. In acute conditions, the nutritional aspect is not important, but it greatly aggravates and complicates the physical complications of excessive alcohol use. It is also important to realize that in addition to its pharmacologic action, most easily noticeable in the central nervous system, alcohol has a metabolic action which, although not clearly perceived, achieves full impact at concentrations considerably lower than those causing measurable impairment of nerve function.

The removal of alcohol is almost entirely by oxidation, principally in the liver, where ethanol is oxidized almost to the exclusion of other, normal substrates. Even a low ethanol concentration induces a maximal metabolic rate in the liver, greatly altering the function of this vital organ. The processes supply the liver with the energy needed for its function, but during ethanol metabolism the strong shift toward reduced conditions caused by ethanol, and the blockage of the citric acid cycle, cause inhibition of glucose formation, a rise in concentrations of reduced metabolites, and decrease in oxidized metabolites of a number of compounds, including steroids, monoamines, and amino acids. Some NAD-dependent dehydrogenase enzymes are also directly inhibited, perhaps more by the first product formed in ethanol oxidation, acetaldehyde, than by ethanol itself. Evidently, there are considerable changes also in peripheral substrate utilization since most of the acetate formed from ethanol in the liver is oxidized in other organs. Most of the alcohol introduced into the organism is finally oxidized to carbon dioxide and water, but a minor proportion of the acetate formed enters into synthetic reactions and is thus incorporated into a variety of compounds in all tissues. Since ethanol is not metabolized in the brain to any significant extent and the blood-brain barrier permits exchange of only a few compounds between brain and blood, the depressant actions of ethanol are not attributable to any of these metabolic changes but evidently are due to a direct action of ethanol molecules. All animals studied contain effective mechanisms for the metabolism of alcohol, probably because of the widespread occurrence of fermentable carbohydrates and various types of yeasts and other micro-organisms capable of fermenting the carbohydrate to alcohol. The faster metabolism and greater surface to volume ratio in small animals result in more rapid metabolism and elimination of alcohol. A lethal effect of this drug requires a blood level of approximately 0.9% in rats compared with about 0.5% in humans (Chapter 2, Table 12, p. 56). An equivalent degree of change in behavioral performance generally also requires a somewhat lower dose in humans than in the rat or mouse.

References p. 839

However, much greater species differences in toxic and effective dosage are prevalent for other drugs.

The effects on physiological functions are generally complex, arising both from metabolic and pharmacological action. Contrary to rather general beliefs, alcohol is not a general vasodilator. For instance, it has no therapeutic value in coronary insufficiency except for psychic effects of mild sedation and decrease in apprehension, and is directly contraindicated in severe cases. In cold exposure, beneficial effects of moderate alcohol doses have been objectively verified, but alcohol impairs physiological defense mechanisms against entry of foreign agents and lowers resistance to infections. Actions of alcohol on fluid and electrolyte balance are generally assumed to be widespread, but there is little evidence for any important actions. The best verified effect is the diuretic action, caused by inhibition of secretion of the antidiuretic hormone from the neurohypophysis. However, this effect reverses to depression of urine production in later stages of intoxication; in chronic alcoholics, overhydration seems to be more common than dehydration. Alcohol also inhibits release of oxytocin from the posterior hypophysis. This effect has led to trials with alcohol as medication for the prevention of spontaneous abortion, with encouraging results. Alcohol in small doses stimulates secretion of epinephrine, and in higher doses causes a generalized stress response, involving the hypophyseal–adrenocortical system. Other endocrine effects in acute intoxication seem to be slight. Even in severe intoxication, the ethanol concentrations attained in the tissues have little direct effects on cells, except for the processes of impulse conduction and transmission in excitable cells. Tissue damage is possible only when high concentrations are reached locally, as after oral administration in the stomach, and around sites of parenteral injection.

Electrophysiological, biochemical, and pharmacological findings, obtained *in vivo* and *in vitro* in a variety of human and animal preparations, vertebrate and invertebrate, lead to an important although as yet somewhat tentative conclusion. The depressant action of alcohol seems to arise primarily through effects on processes involved in the generation of action potentials in nerve and muscle cells. There is little evidence for differences in sensitivity between synaptic transmission and propagation of impulses along the nerve cell membrane. There is some selectivity in action on central inhibitory functions, the association area of the cortex, and the midbrain reticular formation. Also, spinal motor neurons are affected at moderate alcohol concentrations. This widespread impairment of impulse conduction and transmission appears to account for the pervasive action of alcohol and the small difference between the anesthetic and the lethal dose of alcohol. It is also compatible with the suppression of the activation level and the disinhibiting and disruptive effect alcohol has on behavior and performance. There is some evidence that direct action on peripheral synapses accounts for some disturbances caused by alcohol in autonomic function.

Although the consumption of intoxicating doses of alcohol arouses unpleasant, stressful reactions and is almost universally avoided by laboratory animals, intoxication is a frequent consequence of drinking by humans. Several factors may account for this occurrence. One of the principal effects of alcohol intoxication is a general weakening of restraints on behavior. This disinhibitory effect of alcohol is seen in many aspects of behavior, reviewed in Chapter 7. One of the most important consequences of this alcohol effect is a positive feedback by which each response to the drug gives rise to a further, more exaggerated response. Thus even a mild degree of intoxication may override the sober judgment that it is time to stop drinking, and the effects of the further drinks tend to weaken still more the restraints against excessive consumption. Several other factors contribute to this positive feedback. One is the habit of holding and sipping drinks in the social situation, enhanced by the tendency for each member of the group to imitate the drinking behavior by the others. The physiological effects of alcohol may include an increase in thirst, and alcoholic beverages are often the only customarily consumed liquids at a party. Both the effects of alcohol and the action of sipping the drink may reduce the tensions and anxieties evoked by the social situation. These soothing effects reinforce and tend to perpetuate the response of drinking. This effect may especially lead to excessive consumption because of the delay of several minutes before the full effect of a drink is felt. Therefore, the drinker may have already consumed more liquor at the time when the subjectively perceived reactions give warning that any more would be excessive.

The ability of the individual to continue drinking, and thus push the effects of positive feedback to an extreme of intoxication, is enhanced by mechanisms for minimizing and counteracting the alterations caused by the drug. With intoxicating doses, the depressant action of alcohol evokes a compensatory stimulation which is apparent in the form of tissue tolerance at the cellular level and "pulling oneself together" at the behavioral level. This effort to maintain the normal level of functioning is an automatic response to all drugs or other disturbances of the homeostatic balance. As a result, partial recovery from the depressant effects of alcohol occurs even while the blood-alcohol level is still rising.

Various physiological responses to alcohol also show development of tolerance. The diuretic effect disappears when the blood alcohol ceases to rise, even if the blood alcohol is maintained at its peak rather than being allowed to decline. This may be an indication of acute tolerance for this highly reliable physiological response to alcohol. The tendency for intoxicated people to underestimate their performance impairment, or even to believe they are performing better than usual, may be based on the fact that the acute behavioral tolerance usually results in an objective improvement over their performance of a short time before. For example, when blood-alcohol levels of the human subjects were kept at a constant level for three and a half hours, in an experiment by Loomis and West (Chapter 6), the subjects progressively improved in performance and also at the end of that period reported that they expected to perform better than in the prior test. The strong compensatory response to alcohol may account for the fact that a severely intoxicating dose is often necessary to cause detectable performance impairment, so that the margin between an incapacitating dose and an ineffective one may be very small. The compensatory response to counteract the effects of intoxication may be expected to persist after the alcohol has disappeared from the blood. Symptoms of agitation and hypersensitivity, during hangover after acute intoxication and during the withdrawal stage after chronic consumption, are attributable to persistence of the compensatory, excitatory response to the depressant effect of alcohol.

Effects of alcohol may be difficult to predict because of opposite tendencies. The compensatory response, counteracting the depressant action of ethanol, may be accentuated by a stressful situation or a sudden emergency, which causes the intoxicated individual to "pull himself together." The unspecific stress response to a very high alcohol dose might further help to counteract the effects of a severe stressor. It is suggestive that in a study by Wallgren and Tirri (Chapter 7), orally administered alcohol had little effect on performance of emotional, young, female rats with doses as high as 4.5 g/kg. On the other hand, the sedative action of alcohol might alleviate the stressor. The intensity and type of stressor seem likely to be important determinants of whether the depressant alcohol effect relieves the stressful stimulation or is counteracted by it. Another example of opposite tendencies is the effect of alcohol on performance inhibited by punishment or nonreward. The disinhibitory, fear-reducing effect of alcohol enhances the inhibited response in some situations, especially when approach and avoidance tendencies compete directly in the same situation. However, a generalized depressant action of alcohol may enhance the effectiveness of the inhibitory tendency, especially if the animal has been trained to act in one situation and to refrain from acting in another situation. A complexly organized task may aggravate the disruptive effect of alcohol on performance, as found in speed of reaction to stimuli when they are presented occasionally during an ongoing, competing activity, whereas another organized task may be more resistant to detrimental alcohol effects, as found in several tests of sensori-motor coordination compared with more severely detrimental effects of alcohol in the Romberg test of standing steadiness with eyes closed. The swaying elicited by this situation is largely due to the absence of a goal-directed pattern of motor behavior.

Most of the effects of large alcohol doses are detrimental or dangerous. With more moderate doses, the impairment in various types of performance, together with decreased caution and poorer perception of the limits of one's capabilities, lead to many instances of foolhardy behavior, resulting in automobile accidents and other exposures to injury or death. Nash (1966) pointed out that stimulant drugs, such as caffeine, may intensify this danger by increasing the capability and motivation for driving or other active behavior without completely antagonizing the deficiencies in motor coordination and in judgment. Nevertheless, the effects of alcohol may be beneficial in many situations. If it is necessary to undertake dangerous or painful action, alcohol may provide the needed boldness and courage. In a cold environment, alcohol may increase the risk of exposure by decreasing the urge to escape the excessive cold, but if escape is impossible, moderate doses of alcohol have the beneficial function of improving heat balance. The impaired perception of a complex visual scene, under alcohol, may improve the objective accuracy of the perception when the visual context gives rise to a distortion, such as in the Müller–Lyer illusion. Similarly, normal perception is generally facilitated by suppression of images from the subordinate eye which compete with the image from the dominant eye. Alcohol, by weakening this suppression, may disturb normal perception but also may add to the visual information transmitted by the perceptual process. In some circumstances, this additional information is useful and may contribute to the subjective feeling of heightened awareness and sensitivity, reported by some people under the influence of alcohol. Although alcohol generally decreases intellectual capability, several experiments have shown that alcohol can improve intellectual performance in some subjects under certain conditions, primarily by increasing the willingness of people to persist in working on a task which they would ordinarily abandon. This is consistent with the experimental evidence that alcohol may increase tolerance for certain types of stress.

(2) Chronic effects and clinical aspects

Voluntary consumption of ethanol is influenced by its pharmacological, metabolic, nutritional, and taste qualities. In laboratory animals given a continuous choice between an alcohol solution and water, accurate self-regulation of alcohol intake is evidenced by a tendency to consume a constant amount in g/kg/day regardless of variations in alcohol concentration or various treatments which change their fluid intake. However, at concentrations low enough so that most of the fluid intake is from the alcohol bottle, animals generally reduce their alcohol intake rather than increasing their fluid consumption. Large differences are found among species, strains, and individuals in the amount of alcohol consumption in relation to body weight or rate of ethanol metabolism. Some animals maintain chronically a rate of alcohol intake which is close to their maximal metabolic capability, especially if sucrose is included in the alcohol solution. However, they generally regulate the rate of consumption to avoid elevated blood-alcohol concentrations, so that voluntary intoxication has seldom been observed in laboratory animals.

Although rate of ethanol metabolism sets a stringent limit on chronic consumption, variations in the degree of metabolic disturbance caused by alcohol result in further limitation and account for differences in alcohol consumption among individuals under various conditions. A high degree of susceptibility to metabolic disturbance appears to prevent some animals from heavy drinking. Among animals with the metabolic capability, only some choose to drink heavily, perhaps due to greater tolerance for the strong taste of alcohol or greater incentive for the sedative effects. These differences are consistent with genetic evidence that the amount of alcohol consumption is polygenically determined, with greater homogeneity in strains bred for light drinking than for heavy drinking. Variations in nutritional, hormonal, and general metabolic conditions also influence the amount of alcohol consumption. Stressful conditions also may cause a chronic increase in alcohol consumption, presumably by increasing the incentive to obtain the sedative action of alcohol.

Experiments on laboratory animals given an alcohol solution as their only fluid have revealed that rather large quantities of alcohol intake can be tolerated for a long period of time without any detectable adverse effects, provided that intoxication does not occur and nutritional balance is maintained. Many humans also drink moderate amounts of alcohol every day, even with occasional intoxication, without any apparent damage. A steady, consistent pattern of drinking must involve a very large intake of alcohol to be classified as the pathological type of delta alcoholism. Cellular and behavioral tolerance, which was discussed earlier in the present chapter as a compensatory response to the effect of a single alcohol dose, has been demonstrated in laboratory animals to be a strong compensatory response to repeated alcohol doses. Acquisition of tolerance to chronic alcohol intake is also indicated by observations of smaller effects of alcohol on performance of people with a previous history of consuming large quantities of liquor.

One of the consequences of the great sociological and clinical importance of alcohol has been strong interest and active research on its relationships to other drugs. The actions of alcohol, both at the cellular and integrative level of action, resemble those of volatile anesthetics and of barbiturates. All drugs which in their general action resemble alcohol are hypnotics or sedatives. The results of a number of studies suggest that most of the joint actions of alcohol and other drugs arise through interactions at the site of action in the central nervous system. These joint synergistic actions are usually additive in nature, whereas clearly documented instances of potentiation are not known. However, the effects of alcohol on distribution and penetration of drugs, utilized in the common application of alcohol as a solvent and vehicle for other drugs, result in many instances of apparent potentiation in the intact organism, particularly in joint actions at moderate levels of behavioral impairment. Metabolism of other drugs is rarely altered by ethanol, and the few instances are generally due to involvement of NAD-dependent dehydrogenases in the metabolism of the drugs. On the other hand, some therapeutic agents, for instance pyrazol derivatives, inhibit the oxidation of ethanol. Antagonism of alcohol effects is limited to a few strong central stimulants which are dangerous in therapeutic use because of their convulsant properties.

Alcoholism may be defined by three criteria: (a) large quantity of alcohol consumed over a period of years; (b) abnormal, chronic loss of control over drinking, shown by inability to refrain or inability to stop; (c) the drinking causes chronic damage to physical health or social standing. Each of these criteria must generally be present for the person to be regarded as an alcoholic. Data on amount of alcohol consumption (Fig. 1 of Chapter 11, p. 717) show a large amount of overlap between "normal" and "alcoholic" drinkers. Loss of control over drinking is inferred from the drinker's behavior; objective, quantitative measurements are lacking for this criterion. Damage to physical health is seen in only a minority of alcoholics, and damage to social standing depends primarily on the drinker's social and cultural setting. Therefore, no clear-cut distinction is possible between the alcoholic and the heavy drinker whose use of alcohol is controlled and non-pathological. Further evidence for lack of a clear-cut distinction is that the progression toward increasing pathology can be halted and reversed at any stage. Some alcoholics have adopted and maintained a pattern of moderate, controlled drinking.

Physical dependence on alcohol contributes to the craving for liquor and the loss of control over drinking, which are characteristic of alcoholics. Studies of the acute effects of liquor on alcoholics show a prevalently normalizing effect of alcohol, including in many cases an improvement in performance at doses which greatly impair the performance of normal people. Comparisons with other addictive drugs indicate that alcohol has a unique combination of characteristics. The development of physical dependence is slow, requiring the consumption of intoxicating doses during a period of many months. However, the withdrawal syndrome may be severe, even to the point of lethal effect.

Chronic, excessive consumption of alcohol may result in a wide variety of types of physical damage. Clinical experience with diseases of alcoholics has been verified and amplified by experiments on laboratory animals, although the experimental studies have been predominantly on pathology of the liver rather than of the brain and other organ systems. Clinical experience with humans and experimental studies on animals both indicate that the pathological effects are caused by alcohol only indirectly, through the nutritional deficiency which is a consequence of prolonged, excessive drinking. Thus the nutritional rather than pharmacological attribute of alcohol is the most important source of the pathological effects of prolonged intake. When large amounts of alcohol are consumed chronically, supplemental vitamins can remedy the deficit only partially because the large proportion of the liver's activity in metabolizing alcohol curtails the utilization of vitamins and other needed substances.

In the early stages of chronic, excessive drinking, pathological effects are apparent in the severe hangover and other withdrawal symptoms which occur during disappearance of alcohol from the blood. Even after the withdrawal symptoms have disappeared, the alcoholic suffers from feelings of jitteriness, anxiety, and a compulsive craving for liquor. The compensatory response to the effects of alcohol results in tolerance for larger quantities of the drug and also in a normalizing effect of alcohol on mood and performance. These compensatory responses minimize the direct pathological effects of alcohol but also provide the basis for increased craving for alcohol and consumption of increased amounts, thus further elevating the tolerance and dependence. In the early stages of alcoholism, however, the pathological effects appear to be completely reversible. No convincing evidence of permanent physical damage has been reported as a result of chronic, heavy alcohol consumption short of the occurrence of severe, acute alcoholic illness. The compensatory responses are sufficient to cope with the effects of large, severely intoxicating doses of alcohol. The stimulation of liver-cell division and thus storage capacity, resulting from the fatty infiltration during acute intoxication, may enhance the liver's ability to continue functioning normally in spite of damage in the future. This might be the reason for an experimental finding of reduced incidence of liver cirrhosis in rats which were periodically administered intoxicating doses of alcohol. However, growth was more severely retarded in these animals than in a group which consumed the same amount of alcohol in non-intoxicating doses every day.

The later stage of acute alcoholic illness is characterized by loss of the compensatory response to alcohol. Liver damage impairs the metabolism of alcohol, thus decreasing tolerance to the drug. Consumption of alcohol induces acute illness instead of having a normalizing effect. This is a highly dangerous stage of alcoholism, but these adverse reactions to alcohol may have the protective function of counteracting the craving for alcohol. Many alcoholics have abstained and begun to recover only when they experienced these symptoms of acute illness. The severe liver impairment and other organ pathologies at this late stage may result in permanent damage, and life may be endangered by the severe withdrawal syndrome when alcohol consumption ceases. However, the organ systems affected by alcohol appear to have a great capacity for recovery, and many alcoholics have survived the stage of extreme, acute illness with apparently full recovery of their health.

The physical illnesses associated with alcoholism, including liver cirrhosis

References p. 839

and various disorders of the central nervous system, are probably caused primarily by nutritional deficiency and only secondarily by the excess alcohol intake which results in the nutritional deficiency. Since only a minority of alcoholics suffer from these physical complications, and each disease associated with alcoholism occurs in some nondrinkers, the physical illnesses are important as prototypes of the final progression of alcoholism or as confirmatory evidence for a diagnosis rather than as the principal criteria for diagnosis or definition of alcoholism. The diversity among alcoholics should be emphasized. An allegedly typical progression of the disorder through successive stages probably applies only to the gamma type of alcoholic, and stopping or reversal at any stage occurs in many cases. Therefore it is more accurate to describe alcoholism as a disorder, with the behavior of prolonged, excessive drinking as the main characteristic all alcoholics have in common, rather than as a unitary disease. None of the proposed etiological theories of alcoholism seems compatible with the great diversity among alcoholics in physical and personality characteristics. In spite of considerable effort, based on observations and some experimentation, no specific genetic, constitutional, or other biological variables have been conclusively identified as factors predisposing the individual toward alcoholism.

Some characteristics of alcoholics, while not universal, are distinctive enough to deserve special attention in research on this disorder. A self-destructive tendency may be important as an explanation for the persistent seeking of the immediate relief and gratifications obtainable by intoxication, whereas even the less intellectually developed laboratory animals learn to avoid the delayed but more severe aversive consequences of excessive drinking. One of the most striking responses to intoxication, prevalent in alcoholics and rare in normal drinkers, is the occurrence of blackouts or palimpsests, indicated by amnesia after restoration of sobriety for one's experiences and actions while intoxicated. Some alcoholics show this response to rather moderate amounts of alcohol, far short of the dose sufficient to cause stupor or "passing out". This response to alcohol may be one of the best indications of incipient alcoholism and seems to indicate an attempt to keep separated from each other the contradictory desires and self-images associated with drunkenness and sobriety. An adjustive function of this dissociation may be to minimize the disruptive effects of the increasingly pathological drinking behavior on normal motivations and activities. This dissociation is facilitated by the social custom of assigning special settings and times for drinking, and permitting certain expressions of behavior which are normally taboo. The alcoholic's dissociation of the sober from the intoxicated state breaks down only when the drunkenness becomes so constant that he abandons all attempts to control and limit the drinking. A further discussion of alcoholic amnesia, and its relation to dissociation, is given in articles by Washburne (1958) and Storm and Smart (Chapter 11).

Treatment of acute alcohol overdose is so far on a symptomatic, supportive basis. Since the rate of ethanol oxidation is controlled by the fundamental mechanisms of energy-linked regulation of cellular respiration, there is little prospect of improving treatment of alcohol poisoning by radically increasing the rate of removal, except when dialysis can be performed. It is difficult to estimate the possibility of developing an antidote which counteracts the depressant action on the central nervous system. The growing insight into how alcohol disturbs neural function should give a basis for progress in this area.

The difficulty of treating acute alcoholic illness is aggravated by the fact that in many cases the alcoholic comes to the doctor or to the clinic only after reaching a dangerous condition. The patient at this stage is usually suffering from various symptoms of malnutrition, with severe damage to the liver and in many cases to other organs also. Intoxication may precipitate acute symptoms, but the even more severe and dangerous withdrawal symptoms begin within a few hours after the alcoholic stops drinking. No single type of drug or method has yet been established as the optimal treatment for this condition. Different physicians prefer different drugs and procedures. Substitute drugs which induce strong cross-dependence with alcohol have the disadvantages of prolonging the addictive dependence and establishing a new source of addiction, but they may be necessary and are commonly prescribed if the withdrawal symptoms are very severe. Tranquilizing drugs, such as chlorpromazine, are commonly used for less severe illness or after the initial, most acute stage. An instance of a useful contribution of research findings to clinical practice is the administration of glucose to the patients, in order to counteract the hypoglycemia which research has shown to be a concomitant of intoxication and of chronic alcoholism. This particular treatment, which has been introduced fairly recently, is helpful in many cases of acute alcoholic illness. Nutritional supplements offer a slower-acting but important long-term benefit, although their efficacy is far short of the claims by proponents of the hypothesis that alcoholism is caused by a specific nutritional deficiency. Although nutritional treatment has generally been used only for acute alcoholic illness, during the period of hospitalization, it would probably have greater beneficial effect in the long-term rehabilitation of chronic alcoholics.

A special type of acute problem occurs when an intoxicated person suffers an accident which requires major surgery. This combination of conditions is rather frequent, due to the effects of intoxication and the accident-prone nature of alcoholics. Data on the involvement of alcohol in fatal automobile accidents indicate that the intoxicated accident victim is likely to be an alcoholic, at some stage of the malnutrition and general physical deterioration associated with this condition. Even if the intoxication is only acute, with no chronic drinking problem, the lower blood pressure and less efficient myocardial action caused by alcohol impair the victim's resistance to the effects of shock and loss of blood. The risks of surgery are magnified by these effects of alcohol and also by synergism with the depressant action of anesthetics.

In spite of the lack of definitive optimal procedures for treating acute alcoholic intoxication, physicians can and do provide real therapeutic help for patients suffering from this type of illness. Unfortunately, there has been no equivalent development of effective therapy for the craving for alcohol and for the loss of control over drinking which characterize the chronic alcoholic. Different therapists and clinics advocate diverse, often conflicting methods of treatment. None of the therapeutic techniques has been proven substantially more effective than the others, and some studies cast doubt on whether patients given the specified methods of treatment are benefited at all in comparison with alcoholics who are not given formal or systematic therapy.

The therapeutic goal of complete, permanent abstinence from alcohol must counteract both the long-standing craving for liquor and the habit of indulging that craving. The effect of the therapeutic intervention must persist strongly throughout a period of many years. The few experimental comparisons of different methods of therapy indicate a relatively high degree of effectiveness of disulfiram (Antabuse) treatment, aimed at blocking the habitual response of drinking. However, this treatment requires full co-operation from the patient and by itself does nothing to alter the motivation for excessive, uncontrolled drinking. Counter conditioning of the habit by associating alcohol with a painful experience is generally limited to a few training sessions and has only a temporary effect. A more promising method of treatment is the attempt to change the patient's pathological habits and motivations with the aid of the dramatic sensations and perceptions caused by the recently introduced drug, LSD. Although the value of this treatment has been vigorously challenged, a number of positive reports indicate therapeutic effect in some cases, including patients with very poor prognosis. Even if efficacy of LSD treatment were to be proven, it would be doubtful whether the potential benefits for some alcoholics outweigh the danger of exposure to the potent and unpredictable actions of this powerful drug. The need to limit the treatment to a few sessions is a serious disadvantage because the tendency to revert to uncontrolled drinking must be countered continuously during a long time span. Chronic therapy has been tried with many different types of substitute drug, including tranquilizers such as chlorpromazine, sedatives such as chlordiazepoxide or meprobamate, and stimulants such as amphetamine. No type of drug has been generally accepted as the preferred treatment. Since physical debilitation and dietary deficiency are generally concomitants of alcoholism, long-term physical and nutritional therapy might have a strong cumulative effect. However, most patients given a well-balanced diet in the hospital, during treatment of acute alcoholic illness, revert to their usual, inadequate diet when they go home. The influence of diet and general physical health has often been ignored in chronic therapy.

Drugs and other physical interventions can be maximally effective only when they form part of a psychotherapeutic program, and psychotherapy of alcoholics may mean a wide variety of procedures. The routine care and attention by physicians and by all staff members of the clinic or hospital should be regarded as types of psychotherapy. The degree of friendliness, helpfulness, and respect given to the patient undoubtedly has an important effect on the alcoholic's response to treatment. Techniques of group psychotherapy offer important advantages for treatment of alcoholics. Since most drinking is done in a social situation, the pathological features of the alcoholic's behavior are more readily remembered and analyzed in the group session, and the self-awareness and self-control acquired in the therapeutic situation may be expected to transfer more readily to the drinking situation. The fellowship of Alcoholics Anonymous is a group therapy procedure which appears to be effective in many cases but is almost completely inaccessible to research on therapeutic efficacy. Intensive, individual psychotherapy, especially in the form of Freudian psychoanalysis, seems unsuitable and ineffective for most alcoholics.

References p. 839

B. Evaluations and recommendations

Two aspects of the research are evaluated separately in this section. First is the discussion of research methods used in the studies. Second is the discussion of choice of topics, identifying which problems have been overemphasized and which have been neglected. These evaluations represent the opinions of the present authors, rather than an authoritative consensus. We wish to emphasize that in the last several years there has been a great increase in the amount of scientific research on alcohol, together with improvement in the experimental methods, because our discussion emphasizes the failings and shortcomings of recent research, in order to point out to experimenters the areas for potential emphasis and remedy in the coming years.

This book necessarily concentrates mostly on the past by reviewing and evaluating studies which have already been done and reported. However, our principal purpose is to aid future readers in their own research, therapy, administration, teaching, or learning about alcohol. Each reader is expected to integrate the material of this book with other reading and various types of past experience in these activities. The prolonged experience of the present authors in preparing this book has stimulated a number of recommendations for future work on alcohol problems.

(1) Research methods

In recent years, the rapidly increasing volume of alcohol research on biochemical and physiological effects has been accompanied by an improvement in the research methods. The cumulative progress of science has led to important gains in equipment, experimental techniques, and quantitative analyses of the data. Too many of the studies are limited in scope, experimental design, and conclusions, but the aggregate effect of all the research, including the mediocre and minor studies, is a rapid advance in scientific knowledge. Experimental designs and statistical analyses have become more sophisticated and complex, thus enabling scientists to benefit more fully from the increased precision and quantity of the data obtained.

Some available techniques have not been sufficiently exploited in alcohol research. Thus, cell and tissue cultures have hardly been used at all in studies of prolonged alcohol effects. Combination of tissue fractionation with biochemical and ultrastructural techniques, such as autoradiography applied to electron microscopy, should be fruitful in the study of the metabolism and turnover of macromolecular components of various tissues exposed to alcohol both acutely and chronically. In the field of neurobiology, these techniques provide important opportunities for research at the cellular and subcellular level. In exploring the mechanism for the depressant action of ethanol, electrophysiological study should be supplemented with chemical study of the structures involved, extended to model systems such as isolated aggregates of membrane components and artificial membranes.

Biochemical and physiological research techniques have advanced greatly in the last several years. Particularly in the biochemical field, most of the technical approaches available have been applied also to alcohol research. No special techniques are restricted to use in this field, but in all alcohol experiments, attention should be given to the method and conditions of administration of alcohol and the concentration required for the problem under study. It is desirable to try to distinguish pharmacological from purely metabolic mechanisms which mediate effects of alcohol. With few exceptions, such as the use of labeled ethanol for determination of the rate of alcohol metabolism, weaknesses and oversights are more apparent in experimental designs, in the specifications of aims for research, and in the interpretation of implications of results, than in the use of the basic techniques. For instance, peripheral metabolic changes have been studied with the explicit aim of elucidating the basis of behavioral effects of alcohol, although the blood-brain barrier prevents the peripheral changes from being reproduced in the brain. Sweeping generalizations and conclusions have often been made which contrast strongly to the very limited topic studied. Our survey of the literature also has left us with the impression that the conceptual and technical level generally has been more sophisticated in studies of acute than of chronic alcohol effects. Many of the comments made later in this section concerning designs for behavioral experiments also apply to the planning and execution of biochemical and physiological experiments. On the level of integration of the central nervous system, advances should also be possible through application of techniques for computer analysis of EEG-recordings, and utilization of implanted electrodes in freely moving animals for stimulating and recording in various sites and for correlating with overt behavior.

Many of the important questions, especially concerning alcoholism, cannot be answered by laboratory experiments alone. Research efforts should include effective use of the large amount of statistical and clinical

References p. 839

data available on consumption and effects of alcohol in humans. An example of the use of statistical data is the evidence for an inverse relationship between preference for alcohol and preference for sugar, which is supported by experimental findings. Statistical and clinical data have provided important supplements to experimental investigation of the etiology of liver disease in chronic alcoholism. Methods should be developed for improving and extending collection of data on the contribution of alcohol to the medical complications in acute alcoholic illness and chronic alcoholism. For instance, informed education and formulation of goals in alcohol policy would benefit from knowledge about differential effects of various categories of alcoholic beverages. Sociological data provide useful information on involvement of intoxication and alcoholism in murders, other violent crimes, suicides, automobile fatalities, and other accidents. An example is the evidence that in fatal automobile accidents most of the cases of alcohol involvement consist of chronic alcoholics rather than intoxication in normally moderate, controlled drinkers. The preponderance of single-car accidents over collisions in fatal automobile accidents with alcohol involvement (Haddon and Bradess, 1959; Hopkinson and Widdowson, 1964) suggests that alcohol primarily impaired the driver's attention and alertness during uneventful periods rather than impairing ability to maneuver in traffic. The effective use of such information requires direct observation of the habits of people, evaluation of complications against the background of such knowledge, and integration of the data with other information concerning actions of alcohol.

In studies of alcohol effects on behavior, most of the early research, reviewed by Jellinek and McFarland (Chapters 6 and 7), consisted of experiments on a small number of subjects, with no tests of statistical significance of the alcohol effects. In many of these studies there was inadequate control for other factors, such as the practice effect, which might have accounted for differences between the alcohol and control tests. Therefore, Jellinek and McFarland strongly emphasized the shortcomings in the prior research. In subsequent years, most of the experimenters have used a larger number of subjects and have included tests of statistical significance in their data analyses. They have generally eliminated any possible practice effects, by balancing the sequence of alcohol and control tests or by comparing different groups of alcohol and control subjects. The control has generally consisted of a placebo administration rather than a non-drug condition. This is a desirable experimental procedure, even when it is not possible to disguise the difference in taste between the alcohol and the placebo fluid. Accordingly, it has been possible for the present authors to emphasize the conclusions to be made from the various studies, rather than emphasizing discrepancies in the findings and deficiencies of the experimental methods.

However, some shortcomings are prevalent in the recent research. Most of the experiments consist of careful, quantitative measurement of a single type of behavioral performance, with inadequate control of the experimental conditions and generally without any systematic test of the effects of different experimental conditions. Therefore, most of the studies represent small, isolated findings rather than forming part of a coherent structure of growing knowledge. When several tests are given, each one is generally a very brief and superficial measure, given in a fixed sequence which precludes effective comparison among the tests. Some of the early experiments were characterized by thorough, carefully controlled procedures and extensively reported findings on the small number of subjects used. In some of these studies, each subject was tested with several alcohol doses, and with repetitions of the same dose; each test was lengthy and was preceded by many non-drug practice sessions. Perhaps the time has now come when such thorough, careful procedures should be applied to the larger number and greater diversity of subjects generally used in the recent research.

The principal need in future research is for large-scale studies which provide experimental control and systematic variation of a wide range of variables, measuring effects at different levels of response, including biochemical, physiological, and behavioral changes, and conducted on a large enough number of subjects to provide sensitive and reliable tests of the differences among experimental conditions. Experimenters should emphasize efforts to identify the conditions which alter the effect of alcohol and to compare different types of response to alcohol. The precise source of a differential alcohol effect, due to different conditions or differences in the response measured, can be specified only by systematic variation in the same experiment, holding all other conditions constant. Thus it is important to obtain as much information as possible from each experiment. Only by this means will experimenters produce a comprehensive and accurate description of what ethanol really does. Large-scale studies are made more feasible by a general increase in support for research and various technological advances. In particular, the recent development of digital computers enables rapid statistical analyses which formerly were very tedious and time-consuming.

References p. 839

Our specific suggestions for research on acute effects of alcohol are mostly applications of the general need for larger, more comprehensive studies. More experiments are needed with multi-variable factorial designs, testing simultaneously the effects of differences in several variables, which comprise experimental conditions or measures of response, while equating all other variables in the comparison between differences in a particular variable. As much information as possible should be obtained from each subject, including measures of different types of responses and, when feasible, effects of different doses and experimental conditions in several sessions. This is desirable not only to provide a more reliable and efficient test, controlling for individual differences, but also to obtain reliable data on individual differences.

Measurements of blood alcohol have become more common in recent years, due to improvements and innovations in the techniques, both with humans and with laboratory animals (see Chapter 2, pp. 33–35). These should be included whenever feasible; even crude estimates, as from the urine or breath, are preferable to none. Such determinations provide standardized measures of the quantity of alcohol acting on the subjects, thus enabling better comparison with other experiments and also indicating to what extent variations in alcohol effect among individuals and among conditions are attributable to differences in the quantity acting on the subject, after its absorption and before its elimination. Communication of the quantity of alcohol administered and measured would be facilitated by adoption of a more uniform and, in some cases, more complete method of reporting, including g alcohol/kg body weight and percentage blood-alcohol concentration.

In the proposed large-scale studies, comparing alcohol effects under different experimental conditions, general conclusions can be obtained only if these comparisons are made under a wide range of doses and intervals after administration. Previous research has been especially deficient in studying effects of alcohol with low doses and at short intervals after administration. Another important means of enhancing the scope and applicability of future findings would be the development of equivalent situations and measures for comparing alcohol effects on humans and laboratory animals. The subjects have been almost exclusively laboratory animals, in studies of voluntary consumption and of motivational and emotional alterations, and in certain types of physiological response. On the other hand, humans have been used almost exclusively in studies of most motor and sensory effects of alcohol, including tests of performance and EEG recordings. In many research topics it should be possible to apply similar methods and conditions to humans and animals. However, in areas of research where satisfactory techniques have already been developed, the value of future studies can generally be maximized by standardization on the same procedures instead of the strong tendency for different experimenters to establish and maintain various differences in apparatus, procedures, doses of alcohol, and measures of the effects. By using the same methods, the new findings can be compared more precisely with the previous reports, thus enhancing the value of both sets of data. Measurement of blood alcohol in experiments on behavioral performance comprises only one limited application of this type of comparison. Physiological measurements such as heart rate, blood pressure, or galvanic skin response ought to be included more often in behavioral studies.

Our evaluation of the experimental literature impresses us with the value of accurate, objective measurements of alcohol effects. For example, gross observations of ataxia generally show very little alcohol effect except at very high doses, whereas mechanical or photoelectric recordings of standing steadiness or locomotor steadiness show large decreases in performance at moderate alcohol doses. Accurate, objective measurements are particularly necessary for studies on effects of low alcohol doses.

A desirable experimental procedure, for ensuring objective measurements, is to conceal the nature of the treatment both from the recipient and from the experimenter or therapist. This "double-blind" technique has rightly become almost indispensable in clinical evaluations of therapeutic agents. Formidable obstacles to this experimental ideal are imposed by the distinctive taste of alcohol and the necessity for administering rather large quantities. Consequently, experimenters have generally not attempted to disguise the treatment from the subjects. However, accounts of ingenious and apparently effective methods for concealing the treatment from the recipients include rectal administration, intravenous infusion, the use of a strong-tasting beverage as the vehicle for the alcohol and control solution, and inclusion of a small amount of alcohol in the control beverage. There have been very few reports of a double-blind procedure, disguising the treatment from the experimenter also. In general, most of the experimental data appear to yield consistent and valid results, even without concealment of the treatment from the recipient or experimenter. However, the double-blind control is always desirable, and is more important in comparisons of several doses,

References p. 839

especially when low doses are included, and in measurements of subjectively perceived effects.

Comparison of alcohol effects in different experiments will be greatly facilitated if experimenters report a sufficient amount of equivalent information. In all research reports the percentage change in performance caused by alcohol should be stated explicitly or at least easily obtainable from data on performance under alcohol compared with the control condition or control subjects. There should also be a measure of statistical reliability of the alcohol effect, preferably in terms of the percentage of effect which falls within the standard error of measurement. Both of these types of information are essential for effective comparisons of magnitude and reliability of alcohol effects in different experiments and in different conditions of the same experiment. Many of the earlier experimenters failed to test statistical reliability of the alcohol effects, as already noted. Some more recent experimenters have reported on statistical reliability but have given inadequate description of the magnitude of alcohol effect. For example, Eickholt et al. (Chapter 7) and Ideström and Cadenius (1968, Chapter 6) reported alcohol effects exclusively in terms of statistical significance levels. Easterbrook (Chapter 7) presented analysis of variance tables for statistical significance of the difference among various treatments without information on average performance under these conditions, and Nash (Chapters 6, 7) showed the arithmetic magnitude of change in performance caused by alcohol, with the designation of whether the drug effect was at the 5% or 1% level of statistical reliability, without the percentage change caused by alcohol.

In many experiments, performance is measured both before and after alcohol and also both before and after placebo in different subjects or in the same subjects on a different occasion. A sensitive method of analysis, taking advantage of the tendency for consistency of performance by the same subjects, is to compute the percentage difference between pretest and alcohol test, adjusting for the percentage difference between pretest and placebo test. This provides an appropriate measure of the net percentage of alcohol effect, but there has not been standardization on a good index of the error of measurement. Data transformations may be used to provide a closer fit of the distribution of scores to the normal distribution, thereby increasing the accuracy of parametric tests of statistical significance, such as t test and analysis of variance, and reducing the influence of extreme, deviant scores. A logarithmic or reciprocal transformations is often appropriate, but sophisticated data transformation and methods of analysis

should be use donly with caution. Frankenhaeuser *et al.* (Chapter 7) reported
a measure of the difference between drug and placebo scores, divided by
the standard deviation of the placebo scores, but this fails to take into
account the standard deviation of the alcohol scores. For example, in their
data this measure failed to show the greater reliability of alcohol effects
on spatial than on numerical performance due to lower variance among
the spatial performance scores. A more appropriate measure would be the
standard deviation combining the alcohol and placebo conditions, or based
on the variance in the difference scores. Goldberg (1943, Chapters 6, 7)
defined the threshold dose of alcohol as the dose at which the fitted regression
line first diverged from the control baseline, without taking into account
the variability and possible error of the baseline score. A measure of "minimal
effective dose" should be based on the dose at which the response first
becomes reliably different from the control range. The use of a number of
subjects is almost indispensable for obtaining statistically reliable results,
but experimenters should be alert and cautious when averaging data from
different subjects. For example, Ekman *et al.* (1964, Chapter 7) demonstrated
that the linear decrease in blood alcohol during a passage of time appears
to be curvilinear if any zero scores occur, due to differences among individuals
in the time at which the blood-alcohol reaches zero.

A more general deficiency in much of the published research is inadequate
specification of the experimental materials, procedures, and conditions, thus
precluding critical appraisal and restricting the increment to knowledge.
This has been an especially vexing impediment to the task of the present
authors. This deficiency is especially prevalent in studies of joint effects
of alcohol and other drugs. Standardization is badly needed in specifications
to prevent authors from omitting important details. The standardized items
of information should include doses, route of administration, dilution of
alcohol, characteristics of the solvent, duration of administration or ingestion, the time until testing, and the duration of testing. Characteristics of
the subjects and of the test environment should also be specified with
sufficient detail to permit replication of the experiment and evaluation of
the effects of the experimental conditions on the response to alcohol.

The experimenter must be alert to ways in which the alcohol effect might
be influenced by the experimental procedures. In several studies cited in
Chapter 6, effects of alcohol on visual perception were tested by a procedure
of cumulative doses, given at brief intervals (Colson; Lord Charnwood;
Brecher *et al.*). The measurement of the effective dose with this procedure

is complicated by the development of acute tolerance. The degree of over-estimation of the effective dose will depend on the effects of the experimental conditions on the development of acute tolerance. Milner (1968b, Chapter 10), in a test of the lethal effect of alcohol with or without another drug, spaced the alcohol doses 2 hours apart, so that many hours were required for accumulation of the doses to a lethal level. Thus the interaction with the other drug may be due largely to the recurrent stressful experiences rather than to the direct toxicity of alcohol; blood alcohol was not measured. It is greatly preferable to test different doses of alcohol in different subjects, or with sufficient spacing between doses in the same subjects to preclude a direct cumulative effect. Another instance when the procedures influence the alcohol effects is in studies of blood flow in anesthetized animals. The alcohol effects were probably masked by the anesthesia in a study by Smythe et al. (Chapter 4). Likewise, in a study by Sapirstein et al. (Chapter 4), the control animals were under pentobarbital anesthesia. In many physiological experiments it is necessary to anesthetize the animals prior to the alcohol treatment. Comparison of different anesthetics and different degrees of anesthesia might help to separate the alcohol effects from the effects of the anesthetic. For example, local anesthetics should have minimal synergism with systemic alcohol effects.

Measurement of tolerance to alcohol involves methodological problems which have been ignored by most experimenters. In many studies an animal is given a specified amount of alcohol repeatedly for an arbitrarily chosen number of times, followed by various biochemical and physiological tests without any attempt to establish that true tolerance has developed. Clearly, the experimenter should first obtain direct evidence for presence of the condition to be studied. Only a demonstrably stable measure of alcohol effect can be used as a test for the development of tolerance without a control group. A reduction in duration of loss of the righting reflex (sleeping time) has been a frequently used measure. However, it is always desirable to compare the alcohol-habituated group with a control group. This is essential when an improvement in performance can be expected due to practice effects, as in most tests of behavioral performance. When comparing these two groups, the experimenter should equate them not only in the total amount of exposure to the test situation but also in the amount of exposure while under the influence of alcohol. If the habituated group practices under the influence of alcohol, while the control group practices in the placebo condition, the habituated group may perform better in the crucial test under alcohol because this does not involve transfer of the performance from the non-drug to the alcohol condition. The appropriate procedure requires that both the control and experimental group are exposed an equal number of times to the test situation while under the influence of alcohol. This impairs the efficiency with which the development of tolerance can be measured, but it is an essential procedure.

Another topic in which the experimental method has generally been weak is the development of cirrhotic lesions as a result of chronic alcohol intake. The many studies in this field are generally characterized by insufficient control of nutritional intake and insufficient duration of the dietary regimen. Experimenters should undertake research on the difficult topic of chronic alcohol effects only if they are prepared to control the conditions meticulously throughout a span of several months. Research on this topic has also been impeded by a controversy between two groups of investigators involved in polemic efforts to prove or disprove the thesis that alcohol is "toxic" to the liver. In efforts to substantiate their point, which actually is one of semantics rather than of objective fact, both groups have been distracted from effectively taking advantage of important new evidence produced by the other group.

Research on the important clinical problem of therapy of chronic alcoholics is seriously deficient in both specificity and comprehensiveness. A severely critical and highly instructive review of this research is by Hill and Blane (Chapter 11). A particular drawback to all the studies is that the treatment of alcoholics generally included a variety of different procedures, with a different combination of treatments applied to different cases. Even in the few studies comparing different methods of treatment, there was no specification and isolation of a single differential attribute with all other procedures being equated. Valid evaluation of treatment methods also requires the collection of accurate follow-up data on the patients for a period of several years. In contrast to the great amount of attention and care generally devoted to the treatment method, the follow-up phase in most studies has been hasty and perfunctory, with excessively short follow-up periods, inadequate information on the subsequent health or pathology of the patients, and many instances of failure to maintain contact after termination of the treatment period. Because of the episodic nature of gamma alcoholism, several follow-up observations would be preferable. In addition to specificity of the treatment method which is experimentally manipulated, research should be planned to obtain comprehensiveness of the variables studied.

References p. 839

Various conditions which might modify the effectiveness of the treatment method, or additional treatment procedures, should be tested either in a single, large-scale, multi-variable experiment or in a series of smaller experiments.

A more general difficulty in evaluating therapy is the lack of a simple, generally accepted criterion for cure or improvement. Total abstinence from alcohol has traditionally been the goal of the therapy and the criterion for its success. However, this does not necessarily mean any alteration of the craving for liquor and of the inability to control the drinking, which are the principal characteristics of alcoholics. The conflicting, self-destructive motivations, when no longer expressed and aggravated by the excessive drinking, might give rise to alternative, equally pathological modes of behavior or misbehavior. In some cases alcoholism is an expression of a pervasive mental illness, such as schizophrenia, depression, or psychopathic personality. A number of clinical case histories have refuted the prevalent belief that an alcoholic can never return to moderate, controlled drinking. This type of behavior modification appears to be a more extreme difference from alcoholism, and better evidence for cure of the alcoholic's craving and loss of control, than total avoidance of drinking. Thus, some patients classified as "improved" would represent a more favorable outcome than the patients who are "abstinent" throughout the following period. However, in most studies the category of "improved" is more likely to signify resumption of pathological drinking which is minimized by the informant or which has not yet reached the stage of acute alcoholic illness.

(2) Choice of topics

This portion of the concluding chapter summarizes the evaluations and recommendations we have been able to make about research on actions of ethyl alcohol. Emphasis is given to the methods and topics which have been inadequately covered in prior research and thus require special attention in future experiments. In an important area of research, all topics are worth studying, but exaggerated interest in one topic means insufficient attention to others. A balanced effort, with different topics of research advancing at an equivalent pace, is the most effective way for the accumulation of knowledge. Contrary to this desirable balance is the effect of fads and fashions. In science, as in other spheres of life, certain topics become popular, and the intial popularity tends to produce an overemphasis on these particular efforts. It is logical to begin this section with a discussion of such overemphasized topics, which are extensively reviewed in the earlier chapters of this book. After this, we identify some important topics which have been partially or completely neglected in recent research.

The great social interest and importance of alcohol has caused it to be regarded as a topic for social propaganda and practical, remedial actions. Much of this well-meant activity has been characterized by zealousness rather than by good judgment. For instance, often one of the first questions asked is about the causes of alcoholism. The alcohol literature is replete with "explanations" and "theories" of the causation of chronic drinking. However, it is impossible to plan good approaches to this "problem" when there is no satisfactory definition of what alcoholism is. Obviously also, there is little hope of explaining alcoholism on the basis of single biochemical or physiological traits, because whatever else alcoholism may be, it is definitely a form of behavior. As there is no general theory of behavior, there cannot very well be a unified theory of alcoholism either. Thus, many of the studies of the "problem of alcoholism" appear naive and cannot be well planned and executed because the aim is obscure. Therefore, scientists in basic research have generally shunned work with this drug. However, if the objects of a study are defined with sufficient precision, the quality of the work in this field can be as good as in any other area, as has been documented many times in the present review. We would again like to emphasize the value of limited, realistic goals, but such limited studies should preferably be formulated within the frame of a larger strategy of research.

Because of the peripheral status of alcohol in science, scientists in applied and clinical fields have typically undertaken a burst of alcohol research on a particular topic 10 to 20 years after it has been most fashionable in basic research. An example of this tendency is an emphasis in recent alcohol research on biochemical aspects, especially liver metabolism. Similarly, in the study of organ pathologies as a consequence of excessive alcohol intake, biochemical changes in the liver, particularly cirrhosis, have been emphasized at the expense of other organ systems. If this same trend of delayed adoption of fashionable topics continues in alcohol research, we may expect in the next few years an emphasis on cytology, studying the mitochondria. This will imply a still more narrow concentration on mechanisms by which alcohol alters certain limited aspects of physiological functioning. The recent biochemical studies have partly clarified the complex processes by which

References p. 839

alcohol is metabolized and the nature of liver damage which results from prolonged, excessive alcohol intake. The already extensive studies on cellular and especially mitochondrial functioning have provided useful information on the mechanisms by which alcohol alters cellular metabolism. Several aspects are of great interest for basic biochemistry, such as the question of how hydrogen produced in cytoplasmic oxidation is transported into the mitochondria. But our knowledge in the general field of alcohol studies will be increased more by research on some related actions of alcohol which are little understood than by further development of the popular research topics.

In spite of the popularity of research on the liver as affected by alcohol, there has been very little study of the complex interaction among nutritional factors, cell renewal in the liver, and the final development of structural liver damage after chronic alcohol intake. Such studies require the use of biochemical and metabolic techniques which can be applied to alcoholic patients, in comparison with the metabolic reactions of control subjects. However, the immense complexity of the metabolic system creates great difficulties, so that observations on humans must be supplemented by animal experiments which enable more rigid control and sampling of any tissue for specimens. There is not yet a comprehensive theory of the cellular mechanisms by which alcohol contributes to liver disease. Experiments are needed on both the biochemical and ultrastructural effects of ethanol, in samples of liver tissue from human alcoholics and laboratory animals. Another important topic for future research is to test whether the excessive bilirubin often found in the blood in the late stages of cirrhosis is related to alcoholism or solely due to the liver disease. Studies are also needed on the role of liver disease, malnutrition, and malabsorption in the complex effects of chronic alcohol intake on diuresis. We would particularly emphasize the value of research on protein synthesis in the liver. The aggravating effect of dietary fat on the development of alcoholic liver disease may be caused by competition of gluconeogenesis for amino acids also required for cellular repair. Many more studies are needed on changes in peripheral metabolism caused by the process of alcohol oxidation. Only recently has attention been given to lesions which develop in heart and skeletal muscle during chronic alcohol use. Little is known about their etiology, the consequences for physical capability, or the methods and prospects of therapy.

A crucial deficit in our knowledge is about the role of metabolites of alcohol, notably acetaldehyde. The metabolic relationships of ethanol to acetaldehyde, and the effects of acetaldehyde as distinguished from those of ethanol, are important in the analysis of biochemical and cellular process- es. In studies of peripheral vasodilatation caused by alcohol, measurements are needed of metabolic output, heat balance, and time relationship of the flush response after various alcohol doses. Very little is known about interactions of ethanol with endocrinological secretions under various conditions, in humans or animals with different characteristics. Data on effects of alcohol on the intracellular and extracellular water and electrolyte balance are fragmentary and conflicting, perhaps because of insufficient attention to the distinction between effects of low and high doses, or between acute and chronic effects.

One of the valuable resources for research on ethanol is the existence of closely related alcohols, with differences in action related to their slight differences in chemical structure. Comparisons between different alcohols enable the experimenter to study differences in metabolic processes and in duration of action while holding constant the essential features of the pharmacological effects of ethyl alcohol. Chapter 10 reviews the few ex- perimental comparisons of the effects of different alcohols. There have been no studies of the effects of chronic administration of the non-ethyl alcohols. Therefore, this research resource has thus far been exploited very inade- quately. A similar type of experimental comparison would be provided by testing alcohol and a drug with similar effects, such as a barbiturate, in the same experimental situation. Different barbiturates could be used to provide experimental variation in onset and duration of action, but in the few experimental comparisons of alcohol and barbiturates a moderately short-acting barbiturate was used, usually amobarbital or pentobarbital, whose onset and duration of action are approximately the same as those of ethanol.

One of the most serious deficiencies in choice of research topics concerns the functions of the central nervous system, especially effects of alcohol on the brain. Even those theorists who attribute craving for alcohol to nutrition- al or metabolic needs would agree that the most prominent and immediately important effects of ethanol are on the functioning of the central nervous system. The primary action of ethanol apparently is on mechanisms involved in the generation of action potentials. This problem should be pursued by more detailed studies, particularly of changes in central neurons. A distinc- tion between effects on synapses and on other regions of the neuronal membranes should be attempted, as well as study of the membrane structures involved. These are also likely sites of the changes associated with increased tolerance and physical dependence on alcohol. The systems involved in motor control have been very inadequately studied. There are a number of papers on effects of alcohol on nystagmus, but no physiological analysis of the underlying mechanisms. Thus, the action of alcohol on the vestibular apparatus and on the cerebellum should be explored. We also suggest more studies on the mechanisms of alcohol action on the function of the neuro-hypophysis and associated structures.

Ultimately, of course, we should like to correlate the behavioral and the neurophysiological alterations induced by alcohol. Even the most careful mapping of effects on individual systems and functions would not suffice for that. In an excellent and stimulating discussion of the problems involved in explaining behavioral effects of drugs in terms of "mechanisms", Wikler (Chapter 10) pointed out the need for a search for "pattern-specificity" in the drug action. Undoubtedly, differing sensitivity of varying anatomical and functional units within the immensely complex organization of the central nervous system results in a specific and unique pattern for the disturbances caused by ethanol, a pattern which to a larger or smaller proportion can be shared by other agents but always differs in some aspects. Wikler suggested that techniques for simultaneous recording of brain activity and behavior on unrestrained animals should have great prominence in the study of drug action. Regrettably, there is hardly any published work along such lines with ethanol, and we recommend an emphasis on efforts in that direction.

Several aspects of alcohol effects on behavior have not been adequately studied. Jellinek and McFarland (Chapters 6, 7) characterized alcohol as a depressant of all performance capabilities, and many prior claims of stimulant effects were attributed to experimental artifacts or to release of normally inhibited activity. Most subsequent experimenters have accepted their conclusions, and very few recent studies have included tests under conditions, such as low alcohol doses, which would be expected to show the stimulant effects. Alcohol effects have been tested extensively on various types of performances but very seldom on various aspects of the learning process, such as inhibition of the former habit, learning of the new responses, and the motivations and performance capabilities during learning. The findings might improve our understanding of behavior alterations under intoxication, personality changes after repeated intoxications, and the phenomena of "blackout" and of "dissociation" of the intoxicated from the sober condition. Although most experimenters rightly distrust the validity of the subjectively perceived changes in sensations and emotions, reported by human subjects, such introspective accounts may provide useful information which can be related to changes in other types of behavior. The few measurements of subjectively perceived intoxication indicate a high degree of accuracy in that respect.

Forced-feeding of alcohol to laboratory animals permits systematic variation of the amount and spacing of doses and the general nutritive conditions. In studies of the pathological effects of prolonged, excessive intake, the overemphasis on research on pathology of the liver has retarded attention to other organs in studies of the organic complications of alcoholism. Large-scale experiments using this method are necessary to specify whether alcohol causes tissue damage by a direct toxic action, through more indirect changes in metabolic patterns, or because of changes in nutritional balance. Such studies are worth undertaking only if continued for a sufficient duration, usually at least several months, to allow full development of the chronic alcohol effects. Most of the previous experiments have been on the rat, and other species should also be used, in particular the guinea pig because of its apparent high degree of sensitivity to the effects of ethanol (Bourrinet, Chapter 9).

One of the most important topics for research on chronic alcohol effects in laboratory animals is the effect of exposure to intoxicating doses compared with the same total amount of alcohol intake at more frequent intervals, in doses which are small enough so that intoxication is never experienced. Such experiments, simulating the distinction between gamma and delta alcoholics, may provide useful information on the social value of encouraging consumption of weak beverages, such as beer and wine, in preference to the more concentrated distilled spirits. There is little factual evidence for beneficial effects of transition from strong to weak beverages, but general knowledge about the actions of alcohol suggests a link between degree of inebriety and alcoholism, and data such as those presented in Nielsen's (1965) study indicate that beer is definitely less likely to induce physical dependence than more concentrated beverages. On the other hand, complications caused by nutritional imbalance are solely related to the amounts of alcohol ingested and not to specific beverages. Final conclusions concerning the possible value of giving preference to particular types of beverage in education and alcohol policy require much more data on actual habits of consumers of alcoholic beverages. Laboratory studies can never mimic satisfactorily the highly variable and complex patterns of actual usage, extending over periods of many years. Detailed data should be collected on the drinking and eating patterns of human alcoholics, as well as on the pathological changes, throughout the entire span of their years of excessive drinking. The value of such information would fully recompense the time and effort required to obtain it.

Parallel research on human alcoholics and on laboratory animals has been very fruitful in the past and should be extended in future studies. However, research on humans is severely limited by the moral and practical obstacles against experimental manipulation of chronic alcohol consumption, especially in excessive quantities. The findings obtained from the few experiments on voluntary drinking for several weeks by alcoholics or drug addicts are thus especially valuable. The use of this method should be extended to whatever extent is morally and legally permissible. Measurements of biochemical, physiological, neural, and behavioral changes, in alcoholics and normal drinkers, should be used for comparisons between hangover and the withdrawal syndrome in laboratory animals.

In order to broaden the scope of such studies, it will be necessary to develop objective indicators of hangover and the withdrawal syndrome in laboratory animals. To the extent that tolerance, withdrawal symptoms, or other signs of physical dependence can be reproduced experimentally in laboratory animals, they are open for more rigorous and penetrating exploration than is possible in humans. One of the most important tasks in alcohol research is to establish the mechanisms of pharmacological and metabolic dependence. Knowledge of these would put therapy and rehabilitation on a much more rational basis than at present. Unfortunately, experimentation has hardly advanced beyond the initial demonstration that tolerance can be developed in laboratory animals. Only recently has induction of an alcohol withdrawal syndrome in animals been reported (Essig and Lam, Chapter 11). Physiological symptoms such as water consumption, nervous excitability, and elevation of heart rate and of body temperature seem likely to provide easily obtained, valid, reliable measures. Other possible measures are tremor, increased susceptibility to convulsive agents, and reversal of the increased sensitivity by drugs that produce cross-dependence with alcohol. A necessity for further research on these after-effects of alcohol, in both humans and animals, is to quantify the severity of the symptoms rather than merely demonstrate their occurrence. Other methods of research on this topic should include thorough electrophysiological and neurochemical measurements of changes in central nervous functioning, at various stages of prolonged alcohol action and withdrawal. In such studies, careful attention should be given to adequate nutrition and to the doses and times of alcohol administration. It is necessary to use modern techniques for studies of ultrastructure and its alterations in various conditions, for assessment of ion-flux kinetics, for measuring alterations in transmitter and moderator substances, and for study of electrical characteristics of the neurons. At a more integrated level of response, particular attention should be given to central regulation of autonomic functions. Also, the use of cell and tissue cultures is a potentially powerful technique which has seldom been applied to the study of chronic alcohol effects. For example, physical dependence in the central nervous system might be tested by chronic effects of alcohol on nerve cells in culture.

Voluntary consumption of alcoholic beverages is an obviously important topic for study of the motivations for both moderate drinking and alcoholism. Understandably, the early studies were mainly concerned with attempts to induce chronic alcoholism or excessive drinking in laboratory animals, but experimenters have generally been unable to induce voluntary consumption of intoxicating amounts of alcohol by laboratory animals. A technique or condition eliciting this uniquely human type of pathological behavior in "lower" animals would be an important contribution. However, the conditions which influence the amount of moderate, controlled alcohol intake remain important research topics, applicable to the great majority of human drinkers. Chronically heavy drinking is characteristic of many laboratory animals given a continuous choice between an alcohol solution and water. Future experiments should emphasize tests of the pharmacological, nutritional, and gustatory qualities of alcohol as determinants of voluntary consumption. Intraperitoneal or oral administration of alcohol would show the degree to which the alcohol intake adjusts to the amount involuntarily received, and the effect of intoxication could be tested by comparing a large dose administered at long intervals with frequent, small doses. A choice between an alcohol solution and another fluid containing a different drug would enable measurement of the doses which cause equivalent degrees of preference or aversion, and experiments on the conditions which alter the relative preference for the two drugs. In some experiments the alternative fluids should be isocaloric, as in a choice between a 10% v/v ethanol and a 15% w/v sucrose solution. Equating the alternative fluids in both pharmacological and caloric qualities might provide information on the effect of

References p. 839

the taste or smell of the alcohol solution. A strong interest in the identification of genetic variations, seen in such diverse fields as physiology, biochemistry, and psychiatry, has been evident in research on voluntary consumption of alcoholic beverages. Most of the studies thus far have been limited to demonstrations of differences among strains of mice and rats in alcohol choice. It should be possible to relate this genetically determined difference to various physiological and emotional characteristics. Other species should be studied more extensively, especially hamsters because of evidence that they show a high degree of alcohol preference and monkeys because of their closer resemblance to humans. It should be feasible to test moderate human drinkers on various aspects of voluntary alcohol consumption, although such studies must be limited to brief choice tests in the laboratory or only partial control of the variables during a longer time period.

C. Comments on alcohol programs

Some influential authorities on alcohol problems tend to emphasize alcoholism as the overwhelmingly most important problem related to the use of alcoholic beverages. Presumably few would dispute this general view, and many alcoholism programs are limited to a treatment and educational function, as suggested in a report of the North American Association of Alcoholism Programs and American Public Health Association (1966). However, there is widespread appreciation for the value of experimental research, soundly based on the fundamental disciplines, in an alcohol program. Once the decision has been made to include fundamental research in an organized program, it is also important to maintain an open mind in evaluating the significance of various proposals for research. Alcoholism as a subject of investigation cuts across so many boundaries between traditional scientific disciplines that a broad spectrum of research topics should be included in any large research program on alcohol. In view of the methodological and conceptual limitations of scientific work as it is actually conducted, the findings by a specialist, such as a biochemist or a neurophysiologist, cannot give a comprehensive answer to the problems of alcoholism. However, it would be absurd to deny the value of his contribution toward understanding of biochemical or neurophysiological aspects of alcohol effects. Basic findings in research specialties are potentially valuable in building up a comprehensive picture of alcoholism as well as of other problems related to the use of beverage alcohol. Alcoholism research is a field in which the interdisciplinary approach is the only sensible one, and in which there is no basis yet for rating the relative merits of various approaches to the problem except in terms of their inherent soundness as scientific projects. The administrator takes a great responsibility indeed if he deliberately suppresses some specific approaches at the expense of others. There is good reason to challenge any one who claims that he can make a safe prediction about which is the most promising and direct road to advancing our knowledge and understanding.

The interdisciplinary research on alcohol problems requires a large-scale effort by many scientists and clinicians for a long period of time. This is especially true in most studies of therapy of chronic alcoholism. The follow-up studies should continue for several years after treatment, and the slow development of alcoholism requires a correspondingly long time for study of this process in the individual. Another example of the need for a large-scale study is the establishment of different treatment methods at different, equivalent clinics operated by the same agency (Bruun, Chapter 11). This seems preferable to the easier and more common practice of comparing different methods on different patients at the same clinic. When all the patients at the same clinic are treated by the same method, a more consistent and uniform procedure is possible, with the full cooperation of the entire clinic staff, avoiding the premature comparisons among methods which are probably inevitable when the experimenter specifies different methods for different patients at the same clinic. For such research projects, large organizations are needed with adequate financing and a stable basis of support for a number of years.

The principal source of stable support for alcohol research has been in permanent institutions for this purpose. Several such institutions have been especially prominent and influential. One is the Center of Alcohol Studies, founded at Yale University in New Haven, Connecticut, U.S.A., in 1938 and moved to Rutgers University, New Brunswick, New Jersey, U.S.A., in 1962. Another is the Research Laboratories of Alko (the Finnish State Alcohol Monopoly) in Helsinki. A third is the Addiction Research Foundation in Toronto, in the province of Ontario, Canada. A fourth is the Division of Alcohol Studies and Rehabilitation of the Commonwealth of Virginia, U.S.A., in Richmond. A recent organization, with potentially the greatest financial resources for future research, is the National Center for the Prevention and Control of Alcoholism (NCPCA), at Bethesda, Maryland,

U.S.A. This is a component of the National Institute of Mental Health, in the United States Public Health Service.

All of these research organizations are subordinated to the larger aims of their institutions, which place great emphasis on clinical and educational activities. The Rutgers Center of Alcohol Studies publishes the most important periodical in the field of alcohol and alcoholism *(Quarterly Journal of Studies on Alcohol)* and conducts an annual summer school for professional workers on various aspects of the alcoholism problem. Alko supports the Finnish Foundation of Alcohol Studies, for research on the social and clinical aspects of alcohol use. A portion of the revenues to Alko from sale of liquor in Finland is used for an extensive educational program to promote temperance. The Addiction Research Foundation in Toronto strongly emphasizes research on therapy of alcoholics and on cultural and sociological topics, and its program includes research and therapy on all addictive drugs. The Division of Alcohol Studies and Rehabilitation is supported primarily as a medical service for the people of Virginia, with the distinguishing feature of unusually close cooperation between the clinical and research personnel. The NCPCA receives its funds from the United States Congress, which has manifested an increasing concern with the immediate, practical applications as its expenditures for research have rapidly increased to a substantial proportion of the national budget.

In all of these institutions, large and stable support for basic, experimental studies has been possible because of the funds attracted by the social and clinical importance of alcohol. Continued affiliation with such institutions is essential for adequate support of basic research on alcohol in the future. Experimenters should look for the immediate, practical applications of their research and patiently tolerate the almost inevitable lack of full appreciation of the value of basic research among the directors of the institution and the sources of its funds. The practical applications are likely to develop if the program is specifically planned to facilitate such applications. Therefore, every effort should be made to encourage collaboration and contact between people in various branches of research, education, and clinical work. Applications do not develop effectively if authors of research papers simply assume that clinicians will read their published research findings and change their methods accordingly. The institutional facilities should be designed to encourage communication among people who are involved in all aspects of the problem of alcohol and alcoholism.

In addition to such institutional research, the diverse types of alcohol research may be aided with special effectiveness by funds granted by an expert committee to support projects in laboratories which are qualified for research in specialized fields. For example, results in neurophysiology can be obtained more quickly and economically by buying the time of a specialist in this area than by building up a neurophysiological laboratory within the organization founded for alcohol research. This type of function is well fulfilled by research grants to scientists from the United States Public Health Service. The recent establishment of the NCPCA, with funds for such "extramural" research and a committee for awarding research grants, provides a suitable means for identifying and supporting alcohol research conducted by such specialists in various fields. In other countries, however, this type of research support has been severely deficient. Such projects should be attractive to private foundations which wish to support basic research that contributes to public health.

The broad applicability of alcohol problems to various conditions should encourage comprehensive, multidisciplinary activities in alcohol programs. For example, Popham et al. (1968) effectively refuted Pittman's (1968) arguments against the policy of treating both alcoholics and narcotic addicts in the clinics supported by the Addiction Research Foundation in Toronto. The study of addiction to all types of drug is also necessary in basic research on drug dependence. Other public health problems strongly associated with intoxication and alcoholism include suicide, homicide, and automobile accidents. Treatment and research programs for these problems should include special attention to the problem of alcohol.

The twin goals of specificity and comprehensiveness should always be pursued in alcohol research programs. For example, therapy of alcoholics should be studied by experimental manipulation of a single feature of treatment, such as a particular drug, holding constant all other conditions in the experimental and control group of patients. A series of experiments should explore a wide range of conditions which enhance or counteract the therapeutic effectiveness of the drug. Contrary to this desirable research strategy, most studies on therapy of alcoholics have established a number of differences between the experimental and control group, without further research on the effects of the same variables. Even without the benefit of experimental manipulation, much can be learned about alcohol effects from a comprehensive analysis of statistical data, as is exemplified in a discussion by Zylman (1968) on the relationship of drinking to automobile accidents and by Wolfgang and Strohm (1956) on the relationship of alcohol to criminal homicide.

References p. 839

Topics which should receive more emphasis in alcoholism programs are prevention, early detection, and treatment before the physical, social, and emotional damage becomes severe and irreversible. Obstacles to such efforts include the alcoholic's characteristic denial of his problem, the social toleration of heavy drinking, and the Alcoholics Anonymous doctrine that the alcoholic can achieve abstinence only after "hitting bottom". Prevention of alcoholism is emphasized in an article by Terhune (1964) and is also the basis for a controversial suggestion by Chafetz (1966) that children from an early age should be introduced to moderate, controlled consumption of alcoholic beverages. It seems possible that the chief social value of this custom, found in a number of cultures, is the restraining effect on drinking by the adults rather than the development of the habit of moderate drinking in the children. A study by Blane (1968), on excessive drinking by adolescent boys, could lead to the development of effective therapy at this early stage. A method of preventing or alleviating physical damage caused by chronic, excessive drinking would be to diminish the nutritional deficiency giving rise to physical damage in alcoholics by adding supplemental vitamins and minerals to alcoholic beverages. This is technologically feasible and is done commonly with other foods, as in "enriched" white bread.

The dangers and abuses of alcohol, emphasized in research and treatment programs, represent a one-sided view of this drug. Rewarding and beneficial effects of alcohol are indicated by the widespread popularity of alcoholic beverages and by the survival of the custom of drinking in most human societies for numerous generations (Barry, Chapter 11). Alcohol programs should include study of these positive aspects, not for the purpose of justifying the use of alcohol but in order to advance our understanding of the incentives for drinking. Earlier chapters of this review have cited a number of beneficial effects of ethanol on physiological and behavioral functions. Some additional reports of beneficial effects are the use of alcohol intoxication to relieve the symptoms of catatonic schizophrenia in several human patients (Kantarovich and Constantinovich, 1935) and a protective effect of a large ethanol dose against the lethal action of irradiation in mice (Paterson and Matthews, 1951). Instead of making a generalized judgment that alcohol or any other drug is harmful or beneficial, researchers and clinicians should identify the doses, individuals, and other conditions under which it has specific therapeutic and pathological effects.

D. Summary

Ethyl alcohol is classified as a sedative or general depressant drug, and it has a disorganizing action on physiological, neurological, and behavioral processes. However, ethanol has stimulating effects at low doses and at higher doses can cause apparent stimulation by selectively depressing inhibitory functions. In comparison with other drugs, some of the unique properties of alcohol are due to its small, simple molecular structure, a similar mechanism for its metabolism in the liver of all known species, and the substantial amount of calorie value present in pharmacologically effective doses. Important metabolic changes occur even with acute doses below the threshold for measurable impairment of nerve function. The physiological actions of alcohol are varied but relatively unimportant. The metabolic and nutritional effects are important, but the most prominent acute effect is the pharmacological action on the central nervous system, which seems to be a general depressant effect on generation of action potentials in nerve and muscle cells rather than a selective one on synaptic transmission.

The voluntary consumption of intoxicating doses of alcohol, by some humans but not by laboratory animals, may be attributable to various social factors in the drinking situation. A rapid compensatory response to the intoxicating action of alcohol is seen in the development of acute tolerance, so that the same blood-alcohol concentration has less effect during its falling than rising phase. Persistence of this compensatory response after the depressant action of alcohol has disappeared may account for the agitation and hypersensitivity in hangover and withdrawal symptoms. A further expression of the compensatory response is seen when a stressor counteracts the depressant action of alcohol, superseding the sedative action of alcohol in alleviating the stressor. Alcohol may elicit a response inhibited by fear or by nonreward in some conflict situations but cause further depression of behavior in other situations. Although the depressant and disruptive effects of alcohol are generally detrimental to organized behavior, in some situations the motivational, perceptual, and physiological effects of alcohol are beneficial.

Laboratory animals, given a free choice between an alcohol solution and water, generally regulate their alcohol intake in g/kg/day at a stable level but without development of an addictive craving for their preferred amount. Chronic consumption of an alcohol solution as the only fluid has no adverse effects if adequate nutrition and fluid intake are maintained. The pharmacological actions of alcohol resemble those of a number of other central depressants, notably barbiturates, but synergism is generally only additive with little metabolic interaction. There is considerable overlap between alcoholics and nonalcoholics in amount of alcohol consumption, and some alcoholics become moderate, controlled drinkers contrary to the widespread belief that an alcoholic permanently loses control over drinking. The development of physical dependence on alcohol is slow but is evident in the normalizing effect of liquor on alcoholics and the occurrence of withdrawal symptoms which may be severe and dangerous. Cirrhosis of the liver and other physical diseases associated with alcoholism are observed in only a minority of the cases and become irreversible only at a late stage. They are probably caused by nutritional deficiencies associated with chronic, excessive consumption rather than by direct, toxic action of the alcohol. Great diversity among alcoholics in physical and emotional characteristics indicates that no single physiological, nutritional, or psychiatric abnormality is sufficient to account for the etiology of alcoholism. Some typical characteristics of alcoholics, such as a self-destructive tendency, emotional immaturity, and the occurrence of "blackouts", are indications of general susceptibility to pathological behavior or may be consequences rather than causes of the chronic, excessive drinking.

No single treatment for alcohol poisoning or for acute alcohol illness has been universally accepted as the treatment of choice, but a variety of therapeutic measures are available and have been used successfully. Many different types of therapy have been applied to chronic alcoholics, but none of the treatment methods has been proven effective. Aversively protective drugs, such as disulfiram (Antabuse), give evidence for beneficial effects, perhaps because of the long-term therapeutic intervention required, in spite of the limitation that the patient's continuous cooperation is necessary. Therapy sessions with the powerful hallucinogen, LSD, also give some evidence for beneficial effects in spite of the necessarily brief duration of this treatment.

The techniques in alcohol research have improved greatly in recent years, but there are still a number of deficiencies in various aspects of the research. Statistical and clinical data should be used in conjunction with experiments on many of the topics. A particular need is for large-scale experiments with simultaneous manipulation of a number of relevant variables and recording of both physiological and behavioral responses. Accurate, objective measures of alcohol effects are very important. More experiments should include a wide range of doses and time intervals after administration, especially low doses and short intervals, and the double-blind procedure of concealing the dose from both subject and experimenter. Alcohol effects on humans and laboratory animals should be compared by means of parallel experiments using similar techniques on these different species. Many published reports fail to include sufficient information on characteristics of the drug, subjects, and experimental conditions. The percentage change in response from the control to alcohol condition and the standard error of this change should be included in the data reported, but several published reports have given measures of statistical significance without further description of the magnitude of the alcohol effect. There is a danger of obtaining erroneous conclusions from certain research procedures, including cumulative alcohol doses, measurement of alcohol effects in anesthetized animals, and failing to distinguish between the development of physiological tolerance and behavioral tolerance acquired by previous practice in the performance task while under the influence of alcohol.

Research on some important topics has been retarded by a strong influence of fads and fashions for certain topics, such as biochemical actions of alcohol, especially in the liver, and more recently, intracellular mechanisms of alcohol effects. Some aspects of alcohol metabolism in the liver have not been investigated sufficiently, in particular effects of the metabolite, acetaldehyde. The related alcohols should also be compared more extensively with ethanol. Other topics requiring greater research attention include central nervous system effects, especially neuronal and behavioral changes, and correlations of behavioral with neurophysiological effects. Physical dependence should be studied in both human alcoholics and in laboratory animals, with development of techniques for inducing physical dependence in animals and for measuring hangover and withdrawal symptoms. Studies of voluntary consumption should be extended in animals and undertaken in humans who are moderate drinkers.

The multidisciplinary characteristic of alcohol effects requires encouragement and support of a wide variety of research methods and topics in alcohol programs. The large-scale, long-term efforts, needed in many alcohol studies, can best be accomplished in permanent research institutes, such as the Rutgers Center of Alcohol Studies, the Research Laboratories of Alko (the Finnish State Alcohol Monopoly), the Addiction Research Foundation in Toronto, the Division of Alcohol Studies and Rehabilitation of the Commonwealth of Virginia, and the National Center for the Prevention and

References p. 839

Control of Alcoholism (NCPCA). All of these organizations receive their research funds from a governing or outside agency which places greater emphasis on clinical or educational activities than on basic research. In alcohol programs, methods for maximizing communication and collaboration between experimenters and clinicians will greatly benefit the activities of both. Outside such research institutes, there may be particular value in awarding grants for experiments on alcohol to specialists in particular fields. Alcohol research should be included in programs on related problems, such as suicide, homicide, and traffic accidents. Both specificity and comprehensiveness are important goals in research programs. Topics of special potential interest in research programs are prevention, early detection, and early treatment of alcoholism, and beneficial effects of alcohol.

REFERENCES

BLANE, H. T. (1968). Trends in the prevention of alcoholism. *Psychiat. Res. Reports 24*, 1–9.

CHAFETZ, M. E. (1966). Alcohol excess. *Ann. N.Y. Acad. Sci. 133*, 808–813.

HADDON, W., JR. AND BRADESS, V. A. (1959). Alcohol in the single vehicle accident: Experience of Westchester County, New York. *J. Am. Med. Assoc. 169*, 1587–1593.

HOPKINSON, B. R. AND WIDDOWSON, G. M. (1964). Relation of alcohol to road accidents. *Brit. Med. J. 2*, 1569–1570.

KANTOROVICH, N. V. AND CONSTANTINOVICH, S. K. (1935). The effect of alcohol in catatonic syndromes. *Amer. J. Psychiat. 92*, 651–654.

NASH, H. (1966). Psychological effects and alcohol-antagonizing properties of caffeine. *Quart. J. Studies Alc. 27*, 727–734.

NIELSEN, J. (1965). Delirium tremens in Copenhagen. *Acta Psychiat. Scand. 41*, Suppl. 187, 92 pp.

North Amer. Assoc. of Alcoholism Programs and Amer. Public Health Assoc. (1966). Fundamentals and perspectives in alcoholism program evaluation. *Am. J. Public Health 56*, 1142–1152.

PATERSON, E. AND MATTHEWS, J. J. (1951). Protective action of ethyl alcohol on irradiated mice. *Nature 168*, 1126–1127.

PITTMAN, D. J. (1968). The rush to combine: Sociological dissimilarities of alcoholism and drug abuse. *Brit. J. Addict. 62*, 337–343.

POPHAM, R. E., DE LINT, J. E. E. AND SCHMIDT, W. (1968). Some comments on PITTMANN'S "Rush to combine". *Brit. J. Addict. 63*, 25–27.

TERHUNE, W. B. (1964). Prevention of alcoholism. How to drink and stay sober. *N.Y. State J. Med. 64*, 2041–2049.

WASHBURNE, C. (1958). Alcohol, amnesia and awareness. *Quart. J. Studies Alc. 19*, 471–481.

WOLFGANG, M. E. AND STROHM, R. B. (1956). The relationship between alcohol and criminal homicide. *Quart. J. Studies Alc. 17*, 411–425.

ZYLMAN, R. (1968). Accidents, alcohol and single-cause explanations. *Quart. J. Studies Alc.* Suppl. 4, 212–233.

Subject Index

Explanatory note

Since most of the topics in this subject index appear in the text in relation to effects of ethanol, this specification is generally not reiterated in the index term. The summary of each chapter is not indexed, but the concluding Chapter (12) is included in this index, as are also all the terms whose abbreviations are listed on p. xvi of the introductory portion of Volume I and on p. x of the introductory portion of Volume II. In addition to the subject index terms, general topics can be located in the outline of chapter titles, sections and subsections, on pages xi to xiv of the introductory portion of Volume I, and on pages v to viii of the introductory portion of Volume II.